Arizona Statutes

Title 13

Criminal Code

2018 EDITION

ARIZONA LEGISLATURE

Table of Contents

Chapter 1 General Provisions

13-101. Purposes

It is declared that the public policy of this state and the general purposes of the provisions of this title are:
1. To proscribe conduct that unjustifiably and inexcusably causes or threatens substantial harm to individual or public interests;
2. To give fair warning of the nature of the conduct proscribed and of the sentences authorized upon conviction;
3. To define the act or omission and the accompanying mental state which constitute each offense and limit the condemnation of conduct as criminal when it does not fall within the purposes set forth;
4. To differentiate on reasonable grounds between serious and minor offenses and to prescribe proportionate penalties for each;
5. To insure the public safety by preventing the commission of offenses through the deterrent influence of the sentences authorized;
6. To impose just and deserved punishment on those whose conduct threatens the public peace; and
7. To promote truth and accountability in sentencing.

13-101.01. Additional purposes of the criminal law

In order to preserve and protect the rights of crime victims to justice and the right of the people to safety, it is a fundamental purpose of the criminal law to identify and remove from society persons whose conduct continues to threaten public safety through the commission of violent or aggravated felonies after having been convicted twice previously of violent or aggravated felony offenses.

13-102. Applicability of title

A. Except as otherwise provided by law, the procedure governing the accusation, prosecution, conviction and punishment of offenders and offenses is not regulated by this title but by the rules of criminal procedure.
B. This title does not affect any power conferred by law upon a court-martial or other military authority or officer to prosecute and punish conduct and offenders violating military codes or laws, nor any power conferred by law to impose or inflict punishment for contempt.
C. This title does not bar, suspend or otherwise affect any right or liability to damages, penalty, forfeiture or other remedy authorized by law to be recovered or enforced in a civil action, regardless of whether the conduct involved in the proceeding constitutes an offense defined in this title.
D. Except as otherwise expressly provided, or unless the context otherwise requires, the provisions of this title shall govern the construction of and punishment for any offense defined outside this title.

13-103. Abolition of common law offenses and affirmative defenses; definition

A. All common law offenses and affirmative defenses are abolished. No conduct or omission constitutes an offense or an affirmative defense unless it is an offense or an affirmative defense under this title or under another statute or ordinance.
B. For the purposes of this section, "affirmative defense" means a defense that is offered and that attempts to excuse the criminal actions of the accused or another person for whose actions the accused may be deemed to be accountable. Affirmative defense does not include any justification defense pursuant to chapter 4 of this title or any defense that either denies an element of the offense charged or denies responsibility, including alibi, misidentification or lack of intent.

13-104. Rule of construction

The general rule that a penal statute is to be strictly construed does not apply to this title, but the provisions herein must be construed according to the fair meaning of their terms to promote justice and effect the objects of the law, including the purposes stated in section 13-101.

13-105. Definitions

In this title, unless the context otherwise requires:

1. "Absconder" means a probationer who has moved from the probationer's primary residence without permission of the probation officer, who cannot be located within ninety days of the previous contact and against whom a petition to revoke has been filed in the superior court alleging that the probationer's whereabouts are unknown. A probationer is no longer deemed an absconder when the probationer is voluntarily or involuntarily returned to probation service.

2. "Act" means a bodily movement.

3. "Benefit" means anything of value or advantage, present or prospective.

4. "Calendar year" means three hundred sixty-five days' actual time served without release, suspension or commutation of sentence, probation, pardon or parole, work furlough or release from confinement on any other basis.

5. "Community supervision" means that portion of a felony sentence that is imposed by the court pursuant to section 13-603, subsection I and that is served in the community after completing a period of imprisonment or served in prison in accordance with section 41-1604.07.

6. "Conduct" means an act or omission and its accompanying culpable mental state.

7. "Crime" means a misdemeanor or a felony.

8. "Criminal street gang" means an ongoing formal or informal association of persons in which members or associates individually or collectively engage in the commission, attempted commission, facilitation or solicitation of any felony act and that has at least one individual who is a criminal street gang member.

9. "Criminal street gang member" means an individual to whom at least two of the following seven criteria that indicate criminal street gang membership apply:

(a) Self-proclamation.

(b) Witness testimony or official statement.

(c) Written or electronic correspondence.

(d) Paraphernalia or photographs.

(e) Tattoos.

(f) Clothing or colors.

(g) Any other indicia of street gang membership.

10. "Culpable mental state" means intentionally, knowingly, recklessly or with criminal negligence as those terms are defined in this paragraph:

(a) "Intentionally" or "with the intent to" means, with respect to a result or to conduct described by a statute defining an offense, that a person's objective is to cause that result or to engage in that conduct.

(b) "Knowingly" means, with respect to conduct or to a circumstance described by a statute defining an offense, that a person is aware or believes that the person's conduct is of that nature or that the circumstance exists. It does not require any knowledge of the unlawfulness of the act or omission.

(c) "Recklessly" means, with respect to a result or to a circumstance described by a statute defining an offense, that a person is aware of and consciously disregards a substantial and unjustifiable risk that the result will occur or that the circumstance exists. The risk must be of such nature and degree that disregard of such risk constitutes a gross deviation from the standard of conduct that a reasonable person would observe in the situation. A person who creates such a risk but who is unaware of such risk solely by reason of voluntary intoxication also acts recklessly with respect to such risk.

(d) "Criminal negligence" means, with respect to a result or to a circumstance described by a statute defining an offense, that a person fails to perceive a substantial and unjustifiable risk that the result will occur or that the circumstance exists. The risk must be of such nature and degree that the failure to perceive it constitutes a gross deviation from the standard of care that a reasonable person would observe in the situation.

11. "Dangerous drug" means dangerous drug as defined in section 13-3401.

12. "Dangerous instrument" means anything that under the circumstances in which it is used, attempted to be used or threatened to be used is readily capable of causing death or serious physical injury.

13. "Dangerous offense" means an offense involving the discharge, use or threatening exhibition of a deadly weapon or dangerous instrument or the intentional or knowing infliction of serious physical injury on another person.

14. "Deadly physical force" means force that is used with the purpose of causing death or serious physical injury or in the manner of its use or intended use is capable of creating a substantial risk of causing death or serious physical injury.

15. "Deadly weapon" means anything designed for lethal use, including a firearm.

16. "Economic loss" means any loss incurred by a person as a result of the commission of an offense. Economic loss includes lost interest, lost earnings and other losses that would not have been incurred but for the offense. Economic loss does not include losses incurred by the convicted person, damages for pain and suffering, punitive damages or consequential damages.

17. "Enterprise" includes any corporation, association, labor union or other legal entity.

18. "Felony" means an offense for which a sentence to a term of imprisonment in the custody of the state department of corrections is authorized by any law of this state.

19. "Firearm" means any loaded or unloaded handgun, pistol, revolver, rifle, shotgun or other weapon that will or is designed to or may readily be converted to expel a projectile by the action of expanding gases, except that it does not include a firearm in permanently inoperable condition.

20. "Government" means the state, any political subdivision of the state or any department, agency, board, commission, institution or governmental instrumentality of or within the state or political subdivision.

21. "Government function" means any activity that a public servant is legally authorized to undertake on behalf of a government.

22. "Historical prior felony conviction" means:

(a) Any prior felony conviction for which the offense of conviction either:

(i) Mandated a term of imprisonment except for a violation of chapter 34 of this title involving a drug below the threshold amount.

(ii) Involved a dangerous offense.

(iii) Involved the illegal control of a criminal enterprise.

(iv) Involved aggravated driving under the influence of intoxicating liquor or drugs.

(v) Involved any dangerous crime against children as defined in section 13-705.

(b) Any class 2 or 3 felony, except the offenses listed in subdivision (a) of this paragraph, that was committed within the ten years immediately preceding the date of the present offense. Any time spent on absconder status while on probation, on escape status or incarcerated is excluded in calculating if the offense was committed within the preceding ten years. If a court determines a person was not on absconder status while on probation or escape status, that time is not excluded. For the purposes of this subdivision, "escape" means:

(i) A departure from custody or from a juvenile secure care facility, a juvenile detention facility or an adult correctional facility in which the person is held or detained, with knowledge that the departure is not permitted, or the failure to return to custody or detention following a temporary leave granted for a specific purpose or for a limited period.

(ii) A failure to report as ordered to custody or detention to begin serving a term of incarceration.

(c) Any class 4, 5 or 6 felony, except the offenses listed in subdivision (a) of this paragraph, that was committed within the five years immediately preceding the date of the present offense. Any time spent on absconder status while on probation, on escape status or incarcerated is excluded in calculating if the offense was committed within the preceding five years. If a court determines a person was not on absconder status while on probation or escape status, that time is not excluded. For the purposes of this subdivision, "escape" has the same meaning prescribed in subdivision (b) of this paragraph.

(d) Any felony conviction that is a third or more prior felony conviction. For the purposes of this subdivision, "prior felony conviction" includes any offense committed outside the jurisdiction of this state that was punishable by that jurisdiction as a felony.

(e) Any offense committed outside the jurisdiction of this state that was punishable by that jurisdiction as a felony and that was committed within the five years immediately preceding the date of the present offense. Any time spent on absconder status while on probation, on escape status or incarcerated is excluded in calculating if the offense was committed within the preceding five years. If a court determines a person was not on absconder status while on probation or escape status, that time is not excluded. For the purposes of this subdivision, "escape" has the same meaning prescribed in subdivision (b) of this paragraph.

(f) Any offense committed outside the jurisdiction of this state that involved the discharge, use or threatening exhibition of a deadly weapon or dangerous instrument or the intentional or knowing infliction of death or serious physical injury and that was punishable by that jurisdiction as a felony. A person who has been convicted of a felony weapons possession violation in any court outside the jurisdiction of this state that would not be punishable as a felony under the laws of this state is not subject to this paragraph.

23. "Human smuggling organization" means an ongoing formal or informal association of persons in which members or associates individually or collectively engage in the smuggling of human beings.

24. "Intoxication" means any mental or physical incapacity resulting from use of drugs, toxic vapors or intoxicating liquors.

25. "Misdemeanor" means an offense for which a sentence to a term of imprisonment other than to the custody of the state department of corrections is authorized by any law of this state.

26. "Narcotic drug" means narcotic drugs as defined in section 13-3401.

27. "Offense" or "public offense" means conduct for which a sentence to a term of imprisonment or of a fine is provided by any law of the state in which it occurred or by any law, regulation or ordinance of a political subdivision of that state and, if the act occurred in a state other than this state, it would be so punishable under the laws, regulations or ordinances of this state or of a political subdivision of this state if the act had occurred in this state.

28. "Omission" means the failure to perform an act as to which a duty of performance is imposed by law.

29. "Peace officer" means any person vested by law with a duty to maintain public order and make arrests and includes a constable.

30. "Person" means a human being and, as the context requires, an enterprise, a public or private corporation, an unincorporated association, a partnership, a firm, a society, a government, a governmental authority or an individual or entity capable of holding a legal or beneficial interest in property.

31. "Petty offense" means an offense for which a sentence of a fine only is authorized by law.

32. "Physical force" means force used upon or directed toward the body of another person and includes confinement, but does not include deadly physical force.

33. "Physical injury" means the impairment of physical condition.

34. "Possess" means knowingly to have physical possession or otherwise to exercise dominion or control over property.

35. "Possession" means a voluntary act if the defendant knowingly exercised dominion or control over property.

36. "Preconviction custody" means the confinement of a person in a jail in this state or another state after the person is arrested for or charged with a felony offense.

37. "Property" means anything of value, tangible or intangible.

38. "Public servant":

(a) Means any officer or employee of any branch of government, whether elected, appointed or otherwise employed, including a peace officer, and any person participating as an advisor or consultant or otherwise in performing a governmental function.

(b) Does not include jurors or witnesses.

(c) Includes those who have been elected, appointed, employed or designated to become a public servant although not yet occupying that position.

39. "Serious physical injury" includes physical injury that creates a reasonable risk of death, or that causes serious and permanent disfigurement, serious impairment of health or loss or protracted impairment of the function of any bodily organ or limb.

40. "Unlawful" means contrary to law or, where the context so requires, not permitted by law.

41. "Vehicle" means a device in, upon or by which any person or property is, may be or could have been transported or drawn upon a highway, waterway or airway, excepting devices moved by human power or used exclusively upon stationary rails or tracks.

42. "Voluntary act" means a bodily movement performed consciously and as a result of effort and determination.

43. "Voluntary intoxication" means intoxication caused by the knowing use of drugs, toxic vapors or intoxicating liquors by a person, the tendency of which to cause intoxication the person knows or ought to know, unless the person introduces them pursuant to medical advice or under such duress as would afford a defense to an offense.

13-106. Death of convicted defendant; dismissal of appellate and postconviction proceedings

A. On a convicted defendant's death, the court shall dismiss any pending appeal or postconviction proceeding.

B. A convicted defendant's death does not abate the defendant's criminal conviction or sentence of imprisonment or any restitution, fine or assessment imposed by the sentencing court.

13-107. Time limitations

A. A prosecution for any homicide, any conspiracy to commit homicide that results in the death of a person, any offense that is listed in chapter 14 or 35.1 of this title and that is a class 2 felony, any violent sexual assault pursuant to section 13-1423, any violation of section 13-2308.01 or 13-2308.03, any misuse of public monies or a felony involving falsification of public records or any attempt to commit an offense listed in this subsection may be commenced at any time.

B. Except as otherwise provided in this section and section 28-672, prosecutions for other offenses must be commenced within the following periods after actual discovery by the state or the political subdivision having jurisdiction of the offense or discovery by the state or the political subdivision that should have occurred with the exercise of reasonable diligence, whichever first occurs:

1. For a class 2 through a class 6 felony, seven years.

2. For a misdemeanor, one year.

3. For a petty offense, six months.

C. For the purposes of subsection B of this section, a prosecution is commenced when an indictment, information or complaint is filed.

D. The period of limitation does not run during any time when the accused is absent from the state or has no reasonably ascertainable place of abode within the state.

E. The period of limitation does not run for a serious offense as defined in section 13-706 during any time when the identity of the person who commits the offense or offenses is unknown.

F. The time limitation within which a prosecution of a class 6 felony shall commence shall be determined pursuant to subsection B, paragraph 1 of this section, irrespective of whether a court enters a judgment of conviction for or a prosecuting attorney designates the offense as a misdemeanor.

G. If a complaint, indictment or information filed before the period of limitation has expired is dismissed for any reason, a new prosecution may be commenced within six months after the dismissal becomes final even if the period of limitation has expired at the time of the dismissal or will expire within six months of the dismissal.

13-108. Territorial applicability

A. This state has jurisdiction over an offense that a person commits by his own conduct or the conduct of another for which such person is legally accountable if:

1. Conduct constituting any element of the offense or a result of such conduct occurs within this state; or

2. The conduct outside this state constitutes an attempt or conspiracy to commit an offense within this state and an act in furtherance of the attempt or conspiracy occurs within this state; or

3. The conduct within this state constitutes an attempt, solicitation, conspiracy or facilitation to commit or establishes criminal accountability for the commission of an offense in another jurisdiction that is also an offense under the law of this state; or

4. The offense consists of an omission to perform a duty imposed by the law of this state regardless of the location of the defendant at the time of the offense; or

5. The offense is a violation of a statute of this state that prohibits conduct outside the state.

B. When the offense involves a homicide, either the death of the victim or the bodily impact causing death constitutes a result within the meaning of subsection A, paragraph 1. If the body of a homicide victim is found in this state it is presumed that the result occurred in this state.

C. This state includes the land and water and the air space above the land and water.

13-109. Place of trial

A. Criminal prosecutions shall be tried in the county in which conduct constituting any element of the offense or a result of such conduct occurred, unless otherwise provided by law.

B. The following special provisions apply:

1. If conduct constituting an element of an offense or a result constituting an element of an offense occurs in two or more counties, trial of the offense may be held in any of the counties concerned; or

2. A person who in one county solicits, aids, abets or attempts to aid another in the planning or commission of an offense in another county may be tried for the offense in either county; or

3. If an offense is committed in transit and it cannot readily be determined in which county the offense was committed, trial of the offense may be held in any county through or over which the transit occurred; or

4. If the cause of death is inflicted in one county and death ensues in another county, trial of the offense may be held in either county. If the cause of death is inflicted in one county and death ensues out of this state, trial of the offense shall be in the county where the cause was inflicted. If the body of a homicide victim is found in a county, it is presumed that the cause of death was inflicted in that county; or

5. If an offense is committed on the boundary of two or more counties or within one mile of such boundary, trial of the offense may be held in any of the counties concerned; or

6. A person who obtains property unlawfully may be tried in any county in which such person exerts control over the property; or

7. A person who commits a preparatory offense may be tried in any county in which any act that is an element of the offense, including the agreement in conspiracy, is committed.

C. If an offense has been committed within this state and it cannot readily be determined within which county or counties the commission took place, trial may be held in the county in which the defendant resides or, if the defendant has no fixed residence, in the county in which the defendant is apprehended or to which the defendant is extradited.

13-110. Conviction for attempt although crime perpetrated

A person may be convicted of an attempt to commit a crime, although it appears upon the trial that the crime intended or attempted was perpetrated by the person in pursuance of such an attempt, unless the court, in its discretion, discharges the jury and directs the person to be tried for the crime.

13-111. Former jeopardy or acquittal as bar to same or lesser offenses

When the defendant is convicted or acquitted, or has once been placed in jeopardy upon an indictment or information, the conviction, acquittal or jeopardy is a bar to another indictment or information for the offense charged in either, or for an attempt to commit the offense, or for any offense necessarily included therein, of which he might have been convicted under the indictment or information.

13-113. Conviction or acquittal in one county as bar to prosecution in another

Where a person may be tried for an offense in two or more counties, a conviction or acquittal of the offense in one county shall be a bar to a prosecution for the same offense in another county.

13-114. Speedy trial; counsel; witnesses and confrontation

In a criminal action defendant is entitled:
1. To have a speedy public trial by an impartial jury of the county in which the offense is alleged to have been committed.
2. To have counsel.
3. To produce witnesses on his behalf, and to be confronted with the witnesses against him in the presence of the court, except that the testimony or deposition of a witness may be received in evidence at the trial as by law prescribed.

13-115. Presumption of innocence and benefit of doubt; degrees of guilt

A. A defendant in a criminal action is presumed to be innocent until the contrary is proved, and in case of a reasonable doubt whether his guilt is satisfactorily shown, he is entitled to be acquitted.
B. When it appears that a defendant has committed a crime or public offense, and there is reasonable ground of doubt in which of two or more degrees he is guilty, he may be convicted of the lowest of such degrees only.

13-116. Double punishment

An act or omission which is made punishable in different ways by different sections of the laws may be punished under both, but in no event may sentences be other than concurrent. An acquittal or conviction and sentence under either one bars a prosecution for the same act or omission under any other, to the extent the Constitution of the United States or of this state require.

13-117. Defendant as witness; no comment on failure to testify

A. A defendant in a criminal action or proceeding shall not be compelled to be a witness against himself, but may be a witness in his own behalf. If he offers himself as a witness in his own behalf, he may be cross-examined to the same extent and subject to the same rules as any other witness.

B. The defendant's neglect or refusal to be a witness in his own behalf shall not in any manner prejudice him, or be used against him on the trial or proceedings.

13-118. Sexual motivation special allegation; procedures; definition

A. In each criminal case involving an offense other than a sexual offense, the prosecutor may file a special allegation of sexual motivation if sufficient admissible evidence exists that would justify a finding of sexual motivation by a reasonable and objective finder of fact.

B. If the prosecutor files a special allegation of sexual motivation, the state shall prove beyond a reasonable doubt that the defendant committed the offense with a sexual motivation. The trier of fact shall find a special verdict as to whether the defendant committed the offense with a sexual motivation.

C. For purposes of this section "sexual motivation" means that one of the purposes for which the defendant committed the crime was for the purpose of the defendant's sexual gratification.

13-120. Disposition of property taken from defendant; receipts

A. When money or other property is taken from a defendant arrested upon a charge of a crime or public offense, the officer taking it shall at the time make duplicate receipts therefor, specifying particularly the amount of money or the kind of property taken. The officer shall deliver one receipt to the defendant and shall file the other forthwith with the magistrate or clerk of the court to which the officer makes the return of arrest.

B. When such money or property is taken by a police officer of an incorporated city or town, he shall deliver one receipt to the defendant and the other, with the property, forthwith to the clerk or other person in charge of the police office in the city or town.

13-121. Jurisdiction of the court in proceedings subsequent to trial and sentencing

Whenever any further proceedings are instituted before the trial court subsequent to the original trial and sentencing, excepting motions for new trial made within one year after the rendition of the verdict or the finding of the court, the court in the same action shall have jurisdiction to hear such matter only after due proof has been made that notice of such proceeding has been given to the attorney general at least ten days prior to such hearing.

13-122. Action for recovery of public monies

This state or any political subdivision of this state may maintain an action against any person convicted of an offense for the recovery of any public monies paid to the person. Venue for such an action is in the superior court in the county where the monies were paid, where a sale was made or where the defendant resides.

13-123. Certificate of special public importance

In any action for a prosecution involving a dangerous crime against children, the state may file a certificate stating that the case is of special public importance. The clerk shall immediately furnish a copy of the certificate to the chief judge of the superior court in the county in which the action is pending and, after receiving the copy, the chief judge shall immediately designate a judge to hear and determine the action. The judge designated shall, consistent with the rules of criminal procedure, expedite the action and the action shall take precedence over prosecution of any other proceeding.

Chapter 2 General Principles of Criminal Liability

13-201. Requirements for criminal liability

The minimum requirement for criminal liability is the performance by a person of conduct which includes a voluntary act or the omission to perform a duty imposed by law which the person is physically capable of performing.

13-202. Construction of statutes with respect to culpability

A. If a statute defining an offense prescribes a culpable mental state that is sufficient for commission of the offense without distinguishing among the elements of such offense, the prescribed mental state shall apply to each such element unless a contrary legislative purpose plainly appears.

B. If a statute defining an offense does not expressly prescribe a culpable mental state that is sufficient for commission of the offense, no culpable mental state is required for the commission of such offense, and the offense is one of strict liability unless the proscribed conduct necessarily involves a culpable mental state. If the offense is one of strict liability, proof of a culpable mental state will also suffice to establish criminal responsibility.

C. If a statute provides that criminal negligence suffices to establish an element of an offense, that element also is established if a person acts intentionally, knowingly or recklessly. If acting recklessly suffices to establish an element, that element also is established if a person acts intentionally or knowingly. If acting knowingly suffices to establish an element, that element is also established if a person acts intentionally.

13-203. Causal relationship between conduct and result; relationship to mental culpability

A. Conduct is the cause of a result when both of the following exist:

1. But for the conduct the result in question would not have occurred.

2. The relationship between the conduct and result satisfies any additional causal requirements imposed by the statute defining the offense.

B. If intentionally causing a particular result is an element of an offense, and the actual result is not within the intention or contemplation of the person, that element is established if:

1. The actual result differs from that intended or contemplated only in the respect that a different person or different property is injured or affected or that the injury or harm intended or contemplated would have been more serious or extensive than that caused; or

2. The actual result involves similar injury or harm as that intended or contemplated and occurs in a manner which the person knows or should know is rendered substantially more probable by such person's conduct.

C. If recklessly or negligently causing a particular result is an element of an offense, and the actual result is not within the risk of which the person is aware or in the case of criminal negligence, of which the person should be aware, that element is established if:

1. The actual result differs from the probable result only in the respect that a different person or different property is injured or affected or that the injury or harm intended or contemplated would have been more serious or extensive than that caused; or

2. The actual result involves similar injury or harm as the probable result and occurs in a manner which the person knows or should know is rendered substantially more probable by such person's conduct.

13-204. Effect of ignorance or mistake upon criminal liability

A. Ignorance or a mistaken belief as to a matter of fact does not relieve a person of criminal liability unless:

1. It negates the culpable mental state required for commission of the offense; or

2. It supports a defense of justification as defined in chapter 4 of this title.

B. Ignorance or mistake as to a matter of law does not relieve a person of criminal responsibility.

13-205. Affirmative defenses; justification; burden of proof

A. Except as otherwise provided by law, a defendant shall prove any affirmative defense raised by a preponderance of the evidence. Justification defenses under chapter 4 of this title are not affirmative defenses. Justification defenses describe conduct that, if not justified, would constitute an offense but, if justified, does not constitute criminal or wrongful conduct. If evidence of justification pursuant to chapter 4 of this title is presented by the defendant, the state must prove beyond a reasonable doubt that the defendant did not act with justification.

B. This section does not affect the presumption contained in section 13-411, subsection C and section 13-503.

13-206. Entrapment

A. It is an affirmative defense to a criminal charge that the person was entrapped. To claim entrapment, the person must admit by the person's testimony or other evidence the substantial elements of the offense charged.

B. A person who asserts an entrapment defense has the burden of proving the following by clear and convincing evidence:

1. The idea of committing the offense started with law enforcement officers or their agents rather than with the person.

2. The law enforcement officers or their agents urged and induced the person to commit the offense.

3. The person was not predisposed to commit the type of offense charged before the law enforcement officers or their agents urged and induced the person to commit the offense.

C. A person does not establish entrapment if the person was predisposed to commit the offense and the law enforcement officers or their agents merely provided the person with an opportunity to commit the offense. It is not entrapment for law enforcement officers or their agents merely to use a ruse or to conceal their identity. The conduct of law enforcement officers and their agents may be considered in determining if a person has proven entrapment.

Chapter 3 Parties to offenses: Accountability

13-301. Definition of accomplice

In this title, unless the context otherwise requires, "accomplice" means a person, other than a peace officer acting in his official capacity within the scope of his authority and in the line of duty, who with the intent to promote or facilitate the commission of an offense:

1. Solicits or commands another person to commit the offense; or
2. Aids, counsels, agrees to aid or attempts to aid another person in planning or committing an offense.
3. Provides means or opportunity to another person to commit the offense.

13-302. Criminal liability based upon conduct

A person may be guilty of an offense committed by such person's own conduct or by the conduct of another for which such person is criminally accountable as provided in this chapter, or both. In any prosecution, testimony of an accomplice need not be corroborated.

13-303. Criminal liability based upon conduct of another

A. A person is criminally accountable for the conduct of another if:

1. The person is made accountable for such conduct by the statute defining the offense; or
2. Acting with the culpable mental state sufficient for the commission of the offense, such person causes another person, whether or not such other person is capable of forming the culpable mental state, to engage in such conduct; or
3. The person is an accomplice of such other person in the commission of an offense including any offense that is a natural and probable or reasonably foreseeable consequence of the offense for which the person was an accomplice.

B. If causing a particular result is an element of an offense, a person who acts with the kind of culpability with respect to the result that is sufficient for the commission of the offense is guilty of that offense if:

1. The person solicits or commands another person to engage in the conduct causing such result; or
2. The person aids, counsels, agrees to aid or attempts to aid another person in planning or engaging in the conduct causing such result.

13-304. Nondefenses to criminal liability based upon conduct of another

In any prosecution for an offense in which the criminal liability of the accused is based upon the conduct of another under section 13-303 or pursuant to section 13-1003, it is no defense that:

1. The other person has not been prosecuted for or convicted of such offense, or has been acquitted of such offense, or has been convicted of a different offense or degree of offense or has an immunity to prosecution or conviction for such offense; or
2. The accused belongs to a class of persons who by definition of the offense are legally incapable of committing the offense in an individual capacity.

13-305. Criminal liability of enterprises; definitions

A. Notwithstanding any other provisions of law, an enterprise commits an offense if:

1. The conduct constituting the offense consists of a failure to discharge a specific duty imposed by law; or

2. The conduct undertaken in behalf of the enterprise and constituting the offense is engaged in, authorized, solicited, commanded or recklessly tolerated by the directors of the enterprise in any manner or by a high managerial agent acting within the scope of employment; or

3. The conduct constituting the offense is engaged in by an agent of the enterprise while acting within the scope of employment and in behalf of the enterprise; and

(a) The offense is a misdemeanor or petty offense; or

(b) The offense is defined by a statute which imposes criminal liability on an enterprise.

B. As used in this section:

1. "Agent" means any officer, director, employee of an enterprise or any other person who is authorized to act in behalf of the enterprise.

2. "High managerial agent" means an officer of an enterprise or any other agent in a position of comparable authority with respect to the formulation of enterprise policy.

13-306. Criminal liability of an individual for conduct of an enterprise

A person is criminally liable for conduct constituting an offense which such person performs or causes to be performed in the name of or in behalf of an enterprise to the same extent as if such conduct were performed in such person's own name or behalf.

Chapter 4 Justification

13-401. Unavailability of justification defense; justification as defense

A. Even though a person is justified under this chapter in threatening or using physical force or deadly physical force against another, if in doing so such person recklessly injures or kills an innocent third person, the justification afforded by this chapter is unavailable in a prosecution for the reckless injury or killing of the innocent third person.

B. Except as provided in subsection A, justification, as defined in this chapter, is a defense in any prosecution for an offense pursuant to this title.

13-402. Justification; execution of public duty

A. Unless inconsistent with the other sections of this chapter defining justifiable use of physical force or deadly physical force or with some other superseding provision of law, conduct which would otherwise constitute an offense is justifiable when it is required or authorized by law.

B. The justification afforded by subsection A also applies if:

1. A reasonable person would believe such conduct is required or authorized by the judgment or direction of a competent court or tribunal or in the lawful execution of legal process, notwithstanding lack of jurisdiction of the court or defect in the legal process; or

2. A reasonable person would believe such conduct is required or authorized to assist a peace officer in the performance of such officer's duties, notwithstanding that the officer exceeded the officer's legal authority.

13-403. Justification; use of physical force

The use of physical force upon another person which would otherwise constitute an offense is justifiable and not criminal under any of the following circumstances:

1. A parent or guardian and a teacher or other person entrusted with the care and supervision of a minor or incompetent person may use reasonable and appropriate physical force upon the minor or incompetent person when and to the extent reasonably necessary and appropriate to maintain discipline.

2. A superintendent or other entrusted official of a jail, prison or correctional institution may use physical force for the preservation of peace, to maintain order or discipline, or to prevent the commission of any felony or misdemeanor.

3. A person responsible for the maintenance of order in a place where others are assembled or on a common motor carrier of passengers, or a person acting under his direction, may use physical force if and to the extent that a reasonable person would believe it necessary to maintain order, but such person may use deadly physical force only if reasonably necessary to prevent death or serious physical injury.

4. A person acting under a reasonable belief that another person is about to commit suicide or to inflict serious physical injury upon himself may use physical force upon that person to the extent reasonably necessary to thwart the result.

5. A duly licensed physician or a registered nurse or a person acting under his direction, or any other person who renders emergency care at the scene of an emergency occurrence, may use reasonable physical force for the purpose of administering a recognized and lawful form of treatment which is reasonably adapted to promoting the physical or mental health of the patient if:

(a) The treatment is administered with the consent of the patient or, if the patient is a minor or an incompetent person, with the consent of his parent, guardian or other person entrusted with his care and supervision except as otherwise provided by law; or

(b) The treatment is administered in an emergency when the person administering such treatment reasonably believes that no one competent to consent can be consulted and that a reasonable person, wishing to safeguard the welfare of the patient, would consent.

6. A person may otherwise use physical force upon another person as further provided in this chapter.

13-404. Justification; self-defense

A. Except as provided in subsection B of this section, a person is justified in threatening or using physical force against another when and to the extent a reasonable person would believe that physical force is immediately necessary to protect himself against the other's use or attempted use of unlawful physical force.

B. The threat or use of physical force against another is not justified:

1. In response to verbal provocation alone; or

2. To resist an arrest that the person knows or should know is being made by a peace officer or by a person acting in a peace officer's presence and at his direction, whether the arrest is lawful or unlawful, unless the physical force used by the peace officer exceeds that allowed by law; or

3. If the person provoked the other's use or attempted use of unlawful physical force, unless:

(a) The person withdraws from the encounter or clearly communicates to the other his intent to do so reasonably believing he cannot safely withdraw from the encounter; and

(b) The other nevertheless continues or attempts to use unlawful physical force against the person.

13-405. Justification; use of deadly physical force

A. A person is justified in threatening or using deadly physical force against another:

1. If such person would be justified in threatening or using physical force against the other under section 13-404, and

2. When and to the degree a reasonable person would believe that deadly physical force is immediately necessary to protect himself against the other's use or attempted use of unlawful deadly physical force.

B. A person has no duty to retreat before threatening or using deadly physical force pursuant to this section if the person is in a place where the person may legally be and is not engaged in an unlawful act.

13-406. Justification; defense of a third person

A person is justified in threatening or using physical force or deadly physical force against another to protect a third person if, under the circumstances as a reasonable person would believe them to be, such person would be justified under section 13-404 or 13-405 in threatening or using physical force or deadly physical force to protect himself against the unlawful physical force or deadly physical force a reasonable person would believe is threatening the third person he seeks to protect.

13-407. Justification; use of physical force in defense of premises

A. A person or his agent in lawful possession or control of premises is justified in threatening to use deadly physical force or in threatening or using physical force against another when and to the extent that a reasonable person would believe it immediately necessary to prevent or terminate the commission or attempted commission of a criminal trespass by the other person in or upon the premises.

B. A person may use deadly physical force under subsection A only in the defense of himself or third persons as described in sections 13-405 and 13-406.

C. In this section, "premises" means any real property and any structure, movable or immovable, permanent or temporary, adapted for both human residence and lodging whether occupied or not.

13-408. Justification; use of physical force in defense of property

A person is justified in using physical force against another when and to the extent that a reasonable person would believe it necessary to prevent what a reasonable person would believe is an attempt or commission by the other person of theft or criminal damage involving tangible movable property under his possession or control, but such person may use deadly physical force under these circumstances as provided in sections 13-405, 13-406 and 13-411.

13-409. Justification; use of physical force in law enforcement

A person is justified in threatening or using physical force against another if in making or assisting in making an arrest or detention or in preventing or assisting in preventing the escape after arrest or detention of that other person, such person uses or threatens to use physical force and all of the following exist:

1. A reasonable person would believe that such force is immediately necessary to effect the arrest or detention or prevent the escape.

2. Such person makes known the purpose of the arrest or detention or believes that it is otherwise known or cannot reasonably be made known to the person to be arrested or detained.

3. A reasonable person would believe the arrest or detention to be lawful.

13-410. Justification; use of deadly physical force in law enforcement

A. The threatened use of deadly physical force by a person against another is justified pursuant to section 13-409 only if a reasonable person effecting the arrest or preventing the escape would believe the suspect or escapee is:

1. Actually resisting the discharge of a legal duty with deadly physical force or with the apparent capacity to use deadly physical force; or

2. A felon who has escaped from lawful confinement; or

3. A felon who is fleeing from justice or resisting arrest with physical force.

B. The use of deadly physical force by a person other than a peace officer against another is justified pursuant to section 13-409 only if a reasonable person effecting the arrest or preventing the escape would believe the suspect or escapee is actually resisting the discharge of a legal duty with physical force or with the apparent capacity to use deadly physical force.

C. The use of deadly force by a peace officer against another is justified pursuant to section 13-409 only when the peace officer reasonably believes that it is necessary:

1. To defend himself or a third person from what the peace officer reasonably believes to be the use or imminent use of deadly physical force.

2. To effect an arrest or prevent the escape from custody of a person whom the peace officer reasonably believes:

(a) Has committed, attempted to commit, is committing or is attempting to commit a felony involving the use or a threatened use of a deadly weapon.

(b) Is attempting to escape by use of a deadly weapon.

(c) Through past or present conduct of the person which is known by the peace officer that the person is likely to endanger human life or inflict serious bodily injury to another unless apprehended without delay.

(d) Is necessary to lawfully suppress a riot if the person or another person participating in the riot is armed with a deadly weapon.

D. Notwithstanding any other provisions of this chapter, a peace officer is justified in threatening to use deadly physical force when and to the extent a reasonable officer believes it necessary to protect himself against another's potential use of physical force or deadly physical force.

13-411. Justification; use of force in crime prevention; applicability

A. A person is justified in threatening or using both physical force and deadly physical force against another if and to the extent the person reasonably believes that physical force or deadly physical force is immediately necessary to prevent the other's commission of arson of an occupied structure under section 13-1704, burglary in the second or first degree under section 13-1507 or 13-1508, kidnapping under section 13-1304, manslaughter under section 13-1103, second or first degree murder under section 13-1104 or 13-1105, sexual conduct with a minor under section 13-1405, sexual assault under section 13-1406, child molestation under section 13-1410, armed robbery under section 13-1904 or aggravated assault under section 13-1204, subsection A, paragraphs 1 and 2.
B. There is no duty to retreat before threatening or using physical force or deadly physical force justified by subsection A of this section.
C. A person is presumed to be acting reasonably for the purposes of this section if the person is acting to prevent what the person reasonably believes is the imminent or actual commission of any of the offenses listed in subsection A of this section.
D. This section includes the use or threatened use of physical force or deadly physical force in a person's home, residence, place of business, land the person owns or leases, conveyance of any kind, or any other place in this state where a person has a right to be.

13-412. Duress

A. Conduct which would otherwise constitute an offense is justified if a reasonable person would believe that he was compelled to engage in the proscribed conduct by the threat or use of immediate physical force against his person or the person of another which resulted or could result in serious physical injury which a reasonable person in the situation would not have resisted.
B. The defense provided by subsection A is unavailable if the person intentionally, knowingly or recklessly placed himself in a situation in which it was probable that he would be subjected to duress.
C. The defense provided by subsection A is unavailable for offenses involving homicide or serious physical injury.

13-413. No civil liability for justified conduct

No person in this state shall be subject to civil liability for engaging in conduct otherwise justified pursuant to the provisions of this chapter.

13-414. Justification; use of reasonable and necessary means

A correctional officer as defined in section 41-1661 may use all reasonable and necessary means including deadly force to prevent the attempt of a prisoner sentenced to the custody of the state department of corrections to:
1. Escape from custody or from a correctional facility.
2. Take another person as a hostage.
3. Cause serious bodily harm to another person.

13-415. Justification; domestic violence

If there have been past acts of domestic violence as defined in section 13-3601, subsection A against the defendant by the victim, the state of mind of a reasonable person under sections 13-404, 13-405 and 13-406 shall be determined from the perspective of a reasonable person who has been a victim of those past acts of domestic violence.

13-416. Justification; use of reasonable and necessary means; definition

A. A security officer who is employed by a private contractor may use all reasonable and necessary means, including deadly force, to prevent a prisoner in the custody of the private contractor from the following:

1. Escaping from the custody of a law enforcement officer, an authorized custodial agent or a correctional facility.

2. Taking another person as a hostage or causing death or serious bodily harm to another person.

B. Security officers who are described in subsection A and who are employed by private prisons in this state shall meet or exceed the minimal training standards established by the American correctional association.

C. For the purposes of this section, "private contractor" means a person that contracts with any governmental entity to provide detention or incarceration services for prisoners.

13-417. Necessity defense

A. Conduct that would otherwise constitute an offense is justified if a reasonable person was compelled to engage in the proscribed conduct and the person had no reasonable alternative to avoid imminent public or private injury greater than the injury that might reasonably result from the person's own conduct.

B. An accused person may not assert the defense under subsection A if the person intentionally, knowingly or recklessly placed himself in the situation in which it was probable that the person would have to engage in the proscribed conduct.

C. An accused person may not assert the defense under subsection A for offenses involving homicide or serious physical injury.

13-418. Justification; use of force in defense of residential structure or occupied vehicles; definitions

A. Notwithstanding any other provision of this chapter, a person is justified in threatening to use or using physical force or deadly physical force against another person if the person reasonably believes himself or another person to be in imminent peril of death or serious physical injury and the person against whom the physical force or deadly physical force is threatened or used was in the process of unlawfully or forcefully entering, or had unlawfully or forcefully entered, a residential structure or occupied vehicle, or had removed or was attempting to remove another person against the other person's will from the residential structure or occupied vehicle.

B. A person has no duty to retreat before threatening or using physical force or deadly physical force pursuant to this section.

C. For the purposes of this section:

1. "Residential structure" has the same meaning prescribed in section 13-1501.

2. "Vehicle" means a conveyance of any kind, whether or not motorized, that is designed to transport persons or property.

13-419. Presumptions; defense of a residential structure or occupied vehicle; exceptions; definitions

A. A person is presumed to reasonably believe that the threat or use of physical force or deadly force is immediately necessary for the purposes of sections 13-404 through 13-408, section 13-418 and section 13-421 if the person knows or has reason to believe that the person against whom physical force or deadly force is threatened or used is unlawfully or forcefully entering or has unlawfully or forcefully entered and is present in the person's residential structure or occupied vehicle.

B. For the purposes of sections 13-404 through 13-408, section 13-418 and section 13-421, a person who is unlawfully or forcefully entering or who has unlawfully or forcefully entered and is present in a residential structure or occupied vehicle is presumed to pose an imminent threat of unlawful deadly harm to any person who is in the residential structure or occupied vehicle.

C. The presumptions in subsections A and B of this section do not apply if:

1. The person against whom physical force or deadly physical force was threatened or used has the right to be in or is a lawful resident of the residential structure or occupied vehicle, including an owner, lessee, invitee or titleholder, and an order of protection or injunction against harassment has not been filed against that person.

2. The person against whom physical force or deadly physical force was threatened or used is the parent or grandparent, or has legal custody or guardianship, of a child or grandchild sought to be removed from the residential structure or occupied vehicle.

3. The person who threatens or uses physical force or deadly physical force is engaged in an unlawful activity or is using the residential structure or occupied vehicle to further an unlawful activity.

4. The person against whom physical force or deadly physical force was threatened or used is a law enforcement officer who enters or attempts to enter a residential structure or occupied vehicle in the performance of official duties.

D. For the purposes of this section:

1. "Residential structure" has the same meaning prescribed in section 13-1501.

2. "Vehicle" means a conveyance of any kind, whether or not motorized, that is designed to transport persons or property.

13-420. Attorney fees; costs

The court shall award reasonable attorney fees, costs, compensation for lost income and all expenses incurred by a defendant in the defense of any civil action based on conduct otherwise justified pursuant to this chapter if the defendant prevails in the civil action.

13-421. Justification; defensive display of a firearm; definition

A. The defensive display of a firearm by a person against another is justified when and to the extent a reasonable person would believe that physical force is immediately necessary to protect himself against the use or attempted use of unlawful physical force or deadly physical force.

B. This section does not apply to a person who:

1. Intentionally provokes another person to use or attempt to use unlawful physical force.

2. Uses a firearm during the commission of a serious offense as defined in section 13-706 or violent crime as defined in section 13-901.03.

C. This section does not require the defensive display of a firearm before the use of physical force or the threat of physical force by a person who is otherwise justified in the use or threatened use of physical force.

D. For the purposes of this section, "defensive display of a firearm" includes:

1. Verbally informing another person that the person possesses or has available a firearm.

2. Exposing or displaying a firearm in a manner that a reasonable person would understand was meant to protect the person against another's use or attempted use of unlawful physical force or deadly physical force.

3. Placing the person's hand on a firearm while the firearm is contained in a pocket, purse or other means of containment or transport.

Chapter 5 ReSponsibility

13-501. Persons under eighteen years of age; felony charging; definitions

A. The county attorney shall bring a criminal prosecution against a juvenile in the same manner as an adult if the juvenile is fifteen, sixteen or seventeen years of age at the time the alleged offense is committed and the juvenile is accused of any of the following offenses:

1. First degree murder in violation of section 13-1105.

2. Second degree murder in violation of section 13-1104.

3. Forcible sexual assault in violation of section 13-1406.

4. Armed robbery in violation of section 13-1904.

5. Any other violent felony offense.

6. Any felony offense committed by a chronic felony offender.

7. Any offense that is properly joined to an offense listed in this subsection.

B. Except as provided in subsection A of this section, the county attorney may bring a criminal prosecution against a juvenile in the same manner as an adult if the juvenile is at least fourteen years of age at the time the alleged offense is committed and the juvenile is accused of any of the following offenses:

1. A class 1 felony.

2. A class 2 felony.

3. A class 3 felony in violation of any offense in chapters 10 through 17 or chapter 19 or 23 of this title.

4. A class 3, 4, 5 or 6 felony involving a dangerous offense.

5. Any felony offense committed by a chronic felony offender.

6. Any offense that is properly joined to an offense listed in this subsection.

C. A criminal prosecution shall be brought against a juvenile in the same manner as an adult if the juvenile has been accused of a criminal offense and has a historical prior felony conviction.

D. At the time the county attorney files a complaint or indictment the county attorney shall file a notice stating that the juvenile is a chronic felony offender. Subject to subsection E of this section, the notice shall establish and confer jurisdiction over the juvenile as a chronic felony offender.

E. On motion of the juvenile the court shall hold a hearing after arraignment and before trial to determine if a juvenile is a chronic felony offender. At the hearing the state shall prove by a preponderance of the evidence that the juvenile is a chronic felony offender. If the court does not find that the juvenile is a chronic felony offender, the court shall transfer the juvenile to the juvenile court pursuant to section 8-302. If the court finds that the juvenile is a chronic felony offender or if the juvenile does not file a motion to determine if the juvenile is a chronic felony offender, the criminal prosecution shall continue.

F. Except as provided in section 13-921, a person who is charged pursuant to this section shall be sentenced in the criminal court in the same manner as an adult for any offense for which the person is convicted.

G. Unless otherwise provided by law, nothing in this section shall be construed as to confer jurisdiction in the juvenile court over any person who is eighteen years of age or older.

H. For the purposes of this section:

1. "Accused" means a juvenile against whom a complaint, information or indictment is filed.

2. "Chronic felony offender" means a juvenile who has had two prior and separate adjudications and dispositions for conduct that would constitute a historical prior felony conviction if the juvenile had been tried as an adult.

3. "Forcible sexual assault" means sexual assault pursuant to section 13-1406 that is committed without consent as defined in section 13-1401, paragraph 7, subdivision (a).

4. "Other violent felony offense" means:

(a) Aggravated assault pursuant to section 13-1204, subsection A, paragraph 1.

(b) Aggravated assault pursuant to section 13-1204, subsection A, paragraph 2 involving the use of a deadly weapon.

(c) Drive by shooting pursuant to section 13-1209.

(d) Discharging a firearm at a structure pursuant to section 13-1211.

13-502. Insanity test; burden of proof; guilty except insane verdict

A. A person may be found guilty except insane if at the time of the commission of the criminal act the person was afflicted with a mental disease or defect of such severity that the person did not know the criminal act was wrong. A mental disease or defect constituting legal insanity is an affirmative defense. Mental disease or defect does not include disorders that result from acute voluntary intoxication or withdrawal from alcohol or drugs, character defects, psychosexual disorders or impulse control disorders. Conditions that do not constitute legal insanity include but are not limited to momentary, temporary conditions arising from the pressure of the circumstances, moral decadence, depravity or passion growing out of anger, jealousy, revenge, hatred or other motives in a person who does not suffer from a mental disease or defect or an abnormality that is manifested only by criminal conduct.

B. In a case involving the death or serious physical injury of or the threat of death or serious physical injury to another person, if a plea of insanity is made and the court determines that a reasonable basis exists to support the plea, the court may commit the defendant to a secure state mental health facility under the department of health services, a secure county mental health evaluation and treatment facility or another secure licensed mental health facility for up to thirty days for mental health evaluation and treatment. Experts at the mental health facility who are licensed pursuant to title 32, who are familiar with this state's insanity statutes, who are specialists in mental diseases and defects and who are knowledgeable concerning insanity shall observe and evaluate the defendant. The expert or experts who examine the defendant shall submit a written report of the evaluation to the court, the defendant's attorney and the prosecutor. The court shall order the defendant to pay the costs of the mental health facility to the clerk of the court. The clerk of the court shall transmit the reimbursements to the mental health facility for all of its costs. If the court finds the defendant is indigent or otherwise is unable to pay all or any of the costs, the court shall order the county to reimburse the mental health facility for the remainder of the costs. Notwithstanding section 36-545.02, the mental health facility may maintain the reimbursements. If the court does not commit the defendant to a secure state mental health facility, a secure county mental health evaluation and treatment facility or another secure licensed mental health facility, the court shall appoint an independent expert who is licensed pursuant to title 32, who is familiar with this state's insanity statutes, who is a specialist in mental diseases and defects and who is knowledgeable concerning insanity to observe and evaluate the defendant. The expert who examines the defendant shall submit a written report of the evaluation to the court, the defendant's attorney and the prosecutor. The court shall order the defendant to pay the costs of the services of the independent expert to the clerk of the court. The clerk of the court shall transmit the reimbursements to the expert. If the court finds the defendant is indigent or otherwise unable to pay all or any of the costs, the court shall order the county to reimburse the expert for the remainder of the costs. This subsection does not prohibit the defendant or this state from obtaining additional psychiatric examinations by other mental health experts who are licensed pursuant to title 32, who are familiar with this state's insanity statutes, who are specialists in mental diseases and defects and who are knowledgeable concerning insanity.

C. The defendant shall prove the defendant's legal insanity by clear and convincing evidence.

D. If the finder of fact finds the defendant guilty except insane, the court shall determine the sentence the defendant could have received pursuant to section 13-707 or section 13-751, subsection A or the presumptive sentence the defendant could have received pursuant to section 13-702, section 13-703, section 13-704, section 13-705, section 13-706, subsection A, section 13-710 or section 13-1406 if the defendant had not been found insane, and the judge shall sentence the defendant to a term of incarceration in the state department of corrections and shall order the defendant to be placed under the jurisdiction of the psychiatric security review board and committed to a state mental health facility under the department of health services pursuant to section 13-3994 for that term. In making this determination the court shall not consider the sentence enhancements for prior convictions under section 13-703 or 13-704. The court shall expressly identify each act that the defendant committed and separately find whether each act involved the death or physical injury of or a substantial threat of death or physical injury to another person.

E. A guilty except insane verdict is not a criminal conviction for sentencing enhancement purposes under section 13-703 or 13-704.

13-503. Effect of alcohol or drug use

Temporary intoxication resulting from the voluntary ingestion, consumption, inhalation or injection of alcohol, an illegal substance under chapter 34 of this title or other psychoactive substances or the abuse of prescribed medications does not constitute insanity and is not a defense for any criminal act or requisite state of mind.

13-504. Persons under eighteen years of age; juvenile transfer

A. On the motion of a juvenile or on the court's own motion, the court, if a juvenile is being prosecuted in the same manner as an adult pursuant to section 13-501, subsection B, shall hold a hearing to determine if jurisdiction of the criminal prosecution should be transferred to the juvenile court.

B. Notwithstanding subsection A of this section, the court shall hold a hearing if a juvenile is prosecuted in the same manner as an adult pursuant to section 13-501, subsection B for an offense that was committed more than twelve months before the date of the filing of the criminal charge.

C. If the court finds by clear and convincing evidence that public safety and the rehabilitation of the juvenile, if adjudicated delinquent, would be best served by transferring the prosecution to the juvenile court, the judge shall order the juvenile transferred to the juvenile court. On transfer, the court shall order that the juvenile be taken to a place of detention designated by the juvenile court or to that court or shall release the juvenile to the custody of the juvenile's parent or guardian or other person legally responsible for the juvenile. If the juvenile is released to the juvenile's parent or guardian or other person legally responsible for the juvenile, the court shall require that the parent, guardian or other person bring the juvenile to appear before the juvenile court at a designated time. The juvenile court shall then proceed with all further proceedings as if a petition alleging delinquency had been filed with the juvenile court under section 8-301.

D. The court shall consider the following factors in determining whether public safety and the juvenile's rehabilitation, if adjudicated delinquent, would be served by the transfer:

1. The seriousness of the offense involved.

2. The record and previous history of the juvenile, including previous contacts with the court and law enforcement, previous periods of any court ordered probation and the results of that probation.

3. Any previous commitments of the juvenile to juvenile residential placements or other secure institutions.

4. Whether the juvenile was previously committed to the department of juvenile corrections for a felony offense.

5. Whether the juvenile committed another felony offense while the juvenile was a ward of the department of juvenile corrections.

6. Whether the juvenile committed the alleged offense while participating in, assisting, promoting or furthering the interests of a criminal street gang, a criminal syndicate or a racketeering enterprise.

7. The views of the victim of the offense.

8. Whether the degree of the juvenile's participation in the offense was relatively minor but not so minor as to constitute a defense to prosecution.

9. The juvenile's mental and emotional condition.

10. The likelihood of the juvenile's reasonable rehabilitation through the use of services and facilities that are currently available to the juvenile court.

E. At the conclusion of the transfer hearing, the court shall make a written determination whether the juvenile should be transferred to juvenile court. The court shall not defer the decision as to the transfer.

Chapter 6 Classification of offenses and authorized dispositions of offenders

13-601. Classification of offenses

A. Felonies are classified, for the purpose of sentence, into the following six categories:
1. Class 1 felonies.
2. Class 2 felonies.
3. Class 3 felonies.
4. Class 4 felonies.
5. Class 5 felonies.
6. Class 6 felonies.
B. Misdemeanors are classified, for the purpose of sentence, into the following three categories:
1. Class 1 misdemeanors.
2. Class 2 misdemeanors.
3. Class 3 misdemeanors.
C. Petty offenses are not classified.

13-602. Designation of offenses

A. The particular classification of each felony defined in this title is expressly designated in the section or chapter defining it. Any offense defined outside this title which is declared by law to be a felony without either specification of the classification or of the penalty is a class 5 felony.
B. The particular classification of each misdemeanor defined in this title is expressly designated in the section or chapter defining it. Any offense defined outside this title which is declared by law to be a misdemeanor without either specification of the classification or of the penalty is a class 2 misdemeanor.
C. Every petty offense in this title is expressly designated as such. Any offense defined outside this title without either designation as a felony or misdemeanor or specification of the classification or the penalty is a petty offense.
D. Any offense which is declared by law to be a felony, misdemeanor or petty offense without specification of the classification of such offense is punishable according to the penalty prescribed for such offense.
E. Any offense defined within or outside this title without designation as a felony, misdemeanor or petty offense is punishable according to the penalty prescribed for such offense.
F. Any offense defined outside this title with a specification of the classification of such offense is punishable according to the provisions of this title.
G. Any petty offense, class 3 misdemeanor or class 2 misdemeanor, except a violation of title 28, is deemed a minor nontraffic offense for the limited purpose of armed forces recruitment.

13-603. Authorized disposition of offenders

A. Every person convicted of any offense defined in this title or defined outside this title shall be sentenced in accordance with this chapter and chapters 7, 8 and 9 of this title unless otherwise provided by law.
B. If a person is convicted of an offense, the court, if authorized by chapter 9 of this title, may suspend the imposition or execution of sentence and grant such person a period of probation except as otherwise provided by law. The sentence is tentative to the extent that it may be altered or revoked in accordance with chapter 9 of this title, but for all other purposes it is a final judgment of conviction.

C. If a person is convicted of an offense, the court shall require the convicted person to make restitution to the person who is the victim of the crime or to the immediate family of the victim if the victim has died, in the full amount of the economic loss as determined by the court and in the manner as determined by the court or the court's designee pursuant to chapter 8 of this title. Restitution ordered pursuant to this subsection shall be paid to the clerk of the court for disbursement to the victim and is a criminal penalty for the purposes of a federal bankruptcy involving the person convicted of an offense.

D. If the court imposes probation it may also impose a fine as authorized by chapter 8 of this title.

E. If a person is convicted of an offense and not granted a period of probation, or when probation is revoked, any of the following sentences may be imposed:

1. A term of imprisonment authorized by this chapter or chapter 7 of this title.

2. A fine authorized by chapter 8 of this title. The sentence is tentative to the extent it may be modified or revoked in accordance with chapter 8 of this title, but for all other purposes it is a final judgment of conviction. If the conviction is of a class 2, 3 or 4 felony, the sentence cannot consist solely of a fine.

3. Both imprisonment and a fine.

4. Intensive probation, subject to the provisions of chapter 9 of this title.

5. Intensive probation, subject to the provisions of chapter 9 of this title, and a fine.

6. A new term of probation or intensive probation.

F. If an enterprise is convicted of any offense, a fine may be imposed as authorized by chapter 8 of this title.

G. If a person or an enterprise is convicted of any felony, the court may, in addition to any other sentence authorized by law, order the forfeiture, suspension or revocation of any charter, license, permit or prior approval granted to the person or enterprise by any department or agency of the state or of any political subdivision.

H. A court authorized to pass sentence upon a person convicted of any offense defined within or without this title shall have a duty to determine and impose the punishment prescribed for such offense.

I. If a person is convicted of a felony offense and the court sentences the person to a term of imprisonment, the court at the time of sentencing shall impose on the convicted person a term of community supervision. The term of community supervision shall be served consecutively to the actual period of imprisonment if the person signs and agrees to abide by conditions of supervision established by the state department of corrections. Except pursuant to subsection J, the term of community supervision imposed by the court shall be for a period equal to one day for every seven days of the sentence or sentences imposed.

J. In calculating the term of community supervision, all fractions shall be decreased to the nearest month, except for a class 5 or 6 felony which shall not be less than one month.

K. Notwithstanding subsection I, if the court sentences a person to serve a consecutive term of probation immediately after the person serves a term of imprisonment, the court may waive community supervision and order that the person begin serving the term of probation upon the person's release from confinement. The court may retroactively waive the term of community supervision or that part remaining to be served if the community supervision was imposed before July 21, 1997. If the court waives community supervision, the term of probation imposed shall be equal to or greater than the term of community supervision that would have been imposed. If the court does not waive community supervision, the person shall begin serving the term of probation after the person serves the term of community supervision. The state department of corrections shall provide reasonable notice to the probation department of the scheduled release of the inmate from confinement by the department.

L. If at the time of sentencing the court is of the opinion that a sentence that the law requires the court to impose is clearly excessive, the court may enter a special order allowing the person sentenced to petition the board of executive clemency for a commutation of sentence within ninety days after the person is committed to the custody of the state department of corrections. If the court enters a special order regarding commutation, the court shall set forth in writing its specific reasons for concluding that the sentence is clearly excessive. The court shall allow both the state and the victim to submit a written statement on the matter. The court's order, and reasons for its order, and the statements of the state and the victim shall be sent to the board of executive clemency.

13-604. Class 6 felony; designation

A. Notwithstanding any other provision of this title, if a person is convicted of any class 6 felony not involving a dangerous offense and if the court, having regard to the nature and circumstances of the crime and to the history and character of the defendant, is of the opinion that it would be unduly harsh to sentence the defendant for a felony, the court may enter judgment of conviction for a class 1 misdemeanor and make disposition accordingly or may place the defendant on probation in accordance with chapter 9 of this title and refrain from designating the offense as a felony or misdemeanor until the probation is terminated. The offense shall be treated as a felony for all purposes until such time as the court may actually enter an order designating the offense a misdemeanor. This subsection does not apply to any person who stands convicted of a class 6 felony and who has previously been convicted of two or more felonies.

B. If a crime or public offense is punishable in the discretion of the court by a sentence as a class 6 felony or a class 1 misdemeanor, the offense shall be deemed a misdemeanor if the prosecuting attorney files any of the following:

1. An information in superior court designating the offense as a misdemeanor.

2. A complaint in justice court or municipal court designating the offense as a misdemeanor within the jurisdiction of the respective court.

3. A complaint, with the consent of the defendant, before or during the preliminary hearing amending the complaint to charge a misdemeanor.

13-605. Diagnostic commitment

A. If after presentence investigation, the court desires more detailed information as a basis for determining the sentence to be imposed, it may commit the defendant to the custody of the department of corrections. The director of the department of corrections shall accept the commitment only when adequate staff and facilities are available. The notice to the court of acceptance of the commitment shall specify the time and place the defendant is to be received. The commitment shall not exceed ninety days. The department during that period shall conduct a complete study of the prisoner and shall by the expiration of the period of commitment return the prisoner to the court and provide the court with a written report of the results of the study, including whatever recommendations the department believes will be helpful in determining disposition of the case. After receiving the report and recommendations, if the court does not order a further diagnostic commitment under subsection B of this section, it shall sentence the defendant as authorized by section 13-603.

B. If after presentence investigation the court desires more detailed information about the defendant's mental condition, it may commit or refer the defendant to the custody of any diagnostic facility for the performance of psychiatric evaluation. The commitment or referral shall be for a period not to exceed ninety days. Within that period the facility shall return the prisoner to court and transmit to the court a diagnostic report, including whatever recommendations the facility may wish to make. After receiving the report and recommendations, if the court does not order a further diagnostic commitment under subsection A of this section, it shall sentence the defendant as authorized by section 13-603 or invoke the provisions of section 13-606.

C. In an appropriate case the court in its discretion may order diagnostic commitments under both subsections A and B of this section.

D. If after receiving a diagnostic report under subsection A or B of this section the court sentences the defendant to imprisonment, the period of commitment under either or both shall be credited to the sentence imposed.

13-606. Civil commitment after imposition of sentence

A. If, after imposition of sentence authorized by section 13-603 and on the basis of the report and recommendations submitted to the court under subsection B of section 13-605, the court believes that the defendant discloses symptoms of mental disorder, the court may proceed as provided in chapter 5 of title 36.

B. After termination of the commitment in subsection A of this section, the defendant shall be returned to the court for release or to serve the unexpired term imposed as authorized by section 13-

603. The period of confinement pursuant to the civil commitment shall be credited to the sentence imposed.

13-607. Judgment of guilt and sentence document; fingerprint; contents of document; recitations

A. At the time of sentencing a person convicted of a felony offense, a violation of section 13-1802 or 13-1805, a domestic violence offense as defined in section 13-3601 or a violation of chapter 14 of this title or title 28, chapter 4, the court shall execute a judgment of guilt and sentence document or minute order as prescribed by this section.

B. The court or a person appointed by the court shall at the time of sentencing and in open court either permanently affix a defendant's fingerprint to the document or order or obtain and record the defendant's two fingerprint biometric-based identifier in the court case file.

C. The document or order shall recite all of the following in addition to any information deemed appropriate by the court:

1. The defendant's full name and date of birth.

2. The name of the counsel for the defendant or, if counsel was waived, the fact that the defendant knowingly, voluntarily and intelligently waived the defendant's right to counsel after having been fully apprised of the defendant's right to counsel.

3. The name, statutory citation and classification of the offense.

4. Whether there was a finding by the trier of fact that the offense was of a dangerous or repetitive nature pursuant to section 13-703 or 13-704 or was committed while released from confinement pursuant to section 13-708.

5. Whether the basis of the finding of guilt was by trial to a jury or to the court, or by plea of guilty or no contest.

6. That there was a knowing, voluntary and intelligent waiver of the right to a jury trial if the finding of guilt was based on a trial to the court.

7. That there was a knowing, voluntary and intelligent waiver of all pertinent rights if the finding of guilt was based on a plea of guilty or no contest.

8. A certification by the court or the clerk of the court that at the time of sentencing and in open court that either the defendant's fingerprint was permanently affixed to the document or order or the defendant's two fingerprint biometric-based identifier was obtained and recorded in the court case file.

D. The document or order shall be made a permanent part of the public records of the court, and the recitations contained in the document or order are prima facie evidence of the facts stated in the recitations.

E. If the supreme court has authorized the clerk of the court to maintain an electronic court record, the clerk may maintain only an electronic reproduction or image of the original document or order.

13-608. Chronic felony offenders; disposition; notice

A. If a juvenile is prosecuted as a chronic felony offender pursuant to section 13-501, subsection A or B, is convicted of a felony in criminal court and is placed on probation, the juvenile shall be incarcerated in the county jail for a period of not more than one year as a condition of probation.

B. If a juvenile is prosecuted as a chronic felony offender pursuant to section 13-501, subsection A or B in criminal court and is convicted of a felony in criminal court, the court shall provide the following written notice to the juvenile:

You have been convicted as a chronic felony offender and you now have a historical prior felony conviction. You are now on notice that if you commit another felony offense, you will be tried as an adult in the criminal division of the superior court and you will be subject to mandatory sentencing.

C. The failure or inability of the court to provide the notice required by subsection B of this section does not preclude the use of the prior conviction for any purpose otherwise permitted.

13-609. Transfer of criminal justice information; definition

A. If a person is found incompetent by a court pursuant to rule 11, Arizona rules of criminal procedure, the court shall transmit the case information and the date of the incompetency finding to the supreme court. The supreme court shall transmit the case information and the date of the incompetency finding to the department of public safety. The department of public safety shall transmit the case information and the date of the incompetency finding to the national instant criminal background check system.

B. If a person is subsequently found competent, the court shall transmit the case information to the supreme court. The supreme court shall transmit the finding of competency to the department of public safety. The department of public safety shall transmit the finding of competency to the national instant criminal background check system.

C. If a person is found guilty except insane, the court shall transmit the case information and the date of the verdict to the supreme court. The supreme court shall transmit the case information and the date of the verdict to the department of public safety. The department of public safety shall transmit the case information and the date of the verdict to the national instant criminal background check system.

D. On request, the clerk of the court that originally found the defendant incompetent or in which the defendant was found guilty except insane shall provide certified copies of the order to a law enforcement or prosecuting agency that is investigating or prosecuting a prohibited possessor as defined in section 13-3101.

E. For the purposes of this section, "case information" means the person's name, sex and date of birth, the last four digits of the person's social security number, if available, the court case number and the court originating agency identification number.

13-610. DNA testing

A. Within thirty days after a person is sentenced to the state department of corrections or a person who is accepted under the interstate compact for the supervision of parolees and probationers arrives in this state, the state department of corrections shall secure a sufficient sample of blood or other bodily substances for deoxyribonucleic acid testing and extraction from the person if the person was convicted of an offense listed in this section and was sentenced to a term of imprisonment or was convicted of any offense that was committed in another jurisdiction that if committed in this state would be a violation of any offense listed in this section and the person is under the supervision of the state department of corrections. The state department of corrections shall transmit the sample to the department of public safety.

B. Within thirty days after a person is placed on probation and sentenced to a term of incarceration in a county jail detention facility or is detained in a county juvenile detention facility, the county detention facility shall secure a sufficient sample of blood or other bodily substances for deoxyribonucleic acid testing and extraction from the person if the person was convicted of or adjudicated delinquent for an offense listed in this section. The county detention facility shall transmit the sample to the department of public safety.

C. Within thirty days after a person is convicted and placed on probation without a term of incarceration or adjudicated delinquent and placed on probation, the county probation department shall secure a sufficient sample of blood or other bodily substances for deoxyribonucleic acid testing and extraction from the person if the person was convicted of or adjudicated delinquent for an offense listed in this section. The county probation department shall transmit the sample to the department of public safety.

D. Within thirty days after the arrival of a person who is accepted under the interstate compact for the supervision of parolees and probationers and who is under the supervision of a county probation department, the county probation department shall secure a sufficient sample of blood or other bodily substances for deoxyribonucleic acid testing and extraction from the person if the person was convicted of an offense that was committed in another jurisdiction that if committed in this state would be a violation of any offense listed in this section and was sentenced to a term of probation. The county probation department shall transmit the sample to the department of public safety.

E. Within thirty days after a juvenile is committed to the department of juvenile corrections, the department of juvenile corrections shall secure a sufficient sample of blood or other bodily substances for deoxyribonucleic acid testing and extraction from the youth if the youth was adjudicated delinquent for an offense listed in this section and was committed to a secure care facility. The department of juvenile corrections shall transmit the sample to the department of public safety.

F. Within thirty days after the arrival in this state of a juvenile who is accepted by the department of juvenile corrections pursuant to the interstate compact on juveniles and who was adjudicated for an offense that was committed in another jurisdiction that if committed in this state would be a violation of any offense listed in this section, the compact administrator shall request that the sending state impose as a condition of supervision that the juvenile submit a sufficient sample of blood or other bodily substances for deoxyribonucleic acid testing. If the sending state does not impose that condition, the department of juvenile corrections shall request a sufficient sample of blood or other bodily substances for deoxyribonucleic acid testing within thirty days after the juvenile's arrival in this state. The department of juvenile corrections shall transmit the sample to the department of public safety.

G. Notwithstanding subsections A through F, K, L and O of this section, the agency that is responsible for securing a sample pursuant to this section shall not secure the sample if the scientific criminal analysis section of the department of public safety has previously received and is maintaining a sample sufficient for deoxyribonucleic acid testing.

H. The department of public safety shall do all of the following:

1. Conduct or oversee through mutual agreement an analysis of the samples that it receives pursuant to subsections K, L and O of this section.

2. Make and maintain a report of the results of each deoxyribonucleic acid analysis.

3. Maintain samples of blood and other bodily substances for at least thirty-five years.

I. Any sample and the result of any test that is obtained pursuant to this section or section 8-238 may be used only as follows:

1. For law enforcement identification purposes.

2. In a proceeding in a criminal prosecution or juvenile adjudication.

3. In a proceeding under title 36, chapter 37.

J. If the conviction or adjudication of a person who is subject to this section or section 8-238 is overturned on appeal or postconviction relief and a final mandate has been issued, on petition of the person to the superior court in the county in which the conviction occurred, the court shall order that the person's deoxyribonucleic acid profile resulting from that conviction or adjudication be expunged from the Arizona deoxyribonucleic acid identification system established by section 41-2418 unless the person has been convicted or adjudicated delinquent of another offense that would require the person to submit to deoxyribonucleic acid testing pursuant to this section.

K. If a person is arrested for any offense listed in subsection O, paragraph 3 of this section and is transferred by the arresting authority to a state, county or local law enforcement agency or jail, the arresting authority or its designee shall secure a sufficient sample of buccal cells or other bodily substances for deoxyribonucleic acid testing and extraction from the person for the purpose of determining identification characteristics. The arresting authority or its designee shall transmit the sample to the department of public safety.

L. A person who is charged with a felony or misdemeanor offense listed in subsection O, paragraph 3 of this section and who is summoned to appear in court for an initial appearance shall report within five days of release on bail or on the person's own recognizance to the law enforcement agency that investigated the person or its designee and submit a sufficient sample of buccal cells or other bodily substances for deoxyribonucleic acid testing and extraction. The arresting authority or its designee shall transmit the sample to the department of public safety.

M. A person who is subject to subsection K or L of this section or section 8-238 may petition the superior court in the county in which the arrest occurred or the criminal charge was filed to order that the person's deoxyribonucleic acid profile and sample be expunged from the Arizona deoxyribonucleic acid identification system, unless the person has been arrested, charged with or convicted of or adjudicated delinquent of another offense that would require the person to submit to deoxyribonucleic acid testing pursuant to this section, if any of the following applies:

1. The criminal charges are not filed within the applicable period prescribed by section 13-107.

2. The criminal charges are dismissed.

3. The person is acquitted at trial.

N. If any sample that is submitted to the department of public safety under this section or section 8-238 is found to be unacceptable for analysis and use or cannot be used by the department, the department shall require that another sample of blood or other bodily substances be secured pursuant to this section.

O. This section applies to persons who are:

1. Convicted of any felony offense.

2. Adjudicated delinquent for any of the following offenses:

(a) A violation or an attempt to violate any offense in chapter 11 of this title, any felony offense in chapter 14 or 35.1 of this title or section 13-1507, 13-1508 or 13-3608.

(b) Any offense for which a person is required to register pursuant to section 13-3821.

(c) A violation of any felony offense in chapter 34 of this title that may be prosecuted pursuant to section 13-501, subsection B, paragraph 2.

(d) A violation of any felony offense that is listed in section 13-501.

3. Arrested for a violation of any offense in chapter 11 of this title, a violation of section 13-1402, 13-1403, 13-1404, 13-1405, 13-1406, 13-1410, 13-1411, 13-1417, 13-1507, 13-1508, 13-3208, 13-3214, 13-3555 or 13-3608 or a violation of any serious offense as defined in section 13-706 that is a dangerous offense.

Chapter 7 Sentencing and Imprisonment

13-701. Sentence of imprisonment for felony; presentence report; aggravating and mitigating factors; consecutive terms of imprisonment; definition

A. A sentence of imprisonment for a felony shall be a definite term of years and the person sentenced, unless otherwise provided by law, shall be committed to the custody of the state department of corrections.

B. No prisoner may be transferred to the custody of the state department of corrections without a certified copy of the judgment and sentence, signed by the sentencing judge, and a copy of a recent presentence investigation report unless the court has waived preparation of the report.

C. The minimum or maximum term imposed pursuant to section 13-702, 13-703, 13-704, 13-705, 13-708, 13-710, 13-1406, 13-3212 or 13-3419 may be imposed only if one or more of the circumstances alleged to be in aggravation of the crime are found to be true by the trier of fact beyond a reasonable doubt or are admitted by the defendant, except that an alleged aggravating circumstance under subsection D, paragraph 11 of this section shall be found to be true by the court, or in mitigation of the crime are found to be true by the court, on any evidence or information introduced or submitted to the court or the trier of fact before sentencing or any evidence presented at trial, and factual findings and reasons in support of such findings are set forth on the record at the time of sentencing.

D. For the purpose of determining the sentence pursuant to subsection C of this section, the trier of fact shall determine and the court shall consider the following aggravating circumstances, except that the court shall determine an aggravating circumstance under paragraph 11 of this subsection:

1. Infliction or threatened infliction of serious physical injury, except if this circumstance is an essential element of the offense of conviction or has been utilized to enhance the range of punishment under section 13-704.

2. Use, threatened use or possession of a deadly weapon or dangerous instrument during the commission of the crime, except if this circumstance is an essential element of the offense of conviction or has been utilized to enhance the range of punishment under section 13-704.

3. If the offense involves the taking of or damage to property, the value of the property taken or damaged.

4. Presence of an accomplice.

5. Especially heinous, cruel or depraved manner in which the offense was committed.

6. The defendant committed the offense as consideration for the receipt, or in the expectation of the receipt, of anything of pecuniary value.

7. The defendant procured the commission of the offense by payment, or promise of payment, of anything of pecuniary value.

8. At the time of the commission of the offense, the defendant was a public servant and the offense involved conduct directly related to the defendant's office or employment.

9. The victim or, if the victim has died as a result of the conduct of the defendant, the victim's immediate family suffered physical, emotional or financial harm.

10. During the course of the commission of the offense, the death of an unborn child at any stage of its development occurred.

11. The defendant was previously convicted of a felony within the ten years immediately preceding the date of the offense. A conviction outside the jurisdiction of this state for an offense that if committed in this state would be punishable as a felony is a felony conviction for the purposes of this paragraph.

12. The defendant was wearing body armor as defined in section 13-3116.

13. The victim of the offense is at least sixty-five years of age or is a person with a disability as defined in section 38-492, subsection B.

14. The defendant was appointed pursuant to title 14 as a fiduciary and the offense involved conduct directly related to the defendant's duties to the victim as fiduciary.

15. Evidence that the defendant committed the crime out of malice toward a victim because of the victim's identity in a group listed in section 41-1750, subsection A, paragraph 3 or because of the defendant's perception of the victim's identity in a group listed in section 41-1750, subsection A, paragraph 3.

16. The defendant was convicted of a violation of section 13-1102, section 13-1103, section 13-1104, subsection A, paragraph 3 or section 13-1204, subsection A, paragraph 1 or 2 arising from an act that was committed while driving a motor vehicle and the defendant's alcohol concentration at the time of committing the offense was 0.15 or more. For the purposes of this paragraph, "alcohol concentration" has the same meaning prescribed in section 28-101.

17. Lying in wait for the victim or ambushing the victim during the commission of any felony.

18. The offense was committed in the presence of a child and any of the circumstances exists that are set forth in section 13-3601, subsection A.

19. The offense was committed in retaliation for a victim either reporting criminal activity or being involved in an organization, other than a law enforcement agency, that is established for the purpose of reporting or preventing criminal activity.

20. The defendant was impersonating a peace officer as defined in section 1-215.

21. The defendant was in violation of 8 United States Code section 1323, 1324, 1325, 1326 or 1328 at the time of the commission of the offense.

22. The defendant used a remote stun gun or an authorized remote stun gun in the commission of the offense. For the purposes of this paragraph:

(a) "Authorized remote stun gun" means a remote stun gun that has all of the following:

(i) An electrical discharge that is less than one hundred thousand volts and less than nine joules of energy per pulse.

(ii) A serial or identification number on all projectiles that are discharged from the remote stun gun.

(iii) An identification and tracking system that, on deployment of remote electrodes, disperses coded material that is traceable to the purchaser through records that are kept by the manufacturer on all remote stun guns and all individual cartridges sold.

(iv) A training program that is offered by the manufacturer.

(b) "Remote stun gun" means an electronic device that emits an electrical charge and that is designed and primarily employed to incapacitate a person or animal either through contact with electrodes on the device itself or remotely through wired probes that are attached to the device or through a spark, plasma, ionization or other conductive means emitting from the device.

23. During or immediately following the commission of the offense, the defendant committed a violation of section 28-661, 28-662 or 28-663.

24. The defendant was convicted of a violation of section 13-1307 or 13-1308 or section 13-3212, subsection A, paragraph 9 or 10 and the defendant recruited, enticed or obtained the victim from a shelter that is designed to serve runaway youth, foster children, homeless persons or victims of human trafficking, domestic violence or sexual assault.

25. The defendant was convicted of a violation of section 13-1204 and there is evidence that the defendant committed the crime out of malice toward a victim because of the victim's employment as a peace officer.

26. Any other factor that the state alleges is relevant to the defendant's character or background or to the nature or circumstances of the crime.

E. For the purpose of determining the sentence pursuant to subsection C of this section, the court shall consider the following mitigating circumstances:

1. The age of the defendant.

2. The defendant's capacity to appreciate the wrongfulness of the defendant's conduct or to conform the defendant's conduct to the requirements of law was significantly impaired, but not so impaired as to constitute a defense to prosecution.

3. The defendant was under unusual or substantial duress, although not to a degree that would constitute a defense to prosecution.

4. The degree of the defendant's participation in the crime was minor, although not so minor as to constitute a defense to prosecution.

5. During or immediately following the commission of the offense, the defendant complied with all duties imposed under sections 28-661, 28-662 and 28-663.

6. Any other factor that is relevant to the defendant's character or background or to the nature or circumstances of the crime and that the court finds to be mitigating.

F. If the trier of fact finds at least one aggravating circumstance, the trial court may find by a preponderance of the evidence additional aggravating circumstances. In determining what sentence to impose, the court shall take into account the amount of aggravating circumstances and whether the amount of mitigating circumstances is sufficiently substantial to justify the lesser term. If the trier of fact finds aggravating circumstances and the court does not find any mitigating circumstances, the court shall impose an aggravated sentence.

G. The court in imposing a sentence shall consider the evidence and opinions presented by the victim or the victim's immediate family at any aggravation or mitigation proceeding or in the presentence report.

H. This section does not affect any provision of law that imposes the death penalty, that expressly provides for imprisonment for life or that authorizes or restricts the granting of probation and suspending the execution of sentence.

I. The intentional failure by the court to impose the mandatory sentences or probation conditions provided in this title is malfeasance.

J. For the purposes of this section, "trier of fact" means a jury, unless the defendant and the state waive a jury in which case the trier of fact means the court.

13-702. First time felony offenders; sentencing; definition

A. Unless a specific sentence is otherwise provided, the term of imprisonment for a first felony offense shall be the presumptive sentence determined pursuant to subsection D of this section. Except for those felonies involving a dangerous offense or if a specific sentence is otherwise provided, the court may increase or reduce the presumptive sentence within the ranges set by subsection D of this section. Any reduction or increase shall be based on the aggravating and mitigating circumstances listed in section 13-701, subsections D and E and shall be within the ranges prescribed in subsection D of this section.

B. If a person is convicted of a felony without having previously been convicted of any felony and if at least two of the aggravating factors listed in section 13-701, subsection D apply, the court may increase the maximum term of imprisonment otherwise authorized for that offense to an aggravated term. If a person is convicted of a felony without having previously been convicted of any felony and if the court finds at least two mitigating factors listed in section 13-701, subsection E apply, the court may decrease the minimum term of imprisonment otherwise authorized for that offense to a mitigated term.

C. The aggravated or mitigated term imposed pursuant to subsection D of this section may be imposed only if at least two of the aggravating circumstances are found beyond a reasonable doubt to be true by the trier of fact or are admitted by the defendant, except that an aggravating circumstance under section 13-701, subsection D, paragraph 11 shall be found to be true by the court, or in mitigation of the crime are found to be true by the court, on any evidence or information introduced or submitted to the court or the trier of fact before sentencing or any evidence presented at trial, and factual findings and reasons in support of these findings are set forth on the record at the time of sentencing.

D. The term of imprisonment for a presumptive, minimum, maximum, mitigated or aggravated sentence shall be within the range prescribed under this subsection. The terms are as follows:

Felony	Mitigated	Minimum	Presumptive	Maximum	Aggravated
Class 2	3 years	4 years	5 years	10 years	12.5 years
Class 3	2 years	2.5 years	3.5 years	7 years	8.75 years
Class 4	1 year	1.5 years	2.5 years	3 years	3.75 years
Class 5	.5 years	.75 years	1.5 years	2 years	2.5 years
Class 6	.33 years	.5 years	1 year	1.5 years	2 years

E. The court shall inform all of the parties before sentencing occurs of its intent to increase or decrease a sentence to the aggravated or mitigated sentence pursuant this section. If the court fails to inform the parties, a party waives its right to be informed unless the party timely objects at the time of sentencing.

F. For the purposes of this section, "trier of fact" means a jury, unless the defendant and the state waive a jury in which case the trier of fact means the court.

13-703. Repetitive offenders; sentencing

A. If a person is convicted of multiple felony offenses that were not committed on the same occasion but that either are consolidated for trial purposes or are not historical prior felony convictions, the person shall be sentenced as a first time felony offender pursuant to section 13-702 for the first offense, as a category one repetitive offender for the second offense, and as a category two repetitive offender for the third and subsequent offenses.

B. Except as provided in section 13-704 or 13-705, a person shall be sentenced as a category two repetitive offender if the person is at least eighteen years of age or has been tried as an adult and stands convicted of a felony and has one historical prior felony conviction.

C. Except as provided in section 13-704 or 13-705, a person shall be sentenced as a category three repetitive offender if the person is at least eighteen years of age or has been tried as an adult and stands convicted of a felony and has two or more historical prior felony convictions.

D. The presumptive term set by this section may be aggravated or mitigated within the range under this section pursuant to section 13-701, subsections C, D and E.

E. If a person is sentenced as a category one repetitive offender pursuant to subsection A of this section and if at least two aggravating circumstances listed in section 13-701, subsection D apply or at least two mitigating circumstances listed in section 13-701, subsection E apply, the court may impose a mitigated or aggravated sentence pursuant to subsection H of this section.

F. If a person is sentenced as a category two repetitive offender pursuant to subsection A or B of this section and if at least two aggravating circumstances listed in section 13-701, subsection D apply or at least two mitigating circumstances listed in section 13-701, subsection E apply, the court may impose a mitigated or aggravated sentence pursuant to subsection I of this section.

G. If a person is sentenced as a category three repetitive offender pursuant to subsection C of this section and at least two aggravating circumstances listed in section 13-701, subsection D or at least two mitigating circumstances listed in section 13-701, subsection E apply, the court may impose a mitigated or aggravated sentence pursuant to subsection J of this section.

H. A category one repetitive offender shall be sentenced within the following ranges:

Felony	Mitigated	Minimum	Presumptive	Maximum	Aggravated
Class 2	3 years	4 years	5 years	10 years	12.5 years

Felony	Mitigated	Minimum	Presumptive	Maximum	Aggravated
Class 3	2 years	2.5 years	3.5 years	7 years	8.75 years
Class 4	1 year	1.5 years	2.5 years	3 years	3.75 years
Class 5	.5 years	.75 years	1.5 years	2 years	2.5 years
Class 6	.25 years	.5 years	1 year	1.5 years	2 years

I. A category two repetitive offender shall be sentenced within the following ranges:

Felony	Mitigated	Minimum	Presumptive	Maximum	Aggravated
Class 2	4.5 years	6 years	9.25 years	18.5 years	23 years
Class 3	3.25 years	4.5 years	6.5 years	13 years	16.25 years
Class 4	2.25 years	3 years	4.5 years	6 years	7.5 years
Class 5	1 year	1.5 years	2.25 years	3 years	3.75 years
Class 6	.75 years	1 year	1.75 years	2.25 years	2.75 years

J. A category three repetitive offender shall be sentenced within the following ranges:

Felony	Mitigated	Minimum	Presumptive	Maximum	Aggravated
Class 2	10.5 years	14 years	15.75 years	28 years	35 years
Class 3	7.5 years	10 years	11.25 years	20 years	25 years
Class 4	6 years	8 years	10 years	12 years	15 years
Class 5	3 years	4 years	5 years	6 years	7.5 years
Class 6	2.25 years	3 years	3.75 years	4.5 years	5.75 years

K. The aggravated or mitigated term imposed pursuant to subsection H, I or J of this section may be imposed only if at least two of the aggravating circumstances are found beyond a reasonable doubt to be true by the trier of fact or are admitted by the defendant, except that an aggravating circumstance under section 13-701, subsection D, paragraph 11 shall be found to be true by the court, or in mitigation of the crime are found to be true by the court, on any evidence or information introduced or submitted to the court or the trier of fact before sentencing or any evidence presented at trial, and factual findings and reasons in support of these findings are set forth on the record at the time of sentencing.

L. Convictions for two or more offenses committed on the same occasion shall be counted as only one conviction for the purposes of subsections B and C of this section.

M. A person who has been convicted in any court outside the jurisdiction of this state of an offense that was punishable by that jurisdiction as a felony is subject to this section. A person who has been convicted as an adult of an offense punishable as a felony under the provisions of any prior code in this state or the jurisdiction in which the offense was committed is subject to this section. A person who has been convicted of a felony weapons possession violation in any court outside the jurisdiction of this state that would not be punishable as a felony under the laws of this state is not subject to this section.

N. The penalties prescribed by this section shall be substituted for the penalties otherwise authorized by law if an allegation of prior conviction is charged in the indictment or information and admitted or found by the court. The release provisions prescribed by this section shall not be substituted for any penalties required by the substantive offense or a provision of law that specifies a later release or completion of the sentence imposed before release. The court shall allow the allegation of a prior conviction at any time before the date the case is actually tried unless the allegation is filed fewer than twenty days before the case is actually tried and the court finds on the record that the person was in fact prejudiced by the untimely filing and states the reasons for these findings. If the allegation of a prior conviction is filed, the state must make available to the person a copy of any material or information obtained concerning the prior conviction. The charge of previous conviction shall not be read to the jury. For the purposes of this subsection, "substantive offense" means the felony offense that the trier of fact found beyond a reasonable doubt the person committed. Substantive offense does not include allegations that, if proven, would enhance the sentence of imprisonment or fine to which the person otherwise would be subject.

O. A person who is sentenced pursuant to this section is not eligible for suspension of sentence, probation, pardon or release from confinement on any basis, except as specifically authorized by section 31-233, subsection A or B, until the sentence imposed by the court has been served, the person is eligible for release pursuant to section 41-1604.07 or the sentence is commuted.

P. The court shall inform all of the parties before sentencing occurs of its intent to impose an aggravated or mitigated sentence pursuant to subsection H, I or J of this section. If the court fails to inform the parties, a party waives its right to be informed unless the party timely objects at the time of sentencing.

Q. The court in imposing a sentence shall consider the evidence and opinions presented by the victim or the victim's immediate family at any aggravation or mitigation proceeding or in the presentence report.

13-704. Dangerous offenders; sentencing

A. Except as provided in section 13-705, a person who is at least eighteen years of age or who has been tried as an adult and who stands convicted of a felony that is a dangerous offense shall be sentenced to a term of imprisonment as follows:

Felony	Minimum	Presumptive	Maximum
Class 2	7 years	10.5 years	21 years
Class 3	5 years	7.5 years	15 years
Class 4	4 years	6 years	8 years
Class 5	2 years	3 years	4 years
Class 6	1.5 years	2.25 years	3 years

B. Except as provided in section 13-705, a person who is convicted of a class 4, 5 or 6 felony that is a dangerous offense and who has one historical prior felony conviction involving a dangerous offense shall be sentenced to a term of imprisonment as follows:

Felony	Minimum	Presumptive	Maximum
Class 4	8 years	10 years	12 years
Class 5	4 years	5 years	6 years
Class 6	3 years	3.75 years	4.5 years

C. Except as provided in section 13-705 or section 13-706, subsection A, a person who is convicted of a class 4, 5 or 6 felony that is a dangerous offense and who has two or more historical prior felony convictions involving dangerous offenses shall be sentenced to a term of imprisonment as follows:

Felony	Minimum	Presumptive	Maximum
Class 4	12 years	14 years	16 years
Class 5	6 years	7 years	8 years
Class 6	4.5 years	5.25 years	6 years

D. Except as provided in section 13-705 or section 13-706, subsection A, a person who is convicted of a class 2 or 3 felony involving a dangerous offense and who has one historical prior felony conviction that is a class 1, 2 or 3 felony involving a dangerous offense shall be sentenced to a term of imprisonment as follows:

Felony	Minimum	Presumptive	Maximum
Class 2	14 years*	15.75 years	28 years
Class 3	10 years	11.25 years	20 years

E. Except as provided in section 13-705 or section 13-706, subsection A, a person who is convicted of a class 2 or 3 felony involving a dangerous offense and who has two or more historical prior felony convictions that are class 1, 2 or 3 felonies involving dangerous offenses shall be sentenced to a term of imprisonment as follows:

Felony	Minimum	Presumptive	Maximum
Class 2	21 years	28 years	35 years
Class 3	15 years	20 years	25 years

F. A person who is convicted of two or more felony offenses that are dangerous offenses and that were not committed on the same occasion but that are consolidated for trial purposes or that are not historical prior felony convictions shall be sentenced, for the second or subsequent offense, pursuant to this subsection. For a person sentenced pursuant to this subsection, the minimum term prescribed shall be the presumptive term. If the court increases or decreases a sentence pursuant to this subsection, the court shall state on the record the reasons for the increase or decrease. The court shall inform all of the parties before the sentencing occurs of its intent to increase or decrease a sentence pursuant to this subsection. If the court fails to inform the parties, a party waives its right to be informed unless the party timely objects at the time of sentencing. The terms are as follows:

1. For the second dangerous offense:

Felony	Minimum	Maximum	Increased Maximum
Class 2	10.5 years	21 years	26.25 years
Class 3	7.5 years	15 years	18.75 years
Class 4	6 years	8 years	10 years
Class 5	3 years	4 years	5 years
Class 6	2.25 years	3 years	3.75 years

2. For any dangerous offense subsequent to the second dangerous felony offense:

Felony	Minimum	Maximum	Increased Maximum
Class 2	15.75 years	28 years	35 years
Class 3	11.25 years	20 years	25 years

Class 4   10 years   12 years   15 years
Class 5   5 years   6 years   7.5 years
Class 6   3.75 years   4.5 years   5.6 years

G. A person who is sentenced pursuant to subsection A, B, C, D, E or F of this section is not eligible for suspension of sentence, probation, pardon or release from confinement on any basis, except as specifically authorized by section 31-233, subsection A or B, until the sentence imposed by the court has been served, the person is eligible for release pursuant to section 41-1604.07 or the sentence is commuted.

H. The presumptive term authorized by this section may be mitigated or aggravated pursuant to the terms of section 13-701, subsections C, D and E.

I. For the purposes of determining the applicability of the penalties provided in subsection A, D or E of this section for second or subsequent class 2 or 3 felonies, the conviction for any felony committed before October 1, 1978 that, if committed after October 1, 1978, could be a dangerous offense under subsection A, D or E of this section may be designated by the state as a prior felony.

J. Convictions for two or more offenses committed on the same occasion shall be counted as only one conviction for the purposes of subsection A, B, C, D or E of this section.

K. A person who has been convicted in any court outside the jurisdiction of this state of an offense that was punishable by that jurisdiction as a felony is subject to subsection A, B, C, D or E of this section. A person who has been convicted of an offense punishable as a felony under the provisions of any prior code in this state or the jurisdiction in which the offense was committed is subject to subsection A, B, C, D or E of this section. A person who has been convicted of a felony weapons possession violation in any court outside the jurisdiction of this state that would not be punishable as a felony under the laws of this state is not subject to this section.

L. The penalties prescribed by this section shall be substituted for the penalties otherwise authorized by law if an allegation of prior conviction is charged in the indictment or information and admitted or found by the court or if an allegation of dangerous offense is charged in the indictment or information and admitted or found by the trier of fact. The release provisions prescribed by this section shall not be substituted for any penalties required by the substantive offense or provision of law that specifies a later release or completion of the sentence imposed before release. The court shall allow the allegation of a prior conviction or the allegation of a dangerous offense at any time before the date the case is actually tried unless the allegation is filed fewer than twenty days before the case is actually tried and the court finds on the record that the defendant was in fact prejudiced by the untimely filing and states the reasons for these findings. If the allegation of a prior conviction is filed, the state must make available to the defendant a copy of any material or information obtained concerning the prior conviction. The charge of prior conviction shall not be read to the jury. For the purposes of this subsection, "substantive offense" means the felony that the trier of fact found beyond a reasonable doubt the defendant committed. Substantive offense does not include allegations that, if proven, would enhance the sentence of imprisonment or fine to which the defendant otherwise would be subject.

M. Except as provided in section 13-705 or 13-751, if the victim is an unborn child in the womb at any stage of its development, the defendant shall be sentenced pursuant to this section.

13-705. Dangerous crimes against children; sentences; definitions

A. A person who is at least eighteen years of age and who is convicted of a dangerous crime against children in the first degree involving sexual assault of a minor who is twelve years of age or younger or sexual conduct with a minor who is twelve years of age or younger shall be sentenced to life imprisonment and is not eligible for suspension of sentence, probation, pardon or release from confinement on any basis except as specifically authorized by section 31-233, subsection A or B until the person has served thirty-five years or the sentence is commuted. This subsection does not apply to masturbatory contact.

B. Except as otherwise provided in this section, a person who is at least eighteen years of age or who has been tried as an adult and who is convicted of a dangerous crime against children in the first degree involving attempted first degree murder of a minor who is under twelve years of age, second degree murder of a minor who is under twelve years of age, sexual assault of a minor who is under twelve years of age, sexual conduct with a minor who is under twelve years of age or manufacturing methamphetamine under circumstances that cause physical injury to a minor who is under twelve years of age may be sentenced to life imprisonment and is not eligible for suspension of sentence, probation, pardon or release from confinement on any basis except as specifically authorized by section 31-233, subsection A or B until the person has served thirty-five years or the sentence is commuted. If a life sentence is not imposed pursuant to this subsection, the person shall be sentenced to a term of imprisonment as follows:

Minimum   Presumptive   Maximum

13 years   20 years   27 years

C. Except as otherwise provided in this section, a person who is at least eighteen years of age or who has been tried as an adult and who is convicted of a dangerous crime against children in the first degree involving attempted first degree murder of a minor who is twelve, thirteen or fourteen years of age, second degree murder of a minor who is twelve, thirteen or fourteen years of age, sexual assault of a minor who is twelve, thirteen or fourteen years of age, taking a child for the purpose of prostitution, child sex trafficking, sexual conduct with a minor who is twelve, thirteen or fourteen years of age, continuous sexual abuse of a child or manufacturing methamphetamine under circumstances that cause physical injury to a minor who is twelve, thirteen or fourteen years of age or involving or using minors in drug offenses shall be sentenced to a term of imprisonment as follows:

Minimum	Presumptive	Maximum
13 years	20 years	27 years

A person who has been previously convicted of one predicate felony shall be sentenced to a term of imprisonment as follows:

Minimum	Presumptive	Maximum
23 years	30 years	37 years

D. Except as otherwise provided in this section, a person who is at least eighteen years of age or who has been tried as an adult and who is convicted of a dangerous crime against children in the first degree involving aggravated assault, unlawful mutilation, molestation of a child, commercial sexual exploitation of a minor, sexual exploitation of a minor, aggravated luring a minor for sexual exploitation, child abuse or kidnapping shall be sentenced to a term of imprisonment as follows:

Minimum	Presumptive	Maximum
10 years	17 years	24 years

A person who has been previously convicted of one predicate felony shall be sentenced to a term of imprisonment as follows:

Minimum	Presumptive	Maximum
21 years	28 years	35 years

E. Except as otherwise provided in this section, if a person is at least eighteen years of age or has been tried as an adult and is convicted of a dangerous crime against children involving luring a minor for sexual exploitation or unlawful age misrepresentation and is sentenced to a term of imprisonment, the term of imprisonment is as follows and the person is not eligible for release from confinement on any basis except as specifically authorized by section 31-233, subsection A or B until the sentence imposed by the court has been served, the person is eligible for release pursuant to section 41-1604.07 or the sentence is commuted:

Minimum	Presumptive	Maximum
5 years	10 years	15 years

A person who has been previously convicted of one predicate felony shall be sentenced to a term of imprisonment as follows and the person is not eligible for suspension of sentence, probation, pardon or release from confinement on any basis except as specifically authorized by section 31-233, subsection A or B until the sentence imposed by the court has been served, the person is eligible for release pursuant to section 41-1604.07 or the sentence is commuted:

Minimum	Presumptive	Maximum
8 years	15 years	22 years

F. Except as otherwise provided in this section, if a person is at least eighteen years of age or has been tried as an adult and is convicted of a dangerous crime against children involving sexual abuse or bestiality under section 13-1411, subsection A, paragraph 2 and is sentenced to a term of imprisonment, the term of imprisonment is as follows and the person is not eligible for release from confinement on any basis except as specifically authorized by section 31-233, subsection A or B until the sentence imposed by the court has been served, the person is eligible for release pursuant to section 41-1604.07 or the sentence is commuted:

Minimum	Presumptive	Maximum
2.5 years	5 years	7.5 years

A person who has been previously convicted of one predicate felony shall be sentenced to a term of imprisonment as follows and the person is not eligible for suspension of sentence, probation, pardon or release from confinement on any basis except as specifically authorized by section 31-233, subsection A or B until the sentence imposed by the court has been served, the person is eligible for release pursuant to section 41-1604.07 or the sentence is commuted:

Minimum	Presumptive	Maximum
8 years	15 years	22 years

G. The presumptive sentences prescribed in subsections B, C and D of this section or subsections E and F of this section if the person has previously been convicted of a predicate felony may be increased or decreased pursuant to section 13-701, subsections C, D and E.

H. Except as provided in subsection F of this section, a person who is sentenced for a dangerous crime against children in the first degree pursuant to this section is not eligible for suspension of sentence, probation, pardon or release from confinement on any basis except as specifically authorized by section 31-233, subsection A or B until the sentence imposed by the court has been served or commuted.

I. A person who is convicted of any dangerous crime against children in the first degree pursuant to subsection C or D of this section and who has been previously convicted of two or more predicate felonies shall be sentenced to life imprisonment and is not eligible for suspension of sentence, probation, pardon or release from confinement on any basis except as specifically authorized by section 31-233, subsection A or B until the person has served not fewer than thirty-five years or the sentence is commuted.

J. Notwithstanding chapter 10 of this title, a person who is at least eighteen years of age or who has been tried as an adult and who is convicted of a dangerous crime against children in the second degree pursuant to subsection B, C or D of this section is guilty of a class 3 felony and if the person is sentenced to a term of imprisonment, the term of imprisonment is as follows and the person is not eligible for release from confinement on any basis except as specifically authorized by section 31-233, subsection A or B until the person has served the sentence imposed by the court, the person is eligible for release pursuant to section 41-1604.07 or the sentence is commuted:

Minimum   Presumptive   Maximum
5 years   10 years   15 years

K. A person who is convicted of any dangerous crime against children in the second degree and who has been previously convicted of one or more predicate felonies is not eligible for suspension of sentence, probation, pardon or release from confinement on any basis except as specifically authorized by section 31-233, subsection A or B until the sentence imposed by the court has been served, the person is eligible for release pursuant to section 41-1604.07 or the sentence is commuted.

L. Section 13-704, subsection J and section 13-707, subsection B apply to the determination of prior convictions.

M. The sentence imposed on a person by the court for a dangerous crime against children under subsection D of this section involving child molestation or sexual abuse pursuant to subsection F of this section may be served concurrently with other sentences if the offense involved only one victim. The sentence imposed on a person for any other dangerous crime against children in the first or second degree shall be consecutive to any other sentence imposed on the person at any time, including child molestation and sexual abuse of the same victim.

N. In this section, for purposes of punishment an unborn child shall be treated like a minor who is under twelve years of age.

O. A dangerous crime against children is in the first degree if it is a completed offense and is in the second degree if it is a preparatory offense, except attempted first degree murder is a dangerous crime against children in the first degree.

P. For the purposes of this section:

1. "Dangerous crime against children" means any of the following that is committed against a minor who is under fifteen years of age:

(a) Second degree murder.

(b) Aggravated assault resulting in serious physical injury or involving the discharge, use or threatening exhibition of a deadly weapon or dangerous instrument.

(c) Sexual assault.

(d) Molestation of a child.

(e) Sexual conduct with a minor.

(f) Commercial sexual exploitation of a minor.

(g) Sexual exploitation of a minor.

(h) Child abuse as prescribed in section 13-3623, subsection A, paragraph 1.

(i) Kidnapping.

(j) Sexual abuse.

(k) Taking a child for the purpose of prostitution as prescribed in section 13-3206.

(l) Child sex trafficking as prescribed in section 13-3212.

(m) Involving or using minors in drug offenses.

(n) Continuous sexual abuse of a child.

(o) Attempted first degree murder.

(p) Sex trafficking.

(q) Manufacturing methamphetamine under circumstances that cause physical injury to a minor.

(r) Bestiality as prescribed in section 13-1411, subsection A, paragraph 2.

(s) Luring a minor for sexual exploitation.

(t) Aggravated luring a minor for sexual exploitation.

(u) Unlawful age misrepresentation.

(v) Unlawful mutilation.

2. "Predicate felony" means any felony involving child abuse pursuant to section 13-3623, subsection A, paragraph 1, a sexual offense, conduct involving the intentional or knowing infliction of serious physical injury or the discharge, use or threatening exhibition of a deadly weapon or dangerous instrument, or a dangerous crime against children in the first or second degree.

13-706. Serious, violent or aggravated offenders; sentencing; life imprisonment; definitions

A. A person who is at least eighteen years of age or who has been tried as an adult and who is convicted of a serious offense except a drug offense, first degree murder or any dangerous crime against children as defined in section 13-705, whether a completed or preparatory offense, and who has previously been convicted of two or more serious offenses not committed on the same occasion shall be sentenced to life imprisonment and is not eligible for suspension of sentence, probation, pardon or release from confinement on any basis, except as specifically authorized by section 31-233, subsection A or B, until the person has served at least twenty-five years or the sentence is commuted.

B. Unless a longer term of imprisonment or death is the prescribed penalty and notwithstanding any provision that establishes a shorter term of imprisonment, a person who has been convicted of committing or attempting or conspiring to commit any violent or aggravated felony and who has previously been convicted on separate occasions of two or more violent or aggravated felonies not committed on the same occasion shall be sentenced to imprisonment for life and is not eligible for suspension of sentence, probation, pardon or release on any basis except that the person may be eligible for commutation after the person has served at least thirty-five years.

C. In order for the penalty under subsection B of this section to apply, both of the following must occur:

1. The aggravated or violent felonies that comprise the prior convictions shall have been entered within fifteen years of the conviction for the third offense, not including time spent in custody or on probation for an offense or while the person is an absconder.

2. The sentence for the first aggravated or violent felony conviction shall have been imposed before the conduct occurred that gave rise to the second conviction, and the sentence for the second aggravated or violent felony conviction shall have been imposed before the conduct occurred that gave rise to the third conviction.

D. Chapter 3 of this title applies to all offenses under this section.

E. For the purposes of this section, if a person has been convicted of an offense committed in another jurisdiction that if committed in this state would be a violation or attempted violation of any of the offenses listed in this section and that has the same elements of an offense listed in this section, the offense committed in another jurisdiction is considered an offense committed in this state.

F. For the purposes of this section:

1. "Serious offense" means any of the following offenses if committed in this state or any offense committed outside this state that if committed in this state would constitute one of the following offenses:

(a) First degree murder.

(b) Second degree murder.

(c) Manslaughter.

(d) Aggravated assault resulting in serious physical injury or involving the discharge, use or threatening exhibition of a deadly weapon or dangerous instrument.

(e) Sexual assault.

(f) Any dangerous crime against children.

(g) Arson of an occupied structure.

(h) Armed robbery.

(i) Burglary in the first degree.

(j) Kidnapping.

(k) Sexual conduct with a minor under fifteen years of age.

(l) Child sex trafficking.

2. "Violent or aggravated felony" means any of the following offenses:

(a) First degree murder.

(b) Second degree murder.

(c) Aggravated assault resulting in serious physical injury or involving the discharge, use or threatening exhibition of a deadly weapon or dangerous instrument.

(d) Dangerous or deadly assault by prisoner.

(e) Committing assault with intent to incite to riot or participate in riot.

(f) Drive by shooting.

(g) Discharging a firearm at a residential structure if the structure is occupied.

(h) Kidnapping.

(i) Sexual conduct with a minor that is a class 2 felony.

(j) Sexual assault.

(k) Molestation of a child.

(l) Continuous sexual abuse of a child.

(m) Violent sexual assault.

(n) Burglary in the first degree committed in a residential structure if the structure is occupied.

(o) Arson of an occupied structure.

(p) Arson of an occupied jail or prison facility.

(q) Armed robbery.

(r) Participating in or assisting a criminal syndicate or leading or participating in a criminal street gang.

(s) Terrorism.

(t) Taking a child for the purpose of prostitution.

(u) Child sex trafficking.

(v) Commercial sexual exploitation of a minor.

(w) Sexual exploitation of a minor.

(x) Unlawful introduction of disease or parasite as prescribed by section 13-2912, subsection A, paragraph 2 or 3.

13-707. Misdemeanors; sentencing

A. A sentence of imprisonment for a misdemeanor shall be for a definite term to be served other than a place within custody of the state department of corrections. The court shall fix the term of imprisonment within the following maximum limitations:

1. For a class 1 misdemeanor, six months.

2. For a class 2 misdemeanor, four months.

3. For a class 3 misdemeanor, thirty days.

B. A person who is at least eighteen years of age or who has been tried as an adult and who stands convicted of any misdemeanor or petty offense, other than a traffic offense, and who has been convicted of one or more of the same misdemeanors or petty offenses within two years next preceding the date of the present offense shall be sentenced for the next higher class of offense than that for which the person currently is convicted. Time spent incarcerated within the two years next preceding the date of the offense for which a person is currently being sentenced shall not be included in the two years required to be free of convictions.

C. If a person is convicted of a misdemeanor offense and the offense requires enhanced punishment because it is a second or subsequent offense, the court shall determine the existence of the previous conviction. The court shall allow the allegation of a prior conviction to be made in the same manner as the allegation prescribed by section 28-1387, subsection A.

D. A person who has been convicted in any court outside the jurisdiction of this state of an offense that if committed in this state would be punishable as a misdemeanor or petty offense is subject to this section. A person who has been convicted as an adult of an offense punishable as a misdemeanor or petty offense under the provisions of any prior code in this state is subject to this section.

E. The court may direct that a person who is sentenced pursuant to subsection A of this section shall not be released on any basis until the sentence imposed by the court has been served.

13-708. Offenses committed while released from confinement

A. A person who is convicted of any felony involving a dangerous offense that is committed while the person is on probation for a conviction of a felony offense or parole, work furlough, community supervision or any other release or has escaped from confinement for conviction of a felony offense shall be sentenced to imprisonment for not less than the presumptive sentence authorized under this chapter and is not eligible for suspension or commutation or release on any basis until the sentence imposed is served.

B. A person who is convicted of a dangerous offense that is committed while the person is on release or has escaped from confinement for a conviction of a serious offense as defined in section 13-706, an offense resulting in serious physical injury or an offense involving the use or exhibition of a deadly weapon or dangerous instrument shall be sentenced to the maximum sentence authorized under this chapter and is not eligible for suspension or commutation or release on any basis until the sentence imposed is served. If the court finds that at least two substantial aggravating circumstances listed in section 13-701, subsection D apply, the court may increase the maximum sentence authorized under this chapter by up to twenty-five percent.

C. A person who is convicted of any felony offense that is not included in subsection A or B of this section and that is committed while the person is on probation for a conviction of a felony offense or parole, work furlough, community supervision or any other release or escape from confinement for conviction of a felony offense shall be sentenced to a term of not less than the presumptive sentence authorized for the offense and the person is not eligible for suspension of sentence, probation, pardon or release from confinement on any basis except as specifically authorized by section 31-233, subsection A or B until the sentence imposed by the court has been served, the person is eligible for release pursuant to section 41-1604.07 or the sentence is commuted. The release provisions prescribed by this section shall not be substituted for any penalties required by the substantive offense or provision of law that specifies a later release or completion of the sentence imposed before release. For the purposes of this subsection, "substantive offense" means the felony, misdemeanor or petty offense that the trier of fact found beyond a reasonable doubt the defendant committed. Substantive offense does not include allegations that, if proven, would enhance the sentence of imprisonment or fine to which the defendant would otherwise be subject.

D. A person who is convicted of committing any felony offense that is committed while the person is released on bond or on the person's own recognizance on a separate felony offense or while the person is escaped from preconviction custody for a separate felony offense shall be sentenced to a term of imprisonment two years longer than would otherwise be imposed for the felony offense committed while on release. The additional sentence imposed under this subsection is in addition to any enhanced punishment that may be applicable under section 13-703, section 13-704, section 13-1204, subsection C or section 13-714. The person is not eligible for suspension of sentence, probation, pardon or release from confinement on any basis, except as specifically authorized by section 31-233, subsection A or B, until the two years are served, the person is eligible for release pursuant to section 41-1604.07 or the sentence is commuted. The penalties prescribed by this subsection shall be substituted for the penalties otherwise authorized by law if the allegation that the person committed a felony while released on bond or on the person's own recognizance or while escaped from preconviction custody is charged in the indictment or information and admitted or found by the court. The release provisions prescribed by this subsection shall not be substituted for any penalties required by the substantive offense or provision of law that specifies a later release or completion of the sentence imposed before release. The court shall allow the allegation that the person committed a felony while released on bond or on the person's own recognizance on a separate felony offense or while escaped from preconviction custody on a separate felony offense at any time before the case is actually tried unless the allegation is filed fewer than twenty days before the case is actually tried and the court finds on the record that the person was in fact prejudiced by the untimely filing and states the reasons for these findings. The allegation that the person committed a felony while released on bond or on the person's own recognizance or while escaped from preconviction custody shall not be read to the jury. For the purposes of this subsection, "substantive offense" means the felony offense that the trier of fact found beyond a reasonable doubt the person committed. Substantive offense does not include allegations that, if proven, would enhance the sentence of imprisonment or fine to which the person otherwise would be subject.

E. A sentence imposed pursuant to subsection A, B or C of this section shall revoke the convicted person's release if the person was on release and shall be consecutive to any other sentence from which the convicted person had been temporarily released or had escaped, unless the sentence from which the convicted person had been paroled or placed on probation was imposed by a jurisdiction other than this state.

13-709. Offenses committed in school safety zone; sentences; definitions

A. Except as otherwise prescribed in section 13-3411, a person who is convicted of a felony offense that is committed in a school safety zone is guilty of the same class of felony that the person would otherwise be guilty of if the violation had not occurred within a school safety zone, except that the court may impose a sentence that is one year longer than the minimum, maximum and presumptive sentence for that violation if the person is not a criminal street gang member or up to five years longer than the minimum, maximum and presumptive sentence for that violation if the person is a criminal street gang member. The additional sentence imposed under this subsection is in addition to any other enhanced punishment that may be applicable under section 13-703, section 13-704, section 13-706, section 13-708, subsection D or chapter 34 of this title.

B. In addition to any other penalty prescribed by this title, the court may order a person who is subject to subsection A of this section to pay a fine of not less than two thousand dollars and not more than the maximum authorized by chapter 8 of this title.

C. Each school district governing board or its designee, or chief administrative officer in the case of a nonpublic or charter school, may place and maintain permanently affixed signs that are located in a visible manner at the main entrance of each school and that identify the school and its accompanying grounds as a school safety zone. A school may include information regarding the school safety zone boundaries on a sign that identifies the area as a drug free zone and not post separate school safety zone signs.

D. For the purposes of this section:

1. "School" means any public or nonpublic kindergarten program, common school or high school.

2. "School safety zone" means any of the following:

(a) The area within three hundred feet of a school or its accompanying grounds.

(b) Any public property within one thousand feet of a school or its accompanying grounds.

(c) Any school bus.

(d) A bus contracted to transport pupils to any school during the time when the contracted vehicle is transporting pupils on behalf of the school.

(e) A school bus stop.

(f) Any bus stop where school children are awaiting, boarding or exiting a bus contracted to transport pupils to any school.

13-710. Sentence for second degree murder

A. Except as provided in section 13-705 or section 13-706, subsection A, a person who is convicted of second degree murder as defined by section 13-1104 shall be sentenced as follows:

Minimum   Presumptive Maximum

10 calendar years 16 calendar years 25 calendar years

B. Except as provided in section 13-704 or section 13-706, subsection A, a person who is convicted of second degree murder as defined by section 13-1104 and who has previously been convicted of second degree murder or a class 2 or 3 felony involving a dangerous offense shall be sentenced as follows:

Minimum   Presumptive Maximum

15 calendar years 20 calendar years 29 calendar years

C. The presumptive term imposed pursuant to subsections A and B of this section may be mitigated or aggravated pursuant to section 13-701, subsections D and E.

13-711. Consecutive terms of imprisonment

A. Except as otherwise provided by law, if multiple sentences of imprisonment are imposed on a person at the same time, the sentence or sentences imposed by the court shall run consecutively unless the court expressly directs otherwise, in which case the court shall set forth on the record the reason for its sentence.

B. Notwithstanding subsection A, if a person is subject to an undischarged term of imprisonment and is sentenced to an additional term of imprisonment for a felony offense that is committed while the person is under the jurisdiction of the state department of corrections, the sentence imposed by the court shall run consecutively to the undischarged term of imprisonment.

13-712. Calculation of terms of imprisonment

A. A sentence of imprisonment commences when sentence is imposed if the defendant is in custody or surrenders into custody at that time. Otherwise it commences when the defendant becomes actually in custody.

B. All time actually spent in custody pursuant to an offense until the prisoner is sentenced to imprisonment for such offense shall be credited against the term of imprisonment otherwise provided for by this chapter.

C. If a sentence of imprisonment is vacated and a new sentence is imposed on the defendant for the same offense, the new sentence is calculated as if it had commenced at the time the vacated sentence was imposed, and all time served under the vacated sentence shall be credited against the new sentence.

D. If a person serving a sentence of imprisonment escapes from custody, the escape interrupts the sentence. The interruption continues until the person is apprehended and confined for the escape or is confined and subject to a detainer for the escape. Time spent in actual custody prior to return under this subsection shall be credited against the term authorized by law if custody rested on an arrest or surrender for the escape itself, or if the custody arose from an arrest on another charge which culminated in a dismissal or an acquittal, and the person was denied admission to bail pending disposition of that charge because of a warrant lodged against such person arising from the escape.

E. The sentencing court shall include the time of commencement of sentence under subsection A and the computation of time credited against sentence under subsection B, C or D, in the original or an amended commitment order, under procedures established by rule of court.

13-713. Forfeiture of public retirement system benefits; definition

A. Notwithstanding any other law, if a member of a state retirement system or plan is convicted of or pleads no contest to an offense that is a class 1, 2, 3, 4 or 5 felony and that was committed in the course of the member's employment as a public official or for a public employer, the court shall order the person's membership terminated and the person shall forfeit all rights and benefits earned under the state retirement system or plan. A member who forfeits all rights and benefits earned pursuant to this section is entitled to receive, in a lump sum amount, the member's contribution to the state retirement system or plan plus interest as determined by the board of that state retirement system or plan, less any benefits received by the member.

B. An order forfeiting a member's benefits on conviction of an offense listed in subsection A shall not be stayed on the filing of any appeal of the conviction. While an appeal of the conviction is being adjudicated and until a final judgment is issued, for a member who is not receiving benefits, the member and the member's employer are required to continue making contributions to the retirement system or plan and for a member who is receiving benefits, the retirement system or plan shall suspend payments to the member and hold the assets in trust. If the conviction is reversed on final judgment, no rights or benefits shall be forfeited and the member's membership shall be reinstated.

C. Notwithstanding subsection A, the court may award to a spouse, dependent or former spouse of a member who is subject to subsection A some or all of the amount that was forfeited under subsection A. The award under this subsection shall not require the board of the state retirement system or plan to provide any type, form or time of payment of severance, survivor or retirement benefits or any severance, survivor or retirement benefit option that is not provided by the laws governing the state retirement system or plan from which the award is being made. In determining whether to make an award under this subsection, the judge shall consider the totality of circumstances, including:

1. The role, if any, of the person's spouse, dependent or former spouse in connection with the illegal conduct for which the person was convicted.

2. The degree of knowledge, if any, possessed by the person's spouse, dependent or former spouse in connection with the illegal conduct for which the person was convicted.

3. The community property nature of the benefits involved.

4. The extent to which the person's spouse, dependent or former spouse was relying on the forfeited benefits.

D. Notwithstanding subsection H, the court shall order that a person who is subject to forfeiture under this section is ineligible for future membership in any state retirement system or plan.

E. The court shall provide a copy of the order of forfeiture to the state retirement system or plan to which it applies.

F. This section does not apply to a member whose most recent retirement occurs before the effective date of this section, unless the member has resumed making contributions to the state retirement system or plan.

G. Notwithstanding subsection A, a court shall not order the forfeiture of rights and benefits earned under the state retirement system or plan that accrued before the effective date of this section or for a felony committed before the effective date of this section.

H. This section applies only to the state retirement system or plan in which the person was a contributing member at the time the offense was committed.

I. For the purposes of this section, "state retirement system or plan" means the Arizona state retirement system established by title 38, chapter 5, article 2, the elected officials' retirement plan established by title 38, chapter 5, article 3, the public safety personnel retirement system established by title 38, chapter 5, article 4 and the corrections officer retirement plan established by title 38, chapter 5, article 6.

13-714. Offenses committed with intent to promote, further or assist a criminal street gang

A person who is convicted of committing any felony offense with the intent to promote, further or assist any criminal conduct by a criminal street gang shall not be eligible for suspension of sentence, probation, pardon or release from confinement on any basis except as authorized by section 31-233, subsection A or B until the sentence imposed by the court has been served, the person is eligible for release pursuant to section 41-1604.07 or the sentence is commuted. The presumptive, minimum and maximum sentence for the offense shall be increased by three years if the offense is a class 4, 5 or 6 felony or shall be increased by five years if the offense is a class 2 or 3 felony. The additional sentence imposed pursuant to this section is in addition to any enhanced sentence that may be applicable.

13-715. Special sentencing provisions; human smuggling organization

A person who is convicted of committing any felony offense with the intent to promote, further or assist a human smuggling organization that operates for the goal or purpose of human trafficking or human smuggling shall not be eligible for suspension of sentence, probation, pardon or release from confinement on any basis except as authorized by section 31-233, subsection A or B until the sentence imposed by the court has been served, the person is eligible for release pursuant to section 41-1604.07 or the sentence is commuted. The presumptive, minimum and maximum sentence for the offense shall be increased by three years if the offense is a class 4, 5 or 6 felony or shall be increased by five years if the offense is a class 2 or 3 felony. The additional sentence imposed pursuant to this section is in addition to any enhanced sentence that may be applicable.

13-716. Juvenile offenders sentenced to life imprisonment; parole eligibility

Notwithstanding any other law, a person who is sentenced to life imprisonment with the possibility of release after serving a minimum number of calendar years for an offense that was committed before the person attained eighteen years of age is eligible for parole on completion of service of the minimum sentence, regardless of whether the offense was committed on or after January 1, 1994. If granted parole, the person shall remain on parole for the remainder of the person's life except that the person's parole may be revoked pursuant to section 31-415.

Chapter 7.1 Capital Sentencing

13-751. Sentence of death or life imprisonment; aggravating and mitigating circumstances; definition

A. If the state has filed a notice of intent to seek the death penalty and the defendant is:
1. Convicted of first degree murder pursuant to section 13-1105, subsection A, paragraph 1 or 3 and was at least eighteen years of age at the time of the commission of the offense, the defendant shall be sentenced to death or imprisonment in the custody of the state department of corrections for natural life as determined and in accordance with the procedures provided in section 13-752. A defendant who is sentenced to natural life is not eligible for commutation, parole, work furlough, work release or release from confinement on any basis.
2. Convicted of first degree murder pursuant to section 13-1105 and was under eighteen years of age at the time of the commission of the offense, the defendant shall be sentenced to imprisonment in the custody of the state department of corrections for life or natural life, as determined and in accordance with the procedures provided in section 13-752. A defendant who is sentenced to natural life is not eligible for commutation, parole, work furlough, work release or release from confinement on any basis. If the defendant is sentenced to life, the defendant shall not be released on any basis until the completion of the service of twenty-five calendar years if the murdered person was fifteen or more years of age and thirty-five years if the murdered person was under fifteen years of age or was an unborn child.
3. Convicted of first degree murder pursuant to section 13-1105, subsection A, paragraph 2, the defendant shall be sentenced to death or imprisonment in the custody of the state department of corrections for life or natural life as determined and in accordance with the procedures provided in section 13-752. A defendant who is sentenced to natural life is not eligible for commutation, parole, work furlough, work release or release from confinement on any basis. If the defendant is sentenced to life, the defendant shall not be released on any basis until the completion of the service of twenty-five calendar years if the murdered person was fifteen or more years of age and thirty-five years if the murdered person was under fifteen years of age or was an unborn child.

B. At the aggravation phase of the sentencing proceeding that is held pursuant to section 13-752, the admissibility of information relevant to any of the aggravating circumstances set forth in subsection F of this section shall be governed by the rules of evidence applicable to criminal trials. The burden of establishing the existence of any of the aggravating circumstances set forth in subsection F of this section is on the prosecution. The prosecution must prove the existence of the aggravating circumstances beyond a reasonable doubt.

C. At the penalty phase of the sentencing proceeding that is held pursuant to section 13-752, the prosecution or the defendant may present any information that is relevant to any of the mitigating circumstances included in subsection G of this section, regardless of its admissibility under the rules governing admission of evidence at criminal trials. The burden of establishing the existence of the mitigating circumstances included in subsection G of this section is on the defendant. The defendant must prove the existence of the mitigating circumstances by a preponderance of the evidence. If the trier of fact is a jury, the jurors do not have to agree unanimously that a mitigating circumstance has been proven to exist. Each juror may consider any mitigating circumstance found by that juror in determining the appropriate penalty.

D. Evidence that is admitted at the trial and that relates to any aggravating or mitigating circumstances shall be deemed admitted as evidence at a sentencing proceeding if the trier of fact considering that evidence is the same trier of fact that determined the defendant's guilt. The prosecution and the defendant shall be permitted to rebut any information received at the aggravation or penalty phase of the sentencing proceeding and shall be given fair opportunity to present argument as to whether the information is sufficient to establish the existence of any of the circumstances included in subsections F and G of this section.

E. In determining whether to impose a sentence of death or life imprisonment, the trier of fact shall take into account the aggravating and mitigating circumstances that have been proven. The trier of fact shall impose a sentence of death if the trier of fact finds one or more of the aggravating circumstances enumerated in subsection F of this section and then determines that there are no mitigating circumstances sufficiently substantial to call for leniency.

F. The trier of fact shall consider the following aggravating circumstances in determining whether to impose a sentence of death:

1. The defendant has been convicted of another offense in the United States for which under Arizona law a sentence of life imprisonment or death was imposable.

2. The defendant has been or was previously convicted of a serious offense, whether preparatory or completed. Convictions for serious offenses committed on the same occasion as the homicide, or not committed on the same occasion but consolidated for trial with the homicide, shall be treated as a serious offense under this paragraph.

3. In the commission of the offense the defendant knowingly created a grave risk of death to another person or persons in addition to the person murdered during the commission of the offense.

4. The defendant procured the commission of the offense by payment, or promise of payment, of anything of pecuniary value.

5. The defendant committed the offense as consideration for the receipt, or in expectation of the receipt, of anything of pecuniary value.

6. The defendant committed the offense in an especially heinous, cruel or depraved manner.

7. The defendant committed the offense while:

(a) In the custody of or on authorized or unauthorized release from the state department of corrections, a law enforcement agency or a county or city jail.

(b) On probation for a felony offense.

8. The defendant has been convicted of one or more other homicides, as defined in section 13-1101, that were committed during the commission of the offense.

9. The defendant was an adult at the time the offense was committed or was tried as an adult and the murdered person was under fifteen years of age, was an unborn child in the womb at any stage of its development or was seventy years of age or older.

10. The murdered person was an on duty peace officer who was killed in the course of performing the officer's official duties and the defendant knew, or should have known, that the murdered person was a peace officer.

11. The defendant committed the offense with the intent to promote, further or assist the objectives of a criminal street gang or criminal syndicate or to join a criminal street gang or criminal syndicate.

12. The defendant committed the offense to prevent a person's cooperation with an official law enforcement investigation, to prevent a person's testimony in a court proceeding, in retaliation for a person's cooperation with an official law enforcement investigation or in retaliation for a person's testimony in a court proceeding.

13. The offense was committed in a cold, calculated manner without pretense of moral or legal justification.

14. The defendant used a remote stun gun or an authorized remote stun gun in the commission of the offense. For the purposes of this paragraph:

(a) "Authorized remote stun gun" means a remote stun gun that has all of the following:

(i) An electrical discharge that is less than one hundred thousand volts and less than nine joules of energy per pulse.

(ii) A serial or identification number on all projectiles that are discharged from the remote stun gun.

(iii) An identification and tracking system that, on deployment of remote electrodes, disperses coded material that is traceable to the purchaser through records that are kept by the manufacturer on all remote stun guns and all individual cartridges sold.

(iv) A training program that is offered by the manufacturer.

(b) "Remote stun gun" means an electronic device that emits an electrical charge and that is designed and primarily employed to incapacitate a person or animal either through contact with electrodes on the device itself or remotely through wired probes that are attached to the device or through a spark, plasma, ionization or other conductive means emitting from the device.

G. The trier of fact shall consider as mitigating circumstances any factors proffered by the defendant or the state that are relevant in determining whether to impose a sentence less than death, including any aspect of the defendant's character, propensities or record and any of the circumstances of the offense, including but not limited to the following:

1. The defendant's capacity to appreciate the wrongfulness of his conduct or to conform his conduct to the requirements of law was significantly impaired, but not so impaired as to constitute a defense to prosecution.

2. The defendant was under unusual and substantial duress, although not such as to constitute a defense to prosecution.

3. The defendant was legally accountable for the conduct of another under section 13-303, but his participation was relatively minor, although not so minor as to constitute a defense to prosecution.

4. The defendant could not reasonably have foreseen that his conduct in the course of the commission of the offense for which the defendant was convicted would cause, or would create a grave risk of causing, death to another person.

5. The defendant's age.

H. For the purposes of determining whether a conviction of any dangerous crime against children is a serious offense pursuant to this section, an unborn child shall be treated like a minor who is under twelve years of age.

I. In this section, for purposes of punishment an unborn child shall be treated like a minor who is under twelve years of age.

J. For the purposes of this section, "serious offense" means any of the following offenses if committed in this state or any offense committed outside this state that if committed in this state would constitute one of the following offenses:

1. First degree murder.

2. Second degree murder.

3. Manslaughter.

4. Aggravated assault resulting in serious physical injury or committed by the use, threatened use or exhibition of a deadly weapon or dangerous instrument.

5. Sexual assault.

6. Any dangerous crime against children.

7. Arson of an occupied structure.

8. Robbery.

9. Burglary in the first degree.

10. Kidnapping.

11. Sexual conduct with a minor under fifteen years of age.

12. Burglary in the second degree.

13. Terrorism.

13-752. Sentences of death, life imprisonment or natural life; imposition; sentencing proceedings; definitions

A. If the state has filed a notice of intent to seek the death penalty and the defendant is convicted of first degree murder, the trier of fact at the sentencing proceeding shall determine whether to impose a sentence of death in accordance with the procedures provided in this section. If the trier of fact determines that a sentence of death is not appropriate, or if the state has not filed a notice of intent to seek the death penalty, and the defendant is convicted of first degree murder pursuant to section 13-1105, subsection A, paragraph 1 or 3 and was at least eighteen years of age at the time of the commission of the offense, the court shall impose a sentence of natural life. If the defendant was under eighteen years of age at the time of the commission of the offense or if the defendant is convicted of first degree murder pursuant to section 13-1105, subsection A, paragraph 2, the court shall determine whether to impose a sentence of life or natural life.

B. Before trial, the prosecution shall notice one or more of the aggravating circumstances under section 13-751, subsection F.

C. If the trier of fact finds the defendant guilty of first degree murder, the trier of fact shall then immediately determine whether one or more alleged aggravating circumstances have been proven. This proceeding is the aggravation phase of the sentencing proceeding.

D. If the trier of fact finds that one or more of the alleged aggravating circumstances have been proven, the trier of fact shall then immediately determine whether the death penalty should be imposed. This proceeding is the penalty phase of the sentencing proceeding.

E. At the aggravation phase, the trier of fact shall make a special finding on whether each alleged aggravating circumstance has been proven based on the evidence that was presented at the trial or at the aggravation phase. If the trier of fact is a jury, a unanimous verdict is required to find that the aggravating circumstance has been proven. If the trier of fact unanimously finds that an aggravating circumstance has not been proven, the defendant is entitled to a special finding that the aggravating circumstance has not been proven. If the trier of fact unanimously finds no aggravating circumstances, the court shall then determine whether to impose a sentence of life or natural life on the defendant pursuant to subsection A of this section.

F. The penalty phase shall be held immediately after the trier of fact finds at the aggravation phase that one or more of the aggravating circumstances under section 13-751, subsection F have been proven. A finding by the trier of fact that any of the remaining aggravating circumstances alleged has not been proven or the inability of the trier of fact to agree on the issue of whether any of the remaining aggravating circumstances alleged has been proven shall not prevent the holding of the penalty phase.

G. At the penalty phase, the defendant and the state may present any evidence that is relevant to the determination of whether there is mitigation that is sufficiently substantial to call for leniency. In order for the trier of fact to make this determination, regardless of whether the defendant presents evidence of mitigation, the state may present any evidence that demonstrates that the defendant should not be shown leniency including any evidence regarding the defendant's character, propensities, criminal record or other acts.

H. The trier of fact shall determine unanimously whether death is the appropriate sentence. If the trier of fact is a jury and the jury unanimously determines that the death penalty is not appropriate, the court shall determine whether to impose a sentence of life or natural life pursuant to subsection A of this section.

I. If the trier of fact at any prior phase of the trial is the same trier of fact at the subsequent phase, any evidence that was presented at any prior phase of the trial shall be deemed admitted as evidence at any subsequent phase of the trial.

J. At the aggravation phase, if the trier of fact is a jury, the jury is unable to reach a verdict on any of the alleged aggravating circumstances and the jury has not found that at least one of the alleged aggravating circumstances has been proven, the court shall dismiss the jury and shall impanel a new jury. The new jury shall not retry the issue of the defendant's guilt or the issue regarding any of the aggravating circumstances that the first jury found not proved by unanimous verdict. If the new jury is unable to reach a unanimous verdict, the court shall impose a sentence of life or natural life on the defendant.

K. At the penalty phase, if the trier of fact is a jury and the jury is unable to reach a verdict, the court shall dismiss the jury and shall impanel a new jury. The new jury shall not retry the issue of the defendant's guilt or the issue regarding any of the aggravating circumstances that the first jury found by unanimous verdict to be proved or not proved. If the new jury is unable to reach a unanimous verdict, the court shall impose a sentence of life or natural life on the defendant.

L. If the jury that rendered a verdict of guilty is not the jury first impaneled for the aggravation phase, the jury impaneled in the aggravation phase shall not retry the issue of the defendant's guilt. If the jury impaneled in the aggravation phase is unable to reach a verdict on any of the alleged aggravating circumstances and the jury has not found that at least one of the alleged aggravating circumstances has been proven, the court shall dismiss the jury and shall impanel a new jury. The new jury shall not retry the issue of the defendant's guilt or the issue regarding any of the aggravating circumstances that the first jury found not proved by unanimous verdict. If the new jury is unable to reach a unanimous verdict, the court shall impose a sentence of life or natural life on the defendant.

M. Alternate jurors who are impaneled for the trial in a case in which the offense is punishable by death shall not be excused from the case until the completion of the sentencing proceeding.

N. If the sentence of a person who was sentenced to death is overturned, the person shall be resentenced pursuant to this section by a jury that is specifically impaneled for this purpose as if the original sentencing had not occurred.

O. In any case that requires sentencing or resentencing in which the defendant has been convicted of an offense that is punishable by death and in which the trier of fact was a judge or a jury that has since been discharged, the defendant shall be sentenced or resentenced pursuant to this section by a jury that is specifically impaneled for this purpose.

P. The trier of fact shall make all factual determinations required by this section or the Constitution of the United States or this state to impose a death sentence. If the defendant bears the burden of proof, the issue shall be determined in the penalty phase. If the state bears the burden of proof, the issue shall be determined in the aggravation phase.

Q. If the death penalty was not alleged or was alleged but not imposed, the court shall determine whether to impose a sentence of life or natural life pursuant to subsection A of this section. In determining whether to impose a sentence of life or natural life, the court:

1. May consider any evidence introduced before sentencing or at any other sentencing proceeding.

2. Shall consider the aggravating and mitigating circumstances listed in section 13-701 and any statement made by a victim.

R. Subject to section 13-751, subsection B, a victim has the right to be present at the aggravation phase and to present any information that is relevant to the proceeding. A victim has the right to be present and to present information at the penalty phase. At the penalty phase, the victim may present information about the murdered person and the impact of the murder on the victim and other family members and may submit a victim impact statement in any format to the trier of fact.

S. For the purposes of this section:

1. "Trier of fact" means a jury unless the defendant and the state waive a jury, in which case the trier of fact shall be the court.

2. "Victim" means the murdered person's spouse, parent, child, grandparent or sibling, any other person related to the murdered person by consanguinity or affinity to the second degree or any other lawful representative of the murdered person, except if the spouse, parent, child, grandparent, sibling, other person related to the murdered person by consanguinity or affinity to the second degree or other lawful representative is in custody for an offense or is the accused.

13-753. Mental evaluations of capital defendants; hearing; appeal; definitions

A. In any case in which the state files a notice of intent to seek the death penalty, a person who is found to have an intellectual disability pursuant to this section shall not be sentenced to death but shall be sentenced to life or natural life.

B. If the state files a notice of intent to seek the death penalty, the court, unless the defendant objects, shall appoint a prescreening psychological expert in order to determine the defendant's intelligence quotient using current community, nationally and culturally accepted intelligence testing procedures. The prescreening psychological expert shall submit a written report of the intelligence quotient determination to the court within ten days of the testing of the defendant. If the defendant objects to the prescreening, the defendant waives the right to a pretrial determination of status. The waiver does not preclude the defendant from offering evidence of the defendant's intellectual disability in the penalty phase.

C. If the prescreening psychological expert determines that the defendant's intelligence quotient is higher than seventy-five, the notice of intent to seek the death penalty shall not be dismissed on the ground that the defendant has an intellectual disability. If the prescreening psychological expert determines that the defendant's intelligence quotient is higher than seventy-five, the report shall be sealed by the court and be available only to the defendant. The report shall be released on the motion of any party if the defendant introduces the report in the present case or is convicted of an offense in the present case and the sentence is final. A prescreening determination that the defendant's intelligence quotient is higher than seventy-five does not prevent the defendant from introducing evidence of the defendant's intellectual disability or diminished mental capacity at the penalty phase of the sentencing proceeding.

D. If the prescreening psychological expert determines that the defendant's intelligence quotient is seventy-five or less, the trial court, within ten days of receiving the written report, shall order the state and the defendant to each nominate three experts in intellectual disabilities, or jointly nominate a single expert in intellectual disabilities. The trial court shall appoint one expert in intellectual disabilities nominated by the state and one expert in intellectual disabilities nominated by the defendant, or a single expert in intellectual disabilities jointly nominated by the state and the defendant, none of whom made the prescreening determination of the defendant's intelligence quotient. The trial court, in its discretion, may appoint an additional expert in intellectual disabilities who was neither nominated by the state nor the defendant, and who did not make the prescreening determination of the defendant's intelligence quotient. Within forty-five days after the trial court orders the state and the defendant to nominate experts in intellectual disabilities, or on the appointment of such experts, whichever is later, the state and the defendant shall provide to the experts in intellectual disabilities and the court any available records that may be relevant to the defendant's status. The court may extend the deadline for providing records on good cause shown by the state or defendant.

E. Not less than twenty days after receipt of the records provided pursuant to subsection D, or twenty days after the expiration of the deadline for providing the records, whichever is later, each expert in intellectual disability shall examine the defendant using current community, nationally and culturally accepted physical, developmental, psychological and intelligence testing procedures, for the purpose of determining whether the defendant has an intellectual disability. Within fifteen days of examining the defendant, each expert in intellectual disabilities shall submit a written report to the trial court that includes the expert's opinion as to whether the defendant has an intellectual disability.

F. If the scores on all the tests for intelligence quotient administered to the defendant are above seventy, the notice of intent to seek the death penalty shall not be dismissed on the ground that the defendant has an intellectual disability. This does not preclude the defendant from introducing evidence of the defendant's intellectual disability or diminished mental capacity at the penalty phase of the sentencing proceeding.

G. No less than thirty days after the experts in intellectual disabilities submit reports to the court and before trial, the trial court shall hold a hearing to determine if the defendant has an intellectual disability. At the hearing, the defendant has the burden of proving intellectual disability by clear and convincing evidence. A determination by the trial court that the defendant's intelligence quotient is sixty-five or lower establishes a rebuttable presumption that the defendant has an intellectual disability. This subsection does not preclude a defendant with an intelligence quotient of seventy or below from proving intellectual disability by clear and convincing evidence.

H. If the trial court finds that the defendant has an intellectual disability, the trial court shall dismiss the intent to seek the death penalty, shall not impose a sentence of death on the defendant if the defendant is convicted of first degree murder and shall dismiss one of the attorneys appointed under rule 6.2, Arizona rules of criminal procedure, unless the court finds that there is good cause to retain both attorneys. If the trial court finds that the defendant does not have an intellectual disability, the court's finding does not prevent the defendant from introducing evidence of the defendant's intellectual disability or diminished mental capacity at the penalty phase of the sentencing proceeding.

I. Within ten days after the trial court makes a finding on intellectual disability, the state or the defendant may file a petition for special action with the Arizona court of appeals pursuant to the rules of procedure for special actions. The filing of the petition for special action is governed by the rules of procedure for special actions, except that the court of appeals shall exercise jurisdiction and decide the merits of the claims raised.

J. This section applies to all capital sentencing proceedings.

K. For the purposes of this section, unless the context otherwise requires:

1. "Adaptive behavior" means the effectiveness or degree to which the defendant meets the standards of personal independence and social responsibility expected of the defendant's age and cultural group.

2. "Expert in intellectual disabilities" means a psychologist or physician licensed pursuant to title 32, chapter 13, 17 or 19.1 with at least five years' experience in the testing or testing assessment, evaluation and diagnosis of intellectual disabilities.

3. "Intellectual disability" means a condition based on a mental deficit that involves significantly subaverage general intellectual functioning, existing concurrently with significant impairment in adaptive behavior, where the onset of the foregoing conditions occurred before the defendant reached the age of eighteen.

4. "Prescreening psychological expert" means a psychologist licensed pursuant to title 32, chapter 19.1 with at least five years' experience in the testing, evaluation and diagnosis of intellectual disabilities.

5. "Significantly subaverage general intellectual functioning" means a full scale intelligence quotient of seventy or lower. The court in determining the intelligence quotient shall take into account the margin of error for the test administered.

13-754. Capital defendant prescreening evaluation for competency and sanity

A. If the state files a notice of intent to seek the death penalty, unless the defendant objects, the court shall appoint a psychologist or psychiatrist licensed pursuant to title 32, chapter 13, 17 or 19.1 to conduct a prescreening evaluation to determine if reasonable grounds exist to conduct another examination to determine the following:

1. The defendant's competency to stand trial.

2. Whether the defendant was sane at the time the defendant allegedly committed the offense.

B. The court may appoint separate psychological experts to conduct each of the evaluations ordered pursuant to subsection A.

C. The court shall seal any psychological expert's report pursuant to this section, and the report shall only be available to the defendant. The report shall be released on the motion of any party if the defendant introduces the report in the present case, raises a mental health defense at trial or sentencing or is convicted of an offense in the present case and the sentence is final.

D. If the prescreening evaluation indicates that reasonable grounds exist to conduct another examination as prescribed by subsection A, the court shall treat the prescreening evaluation as a preliminary examination pursuant to rule 11.2(c) of the Arizona rules of criminal procedure and shall proceed in accordance with rule 11 of the Arizona rules of criminal procedure.

13-755. Death sentences; supreme court review

A. The supreme court shall review all death sentences. On review, the supreme court shall independently review the trial court's findings of aggravation and mitigation and the propriety of the death sentence.

B. If the supreme court determines that an error was made regarding a finding of aggravation or mitigation, the supreme court shall independently determine if the mitigation the supreme court finds is sufficiently substantial to warrant leniency in light of the existing aggravation. If the supreme court finds that the mitigation is not sufficiently substantial to warrant leniency, the supreme court shall affirm the death sentence. If the supreme court finds that the mitigation is sufficiently substantial to warrant leniency, the supreme court shall impose a life sentence pursuant to section 13-751, subsection A.

C. The independent review required by subsection A does not preclude the supreme court from remanding a case for further action if the trial court erroneously excluded evidence or if the appellate record does not adequately reflect the evidence presented.

13-756. Death sentences; supreme court review

A. The supreme court shall review all death sentences to determine whether the trier of fact abused its discretion in finding aggravating circumstances and imposing a sentence of death.
B. If the supreme court determines that an error occurred in the sentencing proceedings, the supreme court shall determine whether the error was harmless beyond a reasonable doubt. If the supreme court cannot determine whether the error was harmless beyond a reasonable doubt, the supreme court shall remand the case for a new sentencing proceeding.

13-757. Method of infliction of sentence of death; identity of executioners; license suspension

A. The penalty of death shall be inflicted by an intravenous injection of a substance or substances in a lethal quantity sufficient to cause death, under the supervision of the state department of corrections.
B. A defendant who is sentenced to death for an offense committed before November 23, 1992 shall choose either lethal injection or lethal gas at least twenty days before the execution date. If the defendant fails to choose either lethal injection or lethal gas, the penalty of death shall be inflicted by lethal injection.
C. The identity of executioners and other persons who participate or perform ancillary functions in an execution and any information contained in records that would identify those persons is confidential and is not subject to disclosure pursuant to title 39, chapter 1, article 2.
D. If a person who participates or performs ancillary functions in an execution is licensed by a board, the licensing board shall not suspend or revoke the person's license as a result of the person's participation in an execution.

13-758. Persons present at execution of sentence of death; limitation

The director of the state department of corrections or the director's designee shall be present at the execution of all death sentences and shall invite the attorney general and at least twelve reputable citizens of the director's selection to be present at the execution. The director shall, at the request of the defendant, permit clergymen, not exceeding two, whom the defendant names and any persons, relatives or friends, not exceeding five, to be present at the execution. The director may invite peace officers as the director deems expedient to witness the execution. No persons other than those set forth in this section shall be present at the execution nor shall any minor be allowed to witness the execution.

13-759. Death warrant; return

A. After a conviction and sentence of death are affirmed and the first post-conviction relief proceedings have concluded, the supreme court shall issue a warrant of execution that authorizes the director of the state department of corrections to carry out the execution thirty-five days after the supreme court's mandate or order denying review or upon motion by the state. The supreme court shall grant subsequent warrants of execution on a motion by the state. The time for execution shall be fixed for thirty-five days after the state's motion is granted.
B. Upon the execution of a sentence of death, the director of the state department of corrections shall make a return upon the death warrant to the court which pronounced sentence and the supreme court, showing the time, mode and manner in which it was executed.

Chapter 8 Restitution and Fines

13-801. Fines for felonies

A. A sentence to pay a fine for a felony shall be a sentence to pay an amount fixed by the court not more than one hundred fifty thousand dollars.

B. A judgment that the defendant shall pay a fine, with or without the alternative of imprisonment, shall constitute a lien in like manner as a judgment for money rendered in a civil action.

C. This section does not apply to an enterprise.

13-802. Fines for misdemeanors

A. A sentence to pay a fine for a class 1 misdemeanor shall be a sentence to pay an amount, fixed by the court, not more than two thousand five hundred dollars.

B. A sentence to pay a fine for a class 2 misdemeanor shall be a sentence to pay an amount, fixed by the court, not more than seven hundred fifty dollars.

C. A sentence to pay a fine for a class 3 misdemeanor shall be a sentence to pay an amount, fixed by the court, not more than five hundred dollars.

D. A sentence to pay a fine for a petty offense shall be a sentence to pay an amount, fixed by the court, of not more than three hundred dollars.

E. A judgment that the defendant shall pay a fine, with or without the alternative of imprisonment, shall constitute a lien in like manner as a judgment for money rendered in a civil action.

F. This section does not apply to an enterprise.

13-803. Fines against enterprises

A. Except as provided in sections 13-822 and 13-823, a sentence to pay a fine that is imposed on an enterprise for an offense defined in this title or for an offense defined outside this title for which no special enterprise fine is specified shall be a sentence to pay an amount, fixed by the court, of not more than:

1. For a felony, one million dollars.
2. For a class 1 misdemeanor, twenty thousand dollars.
3. For a class 2 misdemeanor, ten thousand dollars.
4. For a class 3 misdemeanor, two thousand dollars.
5. For a petty offense, one thousand dollars.

B. If the court imposes a fine, the court shall impose as a presumptive fine the median of the allowable range under subsection A of this section and the presumptive fine may be mitigated or aggravated pursuant to this section.

C. After considering the factors listed in subsection F of this section, the court shall determine an appropriate fine. If the court deviates from the presumptive fine, the court shall set forth on the record the fine, if any, and how the relevant factors listed in subsection F of this section affected the court's determination.

D. Subsections B, C and F of this section and sections 13-822 and 13-823 do not apply to sentences for misdemeanor violations that are prosecuted in justice court or municipal court, except that the court may consider the factors listed in subsection F of this section and section 13-822 in determining the fine to impose.

E. A judgment that the enterprise shall pay a fine shall constitute a lien in like manner as a judgment for money rendered in a civil action.

F. If the court deviates from the presumptive fine, the court shall base its decision on any evidence or information that was introduced or submitted to it before sentencing or on any evidence that was previously heard at trial and shall consider the following factors, if relevant:

1. The income and assets of the enterprise and the economic impact of the penalty on the enterprise.
2. Any prior criminal, civil or regulatory misconduct by the enterprise.
3. The degree of harm resulting from the offense.
4. Whether the offense resulted in pecuniary gain.
5. Whether the enterprise made good faith efforts to comply with any applicable requirements.
6. The duration of the offense.
7. The role of the directors, officers or principals of the enterprise in the offense.
8. Whether the offense involved an unusually vulnerable victim due to age, physical or mental condition or any other factor that would make the victim particularly susceptible to criminal conduct.
9. Whether the offense involved a threat to a market.
10. Whether the enterprise breached a fiduciary duty in committing the offense.
11. The obligation of the enterprise to pay restitution.

12. Any other factors that the court deems appropriate.

13-804. Restitution for offense causing economic loss; fine for reimbursement of public monies

A. On a defendant's conviction for an offense causing economic loss to any person, the court, in its sole discretion, may order that all or any portion of the fine imposed be allocated as restitution to be paid by the defendant to any person who suffered an economic loss caused by the defendant's conduct.

B. In ordering restitution for economic loss pursuant to section 13-603, subsection C or subsection A of this section, the court shall consider all losses caused by the criminal offense or offenses for which the defendant has been convicted.

C. The court shall not consider the economic circumstances of the defendant in determining the amount of restitution.

D. Restitution payments that are ordered pursuant to section 13-603 and this section shall not be stayed if the defendant files a notice of appeal, and the payments may be held by the court pending the outcome of an appeal.

E. After the court determines the amount of restitution, the court or a staff member designated by the court, including a probation officer, shall specify the manner in which the restitution is to be paid. In deciding the manner in which the restitution is to be paid, the court or a staff member designated by the court, including a probation officer, shall make reasonable efforts to contact any victim who has requested notice pursuant to sections 13-4415 and 13-4417, shall take into account the views of the victim and shall consider the economic circumstances of the defendant. In considering the economic circumstances of the defendant, the court shall consider all of the defendant's assets and income, including workers' compensation and social security benefits. The court shall make all reasonable efforts to ensure that all persons entitled to restitution pursuant to a court order promptly receive full restitution. The court may enter any reasonable order necessary to accomplish this. If a victim has received reimbursement for the victim's economic loss from an insurance company, a crime victim compensation program funded pursuant to section 41-2407 or any other entity, the court shall order the defendant to pay the restitution to that entity. If a victim has received only partial reimbursement for the victim's economic loss, the court shall order the defendant to pay restitution first to the victim and then to the entity that partially reimbursed the victim. If a probation, parole or community supervision officer has reason to believe that court ordered restitution is not being made, the officer shall report to the court supervising the probationer or the board of executive clemency that the defendant has failed to make restitution in a timely manner and the court or the board of executive clemency may revoke the defendant's probation, parole or community supervision.

F. If more than one defendant is convicted of the offense that caused the loss, the defendants are jointly and severally liable for the restitution.

G. If the court does not have sufficient evidence to support a finding of the amount of restitution or the manner in which the restitution should be paid, it may conduct a hearing on the issue according to procedures established by court rule. The court may call the defendant to testify and to produce information or evidence. The state does not represent persons who have suffered economic loss at the hearing but may present evidence or information relevant to the issue of restitution.

H. After making the determinations in subsection B of this section the trial court shall enter a restitution order for each defendant that sets forth all of the following:

1. The total amount of restitution the defendant owes all persons.
2. The total amount of restitution owed to each person.
3. The manner in which the restitution is to be paid.

I. The restitution order under subsection H of this section may be supported by evidence or information introduced or submitted to the court before sentencing or any evidence previously heard by the judge during the proceedings.

J. A restitution lien shall be created in favor of the state for the total amount of the restitution.

K. A restitution lien shall be created in favor of the state for the total amount of the fine, surcharges, assessments, costs, incarceration costs and fees ordered, if any, except that a lien may not be perfected against a titled motor vehicle.

L. Notwithstanding any other law, a restitution lien is created in favor of a victim of the defendant ordered to make restitution. Monies received monthly from the defendant shall be applied first to satisfy the restitution order entered by the court and the payment of any restitution in arrears. Any monies that are owed by this state to a person who is under a restitution order shall be assigned first to discharge the restitution order, including any tax refund that is owed to the defendant.

M. If the defendant, the state or persons entitled to restitution pursuant to a court order disagree with the manner of payment established in subsection E of this section, the defendant, court or person entitled to restitution may petition the court at any time to change the manner in which the restitution is paid. Before modifying the order pertaining to the manner in which the restitution is paid, the court shall give notice and an opportunity to be heard to the defendant, the state and, on request, persons entitled to restitution pursuant to a court order.

13-804.01. Reimbursement of incarceration costs; misdemeanors

A. The court shall order a person who is convicted of a misdemeanor offense and who is sentenced to a term of incarceration to reimburse the political subdivision that is responsible for the costs of the person's incarceration for the incarceration costs.

B. The court may determine the amount of incarceration costs to be paid based on the following factors:

1. The per diem per person cost of incarceration incurred by the political subdivision that incarcerates the person.

2. The person's ability to pay part or all of the incarceration costs.

13-805. Jurisdiction

A. The trial court shall retain jurisdiction of the case as follows:

1. Subject to paragraph 2 of this subsection, for purposes of ordering, modifying and enforcing the manner in which court-ordered payments are made until paid in full or until the defendant's sentence expires.

2. For all restitution orders in favor of a victim, including liens and criminal restitution orders, for purposes of ordering, modifying and enforcing the manner in which payments are made until paid in full.

B. At the time the defendant is ordered to pay restitution by the court, the court may enter a criminal restitution order in favor of each person who is entitled to restitution for the unpaid balance of any restitution order. A criminal restitution order does not affect any other monetary obligation imposed on the defendant pursuant to law.

C. At the time the defendant completes the defendant's period of probation or the defendant's sentence or the defendant absconds from probation or the defendant's sentence, the court shall enter both:

1. A criminal restitution order in favor of the state for the unpaid balance, if any, of any fines, costs, incarceration costs, fees, surcharges or assessments imposed.

2. A criminal restitution order in favor of each person entitled to restitution for the unpaid balance of any restitution ordered, if a criminal restitution order is not issued pursuant to subsection B of this section.

D. The clerk of the court shall notify each person who is entitled to restitution of the criminal restitution order.

E. A criminal restitution order may be recorded and is enforceable as any civil judgment, except that a criminal restitution order does not require renewal pursuant to section 12-1611 or 12-1612. Enforcement of a criminal restitution order by any person who is entitled to restitution or by the state includes the collection of interest that accrues at a rate of ten percent per annum. A criminal restitution order does not expire until paid in full. A filing fee, recording fee or any other charge is not required for recording a criminal restitution order.

F. All monies paid pursuant to a criminal restitution order entered by the court shall be paid to the clerk of the court.

G. Monies received as a result of a criminal restitution order entered pursuant to this section shall be distributed in the following order of priority:

1. Restitution ordered that is reduced to a criminal restitution order.

2. Associated interest.

H. The interest accrued pursuant to subsection E of this section does not apply to fees imposed for collection of the court ordered payments.

I. A criminal restitution order is a criminal penalty for the purposes of a federal bankruptcy involving the defendant.

13-806. Restitution lien

A. The state or any person entitled to restitution pursuant to a court order may file in accordance with this section a restitution lien. A filing fee, recording fee or any other charge is not required for filing a restitution lien.

B. A restitution lien shall be signed by the attorney representing the state in the criminal action or by a magistrate and shall set forth all of the following information:

1. The name and date of birth of the defendant whose property or other interests are subject to the lien.

2. The present residence or principal place of business of the person named in the lien, if known.

3. The criminal proceeding pursuant to which the lien is filed, including the name of the court, the title of the action and the court's file number.

4. The name and address of the attorney representing the state in the proceeding pursuant to which the lien is filed or the name and address of the person entitled to restitution pursuant to a court order filing the lien.

5. A statement that the notice is being filed pursuant to this section.

6. The amount of restitution the defendant in the proceeding has been ordered to pay or an estimated amount of economic loss caused by the offense alleged in the proceeding if no restitution order has been entered yet.

7. A statement that the total amount of restitution owed will change and that the clerk of the court in which the proceeding was or is pending shall maintain a record of the outstanding balance.

C. A prosecutor or a victim in a criminal proceeding in which there was an economic loss may file a request with the court for a preconviction restitution lien after the filing of a misdemeanor complaint or felony information or indictment.

D. A victim in a criminal proceeding may file a restitution lien after restitution is determined and ordered by the trial court following pronouncement of the judgment and sentence.

E. A restitution lien is perfected against interests in personal property by filing the lien with the secretary of state, except that in the case of titled motor vehicles it shall be filed with the department of transportation motor vehicle division. A restitution lien is perfected against interests in real property by filing the lien with the county recorder of the county in which the real property is located. The state or a victim may give the additional notice of the lien as either deems appropriate.

F. The filing of a restitution lien in accordance with this section creates a lien in favor of the state or the victim in all of the following:

1. Any interest of the defendant in real property situated in the county in which the lien is filed then maintained or thereafter acquired in the name of the defendant identified in the lien.

2. Any interest of the defendant in personal property situated in this state then maintained or thereafter acquired in the name of the defendant identified in the lien.

3. Any property identified in the lien to the extent of the defendant's interest in the property.

G. The filing of a restitution lien under this section is notice to all persons dealing with the person or property identified in the lien of the state's or victim's claim. The lien created in favor of the state or the victim in accordance with this section is superior and prior to the claims or interests of any other person, except a person possessing any of the following:

1. A valid lien perfected before the filing of the restitution lien.

2. In the case of real property, an interest acquired and recorded before the filing of the restitution lien.

3. In the case of personal property, an interest acquired before the filing of the restitution lien.

H. This section does not limit the right of the state or any other person entitled to restitution to obtain any order or injunction, receivership, writ, attachment, garnishment or other remedy authorized by law.

I. Following the entry of the judgment and sentence in the criminal case, if the trial court sentences the defendant to pay a fine or awards costs of investigation or prosecution, the state may file a restitution lien pursuant to this section for the amount of the fine or costs, except that a lien may not be perfected against a titled motor vehicle.

J. A criminal restitution lien is a criminal penalty for the purposes of any federal bankruptcy involving the defendant.

K. The court shall order the release of any preconviction restitution lien that has been filed or perfected if the defendant is acquitted or the state does not proceed with the prosecution.

L. A self-service storage facility that forecloses its lien pursuant to section 33-1704 may sell personal property that is subject to a restitution lien. The proceeds from the sale, less the reasonable costs of sale, shall be paid to the restitution lienholder to satisfy the restitution lien as prescribed in section 33-1704. A person who is a good faith purchaser pursuant to section 33-1704 and who purchases personal property that is subject to a restitution lien takes the property free and clear of the rights of the restitution lienholder.

13-807. Civil actions by victims or other persons

A defendant who is convicted in a criminal proceeding is precluded from subsequently denying in any civil proceeding brought by the victim or this state against the criminal defendant the essential allegations of the criminal offense of which he was adjudged guilty, including judgments of guilt resulting from no contest pleas. An order of restitution in favor of a person does not preclude that person from bringing a separate civil action and proving in that action damages in excess of the amount of the restitution order that is actually paid.

13-808. Time and method of payment of fines; conditions of probation; no limitation on restitution and other assessments

A. If a defendant is sentenced to pay a fine alone or in addition to any other sentence, the court or a probation officer or a staff member designated by the court may grant permission for payment to be made within a specified period of time or in specified installments. If no such permission is embodied in the sentence the fine shall be payable immediately.

B. If a defendant sentenced to pay a fine, restitution, penalty, assessment, incarceration cost or surcharge is also sentenced to probation, the court shall make payment of the fine, restitution, penalty, assessment, incarceration cost or surcharge a condition of probation.

C. The amount of restitution, assessments, incarceration costs and surcharges is not limited by the maximum fine that may be imposed under section 13-801 or 13-802.

13-809. Priority of payments; application to traffic offenses; orders to reimburse public monies

A. If a defendant is sentenced to pay a fine or incarceration costs, payment and enforcement of restitution take priority over payment to the state.

B. Section 13-804 does not apply to traffic offenses, except for a violation of section 28-661, 28-662, 28-693, 28-1381, 28-1382 or 28-1383 or any local ordinance relating to the same subject matter of such sections.

C. The court may impose an additional fine on sentencing for any offense to require that the defendant reimburse the law enforcement agency for any public monies paid to any person.

13-810. Consequences of nonpayment of fines, fees, restitution or incarceration costs

A. In addition to any other remedy provided by law, including a writ of execution or other civil enforcement, if a defendant who is sentenced to pay a fine, a fee or incarceration costs defaults in the payment of the fine, fee or incarceration costs or of any installment as ordered, the court, on motion of the prosecuting attorney or on its own motion, shall require the defendant to show cause why the defendant's default should not be treated as contempt and may issue a summons or a warrant of arrest for the defendant's appearance.

B. In addition to any other remedy provided by law, including a writ of execution or other civil enforcement, if a defendant who is ordered to pay restitution defaults in the payment of the restitution or of any installment as ordered, the court, on motion of the prosecuting attorney, on petition of any person entitled to restitution pursuant to a court order or on its own motion, shall require the defendant to show cause why the defendant's default should not be treated as contempt and may issue a summons or a warrant of arrest for the defendant's appearance.

C. In addition to any other remedy provided by law, including a writ of execution or other civil enforcement, the court, on receipt of a petition and issuance of an order to show cause, has jurisdiction to preserve rights over all restitution liens entered pursuant to section 13-806, subsection B, and perfected pursuant to section 13-806, subsection E.

D. At any hearing on the order to show cause the court, the prosecuting attorney or a person entitled to restitution may examine the defendant under oath concerning the defendant's financial condition, employment and assets or on any other matter relating to the defendant's ability to pay restitution.

E. If the court finds that the defendant has wilfully failed to pay a fine, a fee, restitution or incarceration costs or finds that the defendant has intentionally refused to make a good faith effort to obtain the monies required for the payment, the court shall find that the default constitutes contempt and may do one of the following:

1. Order the defendant incarcerated in the county jail until the fine, fee, restitution or incarceration costs, or a specified part of the fine, fee, restitution or incarceration costs, is paid.

2. Revoke the defendant's probation, parole or community supervision and sentence the defendant to prison pursuant to law.

3. Enter an order pursuant to section 13-812. The levy or execution for the collection of a fine, a fee, restitution or incarceration costs does not discharge a defendant who is incarcerated for nonpayment of the fine, fee, restitution or incarceration costs until the amount of the fine, fee, restitution or incarceration costs is collected.

4. Order the defendant to perform community restitution.

F. If the court finds that the default is not wilful and that the defendant cannot pay despite sufficient good faith efforts to obtain the monies, the court may take any lawful action including:

1. Modify the manner in which the restitution, fine, fee or incarceration costs are to be paid.

2. Enter any reasonable order that would assure compliance with the order to pay.

3. Enter an order pursuant to section 13-812. The levy or execution for the collection of a fine, a fee, restitution or incarceration costs does not discharge a defendant incarcerated for nonpayment of the fine, fee, restitution or incarceration costs until the amount of the fine, fee, restitution or incarceration costs is collected.

G. If a fine, a fee, restitution or incarceration costs are imposed on an enterprise it is the duty of the person or persons authorized to make disbursement from the assets of the enterprise to pay them from those assets, and their failure to do so shall be held a contempt unless they make the showing required in subsection A or B of this section.

H. If a defendant is sentenced to pay a fine, a fee, restitution or incarceration costs, the clerk of the sentencing court, on request, shall make the defendant's payment history available to the prosecutor, victim, victim's attorney, probation department and court without cost.

13-811. Disposition of fines

A. Except as provided in subsections B and C of this section, all fines collected in any court, except municipal courts, shall be paid to the county treasurer of the county in which the court is held. All fines collected in the superior court for violation of a city or town ordinance shall be paid to the county treasurer.

B. Except as provided in subsection C of this section, all fines or costs collected in any court for offenses indicted by a state grand jury or for other offenses prosecuted by the attorney general shall be paid to the anti-racketeering revolving fund established by section 13-2314.01.

C. Except as provided in section 13-821, all fines collected in any court for offenses included in chapter 34 of this title and prosecuted by a city prosecutor, a county attorney or the attorney general shall be paid to the drug and gang enforcement fund established by section 41-2402.

13-812. Garnishment for nonpayment of fines, fees, restitution or incarceration costs

A. After a hearing on an order to show cause pursuant to section 13-810, subsection A or B or after a hearing on a petition to revoke probation pursuant to section 13-804, subsection E or the rules of criminal procedure, the court may issue a writ of criminal garnishment for any fine, fee, restitution or incarceration costs.

B. The court may order garnishment for monies that are owed to a victim or the court, the clerk of the court or the prosecuting attorney pursuant to a court order to pay any fine, fee, restitution or incarceration costs. A writ of criminal garnishment applies to any of the following:

1. The defendant's earnings as defined in section 12-1598.

2. Indebtedness that is owed to a defendant by a garnishee for amounts that are not earnings.

3. Monies that are held by a garnishee on behalf of a defendant.

4. The defendant's personal property that is in the possession of a garnishee.

5. If the garnishee is a corporation, shares or securities of a corporation or a proprietary interest in a corporation that belongs to a defendant.

6. The defendant's earnings or monies that are held by the state department of corrections while the defendant is in the custody of the department.

13-813. Issuance of writ of garnishment; service and return of writ

A. The court shall direct the writ of criminal garnishment to the sheriff, the constable or any other officer who is authorized by law to serve process in the county in which the garnishee is alleged to be. The writ shall summon the garnishee to immediately appear to answer the writ before the court issuing the writ. The garnishee shall appear within the time specified in the writ. The writ shall state all of the following:

1. The amount due to the victim or court, clerk of the court or prosecuting attorney as of the date on which the writ is issued.

2. The name and address of the garnishee or the garnishee's authorized agent.

3. The name and address of the victim or the court, clerk of the court or prosecuting attorney presenting the writ.

4. The last known mailing address of the defendant.

B. The victim or the court, the clerk of the court or the prosecuting attorney shall serve the following on the garnishee:

1. Two copies of the writ of garnishment and summons.

2. A copy of the criminal restitution order.

3. Four copies of the answer form.

4. Two copies of the notice to the defendant.

5. Two copies of the instructions to the garnishee.

C. The victim or the court, the clerk of the court or the prosecuting attorney shall serve on the defendant a copy of the writ of garnishment.

D. The victim or the court, the clerk of the court or the prosecuting attorney may serve a copy of the writ of garnishment on the manager or other officer of a banking corporation or association, savings bank, savings and loan association, credit union, trust company or title insurance company to levy monies that are owed pursuant to a writ of criminal garnishment by one of these organizations or to levy credits or other effects that belong to a defendant and that are in the possession of or under the control of one of these organizations. The copy of the writ shall be served at any office or branch that is located in the county in which the service is made. A garnishment is not effective as to any debt owed by a banking corporation or association, savings bank, savings and loan association, credit union, trust company or title insurance company if the account evidencing the indebtedness is carried at an office or branch other than the office or branch named in the writ and at which service is made or, as to credits or other effects in its possession or under its control, at any other office or branch unless the service of the writ is accompanied by twenty-five dollars to be paid to the garnishee for the costs of the search. The writ is effective on the payment of the search fee as to any debt owing by a banking corporation or association, savings bank, savings and loan association, credit union, trust company or title insurance company if the account evidencing the indebtedness is carried at any office or branch located in this state, or as to any credits, property or other effects in its possession or under its control, at any office or branch located in this state.

13-814. Restitution to pawnbrokers and dealers; definitions

A. If the lawful owner of stolen property recovers the property from a pawnbroker or dealer and the person who sold or pledged the property to the pawnbroker or dealer is convicted of a violation of law that is related to the stolen or pledged property, the court shall order the defendant to make restitution to the pawnbroker pursuant to this chapter.
B. For the purposes of this section:
1. "Dealer" has the same meaning prescribed in section 44-1601.
2. "Precious item" has the same meaning prescribed in section 44-1601.
3. "Property" includes a numismatic or bullion gold coin and a precious item.

13-815. Initial lien on earnings

A. If the writ of criminal garnishment is for earnings of the defendant, the writ is a lien on the earnings of the defendant from the date of service on the garnishee until any of the following occurs:
1. An order of continuing lien is entered.
2. If an order is not entered, within forty-five days after the date on which the garnishee files an answer.
3. The writ is quashed or released or becomes ineffective.
B. The garnishee shall not remit any withheld earnings to the party obtaining the writ until the court enters an order pursuant to section 13-818.

13-816. Answer; time and form

A. The garnishee shall answer the writ of criminal restitution in the court issuing the writ within ten days after being served.
B. If the writ of criminal garnishment is for earnings of the defendant, the garnishee shall answer pursuant to section 12-1598.08. If the writ of criminal garnishment is for indebtedness, monies, personal property or shares of stock, the garnishee shall answer pursuant to section 12-1579.

13-817. Objection to garnishment; hearing; discharge of garnishee

A. A party who has an objection to the writ of garnishment or the answer may file a written objection and may request a hearing. The party shall state the grounds for objection in writing and shall deliver copies of the objection to all of the parties to the writ.
B. The court shall hold a hearing on an objection to the writ or the answer within ten days after receiving the request. The court may continue the hearing for good cause on terms the court deems appropriate.
C. The court may discharge the garnishee from the writ of criminal restitution if it appears from the garnishee's answer that the garnishee did not owe earnings to the defendant or have the defendant's indebtedness, monies, property or stock in the garnishee's possession and if no written objection to the answer is filed. The court shall enter an order discharging the garnishee.

13-818. Order on writ of garnishment for money or property

A. If the garnishee's answer shows that the garnishee holds indebtedness or monies of the defendant, the court shall enter an order of criminal garnishment that requires the garnishee to immediately transfer the indebtedness or monies to the victim or to the court, the clerk of the court or the prosecuting attorney who is named in the writ of garnishment.

B. If the garnishee's answer shows that the garnishee holds personal property or stock of the defendant, the court shall enter an order against the garnishee to hold the personal property or stock of the defendant pending service of a writ of special execution pursuant to section 12-1554.

C. The party who obtains the writ of garnishment shall deliver a copy of the order on the writ to the garnishee and the defendant.

D. An order that is entered pursuant to subsection A or B of this section shall not order more money, stocks or property transferred than is reasonably necessary to satisfy the amount of the outstanding balance of the underlying criminal restitution order.

E. A bank deposit made in the name of two or more persons is subject to garnishment pursuant to section 12-1595, except that "judgment creditor" includes a victim or the court, the clerk of the court or the prosecuting attorney that obtains the writ of garnishment and "judgment debtor" includes a criminal defendant.

13-819. Order on writ of garnishment for earnings; continuing lien

A. The party who obtains the writ of garnishment for earnings shall deliver a copy of the order on the writ to the garnishee and the defendant.
B. After service or delivery of the order is made, section 12-1598.10 applies, except that "judgment creditor" includes a victim or the court, the clerk of the court or the prosecuting attorney that obtains the writ of garnishment and "judgment debtor" includes a criminal defendant.
C. Section 12-1598.12 applies to continuing liens for writs of criminal garnishment. Section 12-1598.12 applies to reporting by the party obtaining the writ of criminal garnishment, except that "judgment creditor" includes a victim or the court, the clerk of the court or the prosecuting attorney that obtains the writ of garnishment and "judgment debtor" includes a criminal defendant.

13-820. Contempt proceedings; failure to comply with order

If the garnishee fails to comply with the terms of the order of criminal garnishment within thirty days after receiving the order, the victim or the court, the clerk of the court or the prosecuting attorney may petition the court for an order to show cause why the garnishee should not be held in contempt. If the court finds that the failure was wilful or the result of gross negligence, the court shall find the garnishee in contempt and shall award the petitioner reasonable attorney fees, costs and an additional penalty of not more than five hundred dollars.

13-821. Fines for drug offenses

A. In addition to any other fine or restitution, if a person is convicted of or adjudicated delinquent for a violation of chapter 34 of this title, the court may order the person to pay a fine in one of the following amounts:
1. For a first offense, at least one thousand dollars.
2. For a second or subsequent offense, at least two thousand dollars.
B. The court may suspend the imposition of a fine pursuant to this section if the person agrees to enter a residential drug rehabilitation program approved by the court and to pay for all or a part of the costs associated with the rehabilitation program. On

successfully completing the program, the person may apply to the court for a reduction in the amount of the fine imposed pursuant to this section. If the person establishes to the satisfaction of the court that the person successfully completed the program, the court may reduce the fine by the amount the person paid to participate in the rehabilitation program. If the person fails to complete the program, the court shall enforce the collection of the entire fine that was imposed pursuant to subsection A.

C. The court shall transmit the monies collected pursuant to this section to the supreme court for the purpose of providing drug treatment services to adult probationers through the community punishment program established in title 12, chapter 2, article 11.

13-822. Effective programs to prevent and detect violations of law; fines

A. If based on any evidence or information introduced or submitted to the court before sentencing or on any evidence that was previously heard at trial the court finds by a preponderance of the evidence that an enterprise had an effective program to prevent and detect violations of law in effect at the time the offense was committed, the court shall set forth on the record its factual findings and the reasons in support of its findings and shall reduce the fine imposed pursuant to section 13-803, if any, by twenty-five per cent.

B. An effective program to prevent and detect violations of law requires at a minimum that the enterprise does the following:

1. Establish compliance standards and procedures to be followed by its employees and other agents that are reasonably capable of reducing the prospect of violations of law.

2. Assign specific high-level personnel within the enterprise overall responsibility to oversee compliance with the standards and procedures.

3. Use due care not to delegate substantial discretionary authority to individuals whom the enterprise knows, or should know through the exercise of due diligence, have a propensity to engage in illegal activities.

4. Take steps to communicate effectively its standards and procedures to all employees and other agents, including requiring participation in training programs or disseminating publications that explain in a practical manner what is required.

5. Take reasonable steps to achieve compliance with its standards, including the use of monitoring and auditing systems reasonably designed to detect violations of law by its employees and other agents and having in place and publicizing a reporting system where employees and other agents can report violations of law by others within the enterprise without fear of retribution.

6. Consistently enforce the standards through appropriate disciplinary mechanisms, including, as appropriate, discipline of individuals responsible for the failure to detect a violation.

7. After a violation is detected, take all reasonable steps to respond appropriately to the violation and to prevent further similar violations, including any necessary modifications to its program to prevent and detect violations of law.

C. Relevant factors for determining precise actions necessary for an effective program to prevent and detect violations of law include:

1. The size of the enterprise.

2. The likelihood that certain violations may occur because of the nature of the enterprise's business.

3. The prior history of the enterprise.

D. The failure of an enterprise to incorporate and follow applicable industry practice or the standards called for by any applicable governmental rule weighs against a finding of an effective program to prevent and detect violations of law.

E. An enterprise's failure to prevent or detect violations of law, by itself, does not mean that the program is not effective if the court finds that the enterprise exercised due diligence in establishing and maintaining its program at the time the acts constituting the offense were committed.

F. This section does not apply if any of the following applies:

1. A high managerial agent of the enterprise, a unit of the enterprise with two hundred or more employees and within which the offense was committed or an individual who is responsible for the administration or enforcement of a program to prevent and detect violations of law participated in, condoned or was wilfully ignorant of the offense. It is a rebuttable presumption that the enterprise did not have an effective program to prevent and detect violations of law if an individual with substantial supervisory authority participates in an offense.

2. After becoming aware of an offense, the enterprise unreasonably delayed reporting the offense to the appropriate governmental authorities. An enterprise shall report an offense within seventy-two hours.

3. The enterprise wilfully obstructed or impeded, attempted to obstruct or impede or aided, abetted or encouraged the obstruction of justice during the investigation, prosecution or sentencing of the offense or, with knowledge of the offense, failed to take reasonable steps to prevent the obstruction or impediment or the attempted obstruction or impediment.

4. If the offense is discovered by the government before disclosure by the enterprise unless, under the circumstances of the offense, no high managerial agent knew or could reasonably have known of the conduct constituting the offense.

13-823. Dangerous and repeat enterprise offenders; fines

A. Whether or not an enterprise maintains an effective program to prevent and detect violations of law pursuant to section 13-822, the court may subject an enterprise to five times the maximum fine authorized by section 13-803 if based on any evidence that was introduced before sentencing or that was heard at trial the court finds by a preponderance of the evidence that any of the following applies to the commission of the offense:

1. The offense violated a judicial or administrative order or injunction, other than a violation of a condition of probation or that the enterprise or a separately managed line of business violated a condition of probation by engaging in misconduct similar to that for which it was placed on probation.

2. The offense involved conduct that was malicious or wanton.

3. The offense involved conduct that posed an imminent and substantial hazard to human health or to the environment or resulted in serious actual harm to human health or to the environment and the enterprise continued the conduct after receiving notice.

B. For the purposes of this section, an enterprise is deemed to have received notice if an officer, director or high managerial agent has actual knowledge that the enterprise is engaging in the conduct that constitutes a violation of law and the officer, director or high managerial agent knows or is recklessly indifferent to the fact that the conduct is or may be harmful.

13-824. Community restitution in lieu of fines, fees, assessments or incarceration costs

Notwithstanding any other law, in a municipal or justice court, if a defendant is sentenced to pay a fine, a fee, assessment or incarceration costs and the court finds the defendant is unable to pay all or part of the fine, fee, assessment or incarceration costs, the court may order the defendant to perform community restitution in lieu of the payment for all or part of the fine, fee, assessment or incarceration costs. The amount of community restitution shall be equivalent to the amount of the fine, fee or incarceration costs by crediting any service performed at a rate of ten dollars per hour.

Chapter 9 Probation and Restoration of Civil Rights

13-901. Probation

A. If a person who has been convicted of an offense is eligible for probation, the court may suspend the imposition or execution of sentence and, if so, shall without delay place the person on intensive probation supervision pursuant to section 13-913 or supervised or unsupervised probation on such terms and conditions as the law requires and the court deems appropriate, including participation in any programs authorized in title 12, chapter 2, article 11. If a person is not eligible for probation, imposition or execution of sentence shall not be suspended or delayed. If the court imposes probation, it may also impose a fine as authorized by chapter 8 of this title. If probation is granted the court shall impose a condition that the person waive extradition for any probation revocation procedures and it shall order restitution pursuant to section 13-603, subsection C where there is a victim who has suffered economic loss. When granting probation to an adult the court, as a condition of probation, shall assess a monthly fee of not less than sixty-five dollars unless, after determining the inability of the probationer to pay the fee, the court assesses a lesser fee. This fee is not subject to any surcharge. In justice and municipal courts the fee shall only be assessed when the person is placed on supervised probation. For persons placed on probation in the superior court, the fee shall be paid to the clerk of the superior court and the clerk of the court shall pay all monies collected from this fee to the county treasurer for deposit in the adult probation services fund established by section 12-267. For persons placed on supervised probation in the justice court, the fee shall be paid to the justice court and the justice court shall transmit all of the monies to the county treasurer for deposit in the adult probation services fund established by section 12-267. For persons placed on supervised probation in the municipal court, the fee shall be paid to the municipal court. The municipal court shall transmit all of the monies to the city treasurer who shall transmit the monies to the county treasurer for deposit in the adult probation services fund established by section 12-267. Any amount assessed pursuant to this subsection shall be used to supplement monies used for the salaries of adult probation and surveillance officers and for support of programs and services of the superior court adult probation departments.

B. The period of probation shall be determined according to section 13-902, except that if a person is released pursuant to section 31-233, subsection B and community supervision is waived pursuant to section 13-603, subsection K, the court shall extend the period of probation by the amount of time the director of the state department of corrections approves for the inmate's temporary release.

C. The court, in its discretion, may issue a warrant for the rearrest of the defendant and may modify or add to the conditions or, if the defendant commits an additional offense or violates a condition, may revoke probation in accordance with the rules of criminal procedure at any time before the expiration or termination of the period of probation. If the court revokes the defendant's probation and the defendant is serving more than one probationary term concurrently, the court may sentence the person to terms of imprisonment to be served consecutively.

D. At any time during the probationary term of the person released on probation, any probation officer, without warrant or other process and at any time until the final disposition of the case, may rearrest any person and bring the person before the court.

E. The court, on its own initiative or on application of the probationer, after notice and an opportunity to be heard for the prosecuting attorney and, on request, the victim, may terminate the period of probation or intensive probation and discharge the defendant at a time earlier than that originally imposed if in the court's opinion the ends of justice will be served and if the conduct of the defendant on probation warrants it.

F. When granting probation the court may require that the defendant be imprisoned in the county jail at whatever time or intervals, consecutive or nonconsecutive, the court shall determine, within the period of probation, as long as the period actually spent in confinement does not exceed one year or the maximum period of imprisonment permitted under chapter 7 of this title, whichever is the shorter.

G. If the defendant is placed on lifetime probation and has served one year in the county jail as a term of probation, the court may require that the defendant be additionally imprisoned in the county jail at whatever time or intervals, consecutive or nonconsecutive, the court shall determine, within the period of probation if the defendant's probation is revoked by the court and the defendant is subsequently reinstated on probation. The period actually spent in confinement as a term of being reinstated on probation shall not exceed one year or when including the initial one year period of incarceration imposed as a term of probation, the maximum period of imprisonment permitted under chapter 7 of this title, whichever is the shorter.

H. If restitution is made a condition of probation, the court shall fix the amount of restitution and the manner of performance pursuant to chapter 8 of this title.

I. When granting probation, the court shall set forth at the time of sentencing and on the record the factual and legal reasons in support of each sentence.

J. If the defendant meets the criteria set forth in section 13-901.01 or 13-3422, the court may place the defendant on probation pursuant to either section. If a defendant is placed on probation pursuant to section 13-901.01 or 13-3422, the court may impose any term of probation that is authorized pursuant to this section and that is not in violation of section 13-901.01.

13-901.01. Probation for persons convicted of possession or use of controlled substances or drug paraphernalia; treatment; prevention; education; exceptions; definition

(Caution: 1998 Prop. 105 applies)

A. Notwithstanding any law to the contrary, any person who is convicted of the personal possession or use of a controlled substance or drug paraphernalia is eligible for probation. The court shall suspend the imposition or execution of sentence and place the person on probation.

B. Any person who has been convicted of or indicted for a violent crime as defined in section 13-901.03 is not eligible for probation as provided for in this section but instead shall be sentenced pursuant to chapter 34 of this title.

C. Personal possession or use of a controlled substance pursuant to this section shall not include possession for sale, production, manufacturing or transportation for sale of any controlled substance.

D. If a person is convicted of personal possession or use of a controlled substance or drug paraphernalia, as a condition of probation, the court shall require participation in an appropriate drug treatment or education program administered by a qualified agency or organization that provides such programs to persons who abuse controlled substances. Each person who is enrolled in a drug treatment or education program shall be required to pay for participation in the program to the extent of the person's financial ability.

E. A person who has been placed on probation pursuant to this section and who is determined by the court to be in violation of probation shall have new conditions of probation established by the court. The court shall select the additional conditions it deems necessary, including intensified drug treatment, community restitution, intensive probation, home arrest or any other sanctions except that the court shall not impose a term of incarceration unless the court determines that the person violated probation by committing an offense listed in chapter 34 or 34.1 of this title or an act in violation of an order of the court relating to drug treatment.

F. If a person is convicted a second time of personal possession or use of a controlled substance or drug paraphernalia, the court may include additional conditions of probation it deems necessary, including intensified drug treatment, community restitution, intensive probation, home arrest or any other action within the jurisdiction of the court.

G. At any time while the defendant is on probation, if after having a reasonable opportunity to do so the defendant fails or refuses to participate in drug treatment, the probation department or the prosecutor may petition the court to revoke the defendant's probation. If the court finds that the defendant refused to participate in drug treatment, the defendant shall no longer be eligible for probation under this section but instead shall be sentenced pursuant to chapter 34 of this title.

H. A person is not eligible for probation under this section but instead shall be sentenced pursuant to chapter 34 of this title if the court finds the person either:

1. Had been convicted three times of personal possession of a controlled substance or drug paraphernalia.

2. Refused drug treatment as a term of probation.

3. Rejected probation.

4. Was convicted of the personal possession or use of a controlled substance or drug paraphernalia and the offense involved methamphetamine.

I. Subsections G and H of this section do not prohibit the defendant from being placed on probation pursuant to section 13-901 if the defendant otherwise qualifies for probation under that section.

J. For the purposes of this section, "controlled substance" has the same meaning prescribed in section 36-2501.

13-901.02. Drug treatment and education fund

A. The drug treatment and education fund is established. The administrative office of the supreme court shall administer the fund.

B. Fifty per cent of the monies deposited in the drug treatment and education fund shall be distributed by the administrative office of the supreme court to the superior court probation departments to cover the costs of placing persons in drug education and treatment programs administered by a qualified agency or organization that provides such programs to persons who abuse controlled substances. Such monies shall be allocated to superior court probation departments according to a formula based on probation caseload to be established by the administrative office of the supreme court.

C. Fifty per cent of the monies deposited in the drug treatment and education fund shall be distributed to the Arizona parents commission on drug education and prevention established by section 41-1604.17.

D. The administrative office of the supreme court shall cause to be prepared at the end of each fiscal year after 1997 an accountability report card that details the cost savings realized from the diversion of persons from prisons to probation. A copy of the report shall be submitted to the governor and the legislature, and a copy of the report shall be sent to each public library in the state. Beginning July 1, 2011, the report shall be submitted electronically. The administrative office of the supreme court shall receive reimbursement from the drug treatment and education fund for any administrative costs it incurs in the implementation of this section.

13-901.03. Violent crimes; allegation; definition

A. The allegation that the defendant committed a violent crime shall be charged in the indictment or information and admitted or found by the court. The court shall allow the allegation that the defendant committed a violent crime at any time before the date the case is actually tried unless the allegation is filed fewer than twenty days before the case is actually tried and the court finds on the record that the defendant was in fact prejudiced by the untimely filing and states the reasons for these findings.

B. For the purpose of this section, "violent crime" includes any criminal act that results in death or physical injury or any criminal use of a deadly weapon or dangerous instrument.

13-902. Periods of probation; monitoring; fees

A. Unless terminated sooner, probation may continue for the following periods:

1. For a class 2 felony, seven years.

2. For a class 3 felony, five years.

3. For a class 4 felony, four years.

4. For a class 5 or 6 felony, three years.

5. For a class 1 misdemeanor, three years.

6. For a class 2 misdemeanor, two years.

7. For a class 3 misdemeanor, one year.

B. Notwithstanding subsection A of this section, unless terminated sooner, probation may continue for the following periods:

1. For a violation of section 28-1381 or 28-1382, five years.

2. For a violation of section 28-1383, ten years.

C. If the court has required, as a condition of probation, that the defendant make restitution for any economic loss related to the defendant's offense and that condition has not been satisfied, the court at any time before the termination or expiration of probation may extend the period within the following limits:

1. For a felony, not more than five years.

2. For a misdemeanor, not more than two years.

D. Notwithstanding any other provision of law, justice courts and municipal courts may impose the probation periods specified in subsection A, paragraphs 5, 6 and 7 and subsection B, paragraph 1 of this section.

E. After conviction of a felony offense or an attempt to commit any offense that is included in chapter 14 or 35.1 of this title or section 13-2308.01, 13-2308.03, 13-2923, 13-3212 or 13-3623, if probation is available, probation may continue for a term of not less than the term that is specified in subsection A of this section up to and including life and that the court believes is appropriate for the ends of justice.

F. After conviction of a violation of section 13-3824, subsection A, if a term of probation is imposed and the offense for which the person was required to register was a felony, probation may continue for a term of not less than the term that is specified in subsection A of this section up to and including life and that the court believes is appropriate for the ends of justice.

G. If a person is convicted on or after November 1, 2006 of a dangerous crime against children as defined in section 13-705, a term of probation is imposed, the person is required to register pursuant to section 13-3821 and the person is classified as a level three offender pursuant to section 13-3825, the court shall require global position system or electronic monitoring for the duration of the term of probation. The court may impose a fee on the probationer to offset the cost of the monitoring device required by this subsection. The fee shall be deposited in the adult probation services fund pursuant to section 12-267, subsection A, paragraph 3. This subsection does not preclude global position system or electronic monitoring of any other person who is serving a term of probation.

13-903. Calculation of periods of probation

A. A period of probation commences on the day it is imposed or as designated by the court, and an extended period of probation commences on the day the original period lapses.

B. If a court determines that the defendant violated a condition of the defendant's probation but reinstates probation, the period between the date of the violation and the date of restoration of probation is not computed as part of the period of probation. If it is determined that the defendant is not a violator, there is no interruption of the period.

C. The running of the period of probation shall cease during the unauthorized absence of the defendant from the jurisdiction or from any required supervision and shall resume only upon the defendant's voluntary or involuntary return to the probation service.

D. The running of the period of probation shall cease during the period from the filing of the petition to revoke probation to the termination of revocation of probation proceedings, except that if a court determines that the defendant is not a violator, there is no interruption of the period of probation.

E. If probation is imposed on one who at the time is serving a sentence of imprisonment imposed on a different conviction, service of the sentence of imprisonment shall not satisfy the probation.

F. Time spent in custody under section 13-901, subsection F shall be credited to any sentence of imprisonment imposed upon revocation of probation.

13-904. Suspension of civil rights and occupational disabilities

A. A conviction for a felony suspends the following civil rights of the person sentenced:

1. The right to vote.

2. The right to hold public office of trust or profit.
3. The right to serve as a juror.
4. During any period of imprisonment any other civil rights the suspension of which is reasonably necessary for the security of the institution in which the person sentenced is confined or for the reasonable protection of the public.
5. The right to possess a gun or firearm.
B. Persons sentenced to imprisonment shall not thereby be rendered incompetent as witnesses upon the trial of a criminal action or proceeding, or incapable of making and acknowledging a sale or conveyance of property.
C. A person sentenced to imprisonment is under the protection of the law, and any injury to his person, not authorized by law, is punishable in the same manner as if such person was not convicted and sentenced.
D. The conviction of a person for any offense shall not work forfeiture of any property, except if a forfeiture is expressly imposed by law. All forfeitures to the state, unless expressly imposed by law, are abolished.
E. A person shall not be disqualified from employment by this state or any of its agencies or political subdivisions, nor shall a person whose civil rights have been restored be disqualified to engage in any occupation for which a license, permit or certificate is required to be issued by this state solely because of a prior conviction for a felony or misdemeanor within or without this state. A person may be denied employment by this state or any of its agencies or political subdivisions or a person who has had his civil rights restored may be denied a license, permit or certificate to engage in an occupation by reason of the prior conviction of a felony or misdemeanor if the offense has a reasonable relationship to the functions of the employment or occupation for which the license, permit or certificate is sought.
F. Subsection E of this section is not applicable to any law enforcement agency.
G. Any complaints concerning a violation of subsection E of this section shall be adjudicated in accordance with the procedures set forth in title 41, chapter 6 and title 12, chapter 7, article 6.
H. A person who is adjudicated delinquent under section 8-341 for a felony does not have the right to carry or possess a gun or firearm.

13-905. Restoration of civil rights; persons completing probation

A. A person who has been convicted of two or more felonies and whose period of probation has been completed may have any civil rights which were lost or suspended by the felony conviction restored by the judge who discharges him at the end of the term of probation.
B. On proper application, a person who has been discharged from probation either before or after adoption of this chapter may have any civil rights which were lost or suspended by the felony conviction restored by the superior court judge by whom the person was sentenced or the judge's successors in office from the county in which the person was originally convicted. The clerk of the superior court shall have the responsibility for processing the application on request of the person involved or the person's attorney. The superior court shall serve a copy of the application on the county attorney.
C. If the person was convicted of a dangerous offense under section 13-704, the person may not file for the restoration of the right to possess or carry a gun or firearm. If the person was convicted of a serious offense as defined in section 13-706 the person may not file for the restoration of the right to possess or carry a gun or firearm for ten years from the date of his discharge from probation. If the person was convicted of any other felony offense, the person may not file for the restoration of the right to possess or carry a gun or firearm for two years from the date of the person's discharge from probation.

13-906. Applications by persons discharged from prison

A. On proper application, a person who has been convicted of two or more felonies and who has received an absolute discharge from imprisonment may have any civil rights which were lost or suspended by his conviction restored by the superior court judge by whom the person was sentenced or the judge's successors in office from the county in which the person was originally sentenced.
B. A person who is subject to subsection A of this section may file, no sooner than two years from the date of his absolute discharge, an application for restoration of civil rights that shall be accompanied by a certificate of absolute discharge from the director of the state department of corrections. The clerk of the superior court that sentenced the applicant shall have the responsibility for processing applications for restoration of civil rights upon request of the person involved, the person's attorney or a representative of the state department of corrections. The superior court shall serve a copy of the application on the county attorney.
C. If the person was convicted of a dangerous offense under section 13-704, the person may not file for the restoration of the right to possess or carry a gun or firearm. If the person was convicted of a serious offense as defined in section 13-706, the person may

not file for the restoration of the right to possess or carry a gun or firearm for ten years from the date of his absolute discharge from imprisonment. If the person was convicted of any other felony offense, the person may not file for the restoration of the right to possess or carry a gun or firearm for two years from the date of the person's absolute discharge from imprisonment.

13-907. Setting aside judgment of convicted person on discharge; application; release from disabilities; firearm possession; exceptions

A. Except as provided in subsection E of this section, every person convicted of a criminal offense, on fulfillment of the conditions of probation or sentence and discharge by the court, may apply to the judge, justice of the peace or magistrate who pronounced sentence or imposed probation or such judge, justice of the peace or magistrate's successor in office to have the judgment of guilt set aside. The convicted person shall be informed of this right at the time of discharge.
B. The convicted person or, if authorized in writing, the convicted person's attorney or probation officer may apply to set aside the judgment.
C. If the judge, justice of the peace or magistrate grants the application, the judge, justice of the peace or magistrate shall set aside the judgment of guilt, dismiss the accusations or information and order that the person be released from all penalties and disabilities resulting from the conviction except those imposed by:
1. The department of transportation pursuant to section 28-3304, 28-3306, 28-3307, 28-3308 or 28-3319, except that the conviction may be used as a conviction if the conviction would be admissible had it not been set aside and may be pleaded and proved in any subsequent prosecution of such person by the state or any of its subdivisions for any offense or used by the department of transportation in enforcing section 28-3304, 28-3306, 28-3307, 28-3308 or 28-3319 as if the judgment of guilt had not been set aside.
2. The game and fish commission pursuant to section 17-314 or 17-340.
D. Notwithstanding section 13-905 or 13-906, if a judgment of guilt is set aside pursuant to this section, the person's right to possess a gun or firearm is restored. This subsection does not apply to a person who was convicted of a serious offense as defined in section 13-706.
E. This section does not apply to a person who was convicted of a criminal offense:
1. Involving a dangerous offense.
2. For which the person is required or ordered by the court to register pursuant to section 13-3821.
3. For which there has been a finding of sexual motivation pursuant to section 13-118.
4. In which the victim is a minor under fifteen years of age.
5. In violation of section 28-3473, any local ordinance relating to stopping, standing or operation of a vehicle or title 28, chapter 3, except a violation of section 28-693 or any local ordinance relating to the same subject matter as section 28-693.

13-907.01. Vacating the conviction of a sex trafficking victim; requirements

A. A person who was convicted of a violation of section 13-3214 or a city or town ordinance that has the same or substantially similar elements as section 13-3214 committed before July 24, 2014 may apply to the court that pronounced sentence to vacate the person's conviction. The court shall grant the application and vacate the conviction if the court finds by clear and convincing evidence that the person's participation in the offense was a direct result of being a victim of sex trafficking pursuant to section 13-1307.
B. If the prosecutor does not oppose the application, the court may grant the application and vacate the conviction without a hearing.
C. If the prosecutor opposes the application, the court shall hold a hearing on the application.
D. On vacating the conviction, the court shall:
1. Release the applicant from all penalties and disabilities resulting from the conviction.
2. Enter an order that a notation be made in the court file and in law enforcement and prosecution records that the conviction has been vacated and the person was the victim of a crime.
3. Transmit the order vacating the conviction to the arresting agency, the prosecutor and the department of public safety.
E. A conviction vacated pursuant to this section does not qualify as a historical prior felony conviction and cannot be alleged for any purpose pursuant to section 13-703 or 13-707.
F. Except on an application for employment that requires a fingerprint clearance card pursuant to title 41, chapter 12, article 3.1, a person whose conviction is vacated under this section may in all instances state that the person has never been arrested for,

charged with or convicted of the crime that is the subject of the conviction, including in response to questions on employment, housing, financial aid or loan applications.

13-908. Restoration of civil rights in the discretion of the superior court judge

Except as provided in section 13-912, the restoration of civil rights and the dismissal of the accusation or information under the provisions of this chapter shall be in the discretion of the superior court judge by whom the person was sentenced or his successor in office.

13-909. Restoration of civil rights; persons completing probation for federal offense

A. A person who has been convicted of two or more felonies and whose period of probation has been completed may have any civil rights which were lost or suspended by the felony conviction in a United States district court restored by the presiding judge of the superior court in the county in which the person now resides, on filing of an affidavit of discharge from the judge who discharged him at the end of the term of probation.

B. On proper application, a person who has been discharged from probation either before or after adoption of this chapter may have any civil rights which were lost or suspended by the felony conviction restored by an application filed with the clerk of the superior court in the county in which the person now resides. The clerk of the superior court shall process the application on request of the person involved or the person's attorney.

C. If the person was convicted of an offense which would be a dangerous offense under section 13-704, the person may not file for the restoration of the right to possess or carry a gun or firearm. If the person was convicted of an offense which would be a serious offense as defined in section 13-706 the person may not file for the restoration of the right to possess or carry a gun or firearm for ten years from the date of the person's discharge from probation. If the person was convicted of any other felony offense, the person may not file for the restoration of his right to possess or carry a gun or firearm for two years from the date of his discharge from probation.

13-910. Applications by persons discharged from federal prison

A. On proper application, a person who has been convicted of two or more felonies and who has received an absolute discharge from imprisonment in a federal prison may have any civil rights which were lost or suspended by the conviction restored by the presiding judge of the superior court in the county in which the person now resides.

B. A person who is subject to subsection A of this section may file, no sooner than two years from the date of his absolute discharge, an application for restoration of civil rights that shall be accompanied by a certificate of absolute discharge from the director of the federal bureau of prisons, unless it is shown to be impossible to obtain such certificate. Such application shall be filed with the clerk of the superior court in the county in which the person now resides, and such clerk shall be responsible for processing applications for restoration of civil rights upon request of the person involved or the person's attorney.

C. If the person was convicted of an offense which would be a dangerous offense under section 13-704, the person may not file for the restoration of the right to possess or carry a gun or firearm. If the person was convicted of an offense which would be a serious offense as defined in section 13-706, the person may not file for the restoration of the right to possess or carry a gun or firearm for ten years from the date of the person's absolute discharge from imprisonment. If the person was convicted of any other felony offense, the person may not file for the restoration of the right to possess or carry a gun or firearm for two years from the date of the person's absolute discharge from imprisonment.

13-911. Restoration of civil rights in the discretion of the presiding judge of the superior court

The restoration of civil rights under provisions of sections 13-909 or 13-910 is within the discretion of the presiding judge of the superior court in the county in which the person resides.

13-912. Restoration of civil rights for first offenders; exception

A. Any person who has not previously been convicted of any other felony shall automatically be restored any civil rights that were lost or suspended by the conviction if the person both:

1. Completes a term of probation or receives an absolute discharge from imprisonment.

2. Pays any fine or restitution imposed.

B. This section does not apply to a person's right to possess weapons as defined in section 13-3101 unless the person applies to a court pursuant to section 13-905 or 13-906.

13-912.01. Restoration of civil rights; persons adjudicated delinquent

A. A person who was adjudicated delinquent and whose period of probation has been completed may have the right to possess or carry a gun or firearm restored by the judge who discharges the person at the end of the person's term of probation.

B. A person who was adjudicated delinquent and who has been discharged from probation, on proper application, may have the right to carry or possess a gun or firearm restored by the judge of the juvenile court in the county where the person was adjudicated delinquent or the judge's successors. The clerk of the superior court shall process the application on the request of the person involved or the person's attorney. The applicant shall serve a copy of the application on the county attorney.

C. If the person's adjudication was for a dangerous offense under section 13-704, a serious offense as defined in section 13-706, burglary in the first degree, burglary in the second degree or arson, the person may not file for the restoration of the right to possess or carry a gun or firearm until the person attains thirty years of age. If the person's adjudication was for any other felony offense, the person may not file for the restoration of the right to possess or carry a gun or firearm for two years from the date of the person's discharge.

13-913. Definition of intensive probation

In this chapter, unless the context otherwise requires, "intensive probation" means a program established pursuant to this chapter of highly structured and closely supervised probation which emphasizes the payment of restitution.

13-914. Intensive probation; evaluation; sentence; criteria; limit; conditions

A. An adult probation officer shall prepare a presentence report for every offender who has either:

1. Been convicted of a felony and for whom the granting of probation is not prohibited by law.

2. Violated probation by commission of a technical violation that was not chargeable or indictable as a criminal offense.

B. The adult probation officer shall evaluate the needs of the offender and the offender's risk to the community, including the nature of the offense and criminal history of the offender. If the nature of the offense and the prior criminal history of the offender indicate that the offender should be included in an intensive probation program pursuant to supreme court guidelines for intensive probation, the adult probation officer may recommend to the court that the offender be granted intensive probation.

C. The court may suspend the imposition or execution of the sentence and grant the offender a period of intensive probation in accordance with this chapter. Except for sentences that are imposed pursuant to section 13-3601, the sentence is tentative to the extent that it may be altered or revoked pursuant to this chapter, but for all other purposes it is a final judgment of conviction. This subsection does not preclude the court from imposing a term of intensive probation pursuant to section 13-3601.

D. When granting intensive probation the court shall set forth on the record the factual and legal reasons in support of the sentence.

E. Intensive probation shall be conditioned on the offender:

1. Maintaining employment or full-time student status at a school subject to title 15 or title 32, chapter 30, or a combination of employment and student status, and making progress deemed satisfactory to the probation officer, or being involved in supervised job searches and community restitution work at least six days a week throughout the offender's term of intensive probation.

2. Paying restitution and probation fees of not less than seventy-five dollars unless, after determining the inability of the offender to pay the fee, the court assesses a lesser fee. Probation fees shall be deposited in the adult probation services fund established by section 12-267. Any amount assessed pursuant to this paragraph shall be used to supplement monies used for the salaries of adult probation and surveillance officers and for support of programs and services of the superior court adult probation departments.

3. Establishing a residence at a place approved by the intensive probation team and not changing the offender's residence without the team's prior approval.

4. Remaining at the offender's place of residence at all times except to go to work, to attend school, to perform community restitution and as specifically allowed in each instance by the adult probation officer.

5. Allowing administration of drug and alcohol tests if requested by a member of the intensive probation team.

6. Performing not less than forty hours of community restitution each month. Offenders who are full-time students, employed or in a treatment program approved by the court or the probation department may be exempted or required to perform fewer hours of community restitution. For good cause, the court may reduce the number of community restitution hours performed to not less than twenty hours each month.

7. Meeting any other conditions imposed by the court to meet the needs of the offender and limit the risks to the community, including participation in a program of community punishment authorized in title 12, chapter 2, article 11.

13-916. Intensive probation teams; adult probation officer qualifications; duties; case load limit

A. The chief adult probation officer in each county, with approval of the presiding judge of the superior court, shall appoint intensive probation teams consisting of one adult probation officer and one surveillance officer, two adult probation officers or one adult probation officer and two surveillance officers.

B. A two person intensive probation team shall supervise no more than twenty-five persons at one time, and a three person intensive probation team shall supervise no more than forty persons at one time.

C. The adult probation officers shall meet the bonding requirements and experience and education standards established pursuant to section 12-251.

D. The intensive probation team may serve warrants on, make arrests of and bring before the court persons who have violated the terms of intensive probation.

E. The adult probation and surveillance officers both have the authority of a peace officer in the performance of their duties but are not eligible to participate in the public safety personnel retirement system.

F. The intensive probation team shall:

1. Secure and keep a complete identification record of each person supervised by the team and a written statement of the conditions of the probation.

2. Exercise close supervision and observation over persons sentenced to intensive probation including both of the following:

(a) Visual contact with each probationer at least four times per week.

(b) Weekly verification of the probationer's employment.

3. Obtain and assemble information concerning the conduct of persons sentenced to intensive probation, including weekly arrest records, and report the information to the court.

4. Report to the court if the probationer engages in conduct constituting an offense.

5. Bring a defaulting probationer into court if, in the judgment of the adult probation officer, the probationer's conduct justifies revoking the intensive probation.

6. Monitor the payment of restitution and probation fees and bring into court any probationer who fails to pay restitution or fees.

7. Perform any other responsibilities required by the terms and conditions imposed by the court.

13-917. Modification of supervision

A. The adult probation officer shall periodically examine the needs of each person granted intensive probation and the risks of modifying the level of supervision of the person. The court may at any time modify the level of supervision of a person granted intensive probation, or may transfer the person to supervised probation or terminate the period of intensive probation pursuant to section 13-901, subsection E.

B. The court may issue a warrant for the arrest of a person granted intensive probation. If the person commits an additional offense or violates a condition of probation, the court may revoke intensive probation at any time before the expiration or termination of the period of intensive probation. If a petition to revoke the period of intensive probation is filed and the court finds that the person has committed an additional felony offense or has violated a condition of intensive probation which poses a serious threat or danger to the community, the court shall revoke the period of intensive probation and impose a term of imprisonment as authorized by law. If the court finds that the person has violated any other condition of intensive probation, it shall modify the conditions of intensive probation as appropriate or shall revoke the period of intensive probation and impose a term of imprisonment as authorized by law.

C. The court shall notify the prosecuting attorney, and the victim on request, of any proposed modification of a person's intensive probation if that modification will substantially affect the person's contact with or safety of the victim or if the modification involves restitution or incarceration status.

13-918. Employment; distribution of wages

A. The intensive probation team shall assist each person under its supervision in obtaining employment.

B. The person's wages shall be paid directly to an account established by the chief adult probation officer from which the chief adult probation officer shall make payments for restitution, probation fees, fines and other payments. The balance of the monies shall be placed in an account to be used for or paid to the person or his immediate family in a manner and in such amounts as determined by the chief adult probation officer or the court. Any monies remaining in the account at the time the person successfully completes probation shall be paid to the person.

13-919. Waiver of standards

The requirements of section 13-916, subsection A, subsection B and subsection F, paragraph 2 may be waived for a county if the case load of adult probation officers supervising persons on intensive probation is not more than fifteen persons and the program requires visual contact with each probationer at least one time a week.

13-920. Budget requests

The presiding judge of the superior court shall annually submit a proposed budget for the following fiscal year for the intensive probation program to the supreme court. The supreme court shall include the counties' requests in its annual budget request and shall distribute to the participating counties the monies appropriated by the legislature for intensive probation.

13-921. Probation for defendants under eighteen years of age; dual adult juvenile probation

A. The court may enter a judgment of guilt and place the defendant on probation pursuant to this section if all of the following apply:

1. The defendant is under eighteen years of age at the time the offense is committed.

2. The defendant is convicted of a felony offense.

3. The defendant is not sentenced to a term of imprisonment.

4. The defendant does not have a historical prior felony conviction.

B. If the court places a defendant on probation pursuant to this section, all of the following apply:

1. Except as provided in paragraphs 2, 3 and 4 of this subsection, if the defendant successfully completes the terms and conditions of probation, the court may set aside the judgment of guilt, dismiss the information or indictment, expunge the defendant's record and order the person to be released from all penalties and disabilities resulting from the conviction. The clerk of the court in which the conviction occurred shall notify each agency to which the original conviction was reported that all penalties and disabilities have been discharged and that the defendant's record has been expunged.

2. The conviction may be used as a conviction if it would be admissible pursuant to section 13-703 or 13-704 as if it had not been set aside and the conviction may be pleaded and proved as a prior conviction in any subsequent prosecution of the defendant.

3. The conviction is deemed to be a conviction for the purposes of sections 28-3304, 28-3305, 28-3306 and 28-3320.

4. The defendant shall comply with sections 13-3821 and 13-3822.

C. A defendant who is placed on probation pursuant to this section is deemed to be on adult probation.

D. If a defendant is placed on probation pursuant to this section, the court as a condition of probation may order the defendant to participate in services that are available to the juvenile court.

E. The court may order that a defendant who is placed on probation pursuant to this section be incarcerated in a county jail at whatever time or intervals, consecutive or nonconsecutive, that the court determines. The incarceration shall not extend beyond the period of court ordered probation, and the length of time the defendant actually spends in a county jail shall not exceed one year.

F. In addition to the provisions of this section, the court may apply any of the provisions of section 13-901.

13-923. Persons convicted of sexual offenses; annual probation review hearing; report; notification

A. If requested by the probationer, the court shall conduct a probation hearing at least once a year for a probationer who is under twenty-two years of age and who was convicted of an offense that occurred when the person was under eighteen years of age and that requires the probationer to register pursuant to section 13-3821.

B. This section does not preclude the court from conducting more than one probation review hearing each year.

C. The probation department that is supervising the probationer shall prepare a probation report and submit the report to the court prior to the hearing.

D. The following individuals shall be notified of the hearing:

1. A prosecutor.

2. An attorney for the probationer.

3. Any victim or victim's attorney who has a right to be present and heard pursuant to the victims' bill of rights, article II, section 2.1 of the constitution of this state, title 13, chapter 40 or court rule.

4. The probation officer supervising the probationer.

E. At the hearing, after hearing from those present pursuant to subsection D of this section, the court shall consider the following:

1. Whether to continue, modify or terminate probation.

2. Whether to continue to require, to suspend or to terminate the probationer's registration pursuant to section 13-3821.

3. Whether to continue, defer or terminate community notification pursuant to section 13-3825.

F. The court may hold a prehearing involving the persons listed in subsection D of this section to discuss and advise the court concerning the issues listed in subsection E of this section.

13-924. Probation; earned time credit; applicability

A. The court may adjust the period of a probationer's supervised probation on the recommendation of an adult probation officer for earned time credit.

B. Earned time credit equals twenty days for every thirty days that a probationer does all of the following:

1. Exhibits positive progression toward the goals and treatment of the probationer's case plan.

2. Is current on payments for court ordered restitution and other obligations.

3. Is current in completing community restitution.

C. Any earned time credit awarded pursuant to this section shall be revoked if a probationer is found in violation of a condition of probation.

D. This section does not apply to a probationer who is currently:

1. On lifetime probation.

2. On probation for any class 2 or 3 felony.

3. On probation exclusively for a misdemeanor offense.

4. Required to register pursuant to section 13-3821.

E. This section has no effect on the ability of the court to terminate the period of probation or intensive probation pursuant to section 13-901, subsection E at a time earlier than originally imposed.

13-925. Restoration of right to possess a firearm; mentally ill persons; petition

A. A person may petition the court that entered an order, finding or adjudication that resulted in the person being a prohibited possessor as defined in section 13-3101, subsection A, paragraph 7, subdivision (a) or subject to 18 United States Code section 922(d)(4) or (g)(4) to restore the person's right to possess a firearm.

B. The person or the person's guardian or attorney may file the petition. The petition shall be served on the attorney for the state who appeared in the underlying case.

C. On the filing of the petition the court shall set a hearing. At the hearing, the person shall present psychological or psychiatric evidence in support of the petition. The state shall provide the court with the person's criminal history records, if any. The court shall receive evidence on and consider the following before granting or denying the petition:

1. The circumstances that resulted in the person being a prohibited possessor as defined in section 13-3101, subsection A, paragraph 7, subdivision (a) or subject to 18 United States Code section 922(d)(4) or (g)(4).

2. The person's record, including the person's mental health record and criminal history record, if any.

3. The person's reputation based on character witness statements, testimony or other character evidence.

4. Whether the person is a danger to self or others or has persistent, acute or grave disabilities or whether the circumstances that led to the original order, adjudication or finding remain in effect.

5. Any change in the person's condition or circumstances that is relevant to the relief sought.

6. Any other evidence deemed admissible by the court.

D. The petitioner shall prove by clear and convincing evidence both of the following:

1. The petitioner is not likely to act in a manner that is dangerous to public safety.

2. Granting the requested relief is not contrary to the public interest.

E. At the conclusion of the hearing, the court shall issue findings of fact and conclusions of law.

F. If the court grants the petition for relief, the original order, finding or adjudication is deemed not to have occurred for the purposes of applying section 13-3101, subsection A, paragraph 7, subdivision (a), Public Law 110-180, section 105(a) or 18 United States Code section 922(d)(4) or (g)(4) to that person.

G. The granting of a petition under this section only restores the person's right to possess a firearm and does not apply to and has no effect on any other rights or benefits the person receives.

H. The court shall promptly notify the supreme court and the department of public safety of an order granting a petition under this section. As soon thereafter as practicable the supreme court and the department shall update, correct, modify or remove the person's record in any database that the supreme court or the department maintains and makes available to the national instant criminal background check system consistent with the rules pertaining to the database. Within ten business days after receiving the notification from the court, the department shall notify the United States attorney general that the person no longer falls within the provisions of section 13-3101, subsection A, paragraph 7, subdivision (a) or 18 United States Code section 922(d)(4) or (g)(4).

Chapter 10 Preparatory Offenses

13-1001. Attempt; classifications

A. A person commits attempt if, acting with the kind of culpability otherwise required for commission of an offense, such person:

1. Intentionally engages in conduct which would constitute an offense if the attendant circumstances were as such person believes them to be; or

2. Intentionally does or omits to do anything which, under the circumstances as such person believes them to be, is any step in a course of conduct planned to culminate in commission of an offense; or

3. Engages in conduct intended to aid another to commit an offense, although the offense is not committed or attempted by the other person, provided his conduct would establish his complicity under chapter 3 if the offense were committed or attempted by the other person.

B. It is no defense that it was impossible for the person to aid the other party's commission of the offense, provided such person could have done so had the circumstances been as he believed them to be.

C. Attempt is a:

1. Class 2 felony if the offense attempted is a class 1 felony.

2. Class 3 felony if the offense attempted is a class 2 felony.

3. Class 4 felony if the offense attempted is a class 3 felony.

4. Class 5 felony if the offense attempted is a class 4 felony.

5. Class 6 felony if the offense attempted is a class 5 felony.

6. Class 1 misdemeanor if the offense attempted is a class 6 felony.

7. Class 2 misdemeanor if the offense attempted is a class 1 misdemeanor.

8. Class 3 misdemeanor if the offense attempted is a class 2 misdemeanor.

9. Petty offense if the offense attempted is a class 3 misdemeanor or petty offense.

13-1002. Solicitation; classifications

A. A person, other than a peace officer acting in his official capacity within the scope of his authority and in the line of duty, commits solicitation if, with the intent to promote or facilitate the commission of a felony or misdemeanor, such person commands, encourages, requests or solicits another person to engage in specific conduct which would constitute the felony or misdemeanor or which would establish the other's complicity in its commission.

B. Solicitation is a:

1. Class 3 felony if the offense solicited is a class 1 felony.

2. Class 4 felony if the offense solicited is a class 2 felony.

3. Class 5 felony if the offense solicited is a class 3 felony.

4. Class 6 felony if the offense solicited is a class 4 felony.

5. Class 1 misdemeanor if the offense solicited is a class 5 felony.

6. Class 2 misdemeanor if the offense solicited is a class 6 felony.

7. Class 3 misdemeanor if the offense solicited is a misdemeanor.

13-1003. Conspiracy; classification

A. A person commits conspiracy if, with the intent to promote or aid the commission of an offense, such person agrees with one or more persons that at least one of them or another person will engage in conduct constituting the offense and one of the parties commits an overt act in furtherance of the offense, except that an overt act shall not be required if the object of the conspiracy was to commit any felony upon the person of another, or to commit an offense under section 13-1508 or 13-1704.
B. If a person guilty of conspiracy, as defined in subsection A of this section, knows or has reason to know that a person with whom such person conspires to commit an offense has conspired with another person or persons to commit the same offense, such person is guilty of conspiring to commit the offense with such other person or persons, whether or not such person knows their identity.
C. A person who conspires to commit a number of offenses is guilty of only one conspiracy if the multiple offenses are the object of the same agreement or relationship and the degree of the conspiracy shall be determined by the most serious offense conspired to.
D. Conspiracy to commit a class 1 felony is punishable by a sentence of life imprisonment without possibility of release on any basis until the service of twenty-five years, otherwise, conspiracy is an offense of the same class as the most serious offense which is the object of or result of the conspiracy.
13-1004. Facilitation; classification

A. A person commits facilitation if, acting with knowledge that another person is committing or intends to commit an offense, the person knowingly provides the other person with means or opportunity for the commission of the offense.

B. This section does not apply to peace officers who act in their official capacity within the scope of their authority and in the line of duty.

C. Facilitation is a:

1. Class 5 felony if the offense facilitated is a class 1 felony.

2. Class 6 felony if the offense facilitated is a class 2 or class 3 felony.

3. Class 1 misdemeanor if the offense facilitated is a class 4 or class 5 felony.

4. Class 3 misdemeanor if the offense facilitated is a class 6 felony or a misdemeanor.

13-1005. Renunciation of attempt, solicitation, conspiracy or facilitation; defenses

A. In a prosecution for attempt, conspiracy or facilitation, it is a defense that the defendant, under circumstances manifesting a voluntary and complete renunciation of his criminal intent, gave timely warning to law enforcement authorities or otherwise made a reasonable effort to prevent the conduct or result which is the object of the attempt, conspiracy or facilitation.

B. In a prosecution for solicitation, it is a defense that the defendant, under circumstances manifesting a voluntary and complete renunciation of the defendant's criminal intent completed both of the following acts:
1. Notified the person solicited.
2. Gave timely warning to law enforcement authorities or otherwise made a reasonable effort to prevent the conduct or result solicited.
C. A renunciation is not voluntary and complete within the meaning of this section if it is motivated in whole or in part by:
1. A belief that circumstances exist which increase the probability of immediate detection or apprehension of the accused or another participant in the criminal enterprise or which render more difficult the accomplishment of the criminal purpose; or
2. A decision to postpone the criminal conduct until another time or to transfer the criminal effort to another victim, place or another but similar objective.
D. A warning to law enforcement authorities is not timely within the meaning of this section unless the authorities, reasonably acting upon the warning, would have the opportunity to prevent the conduct or result. An effort is not reasonable within the meaning of this section unless the defendant makes a substantial effort to prevent the conduct or result.

13-1006. Effect of immunity, irresponsibility or incapacity of a party to solicitation, conspiracy or facilitation

A. It is not a defense to a prosecution for solicitation, conspiracy or facilitation that a person solicited, facilitated or with whom the defendant conspired could not be guilty of committing the offense because:
1. Such person is, by definition of the offense, legally incapable in an individual capacity of committing the offense; or
2. Such person is not criminally responsible as defined in chapter 5 of this title, or has an immunity to prosecution or conviction for the commission of the offense; or
3. Such person does not have the state of mind sufficient for the commission of the offense in question.
B. It is not a defense to a prosecution for solicitation or conspiracy that the defendant is, by definition of the offense, legally incapable in an individual capacity of committing the offense that is the object of the solicitation or conspiracy.

13-1101. Definitions

In this chapter, unless the context otherwise requires:
1. "Premeditation" means that the defendant acts with either the intention or the knowledge that he will kill another human being, when such intention or knowledge precedes the killing by any length of time to permit reflection. Proof of actual reflection is not required, but an act is not done with premeditation if it is the instant effect of a sudden quarrel or heat of passion.
2. "Homicide" means first degree murder, second degree murder, manslaughter or negligent homicide.
3. "Person" means a human being.
4. "Adequate provocation" means conduct or circumstances sufficient to deprive a reasonable person of self-control.

13-1102. Negligent homicide; classification

A. A person commits negligent homicide if with criminal negligence the person causes the death of another person, including an unborn child.
B. An offense under this section applies to an unborn child in the womb at any stage of its development. A person may not be prosecuted under this section if any of the following applies:
1. The person was performing an abortion for which the consent of the pregnant woman, or a person authorized by law to act on the pregnant woman's behalf, has been obtained or for which the consent was implied or authorized by law.
2. The person was performing medical treatment on the pregnant woman or the pregnant woman's unborn child.
3. The person was the unborn child's mother.
C. Negligent homicide is a class 4 felony.

Chapter 11 Homicide

13-1103. Manslaughter; classification

A. A person commits manslaughter by:

1. Recklessly causing the death of another person; or

2. Committing second degree murder as prescribed in section 13-1104, subsection A upon a sudden quarrel or heat of passion resulting from adequate provocation by the victim; or

3. Intentionally providing the physical means that another person uses to commit suicide, with the knowledge that the person intends to commit suicide; or

4. Committing second degree murder as prescribed in section 13-1104, subsection A, paragraph 3, while being coerced to do so by the use or threatened immediate use of unlawful deadly physical force upon such person or a third person which a reasonable person in his situation would have been unable to resist; or

5. Knowingly or recklessly causing the death of an unborn child by any physical injury to the mother.

B. An offense under subsection A, paragraph 5 of this section applies to an unborn child in the womb at any stage of its development. A person shall not be prosecuted under subsection A, paragraph 5 of this section if any of the following applies:

1. The person was performing an abortion for which the consent of the pregnant woman, or a person authorized by law to act on the pregnant woman's behalf, has been obtained or for which the consent was implied or authorized by law.

2. The person was performing medical treatment on the pregnant woman or the pregnant woman's unborn child.

3. The person was the unborn child's mother.

C. Manslaughter is a class 2 felony.

13-1104. Second degree murder; classification

A. A person commits second degree murder if without premeditation:

1. The person intentionally causes the death of another person, including an unborn child or, as a result of intentionally causing the death of another person, causes the death of an unborn child; or

2. Knowing that the person's conduct will cause death or serious physical injury, the person causes the death of another person, including an unborn child or, as a result of knowingly causing the death of another person, causes the death of an unborn child; or

3. Under circumstances manifesting extreme indifference to human life, the person recklessly engages in conduct that creates a grave risk of death and thereby causes the death of another person, including an unborn child or, as a result of recklessly causing the death of another person, causes the death of an unborn child.

B. An offense under this section applies to an unborn child in the womb at any stage of its development. A person may not be prosecuted under this section if any of the following applies:

1. The person was performing an abortion for which the consent of the pregnant woman, or a person authorized by law to act on the pregnant woman's behalf, has been obtained or for which the consent was implied or authorized by law.

2. The person was performing medical treatment on the pregnant woman or the pregnant woman's unborn child.

3. The person was the unborn child's mother.

C. Second degree murder is a class 1 felony and is punishable as provided by section 13-705 if the victim is under fifteen years of age or is an unborn child, section 13-706, subsection A or section 13-710.

13-1105. First degree murder; classification

A. A person commits first degree murder if:

1. Intending or knowing that the person's conduct will cause death, the person causes the death of another person, including an unborn child, with premeditation or, as a result of causing the death of another person with premeditation, causes the death of an unborn child.

2. Acting either alone or with one or more other persons the person commits or attempts to commit sexual conduct with a minor under section 13-1405, sexual assault under section 13-1406, molestation of a child under section 13-1410, terrorism under section 13-2308.01, marijuana offenses under section 13-3405, subsection A, paragraph 4, dangerous drug offenses under section 13-3407, subsection A, paragraphs 4 and 7, narcotics offenses under section 13-3408, subsection A, paragraph 7 that equal or exceed the statutory threshold amount for each offense or combination of offenses, involving or using minors in drug offenses under section 13-3409, drive by shooting under section 13-1209, kidnapping under section 13-1304, burglary under section 13-1506, 13-1507 or 13-1508, arson under section 13-1703 or 13-1704, robbery under section 13-1902, 13-1903 or 13-1904, escape under section 13-2503 or 13-2504, child abuse under section 13-3623, subsection A, paragraph 1 or unlawful flight from a pursuing law enforcement vehicle under section 28-622.01 and, in the course of and in furtherance of the offense or immediate flight from the offense, the person or another person causes the death of any person.

3. Intending or knowing that the person's conduct will cause death to a law enforcement officer, the person causes the death of a law enforcement officer who is in the line of duty.

B. Homicide, as prescribed in subsection A, paragraph 2 of this section, requires no specific mental state other than what is required for the commission of any of the enumerated felonies.

C. An offense under subsection A, paragraph 1 of this section applies to an unborn child in the womb at any stage of its development. A person shall not be prosecuted under subsection A, paragraph 1 of this section if any of the following applies:

1. The person was performing an abortion for which the consent of the pregnant woman, or a person authorized by law to act on the pregnant woman's behalf, has been obtained or for which the consent was implied or authorized by law.

2. The person was performing medical treatment on the pregnant woman or the pregnant woman's unborn child.

3. The person was the unborn child's mother.

D. First degree murder is a class 1 felony and is punishable by death or life imprisonment as provided by sections 13-751 and 13-752.

Chapter 12 Assault and Related Offenses

13-1201. Endangerment; classification

A. A person commits endangerment by recklessly endangering another person with a substantial risk of imminent death or physical injury.

B. Endangerment involving a substantial risk of imminent death is a class 6 felony. In all other cases, it is a class 1 misdemeanor.

13-1202. Threatening or intimidating; classification

A. A person commits threatening or intimidating if the person threatens or intimidates by word or conduct:

1. To cause physical injury to another person or serious damage to the property of another; or

2. To cause, or in reckless disregard to causing, serious public inconvenience including, but not limited to, evacuation of a building, place of assembly or transportation facility; or

3. To cause physical injury to another person or damage to the property of another in order to promote, further or assist in the interests of or to cause, induce or solicit another person to participate in a criminal street gang, a criminal syndicate or a racketeering enterprise.

B. Threatening or intimidating pursuant to subsection A, paragraph 1 or 2 is a class 1 misdemeanor, except that it is a class 6 felony if:

1. The offense is committed in retaliation for a victim's either reporting criminal activity or being involved in an organization, other than a law enforcement agency, that is established for the purpose of reporting or preventing criminal activity.

2. The person is a criminal street gang member.

C. Threatening or intimidating pursuant to subsection A, paragraph 3 is a class 3 felony.

13-1203. Assault; classification

A. A person commits assault by:

1. Intentionally, knowingly or recklessly causing any physical injury to another person; or

2. Intentionally placing another person in reasonable apprehension of imminent physical injury; or

3. Knowingly touching another person with the intent to injure, insult or provoke such person.

B. Assault committed intentionally or knowingly pursuant to subsection A, paragraph 1 is a class 1 misdemeanor. Assault committed recklessly pursuant to subsection A, paragraph 1 or assault pursuant to subsection A, paragraph 2 is a class 2 misdemeanor. Assault committed pursuant to subsection A, paragraph 3 is a class 3 misdemeanor.

13-1204. Aggravated assault; classification; definitions

A. A person commits aggravated assault if the person commits assault as prescribed by section 13-1203 under any of the following circumstances:

1. If the person causes serious physical injury to another.

2. If the person uses a deadly weapon or dangerous instrument.

3. If the person commits the assault by any means of force that causes temporary but substantial disfigurement, temporary but substantial loss or impairment of any body organ or part or a fracture of any body part.

4. If the person commits the assault while the victim is bound or otherwise physically restrained or while the victim's capacity to resist is substantially impaired.

5. If the person commits the assault after entering the private home of another with the intent to commit the assault.

6. If the person is eighteen years of age or older and commits the assault on a minor under fifteen years of age.

7. If the person commits assault as prescribed by section 13-1203, subsection A, paragraph 1 or 3 and the person is in violation of an order of protection issued against the person pursuant to section 13-3602 or 13-3624.

8. If the person commits the assault knowing or having reason to know that the victim is any of the following:

(a) A peace officer or a person summoned and directed by the officer.

(b) A constable or a person summoned and directed by the constable while engaged in the execution of any official duties or if the assault results from the execution of the constable's official duties.

(c) A firefighter, fire investigator, fire inspector, emergency medical technician or paramedic engaged in the execution of any official duties or a person summoned and directed by such individual while engaged in the execution of any official duties or if the assault results from the execution of the official duties of the firefighter, fire investigator, fire inspector, emergency medical technician or paramedic.

(d) A teacher or other person employed by any school and the teacher or other employee is on the grounds of a school or grounds adjacent to the school or is in any part of a building or vehicle used for school purposes, any teacher or school nurse visiting a private home in the course of the teacher's or nurse's professional duties or any teacher engaged in any authorized and organized classroom activity held on other than school grounds.

(e) A health care practitioner who is certified or licensed pursuant to title 32, chapter 13, 15, 17 or 25, or a person summoned and directed by the licensed health care practitioner while engaged in the person's professional duties. This subdivision does not apply if the person who commits the assault is seriously mentally ill, as defined in section 36-550, or is afflicted with alzheimer's disease or related dementia.

(f) A prosecutor while engaged in the execution of any official duties or if the assault results from the execution of the prosecutor's official duties.

(g) A code enforcement officer as defined in section 39-123 while engaged in the execution of any official duties or if the assault results from the execution of the code enforcement officer's official duties.

(h) A state or municipal park ranger while engaged in the execution of any official duties or if the assault results from the execution of the park ranger's official duties.

(i) A public defender while engaged in the execution of any official duties or if the assault results from the execution of the public defender's official duties.

(j) A judicial officer while engaged in the execution of any official duties or if the assault results from the execution of the judicial officer's official duties.

9. If the person knowingly takes or attempts to exercise control over any of the following:

(a) A peace officer's or other officer's firearm and the person knows or has reason to know that the victim is a peace officer or other officer employed by one of the agencies listed in paragraph 10, subdivision (a), item (i), (ii), (iii), (iv) or (v) of this subsection.

(b) Any weapon other than a firearm that is being used by a peace officer or other officer or that the officer is attempting to use, and the person knows or has reason to know that the victim is a peace officer or other officer employed by one of the agencies listed in paragraph 10, subdivision (a), item (i), (ii), (iii), (iv) or (v) of this subsection.

(c) Any implement that is being used by a peace officer or other officer or that the officer is attempting to use, and the person knows or has reason to know that the victim is a peace officer or other officer employed by one of the agencies listed in paragraph 10, subdivision (a), item (i), (ii), (iii), (iv) or (v) of this subsection. For the purposes of this subdivision, "implement" means an object that is designed for or that is capable of restraining or injuring an individual. Implement does not include handcuffs.

10. If the person meets both of the following conditions:

(a) Is imprisoned or otherwise subject to the custody of any of the following:

(i) The state department of corrections.

(ii) The department of juvenile corrections.

(iii) A law enforcement agency.

(iv) A county or city jail or an adult or juvenile detention facility of a city or county.

(v) Any other entity that is contracting with the state department of corrections, the department of juvenile corrections, a law enforcement agency, another state, any private correctional facility, a county, a city or the federal bureau of prisons or other federal agency that has responsibility for sentenced or unsentenced prisoners.

(b) Commits an assault knowing or having reason to know that the victim is acting in an official capacity as an employee of any of the entities listed in subdivision (a) of this paragraph.

11. If the person uses a simulated deadly weapon.

B. A person commits aggravated assault if the person commits assault by either intentionally, knowingly or recklessly causing any physical injury to another person, intentionally placing another person in reasonable apprehension of imminent physical injury or knowingly touching another person with the intent to injure the person, and both of the following occur:

1. The person intentionally or knowingly impedes the normal breathing or circulation of blood of another person by applying pressure to the throat or neck or by obstructing the nose and mouth either manually or through the use of an instrument.

2. Any of the circumstances exists that are set forth in section 13-3601, subsection A, paragraph 1, 2, 3, 4, 5 or 6.

C. A person who is convicted of intentionally or knowingly committing aggravated assault on a peace officer pursuant to subsection A, paragraph 1 or 2 of this section shall be sentenced to imprisonment for not less than the presumptive sentence authorized under chapter 7 of this title and is not eligible for suspension of sentence, commutation or release on any basis until the sentence imposed is served.

D. It is not a defense to a prosecution for assaulting a peace officer or a mitigating circumstance that the peace officer was not on duty or engaged in the execution of any official duties.

E. Except pursuant to subsections F and G of this section, aggravated assault pursuant to subsection A, paragraph 1 or 2, paragraph 9, subdivision (a) or paragraph 11 of this section is a class 3 felony except if the aggravated assault is a violation of subsection A, paragraph 1 or 2 of this section and the victim is under fifteen years of age it is a class 2 felony punishable pursuant to section 13-705. Aggravated assault pursuant to subsection A, paragraph 3 or subsection B of this section is a class 4 felony. Aggravated assault pursuant to subsection A, paragraph 9, subdivision (b) or paragraph 10 of this section is a class 5 felony. Aggravated assault pursuant to subsection A, paragraph 4, 5, 6, 7 or 8 or paragraph 9, subdivision (c) of this section is a class 6 felony.

F. Aggravated assault pursuant to subsection A, paragraph 1 or 2 of this section committed on a peace officer is a class 2 felony. Aggravated assault pursuant to subsection A, paragraph 3 of this section committed on a peace officer is a class 3 felony. Aggravated assault pursuant to subsection A, paragraph 8, subdivision (a) of this section committed on a peace officer is a class 5 felony unless the assault results in any physical injury to the peace officer, in which case it is a class 4 felony.

G. Aggravated assault pursuant to:

1. Subsection A, paragraph 1 or 2 of this section is a class 2 felony if committed on a prosecutor.

2. Subsection A, paragraph 3 of this section is a class 3 felony if committed on a prosecutor.

3. Subsection A, paragraph 8, subdivision (f) of this section is a class 5 felony if the assault results in physical injury to a prosecutor.

H. For the purposes of this section:

1. "Judicial officer" means a justice of the supreme court, judge, justice of the peace or magistrate or a commissioner or hearing officer of a state, county or municipal court.

2. "Prosecutor" means a county attorney, a municipal prosecutor or the attorney general and includes an assistant or deputy county attorney, municipal prosecutor or attorney general.

13-1205. Unlawfully administering intoxicating liquors, narcotic drug or dangerous drug; classification

A. A person commits unlawfully administering intoxicating liquors, a narcotic drug or dangerous drug if, for a purpose other than lawful medical or therapeutic treatment, such person knowingly introduces or causes to be introduced into the body of another person, without such other person's consent, intoxicating liquors, a narcotic drug or dangerous drug.

B. Unlawfully administering intoxicating liquors, a narcotic drug or dangerous drug is a class 6 felony.

C. If the victim is a minor, then the offense shall be a class 5 felony.

13-1206. Dangerous or deadly assault by prisoner or juvenile; classification

A person, while in the custody of the state department of corrections, the department of juvenile corrections, a law enforcement agency or a county or city jail, who commits an assault involving the discharge, use or threatening exhibition of a deadly weapon or dangerous instrument or who intentionally or knowingly inflicts serious physical injury upon another person is guilty of a class 2 felony. If the person is an adult or is a juvenile convicted as an adult pursuant to section 8-327 or 13-501 or the rules of procedure for the juvenile court, the person shall not be eligible for suspension of sentence, probation, pardon or release from confinement on any basis until the sentence imposed by the court has been served or commuted. A sentence imposed pursuant to this section shall be consecutive to any other sentence presently being served by the convicted person.

13-1207. Prisoners who commit assault with intent to incite to riot or participate in riot; classification

A. A person, while in the custody of the state department of corrections or a county or city jail, who commits assault on another person with the intent to incite to riot or who participates in a riot is guilty of a class 2 felony.
B. A person who is convicted of a violation of this section shall not be eligible for suspension of sentence, probation, pardon or release from confinement on any basis until the sentence imposed by the court has been served or commuted and the sentence shall be consecutive to any other sentence presently being served by the convicted person.

13-1208. Assault; vicious animals; classification; exception; definition

A. A person who intentionally or knowingly causes any dog to bite and inflict serious physical injury on a human being or otherwise cause serious physical injury to a human being is guilty of a class 3 felony, unless the person would be justified in using physical force or deadly physical force in self-defense or defense of a third person pursuant to chapter 4 of this title.
B. A person who owns a dog that the owner knows or has reason to know has a history of biting or a propensity to cause injury or to otherwise endanger the safety of human beings without provocation or that has been found to be a vicious animal by a court of competent jurisdiction and that bites, inflicts physical injury on or attacks a human being while at large is guilty of a class 5 felony.
C. A person who owns or who is responsible for the care of a dog that the owner or responsible person knows or has reason to know has a history of biting or a propensity to cause injury or to otherwise endanger the safety of human beings without provocation or that has been found to be a vicious animal by a court of competent jurisdiction and who does not take reasonable care to prohibit the dog from escaping to the outside of a residence or enclosed area, yard or structure is guilty of a class 1 misdemeanor.
D. This section does not apply to dogs that are owned or used by a law enforcement agency and that are used in the performance of police work.
E. For the purposes of this section, "reasonable care" means the degree of care that a person of ordinary prudence would exercise in the same or similar circumstances.

13-1209. Drive by shooting; forfeiture; driver license revocation; classification; definitions

A. A person commits drive by shooting by intentionally discharging a weapon from a motor vehicle at a person, another occupied motor vehicle or an occupied structure.
B. Motor vehicles that are used in violation of this section are subject to seizure for forfeiture in the manner provided for in chapter 39 of this title.
C. Notwithstanding title 28, chapter 8, the judge shall order the surrender to the judge of any driver license of the convicted person and, on surrender of the license, shall invalidate or destroy the license and forward the abstract of conviction to the department of transportation with an order of the court revoking the driving privilege of the person for a period of at least one year but not more than five years. On receipt of the abstract of conviction and order, the department of transportation shall revoke the driving privilege of the person for the period of time ordered by the judge.
D. Drive by shooting is a class 2 felony.
E. As used in this section:
1. "Motor vehicle" has the same meaning prescribed in section 28-101.
2. "Occupied structure" has the same meaning prescribed in section 13-3101.

13-1210. Assaults on public safety employees or volunteers and state hospital employees; disease testing; petition; hearing; notice; definitions

A. A public safety employee or volunteer or the employing agency, officer or entity may petition the court for an order authorizing testing of another person for the human immunodeficiency virus, common blood borne diseases or other diseases specified in the petition if there are reasonable grounds to believe an exposure occurred and one of the following applies:

1. The person is charged in any criminal complaint and the complaint alleges that the person interfered with the official duties of the public safety employee or volunteer by biting, scratching, spitting or transferring blood or other bodily fluids on or through the skin or membranes of the public safety employee or volunteer.

2. There is probable cause to believe that the person interfered with the official duties of the public safety employee or volunteer by biting, scratching, spitting or transferring blood or other bodily fluids on or through the skin or membranes of the public safety employee or volunteer and that the person is deceased.

3. There is probable cause to believe that the person bit, scratched, spat or transferred blood or other bodily fluid on or through the skin or membranes of a public safety employee or volunteer who was performing an official duty.

4. The person is arrested, charged or in custody and the public safety employee or volunteer alleges, by affidavit, that the person interfered with the official duties of the public safety employee or volunteer by biting, scratching, spitting or transferring blood or other bodily fluids on or through the skin or membranes of the public safety employee or volunteer.

B. An employee of the Arizona state hospital or the employing agency may petition the court for an order authorizing testing of another person for the human immunodeficiency virus, common blood borne diseases or other diseases specified in the petition if there are reasonable grounds to believe an exposure occurred and the person is a patient who is confined to the Arizona state hospital and who is alleged to have interfered with the official duties of the Arizona state hospital employee by biting, scratching, spitting or transferring blood or other bodily fluids on or through the skin or membranes of the Arizona state hospital employee.

C. The court shall hear the petition promptly. If the court finds that probable cause exists to believe that a possible transfer of blood or other bodily fluids occurred between the person and the public safety employee or volunteer or the Arizona state hospital employee, the court shall order that either:

1. The person provide two specimens of blood for testing.

2. If the person is deceased, the medical examiner draw two specimens of blood for testing.

D. Notwithstanding subsection C, paragraph 2 of this section, on written notice from the agency, officer or entity employing the public safety employee or volunteer, the medical examiner is authorized to draw two specimens of blood for testing during the autopsy or other examination of the deceased person's body. The medical examiner shall release the specimen to the employing agency, officer or entity for testing only after the court issues its order pursuant to subsection C, paragraph 2 of this section. If the court does not issue an order within thirty days after the medical examiner collects the specimen, the medical examiner shall destroy the specimen.

E. Notice of the test results shall be provided as prescribed by the department of health services to the person tested, to the public safety employee or volunteer or the Arizona state hospital employee named in the petition and to the employee's or volunteer's employing agency, officer or entity and, if the person tested is incarcerated or detained, to the officer in charge and the chief medical officer of the facility in which the person is incarcerated or detained.

F. Section 36-665 does not apply to this section.

G. For the purposes of this section:

1. "Arizona state hospital" includes the Arizona community protection and treatment center.

2. "Arizona state hospital employee" means an employee of the Arizona state hospital who has direct patient contact.

3. "Private prison security officer" means a security officer who is employed by a private contractor that contracts with a governmental entity to provide detention or incarceration facility services for offenders.

4. "Public safety employee or volunteer" means a law enforcement officer, any employee or volunteer of a state or local law enforcement agency, a probation officer, a surveillance officer, an adult or juvenile correctional service officer, a detention officer, a private prison security officer, a firefighter or an emergency medical technician.

13-1211. Discharging a firearm at a structure; classification; definitions

A. A person who knowingly discharges a firearm at a residential structure is guilty of a class 2 felony.

B. A person who knowingly discharges a firearm at a nonresidential structure is guilty of a class 3 felony.

C. For the purposes of this section:

1. "Nonresidential structure" means a structure other than a residential structure.

2. "Residential structure" means a movable or immovable or permanent or temporary structure that is adapted for both human residence or lodging.

3. "Structure" means any building, vehicle, railroad car or place with sides and a floor that is separately securable from any other structure attached to it and that is being used for lodging, business or transportation.

13-1212. Prisoner assault with bodily fluids; liability for costs; classification; definition

A. A prisoner commits prisoner assault with bodily fluids if the prisoner throws or projects any bodily fluid at or onto a correctional facility employee or private prison security officer who the prisoner knows or reasonably should know is an employee of a correctional facility or is a private prison security officer.

B. A prisoner who is convicted of a violation of this section is liable for any costs incurred by the correctional facility employee or private prison security officer, including costs incurred for medical expenses or cleaning uniforms.

C. The state department of corrections shall adopt rules for the payment of costs pursuant to subsection B. Monies in the prisoner's trust fund or retention account established by the correctional facility in which the prisoner is incarcerated may be used to pay the costs pursuant to subsection B.

D. A prisoner who violates this section is guilty of a class 6 felony and the sentence imposed for a violation of this section shall run consecutively to any sentence of imprisonment for which the prisoner was confined or to any term of community supervision, probation, parole, work furlough or other release from confinement.

E. For the purposes of this section, "bodily fluids" means saliva, blood, seminal fluid, urine or feces.

13-1213. Aiming a laser pointer at a peace officer or an occupied aircraft; classification; definitions

A. A person commits aiming a laser pointer at a peace officer if the person intentionally or knowingly directs the beam of light from a laser pointer or laser emitting device at another person and the person knows or reasonably should know that the other person is a peace officer.

B. A person commits aiming a laser pointer at an occupied aircraft if the person intentionally or knowingly directs the beam of light from a laser pointer or laser emitting device at an aircraft and the person knows or reasonably should know that the aircraft is occupied.

C. Aiming a laser pointer at a peace officer is a class 1 misdemeanor.

D. Aiming a laser pointer at an occupied aircraft is a class 1 misdemeanor. If the act renders the pilot unable to safely operate the aircraft or causes serious physical injury to any person on board the aircraft it is an assault pursuant to this chapter.

E. For the purposes of this section:

1. "Aircraft" means any vehicle that is designed for flight in the air by buoyancy or by the dynamic action of air on the vehicle's surfaces, including powered airplanes, gliders and helicopters.

2. "Laser pointer or laser emitting device" means any device that is designed or used to amplify electromagnetic radiation by stimulated emission that emits a beam designed to be used by the operator as a pointer or highlighter to indicate, mark or identify a specific position, place, item or object.

13-1214. Unlawful mutilation; classification; definition

A. It is unlawful for a person to:

1. Mutilate a female who is under eighteen years of age.

2. Knowingly transport a female who is under eighteen years of age to another jurisdiction for the purpose of mutilation.

3. Recklessly transport a female who is under eighteen years of age to another jurisdiction where mutilation is likely to occur.

B. In addition to any other penalty prescribed by this title, the court shall order a person who is convicted of a violation of this section to pay a fine of not less than twenty-five thousand dollars.

C. Unlawful mutilation is a class 2 felony, and the person convicted shall be sentenced pursuant to this section and the person is not eligible for suspension of sentence, probation, pardon or release from confinement on any basis except as specifically authorized by section 31 233, subsection A or B until the sentence imposed by the court has been served or commuted. If the victim is under fifteen years of age, unlawful mutilation is punishable pursuant to section 13-705. The presumptive term may be aggravated or mitigated within the range under this section pursuant to section 13-701, subsections C, D and E. The term for a first offense is as follows:

Minimum   Presumptive Maximum
5.25 years 7 years   14 years
The term for a defendant who has one historical prior felony conviction is as follows:
Minimum   Presumptive Maximum
7 years   10.5 years 21 years
The term for a defendant who has two or more historical prior felony convictions is as follows:
Minimum   Presumptive Maximum

14 years   15.75 years 28 years

D. The sentence imposed on a person for unlawful mutilation shall be consecutive to any other unlawful mutilation sentence imposed on the person at any time.

E. The consent of the minor on whom the mutilation is performed or the parents of the minor is not a defense to a prosecution for unlawful mutilation.

F. For the purposes of this section, "mutilate" or "mutilation" means the partial or total removal of the clitoris, prepuce, labia minora, with or without excision of the labia major, the narrowing of the vaginal opening through the creation of a covering seal formed by cutting and repositioning the inner or outer labia, with or without removal of the clitoris, or any harmful procedure to the genitalia, including pricking, piercing, incising, scraping or cauterizing. Mutilate and mutilation do not include procedures performed by a licensed physician that are proven to be medically necessary due to a medically recognized condition.

Chapter 13 Kidnapping and related Offenses

13-1301. Definitions

In this chapter, unless the context otherwise requires:

1. "Relative" means a parent or stepparent, ancestor, descendant, sibling, uncle or aunt, including an adoptive relative of the same degree through marriage or adoption, or a spouse.

2. "Restrain" means to restrict a person's movements without consent, without legal authority, and in a manner which interferes substantially with such person's liberty, by either moving such person from one place to another or by confining such person. Restraint is without consent if it is accomplished by:

(a) Physical force, intimidation or deception; or

(b) Any means including acquiescence of the victim if the victim is a child less than eighteen years old or an incompetent person and the victim's lawful custodian has not acquiesced in the movement or confinement.

13-1302. Custodial interference; child born out of wedlock; defenses; classification

A. A person commits custodial interference if, knowing or having reason to know that the person has no legal right to do so, the person does one of the following:

1. Takes, entices or keeps from lawful custody any child, or any person who is incompetent, and who is entrusted by authority of law to the custody of another person or institution.

2. Before the entry of a court order determining custodial rights, takes, entices or withholds any child from the other parent denying that parent access to any child.

3. If the person is one of two persons who have joint legal custody of a child, takes, entices or withholds from physical custody the child from the other custodian.

4. At the expiration of access rights outside this state, intentionally fails or refuses to return or impedes the return of a child to the lawful custodian.

B. If a child is born out of wedlock, the mother is the legal custodian of the child for the purposes of this section until paternity is established and custody or access is determined by a court.

C. It is a defense to a prosecution pursuant to subsection A, paragraph 2 if both of the following apply:

1. The defendant has begun the process to obtain an order of protection or files a petition for custody within a reasonable period of time and the order of protection or petition states the defendant's belief that the child was at risk if left with the other parent.

2. The defendant is the child's parent and has the right of custody and the defendant either:

(a) Has a good faith and reasonable belief that the taking, enticing or withholding is necessary to protect the child from immediate danger.

(b) Is a victim of domestic violence by the other parent and has a good faith and reasonable belief that the child will be in immediate danger if the child is left with the other parent.

D. Subsection A, paragraphs 2 and 3 do not apply to a person who is the child's parent if both of the following apply:

1. The person has filed an emergency petition regarding custodial rights with the superior court and has received a hearing date from the court.

2. The person has a good faith and reasonable belief that the child will be in immediate danger if the child is left with the other parent.

E. A violation of this section is:

1. A class 3 felony if committed by a person other than the parent or agent of the parent or custodian or agent of the custodian.

2. Notwithstanding paragraph 3 of this subsection, a class 4 felony if the child or incompetent person is taken, enticed or kept from lawful custody out of this state by the parent or agent of the parent or custodian or the agent of the custodian.

3. A class 6 felony if committed by a parent or agent of the parent or custodian or agent of the custodian.

4. A class 1 misdemeanor if the child or incompetent person is voluntarily returned without physical injury by the parent or defendant or the agent of the parent or defendant no later than forty-eight hours after the parent or defendant takes, entices or keeps from lawful custody the child or incompetent person.

13-1303. Unlawful imprisonment; classification; definition

A. A person commits unlawful imprisonment by knowingly restraining another person.

B. In any prosecution for unlawful imprisonment, it is a defense that:

1. The restraint was accomplished by a peace officer or detention officer acting in good faith in the lawful performance of his duty; or

2. The defendant is a relative of the person restrained and the defendant's sole intent is to assume lawful custody of that person and the restraint was accomplished without physical injury.

C. Unlawful imprisonment is a class 6 felony unless the victim is released voluntarily by the defendant without physical injury in a safe place before arrest in which case it is a class 1 misdemeanor.

D. For the purposes of this section, "detention officer" means a person other than an elected official who is employed by a county, city or town and who is responsible for the supervision, protection, care, custody or control of inmates in a county or municipal correctional institution. Detention officer does not include counselors or secretarial, clerical or professionally trained personnel.

13-1304. Kidnapping; classification; consecutive sentence

A. A person commits kidnapping by knowingly restraining another person with the intent to:

1. Hold the victim for ransom, as a shield or hostage; or

2. Hold the victim for involuntary servitude; or

3. Inflict death, physical injury or a sexual offense on the victim, or to otherwise aid in the commission of a felony; or

4. Place the victim or a third person in reasonable apprehension of imminent physical injury to the victim or the third person; or

5. Interfere with the performance of a governmental or political function; or

6. Seize or exercise control over any airplane, train, bus, ship or other vehicle.

B. Kidnapping is a class 2 felony unless the victim is released voluntarily by the defendant without physical injury in a safe place before arrest and before accomplishing any of the further enumerated offenses in subsection A of this section in which case it is a class 4 felony. If the victim is released pursuant to an agreement with the state and without any physical injury, it is a class 3 felony. If the victim is under fifteen years of age kidnapping is a class 2 felony punishable pursuant to section 13-705. The sentence for kidnapping of a victim under fifteen years of age shall run consecutively to any other sentence imposed on the defendant and to any undischarged term of imprisonment of the defendant.

13-1305. Access interference; classification; definition

A. A person commits access interference if, knowing or having reason to know that the person has no legal right to do so, the person knowingly engages in a pattern of behavior that prevents, obstructs or frustrates the access rights of a person who is entitled to access to a child pursuant to a court order.

B. If the child is removed from this state, access interference is a class 5 felony. Otherwise access interference is a class 2 misdemeanor.

C. The enforcement of this section is not limited by the availability of other remedies for access interference.

D. For the purposes of this section "access order" means a court order that is issued pursuant to title 25 and that allows a person to have direct access to a child or incompetent person.

13-1306. Unlawfully obtaining labor or services; classification

A. It is unlawful for a person to knowingly obtain the labor or services of another person by doing any of the following:

1. Causing or threatening to cause bodily injury to that person or another person.

2. Restraining or threatening to restrain that person or another person without lawful authority and against that person's will.

3. Withholding that person's governmental records, identifying information or other personal property.

B. A person who violates this section is guilty of a class 4 felony.

13-1307. Sex trafficking; classification; definitions

A. It is unlawful for a person to knowingly traffic another person who is eighteen years of age or older with either of the following:

1. The intent to cause the other person to engage in any prostitution or sexually explicit performance by deception, force or coercion.

2. The knowledge that the other person will engage in any prostitution or sexually explicit performance by deception, coercion or force.

B. A person who violates this section is guilty of a class 2 felony.

C. For the purposes of this section:

1. "Coercion" includes:

(a) Abusing or threatening to abuse the law or the legal system.

(b) Knowingly destroying, concealing, removing, confiscating, possessing or withholding another person's actual or purported passport or other immigration document, government issued identification document, government record or personal property.

(c) Extortion.

(d) Causing or threatening to cause financial harm to any person.

(e) Facilitating or controlling another person's access to a controlled substance.

2. "Force" includes causing or threatening to cause serious harm to another person or physically restraining or threatening to physically restrain another person.

3. "Sexually explicit performance" means a live or public act or show intended to arouse or satisfy the sexual desires or appeal to the prurient interest of patrons.

4. "Traffic" means to entice, recruit, harbor, provide, transport or otherwise obtain another person.

13-1308. Trafficking of persons for forced labor or services; classification; definitions

A. It is unlawful for a person to either:

1. Knowingly traffic another person with the intent to or knowledge that the other person will be subject to forced labor or services.

2. Knowingly benefit, financially or by receiving anything of value, from participation in a venture that has engaged in an act in violation of section 13-1306, section 13-1307, this section or section 13-3212, subsection A, paragraph 9 or 10.

B. A violation of this section is a class 2 felony.

C. For the purposes of this section:

1. "Forced labor or services":

(a) Means labor or services that are performed or provided by another person and that are obtained through a person's either:

(i) Causing or threatening to cause serious physical injury to any person.

(ii) Restraining or threatening to physically restrain another person.

(iii) Knowingly destroying, concealing, removing, confiscating, possessing or withholding another person's actual or purported passport or other immigration document, government issued identification document, government record or personal property.

(iv) Abusing or threatening to abuse the law or the legal system.

(v) Extortion.

(vi) Causing or threatening to cause financial harm to any person.

(vii) Facilitating or controlling another person's access to a controlled substance.

(b) Does not include ordinary household chores and reasonable disciplinary measures between a parent or legal guardian and the parent's or legal guardian's child.

2. "Traffic" means to entice, recruit, harbor, provide, transport or otherwise obtain another person by deception, coercion or force.

13-1309. Restitution

The court shall order restitution for any violation of section 13-1306, 13-1307 or 13-1308 or section 13-3212, subsection A, paragraph 9 or 10, including the greater of either the gross income or value to the defendant of the victim's labor or services or the value of the victim's labor as guaranteed under the minimum wage and overtime provisions of the fair labor standards act of 1938 (52 Stat. 1060; 29 United States Code sections 201 through 219).

Chapter 14 Sexual Offenses

13-1401. Definitions; factors

A. In this chapter, unless the context otherwise requires:
1. "Oral sexual contact" means oral contact with the penis, vulva or anus.
2. "Position of trust" means a person who is or was any of the following:
(a) The minor's parent, stepparent, adoptive parent, legal guardian or foster parent.
(b) The minor's teacher.
(c) The minor's coach or instructor, whether the coach or instructor is an employee or volunteer.
(d) The minor's clergyman or priest.
(e) Engaged in a sexual or romantic relationship with the minor's parent, adoptive parent, legal guardian, foster parent or stepparent.
3. "Sexual contact" means any direct or indirect touching, fondling or manipulating of any part of the genitals, anus or female breast by any part of the body or by any object or causing a person to engage in such contact.
4. "Sexual intercourse" means penetration into the penis, vulva or anus by any part of the body or by any object or masturbatory contact with the penis or vulva.
5. "Spouse" means a person who is legally married and cohabiting.
6. "Teacher" means a certificated teacher as defined in section 15-501 or any other person who provides instruction to pupils in any school district, charter school or accommodation school, the Arizona state schools for the deaf and the blind or a private school in this state.
7. "Without consent" includes any of the following:
(a) The victim is coerced by the immediate use or threatened use of force against a person or property.
(b) The victim is incapable of consent by reason of mental disorder, mental defect, drugs, alcohol, sleep or any other similar impairment of cognition and such condition is known or should have reasonably been known to the defendant. For the purposes of this subdivision, "mental defect" means the victim is unable to comprehend the distinctively sexual nature of the conduct or is incapable of understanding or exercising the right to refuse to engage in the conduct with another.
(c) The victim is intentionally deceived as to the nature of the act.
(d) The victim is intentionally deceived to erroneously believe that the person is the victim's spouse.
B. The following factors may be considered in determining whether a relationship is currently or was previously a sexual or romantic relationship pursuant to subsection A, paragraph 2, subdivision (e) of this section:
1. The type of relationship.
2. The length of the relationship.
3. The frequency of the interaction between the two persons.
4. If the relationship has terminated, the length of time since the termination.

13-1402. Indecent exposure; exception; classification

A. A person commits indecent exposure if he or she exposes his or her genitals or anus or she exposes the areola or nipple of her breast or breasts and another person is present, and the defendant is reckless about whether the other person, as a reasonable person, would be offended or alarmed by the act.
B. Indecent exposure does not include an act of breast-feeding by a mother.
C. Indecent exposure to a person who is fifteen or more years of age is a class 1 misdemeanor, except that it is a class 6 felony if the defendant has two or more prior convictions for a violation of this section or has one or more prior convictions for a violation of section 13-1406. Indecent exposure to a person who is under fifteen years of age is a class 6 felony.

D. A person who is convicted of a felony violation of this section and who has two or more historical prior felony convictions for a violation of this section or section 13-1403 involving indecent exposure or public sexual indecency to a minor who is under fifteen years of age is guilty of a class 3 felony and shall be sentenced to a term of imprisonment as follows:

Mitigated	Minimum	Presumptive	Maximum	Aggravated
6 years	8 years	10 years	12 years	15 years

E. The presumptive term imposed pursuant to subsection D of this section may be mitigated or aggravated pursuant to section 13-701, subsections D and E.

13-1403. Public sexual indecency; public sexual indecency to a minor; classification

A. A person commits public sexual indecency by intentionally or knowingly engaging in any of the following acts, if another person is present, and the defendant is reckless about whether such other person, as a reasonable person, would be offended or alarmed by the act:
1. An act of sexual contact.
2. An act of oral sexual contact.
3. An act of sexual intercourse.
4. An act of bestiality.
B. A person commits public sexual indecency to a minor if the person intentionally or knowingly engages in any of the acts listed in subsection A of this section and such person is reckless about whether a minor who is under fifteen years of age is present.
C. Public sexual indecency is a class 1 misdemeanor. Public sexual indecency to a minor is a class 5 felony.
D. A person who is convicted of a felony violation of this section and who has two or more historical prior felony convictions for a violation of this section or section 13-1402 involving indecent exposure or public sexual indecency to a minor who is under fifteen years of age shall be sentenced to a term of imprisonment as follows:

Mitigated	Minimum	Presumptive	Maximum	Aggravated
6 years	8 years	10 years	12 years	15 years

E. The presumptive term imposed pursuant to subsection D of this section may be mitigated or aggravated pursuant to section 13-701, subsections D and E.

13-1404. Sexual abuse; classification

A. A person commits sexual abuse by intentionally or knowingly engaging in sexual contact with any person who is fifteen or more years of age without consent of that person or with any person who is under fifteen years of age if the sexual contact involves only the female breast.
B. It is not a defense to a prosecution for a violation of this section that the other person consented if the other person was fifteen, sixteen or seventeen years of age and the defendant was in a position of trust.
C. Sexual abuse is a class 5 felony unless the victim is under fifteen years of age in which case sexual abuse is a class 3 felony punishable pursuant to section 13-705.

13-1405. Sexual conduct with a minor; classification

A. A person commits sexual conduct with a minor by intentionally or knowingly engaging in sexual intercourse or oral sexual contact with any person who is under eighteen years of age.
B. Sexual conduct with a minor who is under fifteen years of age is a class 2 felony and is punishable pursuant to section 13-705. Sexual conduct with a minor who is at least fifteen years of age is a class 6 felony. Sexual conduct with a minor who is at least fifteen years of age is a class 2 felony if the person is or was in a position of trust and the convicted person is not eligible for suspension of sentence, probation, pardon or release from confinement on any basis except as specifically authorized by section 31-233, subsection A or B until the sentence imposed has been served or commuted.

13-1406. Sexual assault; classification; increased punishment

A. A person commits sexual assault by intentionally or knowingly engaging in sexual intercourse or oral sexual contact with any person without consent of such person.

B. Sexual assault is a class 2 felony, and the person convicted shall be sentenced pursuant to this section and the person is not eligible for suspension of sentence, probation, pardon or release from confinement on any basis except as specifically authorized by section 31-233, subsection A or B until the sentence imposed by the court has been served or commuted. If the victim is under fifteen years of age, sexual assault is punishable pursuant to section 13-705. The presumptive term may be aggravated or mitigated within the range under this section pursuant to section 13-701, subsections C, D and E. If the sexual assault involved the intentional or knowing administration of flunitrazepam, gamma hydroxy butyrate or ketamine hydrochloride without the victim's knowledge, the presumptive, minimum and maximum sentence for the offense shall be increased by three years. The additional sentence imposed pursuant to this subsection is in addition to any enhanced sentence that may be applicable. The term for a first offense is as follows:

Minimum   Presumptive Maximum
5.25 years 7 years   14 years

The term for a defendant who has one historical prior felony conviction is as follows:

Minimum   Presumptive Maximum
7 years   10.5 years 21 years

The term for a defendant who has two or more historical prior felony convictions is as follows:

Minimum   Presumptive Maximum
14 years   15.75 years 28 years

C. The sentence imposed on a person for a sexual assault shall be consecutive to any other sexual assault sentence imposed on the person at any time.

D. Notwithstanding section 13-703, section 13-704, section 13-705, section 13-706, subsection A and section 13-708, subsection D, if the sexual assault involved the intentional or knowing infliction of serious physical injury, the person may be sentenced to life imprisonment and is not eligible for suspension of sentence, probation, pardon or release from confinement on any basis except as specifically authorized by section 31-233, subsection A or B until at least twenty-five years have been served or the sentence is commuted. If the person was at least eighteen years of age and the victim was twelve years of age or younger, the person shall be sentenced pursuant to section 13-705.

13-1407. Defenses

A. It is a defense to a prosecution pursuant to sections 13-1404 and 13-1405 involving a minor if the act was done in furtherance of lawful medical practice.

B. It is a defense to a prosecution pursuant to sections 13-1404 and 13-1405 in which the victim's lack of consent is based on incapacity to consent because the victim was fifteen, sixteen or seventeen years of age if at the time the defendant engaged in the conduct constituting the offense the defendant did not know and could not reasonably have known the age of the victim.

C. It is a defense to a prosecution pursuant to section 13-1402, 13-1404, 13-1405 or 13-1406 if the act was done by a duly licensed physician or registered nurse or a person acting under the physician's or nurse's direction, or any other person who renders emergency care at the scene of an emergency occurrence, the act consisted of administering a recognized and lawful form of treatment that was reasonably adapted to promoting the physical or mental health of the patient and the treatment was administered in an emergency when the duly licensed physician or registered nurse or a person acting under the physician's or nurse's direction, or any other person rendering emergency care at the scene of an emergency occurrence, reasonably believed that no one competent to consent could be consulted and that a reasonable person, wishing to safeguard the welfare of the patient, would consent.

D. It is a defense to a prosecution pursuant to section 13-1404 or 13-1405 that the person was the spouse of the other person at the time of commission of the act. It is not a defense to a prosecution pursuant to section 13-1406 that the defendant was the spouse of the victim at the time of commission of the act.

E. It is a defense to a prosecution pursuant to section 13-1404 or 13-1410 that the defendant was not motivated by a sexual interest. It is a defense to a prosecution pursuant to section 13-1404 involving a victim under fifteen years of age that the defendant was not motivated by a sexual interest.

F. It is a defense to a prosecution pursuant to sections 13-1405 and 13-3560 if the victim is fifteen, sixteen or seventeen years of age, the defendant is under nineteen years of age or attending high school and is no more than twenty-four months older than the victim and the conduct is consensual.

13-1408. Adultery; classification; punishment; limitation on prosecution

A. A married person who has sexual intercourse with another than his or her spouse, and an unmarried person who has sexual intercourse with a married person not his or her spouse, commits adultery and is guilty of a class 3 misdemeanor. When the act is committed between parties only one of whom is married, both shall be punished.

B. No prosecution for adultery shall be commenced except upon complaint of the husband or wife.

13-1409. Unlawful sexual conduct; adult probation department employees; juvenile court employees; classification; definitions

A. An adult probation department employee or juvenile court employee commits unlawful sexual conduct if the employee knowingly coerces the victim to engage in sexual contact, oral sexual contact or sexual intercourse by either:

1. Threatening to negatively influence the victim's supervision or release status.

2. Offering to positively influence the victim's supervision or release status.

B. Unlawful sexual conduct with a victim who is under fifteen years of age is a class 2 felony. Unlawful sexual conduct with a victim who is at least fifteen years of age and under eighteen years of age is a class 3 felony. All other unlawful sexual conduct is a class 5 felony.

C. For the purposes of this section:

1. "Adult probation department employee or juvenile court employee" means an employee of an adult probation department or the juvenile court who either:

(a) Through the course of employment, directly provides treatment, care, control or supervision to a victim.

(b) Provides presentence or predisposition reports directly to a court regarding the victim.

2. "Victim" means a person who is either of the following:

(a) Subject to conditions of release or supervision by a court.

(b) A minor who has been referred to the juvenile court.

13-1410. Molestation of a child; classification

A. A person commits molestation of a child by intentionally or knowingly engaging in or causing a person to engage in sexual contact, except sexual contact with the female breast, with a child who is under fifteen years of age.

B. Molestation of a child is a class 2 felony that is punishable pursuant to section 13-705.

13-1411. Bestiality; classification; definition

A. A person commits bestiality by knowingly doing either of the following:

1. Engaging in oral sexual contact, sexual contact or sexual intercourse with an animal.

2. Causing another person to engage in oral sexual contact, sexual contact or sexual intercourse with an animal.

B. In addition to any other penalty imposed for a violation of subsection A of this section, the court may order that the convicted person do any of the following:

1. Undergo a psychological assessment and participate in appropriate counseling at the convicted person's own expense.

2. Reimburse an animal shelter as defined in section 11-1022 for any reasonable costs incurred for the care and maintenance of any animal that was taken to the animal shelter as a result of conduct proscribed by subsection A of this section.

C. This section does not apply to:

1. Accepted veterinary medical practices performed by a licensed veterinarian or veterinary technician.

2. Insemination of animals by the same species, bred for commercial purposes.

3. Accepted animal husbandry practices that provide necessary care for animals bred for commercial purposes.

D. Bestiality is a class 6 felony, except that bestiality pursuant to subsection A, paragraph 2 of this section is a class 3 felony punishable pursuant to section 13-705 if the other person is a minor under fifteen years of age.

E. For the purposes of this section, "animal" means a nonhuman mammal, bird, reptile or amphibian, either dead or alive.

13-1412. Unlawful sexual conduct; peace officers; classification; definitions

A. A peace officer commits unlawful sexual conduct by knowingly engaging in sexual contact, oral sexual contact or sexual intercourse with any person who is in the officer's custody or a person who the officer knows or has reason to know is the subject of an investigation.

B. Unlawful sexual conduct with a victim who is under fifteen years of age is a class 2 felony. Unlawful sexual conduct with a victim who is at least fifteen years of age but less than eighteen years of age is a class 3 felony. All other unlawful sexual conduct is a class 5 felony.

C. This section does not apply to either of the following:

1. Any direct or indirect touching or manipulating of the genitals, anus or female breast that occurs during a lawful search.

2. An officer who is married to or who is in a romantic or sexual relationship with the person at the time of the arrest or investigation. The following factors may be considered in determining whether the relationship between the victim and the defendant is currently a romantic or sexual relationship:

(a) The type of relationship.

(b) The length of the relationship.

(c) The frequency of the interaction between the victim and the defendant.

(d) If the relationship has terminated, the length of time since the termination.

D. For the purposes of this section:

1. "Custody" includes the imposition of actual or constructive restraint pursuant to an on-site arrest, a court order or any contact in which a reasonable person would not feel free to leave. Custody does not include detention in a correctional facility, a juvenile detention facility or a state hospital.

2. "Peace officer" has the same meaning prescribed in section 1-215 but does not include adult or juvenile corrections or detention officers.

13-1413. Capacity of minor sexual assault victim to consent to medical examination

Notwithstanding any other provision of the law, when it is not possible to contact the parents or legal guardian within the short time span in which the examination should be conducted a minor twelve years of age or older alleged to be the victim of a violation of section 13-1406 may give consent to hospital, medical and surgical examination, diagnosis and care in connection with such violation. Such consent shall not be subject to incapacity because of the victim's age. The consent of the parent, parents or legal guardian of such minor shall not be necessary to authorize such hospital, medical and surgical examination, diagnosis and care, and such parent, parents or legal guardian shall not be liable for payment for any services rendered pursuant to this section.

13-1414. Expenses of investigation

Any medical or forensic interview expenses arising out of the need to secure evidence that a person has been the victim of a dangerous crime against children as defined in section 13-705 or a sexual assault shall be paid by the county in which the offense occurred.

13-1415. Human immunodeficiency virus and sexually transmitted disease testing; victim's rights; petition; definitions

A. A defendant, including a defendant who is a minor, who is alleged to have committed a sexual offense or another offense involving significant exposure is subject to a court order that requires the defendant to submit to testing for the human immunodeficiency virus and other sexually transmitted diseases and to consent to the release of the test results to the victim.

B. Pursuant to subsection A of this section, the prosecuting attorney, if requested by the victim, or, if the victim is a minor, by the parent or guardian of the minor, shall petition the court for an order requiring that the person submit a specimen, to be determined by the submitting entity, for laboratory testing by the department of health services or another licensed laboratory for the presence of the human immunodeficiency virus and other sexually transmitted diseases. The court, within ten days, shall determine if sufficient evidence exists to indicate that significant exposure occurred. If the court makes this finding or the act committed against the victim is a sexual offense it shall order that the testing be performed in compliance with rules adopted by the department of health services. The prosecuting attorney shall provide the victim's name and last known address of record to the department of health services for notification purposes. The victim's name and address are confidential, except that the department of health services may disclose the information to a local health department for victim notification purposes.

C. After a specimen has been tested pursuant to subsection B of this section, the laboratory that performed the test shall report the results to the submitting entity.

D. The submitting entity shall provide the results to the department of health services or a local health department. The department of health services or a local health department shall notify the victim of the results of the test conducted pursuant to subsection B of this section and shall counsel the victim regarding the health implications of the results.

E. The submitting entity or the department of health services shall notify the person tested of the results of the test conducted pursuant to subsection B of this section and shall counsel the person regarding the health implications of the results. If the submitting entity does not notify the person tested of the test results, the submitting entity shall provide both the name and last known address of record of the person tested and the test results to the department of health services or a local health department for notification purposes.

F. Notwithstanding any other law, copies of the test results shall be provided only to the victim of the crime, the person tested, the submitting entity and the department of health services.

G. For the purposes of this section:

1. "Sexual offense" means oral sexual contact, sexual contact or sexual intercourse as defined in section 13-1401.

2. "Sexually transmitted diseases" means:

(a) Chlamydia.

(b) Genital herpes.

(c) Gonorrhea.

(d) Syphilis.

(e) Trichomonas.

3. "Significant exposure" means contact of the victim's ruptured or broken skin or mucous membranes with a person's blood or body fluids, other than tears, saliva or perspiration, of a magnitude that the centers for disease control have epidemiologically demonstrated can result in transmission of the human immunodeficiency virus.

4. "Submitting entity" means one of the following:

(a) A local health department.

(b) A health unit of the state department of corrections.

(c) A health unit of any detention facility.

(d) A physician licensed pursuant to title 32, chapter 13, 17 or 29.

13-1416. Admissibility of minor's statement; notice

A. Except as otherwise provided in title 8, a statement made by a minor who is under the age of ten years describing any sexual offense or physical abuse performed with, on or witnessed by the minor, which is not otherwise admissible by statute or court rule, is admissible in evidence in any criminal or civil proceeding if both of the following are true:

1. The court finds, in an in camera hearing, that the time, content and circumstances of the statement provide sufficient indicia of reliability.

2. Either of the following is true:

(a) The minor testifies at the proceedings.

(b) The minor is unavailable as a witness, provided that if the minor is unavailable as a witness, the statement may be admitted only if there is corroborative evidence of the statement.

B. A statement shall not be admitted under this section unless the proponent of the statement makes known to the adverse party his intention to offer the statement and the particulars of the statement sufficiently in advance of the proceedings to provide the adverse party with a fair opportunity to prepare to meet the statement.

13-1417. Continuous sexual abuse of a child; classification

A. A person who over a period of three months or more in duration engages in three or more acts in violation of section 13-1405, 13-1406 or 13-1410 with a child who is under fourteen years of age is guilty of continuous sexual abuse of a child.

B. Continuous sexual abuse of a child is a class 2 felony and is punishable pursuant to section 13-705.

C. To convict a person of continuous sexual abuse of a child, the trier of fact shall unanimously agree that the requisite number of acts occurred. The trier of fact does not need to agree on which acts constitute the requisite number.

D. Any other felony sexual offense involving the victim shall not be charged in the same proceeding with a charge under this section unless the other charged felony sexual offense occurred outside the time period charged under this section or the other felony sexual offense is charged in the alternative. A defendant may be charged with only one count under this section unless more than one victim is involved. If more than one victim is involved, a separate count may be charged for each victim.

13-1418. Sexual misconduct; behavioral health professionals; classification_

A. A behavioral health professional licensed pursuant to title 32, chapter 33 or a psychiatrist or psychologist licensed pursuant to title 32, chapter 13, 17 or 19.1 commits sexual misconduct by intentionally or knowingly engaging in sexual intercourse with a client who is currently under the care or supervision of the licensed behavioral health professional, psychiatrist or psychologist.
B. Sexual misconduct by a licensed behavioral health professional, psychiatrist or psychologist is a class 6 felony.
C. This section does not apply to any act of sexual conduct that occurs between a licensed behavioral health professional, psychiatrist or psychologist and a client after the client has completed a course of treatment or if the client is not under the care of the licensed behavioral health professional, psychiatrist or psychologist.

13-1419. Unlawful sexual conduct; correctional facilities; classification; definition

A. A person commits unlawful sexual conduct by intentionally or knowingly engaging in any act of a sexual nature with an offender who is in the custody of the state department of corrections, the department of juvenile corrections, a private prison facility, a juvenile detention facility or a city or county jail or with an offender who is under the supervision of either department or a city or county. For the purposes of this subsection, "person" means a person who:
1. Is employed by the state department of corrections or the department of juvenile corrections.
2. Is employed by a private prison facility, a juvenile detention facility or a city or county jail.
3. Contracts to provide services with the state department of corrections, the department of juvenile corrections, a private prison facility, a juvenile detention facility or a city or county jail.
4. Is an official visitor, volunteer or agency representative of the state department of corrections, the department of juvenile corrections, a private prison facility, a juvenile detention facility or a city or county jail.
B. This section does not apply to a person who is employed by the state department of corrections, a private prison facility or a city or county jail or who contracts to provide services with the state department of corrections, a private prison facility or a city or county jail or an offender who is on release status if the person was lawfully married to the prisoner or offender on release status before the prisoner or offender was sentenced to the state department of corrections or was incarcerated in a city or county jail.
C. Unlawful sexual conduct with an offender who is under fifteen years of age is a class 2 felony. Unlawful sexual conduct with an offender who is between fifteen and seventeen years of age is a class 3 felony. All other unlawful sexual conduct is a class 5 felony.
D. For the purposes of this section, "any act of a sexual nature":
1. Includes the following:
(a) Any completed, attempted, threatened or requested touching of the genitalia, anus, groin, breast, inner thigh, pubic area or buttocks with the intent to arouse or gratify sexual desire.
(b) Any act of exposing the genitalia, anus, groin, breast, inner thigh, pubic area or buttocks with the intent to arouse or gratify sexual desire.
(c) Any act of photographing, videotaping, filming, digitally recording or otherwise viewing, with or without a device, a prisoner or offender with the intent to arouse or gratify sexual desire, either:
(i) While the prisoner or offender is in a state of undress or partial dress.
(ii) While the prisoner or offender is urinating or defecating.
2. Does not include an act done pursuant to a bona fide medical exam or lawful internal search.

13-1420. Sexual offense; evidence of similar crimes; definition

A. If the defendant is charged with committing a sexual offense, the court may admit evidence that the defendant committed past acts that would constitute a sexual offense and may consider the bearing this evidence has on any matter to which it is relevant.
B. This section does not limit the admission or consideration of evidence under any court rule.
C. For the purposes of this section, "sexual offense" means any of the following:
1. Sexual abuse in violation of section 13-1404.

2. Sexual conduct with a minor in violation of section 13-1405.

3. Sexual assault in violation of section 13-1406.

4. Sexual assault of a spouse if the offense was committed before the effective date of this amendment to this section.

5. Molestation of a child in violation of section 13-1410.

6. Continuous sexual abuse of a child in violation of section 13-1417.

7. Sexual misconduct by a behavioral health professional in violation of section 13-1418.

8. Commercial sexual exploitation of a minor in violation of section 13-3552.

9. Sexual exploitation of a minor in violation of section 13-3553.

13-1421. Evidence relating to victim's chastity; pretrial hearing

A. Evidence relating to a victim's reputation for chastity and opinion evidence relating to a victim's chastity are not admissible in any prosecution for any offense in this chapter. Evidence of specific instances of the victim's prior sexual conduct may be admitted only if a judge finds the evidence is relevant and is material to a fact in issue in the case and that the inflammatory or prejudicial nature of the evidence does not outweigh the probative value of the evidence, and if the evidence is one of the following:

1. Evidence of the victim's past sexual conduct with the defendant.

2. Evidence of specific instances of sexual activity showing the source or origin of semen, pregnancy, disease or trauma.

3. Evidence that supports a claim that the victim has a motive in accusing the defendant of the crime.

4. Evidence offered for the purpose of impeachment when the prosecutor puts the victim's prior sexual conduct in issue.

5. Evidence of false allegations of sexual misconduct made by the victim against others.

B. Evidence described in subsection A shall not be referred to in any statements to a jury or introduced at trial without a court order after a hearing on written motions is held to determine the admissibility of the evidence. If new information is discovered during the course of the trial that may make the evidence described in subsection A admissible, the court may hold a hearing to determine the admissibility of the evidence under subsection A. The standard for admissibility of evidence under subsection A is by clear and convincing evidence.

13-1422. Adult oriented businesses; location; hours of operation; injunction; classification; definitions

A. An adult oriented business shall not be located within one-fourth mile of a child care facility, a private, public or charter school, a public playground, a public recreational facility, a residence or a place of worship. For the purposes of this subsection, measurements shall be made in a straight line in all directions, without regard to intervening structures or objects, from the nearest point on the property line of a parcel containing an adult oriented business to the nearest point on the property line of a parcel containing a child care facility, a private, public or charter school, a public playground, a public recreational facility, a residence or a place of worship. An adult oriented business lawfully operating in conformity with this section does not violate this section if a child care facility, a private, public or charter school, a public playground, a public recreational facility, a residence or a place of worship subsequently locates within one-fourth mile of the adult oriented business.

B. An adult arcade, adult bookstore or video store, adult cabaret, adult motion picture theater, adult theater, escort agency or nude model studio shall not remain open at any time between the hours of 1:00 a.m. and 8:00 a.m. on Monday through Saturday and between the hours of 1:00 a.m. and 12:00 noon on Sunday.

C. Subsection A of this section does not prohibit counties or municipalities from enacting and enforcing ordinances that regulate the location of adult oriented businesses.

D. Subsection B of this section does not prohibit counties or municipalities from enacting and enforcing ordinances that regulate an adult arcade, adult bookstore or video store, adult cabaret, adult motion picture theater, adult theater, escort agency or nude model studio in a manner that is at least as restrictive as subsection B of this section.

E. If there is reason to believe that a violation of subsection A of this section is being committed in any county or city, the county attorney of the county shall, or a citizen of this state who resides in the county or city in the citizen's own name may, maintain an action to abate and prevent the violation and to enjoin perpetually any person who is committing the violation and the owner, lessee or agent of the building or place in or on which the violation is occurring from directly or indirectly committing or permitting the violation.

F. A violation of subsection A or B of this section is a class 1 misdemeanor. Each day of violation constitutes a separate offense.

G. For the purposes of this section:

1. "Adult arcade" has the same meaning prescribed in section 11-811.

2. "Adult bookstore or video store" has the same meaning prescribed in section 11-811.

3. "Adult cabaret" excludes any establishment licensed under title 4 and includes any nightclub, bar, restaurant or other similar commercial establishment that regularly features:

(a) Persons who appear in a state of nudity or who are seminude.

(b) Live performances that are characterized by the exposure of specific anatomical areas or specific sexual activities.

(c) Films, motion pictures, videocassettes, slides or other photographic reproductions that are characterized by the depiction or description of specific sexual activities or specific anatomical areas.

4. "Adult motion picture theater" has the same meaning prescribed in section 11-811.

5. "Adult oriented business" has the same meaning prescribed in section 11-811.

6. "Adult theater" has the same meaning prescribed in section 11-811.

7. "Escort" means a person who for consideration agrees or offers to act as a companion, guide or date for another person or who agrees or offers to privately model lingerie or to privately perform a striptease for another person.

8. "Escort agency" means a person or business association that furnishes, offers to furnish or advertises the furnishing of escorts as one of its primary business purposes for any fee, tip or other consideration.

9. "Nude model studio" has the same meaning prescribed in section 11-811.

10. "Nude", "nudity" or "state of nudity" has the same meaning prescribed in section 11-811.

11. "Place of worship" means a structure where persons regularly assemble for worship, ceremonies, rituals and education relating to a particular form of religious belief and which a reasonable person would conclude is a place of worship by reason of design, signs or architectural or other features.

12. "Residence" means a permanent dwelling place.

13. "Seminude" has the same meaning prescribed in section 11-811.

14. "Specific anatomical areas" has the same meaning prescribed in section 11-811.

15. "Specific sexual activities" has the same meaning prescribed in section 11-811.

13-1423. Violent sexual assault; natural life sentence

A. A person is guilty of violent sexual assault if in the course of committing an offense under section 13-1404, 13-1405, 13-1406 or 13-1410 the offense involved the discharge, use or threatening exhibition of a deadly weapon or dangerous instrument or involved the intentional or knowing infliction of serious physical injury and the person has a historical prior felony conviction for a sexual offense under this chapter or any offense committed outside this state that if committed in this state would constitute a sexual offense under this chapter.

B. Notwithstanding section 13-703, section 13-704, section 13-705, section 13-706, subsection A and section 13-708, subsection D, a person who is guilty of a violent sexual assault shall be sentenced to life imprisonment and the court shall order that the person not be released on any basis for the remainder of the person's natural life.

13-1424. Voyeurism; classification

A. It is unlawful to knowingly invade the privacy of another person without the knowledge of the other person for the purpose of sexual stimulation.

B. It is unlawful for a person to disclose, display, distribute or publish a photograph, videotape, film or digital recording that is made in violation of subsection A of this section without the consent or knowledge of the person depicted.

C. For the purposes of this section, a person's privacy is invaded if both of the following apply:

1. The person has a reasonable expectation that the person will not be photographed, videotaped, filmed, digitally recorded or otherwise viewed or recorded.

2. The person is photographed, videotaped, filmed, digitally recorded or otherwise viewed, with or without a device, either:

(a) While the person is in a state of undress or partial dress.

(b) While the person is engaged in sexual intercourse or sexual contact.

(c) While the person is urinating or defecating.

(d) In a manner that directly or indirectly captures or allows the viewing of the person's genitalia, buttock or female breast, whether clothed or unclothed, that is not otherwise visible to the public.

D. This section does not apply to any of the following:

1. Photographing, videotaping, filming or digitally recording for security purposes if notice of the use of the photographing, videotaping, filming or digital recording equipment is clearly posted in the location and the location is one in which the person has a reasonable expectation of privacy.

2. Photographing, videotaping, filming or digitally recording by correctional officials for security reasons or in connection with the investigation of alleged misconduct of persons on the premises of a jail or prison.

3. Photographing, videotaping, filming or digitally recording by law enforcement officers pursuant to an investigation, which is otherwise lawful.

4. The use of a child monitoring device as defined in section 13-3001.

E. A violation of subsection A or B of this section is a class 5 felony, except that a violation of subsection B of this section is a class 4 felony if the person depicted is recognizable.

13-1425. Unlawful disclosure of images depicting states of nudity or specific sexual activities; classification; definitions

A. It is unlawful for a person to intentionally disclose an image of another person who is identifiable from the image itself or from information displayed in connection with the image if all of the following apply:

1. The person in the image is depicted in a state of nudity or is engaged in specific sexual activities.

2. The depicted person has a reasonable expectation of privacy. Evidence that a person has sent an image to another person using an electronic device does not, on its own, remove the person's reasonable expectation of privacy for that image.

3. The image is disclosed with the intent to harm, harass, intimidate, threaten or coerce the depicted person.

B. This section does not apply to any of the following:

1. The reporting of unlawful conduct.

2. Lawful and common practices of law enforcement, criminal reporting, legal proceedings or medical treatment.

3. Images involving voluntary exposure in a public or commercial setting.

4. An interactive computer service, as defined in 47 United States Code section 230(f)(2), or an information service, as defined in 47 United States Code section 153, with regard to content wholly provided by another party.

5. Any disclosure that is made with the consent of the person who is depicted in the image.

C. A violation of this section is a class 5 felony, except that a violation of this section is a:

1. Class 4 felony if the image is disclosed by electronic means.

2. Class 1 misdemeanor if a person threatens to disclose but does not disclose an image that if disclosed would be a violation of this section.

D. For the purposes of this section:

1. "Disclose" means display, distribute, publish, advertise or offer.

2. "Disclosed by electronic means" means delivery to an e-mail address, mobile device, tablet or other electronic device and includes disclosure on a website.

3. "Harm" means physical injury, financial injury or serious emotional distress.

4. "Image" means a photograph, videotape, film or digital recording.

5. "Reasonable expectation of privacy" means the person exhibits an actual expectation of privacy and the expectation is reasonable.

6. "Specific sexual activities" has the same meaning prescribed in section 11-811, subsection D, paragraph 18, subdivisions (a) and (b).

7. "State of nudity" has the same meaning prescribed in section 11-811, subsection D, paragraph 14, subdivision (a).

13-1426. Sexual assault investigations; collected biological evidence testing; definitions

A. A health care facility that obtains written consent to release sexual assault kit evidence shall notify the investigating law enforcement agency, if known, or the law enforcement agency that has jurisdiction in that portion of the local unit of government in which the health care facility is located within forty-eight hours after the sexual assault kit evidence collection.

B. A law enforcement agency that receives notice pursuant to subsection A of this section must take possession of the sexual assault kit evidence from the health care facility within five business days after notification.

C. The investigating law enforcement agency must submit the sexual assault kit evidence to a public accredited crime laboratory for forensic analysis within fifteen business days after its receipt in all cases in which a victim reports to law enforcement and law enforcement determines that a crime occurred.

D. All sexual assault examination kits that are submitted for analysis must be analyzed as soon as practicable if sufficient personnel and resources are available.

E. The public accredited crime laboratory shall ensure that all eligible DNA profiles are uploaded into:

1. Databases that are maintained by the state law enforcement agency, if the DNA profile meets the requirements of the state database comparison policies.

2. Databases that are maintained by municipal law enforcement agencies, if the DNA profile meets the requirements of the municipal crime laboratory comparison policies.

3. The combined DNA index system database established by the federal bureau of investigation, if the DNA profile meets the requirements of the bureau's comparison policies.

F. A public accredited crime laboratory may contract with a private accredited crime laboratory, as appropriate, to perform the analysis that is required by this section, subject to the necessary quality assurance reviews by the public accredited crime laboratory.

G. The failure of a law enforcement agency to submit a request for analysis within the time limits prescribed by this section does not constitute grounds in any criminal or civil proceeding to challenge the validity of a DNA evidence association and a court may not exclude any evidence obtained from the sexual assault examination kit on those grounds.

H. A person who is accused or convicted of committing a crime against a victim does not have standing to object to any failure to comply with this section and such failure is not grounds for setting aside a conviction or sentence.

I. This section does not establish a private right of action or claim on the part of any individual, entity or agency against any law enforcement agency or any contractor of a law enforcement agency.

J. For the purposes of this section:

1. "Law enforcement agency" means the police department of any state, county, municipality or postsecondary educational institution or for any agency that has an agreement in place for evidence analysis.

2. "Public accredited crime laboratory" means a crime laboratory that is established pursuant to section 41-1771 or a municipal crime laboratory.

13-1427. Sexual assault kits; annual report; definitions

A. On or before August 30 of each year, each law enforcement agency shall report to the department of public safety on a form prescribed by the department of public safety:

1. The number of sexual assault kits that the agency received.

2. The number of sexual assault kits that were submitted to a public accredited crime laboratory for analysis.

3. The number of sexual assault kits that were not submitted to a public accredited crime laboratory for analysis.

4. The reason or reasons for not submitting evidence from each sexual assault kit to a public accredited crime laboratory for analysis.

B. On or before August 30 of each year, each public accredited crime laboratory shall report to the department of public safety:

1. The number of sexual assault kits that the laboratory received.

2. The number of sexual assault kits that were not analyzed and the reason or reasons that the kits were not analyzed.

C. On or before December 1 of each year, the department of public safety shall report to the governor, the president of the senate and the speaker of the house of representatives on the compilation of the reports that are received from each public accredited crime laboratory and each law enforcement agency pursuant to subsections A and B of this section. The report must include any reconciliation and recommendations for increased compliance if necessary. The department of public safety shall post the reports on the department's website.

D. For the purposes of this section, "law enforcement agency" and "public accredited crime laboratory" have the same meanings prescribed in section 13-1426.

Chapter 15 Criminal Trespass and Burglary

13-1501. Definitions

In this chapter, unless the context otherwise requires:

1. "Critical public service facility" means:

(a) A structure or fenced yard that is posted with signage indicating it is a felony to trespass or signage indicating high voltage or high pressure and is used by a rail, bus, air or other mass transit provider, a public or private utility, any municipal corporation, city, town or other political subdivision that is organized under state law and that generates, transmits, distributes or otherwise provides natural gas, liquefied petroleum gas, electricity or a combustible substance for a delivery system that is not a retail-only facility, a telecommunications carrier or telephone company, a municipal provider as defined in section 45-561, a law enforcement agency, a public or private fire department or an emergency medical service provider.

(b) A structure or fenced yard or any equipment or apparatus that is posted with signage indicating it is a felony to trespass or signage indicating high voltage or high pressure and is used to manufacture, extract, transport, distribute or store gas, including natural gas or liquefied petroleum gas, oil, electricity, water or hazardous materials, unless it is a retail-only facility.

2. "Enter or remain unlawfully" means an act of a person who enters or remains on premises when the person's intent for so entering or remaining is not licensed, authorized or otherwise privileged except when the entry is to commit theft of merchandise displayed for sale during normal business hours, when the premises are open to the public and when the person does not enter any unauthorized areas of the premises.

3. "Entry" means the intrusion of any part of any instrument or any part of a person's body inside the external boundaries of a structure or unit of real property.

4. "Fenced commercial yard" means a unit of real property that is surrounded completely by fences, walls, buildings or similar barriers, or any combination of fences, walls, buildings or similar barriers, and that is zoned for business operations or where livestock, produce or other commercial items are located.

5. "Fenced residential yard" means a unit of real property that immediately surrounds or is adjacent to a residential structure and that is enclosed by a fence, wall, building or similar barrier or any combination of fences, walls, buildings or similar barriers.

6. "Fenced yard" means a unit of real property that is surrounded by fences, walls, buildings or similar barriers or any combination of fences, walls, buildings or similar barriers.

7. "In the course of committing" means any acts that are performed by an intruder from the moment of entry to and including flight from the scene of a crime.

8. "Manipulation key" means a key, device or instrument, other than a key that is designed to operate a specific lock, that can be variably positioned and manipulated in a vehicle keyway to operate a lock or cylinder, including a wiggle key, jiggle key or rocker key.

9. "Master key" means a key that operates all the keyed locks or cylinders in a similar type or group of locks.

10. "Nonresidential structure" means any structure other than a residential structure and includes a retail establishment.

11. "Residential structure" means any structure, movable or immovable, permanent or temporary, that is adapted for both human residence and lodging whether occupied or not.

12. "Structure" means any device that accepts electronic or physical currency and that is used to conduct commercial transactions, any vending machine or any building, object, vehicle, railroad car or place with sides and a floor that is separately securable from any other structure attached to it and that is used for lodging, business, transportation, recreation or storage.

13. "Vending machine" means a machine that dispenses merchandise or service through the means of currency, coin, token, credit card or other nonpersonal means of accepting payment for merchandise or service received.

13-1502. Criminal trespass in the third degree; classification

A. A person commits criminal trespass in the third degree by:

1. Knowingly entering or remaining unlawfully on any real property after a reasonable request to leave by a law enforcement officer, the owner or any other person having lawful control over such property, or reasonable notice prohibiting entry.

2. Knowingly entering or remaining unlawfully on the right-of-way for tracks, or the storage or switching yards or rolling stock of a railroad company.

B. Pursuant to subsection A, paragraph 1 of this section, a request to leave by a law enforcement officer acting at the request of the owner of the property or any other person having lawful control over the property has the same legal effect as a request made by the property owner or other person having lawful control of the property.

C. Criminal trespass in the third degree is a class 3 misdemeanor.

13-1503. Criminal trespass in the second degree; classification

A. A person commits criminal trespass in the second degree by knowingly entering or remaining unlawfully in or on any nonresidential structure or in any fenced commercial yard.

B. Criminal trespass in the second degree is a class 2 misdemeanor.

13-1504. Criminal trespass in the first degree; classification

A. A person commits criminal trespass in the first degree by knowingly:
1. Entering or remaining unlawfully in or on a residential structure.
2. Entering or remaining unlawfully in a fenced residential yard.
3. Entering any residential yard and, without lawful authority, looking into the residential structure thereon in reckless disregard of infringing on the inhabitant's right of privacy.
4. Entering unlawfully on real property that is subject to a valid mineral claim or lease with the intent to hold, work, take or explore for minerals on the claim or lease.
5. Entering or remaining unlawfully on the property of another and burning, defacing, mutilating or otherwise desecrating a religious symbol or other religious property of another without the express permission of the owner of the property.
6. Entering or remaining unlawfully in or on a critical public service facility.
B. Criminal trespass in the first degree under subsection A, paragraph 6 of this section is a class 5 felony. Criminal trespass in the first degree under subsection A, paragraph 1 or 5 of this section is a class 6 felony. Criminal trespass in the first degree under subsection A, paragraph 2, 3 or 4 of this section is a class 1 misdemeanor.

13-1505. Possession of burglary tools; master key; manipulation key; classification

A. A person commits possession of burglary tools by:
1. Possessing any explosive, tool, instrument or other article adapted or commonly used for committing any form of burglary as defined in sections 13-1506, 13-1507 and 13-1508 and intending to use or permit the use of such an item in the commission of a burglary.
2. Buying, selling, transferring, possessing or using a motor vehicle manipulation key or master key.
B. Subsection A, paragraph 2 of this section does not apply to a person who either:
1. Uses a master key in the course of the person's lawful business or occupation, including licensed vehicle dealers and manufacturers, key manufacturers who are engaged in the business of designing, making, altering, duplicating or repairing locks or keys, locksmiths, loan institutions that finance vehicles and law enforcement.
2. Transfers, possesses or uses no more than one manipulation key, unless the manipulation key is transferred, possessed or used with the intent to commit any theft or felony.
C. Possession of burglary tools is a class 6 felony.

13-1506. Burglary in the third degree; classification

A. A person commits burglary in the third degree by:
1. Entering or remaining unlawfully in or on a nonresidential structure or in a fenced commercial or residential yard with the intent to commit any theft or any felony therein.
2. Making entry into any part of a motor vehicle by means of a manipulation key or master key, with the intent to commit any theft or felony in the motor vehicle.
B. Burglary in the third degree is a class 4 felony.

13-1507. Burglary in the second degree; classification

A. A person commits burglary in the second degree by entering or remaining unlawfully in or on a residential structure with the intent to commit any theft or any felony therein.
B. Burglary in the second degree is a class 3 felony.

13-1508. Burglary in the first degree; classification

A. A person commits burglary in the first degree if such person or an accomplice violates the provisions of either section 13-1506 or 13-1507 and knowingly possesses explosives, a deadly weapon or a dangerous instrument in the course of committing any theft or any felony.

B. Burglary in the first degree of a nonresidential structure or a fenced commercial or residential yard is a class 3 felony. It is a class 2 felony if committed in a residential structure.

13-1509. Willful failure to complete or carry an alien registration document; exception; authenticated records; classification

A. In addition to any violation of federal law, a person is guilty of willful failure to complete or carry an alien registration document if the person is in violation of 8 United States Code section 1304(e) or 1306(a).

B. In the enforcement of this section, an alien's immigration status may be determined by:

1. A law enforcement officer who is authorized by the federal government to verify or ascertain an alien's immigration status.

2. The United States immigration and customs enforcement or the United States customs and border protection pursuant to 8 United States Code section 1373(c).

C. A law enforcement official or agency of this state or a county, city, town or other political subdivision of this state may not consider race, color or national origin in the enforcement of this section except to the extent permitted by the United States or Arizona Constitution.

D. A person who is sentenced pursuant to this section is not eligible for suspension of sentence, probation, pardon, commutation of sentence, or release from confinement on any basis except as authorized by section 31-233, subsection A or B until the sentence imposed by the court has been served or the person is eligible for release pursuant to section 41-1604.07.

E. In addition to any other penalty prescribed by law, the court shall order the person to pay jail costs.

F. This section does not apply to a person who maintains authorization from the federal government to remain in the United States.

G. Any record that relates to the immigration status of a person is admissible in any court without further foundation or testimony from a custodian of records if the record is certified as authentic by the government agency that is responsible for maintaining the record.

H. A violation of this section is a class 1 misdemeanor, except that the maximum fine is one hundred dollars and for a first violation of this section the court shall not sentence the person to more than twenty days in jail and for a second or subsequent violation the court shall not sentence the person to more than thirty days in jail.

13-1601. Definitions

In this chapter, unless the context otherwise requires:

1. "Damaging" means damage as defined in section 13-1701.

2. "Defacing" means any unnecessary act of substantially marring any surface or place, by any means, or any act of putting up, affixing, fastening, printing or painting any notice on any structure, without permission from the owner.

3. "Litter" includes any rubbish, refuse, waste material, offal, paper, glass, cans, bottles, organic or inorganic trash, debris, filthy or odoriferous objects, dead animals or any foreign substance of whatever kind or description, including junked or abandoned vehicles, whether or not any of these items are of value.

4. "Property of another" means property in which any person other than the defendant has an interest, including community property and other property in which the defendant also has an interest and, for damage caused by theft of scrap metal, the property of other persons damaged directly or indirectly as a result of the acts of the defendant.

5. "Tamper" means any act of interference.

6. "Tampering with utility property" means any of the following if committed against property that is owned or operated by a utility for the purposes of transmission or distribution:

(a) Rearranging, damaging, altering, interfering with or otherwise preventing the performance of a normal or customary function of utility property.

(b) Connecting any wire, conduit or device to any utility property without authorization.

(c) Defacing, puncturing, removing, reversing or altering any utility property.

(d) Preventing any meter from properly measuring or registering.

(e) Taking, receiving, using or converting to personal use or the use of another any utility service that has not been measured or authorized.

(f) Diverting or changing the intended course or path of the utility service without the authorization or consent of the utility.

(g) Causing, procuring, permitting, aiding or abetting any person to do any of the acts listed in this paragraph.

7. "Utility" means any enterprise, public or private, that provides gas, electric, irrigation, steam, water, water conservation, sewer or communications services, as well as any common carrier on land, rail, sea or air.

Chapter 16 Criminal Damage to Property

13-1602. Criminal damage; classification

A. A person commits criminal damage by:

1. Recklessly defacing or damaging property of another person.

2. Recklessly tampering with property of another person so as substantially to impair its function or value.

3. Recklessly damaging property of a utility.

4. Recklessly parking any vehicle in such a manner as to deprive livestock of access to the only reasonably available water.

5. Recklessly drawing or inscribing a message, slogan, sign or symbol that is made on any public or private building, structure or surface, except the ground, and that is made without permission of the owner.

6. Intentionally tampering with utility property.

B. Criminal damage is punished as follows:

1. Criminal damage is a class 4 felony if the person recklessly damages property of another in an amount of ten thousand dollars or more.

2. Criminal damage is a class 4 felony if the person recklessly damages the property of a utility in an amount of five thousand dollars or more or if the person intentionally tampers with utility property and the damage causes an imminent safety hazard to any person.

3. Criminal damage is a class 5 felony if the person recklessly damages property of another in an amount of two thousand dollars or more but less than ten thousand dollars or if the damage is inflicted to promote, further or assist any criminal street gang or criminal syndicate with the intent to intimidate and the person is not subject to paragraph 1 or 2 of this subsection.

4. Criminal damage is a class 6 felony if the person recklessly damages property of another in an amount of one thousand dollars or more but less than two thousand dollars.

5. Criminal damage is a class 1 misdemeanor if the person recklessly damages property of another in an amount of more than two hundred fifty dollars but less than one thousand dollars.

6. In all other cases criminal damage is a class 2 misdemeanor.

C. For a violation of subsection A, paragraph 5 of this section, in determining the amount of damage to property, damages include reasonable labor costs of any kind, reasonable material costs of any kind and any reasonable costs that are attributed to equipment that is used to abate or repair the damage to the property.

13-1603. Criminal littering or polluting; classification

A. A person commits criminal littering or polluting if the person without lawful authority does any of the following:

1. Throws, places, drops or permits to be dropped on public property or property of another that is not a lawful dump any litter, destructive or injurious material that the person does not immediately remove.

2. Discharges or permits to be discharged any sewage, oil products or other harmful substances into any waters or onto any shorelines within this state.

3. Dumps any earth, soil, stones, ores or minerals on any land.

B. Criminal littering or polluting is punishable as follows:

1. A class 6 felony if the act is a knowing violation of subsection A in which the amount of litter or other prohibited material or substance exceeds three hundred pounds in weight or one hundred cubic feet in volume or is done in any quantity for a commercial purpose.

2. A class 1 misdemeanor if the act is a knowing violation of subsection A, paragraph 1 in which the amount of litter or prohibited material or substance is more than one hundred pounds in weight but less than three hundred pounds in weight or more than thirty-five cubic feet in volume but less than one hundred cubic feet in volume and is not done for a commercial purpose.

3. A class 1 misdemeanor if the act is not punishable under paragraph 1 of this subsection and involves placing any destructive or injurious material on or within fifty feet of a highway, beach or shoreline of any body of water used by the public.

4. A class 2 misdemeanor if the act is not punishable under paragraph 1, 2 or 3 of this subsection.

C. If a fine is assessed for a violation of subsection A, paragraph 1 or 2, one hundred per cent of any assessed fine shall be deposited in the general fund of the county in which the fine was assessed. At least fifty per cent of the fine shall be used by the county for the purposes of illegal dumping cleanup.

13-1604. Aggravated criminal damage; classification

A. A person commits aggravated criminal damage by intentionally or recklessly without the express permission of the owner:
1. Defacing, damaging or in any way changing the appearance of any building, structure, personal property or place used for worship or any religious purpose.
2. Defacing or damaging any building, structure or place used as a school or as an educational facility.
3. Defacing, damaging or tampering with any cemetery, mortuary or personal property of the cemetery or mortuary or other facility used for the purpose of burial or memorializing the dead.
4. Defacing, damaging or tampering with any utility or agricultural infrastructure or property, construction site or existing structure for the purpose of obtaining nonferrous metals.
B. Aggravated criminal damage is punishable as follows:
1. If the person intentionally or recklessly does any act described in subsection A of this section that causes damage to the property of another in an amount of ten thousand dollars or more, aggravated criminal damage:
(a) Resulting from actions described in subsection A, paragraph 1, 2 or 3 of this section is a class 4 felony.
(b) Resulting from actions described in subsection A, paragraph 4 of this section is a class 3 felony.
2. If the person intentionally or recklessly damages property of another in an amount of one thousand five hundred dollars or more but less than ten thousand dollars, aggravated criminal damage:
(a) Resulting from actions described in subsection A, paragraph 1, 2 or 3 of this section is a class 5 felony.
(b) Resulting from actions described in subsection A, paragraph 4 of this section is a class 4 felony.
3. In all other cases aggravated criminal damage is:
(a) A class 6 felony if it results from actions described in subsection A, paragraph 1, 2 or 3 of this section.
(b) A class 5 felony if it results from actions described in subsection A, paragraph 4 of this section.
C. In determining the amount of damage to property, damages include the cost of repair or replacement of the property that was damaged, the cost of the loss of crops and livestock, reasonable labor costs of any kind, reasonable material costs of any kind and any reasonable costs that are attributed to equipment that is used to abate or repair the damage to the property.

13-1605. Aggregation of amounts of damage

Amounts of damage caused pursuant to one scheme or course of conduct, whether to property of one or more persons, may be aggregated in the indictment or information at the discretion of this state in determining the classification of an offense in violation of this chapter.

13-1701. Definitions

In this chapter, unless the context otherwise requires:
1. "Damage" means any physical or visual impairment of any surface.
2. "Occupied structure" means any structure as defined in paragraph 4 in which one or more human beings either is or is likely to be present or so near as to be in equivalent danger at the time the fire or explosion occurs. The term includes any dwelling house, whether occupied, unoccupied or vacant.
3. "Property" means anything other than a structure which has value, tangible or intangible, public or private, real or personal, including documents evidencing value or ownership.
4. "Structure" means any building, object, vehicle, watercraft, aircraft or place with sides and a floor, used for lodging, business, transportation, recreation or storage.
5. "Wildland" means any brush covered land, cutover land, forest, grassland or woods.

13-1702. Reckless burning; classification

A. A person commits reckless burning by recklessly causing a fire or explosion which results in damage to an occupied structure, a structure, wildland or property.

B. Reckless burning is a class 1 misdemeanor.

13-1703. Arson of a structure or property; classification

A. A person commits arson of a structure or property by knowingly and unlawfully damaging a structure or property by knowingly causing a fire or explosion.

B. Arson of a structure is a class 4 felony. Arson of property is a class 4 felony if the property had a value of more than one thousand dollars. Arson of property is a class 5 felony if the property had a value of more than one hundred dollars but not more than one thousand dollars. Arson of property is a class 1 misdemeanor if the property had a value of one hundred dollars or less.

13-1704. Arson of an occupied structure; classification

A. A person commits arson of an occupied structure by knowingly and unlawfully damaging an occupied structure by knowingly causing a fire or explosion.

B. Arson of an occupied structure is a class 2 felony.

13-1705. Arson of an occupied jail or prison facility; classification.

A. A person commits arson of an occupied jail or prison facility by knowingly causing a fire or explosion which results in physical damage to the jail or prison facility.

B. Arson of an occupied jail or prison facility is a class 4 felony.

Chapter 17 Arson

13-1706. Burning of wildlands; exceptions; classification

A. It is unlawful for any person, without lawful authority, to intentionally, knowingly, recklessly or with criminal negligence to set or cause to be set on fire any wildland other than the person's own or to permit a fire that was set or caused to be set by the person to pass from the person's own grounds to the grounds of another person.

B. This section does not apply to any of the following:

1. Open burning that is lawfully conducted in the course of agricultural operations.

2. Fire management operations that are conducted by a political subdivision.

3. Prescribed or controlled burns that are conducted with written authority from the state forester.

4. Lawful activities that are conducted pursuant to any rule, regulation or policy that is adopted by a state, tribal or federal agency.

5. In absence of a fire ban or other burn restrictions to a person on public lands, setting a fire for purposes of cooking or warming that does not spread sufficiently from its source to require action by a fire control agency.

C. A person who violates this section is guilty of an offense as follows:

1. If done with criminal negligence, the offense is a class 2 misdemeanor.

2. If done recklessly, the offense is a class 1 misdemeanor.

3. If done intentionally or knowingly and the person knows or reasonably should know that the person's conduct violates any order or rule that is issued by a governmental entity and that prohibits, bans, restricts or otherwise regulates fires during periods of extreme fire hazard, the offense is a class 6 felony.

4. If done intentionally and the person's conduct places another person in danger of death or serious bodily injury or places any building or occupied structure of another person in danger of damage, the offense is a class 3 felony.

13-1707. Unlawful cross burning; classification

A. It is unlawful for a person to burn or cause to be burned a cross on the property of another person without that person's permission or on a highway or any other public place with the intent to intimidate any person or group of persons. The intent to intimidate may not be inferred solely from the act of burning a cross, but shall be proven by independent evidence.
B. A person who violates this section is guilty of a class 1 misdemeanor.

13-1708. Unlawful symbol burning; classification

A. It is unlawful for a person to burn or cause to be burned any symbol not addressed by section 13-1707 on the property of another person without that person's permission or on a highway or any other public place with the intent to intimidate any person or group of persons. The intent to intimidate may not be inferred solely from the act of burning the symbol, but shall be proven by independent evidence.
B. A person who violates this section is guilty of a class 1 misdemeanor.

13-1709. Emergency response and investigation costs; civil liability; definitions

A. A person who commits an act in violation of this chapter that results in an appropriate emergency response or investigation and who is convicted of the violation may be liable for the expenses that are incurred incident to the emergency response and the investigation of the commission of the offense.
B. The court may assess and collect the expenses prescribed in subsection A. The court shall state the amount of these expenses as a separate item in any final judgment, order or decree.
C. The expenses are a debt of the person. The public agency, for profit entity or nonprofit entity that incurred the expenses may collect the debt proportionally. The liability that is imposed under this section is in addition to and not in limitation of any other liability that may be imposed. If a person is subject to liability under this section and is married, only the separate property of the person is subject to liability.
D. There shall be no duty under a policy of liability insurance to defend or indemnify any person found liable for any expenses under this section.
E. For the purposes of this section:
1. "Expenses" means reasonable costs that are directly incurred by a public agency, for profit entity or nonprofit entity that makes an appropriate emergency response to an incident or an investigation of the commission of the offense, including the costs of providing police, fire fighting, rescue and emergency medical services at the scene of the incident and the salaries of the persons who respond to the incident but excluding charges assessed by an ambulance service that is regulated pursuant to title 36, chapter 21.1, article 2.
2. "Public agency" means this state, any city, county, municipal corporation or district, any Arizona federally recognized native American tribe or any other public authority that is located in whole or in part in this state and that provides police, fire fighting, medical or other emergency services.

Chapter 18 Theft

13-1801. Definitions

A. In this chapter, unless the context otherwise requires:
1. "Check" means any check, draft or other negotiable or nonnegotiable instrument of any kind.
2. "Control" or "exercise control" means to act so as to exclude others from using their property except on the defendant's own terms.
3. "Credit" means an express agreement with the drawee for the payment of a check.
4. "Deprive" means to withhold the property interest of another either permanently or for so long a time period that a substantial portion of its economic value or usefulness or enjoyment is lost, to withhold with the intent to restore it only on payment of any reward or other compensation or to transfer or dispose of it so that it is unlikely to be recovered.

5. "Draw" means making, drawing, uttering, preparing, writing or delivering a check.

6. "Funds" means money or credit.

7. "Issue" means to deliver or cause to be delivered a check to a person who thereby acquires a right against the drawer with respect to the check. A person who draws a check with the intent that it be so delivered is deemed to have issued it if the delivery occurs.

8. "Material misrepresentation" means a pretense, promise, representation or statement of present, past or future fact that is fraudulent and that, when used or communicated, is instrumental in causing the wrongful control or transfer of property or services. The pretense may be verbal or it may be a physical act.

9. "Means of transportation" means any vehicle.

10. "Obtain" means to bring about or to receive the transfer of any interest in property, whether to a defendant or to another, or to secure the performance of a service or the possession of a trade secret.

11. "Pass" means, for a payee, holder or bearer of a check that previously has been or purports to have been drawn and issued by another, to deliver a check, for a purpose other than collection, to a third person who by delivery acquires a right with respect to the check.

12. "Property" means any thing of value, tangible or intangible, including trade secrets.

13. "Property of another" means property in which any person other than the defendant has an interest on which the defendant is not privileged to infringe, including property in which the defendant also has an interest, notwithstanding the fact that the other person might be precluded from civil recovery because the property was used in an unlawful transaction or was subject to forfeiture as contraband. Property in possession of the defendant is not deemed property of another person who has only a security interest in the property, even if legal title is in the creditor pursuant to a security agreement.

14. "Services" includes labor, professional services, transportation, cable television, computer or communication services, gas or electricity services, accommodation in hotels, restaurants or leased premises or elsewhere, admission to exhibitions and use of vehicles or other movable property.

15. "Value" means the fair market value of the property or services at the time of the theft. The value of ferrous metal or nonferrous metal, as defined in section 44-1641, is the average fair market value of the metal in the local area together with the repair or replacement value of any property from which the metal was removed at the time of the theft. Written instruments that do not have a readily ascertained market value have as their value either the face amount of indebtedness less the portion satisfied or the amount of economic loss involved in deprivation of the instrument, whichever is greater. When property has an undeterminable value the trier of fact shall determine its value and, in reaching its decision, may consider all relevant evidence, including evidence of the property's value to its owner.

B. In determining the classification of the offense, the state may aggregate in the indictment or information amounts taken in thefts committed pursuant to one scheme or course of conduct, whether the amounts were taken from one or several persons.

13-1802. Theft; classification; definitions

A. A person commits theft if, without lawful authority, the person knowingly:

1. Controls property of another with the intent to deprive the other person of such property; or

2. Converts for an unauthorized term or use services or property of another entrusted to the defendant or placed in the defendant's possession for a limited, authorized term or use; or

3. Obtains services or property of another by means of any material misrepresentation with intent to deprive the other person of such property or services; or

4. Comes into control of lost, mislaid or misdelivered property of another under circumstances providing means of inquiry as to the true owner and appropriates such property to the person's own or another's use without reasonable efforts to notify the true owner; or

5. Controls property of another knowing or having reason to know that the property was stolen; or

6. Obtains services known to the defendant to be available only for compensation without paying or an agreement to pay the compensation or diverts another's services to the person's own or another's benefit without authority to do so; or

7. Controls the ferrous metal or nonferrous metal of another with the intent to deprive the other person of the metal; or

8. Controls the ferrous metal or nonferrous metal of another knowing or having reason to know that the metal was stolen; or

9. Purchases within the scope of the ordinary course of business the ferrous metal or nonferrous metal of another person knowing that the metal was stolen.

B. A person commits theft if, without lawful authority, the person knowingly takes control, title, use or management of a vulnerable adult's property while acting in a position of trust and confidence and with the intent to deprive the vulnerable adult of the property. Proof that a person took control, title, use or management of a vulnerable adult's property without adequate consideration to the vulnerable adult may give rise to an inference that the person intended to deprive the vulnerable adult of the property.

C. It is an affirmative defense to any prosecution under subsection B of this section that either:

1. The property was given as a gift consistent with a pattern of gift giving to the person that existed before the adult became vulnerable.

2. The property was given as a gift consistent with a pattern of gift giving to a class of individuals that existed before the adult became vulnerable.

3. The superior court approved the transaction before the transaction occurred.

D. The inferences set forth in section 13-2305 apply to any prosecution under subsection A, paragraph 5 of this section.

E. At the conclusion of any grand jury proceeding, hearing or trial, the court shall preserve any trade secret that is admitted in evidence or any portion of a transcript that contains information relating to the trade secret pursuant to section 44-405.

F. Subsection B of this section does not apply to an agent who is acting within the scope of the agent's duties as or on behalf of a health care institution that is licensed pursuant to title 36, chapter 4 and that provides services to the vulnerable adult.

G. Theft of property or services with a value of twenty-five thousand dollars or more is a class 2 felony. Theft of property or services with a value of four thousand dollars or more but less than twenty-five thousand dollars is a class 3 felony. Theft of property or services with a value of three thousand dollars or more but less than four thousand dollars is a class 4 felony, except that theft of any vehicle engine or transmission is a class 4 felony regardless of value. Theft of property or services with a value of two thousand dollars or more but less than three thousand dollars is a class 5 felony. Theft of property or services with a value of one thousand dollars or more but less than two thousand dollars is a class 6 felony. Theft of any property or services valued at less than one thousand dollars is a class 1 misdemeanor, unless the property is taken from the person of another, is a firearm or is an animal taken for the purpose of animal fighting in violation of section 13-2910.01, in which case the theft is a class 6 felony.

H. A person who is convicted of a violation of subsection A, paragraph 1 or 3 of this section that involved property with a value of one hundred thousand dollars or more is not eligible for suspension of sentence, probation, pardon or release from confinement on any basis except pursuant to section 31-233, subsection A or B until the sentence imposed by the court has been served, the person is eligible for release pursuant to section 41-1604.07 or the sentence is commuted.

I. For the purposes of this section, the value of ferrous metal or nonferrous metal includes the amount of any damage to the property of another caused as a result of the theft of the metal.

J. In an action for theft of ferrous metal or nonferrous metal:

1. Unless satisfactorily explained or acquired in the ordinary course of business by an automotive recycler as defined and licensed pursuant to title 28, chapter 10 or by a scrap metal dealer as defined in section 44-1641, proof of possession of scrap metal that was recently stolen may give rise to an inference that the person in possession of the scrap metal was aware of the risk that it had been stolen or in some way participated in its theft.

2. Unless satisfactorily explained or sold in the ordinary course of business by an automotive recycler as defined and licensed pursuant to title 28, chapter 10 or by a scrap metal dealer as defined in section 44-1641, proof of the sale of stolen scrap metal at a price substantially below its fair market value may give rise to an inference that the person selling the scrap metal was aware of the risk that it had been stolen.

K. For the purposes of this section:

1. "Adequate consideration" means the property was given to the person as payment for bona fide goods or services provided by the person and the payment was at a rate that was customary for similar goods or services in the community that the vulnerable adult resided in at the time of the transaction.

2. "Ferrous metal" and "nonferrous metal" have the same meanings prescribed in section 44-1641.

3. "Pattern of gift giving" means two or more gifts that are the same or similar in type and monetary value.

4. "Position of trust and confidence" has the same meaning prescribed in section 46-456.

5. "Property" includes all forms of real property and personal property.

6. "Vulnerable adult" has the same meaning prescribed in section 46-451.

13-1803. Unlawful use of means of transportation; classification

A. A person commits unlawful use of means of transportation if, without intent permanently to deprive, the person either:

1. Knowingly takes unauthorized control over another person's means of transportation.

2. Knowingly is transported or physically located in a vehicle that the person knows or has reason to know is in the unlawful possession of another person pursuant to paragraph 1 or section 13-1814.

B. A violation of subsection A, paragraph 1 of this section is a class 5 felony.

C. A violation of subsection A, paragraph 2 of this section is a class 6 felony.

13-1804. Theft by extortion; classification

A. A person commits theft by extortion by knowingly obtaining or seeking to obtain property or services by means of a threat to do in the future any of the following:
1. Cause physical injury to anyone by means of a deadly weapon or dangerous instrument or cause death or serious physical injury to anyone.
2. Cause physical injury to anyone except as provided in paragraph 1 of this subsection.
3. Cause damage to property.
4. Engage in other conduct constituting an offense.
5. Accuse anyone of a crime or bring criminal charges against anyone.
6. Expose a secret or an asserted fact, whether true or false, tending to subject anyone to hatred, contempt or ridicule or to impair the person's credit or business.
7. Take or withhold action as a public servant or cause a public servant to take or withhold action.
8. Cause anyone to part with any property.
9. Take or withhold action regarding an alleged claim of easement or other right of access to an adjoining property if both of the following occur:
(a) The claimant's property interest is the result of a tax lien purchase or foreclosure pursuant to title 42, chapter 18.
(b) The fair market value of the claimant's property is equal to or less than the amount paid by the claimant for the purchase of the tax lien or foreclosure, including taxes paid after the lien purchase and any costs and attorney fees paid in connection with the lien foreclosure. For the purposes of this subdivision, "fair market value" means the fair market value as defined in section 33-814, subsection A as of the date of the theft.
B. It is an affirmative defense to a prosecution under subsection A, paragraph 5, 6 or 7 that the property obtained by threat of the accusation, exposure, lawsuit or other invocation of official action was lawfully claimed either as:
1. Restitution or indemnification for harm done under circumstances to which the accusation, exposure, lawsuit or other official action relates.
2. Compensation for property that was lawfully obtained or for lawful services.
C. Theft by extortion as defined in subsection A, paragraph 1 is a class 2 felony. Otherwise, theft by extortion is a class 4 felony.

13-1805. Shoplifting; detaining suspect; defense to wrongful detention; civil action by merchant; public services; classification

A. A person commits shoplifting if, while in an establishment in which merchandise is displayed for sale, the person knowingly obtains such goods of another with the intent to deprive that person of such goods by:
1. Removing any of the goods from the immediate display or from any other place within the establishment without paying the purchase price; or
2. Charging the purchase price of the goods to a fictitious person or any person without that person's authority; or
3. Paying less than the purchase price of the goods by some trick or artifice such as altering, removing, substituting or otherwise disfiguring any label, price tag or marking; or
4. Transferring the goods from one container to another; or
5. Concealment.
B. A person is presumed to have the necessary culpable mental state pursuant to subsection A of this section if the person does either of the following:
1. Knowingly conceals on himself or another person unpurchased merchandise of any mercantile establishment while within the mercantile establishment.
2. Uses an artifice, instrument, container, device or other article to facilitate the shoplifting.
C. A merchant, or a merchant's agent or employee, with reasonable cause, may detain on the premises in a reasonable manner and for a reasonable time any person who is suspected of shoplifting as prescribed in subsection A of this section for questioning or summoning a law enforcement officer.
D. Reasonable cause is a defense to a civil or criminal action against a peace officer, a merchant or an agent or employee of the merchant for false arrest, false or unlawful imprisonment or wrongful detention.

E. If a minor engages in conduct that violates subsection A of this section, notwithstanding the fact that the minor may not be held responsible because of the person's minority, any merchant who is injured by the shoplifting of the minor may bring a civil action against the parent or legal guardian of the minor under either section 12-661 or 12-692.

F. Any merchant who is injured by the shoplifting of an adult or emancipated minor in violation of subsection A of this section may bring a civil action against the adult or emancipated minor pursuant to section 12-691.

G. In imposing sentence on a person who is convicted of violating this section, the court may require any person to perform public services designated by the court in addition to or in lieu of any fine that the court might impose.

H. Shoplifting property with a value of two thousand dollars or more, shoplifting property during any continuing criminal episode or shoplifting property if done to promote, further or assist any criminal street gang or criminal syndicate is a class 5 felony. Shoplifting property with a value of one thousand dollars or more but less than two thousand dollars is a class 6 felony. Shoplifting property valued at less than one thousand dollars is a class 1 misdemeanor, unless the property is a firearm in which case the shoplifting is a class 6 felony. For the purposes of this subsection, "continuing criminal episode" means theft of property with a value of one thousand five hundred dollars or more if committed during at least three separate incidences within a period of ninety consecutive days.

I. A person who in the course of shoplifting uses an artifice, instrument, container, device or other article with the intent to facilitate shoplifting or who commits shoplifting and who has previously committed or been convicted within the past five years of two or more offenses involving burglary, shoplifting, robbery, organized retail theft or theft is guilty of a class 4 felony.

13-1806. Unlawful failure to return rented or leased property; notice; classification

A. A person commits unlawful failure to return rented property if, without notice to and permission of the lessor of the property, the person knowingly fails without good cause to return the property within seventy-two hours after the time provided for return in the rental agreement.

B. If the property is not leased on a periodic tenancy basis, the person who rents out the property shall include the following information, clearly written as part of the terms of the rental agreement:

1. The date and time the property is required to be returned.

2. The maximum penalties if the property is not returned within seventy-two hours of the date and time listed in paragraph 1.

C. If the property is leased on a periodic tenancy basis without a fixed expiration or return date the lessor shall include within the lease clear written notice that the lessee is required to return the property within seventy-two hours from the date and time of the failure to pay any periodic lease payment required by the lease.

D. It is a defense to prosecution under this section that the defendant was physically incapacitated and unable to request or obtain permission of the lessor to retain the property or that the property itself was in such a condition, through no fault of the defendant, that it could not be returned to the lessor within such time.

E. Unlawful failure to return rented or leased property if the property is a motor vehicle is a class 5 felony. In all other cases, unlawful failure to return rented or leased property is a class 1 misdemeanor.

13-1807. Issuing a bad check; violation; classification

A. A person commits issuing a bad check if the person issues or passes a check knowing that the person does not have sufficient funds in or on deposit with the bank or other drawee for the payment in full of the check as well as all other checks outstanding at the time of issuance.

B. Any of the following is a defense to prosecution under this section:

1. The payee or holder knows or has been expressly notified before the drawing of the check or has reason to believe that the drawer did not have on deposit or to the drawer's credit with the drawee sufficient funds to ensure payment on its presentation.

2. The check is postdated and sufficient funds are on deposit with the drawee on such later date for the payment in full of the check.

3. Insufficiency of funds results from an adjustment to the person's account by the credit institution without notice to the person.

C. Nothing in this section prohibits prosecution for any other applicable criminal offense.

D. Except as provided in subsection E of this section, issuing a bad check is a class 1 misdemeanor.

E. Issuing a bad check in an amount of five thousand dollars or more is a class 6 felony if the person fails to pay the full amount of the check, including accrued interest at the rate of twelve per cent per year and any other applicable fees pursuant to this chapter, within sixty days after receiving notice pursuant to section 13-1808.

13-1808. Presumptions relating to issuing a bad check; proof of presentation; nonpayment; protest; notice

A. For the purposes of this chapter, the issuer's knowledge of insufficient funds may be presumed if either:

1. The issuer had no account or a closed account with the bank or other drawee at the time the issuer issued the check.

2. Payment was refused by the bank or other drawee for lack of funds on presentation within thirty days after issue and the issuer failed to pay the holder in full the amount due on the check, together with reasonable costs, within twelve days after receiving notice of that refusal.

B. If a person obtained property or secured performance of services by issuing or passing a check when the issuer did not have sufficient funds in or on deposit with the bank or other drawee for the payment in full of the check as well as all other checks then outstanding, the person's intent to deprive the owner of property or to avoid payment for service under section 13-1802 may be presumed if either:

1. The issuer had no account or a closed account with the bank or other drawee at the time the issuer issued the check.

2. Payment was refused by the bank or other drawee for lack of funds on presentation within thirty days after issue and the issuer failed to pay the holder in full the amount due on the check, together with reasonable costs, within twelve days after receiving notice of that refusal.

C. Nothing in this section prevents the prosecution from establishing the requisite intent by direct evidence.

D. Notice may be actual notice or notice in writing that is sent by registered or certified mail, return receipt requested, or by regular mail that is supported by an affidavit of service by mailing. Written notice shall be addressed to the issuer at the issuer's address shown on any of the following:

1. The check.

2. The records of the bank or other drawee.

3. The records of the person to whom the check is issued or passed.

E. The form of notice shall be substantially as follows:

Notice of dishonored check

Date:_____

Name of issuer:_____

Street address:_____
City and state:_____

You are, according to law, hereby notified that a check or instrument numbered _____, dated _____, 19_____, drawn on _____ in the amount of _____
(bank or other drawee)

and payable to _____ has been dishonored.

Pursuant to Arizona law, you have twelve days from receipt of this notice to pay or tender to_____ the full amount
              (holder)
of the check or instrument, together with all reasonable costs and protest fees of _____, the total amount due being
_____. Unless this amount is paid in full within the specified time above, the holder of the check or instrument may turn over the dishonored check or instrument and all other available information relating to this incident to the county attorney for criminal prosecution.

F. If written notice is given in accordance with this section, it is presumed that the notice was received no later than five days after it was sent.

13-1809. Jurisdiction; restitution; fees; deferred prosecution

A. The county attorney may prosecute any violation of section 13-1807. If the defendant is alleged to have committed multiple violations of section 13-1807 within the same county, the county attorney may file a complaint charging all of the violations that have not previously been filed in the justice of the peace precinct in which the greatest number of violations are alleged to have occurred.

B. A person who is charged with an offense under this chapter may make restitution for the bad checks. Restitution shall be made through the prosecutor's office if collection and processing were initiated through that office. Restitution shall include at a minimum the face amount of the check. The fact that restitution to the party injured is made and that any costs of filing with the county attorney are paid is a mitigating factor in any imposition of punishment for any violation of this chapter. On sentencing, the court may require any person convicted under this chapter to make restitution in an amount not to exceed twice the amount of the dishonored check or fifty dollars, whichever is greater, together with all applicable costs and fees. This is in addition to any other punishment imposed under this chapter.

C. A county attorney may collect a fee if the county attorney's office collects and processes a check if the check is issued or passed in a manner that makes the issuance or passing an offense under section 13-1802, 13-1807 or 13-2310 or has been forged under section 13-2002.

D. The county attorney may collect the fee from any person who is a party to an offense described in this section.

E. The amount of the fee for each check shall not exceed:

1. Seventy-five dollars if the face amount of the check does not exceed one hundred dollars.

2. One hundred dollars if the face amount of the check is greater than one hundred dollars but does not exceed three hundred dollars.

3. One hundred twenty-five dollars if the face amount of the check is greater than three hundred dollars but does not exceed one thousand dollars.

4. Twenty per cent of the face amount of the check if the check is greater than one thousand dollars.

F. If the person from whom the fee is collected was a party to the offense of forgery under section 13-2002 and the offense was committed by altering the face amount of the check, the face amount as altered governs for the purpose of determining the amount of the fee prescribed in subsection E of this section.

13-1810. Deferred prosecution of bad check cases

A. Each county attorney may create within his office a deferred prosecution program for bad check cases.

B. The county attorney may refer a bad check case to the bad check deferred prosecution program. This chapter does not limit the power of the county attorney to prosecute bad check complaints.

C. On receipt of a bad check case, the county attorney shall determine if the case is one which is appropriate to be referred to the bad check deferred prosecution program. In determining whether to refer a case to the bad check deferred prosecution program, the county attorney shall consider the following guidelines:

1. The amount of the bad check.

2. If there is a prior criminal record of the defendant.

3. The number of bad check complaints against the defendant previously received by the county attorney.

4. Whether or not there are other bad check complaints currently pending against the defendant.

5. The strength of the evidence of intent to defraud the victim.

D. On referral of a complaint to the bad check deferred prosecution program, a notice of the complaint shall be forwarded by mail to the defendant. The notice shall contain all of the following:

1. The date and amount of the check.

2. The name of the payee.

3. The date before which the defendant must contact the office of the county attorney concerning the complaint.

4. A statement of the penalty for issuance of a bad check.

E. The county attorney may enter into a written agreement with the defendant to defer prosecution on the bad check for a period to be determined by the county attorney, not to exceed one year for misdemeanors, pending all of the following:

1. Completion of the bad check deferred prosecution school program conducted by the county attorney or a private entity under contract with the county attorney.

2. Full restitution being made to the victim of the bad check, as specified in section 13-1809, subsection B.

3. Full payment of fees due under section 13-1809.

F. For each check, monies received from a person pursuant to section 13-1809 shall be applied first to satisfy restitution to the victim.

13-1811. County bad check trust fund; use of fund

A. The board of supervisors of a county shall establish a county bad check trust fund in the county treasury. The county attorney shall administer the fund under the conditions and for the purposes provided by this section.

B. The county attorney shall transmit to the county treasurer for deposit in the county bad check trust fund any fees that are collected pursuant to sections 13-1809 and 13-1810, any investigation and prosecution costs and any monies that are obtained as a result of a forfeiture and that are recovered for the county through enforcement of section 13-1802, 13-1807, 13-2002 or 13-2310, whether by final judgment, settlement or otherwise.

C. Monies that are collected by the county attorney pursuant to a prosecution under section 13-1802, 13-1807, 13-2002 or 13-2310 and that are not claimed by a victim within one hundred eighty days after the monies are collected shall be disposed of pursuant to section 12-941, except that the monies shall be transmitted to the county treasurer for deposit in the county bad check trust fund.

D. The county attorney shall transmit to the county treasurer for deposit in the county bad check trust fund any grant monies that the county attorney receives for the investigation or prosecution of bad check cases from a political subdivision of this state, any department or agency of the United States or another state, any foundation or any corporation.

E. The monies in the fund shall be used only for the expenditures associated with the investigation, prosecution and deferred prosecution of offenses pursuant to sections 13-1802, 13-1807, 13-2002 and 13-2310.

F. On or before January 15, April 15, July 15 and October 15, the county attorney shall file with the board of supervisors a report for the previous calendar quarter. The report shall set forth the source of all monies for and all expenditures from the fund. The report shall not include any identifying information about specific investigations or prosecutions.

13-1812. Bank records; subpoenas; affidavit of dishonor; affidavit of loss

A. The county attorney may issue a subpoena duces tecum to a financial institution to obtain account records or affidavits of dishonor in an investigation or prosecution of any violation of section 13-1802, 13-1807, 13-2002, 13-2310 or 13-2311. This section does not prevent the county attorney from obtaining a grand jury subpoena duces tecum for any of the suspect's records that are held by a financial institution.

B. The subpoena shall identify the subject of the investigation, the account or accounts under investigation and a specific time period that is relevant to the investigation or prosecution.

C. Account records may include copies of any account agreement between the drawee financial institution and the subject of the investigation, signature cards, monthly statements, correspondence or other records of communication between the financial institution and the subject of the investigation.

D. An authorized representative of a drawee financial institution may certify bank records that are obtained by subpoena if all of the following apply:

1. The bank records are the regular account records that are used and kept by the drawee financial institution.

2. The bank records are made at or near the time the underlying transactions occur in the ordinary course of business.

3. The bank records are made from information that is transmitted by a person who has firsthand knowledge acquired in the course of the drawee financial institution's regular course of business.

E. At a trial for a violation of section 13-1802, 13-1807, 13-2002 or 13-2310, certified bank records that are obtained by subpoena may be introduced in evidence and constitute prima facie evidence of the facts contained in the records.

F. At a trial for a violation of section 13-1802, 13-1807, 13-2002 or 13-2310, an affidavit of dishonor may be introduced in evidence and constitutes prima facie evidence of either:

1. The refusal of a drawee financial institution to pay a check because the drawer had no account or a closed account with the drawee at the time a check was issued or passed.

2. The refusal of a drawee financial institution to pay a check because of insufficiency of the drawer's funds at the time a check was issued or passed.

G. A certification of bank records or an affidavit of dishonor that is acknowledged by any notary public or other officer who is authorized by law to take acknowledgments shall be received in evidence without further proof of its authenticity.

13-1813. Unlawful failure to return a motor vehicle subject to a security interest; notice; classification

A. A person commits unlawful failure to return a motor vehicle subject to a security interest if all of the following apply:

1. The person fails to make a payment on the lien for more than ninety days.

2. The secured creditor notifies the owner in writing, by certified mail return receipt requested, that the owner is ninety days late in making a payment and is in default. The notice shall include the following:

(a) A statement stating:

"You are now in default on loan agreement #_____. If you fail to return the _____ (year of vehicle, make, model) within thirty days you will be subject to criminal prosecution."

(b) The business address and hours of operation for return of the vehicle.

(c) The maximum penalties for unlawful failure to return a motor vehicle subject to a security interest.

3. The owner fails to cure the default within thirty days.

4. With the intent to hinder or prevent the enforcement of the secured creditor's security interest, the owner knowingly fails to do either of the following:

(a) Return the motor vehicle to the secured creditor.

(b) Allow the secured creditor to take possession of the motor vehicle.

B. The original contract creating the security interest in the motor vehicle shall contain the following information:

1. A statement that it is unlawful to fail to return a motor vehicle subject to a security interest within thirty days after receiving notice of default.

2. A statement that notice of default will be mailed to the address on the loan agreement and that it is the responsibility of the owner to keep the listed address current.

3. The maximum penalty for unlawful failure to return a motor vehicle subject to a security interest.

C. It is a defense to prosecution under this section that:

1. The owner was physically incapacitated and unable to request or obtain permission of the secured creditor to retain the motor vehicle.

2. The motor vehicle itself was in a condition, through no intentional fault of the defendant, that it could not be returned to the secured creditor within the specified time.

3. The owner has a security interest pursuant to section 47-2711, subsection C.

D. If a law enforcement agency seizes the vehicle, the secured creditor shall be responsible for all towing, storage and related fees or charges.

E. A vehicle that is not returned pursuant to this section is a stolen vehicle for purposes of section 28-4845.

F. Unlawful failure to return a motor vehicle subject to a property interest is a class 6 felony.

13-1814. Theft of means of transportation; affidavit; classification

A. A person commits theft of means of transportation if, without lawful authority, the person knowingly does one of the following:

1. Controls another person's means of transportation with the intent to permanently deprive the person of the means of transportation.

2. Converts for an unauthorized term or use another person's means of transportation that is entrusted to or placed in the defendant's possession for a limited, authorized term or use.

3. Obtains another person's means of transportation by means of any material misrepresentation with intent to permanently deprive the person of the means of transportation.

4. Comes into control of another person's means of transportation that is lost or misdelivered under circumstances providing means of inquiry as to the true owner and appropriates the means of transportation to the person's own or another's use without reasonable efforts to notify the true owner.

5. Controls another person's means of transportation knowing or having reason to know that the property is stolen.

B. The inferences set forth in section 13-2305 apply to any prosecution under subsection A, paragraph 5 of this section.

C. A person who alleges that a theft of means of transportation has occurred shall attest to that fact by signing an affidavit that is provided by the law enforcement officer or agency when the report is taken in person or by signing and notarizing an affidavit that is provided by the law enforcement agency if the report is taken other than in person. If the affidavit is not taken in person by a law enforcement officer or agency, the person who alleges that a theft of means of transportation has occurred shall mail or deliver the signed and notarized affidavit to the appropriate local law enforcement agency within seven days after reporting the theft. If the appropriate law enforcement agency does not receive the signed and notarized affidavit within thirty days after the initial report, the vehicle information shall be removed from the databases of the national crime information center and the Arizona criminal justice information system. The affidavit provided by the law enforcement agency shall indicate that a person who falsely reports a theft of means of transportation may be subject to criminal prosecution.

D. Theft of means of transportation is a class 3 felony.

13-1815. Unlawful use of power of attorney; classification

A. An agent who holds a principal's power of attorney pursuant to title 14, chapter 5, article 5 and who uses or manages the principal's assets or property with the intent to unlawfully deprive that person of the asset or property is guilty of theft.

B. A violation of this section carries the same classification as theft pursuant to section 13-1802.

13-1816. Unlawful use, possession or removal of theft detection shielding devices; classification; definition

A. A person commits unlawful use of a theft detection shielding device if the person knowingly manufacturers, sells, offers for sale or distributes in any way a laminated or coated bag or device unique to and marketed for shielding and intended to shield merchandise from detection by an electronic or magnetic theft alarm sensor.

B. A person commits unlawful possession of a theft detection shielding device if, with the intent to commit theft or shoplifting, the person knowingly possesses any laminated or coated bag or device unique to and marketed for shielding and intended to shield merchandise from detection by an electronic or magnetic theft alarm sensor.

C. A person commits unlawful possession of a theft detection device remover if the person knowingly possesses any tool or device that is designed to allow the removal of any theft detection device from any merchandise and the person intended to use the tool to remove any theft detection device from any merchandise without the permission of the merchant or person who owns or holds the merchandise.

D. A person commits unlawful removal of a theft detection device if the person intentionally removes the device from merchandise before purchasing that merchandise.

E. A violation of this section is a class 6 felony.

F. For the purposes of this section, "merchant" means a person who offers for sale or exchange at least six like items of new and unused personal property in this state.

13-1817. Unlawful possession, use or alteration of a retail sales receipt or universal product code label; classification; definition

A. It is unlawful for a person to intentionally cheat or defraud a merchant by doing any of the following:
1. Possessing at least fifteen fraudulent retail sales receipts or universal product code labels or possessing a device that manufactures fraudulent retail sales receipts or universal product code labels.
2. Possessing, using, uttering, transferring, making, altering, counterfeiting or reproducing a retail sales receipt or a universal product code label.
B. A violation of subsection A, paragraph 1 is a class 5 felony. A violation of subsection A, paragraph 2 is a class 6 felony and, in addition to any other fine authorized by law, the court may impose a fine of not more than three times the value represented on the retail sales receipt or the retail price represented by the original universal product code label.
C. For the purposes of this section, "merchant" means a person who offers for sale or exchange at least six like items of new and unused personal property in this state.

13-1818. Misappropriation of charter school monies; violation; classification

A. A person commits misappropriation of charter school monies if without lawful authority and with an intent to defraud the person converts monies provided by this state under a charter school contract in a manner that does not further the purposes of the charter and is not reasonably related to the business of the charter school.

B. A violation of subsection A is a class 4 felony, except that if the amount of monies converted is twenty-five thousand dollars or more a violation of subsection A is a class 2 felony.

13-1819. Organized retail theft; classification

A. A person commits organized retail theft if the person acting alone or in conjunction with another person does any of the following:

1. Removes merchandise from a retail establishment without paying the purchase price with the intent to resell or trade the merchandise for money or for other value.

2. Uses an artifice, instrument, container, device or other article to facilitate the removal of merchandise from a retail establishment without paying the purchase price.

B. Organized retail theft is a class 4 felony.

13-1820. Theft of trade secrets; classification; definition

A. A person commits theft of trade secrets if, with the intent to deprive or withhold the exclusive control of a trade secret from its owner or with the intent to make any use of a trade secret, the person does any of the following:

1. Takes, transmits, exhibits, conveys, alters, destroys, conceals or uses a trade secret without the permission of the owner.

2. Makes or causes to be made a copy of a trade secret without the permission of the owner.

3. Receives, purchases or possesses a trade secret, knowing that the trade secret has been obtained by means described in paragraph 1 or 2 of this subsection.

B. It is not a defense to a prosecution for theft of trade secrets that the person charged returned or intended to return the trade secret that was stolen, copied or obtained from another.

C. A violation of this section is a class 5 felony.

D. For the purposes of this section, "trade secrets" means information, without regard to form, including a formula, pattern, compilation, program, device, method, technique, plan, drawing, design or process that both:

1. Derives independent economic value, actual or potential, from not being generally known to and not being readily ascertainable by proper means by other persons who can obtain economic value from its disclosure or use.

2. Is the subject of efforts to maintain its secrecy that are reasonable under the circumstances.

Chapter 19 Robbery

13-1901. Definitions

In this chapter, unless the context otherwise requires:

1. "Force" means any physical act directed against a person as a means of gaining control of property.

2. "In the course of committing" includes any of the defendant's acts beginning with the initiation and extending through the flight from a robbery.

3. "Property of another" means property of another as defined in section 13-1801.

4. "Threat" means a verbal or physical menace of imminent physical injury to a person.

13-1902. Robbery; classification

A. A person commits robbery if in the course of taking any property of another from his person or immediate presence and against his will, such person threatens or uses force against any person with intent either to coerce surrender of property or to prevent resistance to such person taking or retaining property.

B. Robbery is a class 4 felony.

3-1903. Aggravated robbery; classification

A. A person commits aggravated robbery if in the course of committing robbery as defined in section 13-1902, such person is aided by one or more accomplices actually present.

B. Aggravated robbery is a class 3 felony.

13-1904. Armed robbery; classification

A. A person commits armed robbery if, in the course of committing robbery as defined in section 13-1902, such person or an accomplice:

1. Is armed with a deadly weapon or a simulated deadly weapon; or

2. Uses or threatens to use a deadly weapon or dangerous instrument or a simulated deadly weapon.

B. Armed robbery is a class 2 felony.

Chapter 20 Forgery and Related Offenses

13-2001. Definitions

In this chapter, unless the context otherwise requires:

1. "Access device" means any card, token, code, account number, electronic serial number, mobile or personal identification number, password, encryption key, biometric identifier or other means of account access, including a canceled or revoked access device, that can be used alone or in conjunction with another access device to obtain money, goods, services, computer or network access or any other thing of value or that can be used to initiate a transfer of any thing of value.

2. "Coin machine" means a coin box, turnstile, vending machine or other mechanical, electrical or electronic device or receptacle that is designed to receive a coin or bill of a certain denomination or a token made for such purpose and that, in return for the insertion or deposit of the coin, bill or token, automatically offers, provides, assists in providing or permits the acquisition or use of some property or service.

3. "Complete written instrument" means a written instrument that purports to be genuine and fully drawn with respect to every essential feature.

4. "Entity identifying information" includes, if the entity is a person other than a human being, any written document or electronic data that does or purports to provide information concerning the entity's name, address, telephone number, employer identification number, account number or electronic serial number, the identifying number of the entity's depository account or any other information or data that is unique to, assigned to or belongs to the entity and that is intended to be used to access services, funds or benefits of any kind that the entity owns or to which the entity is entitled.

5. "Falsely alters a written instrument" means to change a complete or incomplete written instrument, without the permission of anyone entitled to grant it, by means of counterfeiting, washing, erasure, obliteration, deletion, insertion of new matter, connecting together different parts of the whole of more than one genuine instrument or transposition of matter or in any other manner, so that the altered instrument falsely appears or purports to be in all respects an authentic creation of its ostensible maker or authorized by him.

6. "Falsely completes a written instrument" means to transform an incomplete written instrument into a complete one by adding, inserting or changing matter without the permission of anyone entitled to grant it, so that the complete written instrument falsely appears or purports to be in all respects an authentic creation of its ostensible maker or authorized by him.

7. "Falsely makes a written instrument" means to make or draw a complete or incomplete written instrument that purports to be an authentic creation of its ostensible maker but that is not either because the ostensible maker is fictitious, or because, if real, the ostensible maker did not authorize the making or drawing of the written instrument.

8. "Forged instrument" means a written instrument that has been falsely made, completed or altered.

9. "Incomplete written instrument" means a written instrument that contains some matter by way of content or authentication but that requires additional matter to render it a complete written instrument.

10. "Personal identifying information" means any written document or electronic data that does or purports to provide information concerning a name, signature, electronic identifier or screen name, electronic mail signature, address or account, biometric identifier, driver or professional license number, access device, residence or mailing address, telephone number, employer, student or military identification number, social security number, tax identification number, employment information, citizenship status or alien identification number, personal identification number, photograph, birth date, savings, checking or other financial account number, credit card, charge card or debit card number, mother's maiden name, fingerprint or retinal image, the image of an iris or deoxyribonucleic acid or genetic information.

11. "Slug" means an object, article or device that by virtue of its size, its shape or any other quality is capable of being inserted, deposited or otherwise used in a coin machine as a fraudulent substitute for a genuine token, lawful coin or bill of the United States.

12. "Written instrument" means either:

(a) Any paper, document or other instrument that contains written or printed matter or its equivalent.

(b) Any token, stamp, seal, badge, trademark, graphical image, access device or other evidence or symbol of value, right, privilege or identification.

13-2002. Forgery; classification

A. A person commits forgery if, with intent to defraud, the person:

1. Falsely makes, completes or alters a written instrument; or

2. Knowingly possesses a forged instrument; or

3. Offers or presents, whether accepted or not, a forged instrument or one that contains false information.

B. The possession of five or more forged instruments may give rise to an inference that the instruments are possessed with an intent to defraud.

C. Forgery is a class 4 felony, except that if the forged instrument is used in connection with the purchase, lease or renting of a dwelling that is used as a drop house, it is a class 3 felony. For the purposes of this subsection, "drop house" means property that is used to facilitate smuggling pursuant to section 13-2319.

13-2003. Criminal possession of a forgery device; classification

A. A person commits criminal possession of a forgery device if the person either:

1. Makes or possesses with knowledge of its character and with intent to commit fraud any plate, die, or other device, apparatus, equipment, software, access device, article, material, good, property or supply specifically designed or adapted for use in forging written instruments.

2. Makes or possesses any device, apparatus, equipment, software, access device, article, material, good, property or supply adaptable for use in forging written instruments with intent to use it or to aid or permit another to use it for purposes of forgery.

B. Subsection A, paragraph 1 does not apply to peace officers or prosecutors in the performance of their duties.

C. A violation of subsection A, paragraph 1 is a class 6 felony. A violation of subsection A, paragraph 2 is a class 5 felony.

13-2004. Criminal simulation; classification

A. A person commits criminal simulation if, with intent to defraud, such person makes, alters, or presents or offers, whether accepted or not, any object so that it appears to have an antiquity, rarity, source, authorship or value that it does not in fact possess.

B. Criminal simulation is a class 6 felony.

13-2005. Obtaining a signature by deception; classification

A. A person commits obtaining a signature by deception if, with intent to defraud, such person obtains the signature of another person to a written instrument by knowingly misrepresenting or omitting any fact material to the instrument or transaction.

B. Obtaining a signature by deception is a class 1 misdemeanor.

13-2006. Criminal impersonation; classification

A. A person commits criminal impersonation by:
1. Assuming a false identity with the intent to defraud another; or
2. Pretending to be a representative of some person or organization with the intent to defraud; or
3. Pretending to be, or assuming a false identity of, an employee or a representative of some person or organization with the intent to induce another person to provide or allow access to property. This paragraph does not apply to peace officers in the performance of their duties.
B. Criminal impersonation is a class 6 felony.

13-2007. Unlawful use of slugs; classification

A. A person commits unlawful use of slugs if:
1. With intent to defraud the supplier of property or a service sold or offered by means of a coin machine, such person inserts, deposits or otherwise uses a slug in such machine; or
2. Such person makes, possesses, offers for sale or disposes of a slug with intent to enable a person to use it fraudulently in a coin machine.
B. Unlawful use of slugs is a class 2 misdemeanor.

13-2008. Taking identity of another person or entity; classification

A. A person commits taking the identity of another person or entity if the person knowingly takes, purchases, manufactures, records, possesses or uses any personal identifying information or entity identifying information of another person or entity, including a real or fictitious person or entity, without the consent of that other person or entity, with the intent to obtain or use the other person's or entity's identity for any unlawful purpose or to cause loss to a person or entity whether or not the person or entity actually suffers any economic loss as a result of the offense, or with the intent to obtain or continue employment.
B. On the request of a person or entity, a peace officer in any jurisdiction in which an element of an offense under this section is committed, a result of an offense under this section occurs or the person or entity whose identity is taken or accepted resides or is located shall take a report. The peace officer may provide a copy of the report to any other law enforcement agency that is located in a jurisdiction in which a violation of this section occurred.
C. If a defendant is alleged to have committed multiple violations of this section within the same county, the prosecutor may file a complaint charging all of the violations and any related charges under other sections that have not been previously filed in any precinct in which a violation is alleged to have occurred. If a defendant is alleged to have committed multiple violations of this section within the state, the prosecutor may file a complaint charging all of the violations and any related charges under other sections that have not been previously filed in any county in which a violation is alleged to have occurred.
D. This section does not apply to a violation of section 4-241 by a person who is under twenty-one years of age.
E. Taking the identity of another person or entity is a class 4 felony.

13-2009. Aggravated taking identity of another person or entity; knowingly accepting the identity of another person; classification

A. A person commits aggravated taking the identity of another person or entity if the person knowingly takes, purchases, manufactures, records, possesses or uses any personal identifying information or entity identifying information of either:
1. Three or more other persons or entities, including real or fictitious persons or entities, without the consent of the other persons or entities, with the intent to obtain or use the other persons' or entities' identities for any unlawful purpose or to cause loss to the persons or entities whether or not the persons or entities actually suffer any economic loss.
2. Another person or entity, including a real or fictitious person or entity, without the consent of that other person or entity, with the intent to obtain or use the other person's or entity's identity for any unlawful purpose and causes another person or entity to suffer an economic loss of one thousand dollars or more.

3. Another person, including a real or fictitious person, with the intent to obtain employment.

B. A person commits knowingly accepting the identity of another person if the person, in hiring an employee, knowingly does both of the following:

1. Accepts any personal identifying information of another person from an individual and knows that the individual is not the actual person identified by that information.

2. Uses that identity information for the purpose of determining whether the individual who presented that identity information has the legal right or authorization under federal law to work in the United States as described and determined under the processes and procedures under 8 United States Code section 1324a.

C. In an action for aggravated taking the identity of another person or entity under subsection A, paragraph 1 of this section, proof of possession out of the regular course of business of the personal identifying information or entity identifying information of three or more other persons or entities may give rise to an inference that the personal identifying information or entity identifying information of the three or more other persons or entities was possessed for an unlawful purpose.

D. This section does not apply to a violation of section 4-241 by a person who is under twenty-one years of age.

E. Aggravated taking the identity of another person or entity or knowingly accepting the identity of another person is a class 3 felony.

13-2010. Trafficking in the identity of another person or entity; classification

A. A person commits trafficking in the identity of another person or entity if the person knowingly sells, transfers or transmits any personal identifying information or entity identifying information of another person or entity, including a real or fictitious person or entity, without the consent of the other person or entity for any unlawful purpose or to cause loss to the person or entity whether or not the other person or entity actually suffers any economic loss, or allowing another person to obtain or continue employment.

B. This section does not apply to a violation of section 4-241 by a person who is under twenty-one years of age.

C. Trafficking in the identity of another person or entity is a class 2 felony.

13-2011. Admission tickets; fraudulent creation or possession; classification

A. It is unlawful for a person, with intent to defraud, to forge, alter or possess any ticket, token or paper that is designed for admission to or for the rendering of services by any sports, amusement, concert or other facility that offers services to the general public.

B. A person who violates this section is guilty of a class 1 misdemeanor.

Chapter 21 Credit Card Fraud

13-2101. Definitions

In this chapter, unless the context otherwise requires:

1. "Cancelled or revoked credit card" means a credit card that is no longer valid because permission to use it has been suspended, revoked or terminated by the issuer of the credit card by written notice sent by certified or registered mail addressed to the person to whom the credit card was issued at the person's last known address. Proof that the written notice has been deposited as certified or registered matter in the United States mail addressed to the person to whom the credit card was issued at the person's last known address gives rise to an inference that the written notice has been given to the cardholder.

2. "Cardholder" means any person who is either:

(a) Named on the face of a credit card to whom or for whose benefit the credit card is issued by an issuer.

(b) In possession of a credit card with the consent of the person to whom the credit card was issued.

3. "Credit card" means:

(a) Any instrument or device, whether known as a credit card, charge card, credit plate, courtesy card or identification card or by any other name, that is issued with or without fee by an issuer for the use of the cardholder in obtaining money, goods, services or anything else of value, either on credit or in possession or in consideration of an undertaking or guaranty by the issuer of the payment of a check drawn by the cardholder, on a promise to pay in part or in full therefor at a future time, whether or not all or any part of the indebtedness that is represented by the promise to make deferred payment is secured or unsecured.

(b) A debit card, electronic benefit transfer card or other access instrument or device, other than a check that is signed by the holder or other authorized signatory on the deposit account, that draws funds from a deposit account in order to obtain money, goods, services or anything else of value.

(c) A stored value card, smart card or other instrument or device that enables a person to obtain goods, services or anything else of value through the use of value stored on the card, instrument or device.

(d) The number that is assigned to the card, instrument or device described in subdivision (a), (b) or (c) of this paragraph even if the physical card, instrument or device is not used or presented.

4. "Expired credit card" means a credit card that is no longer valid because the term shown on the credit card has elapsed.

5. "Incomplete credit card" means a credit card on which part of the matter, other than the signature of the cardholder, which an issuer requires to appear before it can be used by a cardholder, has not been stamped, embossed, imprinted or written.

6. "Issuer" means any business organization, state agency or financial institution, or its duly authorized agent, that issues a credit card.

7. "Merchant" means a person who is authorized under a written contract with a participating party to furnish money, goods, services or anything else of value on presentation of a credit card by a cardholder.

8. "Participating party" means a business organization or financial institution that is obligated or permitted by contract to acquire by electronic transmission or other means from a merchant a sales slip or sales draft or instrument for the payment of money evidencing a credit card transaction and from whom an issuer is obligated or permitted by contract to acquire by electronic transmission or other means such sales slip, sales draft or instrument for the payment of money evidencing a credit card transaction.

9. "Receives" or "receiving" means acquiring possession or control of a credit card or accepting a credit card as security for a loan.

10. "Reencoder" means an electronic device that places encoded information from the magnetic strip or stripe of a credit card onto the magnetic strip or stripe of a different credit card.

11. "Scanning device" means a scanner, reader or other electronic device that is used to access, read, scan, obtain, memorize, transmit or store, temporarily or permanently, information that is encoded on a magnetic strip or stripe of a credit card.

13-2102. Theft of a credit card or obtaining a credit card by fraudulent means; classification

A. A person commits theft of a credit card or obtaining a credit card by fraudulent means if the person:
1. Controls a credit card without the cardholder's or issuer's consent through conduct prescribed in section 13-1802 or 13-1804; or
2. Sells, transfers or conveys a credit card with the intent to defraud; or
3. With intent to defraud, obtains possession, care, custody or control over a credit card as security for debt.
B. Theft of a credit card or obtaining a credit card by fraudulent means is a class 5 felony.

13-2103. Receipt of anything of value obtained by fraudulent use of a credit card; classification

A. A person, being a third party, commits receipt of anything of value obtained by fraudulent use of a credit card by buying or receiving or attempting to buy or receive money, goods, services or any other thing of value obtained in violation of section 13-2105, knowing or believing that it was so obtained.
B. Receipt of anything of value obtained by fraudulent use of a credit card is a class 1 misdemeanor if the value of the property bought or received or attempted to be bought or received is less than two hundred fifty dollars. If the value of the property bought or received or attempted to be bought or received is two hundred fifty dollars or more but less than one thousand dollars the offense is a class 6 felony. If the value of the property bought or received or attempted to be bought or received is one thousand dollars or more the offense is a class 5 felony. Amounts obtained by fraudulent use of a credit card pursuant to one scheme or course of conduct, whether from one or several persons, may be aggregated in determining the classification of offense.

13-2104. Forgery of credit card; classification

A. A person commits forgery of a credit card if the person:
1. With intent to defraud, alters any credit card, falsely makes, manufactures, fabricates or causes to be made, manufactured or fabricated an instrument or device purporting to be a credit card without the express authorization of an issuer to do so, or falsely embosses or alters a credit card, or instrument or device purporting to be a credit card, or utters such a credit card or instrument or device purporting to be a credit card; or

2. Other than the cardholder, with intent to defraud, signs the name of any actual or fictitious person to a credit card or instrument for the payment of money which evidences a credit card transaction.

B. Forgery of a credit card is a class 4 felony.

13-2105. Fraudulent use of a credit card; classification

A. A person commits fraudulent use of a credit card if the person:

1. With intent to defraud, uses, for the purposes of obtaining or attempting to obtain money, goods, services or any other thing of value, a credit card or credit card number obtained or retained in violation of this chapter or a credit card or credit card number which the person knows is forged, expired, cancelled or revoked; or

2. Obtains or attempts to obtain money, goods, services or any other thing of value by representing, without the consent of the cardholder, that the person is the holder to a specified card or by representing that the person is the holder of a credit card and the card has not in fact been issued.

B. Fraudulent use of a credit card is a class 1 misdemeanor. If the value of all money, goods, services and other things of value obtained or attempted to be obtained in violation of this section is two hundred fifty dollars or more but less than one thousand dollars in any consecutive six-month period the offense is a class 6 felony. If the value of all money, goods, services and other things of value obtained or attempted to be obtained in violation of this section is one thousand dollars or more in any consecutive six-month period the offense is a class 5 felony.

13-2106. Possession of machinery, plate or other contrivance or incomplete credit card; classification

A. A person commits possession of machinery, plate or other contrivance or incomplete credit card if such person:

1. Possesses an incomplete credit card with intent to complete it without the express consent of the issuer.

2. Possesses, with intent to defraud and with knowledge of its character, any machinery, plate or any other contrivance designed to reproduce an instrument or device purporting to be the credit card of an issuer who has not consented to the preparation of such credit card.

B. Possession of machinery, plate or other contrivance or incomplete credit card in subsection A, paragraph 1 is a class 1 misdemeanor and a class 6 felony in subsection A, paragraph 2.

13-2107. False statement as to financial condition or identity; classification

A. A person commits false statement as to financial condition or identity if the person makes or causes to be made, either directly or indirectly, any false statement in writing as to a material fact, knowing it to be false, with the intent that it be relied on respecting the identity of that person or of any other person, firm or corporation or the financial condition of that person or of any other person, firm or corporation, for the purpose of procuring the issuance of a credit card.

B. False statement as to financial condition or identity is a class 5 felony.

13-2108. Fraud by person authorized to provide goods or services; classification

A. A person commits fraud by a person authorized to provide goods or services if such person knowingly:

1. Furnishes money, goods, services or any other thing of value upon presentation of a credit card obtained or retained in violation of section 13-2102 or a credit card which such person knows is forged, expired, cancelled or revoked.

2. Fails to furnish money, goods, services or any other thing of value which such person represents in writing to the issuer or a participating party that such person has furnished, and who receives any payment therefor.

B. Except as provided in subsections C and D, fraud by a person authorized to provide goods or services in subsection A, paragraphs 1 and 2 is a class 1 misdemeanor.

C. If the payment received by the person for all money, goods, services or other things of value furnished in violation of subsection A, paragraph 1 exceeds one hundred dollars in any consecutive six-month period, the offense is a class 6 felony.

D. If the difference between the value of all monies, goods, services or any other thing of value actually furnished and the payment or payments received by the person therefor upon such representation in violation of subsection A, paragraph 2 exceeds one hundred dollars in any consecutive six-month period, the offense is a class 6 felony.

13-2109. Credit card transaction record theft; classification

A. A person commits credit card transaction record theft by:
1. If the person is a merchant, knowingly presenting for payment to a participating party, with intent to defraud, a credit card transaction record of a sale that was not made by the merchant.
2. Knowingly and without the participating party's authorization commanding, encouraging, requesting or soliciting a merchant to present for payment to the participating party a credit card transaction record of a sale that was not made by the merchant.
B. In order to determine the classification of the offense, the state may aggregate in the indictment or information amounts that were taken from one or more persons in credit card transaction record theft that was committed pursuant to one scheme or course of conduct.
C. Credit card transaction record theft with a value of twenty-five thousand dollars or more is a class 2 felony. Credit card transaction record theft with a value of at least three thousand dollars but less than twenty-five thousand dollars is a class 3 felony. Credit card transaction record theft with a value of at least two thousand dollars but less than three thousand dollars is a class 4 felony. Credit card transaction record theft with a value of at least one thousand dollars but less than two thousand dollars is a class 5 felony. Credit card transaction record theft with a value of at least five hundred dollars but less than one thousand dollars is a class 6 felony. Credit card transaction record theft with a value of less than five hundred dollars is a class 1 misdemeanor.
D. A person who is convicted of a violation of this section that involved an amount of at least one hundred thousand dollars is not eligible for suspension of sentence, probation, pardon, or release from confinement on any other basis except pursuant to section 31-233, subsection A or B until the sentence imposed by the court has been served, the person is eligible for release pursuant to section 41-1604.07 or the sentence is commuted.

13-2110. Unlawful possession or use of scanning device or reencoder; classification

A. It is unlawful for a person to use a scanning device or reencoder without the permission of the cardholder of the credit card from which the information is being scanned or reencoded and with the intent to defraud the cardholder, the issuer or a merchant.
B. It is unlawful for a person to intentionally or knowingly make or possess with the intent to commit fraud any device, apparatus, equipment, software, article, material, good, property or supply that is specifically designed or adapted for use as or in a scanning device or a reencoder.
C. Subsection B of this section does not apply to peace officers or prosecutors in the performance of their duties.
D. A person who violates this section is guilty of a class 4 felony.

Chapter 22 Business and Commercial Fraud

13-2201. Definitions

In this chapter, unless the context otherwise requires:
1. "Adulterated" means varying from the standard of composition or quality prescribed by statute or administrative regulation or, if none, as set by established commercial usage.
2. "Fiduciary" means a trustee, guardian, executor, administrator, receiver or any other person carrying on functions of trust on behalf of another person, corporation or organization.
3. "Financial institution" means a bank, insurance company, credit union, savings and loan association, investment trust or other organization held out to the public as a place of deposit for funds or medium of savings or collective investment.
4. "Insolvent" means that, for any reason, a financial institution is unable to pay its obligations in the ordinary or usual course of business or the present fair salable value of its assets is less than the amount that will be required to pay its probable liabilities on its existing debts as they become absolute and matured.
5. "Mislabeled" means:
(a) Varying from the standard of truth or disclosure in labeling prescribed by statute or administrative regulation or, if none, as set by established commercial usage; or
(b) Represented as being another person's product, though otherwise labeled accurately as to quality and quantity.
6. "Misleading statement" means an offer to sell property or services when the offerer does not intend to sell or provide the advertised property or services:

(a) At a price equal to or lower than the price offered; or

(b) In a quantity sufficient to meet the reasonably expected public demand, unless the quantity available is specifically stated in the advertisement; or

(c) At all.

7. "Security interest" means an interest in personal property or fixtures pursuant to title 47, chapter 9.

13-2202. Deceptive business practices; classification

A. A person commits deceptive business practices if in the course of engaging in a business, occupation or profession such person recklessly:

1. Uses or possesses for use a false weight or measure or any other device for falsely determining or recording any quality or quantity; or

2. Sells, offers or exposes for sale or delivers less than the represented quantity of any commodity or service; or

3. Takes or attempts to take more than the represented quantity of any goods or service when as buyer such person furnishes the weight or measure; or

4. Sells, offers or exposes for sale adulterated goods or services; or

5. Sells, offers or exposes for sale mislabeled goods or services.

B. Deceptive business practices is a class 1 misdemeanor.

13-2203. False advertising; classification

A. A person commits false advertising if, in connection with the promotion of the sale of property or services, such person recklessly causes to be made or makes a false or misleading statement in any advertisement.

B. False advertising is a class 1 misdemeanor.

13-2204. Defrauding secured creditors; definition; classification

A. A person commits defrauding secured creditors if the person knowingly destroys, removes, conceals, encumbers, converts, sells, obtains, transfers, controls or otherwise deals with property subject to a security interest with the intent to hinder or prevent the enforcement of that interest.

B. For the purposes of this section, "control" has the same meaning as prescribed by section 13-1801.

C. Defrauding secured creditors is a class 6 felony.

13-2205. Defrauding judgment creditors; classification

A. A person commits defrauding judgment creditors if such person secretes, assigns, conveys or otherwise disposes of his property with the intent to defraud a judgment creditor or to prevent that property from being subjected to payment of a judgment.

B. Defrauding judgment creditors is a class 6 felony.

13-2206. Fraud in insolvency; classification

A. A person commits fraud in insolvency if, when proceedings have been or are about to be instituted for the appointment of a trustee, receiver or other person entitled to administer property for the benefit of creditors or when any other assignment, composition or liquidation for the benefit of creditors has been or is about to be made, such person:

1. Destroys, removes, conceals, encumbers, transfers or otherwise harms or reduces the value of the property with intent to defeat or obstruct the operation of any law relating to the administration of property for the benefit of creditors; or

2. Knowingly falsifies any writing or record relating to the property; or

3. Knowingly misrepresents or refuses to disclose to a receiver or other person entitled to administer property for the benefit of creditors the existence, amount or location of the property or any other information which he could be legally required to furnish to such administration; or

4. Obtains any substantial part of or interest in the debtor's estate with intent to defraud any creditor.

B. Fraud in insolvency is a class 6 felony.

13-2207. Receiving deposits in an insolvent financial institution; classification

A. A person commits receiving deposits in an insolvent financial institution if, as an officer, manager or other person participating in the direction of a financial institution, such person receives or permits the receipt of a deposit, premium payment or investment in the institution in excess of the amount insured by the federal deposit insurance corporation, the federal savings and loan insurance corporation or the national credit union administration knowing that the institution is insolvent.

B. It is a defense to prosecution under this section that the person making the deposit, premium payment or investment was fully informed of the financial condition of the institution.

C. Receiving deposits in an insolvent financial institution is a class 5 felony.

13-2208. Usury; classification

A. A person commits usury by knowingly engaging in or directly or indirectly providing financing for the business of making loans at a higher rate of interest or consideration than authorized by law.

B. Usury is a class 1 misdemeanor.

Chapter 23 Organized Crime , Fraud and Terrorism

13-2301. Definitions

A. For the purposes of sections 13-2302, 13-2303 and 13-2304:

1. "Collect an extension of credit" means to induce in any way any person to make repayment of that extension.

2. "Creditor" means any person making an extension of credit or any person claiming by, under or through any person making an extension of credit.

3. "Debtor" means any person to whom an extension of credit is made or any person who guarantees the repayment of an extension of credit, or in any manner undertakes to indemnify the creditor against loss resulting from the failure of any person to whom an extension is made to repay the extension.

4. "Extend credit" means to make or renew any loan or to enter into any agreement, tacit or express, whereby the repayment or satisfaction of any debt or claim, whether acknowledged or disputed, valid or invalid, and however arising, may or shall be deferred.

5. "Extortionate extension of credit" means any extension of credit with respect to which it is the understanding of the creditor and the debtor at the time the extension is made that delay in making repayment or failure to make repayment could result in the use of violence or other criminal means to cause harm to the person or the reputation or property of any person.

6. "Extortionate means" means the use, or an express or implicit threat of use, of violence or other criminal means to cause harm to the person or the reputation or property of any person.

7. "Repayment of any extension of credit" means the repayment, satisfaction or discharge in whole or in part of any debt or claim, acknowledged or disputed, valid or invalid, resulting from or in connection with that extension of credit.

B. For the purposes of section 13-2305, 13-2306 or 13-2307:

1. "Dealer in property" means a person who buys and sells property as a business.

2. "Stolen property" means property of another as defined in section 13-1801 that has been the subject of any unlawful taking.

3. "Traffic" means to sell, transfer, distribute, dispense or otherwise dispose of stolen property to another person, or to buy, receive, possess or obtain control of stolen property, with the intent to sell, transfer, distribute, dispense or otherwise dispose of the property to another person.

C. For the purposes of this chapter:

1. "Animal activity" means a commercial enterprise that uses animals for food, clothing or fiber production, agriculture or biotechnology.

2. "Animal facility" means a building or premises where a commercial activity in which the use of animals is essential takes place, including a zoo, rodeo, circus, amusement park, hunting preserve and horse and dog event.

3. "Animal or ecological terrorism" means any felony in violation of section 13-2312, subsection B that involves at least three persons acting in concert, that involves the intentional or knowing infliction of property damage in an amount of more than ten thousand dollars to the property that is used by a person for the operation of a lawfully conducted animal activity or to a commercial enterprise that is engaged in a lawfully operated animal facility or research facility and that involves either:

(a) The use of a deadly weapon or dangerous instrument.

(b) The intentional or knowing infliction of serious physical injury on a person engaged in a lawfully conducted animal activity or participating in a lawfully conducted animal facility or research facility.

4. "Biological agent" means any microorganism, virus, infectious substance or biological product that may be engineered through biotechnology or any naturally occurring or bioengineered component of any microorganism, virus, infectious substance or biological product and that is capable of causing any of the following:

(a) Death, disease or physical injury in a human, animal, plant or other living organism.

(b) The deterioration or contamination of air, food, water, equipment, supplies or material of any kind.

5. "Combination" means persons who collaborate in carrying on or furthering the activities or purposes of a criminal syndicate even though such persons may not know each other's identity, membership in the combination changes from time to time or one or more members may stand in a wholesaler-retailer or other arm's length relationship with others as to activities or dealings between or among themselves in an illicit operation.

6. "Communication service provider" has the same meaning prescribed in section 13-3001.

7. "Criminal syndicate" means any combination of persons or enterprises engaging, or having the purpose of engaging, on a continuing basis in conduct that violates any one or more provisions of any felony statute of this state.

8. "Explosive agent" means an explosive as defined in section 13-3101 and flammable fuels or fire accelerants in amounts over fifty gallons but excludes:

(a) Fireworks as defined in section 36-1601.

(b) Firearms.

(c) A propellant actuated device or propellant actuated industrial tool.

(d) A device that is commercially manufactured primarily for the purpose of illumination.

(e) A rocket having a propellant charge of less than four ounces.

9. "Material support or resources" includes money or other financial securities, financial services, lodging, sustenance, training, safehouses, false documentation or identification, communications equipment, facilities, weapons, lethal substances, explosives, personnel, transportation, disguises and other physical assets but does not include medical assistance, legal assistance or religious materials.

10. "Public establishment" means a structure, vehicle or craft that is owned, leased or operated by any of the following:

(a) This state or a political subdivision as defined in section 38-502.

(b) A public agency as defined in section 38-502.

(c) The federal government.

(d) A health care institution as defined in section 36-401.

11. "Research facility" means a laboratory, institution, medical care facility, government facility, public or private educational institution or nature preserve at which a scientific test, experiment or investigation involving the use of animals is lawfully carried out, conducted or attempted.

12. "Terrorism" means any felony, including any completed or preparatory offense, that involves the use of a deadly weapon or a weapon of mass destruction or the intentional or knowing infliction of serious physical injury with the intent to do any of the following:

(a) Influence the policy or affect the conduct of this state or any of the political subdivisions, agencies or instrumentalities of this state.

(b) Cause substantial damage to or substantial interruption of public communications, communication service providers, public transportation, common carriers, public utilities, public establishments or other public services.

(c) Intimidate or coerce a civilian population and further the goals, desires, aims, public pronouncements, manifestos or political objectives of any terrorist organization.

13. "Terrorist organization" means any organization that is designated by the United States department of state as a foreign terrorist organization under section 219 of the immigration and nationality act (8 United States Code section 1189).

14. "Toxin" means the toxic material of plants, animals, microorganisms, viruses, fungi or infectious substances or a recombinant molecule, whatever its origin or method of reproduction, including:

(a) Any poisonous substance or biological product that may be engineered through biotechnology and that is produced by a living organism.

(b) Any poisonous isomer or biological product, homolog or derivative of such a substance.

15. "Vector" means a living organism or molecule, including a recombinant molecule or biological product that may be engineered through biotechnology, that is capable of carrying a biological agent or toxin to a host.

16. "Weapon of mass destruction" means:

(a) Any device or object that is designed or that the person intends to use to cause multiple deaths or serious physical injuries through the use of an explosive agent or the release, dissemination or impact of a toxin, biological agent or poisonous chemical, or its precursor, or any vector.

(b) Except as authorized and used in accordance with a license, registration or exemption by the department of health services pursuant to section 30-672, any device or object that is designed or that the person intends to use to release radiation or radioactivity at a level that is dangerous to human life.

D. For the purposes of sections 13-2312, 13-2313, 13-2314 and 13-2315, unless the context otherwise requires:

1. "Control", in relation to an enterprise, means the possession of sufficient means to permit substantial direction over the affairs of an enterprise and, in relation to property, means to acquire or possess.

2. "Enterprise" means any corporation, partnership, association, labor union or other legal entity or any group of persons associated in fact although not a legal entity.

3. "Financial institution" means any business under the jurisdiction of the department of financial institutions or a banking or securities regulatory agency of the United States, a business coming within the definition of a bank, financial agency or financial institution as prescribed by 31 United States Code section 5312 or 31 Code of Federal Regulations section 1010.100 or a business under the jurisdiction of the securities division of the corporation commission, the state real estate department or the department of insurance.

4. "Racketeering" means any act, including any preparatory or completed offense, that is chargeable or indictable under the laws of the state or country in which the act occurred and, if the act occurred in a state or country other than this state, that would be chargeable or indictable under the laws of this state if the act had occurred in this state, and that would be punishable by imprisonment for more than one year under the laws of this state and, if the act occurred in a state or country other than this state, under the laws of the state or country in which the act occurred, regardless of whether the act is charged or indicted, and the act involves either:

(a) Terrorism, animal terrorism or ecological terrorism that results or is intended to result in a risk of serious physical injury or death.

(b) Any of the following acts if committed for financial gain:

(i) Homicide.

(ii) Robbery.

(iii) Kidnapping.

(iv) Forgery.

(v) Theft.

(vi) Bribery.

(vii) Gambling.

(viii) Usury.

(ix) Extortion.

(x) Extortionate extensions of credit.

(xi) Prohibited drugs, marijuana or other prohibited chemicals or substances.

(xii) Trafficking in explosives, weapons or stolen property.

(xiii) Participating in a criminal syndicate.

(xiv) Obstructing or hindering criminal investigations or prosecutions.

(xv) Asserting false claims, including false claims asserted through fraud or arson.

(xvi) Intentional or reckless false statements or publications concerning land for sale or lease or sale of subdivided lands or sale and mortgaging of unsubdivided lands.

(xvii) Resale of realty with intent to defraud.

(xviii) Intentional or reckless fraud in the purchase or sale of securities.

(xix) Intentional or reckless sale of unregistered securities or real property securities.

(xx) A scheme or artifice to defraud.

(xxi) Obscenity.

(xxii) Sexual exploitation of a minor.

(xxiii) Prostitution.

(xxiv) Restraint of trade or commerce in violation of section 34-252.

(xxv) Terrorism.

(xxvi) Money laundering.

(xxvii) Obscene or indecent telephone communications to minors for commercial purposes.

(xxviii) Counterfeiting marks as proscribed in section 44-1453.

(xxix) Animal terrorism or ecological terrorism.

(xxx) Smuggling of human beings.

(xxxi) Child sex trafficking.

(xxxii) Sex trafficking.

(xxxiii) Trafficking of persons for forced labor or services.

(xxxiv) Manufacturing, selling or distributing misbranded drugs in violation of section 13-3406, subsection A, paragraph 9.

5. "Records" means any book, paper, writing, computer program, data, image or information that is collected, recorded, preserved or maintained in any form of storage medium.

6. "Remedy racketeering" means to enter a civil judgment pursuant to this chapter or chapter 39 of this title against property or a person who is subject to liability, including liability for injury to the state that is caused by racketeering or by actions in concert with racketeering.

E. For the purposes of sections 13-2316, 13-2316.01 and 13-2316.02:

1. "Access" means to instruct, communicate with, store data in, retrieve data from or otherwise make use of any resources of a computer, computer system or network.

2. "Access device" means any card, token, code, account number, electronic serial number, mobile or personal identification number, password, encryption key, biometric identifier or other means of account access, including a canceled or revoked access device, that can be used alone or in conjunction with another access device to obtain money, goods, services, computer or network access or any other thing of value or that can be used to initiate a transfer of any thing of value.

3. "Computer" means an electronic device that performs logic, arithmetic or memory functions by the manipulations of electronic or magnetic impulses and includes all input, output, processing, storage, software or communication facilities that are connected or related to such a device in a system or network.

4. "Computer contaminant" means any set of computer instructions that is designed to modify, damage, destroy, record or transmit information within a computer, computer system or network without the intent or permission of the owner of the information, computer system or network. Computer contaminant includes a group of computer instructions, such as viruses or worms, that is self-replicating or self-propagating and that is designed to contaminate other computer programs or computer data, to consume computer resources, to modify, destroy, record or transmit data or in some other fashion to usurp the normal operation of the computer, computer system or network.

5. "Computer program" means a series of instructions or statements, in a form acceptable to a computer, that permits the functioning of a computer system in a manner designed to provide appropriate products from the computer system.

6. "Computer software" means a set of computer programs, procedures and associated documentation concerned with the operation of a computer system.

7. "Computer system" means a set of related, connected or unconnected computer equipment, devices and software, including storage, media and peripheral devices.

8. "Critical infrastructure resource" means any computer or communications system or network that is involved in providing services necessary to ensure or protect the public health, safety or welfare, including services that are provided by any of the following:

(a) Medical personnel and institutions.

(b) Emergency services agencies.

(c) Public and private utilities, including water, power, communications and transportation services.

(d) Fire departments, districts or volunteer organizations.

(e) Law enforcement agencies.

(f) Financial institutions.

(g) Public educational institutions.

(h) Government agencies.

9. "False or fraudulent pretense" means the unauthorized use of an access device or the use of an access device to exceed authorized access.

10. "Financial instrument" means any check, draft, money order, certificate of deposit, letter of credit, bill of exchange, credit card or marketable security or any other written instrument as defined in section 13-2001 that is transferable for value.

11. "Network" includes a complex of interconnected computer or communication systems of any type.

12. "Property" means financial instruments, information, including electronically produced data, computer software and programs in either machine or human readable form, and anything of value, tangible or intangible.

13. "Proprietary or confidential computer security information" means information about a particular computer, computer system or network that relates to its access devices, security practices, methods and systems, architecture, communications facilities, encryption methods and system vulnerabilities and that is not made available to the public by its owner or operator.

14. "Services" includes computer time, data processing, storage functions and all types of communication functions.

13-2302. Making extortionate extensions of credit; classification

A. Any person who makes an extortionate extension of credit is guilty of a class 5 felony.

B. In any prosecution pursuant to this section, if it is shown that all of the following factors were present in connection with the extension of credit, there is prima facie evidence that the extension of credit was extortionate:

1. The repayment of the extension of credit, or the performance of any promise given in consideration thereof, would be unenforceable at the time the extension of credit was made through civil judicial processes against the debtor in the county within which the debtor, if a natural person, resided or in every county within which the debtor, if other than a natural person, was incorporated, or qualified to do business.

2. The extension of credit was made at a rate of interest in excess of an annual rate of forty-five per cent calculated according to the actuarial method of allocating payments made on a debt between principal and interest, pursuant to which a payment is applied first to the accumulated interest and the balance is applied to the unpaid principal.

3. At the time the extension of credit was made, the debtor reasonably believed that either of the following:

(a) One or more extensions of credit by the creditor had been collected or attempted to be collected by extortionate means, or the nonrepayment had been punished by extortionate means.

(b) The creditor had a reputation for the use of extortionate means to collect extensions of credit or to punish the nonrepayment thereof.

4. Upon the making of the extension of credit, the total of the extensions of credit by the creditor to the debtor then outstanding, including any unpaid interest or similar charges, exceeded one hundred dollars.

C. In any prosecution pursuant to this section, if evidence has been introduced tending to show the existence of any of the circumstances described in subsection B, paragraph 1 or 2, and direct evidence of the actual belief of the debtor as to the creditor's collection practices is not available, then for the purpose of showing the understanding of the debtor and the creditor at the time the extension of credit was made, the court may in its discretion allow evidence to be introduced tending to show the reputation as to collection practices of the creditor in any community of which the debtor was a member at the time of the extension.

13-2303. Financing extortionate extensions of credit

A person who knowingly advances money or property, whether as a gift, loan, investment, pursuant to a partnership or profit sharing agreement or otherwise, to any person, with reasonable grounds to believe that it is the intention of that person to use the money or property so advanced, directly or indirectly, for the purpose of making extortionate extensions of credit, is guilty of a class 2 felony.

13-2304. Collection of extensions of credit by extortionate means

A. A person who knowingly participates in any way in the use of any extortionate means to collect or attempt to collect any extensions of credit or to punish any person for the nonrepayment thereof is guilty of a class 4 felony.

B. In any prosecution pursuant to this section, for the purpose of showing an implicit threat as a means of collection, evidence may be introduced tending to show that one or more extensions of credit by the creditor were, to the knowledge of the person against whom the implicit threat was alleged to have been made, collected or attempted to be collected by extortionate means or that the nonrepayment was punished by extortionate means.

C. In any prosecution pursuant to this section, if evidence has been introduced tending to show the existence at the time the extension of credit in question was made of the circumstances described in section 13-2302, subsection B, paragraph 1 or 2, and direct evidence of the actual belief of the debtor as to the creditor's collection practices is not available, then for the purpose of showing that words or other means of communication, shown to have been employed as a means of collection, in fact carried an express or implicit threat, the court may in its discretion allow evidence to be introduced tending to show the reputation of the defendant in any community of which the person against whom the alleged threat was made was a member at the time of the collection or attempt at collection.

13-2305. Permissible inferences

In an action for trafficking in stolen property:
1. Proof of possession of property recently stolen, unless satisfactorily explained, may give rise to an inference that the person in possession of the property was aware of the risk that it had been stolen or in some way participated in its theft.
2. Proof of the purchase or sale of stolen property at a price substantially below its fair market value, unless satisfactorily explained, may give rise to an inference that the person buying or selling the property was aware of the risk that it had been stolen.
3. Proof of the purchase or sale of stolen property by a dealer in property, out of the regular course of business, or without the usual indicia of ownership other than mere possession, unless satisfactorily explained, may give rise to an inference that the person buying or selling the property was aware of the risk that it had been stolen.

13-2306. Possession of altered property; classification

A. A person who is a dealer in property and recklessly possesses property the permanent identifying features of which, including serial numbers or labels, have been removed or in any fashion altered is guilty of a class 6 felony.

B. It is a defense to a prosecution under this section that a person has lawfully obtained a special serial number pursuant to section 28-2165 or lawfully possesses the usual indicia of ownership in addition to mere possession or has obtained the consent of the manufacturer of the property.

13-2307. Trafficking in stolen property; classification

A. A person who recklessly traffics in the property of another that has been stolen is guilty of trafficking in stolen property in the second degree.

B. A person who knowingly initiates, organizes, plans, finances, directs, manages or supervises the theft and trafficking in the property of another that has been stolen is guilty of trafficking in stolen property in the first degree.

C. Trafficking in stolen property in the second degree is a class 3 felony. Trafficking in stolen property in the first degree is a class 2 felony.

13-2308. Participating in or assisting a criminal syndicate; classification

A. A person commits participating in a criminal syndicate by:
1. Intentionally organizing, managing, directing, supervising or financing a criminal syndicate with the intent to promote or further the criminal objectives of the syndicate; or
2. Knowingly inciting or inducing others to engage in violence or intimidation to promote or further the criminal objectives of a criminal syndicate; or
3. Furnishing advice or direction in the conduct, financing or management of a criminal syndicate's affairs with the intent to promote or further the criminal objectives of a criminal syndicate; or
4. Intentionally promoting or furthering the criminal objectives of a criminal syndicate by inducing or committing any act or omission by a public servant in violation of his official duty; or
5. Hiring, engaging or using a minor for any conduct preparatory to or in completion of any offense in this section.
B. A person shall not be convicted pursuant to subsection A of this section on the basis of accountability as an accomplice unless he participates in violating this section in one of the ways specified.

C. A person commits assisting a criminal syndicate by committing any felony offense, whether completed or preparatory, with the intent to promote or further the criminal objectives of a criminal syndicate.

D. Except as provided in subsection E or F of this section, participating in a criminal syndicate is a class 2 felony.

E. A violation of subsection A, paragraph 5 of this section is a class 2 felony and the person convicted is not eligible for probation, pardon, suspension of sentence or release on any basis until the person has served the sentence imposed by the court or the sentence is commuted.

F. Assisting a criminal syndicate is a class 4 felony.

G. Use of a common name or common identifying sign or symbol shall be admissible and may be considered in proving the combination of persons or enterprises required by this section.

13-2308.01. Terrorism; classification

A. It is unlawful for a person to intentionally or knowingly do any of the following:

1. Engage in an act of terrorism.

2. Organize, manage, direct, supervise or finance an act of terrorism.

3. Solicit, incite or induce others to promote or further an act of terrorism.

4. Without lawful authority or when exceeding lawful authority, manufacture, sell, deliver, display, use, make accessible to others, possess or exercise control over a weapon of mass destruction knowing or having reason to know that the device or object involved is a weapon of mass destruction.

5. Make property available to another, by transaction, transportation or otherwise, knowing or having reason to know that the property is intended to facilitate an act of terrorism.

6. Provide advice, assistance or direction in the conduct, financing or management of an act of terrorism knowing or having reason to know that an act of terrorism has occurred or may result by:

(a) Harboring or concealing any person or property.

(b) Warning any person of impending discovery, apprehension, prosecution or conviction. This subdivision does not apply to a warning that is given in connection with an effort to bring another person into compliance with the law.

(c) Providing any person with material support or resources or any other means of avoiding discovery, apprehension, prosecution or conviction.

(d) Concealing or disguising the nature, location, source, ownership or control of material support or resources.

(e) Preventing or obstructing by means of force, deception or intimidation anyone from performing an act that might aid in the discovery, apprehension, prosecution or conviction of any person or that might aid in the prevention of an act of terrorism.

(f) Suppressing by any act of concealment, alteration or destruction any physical evidence that might aid in the discovery, apprehension, prosecution or conviction of any person or that might aid in the prevention of an act of terrorism.

(g) Concealing the identity of any person.

7. Provide advice, assistance or direction in the conduct, financing or management of a terrorist organization.

B. A violation of this section is a class 2 felony.

C. A person who is convicted of a violation of this section may be sentenced to imprisonment in the custody of the state department of corrections for life or natural life. A defendant who is sentenced to natural life is not eligible for commutation, parole, work furlough, work release or release from confinement on any basis for the remainder of the defendant's natural life. A defendant who is sentenced to life is not eligible for suspension of sentence, probation, pardon or release from confinement on any basis except as specifically authorized by section 13-716 or section 31-233, subsection A or B until the completion of the service of twenty-five calendar years or the sentence is commuted. If the defendant is not sentenced to life or natural life, the defendant shall be sentenced to a term of imprisonment as follows:

Minimum	Presumptive	Maximum
10 calendar years	16 calendar years	25 calendar years

13-2308.02. Making a terrorist threat; false reporting of terrorism; liability for expenses; classification; definitions

A. It is unlawful for a person to threaten to commit an act of terrorism and communicate the threat to any other person.

B. It is unlawful for a person to knowingly make a false report of an act of terrorism and communicate the false report to any other person.

C. It is not a defense to a prosecution under this section that the person did not have the intent or capability of committing the act of terrorism.

D. A person who is convicted of a violation of this section is liable for the expenses that are incurred incident to the response to or the investigation of the commission of the terrorist threat or the false report of terrorism. If the person is a juvenile who is adjudicated delinquent for a violation of this section, the court may order the juvenile to pay the expenses incurred under this subsection as restitution. The expenses are a debt of the person. The public agency, for-profit entity or not-for-profit entity that incurred the expenses may collect the debt proportionally. The liability that is imposed under this subsection is in addition to any other liability that may be imposed.

E. A violation of this section is a class 3 felony.

F. For the purposes of this section:

1. "Expenses":

(a) Means any reasonable costs that are directly incurred by a public agency, for-profit entity or not-for-profit entity that makes an appropriate response to an incident or an investigation of the commission of the terrorist threat or a false report of terrorism.

(b) Includes the costs of providing police, firefighting, rescue and emergency medical services at the scene of an incident and the salaries of the persons who respond to the incident.

(c) Does not include any charges that are assessed by an ambulance service that is regulated pursuant to title 36, chapter 21.1, article 2.

2. "Public agency" has the same meaning prescribed in section 38-502 and includes the federal government, any Arizona federally recognized native American tribe or any other public authority that is located in whole or in part in this state.

13-2308.03. Unlawful use of infectious biological substance or radiological agent; classification; definitions

A. It is unlawful for a person to intentionally cause injury to another person by means of an infectious biological substance or a radiological agent.

B. It is unlawful for a person to intentionally or knowingly do any of the following:

1. Possess, with the intent to injure another person, an infectious biological substance or a radiological agent.

2. Manufacture, sell, give, distribute or use an infectious biological substance or a radiological agent with the intent to injure another person.

3. Destroy or damage or attempt to destroy or damage any facility, equipment or material involved in the sale, manufacture, storage or distribution of an infectious biological substance or a radiological agent with the intent to injure another by the release of the substance or agent.

4. Give or send to another person or place in a public or private place a simulated infectious biological substance or a radiological agent with the intent to terrify, intimidate, threaten or harass. The placing or sending of a simulated infectious biological substance or radiological agent without written notice attached to the substance or agent in a conspicuous place that the substance or agent has been rendered inert and is possessed for a curio or relic collection, display or other similar purpose is prima facie evidence of an intent to terrify, intimidate, threaten or harass.

5. Transport any radiological isotope or agent for the purpose of committing another act in violation of this section.

6. Adulterate or misbrand any radiological isotope.

7. Manufacture, hold, sell or offer to sell any radiological isotope that is adulterated or misbranded.

8. Alter, mutilate, destroy, obliterate or remove any part of the labeling of a radiological isotope.

9. Engage in any other act with respect to a radiological isotope if the act is done when the article is possessed, transferred, transported or held for sale and results in the article being adulterated or misbranded.

C. The possession of an infectious biological substance or a radiological agent, unless satisfactorily explained, may give rise to an inference that the person who is in possession of the substance or agent is aware of the risk that the substance or agent may be used to commit an act in violation of this section.

D. This section does not apply to any person who is permitted or licensed pursuant to title 30, chapter 4 and 10 Code of Federal Regulations part 30, a member or employee of the armed forces of the United States, a federal or state governmental agency or any political subdivision of a state, a charitable, scientific or educational institution or a private entity if both of the following apply:

1. The person is engaged in lawful activity within the scope of the person's employment and the person is otherwise duly authorized or licensed to manufacture, possess, sell, deliver, display, use, exercise control over or make accessible to others any weapon of mass destruction, infectious biological substance or radiological agent or to otherwise engage in any activity described in this paragraph.

2. The person is in compliance with all applicable federal and state laws in doing so.

E. A violation of this section is a class 2 felony. A person who is convicted of a violation of subsection A or subsection B, paragraph 1 or 2 of this section is not eligible for suspension of sentence, probation, pardon or release from confinement on any basis until the person has served the sentence imposed by the court or the sentence is commuted.

F. For the purposes of this section:

1. "Infectious biological substance":

(a) Includes any bacteria, virus, fungus, protozoa, prion, toxin or material found in nature that is capable of causing death or serious physical injury.

(b) Does not include human immunodeficiency virus, syphilis or hepatitis.

2. "Radiological agent" includes any substance that is able to release radiation at levels that are capable of causing death or serious bodily injury or at any level if used with the intent to terrify, intimidate, threaten or harass.

13-2309. Bribery of participants in professional or amateur games, sports, horse races, dog races, contests; classification

Whoever knowingly gives, promises or offers to any professional or amateur baseball, football, hockey, polo, tennis, horse race, dog race or basketball player or boxer or any player or referee or other official who participates or expects to participate in any professional or amateur game or sport, or to any manager, coach or trainer of any team or participant or prospective participant in any such game, contest or sport, any benefit with intent to influence him to lose or try to lose or cause to be lost or to limit his or his team's margin of victory or defeat, or in the case of a referee or other official to affect his decisions or the performance of his duties in any way, in a baseball, football, hockey or basketball game, boxing, tennis, horse race, dog race, or polo match, or any professional or amateur sport, or game, in which such player or participant or referee or other official is taking part or expects to take part, or has any duty or connection therewith, is guilty of a class 4 felony.

13-2310. Fraudulent schemes and artifices; classification; definition

A. Any person who, pursuant to a scheme or artifice to defraud, knowingly obtains any benefit by means of false or fraudulent pretenses, representations, promises or material omissions is guilty of a class 2 felony.

B. Reliance on the part of any person shall not be a necessary element of the offense described in subsection A of this section.

C. A person who is convicted of a violation of this section that involved a benefit with a value of one hundred thousand dollars or more is not eligible for suspension of sentence, probation, pardon or release from confinement on any basis except pursuant to section 31-233, subsection A or B until the sentence imposed by the court has been served, the person is eligible for release pursuant to section 41-1604.07 or the sentence is commuted.

D. The state shall apply the aggregation prescribed by section 13-1801, subsection B to violations of this section in determining the applicable punishment.

E. As used in this section, "scheme or artifice to defraud" includes a scheme or artifice to deprive a person of the intangible right of honest services.

13-2311. Fraudulent schemes and practices; wilful concealment; classification

A. Notwithstanding any provision of the law to the contrary, in any matter related to the business conducted by any department or agency of this state or any political subdivision thereof, any person who, pursuant to a scheme or artifice to defraud or deceive, knowingly falsifies, conceals or covers up a material fact by any trick, scheme or device or makes or uses any false writing or document knowing such writing or document contains any false, fictitious or fraudulent statement or entry is guilty of a class 5 felony.

B. For the purposes of this section, "agency" includes a public agency as defined by section 38-502, paragraph 6.

13-2312. Illegal control of an enterprise; illegally conducting an enterprise; classification

A. A person commits illegal control of an enterprise if such person, through racketeering or its proceeds, acquires or maintains, by investment or otherwise, control of any enterprise.

B. A person commits illegally conducting an enterprise if such person is employed by or associated with any enterprise and conducts such enterprise's affairs through racketeering or participates directly or indirectly in the conduct of any enterprise that the person knows is being conducted through racketeering.

C. A person violates this section if the person hires, engages or uses a minor for any conduct preparatory to or in completion of any offense in this section.

D. A knowing violation of subsection A or B is a class 3 felony. A knowing violation of subsection C is a class 2 felony and the person is not eligible for probation, pardon, suspension of sentence or release on any basis until the person has served the sentence imposed by the court or the sentence is commuted.

13-2313. Judicial powers over racketeering criminal cases

During the pendency of any criminal case charging an offense included in the definition of racketeering in section 13-2301, subsection D, paragraph 4 or a violation of section 13-2312, the superior court may, in addition to its other powers, issue an order pursuant to section 13-2314, subsections B and C. Upon conviction of a person for an offense included in the definition of racketeering in section 13-2301, subsection D, paragraph 4 or a violation of section 13-2312, the superior court may, in addition to its other powers of disposition, issue an order pursuant to section 13-2314.

13-2314. Racketeering; civil remedies by this state; definitions

A. The attorney general or a county attorney may file an action in superior court on behalf of a person who sustains injury to his person, business or property by racketeering as defined by section 13-2301, subsection D, paragraph 4 or by a violation of section 13-2312 for the recovery of treble damages and the costs of the suit, including reasonable attorney fees, or to prevent, restrain or remedy racketeering as defined by section 13-2301, subsection D, paragraph 4 or a violation of section 13-2312. If the person against whom a racketeering claim has been asserted, including a forfeiture action or lien, prevails on that claim, the person may be awarded costs and reasonable attorney fees incurred in defense of that claim. In actions filed by the state or a county, awards of costs and reasonable attorney fees are to be assessed against and paid from monies acquired pursuant to sections 13-2314.01 and 13-2314.03.

B. The superior court has jurisdiction to prevent, restrain and remedy racketeering as defined by section 13-2301, subsection D, paragraph 4 or a violation of section 13-2312 after making provision for the rights of any person who sustained injury to his person, business or property by the racketeering conduct and after a hearing or trial, as appropriate, by issuing appropriate orders.

C. Before a determination of liability the orders may include issuing seizure warrants, entering findings of probable cause for in personam or in rem forfeiture, entering restraining orders or prohibitions or taking such other actions, including the acceptance of satisfactory performance bonds, the creation of receiverships and the enforcement of constructive trusts, in connection with any property or other interest subject to forfeiture, damages or other remedies or restraints pursuant to this section as the court deems proper.

D. Following a determination of liability the orders may include:

1. Ordering any person to divest himself of any interest, direct or indirect, in any enterprise.

2. Imposing reasonable restrictions on the future activities or investments of any person, including prohibiting any person from engaging in the same type of endeavor as the enterprise engaged in, the activities of which affect the laws of this state, to the extent the constitutions of the United States and this state permit.

3. Ordering dissolution or reorganization of any enterprise.

4. Ordering the payment of treble damages to those persons injured by racketeering as defined by section 13-2301, subsection D, paragraph 4 or a violation of section 13-2312.

5. Ordering the payment of all costs and expenses of the prosecution and investigation of any offense included in the definition of racketeering in section 13-2301, subsection D, paragraph 4 or a violation of section 13-2312, civil and criminal, including reasonable attorney fees, to be paid to the general fund of the state or the county which brings the action.

6. In personam forfeiture pursuant to chapter 39 of this title to the general fund of the state or county, as appropriate, to the extent that forfeiture is not inconsistent with protecting the rights of any person who sustained injury to his person, business or property by the racketeering conduct, of the interest of a person in:

(a) Any property or interest in property acquired or maintained by the person in violation of section 13-2312.

(b) Any interest in, security of, claims against or property, office, title, license or contractual right of any kind affording a source of influence over any enterprise or other property that the person has acquired or maintained an interest in or control of, conducted or participated in the conduct of in violation of section 13-2312.

(c) All proceeds traceable to an offense included in the definition of racketeering in section 13-2301, subsection D, paragraph 4 and held by the person and all monies, negotiable instruments, securities and other property used or intended to be used by the person in any manner or part to facilitate commission of the offense and that the person either owned or controlled for the purpose of that use.

(d) Any other property up to the value of the subject property described in subdivision (a), (b) or (c) of this paragraph.

7. Payment to the general fund of the state or county as appropriate of an amount equal to the gain that was acquired or maintained through an offense included in the definition of racketeering in section 13-2301, subsection D, paragraph 4 or a violation of section 13-2312 or that any person is liable for under this section.

E. A person who is liable for conduct described in subsection D, paragraph 6, subdivision (a), (b) or (c) of this section is liable for the total value of all interests in property described in those subdivisions. The court shall enter an order of forfeiture against the person in the amount of the total value of all those interests less the value of any interests that are forfeited before or at the time of the entry of the final judgment.

F. A person or enterprise that acquires any property through an offense included in the definition of racketeering in section 13-2301, subsection D, paragraph 4 or through a violation of section 13-2312 is an involuntary trustee. The involuntary trustee and any other person or enterprise, except a bona fide purchaser for value who is reasonably without notice of the unlawful conduct and who is not knowingly taking part in an illegal transaction, hold the property, its proceeds and its fruits in constructive trust for the benefit of persons entitled to remedies under this section.

G. In addition to an action under this section the attorney general or a county attorney may file an in rem action pursuant to chapter 39 of this title for forfeiture, to the extent that forfeiture is not inconsistent with protecting the rights of any person who sustained injury to his person, business or property by the racketeering conduct, of:

1. Any property or interest in property acquired or maintained by a person in violation of section 13-2312.

2. Any interest in, security of, claims against or property, office, title, license or contractual right of any kind affording a source of influence over any enterprise or other property that a person has acquired or maintained an interest in or control of, conducted or participated in the conduct of in violation of section 13-2312.

3. All proceeds traceable to an offense included in the definition of racketeering in section 13-2301, subsection D, paragraph 4 and all monies, negotiable instruments, securities and other property used or intended to be used in any manner or part to facilitate the commission of the offense.

H. A defendant convicted in any criminal proceeding shall be precluded from subsequently denying the essential allegations of the criminal offense of which he was convicted in any civil proceeding. For the purposes of this subsection, a conviction may result from a verdict or plea including a no contest plea.

I. Notwithstanding any law creating a lesser period, the initiation of civil proceedings related to violations of any offense included in the definition of racketeering in section 13-2301, subsection D, paragraph 4 or a violation of section 13-2312, including procedures pursuant to chapter 39 of this title, shall be commenced within seven years after actual discovery of the violation.

J. In any civil action brought pursuant to this section, the attorney general or a county attorney may file with the clerk of the superior court a certificate stating that the case is of special public importance. A copy of that certificate shall be furnished immediately by such clerk to the chief judge or presiding chief judge of the superior court in the county in which such action is pending, and, upon receipt of such copy, the judge shall immediately designate a judge to hear and determine the action. The judge so designated shall promptly assign such action for hearing, participate in the hearings and determination and cause the action to be expedited.

K. The standard of proof in actions brought pursuant to this section is the preponderance of the evidence test, except that the standard of proof for an order under subsection D, paragraph 6 of this section is the standard of proof that is applicable for an in personam forfeiture as set forth in chapter 39 of this title and the standard of proof for an in rem forfeiture under subsection G of this section is the standard of proof that is applicable to an in rem forfeiture as set forth in chapter 39 of this title.

L. A civil action authorized by this section, including proceedings pursuant to chapter 39 of this title, is remedial and not punitive and does not limit and is not limited by any other previous or subsequent civil or criminal action under this title or any other provision of law. Civil remedies provided under this title are supplemental and not mutually exclusive.

M. The attorney general may appear as amicus curiae in any proceeding in which a claim under this section has been asserted, including proceedings pursuant to chapter 39 of this title, or in which the court is interpreting this chapter or chapter 39 of this title. A party who files a notice of appeal from a civil action brought under this chapter or chapter 39 of this title shall serve the notice and one copy of the appellant's brief on the attorney general at the time the person files the appellant's brief with the court. This requirement is jurisdictional.

N. For the purposes of this section and section 13-2312:

1. "Acquire" means for a person to do any of the following:

(a) Possess.

(b) Act so as to exclude other persons from using their property except on his own terms.

(c) Bring about or receive the transfer of any interest in property, whether to himself or to another person, or to secure performance of a service.

2. "Gain" means any benefit, interest or property of any kind without reduction for expenses of acquiring or maintaining it or incurred for any other reason.

3. "Proceeds" includes any interest in property of any kind acquired through or caused by an act or omission, or derived from the act or omission, directly or indirectly, and any fruits of this interest, in whatever form.

13-2314.01. Anti-racketeering revolving fund; use of fund; reports; audit

A. The anti-racketeering revolving fund is established. The attorney general shall administer the fund under the conditions and for the purposes provided by this section. Monies in the fund are exempt from the lapsing provisions of section 35-190.

B. Any prosecution and investigation costs, including attorney fees, recovered for the state by the attorney general as a result of enforcement of civil and criminal statutes pertaining to any offense included in the definition of racketeering in section 13-2301, subsection D, paragraph 4 or section 13-2312, whether by final judgment, settlement or otherwise, shall be deposited in the fund established by this section.

C. Any monies received by any department or agency of this state or any political subdivision of this state from any department or agency of the United States or another state as a result of participation in any investigation or prosecution, whether by final judgment, settlement or otherwise, shall be deposited in the fund established by this section or, if the recipient is a political subdivision of this state, may be deposited in the fund established pursuant to section 13-2314.03.

D. Any monies obtained as a result of a forfeiture by any department or agency of this state under this title or under federal law shall be deposited in the fund established by this section. Any monies or other property obtained as a result of a forfeiture by any political subdivision of this state or the federal government may be deposited in the fund established by this section. Monies deposited in the fund pursuant to this section or section 13-4315 shall accrue interest and shall be held for the benefit of the agency or agencies responsible for the seizure or forfeiture to the extent of their contribution.

E. Except as provided in subsections G and H of this section, the monies and interest shall be distributed within thirty days of application to the agency or agencies responsible for the seizure or forfeiture. The agency or agencies applying for monies must submit an application in writing to the attorney general that includes a description of what the requested monies will be used for. The attorney general may deny an application that requests monies for a purpose that is not authorized by this section, section 13-4315 or federal law. Monies in the fund used by the attorney general for capital projects in excess of one million dollars are subject to review by the joint committee on capital review.

F. Monies in the fund may be used for the following:

1. The funding of gang prevention programs, substance abuse prevention programs, substance abuse education programs, programs that provide assistance to victims of a criminal offense that is listed in section 13-2301 and witness protection pursuant to section 41-196 or for any purpose permitted by federal law relating to the disposition of any property that is transferred to a law enforcement agency.

2. The investigation and prosecution of any offense included in the definition of racketeering in section 13-2301, subsection D, paragraph 4 or section 13-2312, including civil enforcement.

3. The payment of the relocation expenses of any law enforcement officer and the officer's immediate family if the law enforcement officer is the victim of a bona fide threat that occurred because of the law enforcement officer's duties.

4. The costs of the reports, audits and application approvals that are required by this section.

G. On or before January 28, April 28, July 28 and October 28 of each year, each department or agency of this state receiving monies pursuant to this section or section 13-2314.03 or 13-4315 or from any department or agency of the United States or another state as a result of participation in any investigation or prosecution shall file with the attorney general, the board of supervisors if the sheriff received the monies and the city or town council if the city's or town's department received the monies a report for the previous calendar quarter. The report shall be in an electronic form that is prescribed by the Arizona criminal justice commission and approved by the director of the joint legislative budget committee. The report shall set forth the sources of all monies and all expenditures as required by subsection K of this section. The report shall not include any identifying information about specific investigations. If a department or agency of this state fails to file a report within forty-five days after the report is due and there is no good cause as determined by the Arizona criminal justice commission, the attorney general shall make no expenditures from the fund for the benefit of the department or agency until the report is filed. The attorney general is responsible for collecting all reports from departments and agencies of this state and transmitting the reports to the Arizona criminal justice commission at the time that the report required pursuant to subsection H of this section is submitted.

H. On or before February 21, May 21, August 21 and November 21 of each year, the attorney general shall file with the Arizona criminal justice commission a report for the previous calendar quarter. The report shall be in an electronic form that is prescribed by the Arizona criminal justice commission and approved by the director of the joint legislative budget committee. The report shall set forth the sources of all monies and all expenditures as required by subsections J and K of this section. The report shall not include any identifying information about specific investigations. If the attorney general fails to file a report within sixty days after the report is due and there is no good cause as determined by the Arizona criminal justice commission, the attorney general shall make no expenditures from the fund for the benefit of the attorney general until the report is filed. If a political subdivision of this state fails to file a report with the county attorney pursuant to section 13-2314.03 within forty-five days after the report is due and there is no good cause as determined by the Arizona criminal justice commission, the attorney general shall make no expenditures from the fund for the benefit of the political subdivision until the report is filed.

I. On or before the last day of February, May, August and November of each year, the Arizona criminal justice commission shall compile the attorney general report and the reports of all departments and agencies of this state into a single comprehensive report for the previous calendar quarter and shall submit an electronic copy of the report to the governor, the director of the department of administration, the president of the senate, the speaker of the house of representatives, the director of the joint legislative budget committee and the secretary of state.

J. The report that is required by subsection H of this section must include all of the following information if monies were obtained as a result of a forfeiture:

1. The name of the law enforcement agency that seized the property.

2. The date of the seizure for forfeiture.

3. The type of property seized and a description of the property seized, including, if applicable, the make, the model and the serial number of the property.

4. The location of the original seizure by law enforcement.

5. The estimated value of the property seized for forfeiture, not excluding encumbrances.

6. The criminal statute that allowed the seizure for forfeiture.

7. The criminal statute charged in any criminal case that is related to the forfeiture case, if known at the time of the report.

8. The court case number of any criminal case that is related to the forfeiture case, if known at the time of the report.

9. The outcome of any criminal case that is related to the forfeiture case, if known at the time of the report.

10. If the property was seized by a state agency and submitted for state forfeiture proceedings but was transferred to federal authorities for forfeiture proceedings, the reason for the federal transfer.

11. The forfeiture case number.

12. The method of forfeiture proceeding, including whether it was criminal or civil, and if civil, whether the civil forfeiture was judicial or uncontested pursuant to section 13-4309.

13. The venue of the forfeiture action.

14. Whether a person or entity filed a claim or counterclaim or submitted a petition asserting an interest in the property as an owner, interest holder or injured person.

15. Whether the owner, interest holder or injured person was assisted by an attorney in the forfeiture case.

16. The date of the forfeiture decision.

17. Whether there was a forfeiture settlement agreement.

18. Whether the property was awarded or partially awarded to the owner, partial owner or injured person or if the property was forfeited to the state.

19. Whether the property was sold, destroyed or retained by law enforcement.

20. The earliest date that the property was disposed of or sent for disposition.

21. The net amount of monies received from the forfeiture.

22. The estimated administrative and storage costs and any other costs, including any costs of litigation.

23. The amount of attorney fees, costs, expenses and damages awarded and to whom the fees, costs, expenses or damages were awarded.

K. The reports that are required by subsections G and H of this section must include the following information with regard to all expenditures made from the fund for:

1. Crime, gang and substance abuse prevention programs.

2. Any injured person as defined in section 13-4301.

3. Witness protection.

4. Investigation costs, including informant fees and buy money.

5. Regular-time salaries, overtime pay and employee benefits of prosecutors.

6. Regular-time salaries, overtime pay and employee benefits of sworn law enforcement agency personnel other than prosecutors.

7. Regular-time salaries, overtime pay and employee benefits of unsworn law enforcement agency personnel other than prosecutors.

8. Professional or outside services, including services related to auditing, outside attorney fees, court reporting, expert witnesses and other court costs.

9. Travel and meals.

10. Training.

11. Conferences.

12. Vehicles purchased or leased.

13. Vehicle maintenance.

14. Canines, firearms and related equipment, including tactical gear.

15. Other capital expenditures, including furniture, computers and office equipment.

16. External publications and communications.

17. Other operating expenses, including office supplies, postage and printing. Expenses listed under this paragraph must be separately categorized.

L. Beginning in 2018 and every other year thereafter, the auditor general shall conduct a performance audit, as defined in section 41-1278, and a financial audit of the attorney general's use of monies in the fund. The audits must include all expenditures that were made by the attorney general's office from the fund for the previous two years. The auditor general shall submit copies of the performance and financial audits to the president of the senate, the speaker of the house of representatives and the chairpersons of the senate judiciary committee and the house of representatives judiciary and public safety committee, or their successor committees. The attorney general shall pay any fees and costs of the audits under this section from the fund.

13-2314.02. Racketeering lien; content; filing; notice; effect

A. The state, upon filing a civil action under section 13-2314, upon seizure for forfeiture under chapter 39 of this title or upon charging an offense included in the definition of racketeering in section 13-2301, subsection D, paragraph 4 or a violation of section 13-2312, may file a racketeering lien in accordance with this section. A filing fee or other charge is not required for filing a racketeering lien.

B. A racketeering lien shall be signed by the attorney general or the county attorney representing the state in the action and shall set forth the following information:

1. The name of the defendant whose property or interest in property is to be subject to the lien, including as the defendant the name of any corporation, partnership, trust or other entity, including nominees, that are owned or controlled by the defendant.

2. In the discretion of the attorney general or county attorney filing the lien, any aliases or fictitious names of the defendant named in the lien.

3. If known to the attorney general or county attorney filing the lien, the present residence or principal place of business and the date of birth of the person named in the lien.

4. A reference to the proceeding pursuant to which the lien is filed, including the name of the court, the title of the action and the court's file number for the proceeding, if any.

5. The name and address of the attorney representing the state in the proceeding pursuant to which the lien is filed.

6. A statement that the notice is being filed pursuant to this section.

7. The amount which the state claims in the action or, with respect to property or an interest in property which the state asserts is subject to forfeiture, a description of the property or interest in property.

8. If known to the attorney general or county attorney filing the lien, a description of property in which the defendant has an interest which is available to satisfy a judgment entered in favor of the state.

9. Such other information as the attorney general or county attorney filing the lien deems appropriate.

C. The attorney general or the county attorney filing the lien may amend a lien filed under this section at any time by filing an amended racketeering lien in accordance with this section which identifies the prior lien amended. If the action in which the lien was filed is subsequently dismissed, the attorney general or county attorney filing the lien shall file a notice of release of the lien within twenty days after the final order of dismissal. The notice of release shall be filed with the same agency with which the original lien was filed.

D. The attorney general or the county attorney filing the lien shall, as soon as practical after filing a racketeering lien, furnish to any person named in the lien a notice of the filing of the lien. Failure to furnish notice under this subsection does not invalidate or otherwise affect a racketeering lien filed in accordance with this section.

E. In an action in which a racketeering lien has been filed covering property, a hearing seeking to release or extinguish the lien may be requested by the person named in the racketeering lien or a person claiming to possess a valid lien or an interest under subsection J of this section with respect to property covered in the lien.

F. After the person requests a hearing, the court shall enter an order to show cause setting a hearing date. The hearing date shall be at least five days but not more than ten days from the date the hearing was requested. The order to show cause setting the hearing and a copy of the entire hearing request shall be personally served on the filing agency by the person requesting the hearing as soon as possible but not less than five days before the date of the hearing. The filing agency is entitled to obtain discovery from and demand disclosure pursuant to rule 26.1 of the rules of civil procedure from a person requesting a hearing pursuant to this section.

G. If the person filing the request for a hearing pursuant to this section shows that the person possesses a valid lien or interest under subsection J of this section with respect to the property described in the request and either that probable cause does not then exist to support the racketeering lien and the property is not otherwise subject to attachment or encumbrance by the filing agency, the court shall enter an order extinguishing the racketeering lien or releasing the person's property interest, from the racketeering lien or shall enter any other order adequately protecting the person's rights, lien or interest. If the person filing the request for a hearing pursuant to this section establishes that probable cause does not exist to support the racketeering lien or forfeiture action and the lawsuit is not well grounded in fact, the court shall award the person costs and reasonable attorney fees to be assessed against and paid from monies acquired pursuant to sections 13-2314.01 and 13-2314.03.

H. A racketeering lien is perfected against interests in personal property by filing the lien with the secretary of state, except that in the case of titled motor vehicles and trailers it shall be filed with the motor vehicle division of the department of transportation. A racketeering lien is perfected against interests in real property by filing the lien with the county recorder of the county in which the real property is located. The state may give such additional notice of the lien as it deems appropriate.

I. The filing of a racketeering lien in accordance with this section creates a lien in favor of the state in all of the following:

1. Any interest of the defendant, in real property situated in the county in which the lien is filed, then maintained or thereafter acquired in the name of the defendant identified in the lien.

2. Any interest of the defendant, in personal property situated in this state, then maintained or thereafter acquired in the name of the defendant identified in the lien.

3. Any property identified in the lien to the extent of the defendant's interest therein.

J. The filing of a racketeering lien under this section is notice to all persons dealing with the person or property identified in the lien of the state's claim. The lien created in favor of the state in accordance with this section is superior and prior to the claims or interests of any other person, except a person possessing an interest that is exempt from forfeiture under chapter 39 of this title that is:

1. A valid lien perfected prior to the filing of the racketeering lien.

2. In the case of real property, an interest acquired and recorded prior to the filing of the racketeering lien.

3. In the case of personal property, an interest acquired prior to the filing of the racketeering lien.

4. In the case of community property, an interest acquired prior to the filing of the racketeering lien by a spouse whose own personal conduct does not provide a basis for the filing of the racketeering lien.

K. Upon entry of judgment in favor of the state, the state may proceed to execute thereon as in the case of any other judgment, except that:

1. In order to preserve the state's lien priority as provided in this section the state shall, in addition to such other notice as is required by law, give at least thirty days' notice of such execution to any person possessing at the time such notice is given an interest recorded subsequent to the date the state's lien was perfected.

2. If a person's property or interest in property has been released from the racketeering lien, the property or interest in property released from the lien shall not be subject to any judgment liens or any order or injunction, receivership, writ, attachment, garnishment or other remedy authorized under section 13-2314 or available under chapter 39 of this title as a result of an act or omission occurring prior to the filing of the released lien and known to the filing agency at the time the lien was filed.

L. This section shall not limit the right of the state to obtain any order or injunction, receivership, writ, attachment, garnishment or other remedy authorized under section 13-2314 or appropriate to protect the interests of the state or available under other applicable law, including, without limitation, title 44, chapter 8, article 1 and chapter 39 of this title.

13-2314.03. County anti-racketeering revolving fund; use of fund; reports

A. The board of supervisors of a county shall establish a county anti-racketeering revolving fund administered by the county attorney under the conditions and for the purposes provided by this section.

B. Any prosecution and investigation costs, including attorney fees, recovered for the county as a result of enforcement of civil and criminal statutes pertaining to any offense included in the definition of racketeering in section 13-2301, subsection D, paragraph 4 or section 13-2312, whether by final judgment, settlement or otherwise, shall be deposited in the fund established by the board of supervisors.

C. Any monies received by any department or agency of this state or any political subdivision of this state from any department or agency of the United States or another state as a result of participation in any investigation or prosecution, whether by final judgment, settlement or otherwise, shall be deposited in the fund established pursuant to this section or in the fund established by section 13-2314.01.

D. Any monies obtained as a result of a forfeiture by the county attorney under this title or under federal law shall be deposited in the fund established pursuant to this section. Any monies or other property obtained as a result of a forfeiture by any political subdivision of this state or the federal government may be deposited in the fund established pursuant to this section or in the fund established by section 13-2314.01. Monies deposited in the fund pursuant to this section or section 13-4315 shall accrue interest and shall be held for the benefit of the agency or agencies responsible for the seizure or forfeiture to the extent of their contribution.

E. Except as provided in subsections G and H of this section, the monies and interest shall be distributed to the agency or agencies responsible for the seizure or forfeiture within thirty days of application. The agency or agencies applying for monies must submit an application in writing to the county attorney that includes a description of what the requested monies will be used for. The county attorney may deny an application that requests monies for a purpose that is not authorized by this section, section 13-4315 or federal law. Except in an emergency, before the county attorney's office may use any monies from the fund, the county attorney shall submit an application that includes a description of what the requested monies will be used for to the board of supervisors. The board of supervisors shall approve the county attorney's use of the monies if the purpose is authorized by this section, section 13-4315 or federal law. If an application is not submitted to the board of supervisors before the county attorney's office uses monies from the fund because of an emergency, the application must be submitted to the board of supervisors within a reasonable amount of time after the monies are used. The board of supervisors, at its next meeting, shall review and ratify, if appropriate, the county attorney's use of the monies. The board of supervisors may retain outside counsel, if necessary, to approve, review or ratify the county attorney's use of the monies.

F. Monies in the fund may be used for the funding of gang prevention programs, substance abuse prevention programs, substance abuse education programs, programs that provide assistance to victims of a criminal offense that is listed in section 13-2301 and witness protection pursuant to section 11-536 or for any purpose permitted by federal law relating to the disposition of any property that is transferred to a law enforcement agency. Monies in the fund may be used for the investigation and prosecution of any offense included in the definition of racketeering in section 13-2301, subsection D, paragraph 4 or section 13-2312, including civil enforcement, and for the costs of the reports and application and expenditure reviews and approvals that are required by this section.

G. On or before February 21, May 21, August 21 and November 21 of each year, the county attorney shall file with the Arizona criminal justice commission a report for the previous calendar quarter. The report shall be in an electronic form that is prescribed by the Arizona criminal justice commission and approved by the director of the joint legislative budget committee. The report shall set forth the sources of all monies and all expenditures as required by subsections J and K of this section. The report shall not include any identifying information about specific investigations. If the county attorney fails to file a report within sixty days after it is due and there is no good cause as determined by the Arizona criminal justice commission, the county attorney shall make no expenditures from the fund for the benefit of the county attorney until the report is filed.

H. On or before January 28, April 28, July 28 and October 28 of each year, each political subdivision of this state receiving monies pursuant to this section or section 13-2314.01 or 13-4315 or from any department or agency of the United States or another state as a result of participating in any investigation or prosecution shall file with the board of supervisors of the county in which the political subdivision is located, each city or town council in which the political subdivision is located and the county attorney of the county in which the political subdivision is located a report for the previous calendar quarter. The report shall be in an electronic form that is prescribed by the Arizona criminal justice commission and approved by the director of the joint legislative budget committee. The report shall set forth the sources of all monies and all expenditures as required by subsection K of this section. The report shall not include any identifying information about specific investigations. If a political subdivision of this state fails to file a report within forty-five days after the report is due and there is no good cause as determined by the Arizona criminal justice commission, the county attorney shall make no expenditures from the fund for the benefit of the political subdivision until the report is filed. The county attorney shall be responsible for collecting all reports from political subdivisions within that county and transmitting the reports to the Arizona criminal justice commission at the time that the county report required pursuant to subsection G of this section is submitted.

I. On or before the last day of February, May, August and November of each year, the Arizona criminal justice commission shall compile all county attorney reports into a single comprehensive report for the previous calendar quarter and all political subdivision reports into a single comprehensive report for the previous calendar quarter and submit an electronic copy of each comprehensive report to the governor, the president of the senate, the speaker of the house of representatives, the director of the joint legislative budget committee and the secretary of state.

J. The report that is required by subsection G of this section must include all of the following information if monies were obtained as a result of a forfeiture:

1. The name of the law enforcement agency that seized the property.

2. The date of the seizure for forfeiture.

3. The type of property seized and a description of the property seized, including, if applicable, the make, the model and the serial number of the property.

4. The location of the original seizure by law enforcement.

5. The estimated value of the property seized for forfeiture, not excluding encumbrances.

6. The criminal statute that allowed the seizure for forfeiture.

7. The criminal statute charged in any criminal case that is related to the forfeiture case, if known at the time of the report.

8. The court case number of any criminal case that is related to the forfeiture case, if known at the time of the report.

9. The outcome of any criminal case that is related to the forfeiture case, if known at the time of the report.

10. If the property was seized by a state agency and submitted for state forfeiture proceedings but was transferred to federal authorities for forfeiture proceedings, the reason for the federal transfer.

11. The forfeiture case number.

12. The method of forfeiture proceeding, including whether it was criminal or civil, and if civil, whether the civil forfeiture was judicial or uncontested pursuant to section 13-4309.

13. The venue of the forfeiture action.

14. Whether a person or entity filed a claim or counterclaim or submitted a petition asserting an interest in the property as an owner, interest holder or injured person.

15. Whether the owner, interest holder or injured person was assisted by an attorney in the forfeiture case.

16. The date of the forfeiture decision.

17. Whether there was a forfeiture settlement agreement.

18. Whether the property was awarded or partially awarded to the owner, partial owner or injured person or if the property was forfeited to the state.

19. Whether the property was sold, destroyed or retained by law enforcement.

20. The earliest date that the property was disposed of or sent for disposition.

21. The net amount of monies received from the forfeiture.

22. The estimated administrative and storage costs and any other costs, including any costs of litigation.

23. The amount of attorney fees, costs, expenses and damages awarded and to whom the fees, costs, expenses or damages were awarded.

K. The reports that are required by subsections G and H of this section must include the following information with regard to all expenditures made from the fund for:

1. Crime, gang and substance abuse prevention programs.

2. Any injured person as defined in section 13-4301.

3. Witness protection.

4. Investigation costs, including informant fees and buy money.

5. Regular-time salaries, overtime pay and employee benefits of prosecutors.

6. Regular-time salaries, overtime pay and employee benefits of sworn law enforcement agency personnel other than prosecutors.

7. Regular-time salaries, overtime pay and employee benefits of unsworn law enforcement agency personnel other than prosecutors.

8. Professional or outside services, including services related to auditing, outside attorney fees, court reporting, expert witnesses and other court costs.

9. Travel and meals.

10. Training.

11. Conferences.

12. Vehicles purchased or leased.

13. Vehicle maintenance.

14. Canines, firearms and related equipment, including tactical gear.

15. Other capital expenditures, including furniture, computers and office equipment.

16. External publications and communications.

17. Other operating expenses, including office supplies, postage and printing. Expenses listed under this paragraph must be separately categorized.

18. Any emergency use when monies were used from the fund before an application to use the monies was approved.

13-2314.04. Racketeering; unlawful activity; civil remedies by private cause of action; definitions

A. A person who sustains reasonably foreseeable injury to his person, business or property by a pattern of racketeering activity, or by a violation of section 13-2312 involving a pattern of racketeering activity, may file an action in superior court for the recovery of up to treble damages and the costs of the suit, including reasonable attorney fees for trial and appellate representation. If the person against whom a racketeering claim has been asserted, including a lien, prevails on that claim, the person may be awarded costs and reasonable attorney fees incurred in defense of that claim. No person may rely on any conduct that would have been actionable as fraud in the purchase or sale of securities to establish an action under this section except an action against a person who is convicted of a crime in connection with the fraud, in which case the period to initiate a civil action starts to run on the date on which the conviction becomes final.

B. The superior court has jurisdiction to prevent, restrain and remedy a pattern of racketeering activity or a violation of section 13-2312 involving a pattern of racketeering activity, after making provision for the rights of all innocent persons affected by the violation and after a hearing or trial, as appropriate, by issuing appropriate orders.

C. Before a determination of liability these orders may include, but are not limited to, entering restraining orders or prohibitions or taking such other actions, including the acceptance of satisfactory performance bonds, the creation of receiverships and the enforcement of constructive trusts, in connection with any property or other interest subject to damage or other remedies or restraints pursuant to this section as the court deems proper.

D. After a determination of liability these orders may include, but are not limited to:

1. Ordering any person to divest himself of any interest, direct or indirect, in any enterprise.

2. Imposing reasonable restrictions on the future activities or investments of any person, including prohibiting any person from engaging in the same type of endeavor as the enterprise engaged in, the activities of which affect the laws of this state, to the extent the constitutions of the United States and this state permit.

3. Ordering dissolution or reorganization of any enterprise.

4. Ordering the payment of up to treble damages to those persons injured by a pattern of racketeering activity or a violation of section 13-2312 involving a pattern of racketeering activity.

5. Prejudgment interest on damages, except that prejudgment interest may not be awarded on any increase in the damages authorized under paragraph 4 of this subsection.

6. A person or enterprise that acquires any property through an offense included in the definition of racketeering in section 13-2301, subsection D or a violation of section 13-2312 is an involuntary trustee. The involuntary trustee and any other person or enterprise, except a bona fide purchaser for value who is reasonably without notice of the unlawful conduct and who is not knowingly taking part in an illegal transaction, hold the property, its proceeds and its fruits in constructive trust for the benefit of persons entitled to remedies under this section.

E. A defendant convicted in any criminal proceeding is precluded from subsequently denying the essential allegations of the criminal offense of which the defendant was convicted in any civil proceedings. For the purpose of this subsection, a conviction may result from a verdict or plea including a no contest plea.

F. Notwithstanding any law prescribing a lesser period but subject to subsection A of this section, the initiation of civil proceedings pursuant to this section shall be commenced within three years from the date the violation was discovered, or should have been discovered with reasonable diligence, and ten years after the events giving rise to the cause of action, whichever comes first.

G. The standard of proof in actions brought pursuant to this section is the preponderance of evidence test.

H. A person who files an action under this section shall serve notice and one copy of the pleading on the attorney general within thirty days after the action is filed with the superior court. This requirement is jurisdictional. The notice shall identify the action, the person and the person's attorney. Service of the notice does not limit or otherwise affect the right of the state to maintain an action under section 13-2314 or to intervene in a pending action nor does it authorize the person to name this state or the attorney general as a party to the action.

I. On timely application, the attorney general may intervene in any civil action or proceeding brought under this section if the attorney general certifies that in the attorney general's opinion the action is of special public importance. On intervention, the attorney general may assert any available claim and is entitled to the same relief as if the attorney general has instituted a separate action.

J. In addition to the state's right to intervene as a party in any action under this section, the attorney general may appear as amicus curiae in any proceeding in which a claim under this section has been asserted or in which a court is interpreting section 13-2301, 13-2312, 13-2313, 13-2314.01, 13-2314.02 or 13-2315 or this section.

K. A civil action authorized by this section is remedial and not punitive and does not limit and is not limited by any other previous or subsequent civil or criminal action under this title or any other provision of law. Civil remedies provided under this title are supplemental and not mutually exclusive, except that a person may not recover, for an action brought pursuant to this section, punitive damages or emotional injury damages in the absence of bodily injury.

L. A natural person shall not be held liable in damages or for other relief pursuant to this section based on the conduct of another unless the fact finder finds by a preponderance of the evidence that the natural person authorized, requested, commanded, ratified or recklessly tolerated the unlawful conduct of the other. An enterprise shall not be held liable in damages or for other relief pursuant to this section based on the conduct of an agent, unless the fact finder finds by a preponderance of the evidence that a director or high managerial agent performed, authorized, requested, commanded, ratified or recklessly tolerated the unlawful conduct of the agent. A bank or savings and loan association insured by the federal deposit insurance corporation or a credit union insured by the national credit union administration shall not be held liable in damages or for other relief pursuant to this section for conduct proscribed by section 13-2317, subsection B, paragraph 1, based on acquiring or maintaining an interest in or transporting, transacting, transferring or receiving funds belonging to a person other than the person presenting the funds, unless the fact finder finds by a preponderance of the evidence that the person or agent acquiring or maintaining an interest in or transporting, transacting, transferring or receiving the funds on behalf of the defendant did so knowing that the funds were the proceeds of an offense and that a director or high managerial agent performed, authorized, requested, commanded, ratified or recklessly tolerated the unlawful conduct of the person or agent. A person or enterprise shall not be held liable in damages or for other relief pursuant to this section unless the fact finder makes particularized findings sufficient to permit full and complete review of the record, if any, of the conduct of the person. A natural person or enterprise shall not be held liable in damages for recklessly tolerating the unlawful conduct of another person or agent if the other person or agent engaged in unlawful conduct proscribed by section 13-2301, subsection D, paragraph 4, subdivision (b), item (xvi), (xviii), (xix) or (xx) and the unlawful conduct involved the purchase or sale of securities.

M. Notwithstanding subsection A of this section, a court shall not award costs, including attorney fees, if the award would be unjust because of special circumstances, including the relevant disparate economic position of the parties or the disproportionate amount of the costs, including attorney fees, to the nature of the damage or other relief obtained.

N. If the court determines that the filing of any pleading, motion or other paper under this section was frivolous or that any civil action or proceeding was brought or continued under this section in bad faith, vexatiously, wantonly or for an improper or oppressive reason, it shall award a proper sanction to deter this conduct in the future that may include the costs of the civil action or proceeding, including the costs of investigation and reasonable attorney fees in the trial and appellate courts.

O. Notwithstanding any other law, a complaint, counterclaim, answer or response filed by a person in connection with a civil action or proceeding under this section shall be verified by at least one party or the party's attorney. If the person is represented by an attorney, at least one attorney of record shall sign any pleading, motion or other paper in the attorney's individual name and shall state the attorney's address.

P. The verification by a person or the person's attorney and the signature by an attorney required by subsection O of this section constitute a certification by the person or the person's attorney that the person or the person's attorney has carefully read the pleading, motion or other paper and, based on a reasonable inquiry, believes all of the following:

1. It is well grounded in fact.

2. It is warranted by existing law or there is a good faith argument for the extension, modification or reversal of existing law.

3. It is not made for any bad faith, vexatious, wanton, improper or oppressive reason, including to harass, to cause unnecessary delay, to impose a needless increase in the cost of litigation or to force an unjust settlement through the serious character of the averment.

Q. If any pleading, motion or other paper is signed in violation of the certification provisions of subsection P of this section, the court, on its own motion or on the motion of the other party and after a hearing and appropriate findings of fact, shall impose on the person who verified it or the attorney who signed it, or both, a proper sanction to deter this conduct in the future, including the costs of the proceeding under subsection N of this section.

R. If any pleading, motion or other paper includes an averment of fraud or coercion, it shall state these circumstances with particularity with respect to each defendant.

S. In any civil action or proceeding under this section in which the pleading, motion or other paper does not allege a crime of violence as a racketeering act:

1. The term "racketeer" shall not be used in referring to any person.

2. The terms used to refer to acts of racketeering or a pattern of racketeering activity shall be "unlawful acts" or "a pattern of unlawful activity".

T. In this section, unless the context otherwise requires:

1. "Acquire" means for a person to do any of the following:

(a) Possess.

(b) Act so as to exclude another person from using the person's property except on the person's own terms.

(c) Bring about or receive the transfer of any interest in property, whether to himself or to another person, or to secure performance of a service.

2. "Gain" means any benefit, interest or property of any kind without reduction for expenses of acquiring or maintaining it or incurred for any other reason.

3. "Pattern of racketeering activity" means either:

(a) At least two acts of racketeering as defined in section 13-2301, subsection D, paragraph 4, subdivision (b), item (iv), (v), (vi), (vii), (viii), (ix), (x), (xiii), (xv), (xvi), (xvii), (xviii), (xix), (xx), (xxiv) or (xxvi) that meet the following requirements:

(i) The last act of racketeering activity that is alleged as the basis of the claim occurred within five years of a prior act of racketeering.

(ii) The acts of racketeering that are alleged as the basis of the claim were related to each other or to a common external organizing principle, including the affairs of an enterprise. Acts of racketeering are related if they have the same or similar purposes, results, participants, victims or methods of commission or are otherwise interrelated by distinguishing characteristics.

(iii) The acts of racketeering that are alleged as the basis of the claim were continuous or exhibited the threat of being continuous.

(b) A single act of racketeering as defined in section 13-2301, subsection D, paragraph 4, subdivision (b), item (i), (ii), (iii), (xi), (xii), (xiv), (xxi), (xxii), (xxiii), (xxv), (xxvii) or (xxviii).

4. "Proceeds" means any interest in property of any kind acquired through or caused by an act or omission, or derived from the act or omission, directly or indirectly, and any fruits of this interest, in whatever form.

13-2315. Racketeering; investigation of records; confidentiality; court enforcement; immunity; classification

A. A custodian of the records of a financial institution as defined in section 13-2301 shall, at no expense to the financial institution, produce for inspection or copying the records in the custody of such financial institution when requested to be inspected by the attorney general or a county attorney authorized by the attorney general, provided such person requesting such information signs and submits a sworn statement to the custodian that the request is made in order to investigate racketeering as defined by section 13-2301, subsection D, paragraph 4 or a violation of section 13-2312. Such records may be removed from the premises of the financial institution only for the purpose of copying the records and shall be returned within forty-eight hours. The attorney general or an authorized county attorney or any peace officer designated by such county attorney or the attorney general shall be prohibited from using or releasing such information except in the proper discharge of official duties. The furnishing of records in compliance with this section by a custodian of records shall be a bar to civil or criminal liability against such custodian or financial institution in any action brought alleging violation of the confidentiality of such records.

B. The attorney general or the authorized county attorney may petition the superior court for enforcement of this section in the event of noncompliance with the request for inspection. Enforcement shall be granted if the request is reasonable and the attorney general or the authorized county attorney has reasonable grounds to believe the records sought to be inspected are relevant to a civil or criminal investigation of an offense included in the definition of racketeering in section 13-2301, subsection D, paragraph 4 or a violation of section 13-2312.

C. The investigation authority granted pursuant to the provisions of this section may not be exercised by a county attorney in the absence of authorization by the attorney general.

D. Nothing in this section precludes a financial institution or an officer, employee or agent of a financial institution from notifying the attorney general or a county attorney of information which may be relevant to a possible racketeering violation. A person who reports the information to the attorney general or a county attorney is immune from civil liability for the release of the information.

E. Any person releasing information obtained pursuant to this section, except in the proper discharge of official duties, is guilty of a class 2 misdemeanor.

13-2316. Computer tampering; venue; forfeiture; classification

A. A person who acts without authority or who exceeds authorization of use commits computer tampering by:

1. Accessing, altering, damaging or destroying any computer, computer system or network, or any part of a computer, computer system or network, with the intent to devise or execute any scheme or artifice to defraud or deceive, or to control property or services by means of false or fraudulent pretenses, representations or promises.

2. Knowingly altering, damaging, deleting or destroying computer programs or data.

3. Knowingly introducing a computer contaminant into any computer, computer system or network.

4. Recklessly disrupting or causing the disruption of computer, computer system or network services or denying or causing the denial of computer or network services to any authorized user of a computer, computer system or network.

5. Recklessly using a computer, computer system or network to engage in a scheme or course of conduct that is directed at another person and that seriously alarms, torments, threatens or terrorizes the person. For the purposes of this paragraph, the conduct must both:

(a) Cause a reasonable person to suffer substantial emotional distress.

(b) Serve no legitimate purpose.

6. Preventing a computer user from exiting a site, computer system or network-connected location in order to compel the user's computer to continue communicating with, connecting to or displaying the content of the service, site or system.

7. Knowingly obtaining any information that is required by law to be kept confidential or any records that are not public records by accessing any computer, computer system or network that is operated by this state, a political subdivision of this state, a health care provider as defined in section 12-2291, a clinical laboratory as defined in section 36-451 or a person or entity that provides services on behalf of a health care provider or a clinical laboratory.

8. Knowingly accessing any computer, computer system or network or any computer software, program or data that is contained in a computer, computer system or network.

B. In addition to section 13-109, a prosecution for a violation of this section may be tried in any of the following counties:

1. The county in which the victimized computer, computer system or network is located.

2. The county in which the computer, computer system or network that was used in the commission of the offense is located or in which any books, records, documents, property, financial instruments, computer software, data, access devices or instruments of the offense were used.

3. The county in which any authorized user was denied service or in which an authorized user's service was interrupted.

4. The county in which critical infrastructure resources were tampered with or affected.

C. On conviction of a violation of this section, the court shall order that any computer system or instrument of communication that was owned or used exclusively by the defendant and that was used in the commission of the offense be forfeited and sold, destroyed or otherwise properly disposed.

D. A violation of subsection A, paragraph 6 of this section constitutes an unlawful practice under section 44-1522 and is in addition to all other causes of action, remedies and penalties that are available to this state. The attorney general may investigate and take appropriate action pursuant to title 44, chapter 10, article 7.

E. Computer tampering pursuant to subsection A, paragraph 1 of this section is a class 3 felony. Computer tampering pursuant to subsection A, paragraph 2, 3 or 4 of this section is a class 4 felony, unless the computer, computer system or network tampered with is a critical infrastructure resource, in which case it is a class 2 felony. Computer tampering pursuant to subsection A, paragraph 5 of this section is a class 5 felony. Computer tampering pursuant to subsection A, paragraph 7 or 8 of this section is a class 6 felony.

13-2316.01. Unlawful possession of an access device; classification

A. A person commits unlawful possession of an access device by knowingly possessing, trafficking in, publishing or controlling an access device without the consent of the issuer, owner or authorized user and with the intent to use or distribute that access device.

B. The possession, trafficking, publishing or control of five or more access devices without the consent of the issuer, owner or authorized user may give rise to an inference that the person possessing, trafficking in, publishing or controlling the access devices intended to use or distribute the devices.

C. Unlawful possession of one hundred or more access devices is a class 4 felony. Unlawful possession of five or more but fewer than one hundred access devices is a class 5 felony. Unlawful possession of fewer than five access devices is a class 6 felony.

13-2316.02. Unauthorized release of proprietary or confidential computer security information; exceptions; classification

A. A person commits unauthorized release of proprietary or confidential computer security information by communicating, releasing or publishing proprietary or confidential computer security information, security-related measures, algorithms or encryption devices relating to a particular computer, computer system or network without the authorization of its owner or operator.

B. The following are exempt from this section:

1. The release by publishers, vendors, users and researchers of warnings or information about security measures or defects in software, hardware or encryption products if the release of the warnings or information is not specific to a particular owner's or operator's computer, computer system or network.

2. The release of security information among the authorized users of a computer, computer system or network or the notification to the owner or operator of a computer, computer system or network of a perceived security threat.

3. The release of security information in connection with the research, development and testing of security-related measures, products or devices if the release of the security information is not specific to a particular owner's or operator's computer, computer system or network.

C. At the conclusion of any grand jury, hearing or trial, the court shall preserve pursuant to section 44-405 any proprietary computer security information that was admitted in evidence or any portion of a transcript that contains information relating to proprietary computer security information.

D. Unauthorized release of proprietary or confidential computer security information is a class 6 felony, unless the security information relates to a critical infrastructure resource, in which case it is a class 4 felony.

13-2317. Money laundering; classification; definitions

A. A person is guilty of money laundering in the first degree if the person does any of the following:

1. Knowingly initiates, organizes, plans, finances, directs, manages, supervises or is in the business of money laundering in violation of subsection B of this section.

2. Violates subsection B of this section in the course of or for the purpose of facilitating terrorism or murder.

B. A person is guilty of money laundering in the second degree if the person does any of the following:

1. Acquires or maintains an interest in, transacts, transfers, transports, receives or conceals the existence or nature of racketeering proceeds knowing or having reason to know that they are the proceeds of an offense.

2. Makes property available to another by transaction, transportation or otherwise knowing that it is intended to be used to facilitate racketeering.

3. Conducts a transaction knowing or having reason to know that the property involved is the proceeds of an offense and with the intent to conceal or disguise the nature, location, source, ownership or control of the property or the intent to facilitate racketeering.

4. Intentionally or knowingly makes a false statement, misrepresentation or false certification or makes a false entry or omits a material entry in any application, financial statement, account record, customer receipt, report or other document that is filed or required to be maintained or filed under title 6, chapter 12.

5. Intentionally or knowingly evades or attempts to evade any reporting requirement under section 6-1241, whether by structuring transactions as described in 31 Code of Federal Regulations chapter X, by causing any financial institution, money transmitter, trade or business to fail to file the report, by failing to file a required report or record or by any other means.

6. Intentionally or knowingly provides any false information or fails to disclose information that causes any licensee, authorized delegate, money transmitter, trade or business to either:

(a) Fail to file any report or record that is required under section 6-1241.

(b) File such a report or record that contains a material omission or misstatement of fact.

7. Intentionally or knowingly falsifies, conceals, covers up or misrepresents or attempts to falsify, conceal, cover up or misrepresent the identity of any person in connection with any transaction with a financial institution or money transmitter.

8. In connection with a transaction with a financial institution or money transmitter, intentionally or knowingly makes, uses, offers or presents or attempts to make, use, offer or present, whether accepted or not, a forged instrument, a falsely altered or completed written instrument or a written instrument that contains any materially false personal identifying information.

9. If the person is a money transmitter, a person engaged in a trade or business or any employee of a money transmitter or a person engaged in a trade or business, intentionally or knowingly accepts false personal identifying information from any person or otherwise knowingly incorporates false personal identifying information into any report or record that is required by section 6-1241.

10. Intentionally conducts, controls, manages, supervises, directs or owns all or part of a money transmitting business for which a license is required by title 6, chapter 12 unless the business is licensed pursuant to title 6, chapter 12 and complies with the money transmitting business registration requirements under 31 United States Code section 5330.

C. A person is guilty of money laundering in the third degree if the person intentionally or knowingly does any of the following:

1. In the course of any transaction transmitting money, confers or agrees to confer anything of value on a money transmitter or any employee of a money transmitter that is intended to influence or reward any person for failing to comply with any requirement under title 6, chapter 12.

2. Engages in the business of receiving money for transmission or transmitting money, as an employee or otherwise, and receives anything of value upon an agreement or understanding that it is intended to influence or benefit the person for failing to comply with any requirement under title 6, chapter 12.

D. In addition to any other criminal or civil remedy, if a person violates subsection A or B of this section as part of a pattern of violations that involve a total of one hundred thousand dollars or more in any twelve month period, the person is subject to forfeiture of substitute assets in an amount that is three times the amount that was involved in the pattern, including conduct that occurred before and after the twelve month period.

E. Money laundering in the third degree is a class 6 felony. Money laundering in the second degree is a class 3 felony. Money laundering in the first degree is a class 2 felony.

F. For the purposes of this section:

1. The following terms have the same meaning prescribed in section 6-1201:

(a) "Authorized delegate".

(b) "Licensee".

(c) "Money accumulation business".

(d) "Money transmitter".

(e) "Trade or business".

(f) "Transmitting money".

2. The following terms have the same meaning prescribed in section 13-2001:

(a) "Falsely alters a written instrument".

(b) "Falsely completes a written instrument".

(c) "Falsely makes a written instrument".

(d) "Forged instrument".

(e) "Personal identifying information".

(f) "Written instrument".

3. The following terms have the same meaning prescribed in section 13-2301:

(a) "Financial institution".

(b) "Financial instrument".

(c) "Racketeering", except that for the purposes of civil remedies sought by the attorney general, racketeering includes any act, regardless of whether the act would be chargeable or indictable under the laws of this state or whether the act is charged or indicted, that is committed for financial gain, punishable by imprisonment for more than one year under the laws of the United States and described in section 274(a)(1)(A)(i), (ii) or (iii) or (a)(2) of the immigration and nationality act (8 United States Code section 1324(a)(1)(A)(i), (ii) or (iii) or (a)(2)) if persons acting in concert in the conduct acquire a total of more than five thousand dollars through the conduct in a one month period. For the purpose of forfeiture of property other than real property, the conduct must involve more than three aliens in a one month period. For the purpose of forfeiture of real property, the conduct must involve more than fifteen aliens in a one month period.

4. The following terms have the same meaning prescribed in section 13-2314:

(a) "Acquire".

(b) "Proceeds".

G. For the purposes of this section:

1. "Offense" has the same meaning prescribed in section 13 105 and includes conduct for which a sentence to a term of incarceration is provided by any law of the United States.

2. "Superintendent" has the same meaning prescribed in section 6-101.

3. "Transaction" means a purchase, sale, trade, loan, pledge, investment, gift, transfer, transmission, delivery, deposit, withdrawal, payment, transfer between accounts, exchange of currency, extension of credit, purchase or sale of any financial instrument or any other acquisition or disposition of property by whatever means.

13-2318. Civil judgments; injury to the state

The court shall not reduce or increase the judgment in a civil action under this title because of the imposition or failure to impose a sanction in a separate criminal prosecution involving the same conduct but shall determine the civil judgment solely according to the civil remedies that are provided under this chapter and chapter 39 of this title, including the amount of injury to the state. Injury to the state includes:

1. The expenditure of any public monies, including the expenses of law enforcement and prosecutors in pursuing civil and criminal remedies.

2. The amount of money or the value of other property that is exchanged or that would foreseeably be exchanged for prohibited drugs, marijuana or other prohibited chemicals or substances or that is used, made available to another or otherwise involved in a violation of section 13-2317. The exchange of a prohibited chemical or substance for gain is a foreseeable consequence of the manufacture, production, transportation or sale of the prohibited chemical or substance.

3. The acquisition or gain of proceeds as defined in section 13-2314 of any offense included in the definition of racketeering as defined in section 13-2301, subsection D, paragraph 4.

13-2319. Smuggling; classification; definitions

A. It is unlawful for a person to intentionally engage in the smuggling of human beings for profit or commercial purpose.

B. A violation of this section is a class 4 felony.

C. Notwithstanding subsection B of this section, a violation of this section:

1. Is a class 2 felony if the human being who is smuggled is under eighteen years of age and is not accompanied by a family member over eighteen years of age or the offense involved the use of a deadly weapon or dangerous instrument.

2. Is a class 3 felony if the offense involves the use or threatened use of deadly physical force and the person is not eligible for suspension of sentence, probation, pardon or release from confinement on any other basis except pursuant to section 31-233, subsection A or B until the sentence imposed by the court is served, the person is eligible for release pursuant to section 41-1604.07 or the sentence is commuted.

D. Chapter 10 of this title does not apply to a violation of subsection C, paragraph 1 of this section.

E. Notwithstanding any other law, in the enforcement of this section a peace officer may lawfully stop any person who is operating a motor vehicle if the officer has reasonable suspicion to believe the person is in violation of any civil traffic law.

F. For the purposes of this section:

1. "Family member" means the person's parent, grandparent, sibling or any other person who is related to the person by consanguinity or affinity to the second degree.

2. "Procurement of transportation" means any participation in or facilitation of transportation and includes:

(a) Providing services that facilitate transportation including travel arrangement services or money transmission services.

(b) Providing property that facilitates transportation, including a weapon, a vehicle or other means of transportation or false identification, or selling, leasing, renting or otherwise making available a drop house as defined in section 13-2322.

3. "Smuggling of human beings" means the transportation, procurement of transportation or use of property or real property by a person or an entity that knows or has reason to know that the person or persons transported or to be transported are not United States citizens, permanent resident aliens or persons otherwise lawfully in this state or have attempted to enter, entered or remained in the United States in violation of law.

13-2320. Residential mortgage fraud; classification; definitions

A. A person commits residential mortgage fraud if, with the intent to defraud, the person does any of the following:

1. Knowingly makes any deliberate misstatement, misrepresentation or material omission during the mortgage lending process that is relied on by a mortgage lender, borrower or other party to the mortgage lending process.

2. Knowingly uses or facilitates the use of any deliberate misstatement, misrepresentation or material omission during the mortgage lending process that is relied on by a mortgage lender, borrower or other party to the mortgage lending process.

3. Receives any proceeds or other monies in connection with a residential mortgage loan that the person knows resulted from a violation of paragraph 1 or 2 of this subsection.

4. Files or causes to be filed with the office of the county recorder of any county of this state any residential mortgage loan document that the person knows to contain a deliberate misstatement, misrepresentation or material omission.

B. An offense involving residential mortgage fraud shall not be based solely on information that is lawfully disclosed under federal disclosure laws, regulations and interpretations related to the mortgage lending process.

C. This section does not apply to a person who is not aware that the information that is relied on by the mortgage lender, borrower or other party to the mortgage lending process is a deliberate misstatement, misrepresentation or material omission.

D. A person who violates this section is guilty of a class 4 felony, except that a person who engages or participates in a pattern of residential mortgage fraud or who conspires to engage or participate in a pattern of residential mortgage fraud is guilty of a class 2 felony.

E. For the purposes of this section:

1. "Mortgage lending process" means the process through which a person seeks or obtains a residential mortgage loan including solicitation, application, origination, negotiation of terms, third-party provider services, underwriting, signing, closing and funding of the loan.

2. "Pattern of residential mortgage fraud" means one or more violations of subsection A that involve two or more residential properties and that have the same or similar intents, results, accomplices, victims or methods of commission or are otherwise interrelated by distinguishing characteristics.

3. "Residential mortgage loan" means a loan or agreement to extend credit to a person that is secured by a deed to secure debt, security deed, mortgage, security interest, deed of trust or other document representing a security interest or lien on any interest in one to four family residential property and includes the renewal or refinancing of any loan.

13-2321. Participating in or assisting a criminal street gang; classification

A. A person commits participating in a criminal street gang by any of the following:

1. Intentionally organizing, managing, directing, supervising or financing a criminal street gang with the intent to promote or further the criminal objectives of the criminal street gang.

2. Knowingly inciting or inducing others to engage in violence or intimidation to promote or further the criminal objectives of a criminal street gang.

3. Furnishing advice or direction in the conduct, financing or management of a criminal street gang's affairs with the intent to promote or further the criminal objectives of a criminal street gang.

4. Intentionally promoting or furthering the criminal objectives of a criminal street gang by inducing or committing any act or omission by a public servant in violation of the public servant's official duty.

B. A person commits assisting a criminal street gang by committing any felony offense, whether completed or preparatory for the benefit of, at the direction of or in association with any criminal street gang.

C. Participating in a criminal street gang is a class 2 felony.

D. Assisting a criminal street gang is a class 3 felony.

E. Use of a common name or common identifying sign or symbol shall be admissible and may be considered in proving the existence of a criminal street gang or membership in a criminal street gang.

13-2322. Unlawful transactions involving drop house properties; classification; definition

A. A person or company that owns, sells, leases or brokers a transaction involving property or real property that the person or company knows will be used as a drop house is guilty of a class 4 felony.

B. It is a defense to a prosecution pursuant to this section if both of the following apply:

1. The person or company acquires actual knowledge that the property or real property is being used as a drop house after the person or company acquires ownership of, sells, leases or brokers a transaction involving the property or real property.

2. The person or company reports this information to a law enforcement agency.

C. For the purposes of this section, "drop house" means property or real property that is used to facilitate smuggling pursuant to section 13 2319.

13-2323. Participating in or assisting a human smuggling organization; classification

A. A person commits participating in a human smuggling organization by any of the following:

1. Intentionally organizing, managing, directing, supervising or financing a human smuggling organization with the intent to promote or further the criminal objectives of the human smuggling organization.

2. Knowingly directing or instructing others to engage in violence or intimidation to promote or further the criminal objectives of a human smuggling organization.

3. Furnishing advice or direction in the conduct, financing or management of a human smuggling organization's affairs with the intent to promote or further the criminal objectives of a human smuggling organization.

4. Intentionally promoting or furthering the criminal objectives of a human smuggling organization by inducing or committing any act or omission by a public servant in violation of the public servant's official duty.

B. A person commits assisting a human smuggling organization by committing any felony offense, whether completed or preparatory, at the direction of or in association with any human smuggling organization.

C. Participating in a human smuggling organization is a class 2 felony.

D. Assisting a human smuggling organization is a class 3 felony.

Chapter 24 Obstruction of Public Administration

13-2401. Personal information on the world wide web; exception; classification; definitions

A. It is unlawful for a person to knowingly make available on the world wide web the personal information of a peace officer, justice, judge, commissioner, public defender, employee of the department of child safety who has direct contact with families in the course of employment or prosecutor if the dissemination of the personal information poses an imminent and serious threat to the peace officer's, justice's, judge's, commissioner's, public defender's, department of child safety employee's or prosecutor's safety or the safety of that person's immediate family and the threat is reasonably apparent to the person making the information available on the world wide web to be serious and imminent.

B. It is not a violation of this section if an employee of a county recorder, county treasurer or county assessor publishes personal information, in good faith, on the website of the county recorder, county treasurer or county assessor in the ordinary course of carrying out public functions.

C. A violation of subsection A is a class 5 felony.

D. For the purposes of this section:

1. "Commissioner" means a commissioner of the superior court.

2. "Immediate family" means a peace officer's, justice's, judge's, commissioner's, public defender's or prosecutor's spouse, child or parent and any other adult who lives in the same residence as the person.

3. "Judge" means a judge of the United States district court, the United States court of appeals, the United States magistrate court, the United States bankruptcy court, the Arizona court of appeals, the superior court or a municipal court.

4. "Justice" means a justice of the United States or Arizona supreme court or a justice of the peace.

5. "Personal information" means a peace officer's, justice's, judge's, commissioner's, public defender's or prosecutor's home address, home telephone number, pager number, personal photograph, directions to the person's home or photographs of the person's home or vehicle.

6. "Prosecutor" means a county attorney, a municipal prosecutor, the attorney general or a United States attorney and includes an assistant or deputy United States attorney, county attorney, municipal prosecutor or attorney general.

7. "Public defender" means a federal public defender, county public defender, county legal defender or county contract indigent defense counsel and includes an assistant or deputy federal public defender, county public defender or county legal defender.

13-2402. Obstructing governmental operations; classification

A. A person commits obstructing governmental operations if, by using or threatening to use violence or physical force, such person knowingly obstructs, impairs or hinders:

1. The performance of a governmental function by a public servant acting under color of his official authority; or

2. The enforcement of the penal law or the preservation of the peace by a peace officer acting under color of his official authority.

B. This section does not apply to the obstruction, impairment or hinderance of the making of an arrest.

C. Obstructing governmental operations is a class 1 misdemeanor.

13-2403. Refusing to aid a peace officer; classification

A. A person commits refusing to aid a peace officer if, upon a reasonable command by a person reasonably known to be a peace officer, such person knowingly refuses or fails to aid such peace officer in:

1. Effectuating or securing an arrest; or

2. Preventing the commission by another of any offense.

B. A person who complies with this section by aiding a peace officer shall not be held liable to any person for damages resulting therefrom, provided such person acted reasonably under the circumstances known to him at the time.

C. Refusing to aid a peace officer is a class 1 misdemeanor.

13-2404. Refusing to assist in fire control; classification

A. A person commits refusing to assist in fire control if:

1. Upon a reasonable command by a person reasonably known to be a fireman, such person knowingly refuses to aid in extinguishing a fire or in protecting property at the scene of a fire; or

2. Upon command by a person reasonably known to be a fireman or peace officer, such person knowingly disobeys an order or regulation relating to the conduct of persons in the vicinity of a fire.

B. In this section, "fireman" means any officer of the fire department, the state forester or his deputies or any other person vested by law with the duty to extinguish fires.

C. A person who complies with this section by assisting in fire control shall not be held liable to any person for damages resulting therefrom, if such person acted reasonably under the circumstances known to him at the time.

D. Refusing to assist in fire control is a class 1 misdemeanor.

13-2405. Compounding; classification

A. A person commits compounding if such person knowingly accepts or agrees to accept any pecuniary benefit as consideration for:

1. Refraining from seeking prosecution of an offense; or

2. Refraining from reporting to law enforcement authorities the commission or suspected commission of any offense or information relating to the offense.

B. Subsection A shall apply in all cases except those which are compromised by leave of court as provided by law.

C. Compounding is a class 6 felony if the crime compounded is a felony. If the crime compounded is not a felony, compounding is a class 3 misdemeanor.

13-2406. Impersonating a public servant; classification; definition

A. A person commits impersonating a public servant if such person pretends to be a public servant and engages in any conduct with the intent to induce another to submit to his pretended official authority or to rely on his pretended official acts.

B. It is no defense to a prosecution under this section that the office the person pretended to hold did not in fact exist or that the pretended office did not in fact possess the authority claimed for it.

C. Impersonating a public servant is a class 1 misdemeanor.

D. For the purposes of this section, "public servant" includes a notary public.

13-2407. Tampering with a public record; classification

A. A person commits tampering with a public record if, with the intent to defraud or deceive, such person knowingly:

1. Makes or completes a written instrument, knowing that it has been falsely made, which purports to be a public record or true copy thereof or alters or makes a false entry in a written instrument which is a public record or a true copy of a public record; or

2. Presents or uses a written instrument which is or purports to be a public record or a copy of such public record, knowing that it has been falsely made, completed or altered or that a false entry has been made, with intent that it be taken as genuine; or

3. Records, registers or files or offers for recordation, registration or filing in a governmental office or agency a written statement which has been falsely made, completed or altered or in which a false entry has been made or which contains a false statement or false information; or

4. Destroys, mutilates, conceals, removes or otherwise impairs the availability of any public record; or

5. Refuses to deliver a public record in such person's possession upon proper request of a public servant entitled to receive such record for examination or other purposes.

B. In this section "public record" means all official books, papers, written instruments or records created, issued, received or kept by any governmental office or agency or required by law to be kept by others for the information of the government.

C. Tampering with a public record is a class 6 felony.

13-2408. Securing the proceeds of an offense; classification

A. A person commits securing the proceeds of an offense if, with intent to assist another in profiting or benefiting from the commission of an offense, such person aids the person in securing the proceeds of the offense.

B. Securing the proceeds of an offense is a class 6 felony if the person assisted committed a felony. Securing the proceeds of an offense is a class 2 misdemeanor if the person assisted committed a misdemeanor.

13-2409. Obstructing criminal investigations or prosecutions; classification

A person who knowingly attempts by means of bribery, misrepresentation, intimidation or force or threats of force to obstruct, delay or prevent the communication of information or testimony relating to a violation of any criminal statute to a peace officer, magistrate, prosecutor or grand jury or who knowingly injures another in his person or property on account of the giving by the latter or by any other person of any such information or testimony to a peace officer, magistrate, prosecutor or grand jury is guilty of a class 5 felony, except that it is a class 3 felony if the person commits the offense with the intent to promote, further or assist a criminal street gang.

13-2410. Obstructing officer from collecting public money; classification

A person who knowingly obstructs or hinders a public officer from collecting revenue, taxes or other money in which this state or a county, city or town has an interest and that the officer is authorized to collect by law is guilty of a class 2 misdemeanor.

13-2411. Impersonating a peace officer; classification; definition

A. A person commits impersonating a peace officer if the person, without lawful authority, pretends to be a peace officer and engages in any conduct with the intent to induce another to submit to the person's pretended authority or to rely on the person's pretended acts.

B. It is not a defense to a prosecution under this section that the law enforcement agency the person pretended to represent did not in fact exist or that the law enforcement agency the person pretended to represent did not in fact possess the authority claimed for it.

C. Impersonating a peace officer is a class 6 felony, except that impersonating a peace officer during the commission of any of the following felonies is a class 4 felony:

1. Negligent homicide.
2. Manslaughter.
3. First degree murder.
4. Second degree murder.
5. Assault.
6. Aggravated assault.
7. Sexual assault.
8. Violent sexual assault.
9. Sexual abuse.
10. Unlawfully administering intoxicating liquors, narcotic drugs or dangerous drugs.
11. Attack by a person's vicious animal as prescribed in section 13-1208.
12. Drive by shooting.
13. Discharging a firearm at a structure.
14. Aggravated criminal damage.
15. Theft.
16. Theft by extortion.
17. Theft of a credit card or obtaining a credit card by fraudulent means.
18. Misconduct involving weapons.
19. Misconduct involving explosives.

20. Depositing explosives.

21. Procuring or placing persons in a house of prostitution.

22. Dangerous crimes against children as prescribed in section 13-705.

23. Burglary.

24. Arson.

25. Kidnapping.

26. Robbery.

D. For the purposes of this section, "peace officer" has the same meaning prescribed in section 1-215 and includes any federal law enforcement officer or agent who has the power to make arrests pursuant to federal law.

13-2412. Refusing to provide truthful name when lawfully detained; classification

A. It is unlawful for a person, after being advised that the person's refusal to answer is unlawful, to fail or refuse to state the person's true full name on request of a peace officer who has lawfully detained the person based on reasonable suspicion that the person has committed, is committing or is about to commit a crime. A person detained under this section shall state the person's true full name, but shall not be compelled to answer any other inquiry of a peace officer.

B. A person who violates this section is guilty of a class 2 misdemeanor.

Chapter 25 Escape and Related Offenses

13-2501. Definitions

In this chapter, unless the context otherwise requires:

1. "Contraband" means any dangerous drug, narcotic drug, marijuana, intoxicating liquor of any kind, deadly weapon, dangerous instrument, explosive, wireless communication device, multimedia storage device or other article whose use or possession would endanger the safety, security or preservation of order in a correctional facility or a juvenile secure care facility as defined in section 41-2801, or of any person within a correctional or juvenile secure care facility.

2. "Correctional facility" means any place used for the confinement or control of a person:

(a) Charged with or convicted of an offense; or

(b) Held for extradition; or

(c) Pursuant to an order of court for law enforcement purposes.

Lawful transportation or movement incident to correctional facility confinement pursuant to this paragraph is within the control of a correctional facility. For the purposes of this chapter, being within the control of a correctional facility does not include release on parole, on community supervision, on probation or by other lawful authority on the condition of subsequent personal appearance at a designated place and time.

3. "Custody" means the imposition of actual or constructive restraint pursuant to an on-site arrest or court order but does not include detention in a correctional facility, juvenile detention center or state hospital.

4. "Escape" means departure from custody or from a juvenile secure care facility as described in section 41-2816, a juvenile detention facility or an adult correctional facility in which a person is held or detained with knowledge that such departure is unpermitted or failure to return to custody or detention following a temporary leave granted for a specific purpose or for a limited period.

13-2502. Escape in the third degree; classification

A. A person commits escape in the third degree if, having been arrested for, charged with or found guilty of a misdemeanor or petty offense, such person knowingly escapes or attempts to escape from custody.

B. Escape in the third degree is a class 6 felony.

13-2503. Escape in the second degree; classification

A. A person commits escape in the second degree by knowingly:

1. Escaping or attempting to escape from a juvenile secure care facility, a juvenile detention facility or an adult correctional facility; or

2. Escaping or attempting to escape from custody imposed as a result of having been arrested for, charged with or found guilty of a felony; or

3. Escaping or attempting to escape from the Arizona state hospital if the person was committed to the hospital for treatment pursuant to section 8-291.09, 13-502, 13-3994, 13-4507, 13-4512 or 31-226 or rule 11 of the Arizona rules of criminal procedure; or

4. Escaping or attempting to escape from the Arizona state hospital if the person was committed to the hospital for treatment pursuant to title 36, chapter 37.

B. Escape in the second degree pursuant to subsection A, paragraph 1, 2 or 4 of this section is a class 5 felony, and the sentence imposed for a violation of this section shall run consecutively to any sentence of imprisonment for which the person was confined or to any term of community supervision for the sentence including probation, parole, work furlough or any other release. Escape in the second degree pursuant to subsection A, paragraph 3 of this section is a class 2 misdemeanor.

13-2504. Escape in the first degree; classification

A. A person commits escape in the first degree by knowingly escaping or attempting to escape from custody or a juvenile secure care facility, juvenile detention facility or an adult correctional facility by:

1. Using or threatening the use of physical force against another person; or

2. Using or threatening to use a deadly weapon or dangerous instrument against another person.

B. Escape in the first degree is a class 4 felony, and the sentence imposed for a violation of this section shall run consecutively to any sentence of imprisonment for which the person was confined or to any term of community supervision for the sentence including probation, parole, work furlough or any other release.

13-2505. Promoting prison contraband; exceptions; x-radiation; body scans; classification

A. A person, not otherwise authorized by law, commits promoting prison contraband:

1. By knowingly taking contraband into a correctional facility or the grounds of a correctional facility; or

2. By knowingly conveying contraband to any person confined in a correctional facility; or

3. By knowingly making, obtaining or possessing contraband while being confined in a correctional facility or while being lawfully transported or moved incident to correctional facility confinement.

B. Any person who has reasonable grounds to believe there has been a violation or attempted violation of this section shall immediately report the violation or attempted violation to the official in charge of the facility or to a peace officer.

C. Notwithstanding any law to the contrary, any person who is convicted of a violation of this section is prohibited from being employed by this state or any of its agencies or political subdivisions until the person's civil rights have been restored pursuant to chapter 9 of this title.

D. This section does not apply to any of the following:

1. A prisoner who possesses or carries any tool, instrument or implement used by him at the direction or with the permission of prison officials.

2. Contraband located at the place where a person is on home arrest.

3. Contraband authorized by the correctional facility policies and used at the direction or with the permission of prison officials.

E. The state department of corrections or a county jail may request a licensed practitioner as defined in section 32-2801 to order that x-radiation be performed on any inmate if there is reason to believe the inmate is in possession of any contraband.

F. The state department of corrections or a county jail, in compliance with generally accepted health and safety standards, may perform a body scan of an inmate by using low-dose ionizing radiation without an order from a licensed practitioner to prevent any contraband from entering into a correctional facility.

G. Promoting prison contraband if the contraband is a deadly weapon, dangerous instrument or explosive is a class 2 felony. Promoting prison contraband if the contraband is a dangerous drug, narcotic drug or marijuana is a class 2 felony. In all other cases promoting prison contraband is a class 5 felony. Failure to report a violation or attempted violation of this section is a class 5 felony.

13-2506. Failure to appear in the second degree; classification

A. A person commits failure to appear in the second degree if, having either:

1. Been required by law to appear in connection with any misdemeanor or petty offense, the person knowingly fails to appear as required, regardless of the disposition of the charge requiring the appearance.

2. Given a written promise to appear in court or been personally served with a written notice to appear on a designated date pursuant to section 13-3903, the person thereafter fails to appear, personally or by counsel.

B. Failure to appear in the second degree pursuant to subsection A, paragraph 1 of this section is a class 1 misdemeanor. Failure to appear in the second degree pursuant to subsection A, paragraph 2 of this section is a class 2 misdemeanor.

13-2507. Failure to appear in the first degree; classification

A. A person commits failure to appear in the first degree if, having been required by law to appear in connection with any felony, such person knowingly fails to appear as required, regardless of the disposition of the charge requiring the appearance.

B. Failure to appear in the first degree is a class 5 felony.

13-2508. Resisting arrest; classification; definition

A. A person commits resisting arrest by intentionally preventing or attempting to prevent a person reasonably known to him to be a peace officer, acting under color of such peace officer's official authority, from effecting an arrest by:

1. Using or threatening to use physical force against the peace officer or another.

2. Using any other means creating a substantial risk of causing physical injury to the peace officer or another.

3. Engaging in passive resistance.

B. Resisting arrest pursuant to subsection A, paragraph 1 or 2 of this section is a class 6 felony. Resisting arrest pursuant to subsection A, paragraph 3 of this section is a class 1 misdemeanor.

C. For the purposes of this section, "passive resistance" means a nonviolent physical act or failure to act that is intended to impede, hinder or delay the effecting of an arrest.

13-2509. Resisting an order directing, regulating or controlling motor vehicle; classification

A. A person commits resisting an order directing, regulating or controlling a motor vehicle by knowingly failing to obey an order of a person reasonably known to him to be a peace officer, acting under color of such officer's official authority, directing, regulating or controlling his vehicle.

B. Resisting an order directing, regulating or controlling a motor vehicle is a class 2 misdemeanor.

13-2510. Hindering prosecution; definition

For purposes of sections 13-2511 and 13-2512 a person renders assistance to another person by knowingly:

1. Harboring or concealing the other person; or

2. Warning the other person of impending discovery, apprehension, prosecution or conviction. This does not apply to a warning given in connection with an effort to bring another into compliance with the law; or

3. Providing the other person with money, transportation, a weapon, a disguise or other similar means of avoiding discovery, apprehension, prosecution or conviction; or

4. Preventing or obstructing by means of force, deception or intimidation anyone from performing an act that might aid in the discovery, apprehension, prosecution or conviction of the other person; or

5. Suppressing by an act of concealment, alteration or destruction any physical evidence that might aid in the discovery, apprehension, prosecution or conviction of the other person; or

6. Concealing the identity of the other person.

13-2511. Hindering prosecution in the second degree; classification

A. A person commits hindering prosecution in the second degree if, with the intent to hinder the apprehension, prosecution, conviction or punishment of another for any misdemeanor or petty offense, such person renders assistance to such person.

B. Hindering prosecution in the second degree is a class 1 misdemeanor.

13-2512. Hindering prosecution in the first degree; classification

A. A person commits hindering prosecution in the first degree if, with the intent to hinder the apprehension, prosecution, conviction or punishment of another for any felony, the person renders assistance to the other person.
B. Hindering prosecution in the first degree is a class 5 felony, except that it is a class 3 felony if either:
1. The person knows or has reason to know that the offense involves terrorism or murder.
2. The person commits the offense with the intent to promote, further or assist a criminal street gang.

13-2513. Failure to discharge duties; classification; definition

A. A person who has custodial responsibility and who intentionally fails to discharge those duties is guilty of a class 1 misdemeanor if that failure results in any of the following:
1. The escape of a prisoner.
2. Serious physical injury to or the death of any other person or prisoner.
B. For the purposes of this section, "custodial responsibility" means having responsibility for the care, management or control of a prisoner who is committed to the state department of corrections.

13-2514. Promoting secure care facility contraband; classifications

A. A person, not otherwise authorized by law, commits promoting secure care facility contraband by knowingly doing any of the following:
1. Taking contraband onto the grounds of or into a secure care facility under the jurisdiction of the department of juvenile corrections.
2. Conveying contraband to any person confined in a secure care facility under the jurisdiction of the department of juvenile corrections.
3. Making, obtaining or possessing contraband while being confined in a secure care facility under the jurisdiction of the department of juvenile corrections.
B. Except for information protected under attorney client privilege, any person who has reasonable grounds to believe there has been a violation or attempted violation of this section shall immediately report the violation or attempted violation to the official in charge of the facility or to a peace officer.
C. Promoting secure care facility contraband if the contraband is a deadly weapon, dangerous instrument or explosive is a class 2 felony. Promoting secure care facility contraband if the contraband is a dangerous drug, narcotic drug or marijuana is a class 2 felony. In all other cases promoting secure care facility contraband is a class 5 felony. Failure to report a violation or attempted violation of this section is a class 5 felony.
D. Notwithstanding any law to the contrary, any person convicted of a violation of this section shall be prohibited from employment by this state or any of its agencies or political subdivisions until the person's civil rights have been restored pursuant to chapter 9 of this title.

Chapter 26 Bribery

13-2601. Definition

In this chapter, unless the context otherwise requires:
1. "Employee" includes a person employed by an enterprise or an agent or fiduciary of a principal.
2. "Employer" includes an enterprise or principal.
3. "Party officer" means a person who holds any position or office in a political party, whether by election, appointment or otherwise.

13-2602. Bribery of a public servant or party officer; classification

A. A person commits bribery of a public servant or party officer if with corrupt intent:

1. Such person offers, confers or agrees to confer any benefit upon a public servant or party officer with the intent to influence the public servant's or party officer's vote, opinion, judgment, exercise of discretion or other action in his official capacity as a public servant or party officer; or

2. While a public servant or party officer, such person solicits, accepts or agrees to accept any benefit upon an agreement or understanding that his vote, opinion, judgment, exercise of discretion or other action as a public servant or party officer may thereby be influenced.

B. It is no defense to a prosecution under this section that a person sought to be influenced was not qualified to act in the desired way because such person had not yet assumed office, lacked jurisdiction or for any other reason.

C. Bribery of a public servant or party officer is a class 4 felony.

13-2603. Trading in public office; classification

A. A person commits trading in public office if with corrupt intent:

1. Such person offers, confers or agrees to confer any benefit upon a public servant or party officer upon an agreement or understanding that he will or may be appointed to a public office or designated or nominated as a candidate for public office; or

2. While a public servant or party officer, such person solicits, accepts or agrees to accept any benefit from another upon an agreement or understanding that that person will or may be appointed to a public office or designated or nominated as a candidate for public office.

B. This section does not apply to contributions to political campaign funds or other similar political contributions made without corrupt intent.

C. Trading in public office is a class 6 felony.

13-2604. Forfeiture and disqualification from office

Notwithstanding the provisions of sections 13-904 and 13-912, a person convicted of violating section 13-2602 or 13-2603 shall forever be disqualified from becoming a public servant and shall, if such person is a public servant at the time of his conviction, forfeit his office.

13-2605. Commercial bribery; classification; exception

A. A person commits commercial bribery if:

1. Such person confers any benefit on an employee without the consent of such employee's employer, corruptly intending that such benefit will influence the conduct of the employee in relation to the employer's commercial affairs, and the conduct of the employee causes economic loss to the employer.

2. While an employee of an employer such employee accepts any benefit from another person, corruptly intending that such benefit will influence his conduct in relation to the employer's commercial affairs, and such conduct causes economic loss to the employer or principal.

B. Commercial bribery is a class 5 felony if the value of the benefit is more than one thousand dollars. Commercial bribery is a class 6 felony if the value of the benefit is not more than one thousand dollars but not less than one hundred dollars. Commercial bribery is a class 1 misdemeanor if the value of the benefit is less than one hundred dollars.

C. This section shall not be construed to prohibit a person from recruiting an employee of another employer unless, pursuant to an agreement between such person and the employee that such employee engage in conduct which will cause economic loss to his employer, such employee engages in conduct while an employee of his original employer and such conduct causes economic loss to the employer.

13-2606. Offer to exert improper influence on public officer or employee for consideration; classification

A person who intentionally or knowingly obtains or seeks to obtain any benefit from another person upon a claim or representation that he can or will improperly influence the action of a public servant is guilty of a class 4 felony.

Chapter 27 Perjury and Related Offenses

13-2701. Definitions

In this chapter, unless the context otherwise requires:
1. "Material" means that which could have affected the course or outcome of any proceeding or transaction. Whether a statement is material in any given factual situation is a question of law.
2. "Statement" means any representation of fact and includes a representation of opinion, belief or other state of mind where the representation clearly relates to state of mind apart from or in addition to any facts which are the subject of the representation.
3. "Sworn statement" means any statement knowingly given under oath or affirmation attesting to the truth of what is stated, including a notarized statement whether or not given in connection with an official proceeding.

13-2702. Perjury; classification

A. A person commits perjury by making either:
1. A false sworn statement in regard to a material issue, believing it to be false.
2. A false unsworn declaration, certificate, verification or statement in regard to a material issue that the person subscribes as true under penalty of perjury, believing it to be false.
B. Perjury is a class 4 felony.

13-2703. False swearing; classification

A. A person commits false swearing by making a false sworn statement, believing it to be false.
B. False swearing is a class 6 felony.

13-2704. Unsworn falsification; classification

A. A person commits unsworn falsification by knowingly:
1. Making any statement that he believes to be false, in regard to a material issue, to a public servant in connection with an application for any benefit, privilege or license.
2. Making any statement that he believes to be false in regard to a material issue to a public servant in connection with any official proceeding as defined in section 13-2801.
B. Unsworn falsification pursuant to paragraph 1, subsection A, is a class 2 misdemeanor. Unsworn falsification pursuant to subsection A, paragraph 2 is a class 1 misdemeanor.

13-2705. Perjury by inconsistent statements

When a person has made inconsistent statements under oath, both having been made within the period of the statute of limitations, the prosecution may proceed by setting forth the inconsistent statements in a single charge alleging in the alternative that one or the other was false and not believed by the defendant. In such case it shall not be necessary for the prosecution to prove which statement was false but only that one or the other was false and not believed by the defendant to be true.

13-2706. Limitation on defenses

A. It is no defense to a prosecution under this chapter that:
1. The statement was inadmissible under the rules of evidence; or
2. The oath or affirmation was taken or administered in an irregular manner; or
3. The defendant mistakenly believed the false statement to be immaterial.
B. The provisions of law which declare that evidence obtained upon examination of a person as a witness cannot be received against him in a criminal proceeding do not forbid giving such evidence against the person upon any proceedings founded upon a charge of perjury committed in such examination.

Proof of guilt beyond a reasonable doubt is sufficient for perjury or false swearing and it shall not be necessary that proof be made by a particular number of witnesses or by documentary or other type of evidence.

Chapter 28 Interference with Judicial and other Proceedings

13-2801. Definitions

In this chapter, unless the context otherwise requires:
1. "Juror" means any person who is a member of any impaneled jury or grand jury, and includes any person who has been drawn or summoned to attend as a prospective juror.
2. "Official proceeding" means a proceeding heard before any legislative, judicial, administrative or other governmental agency or official authorized to hear evidence under oath.
3. "Physical evidence" means any article, object, document, record or other thing of physical substance.
4. "Testimony" means oral or written statements, documents or any other material that may be offered by a witness in an official proceeding.
5. "Threat" means a threat proscribed by section 13-1804, subsection A.

13-2802. Influencing a witness; classification

A. A person commits influencing a witness if such person threatens a witness or offers, confers or agrees to confer any benefit upon a witness in any official proceeding or a person he believes may be called as a witness with intent to:
1. Influence the testimony of that person; or
2. Induce that person to avoid legal process summoning him to testify; or
3. Induce that person to absent himself from any official proceeding to which he has been legally summoned.
B. Influencing a witness is a class 5 felony.

13-2803. Receiving a bribe by a witness; classification

A. A witness in an official proceeding or a person who believes he may be called as a witness commits receiving a bribe by a witness if such person knowingly solicits, accepts or agrees to accept any benefit upon an agreement or understanding that:
1. His testimony will thereby be influenced; or
2. He will attempt to avoid legal process summoning him to testify; or
3. He will absent himself from any official proceeding to which he has been legally summoned.
B. Receiving a bribe by a witness is a class 5 felony.

13-2804. Tampering with a witness; classification

A. A person commits tampering with a witness if the person knowingly communicates, directly or indirectly, with a witness in any official proceeding or a person he believes may be called as a witness to do any of the following:

1. Unlawfully withhold any testimony.

2. Testify falsely.

3. Absent himself from any official proceeding to which he has been legally summoned.

4. Evade a summons or subpoena.

B. Tampering with a witness is a class 6 felony.

13-2805. Influencing a juror; classification

A. A person commits influencing a juror if such person threatens a juror or offers, confers or agrees to confer a benefit upon a juror with the intent to influence the juror's vote, opinion, decision or other action as a juror.
B. Influencing a juror is a class 4 felony.

13-2806. Receiving a bribe by a juror; classification

A. A juror commits receiving a bribe by a juror if such person knowingly solicits, accepts or agrees to accept any benefit upon an agreement or understanding that his vote, opinion, decision or other action as a juror may be influenced.
B. Receiving a bribe by a juror is a class 5 felony.

13-2807. Jury tampering; classification

A. A person commits jury tampering if, with intent to influence a juror's vote, opinion, decision or other action in a case, such person directly or indirectly, communicates with a juror other than as part of the normal proceedings of the case.
B. Jury tampering is a class 6 felony.

13-2808. Misconduct by a juror; classification

A. A juror commits misconduct by a juror if, in relation to an action or proceeding pending or about to be brought before him, such person knowingly:
1. Allows an unauthorized communication to be made to him; or
2. Makes a promise or agreement to decide for or against any party to the proceeding other than as part of jury deliberation.
B. Misconduct by a juror is a class 6 felony.

13-2809. Tampering with physical evidence; classification

A. A person commits tampering with physical evidence if, with intent that it be used, introduced, rejected or unavailable in an official proceeding which is then pending or which such person knows is about to be instituted, such person:
1. Destroys, mutilates, alters, conceals or removes physical evidence with the intent to impair its verity or availability; or
2. Knowingly makes, produces or offers any false physical evidence; or
3. Prevents the production of physical evidence by an act of force, intimidation or deception against any person.
B. Inadmissibility of the evidence in question is not a defense.
C. Tampering with physical evidence is a class 6 felony.

13-2810. Interfering with judicial proceedings; classification

A. A person commits interfering with judicial proceedings if such person knowingly:
1. Engages in disorderly, disrespectful or insolent behavior during the session of a court which directly tends to interrupt its proceedings or impairs the respect due to its authority; or
2. Disobeys or resists the lawful order, process or other mandate of a court; or
3. Refuses to be sworn or affirmed as a witness in any court proceeding; or
4. Publishes a false or grossly inaccurate report of a court proceeding; or
5. Refuses to serve as a juror unless exempted by law; or

6. Fails inexcusably to attend a trial at which he has been chosen to serve as a juror.
B. Interfering with judicial proceedings is a class 1 misdemeanor.

13-2812. Unlawful grand jury disclosure; classification

A. A person commits unlawful grand jury disclosure if the person knowingly discloses to another the nature or substance of any grand jury testimony or any decision, result or other matter attending a grand jury proceeding, except in the proper discharge of official duties, at the discretion of the prosecutor to inform a victim of the status of the case or when permitted by the court in furtherance of justice.
B. Unlawful grand jury disclosure is a class 1 misdemeanor.

13-2813. Unlawful disclosure of an indictment, information or complaint; classification

A. A person commits unlawful disclosure of an indictment, information or complaint if the person knowingly discloses the fact that an indictment, information or complaint has been found or filed before the accused person is in custody or has been served with a summons, except in the proper discharge of official duties, at the discretion of the prosecutor to inform a victim of the status of the case or as authorized by the court in furtherance of justice.
B. This section does not apply to offenses that are created by city or county ordinance.
C. Unlawful disclosure of an indictment, information or complaint is a class 1 misdemeanor.

13-2814. Simulating legal process; classification

A. A person commits simulating legal process if such person knowingly sends or delivers to another any document falsely purporting to be an order or other document that simulates civil or criminal process.
B. Simulating legal process is a class 2 misdemeanor.

Chapter 29 Offenses Against Public Order

13-2901. Definitions

In this chapter, unless the context otherwise requires:
1. "Marijuana" means all parts of any plant of the genus cannabis, from which the resin has not been extracted, whether growing or not, and the seeds of such plant. Marijuana does not include the mature stalks of such plant, or the sterilized seed of such plant which is incapable of germination.
2. "Public" means affecting or likely to affect a substantial group of persons.

13-2902. Unlawful assembly; classification

A. A person commits unlawful assembly by:
1. Assembling with two or more other persons with the intent to engage in conduct constituting a riot as defined in section 13-2903; or
2. Being present at an assembly of two or more other persons who are engaged in or who have the readily apparent intent to engage in conduct constituting a riot as defined in section 13-2903 and knowingly remaining there and refusing to obey an official order to disperse.
B. Unlawful assembly is a class 1 misdemeanor.

13-2903. Riot; classification

A. A person commits riot if, with two or more other persons acting together, such person recklessly uses force or violence or threatens to use force or violence, if such threat is accompanied by immediate power of execution, which disturbs the public peace.

B. Riot is a class 5 felony.

13-2904. Disorderly conduct; classification

A. A person commits disorderly conduct if, with intent to disturb the peace or quiet of a neighborhood, family or person, or with knowledge of doing so, such person:
1. Engages in fighting, violent or seriously disruptive behavior; or
2. Makes unreasonable noise; or
3. Uses abusive or offensive language or gestures to any person present in a manner likely to provoke immediate physical retaliation by such person; or
4. Makes any protracted commotion, utterance or display with the intent to prevent the transaction of the business of a lawful meeting, gathering or procession; or
5. Refuses to obey a lawful order to disperse issued to maintain public safety in dangerous proximity to a fire, a hazard or any other emergency; or
6. Recklessly handles, displays or discharges a deadly weapon or dangerous instrument.
B. Disorderly conduct under subsection A, paragraph 6 is a class 6 felony. Disorderly conduct under subsection A, paragraph 1, 2, 3, 4 or 5 is a class 1 misdemeanor.

13-2905. Loitering; classification

A. A person commits loitering if such person intentionally:
1. Is present in a public place and in an offensive manner or in a manner likely to disturb the public peace solicits another person to engage in any sexual offense.
2. Is present in a transportation facility and after a reasonable request to cease or unless specifically authorized to do so solicits or engages in any business, trade or commercial transactions involving the sale of merchandise or services.
3. Is present in a public place, unless specifically authorized by law, to gamble with any cards, dice or other similar gambling devices.
4. Is present in or about a school, college or university building or grounds after a reasonable request to leave and either does not have any reason or relationship involving custody of or responsibility for a pupil or student or any other specific legitimate reason for being there or does not have written permission to be there from anyone authorized to grant permission.
5. Except as provided in section 13-3969, subsection A, solicits bail bond business inside a court building or immediately around or near the entrance of a county or city jail. For the purposes of this paragraph, "solicit" includes handing out business cards or any printed material or displaying any electronic devices related to bail bonds, verbally asking a person if the person needs a bail bond and recruiting another person to solicit bail bond business.
B. Loitering under subsection A, paragraph 4 is a class 1 misdemeanor. Loitering under subsection A, paragraphs 1, 2, 3 and 5 is a class 3 misdemeanor.

13-2906. Obstructing a highway or other public thoroughfare; classification; definition

A. A person commits obstructing a highway or other public thoroughfare if the person, alone or with other persons, does any of the following:
1. Having no legal privilege to do so, recklessly interferes with the passage of any highway or public thoroughfare by creating an unreasonable inconvenience or hazard.
2. Intentionally activates a pedestrian signal on a highway or public thoroughfare if the person's reason for activating the signal is not to cross the highway or public thoroughfare but to do both of the following:
(a) Stop the passage of traffic on the highway or public thoroughfare.
(b) Solicit a driver for a donation or business.
3. After receiving a verbal warning to desist, intentionally interferes with passage on a highway or other public thoroughfare or entrance into a public forum that results in preventing other persons from gaining access to a governmental meeting, a governmental hearing or a political campaign event.

B. Obstructing a highway or other public thoroughfare under subsection A, paragraph 3 of this section is a class 1 misdemeanor. Obstructing a highway or other public thoroughfare under subsection A, paragraph 1 or 2 of this section is a class 3 misdemeanor.

C. For the purposes of this section, "public forum" has the same meaning prescribed in section 15-1861.

13-2907. False reporting; emergency response costs; classification; definitions

A. A person commits false reporting by initiating or circulating a report of a bombing, fire, offense or other emergency knowing that such report is false and intending:

1. That it will cause action of any sort by an official or volunteer agency organized to deal with emergencies; or

2. That it will place a person in fear of imminent serious physical injury; or

3. That it will prevent or interrupt the occupation of any building, room, place of assembly, public place or means of transportation.

B. A person who commits a violation of this section that results in an emergency response or investigation of false reporting and who is convicted of a violation of this section is liable for the expenses that are incurred incident to the emergency response or the investigation of the commission of false reporting, except that if the person is a juvenile who is adjudicated delinquent of a violation of this section, the court may order the juvenile to pay the expenses incurred under this subsection as restitution. The expenses are a debt of the person. The public agency, for profit entity or not-for-profit entity that incurred the expenses may collect the debt proportionally. The liability that is imposed under this subsection is in addition to any other liability that may be imposed.

C. False reporting is a class 1 misdemeanor, except that a second or subsequent violation is a class 6 felony.

D. For the purposes of this section:

1. "Expenses" means any reasonable costs that are directly incurred by a public agency, for profit entity or not-for-profit entity that makes an appropriate emergency response to an incident or an investigation of the commission of false reporting. Expenses includes the costs of providing police, fire fighting, rescue and emergency medical services at the scene of an incident and the salaries of the persons who respond to the incident. Expenses does not include any charges that are assessed by an ambulance service that is regulated pursuant to title 36, chapter 21.1, article 2.

2. "Public agency" means this state, any city, county, municipal corporation or district, any Arizona federally recognized native American tribe or any other public authority that is located in whole or in part in this state and that provides police, fire fighting, medical or other emergency services.

13-2907.01. False reporting to law enforcement agencies; classification

A. It is unlawful for a person to knowingly make to a law enforcement agency of either this state or a political subdivision of this state a false, fraudulent or unfounded report or statement or to knowingly misrepresent a fact for the purpose of interfering with the orderly operation of a law enforcement agency or misleading a peace officer.

B. Violation of this section is a class 1 misdemeanor.

13-2907.02. False reporting of child abuse or neglect; classification

A person who knowingly and intentionally makes a false report of child abuse or neglect knowing the report is false or a person who coerces another person to make a false report of child abuse or neglect knowing the report is false is guilty of a class 1 misdemeanor.

13-2907.03. False reporting of sexual assault involving a spouse; classification

A person who intentionally makes a false report of sexual assault involving a spouse knowing the report is false or a person who coerces another person to make a false report of sexual assault involving a spouse knowing the report is false is guilty of a class 1 misdemeanor.

13-2907.04. False reporting of vulnerable adult abuse; classification

A. It is unlawful for a person to intentionally make a false report of vulnerable adult abuse or neglect to a law enforcement agency or to another person who is required by law to report the information to a law enforcement agency.

B. A violation of this section is a class 1 misdemeanor.

13-2907.05. False reporting of an offense involving corrections or probation employees; classification

A person who intentionally makes a false report of an offense listed in section 13-1409 or 13-1419 knowing the report is false or a person who coerces another person to make a false report of an offense listed in section 13-1409 or 13-1419 knowing the report is false is guilty of a class 1 misdemeanor.

13-2908. Criminal nuisance; classification

A. A person commits criminal nuisance:
1. If, by conduct either unlawful in itself or unreasonable under the circumstances, such person recklessly creates or maintains a condition which endangers the safety or health of others.
2. By knowingly conducting or maintaining any premises, place or resort where persons gather for purposes of engaging in unlawful conduct.
B. Criminal nuisance is a class 3 misdemeanor.

13-2909. Residential picketing; classification

A. A person commits residential picketing if, with intent to harass, annoy or alarm another person, such person intentionally engages in picketing or otherwise demonstrates before or about the residence or dwelling place of an individual, other than a residence or dwelling place also used as the principal place of business of such individual.
B. Residential picketing is a class 3 misdemeanor.

13-2910. Cruelty to animals; interference with working or service animal; classification; definitions

A. A person commits cruelty to animals if the person does any of the following:
1. Intentionally, knowingly or recklessly subjects any animal under the person's custody or control to cruel neglect or abandonment.
2. Intentionally, knowingly or recklessly fails to provide medical attention necessary to prevent protracted suffering to any animal under the person's custody or control.
3. Intentionally, knowingly or recklessly inflicts unnecessary physical injury to any animal.
4. Recklessly subjects any animal to cruel mistreatment.
5. Intentionally, knowingly or recklessly kills any animal under the custody or control of another person without either legal privilege or consent of the owner.
6. Recklessly interferes with, kills or harms a working or service animal without either legal privilege or consent of the owner.
7. Intentionally, knowingly or recklessly leaves an animal unattended and confined in a motor vehicle and physical injury to or death of the animal is likely to result.
8. Intentionally or knowingly subjects any animal under the person's custody or control to cruel neglect or abandonment that results in serious physical injury to the animal.
9. Intentionally or knowingly subjects any animal to cruel mistreatment.
10. Intentionally or knowingly interferes with, kills or harms a working or service animal without either legal privilege or consent of the owner.
11. Intentionally or knowingly allows any dog that is under the person's custody or control to interfere with, kill or cause physical injury to a service animal.
12. Recklessly allows any dog that is under the person's custody or control to interfere with, kill or cause physical injury to a service animal.
13. Intentionally or knowingly obtains or exerts unauthorized control over a service animal with the intent to deprive the service animal handler of the service animal.
B. It is a defense to subsection A of this section if:
1. Any person exposes poison to be taken by a dog that has killed or wounded livestock or poison to be taken by predatory animals on premises owned, leased or controlled by the person for the purpose of protecting the person or the person's livestock or poultry, the treated property is kept posted by the person who authorized or performed the treatment until the poison has been removed

and the poison is removed by the person exposing the poison after the threat to the person or the person's livestock or poultry has ceased to exist. The posting required shall provide adequate warning to persons who enter the property by the point or points of normal entry. The warning notice that is posted shall be readable at a distance of fifty feet, shall contain a poison statement and symbol and shall state the word "danger" or "warning".

2. Any person uses poisons in and immediately around buildings owned, leased or controlled by the person for the purpose of controlling wild and domestic rodents as otherwise allowed by the laws of the state, excluding any fur-bearing animals as defined in section 17-101.

C. This section does not prohibit or restrict:

1. The taking of wildlife or other activities permitted by or pursuant to title 17.

2. Activities permitted by or pursuant to title 3.

3. Activities regulated by the Arizona game and fish department or the Arizona department of agriculture.

D. A peace officer, animal control enforcement agent or animal control enforcement deputy may use reasonable force to open a vehicle to rescue an animal if the animal is left in the vehicle as prescribed in subsection A, paragraph 7 of this section.

E. A person who is convicted of a violation of subsection A, paragraph 6 or 10 of this section is liable as follows:

1. If the working or service animal was killed or disabled, to the owner or agency that owns the working or service animal and that employs the handler or to the owner or handler for the replacement and training costs of the working or service animal and for any veterinary bills.

2. To the owner or agency that owns a working or service animal for the salary of the handler for the period of time that the handler's services are lost to the owner or agency.

3. To the owner for the owner's contractual losses with the agency.

F. An incorporated city or town or a county may adopt an ordinance with misdemeanor provisions at least as stringent as the misdemeanor provisions of this section, except that any ordinance adopted shall not prohibit or restrict any activity involving a dog, whether the dog is restrained or not, if the activity is directly related to the business of shepherding or herding livestock and the activity is necessary for the safety of a human, the dog or livestock or is permitted by or pursuant to title 3.

G. A person who violates subsection A, paragraph 1, 2, 3, 4, 5, 6, 7 or 12 of this section is guilty of a class 1 misdemeanor. A person who violates subsection A, paragraph 8, 9, 10, 11 or 13 of this section is guilty of a class 6 felony.

H. For the purposes of this section:

1. "Animal" means a mammal, bird, reptile or amphibian.

2. "Cruel mistreatment" means to torture or otherwise inflict unnecessary serious physical injury on an animal or to kill an animal in a manner that causes protracted suffering to the animal.

3. "Cruel neglect" means to fail to provide an animal with necessary food, water or shelter.

4. "Handler" means a law enforcement officer or any other person who has successfully completed a course of training prescribed by the person's agency or the service animal owner and who used a specially trained animal under the direction of the person's agency or the service animal owner.

5. "Service animal" means an animal that has completed a formal training program, that assists its owner in one or more daily living tasks that are associated with a productive lifestyle and that is trained to not pose a danger to the health and safety of the general public.

6. "Working animal" means a horse or dog that is used by a law enforcement agency, that is specially trained for law enforcement work and that is under the control of a handler.

13-2910.01. Animal fighting; classification

A. A person commits animal fighting by knowingly:

1. Owning, possessing, keeping or training any animal if the person knows or has reason to know that the animal will engage in an exhibition of fighting with another animal.

2. For amusement or gain, causing any animal to fight with another animal, or causing any animals to injure each other.

3. Permitting any act in violation of paragraph 1 or 2 to be done on any premises under the person's charge or control.

B. This section does not:

1. Prohibit or restrict activities permitted by or pursuant to title 3.

2. Apply to animals that are trained to protect livestock from predation and that engage in actions to protect livestock.

C. Animal fighting is a class 5 felony.

13-2910.02. Presence at animal fight; classification

Any person who is knowingly present at any place or building where preparations are being made for an exhibition of the fighting of animals, or who is present at such exhibition, is guilty of a class 6 felony.

13-2910.03. Cockfighting; classification

(Caution: 1998 Prop. 105 applies)

A. A person commits cockfighting by knowingly:
1. Owning, possessing, keeping or training any cock with the intent that such cock engage in an exhibition of fighting with another cock.
2. For amusement or gain, causing any cock to fight with another cock or causing any cocks to injure each other.
3. Permitting any act in violation of paragraph 1 or 2 to be done on any premises under his charge or control.
B. Cockfighting is a class 5 felony.
C. For purposes of this section and section 13-2910.04, cock means any male chicken, including game fowl except wildlife as defined in Arizona Revised Statutes section 17-101.

13-2910.04. Presence at cockfight; classification

(Caution: 1998 Prop. 105 applies)

Any person who is knowingly present at any place or building where preparations are being made for an exhibition of the fighting of cocks, or is present at such exhibition, is guilty of a class 1 misdemeanor.

13-2910.05. Exempt activities

(Caution: 1998 Prop. 105 applies)

Activity involving the possession, training, exhibition or use of an animal in the otherwise lawful pursuits of hunting, ranching, farming, rodeos, shows and security services shall be exempt from the provisions of sections 13-2910.01, 13-2910.02, 13-2910.03 and 13-2910.04.

13-2910.06. Defense to cruelty to animals and bird fighting

(Caution: 1998 Prop. 105 applies)

It is a defense to sections 13-2910, 13-2910.01, 13-2910.02, 13-2910.03 and 13-2910.04 that the activity charged involves the possession, training, exhibition or use of a bird or animal in the otherwise lawful sports of falconry, animal hunting, rodeos, ranching or the training or use of hunting dogs.

13-2910.07. Cruel and inhumane confinement of a pig during pregnancy or of a calf raised for veal

(Caution: 1998 Prop. 105 applies)

A. Notwithstanding any other provision of title 3 or title 13, a person shall not tether or confine any pig during pregnancy or any calf raised for veal, on a farm, for all or the majority of any day, in a manner that prevents such animal from:
1. Lying down and fully extending his or her limbs; or
2. Turning around freely.

B. This section shall not apply to:

1. Pigs or calves during transportation.

2. Pigs or calves in rodeo exhibitions, state or county fair exhibitions, or other similar exhibitions.

3. The killing of pigs or calves according to the provisions of chapter 13, title 3 and other applicable law and regulations.

4. Pigs or calves involved in lawful scientific or agricultural research.

5. Pigs or calves while undergoing an examination, test, treatment or operation for veterinary purposes.

6. A pig during the seven day period prior to the pig's expected date of giving birth.

C. A person who violates this section is guilty of a class 1 misdemeanor.

D. The following definitions shall govern this section:

1. "Calf" means a calf of the bovine species.

2. "Calf raised for veal" means a calf raised with the intent of selling, marketing or distributing the meat, organs or any part of such calf as a food product described as "veal."

3. "Farm" means the land, buildings, support facilities, and other equipment that is wholly or partially used for the production of animals for food or fiber.

4. "Pig" means any animal of the porcine species.

5. "Turning around freely" means having the ability to turn around in a complete circle without any impediment, including a tether, or, in the case of an enclosure (including what is commonly described as a "gestation crate" for pigs and a "veal crate" for calves) without touching any side of the enclosure.

13-2910.08. The humane treatment of farm animals fund

(Conditionally Eff. Caution: 1998 Prop. 105 applies)

The "humane treatment of farm animals fund" is hereby established to be administered by the attorney general under the conditions and for the purposes provided by this section. Upon receipt, the attorney general shall deposit in the fund any monies received for the state as a result of enforcement of the humane treatment of farm animals act and any monies received by the attorney general as a money donation to the fund from any public or private group, society, association or individual. The monies in the fund shall be used only for mandatory expenditures, if any, required by the humane treatment of farm animals act and administration of the fund. Monies in the fund are not subject to legislative appropriation. The fund is exempt from statutory provisions relating to lapsing of appropriations and shall not revert to the general fund.

13-2910.09. Equine tripping; classification; definitions

A. A person who knowingly or intentionally trips an equine for entertainment or sport is guilty of a class 1 misdemeanor.

B. A person who is convicted of a first violation of this section:

1. Shall be sentenced to serve not less than forty-eight consecutive hours in jail and is not eligible for probation or suspension of execution of sentence unless the entire sentence is served.

2. Shall pay a fine of not less than one thousand dollars.

C. A person who is convicted of a second violation of this section:

1. Shall be sentenced to serve not less than thirty consecutive days in jail and is not eligible for probation or suspension of execution of sentence unless the entire sentence is served.

2. Shall pay a fine of not less than two thousand dollars.

D. A person who is convicted of a third or subsequent violation of this section:

1. Shall be sentenced to serve not less than ninety consecutive days in jail and is not eligible for probation or suspension of execution of sentence unless the entire sentence is served.

2. Shall pay a fine of not less than two thousand dollars.

E. This section does not apply to any jumping or steeplechase events, racing, training, branding, show events, calf or steer roping events, bulldogging or steer wrestling events or any other traditional western rodeo events, including barrel racing, bareback or saddled bronc riding or other similar activities or events.

F. For the purposes of this section:

1. "Equine" means a horse, pony, mule, donkey or hinny.

2. "Trips" means knowingly or intentionally causing an equine to lose its balance or fall by use of a wire, pole, stick or rope or any other object or by any other means.

13-2911. Interference with or disruption of an educational institution; violation; classification; definitions

A. A person commits interference with or disruption of an educational institution by doing any of the following:
1. Intentionally, knowingly or recklessly interfering with or disrupting the normal operations of an educational institution by either:
(a) Threatening to cause physical injury to any employee or student of an educational institution or any person on the property of an educational institution.
(b) Threatening to cause damage to any educational institution, the property of any educational institution or the property of any employee or student of an educational institution.
2. Intentionally or knowingly entering or remaining on the property of any educational institution for the purpose of interfering with the lawful use of the property or in any manner as to deny or interfere with the lawful use of the property by others.
3. Intentionally or knowingly refusing to obey a lawful order given pursuant to subsection C of this section.
B. To constitute a violation of this section, the acts that are prohibited by subsection A, paragraph 1 of this section are not required to be directed at a specific individual, a specific educational institution or any specific property of an educational institution.
C. The chief administrative officer of an educational institution or an officer or employee designated by the chief administrative officer to maintain order may order a person to leave the property of the educational institution if the officer or employee has reasonable grounds to believe either that:
1. Any person or persons are committing any act that interferes with or disrupts the lawful use of the property by others at the educational institution.
2. Any person has entered on the property of an educational institution for the purpose of committing any act that interferes with or disrupts the lawful use of the property by others at the educational institution.
D. The appropriate governing board of every educational institution shall adopt rules pursuant to title 41, chapter 6 for the maintenance of public order on all property of any educational institution under its jurisdiction that is used for educational purposes and shall provide a program for the enforcement of its rules. The rules shall govern the conduct of students, faculty and other staff and all members of the public while on the property of the educational institution. Penalties for violations of the rules shall be clearly set forth and enforced. Penalties shall include provisions for the ejection of a violator from the property and, in the case of a student, faculty member or other staff violator, the violator's suspension or expulsion or any other appropriate disciplinary action. A governing board shall amend its rules as necessary to ensure the maintenance of public order. Any deadly weapon, dangerous instrument or explosive that is used, displayed or possessed by a person in violation of a rule adopted pursuant to this subsection shall be forfeited and sold or otherwise disposed of pursuant to section 13-3105 and chapter 39 of this title. This subsection does not do either of the following:
1. Preclude school districts from conducting approved gun safety programs on school campuses.
2. Apply to private universities, colleges, high schools or common schools or other private educational institutions.
E. An educational institution is not eligible to receive any state aid or assistance unless rules are adopted in accordance with this section.
F. This section does not prevent or limit the authority of the governing board of any educational institution to discharge any employee or expel, suspend or otherwise punish any student for any violation of its rules, even though the violation is unlawful under this chapter or is otherwise an offense.
G. This section may be enforced by any peace officer in this state wherever and whenever a violation occurs.
H. Restitution under sections 8-341, 8-345 and 13-603 applies to any financial loss that is suffered by a person or educational institution as a result of a violation of this section.
I. Notwithstanding section 15-341 and subsection D of this section, the governing board of an educational institution may not adopt or enforce any policy or rule that prohibits the lawful possession or carrying of a deadly weapon on a public right-of-way by a person or on or within a person's means of transportation.
J. Interference with or disruption of an educational institution pursuant to subsection A, paragraph 1 of this section is a class 6 felony. Interference with or disruption of an educational institution pursuant to subsection A, paragraph 2 or 3 of this section is a class 1 misdemeanor.
K. For the purposes of this section:
1. "Educational institution" means, except as otherwise provided, any university, college, community college, high school or common school in this state.

2. "Governing board" means the body, whether appointed or elected, that has responsibility for the maintenance and government of an educational institution.

3. "Interference with or disruption of" includes any act that might reasonably lead to the evacuation or closure of any property of the educational institution or the postponement, cancellation or suspension of any class or other school activity. For the purposes of this paragraph, an actual evacuation, closure, postponement, cancellation or suspension is not required for the act to be considered an interference or disruption.

4. "Property of an educational institution" means all land, buildings and other facilities that are owned, operated or controlled by the governing board of an educational institution and that are devoted to educational purposes.

5. "Public right-of-way" means any highway, street, road, thoroughfare, path, alley or other right-of-way that is publicly accessible and that is established and maintained by this state or a political subdivision of this state. Public right-of-way does not include property of an educational institution.

13-2912. Unlawful introduction of disease or parasite; classification

A. It is unlawful for a person to knowingly introduce into this state a disease or parasite of animals or poultry that constitutes a threat to:

1. Livestock or poultry industry in this state.
2. Human health.
3. Human life.

B. This section does not apply to research conducted by government or educational institutions.

C. A violation of subsection A:

1. Paragraph 1 is a class 5 felony.
2. Paragraph 2 is a class 4 felony.
3. Paragraph 3 is a class 2 felony.

13-2913. Unlawful violation of fire ban; classification

A. It is unlawful for a person to enter or remain in any public building or on any public property in violation of any order or rule that is issued by any officer or agency having the power of control, management or supervision of the building or property and that relates to the control and limitation of fires, including any prohibition, restriction or ban on fires, any provision to avert the start of or lessen the likelihood of wildfire and the designation of any place where fires are permitted, restricted, prohibited or banned.

B. A person who violates this section is guilty of a class 2 misdemeanor.

13-2914. Aggressive solicitation; classification; definitions

A. It is unlawful for a person to solicit any money or other thing of value or solicit the sale of goods or services:

1. Within fifteen feet of any bank entrance or exit or any automated teller machine if the person does not have permission to be there from the bank or the owner of the property on which the automated teller machine is located.

2. In a public area by:

(a) Intentionally, knowingly or recklessly making any physical contact with or touching another person in the course of the solicitation without the person's consent.

(b) Approaching or following the person being solicited in a manner that is intended or is likely to cause a reasonable person to fear imminent bodily harm to oneself or another or damage to or loss of property or that is reasonably likely to intimidate the person being solicited into responding affirmatively to the solicitation.

(c) Continuing to solicit the person after the person being solicited has clearly communicated a request that the solicitation stop.

(d) Intentionally, knowingly or recklessly obstructing the safe or free passage of the person being solicited or requiring the person to take evasive action to avoid physical contact with the person making the solicitation. This subdivision does not apply to acts that are authorized as an exercise of one's constitutional right to picket or protest.

(e) Intentionally, knowingly or recklessly using obscene or abusive language or gestures that are intended or likely to cause a reasonable person to fear imminent bodily harm or that are reasonably likely to intimidate the person being solicited into responding affirmatively to the solicitation.

B. A violation of this section is a petty offense.

C. For the purposes of this section:

1. "Automated teller machine" has the same meaning prescribed in section 6-101.
2. "Bank" means a bank, credit union or other similar financial institution.
3. "Public area" means an area that the public or a substantial group of persons has access to and includes alleys, bridges, buildings, driveways, parking lots, parks, playgrounds, plazas, sidewalks and streets open to the general public, and the doorways and entrances to buildings and dwellings and the grounds enclosing them.
4. "Solicit" means using any means of communication, including by spoken, written or printed word, to request an immediate donation or exchange of money or other thing of value from another person regardless of the solicitor's purpose or intended use of the money or other thing of value.

13-2915. Preventing use of telephone in emergency; false representation of emergency; classification; definitions

A. It is unlawful for a person to do any of the following:
1. Knowingly refuse to yield or surrender the use of a party line to another person to report a fire or summon police or medical or other aid in case of emergency.
2. Ask for or request the use of a party line on the pretext that an emergency exists, knowing that no emergency in fact exists.
3. Intentionally prevent or interfere with the use of a telephone by another person in an emergency situation.
B. Every telephone directory that is compiled and distributed to subscribers shall contain a notice explaining this section. The notice shall be printed in type that is no smaller than any other type on the same page, other than headings, and shall be preceded by the word "warning". This subsection does not apply to directories that are distributed solely for business advertising purposes, commonly known as classified directories.
C. This section does not require a person to allow another person to enter the person's home or place of residence for the purpose of using a telephone in an emergency situation.
D. A person who violates this section is guilty of a class 2 misdemeanor.
E. For the purposes of this section:
1. "Emergency" means a situation in which property or human life is in jeopardy and the prompt summoning of aid is essential.
2. "Emergency situation" means a situation in which both of the following apply:
(a) Human health, life or safety is in jeopardy and the prompt summoning of aid is essential.
(b) It is reasonable to believe that a domestic violence offense pursuant to section 13-3601 is being, has been or is about to be committed.
3. "Party line" means a subscriber's line telephone circuit, consisting of two or more main telephone stations connected therewith, each station with a distinctive ring or telephone number.

13-2916. Use of an electronic communication to terrify, intimidate, threaten or harass; applicability; classification; definition

A. It is unlawful for any person, with intent to terrify, intimidate, threaten or harass a specific person or persons, to do any of the following:
1. Direct any obscene, lewd or profane language or suggest any lewd or lascivious act to the person in an electronic communication.
2. Threaten to inflict physical harm to any person or property in any electronic communication.
3. Otherwise disturb by repeated anonymous, unwanted or unsolicited electronic communications the peace, quiet or right of privacy of the person at the place where the communications were received.
B. Any offense committed by use of an electronic communication as set forth in this section is deemed to have been committed at either the place where the communications originated or at the place where the communications were received.
C. This section does not apply to constitutionally protected speech or activity or to any other activity authorized by law.
D. Any person who violates this section is guilty of a class 1 misdemeanor.
E. For the purposes of this section, "electronic communication" means a wire line, cable, wireless or cellular telephone call, a text message, an instant message or electronic mail.

13-2917. Public nuisance; abatement; classification

A. It is a public nuisance, and is no less a nuisance because the extent of the annoyance or damage inflicted is unequal, for anything:

1. To be injurious to health, indecent, offensive to the senses or an obstruction to the free use of property that interferes with the comfortable enjoyment of life or property by an entire community or neighborhood or by a considerable number of persons.

2. To unlawfully obstruct the free passage or use, in the customary manner, of any navigable lake, river, bay, stream, canal or basin, or any public park, square, street or highway.

B. It is a public nuisance for any person to sell, offer to sell, transfer, trade or disseminate any item which is obscene as defined in section 13-3501, within two thousand feet, measured in a straight line, of the nearest boundary line of any of the following:

1. Any building used as a private or public elementary or high school.

2. Any public park.

3. Any residence district as defined in section 28-101.

C. The county attorney, the attorney general or the city attorney may bring an action in superior court to abate, enjoin and prevent the activity described in subsections A and B of this section.

D. Any person who knowingly maintains or commits a public nuisance or who knowingly fails or refuses to perform any legal duty relating to the removal of a public nuisance is guilty of a class 2 misdemeanor.

13-2918. Interference with emergency transmission on citizens' band radio frequency; presumption; definition; classification

A. It is unlawful for a person to recklessly interrupt, impede or otherwise interfere with the transmission of an emergency communication over a citizens' band radio frequency.

B. A person is presumed to have acted recklessly if he interrupts, impedes or interferes with the transmission of a communication on a channel dedicated to use for emergency communications.

C. As used in this section "emergency" means a situation in which a person is or is reasonably believed by the person transmitting the communication to be in imminent danger of serious physical injury or in which property is or is reasonably believed by the person transmitting the communication to be in imminent danger of damage or destruction.

D. A person who violates this section is guilty of a class 1 misdemeanor.

13-2919. Automated telephone solicitation; violation; classification

A. A person shall not use an automated system for the selection and dialing of telephone numbers and the playing of a recorded message or sending a text message for the purpose of soliciting persons to purchase goods or services or requesting survey information if the results are to be used directly for the purpose of soliciting persons to purchase goods or services.

B. This section does not apply if a recorded message or text message is received under any of the following circumstances:

1. With prior express invitation or permission by the recipient.

2. By a recipient who has an existing business relationship with the sender.

C. A person who violates this section is guilty of a class 2 misdemeanor.

13-2920. Advertisements and required preamble message for telephone information services; telecommunications corporation compensation; definitions; classification

A. An information access telephone service provider shall not provide or sponsor an advertisement, publication or other communication regarding information access telephone service that does not clearly and conspicuously display the price for each call or for each minute of the call or provide or sponsor a television or radio advertisement that does not include a clearly audible voice announcement of the price for each call or for each minute of the call.

B. Information access telephone service providers shall begin each information access telephone service call with a clear statement, without charge, of whether the call is billed on a per minute or a per call basis and the price for the call or for each minute of the call.

C. Information access telephone service providers shall compensate any telecommunications corporation transporting the provider's service for all charges associated with blocking information access telephone services, and shall make arrangements with the telecommunications corporation for a one time adjustment per residential customer account for an information access telephone service charge if the adjustments involve calls made by minors without authorization or involve claims of fraud, theft or misrepresentation. An adjustment pursuant to this subsection, except for billing and transport charges, shall be charged to the information access telephone service provider who shall not attempt private collection of any adjustments to customers' accounts made by a telecommunications corporation.

D. An information access telephone service provider shall not provide an information access telephone service which describes or depicts, directly or indirectly, sexual conduct or activity or which contains sexually suggestive content unless access to such service is restricted to persons eighteen years of age or older and requires that the service is provided by subscription through the information access telephone service provider.

E. An information access telephone service provider shall not provide recorded announcements or live programs which forward or refer callers to telephone numbers which are not 976 service or 676 service for the purpose of the type of services provided by 976 service or 676 service.

F. In this section:

1. "Information access telephone service" means telephone service and facilities which provide access to a provider-sponsored prerecorded or live announcement or program and which is commonly referred to as "976 service" or "676 service".

2. "Provider" means a person, partnership, corporation or organization that contracts with a telecommunications corporation to transport telephone calls, bill customers or collect charges for a prerecorded or live announcement or program.

3. "Adjustment" means a waiver of all unpaid charges incurred by the residential customer for information access telephone services up to the time the customer contacts the telecommunications corporation and requests the adjustment.

G. A person who violates this section is guilty of a class 3 misdemeanor.

13-2921. Harassment; classification; definition

A. A person commits harassment if, with intent to harass or with knowledge that the person is harassing another person, the person:

1. Anonymously or otherwise contacts, communicates or causes a communication with another person by verbal, electronic, mechanical, telegraphic, telephonic or written means in a manner that harasses.

2. Continues to follow another person in or about a public place for no legitimate purpose after being asked to desist.

3. Repeatedly commits an act or acts that harass another person.

4. Surveils or causes another person to surveil a person for no legitimate purpose.

5. On more than one occasion makes a false report to a law enforcement, credit or social service agency.

6. Interferes with the delivery of any public or regulated utility to a person.

B. A person commits harassment against a public officer or employee if the person, with intent to harass, files a nonconsensual lien against any public officer or employee that is not accompanied by an order or a judgment from a court of competent jurisdiction authorizing the filing of the lien or is not issued by a governmental entity or political subdivision or agency pursuant to its statutory authority, a validly licensed utility or water delivery company, a mechanics' lien claimant or an entity created under covenants, conditions, restrictions or declarations affecting real property.

C. Harassment under subsection A is a class 1 misdemeanor. Harassment under subsection B is a class 5 felony.

D. This section does not apply to an otherwise lawful demonstration, assembly or picketing.

E. For the purposes of this section, "harassment" means conduct that is directed at a specific person and that would cause a reasonable person to be seriously alarmed, annoyed or harassed and the conduct in fact seriously alarms, annoys or harasses the person.

13-2921.01. Aggravated harassment; classification; definition

A. A person commits aggravated harassment if the person commits harassment as provided in section 13-2921 and any of the following applies:

1. A court has issued an order of protection or an injunction against harassment against the person and in favor of the victim of harassment and the order or injunction has been served and is still valid.

2. The person has previously been convicted of an offense included in section 13-3601.

B. The victim of any previous offense shall be the same as in the present offense.

C. A person who violates subsection A, paragraph 1 of this section is guilty of a class 6 felony. A person who commits a second or subsequent violation of subsection A, paragraph 1 of this section is guilty of a class 5 felony. A person who violates subsection A, paragraph 2 of this section is guilty of a class 5 felony.

D. For the purposes of this section, "convicted" means a person who was convicted of an offense included in section 13-3601 or who was adjudicated delinquent for conduct that would constitute a historical prior felony conviction if the juvenile had been tried as an adult for an offense included in section 13-3601.

13-2922. Interference with transmissions on public safety land mobile radio frequencies; classification; definitions

A. It is unlawful for a person to recklessly interrupt, impede or otherwise directly interfere with emergency communications over a public safety land mobile radio frequency communications network or system created for emergency communications.

B. It is unlawful for a person to recklessly interrupt, impede or otherwise interfere with the transmission of a nonemergency communication over a public safety land mobile radio frequency that is dedicated to the dispatch of police, fire or emergency medical response personnel to the scene of an emergency or dedicated to use for emergency communications.

C. A person who violates subsection A is guilty of a class 6 felony. A person who violates subsection B is guilty of a class 1 misdemeanor.

D. As used in this section:

1. "Emergency" means a situation in which a person is or is reasonably believed by the person transmitting the communication to be in imminent danger of serious physical injury or in which property is or is reasonably believed by the person transmitting the communication to be in imminent danger of damage or destruction.

2. "Public safety land mobile radio frequency" means a frequency prescribed in 47 Code of Federal Regulations part 90, subpart B and part 97, subpart A.

3. "Public safety land mobile radio frequency communications network or system" means those radio services and emergency communications systems that are prescribed in 47 Code of Federal Regulations part 90, subpart B and part 97, subpart A.

13-2923. Stalking; classification; exceptions; definitions

A. A person commits stalking if the person intentionally or knowingly engages in a course of conduct that is directed toward another person and if that conduct causes the victim to:
1. Suffer emotional distress or reasonably fear that either:
(a) The victim's property will be damaged or destroyed.
(b) Any of the following will be physically injured:
(i) The victim.
(ii) The victim's family member, domestic animal or livestock.
(iii) A person with whom the victim has or has previously had a romantic or sexual relationship.
(iv) A person who regularly resides in the victim's household or has resided in the victim's household within the six months before the last conduct occurred.
2. Reasonably fear death or the death of any of the following:
(a) The victim's family member, domestic animal or livestock.
(b) A person with whom the victim has or has previously had a romantic or sexual relationship.
(c) A person who regularly resides in the victim's household or has resided in the victim's household within the six months before the last conduct occurred.
B. This section does not apply to an interactive computer service, as defined in 47 United States Code section 230(f)(2), or to an information service or telecommunications service, as defined in 47 United States Code section 153, for content that is provided by another person.

C. Stalking under subsection A, paragraph 1 of this section is a class 5 felony. Stalking under subsection A, paragraph 2 of this section is a class 3 felony.

D. For the purposes of this section:

1. "Course of conduct":

(a) Means directly or indirectly, in person or through one or more third persons or by any other means, to do any of the following:

(i) Maintain visual or physical proximity to a specific person or direct verbal, written or other threats, whether express or implied, to a specific person on two or more occasions over a period of time, however short.

(ii) Use any electronic, digital or global positioning system device to surveil a specific person or a specific person's internet or wireless activity continuously for twelve hours or more or on two or more occasions over a period of time, however short, without authorization.

(iii) Communicate, or cause to be communicated, on more than one occasion words, images or language by or through the use of electronic mail or an electronic communication that is directed at a specific person without authorization and without a legitimate purpose.

(b) Does not include constitutionally protected activity or other activity authorized by law, the other person, the other person's authorized representative or if the other person is a minor, the minor's parent or guardian.

2. "Emotional distress" means significant mental suffering or distress that may, but does not have to, require medical or other professional treatment or counseling.

13-2924. Unlawful solicitation of tort victims; classification; definitions

A. Except as otherwise provided by law, a person commits unlawful solicitation of a tort victim if the person knowingly does any of the following at the scene of any accident that may result in a civil action, criminal action or claim for tort damages by or against another person:

1. Solicits a tort victim if the person receives or expects to receive compensation as a result of the solicitation.

2. Offers or provides compensation to another person for the solicitation of a tort victim.

3. Requests or accepts compensation for the solicitation of a tort victim.

B. This section does not prohibit or restrict any of the following:

1. The solicitation of motor vehicle repair or storage services by a towing company.

2. Police, fire or emergency medical personnel who are engaged in activity which is within the normal scope of duty for their respective occupation or profession.

3. The tort victim from communicating with the tort victim's insurer regarding the investigation of a claim or settlement of any property damage claim.

C. The tort victim may void any contract, agreement or obligation that is made, obtained, procured or incurred in violation of this section.

D. A person who violates this section is guilty of a class 1 misdemeanor.

E. For the purposes of this section:

1. "Compensation" means the direct or indirect promise or payment of any fee, salary, wage, commission, bonus, rebate, refund, dividend or discount.

2. "Solicit" or "solicitation" means directly or indirectly either:

(a) Touting, promoting, recommending, suggesting or offering services or goods to a tort victim.

(b) Selecting, obtaining or procuring services or goods for a tort victim.

3. "Tort victim" means any of the following:

(a) A person whose property has been damaged as a result of any accident that may result in a civil action, criminal action or claim for tort damages by or against another person.

(b) A person who has been injured or killed as a result of any accident that may result in a civil action, criminal action or claim for tort damages by or against another person.

(c) A parent, guardian, spouse, sibling or child of a person who has died as a result of any accident that may result in a civil action, criminal action or claim for tort damages by or against another person.

13-2926. Abandonment or concealment of a dead body; classification

A. It is unlawful for a person to knowingly move a dead human body or parts of a human body with the intent to abandon or conceal the dead human body or parts.

B. This section does not apply to the disposition, transportation or other handling of dead human remains for any purpose authorized under title 32, chapter 12, title 32, chapter 20, article 6 and title 36, chapters 3 and 7.
C. A person who violates this section is guilty of a class 5 felony.

13-2927. Unlawful feeding of wildlife; classification

A. A person commits unlawful feeding of wildlife by intentionally, knowingly or recklessly feeding, attracting or otherwise enticing wildlife into an area, except for:
1. Persons lawfully taking or holding wildlife pursuant to title 17 or pursuant to rules or orders of the Arizona game and fish commission.
2. Public employees or authorized agents acting within the scope of their authority for public safety or for wildlife management purposes.
3. Normal agricultural or livestock operational practices.
4. Tree squirrels or birds.
B. This section applies in a county with a population of more than two hundred eighty thousand persons.
C. Unlawful feeding of wildlife is a petty offense.

13-2928. Unlawful stopping to hire and pick up passengers for work; unlawful application, solicitation or employment; classification; definitions

A. It is unlawful for an occupant of a motor vehicle that is stopped on a street, roadway or highway to attempt to hire or hire and pick up passengers for work at a different location if the motor vehicle blocks or impedes the normal movement of traffic.
B. It is unlawful for a person to enter a motor vehicle that is stopped on a street, roadway or highway in order to be hired by an occupant of the motor vehicle and to be transported to work at a different location if the motor vehicle blocks or impedes the normal movement of traffic.
C. It is unlawful for a person who is unlawfully present in the United States and who is an unauthorized alien to knowingly apply for work, solicit work in a public place or perform work as an employee or independent contractor in this state.
D. A law enforcement official or agency of this state or a county, city, town or other political subdivision of this state may not consider race, color or national origin in the enforcement of this section except to the extent permitted by the United States or Arizona Constitution.
E. In the enforcement of this section, an alien's immigration status may be determined by:
1. A law enforcement officer who is authorized by the federal government to verify or ascertain an alien's immigration status.
2. The United States immigration and customs enforcement or the United States customs and border protection pursuant to 8 United States Code section 1373(c).
F. A violation of this section is a class 1 misdemeanor.
G. For the purposes of this section:
1. "Solicit" means verbal or nonverbal communication by a gesture or a nod that would indicate to a reasonable person that a person is willing to be employed.
2. "Unauthorized alien" means an alien who does not have the legal right or authorization under federal law to work in the United States as described in 8 United States Code section 1324a(h)(3).

13-2929. Unlawful transporting, moving, concealing, harboring or shielding of unlawful aliens; vehicle impoundment; exception; classification

A. It is unlawful for a person who is in violation of a criminal offense to:
1. Transport or move or attempt to transport or move an alien in this state, in furtherance of the illegal presence of the alien in the United States, in a means of transportation if the person knows or recklessly disregards the fact that the alien has come to, has entered or remains in the United States in violation of law.
2. Conceal, harbor or shield or attempt to conceal, harbor or shield an alien from detection in any place in this state, including any building or any means of transportation, if the person knows or recklessly disregards the fact that the alien has come to, has entered or remains in the United States in violation of law.

3. Encourage or induce an alien to come to or reside in this state if the person knows or recklessly disregards the fact that such coming to, entering or residing in this state is or will be in violation of law.

B. A means of transportation that is used in the commission of a violation of this section is subject to mandatory vehicle immobilization or impoundment pursuant to section 28-3511.

C. A law enforcement official or agency of this state or a county, city, town or other political subdivision of this state may not consider race, color or national origin in the enforcement of this section except to the extent permitted by the United States or Arizona Constitution.

D. In the enforcement of this section, an alien's immigration status may be determined by:

1. A law enforcement officer who is authorized by the federal government to verify or ascertain an alien's immigration status.

2. The United States immigration and customs enforcement or the United States customs and border protection pursuant to 8 United States Code section 1373(c).

E. This section does not apply to a child safety worker acting in the worker's official capacity or a person who is acting in the capacity of a first responder, an ambulance attendant or an emergency medical technician and who is transporting or moving an alien in this state pursuant to title 36, chapter 21.1.

F. A person who violates this section is guilty of a class 1 misdemeanor and is subject to a fine of at least one thousand dollars, except that a violation of this section that involves ten or more illegal aliens is a class 6 felony and the person is subject to a fine of at least one thousand dollars for each alien who is involved.

13-2930. Unlawful funeral or burial protest activities; classification; definition

A. A person shall not picket or engage in other protest activities, and an association or corporation shall not cause picketing or other protest activities to occur, within three hundred feet of the property line of any residence, cemetery, funeral home, church, synagogue or other establishment during or within one hour before or one hour after the conducting of a funeral or burial service at that place.

B. A person who violates this section is guilty of a class 1 misdemeanor.

C. For the purposes of this section, "other protest activities" means any action that is disruptive or that is undertaken to disrupt or disturb a funeral or burial service.

Chapter 30 Eavesdroppings and Communications

13-3001. Definitions

In this chapter, unless the context otherwise requires:

1. "Aural transfer" means a communication containing the human voice at any point between and including the point of origin and the point of reception.

2. "Child monitoring device" means a device that is capable of transmitting an audio or audiovisual signal and that is installed or used in a residence for child supervision or safety monitoring by any parent, guardian or other responsible person in the person's own residence.

3. "Communication service provider" means any person who is engaged in providing a service that allows its users to send or receive oral, wire or electronic communications or computer services.

4. "Electronic communication" means any transfer of signs, signals, writing, images, sounds, data or intelligence of any nature that is transmitted in whole or in part by a wire, radio, electromagnetic, photoelectronic or photooptical system but that does not include any of the following:

(a) Any wire or oral communication.

(b) Any communication made through a tone-only paging device.

(c) Any communication from a tracking device.

5. "Electronic communication system" means any communication or computer facilities or related electronic equipment for the transmission, processing or electronic storage of electronic communications.

6. "Electronic storage" means either of the following:

(a) Any temporary, intermediate storage of a wire or electronic communication incidental to the electronic transmission.

(b) Any storage of the communication by an electronic communication service provider for purposes of backup protection of the communication.

7. "Intercept" means the aural or other acquisition of the contents of any wire, electronic or oral communication through the use of any electronic, mechanical or other device.

8. "Oral communication" means a spoken communication that is uttered by a person who exhibits an expectation that the communication is not subject to interception under circumstances justifying the expectation but does not include any electronic communication.

9. "Pen register" means a device or process that records or decodes electronic or other impulses that identify the numbers dialed or otherwise transmitted on the telephone line or communication facility to which the device is attached or the dialing, routing, addressing or signaling information that is transmitted by an instrument or facility from which a wire or electronic communication is transmitted but does not include the contents of any communication, except when used in connection with a court order issued pursuant to section 13-3010 or 13-3012. A pen register does not include a publicly available device or process that is otherwise not unlawful.

10. "Person" means any individual, enterprise, public or private corporation, unincorporated association, partnership, firm, society, governmental authority or entity, including the subscriber to the communication service involved, and any law enforcement officer.

11. "Readily accessible to the general public" means a radio communication that is not:

(a) Scrambled or encrypted.

(b) Transmitted using modulation techniques with essential parameters that have been withheld from the public to preserve the privacy of the communication.

(c) Carried on a subcarrier or other signal subsidiary to a radio transmission.

(d) Transmitted over a communication system provided by a common carrier, unless the communication is a tone-only paging system communication.

(e) Transmitted on frequencies allocated under part 25, subpart D, E or F or part 74 or part 94 of the rules of the federal communications commission. If a communication transmitted on a frequency allocated under part 74 is not exclusively allocated to broadcast auxiliary services, the communication is a two-way voice communication system by radio.

12. "Remote computing service" means providing to the public any computer storage or processing services by means of an electronic communication system.

13. "Trap and trace device" means a device or process that captures the incoming electronic or other impulses that identify the originating number of an instrument or device from which a wire or electronic communication was transmitted or the dialing, routing, addressing and signaling information that is reasonably likely to identify the source of a wire or electronic communication but does not include the content of any communication, except when used in connection with a court order issued pursuant to section 13-3010 or 13-3012. A trap and trace device does not include a publicly available device or process that is otherwise not unlawful.

14. "Wire communication" means any aural transfer that is made in whole or in part through the use of facilities for the transmission of communications by the aid of any wire, cable or other like connection between the point of origin and the point of reception, including the use of a connection in a switching station, and that is furnished or operated by any person who is engaged in providing or operating the facilities for the transmission of communications.

13-3002. False or forged messages; classification

A. It is unlawful for a person:

1. Knowingly to send to any person by telegraph or telephone a false or forged message, purporting to be from a telegraph or telephone office, or from any other person.

2. Knowingly to deliver or cause to be delivered to any person a false or forged message, falsely purporting to have been received by telegraph or telephone.

3. To furnish or conspire to furnish, or cause to be furnished to an agent, operator or employee, to be sent by telegraph or telephone, or to be delivered, a message, knowing it is false or forged, with intent to deceive, injure or defraud another.

B. A person who violates this section is guilty of a class 1 misdemeanor.

13-3003. Opening, reading or publishing sealed letter of another without authority; classification

A person who knowingly opens or reads or causes to be read a sealed letter not addressed to himself, without being authorized so to do either by the writer of such letter, or by the person to whom it is addressed, or a person who, without like authority, publishes the contents of such letter, knowing it to have been unlawfully opened, is guilty of a class 2 misdemeanor.

13-3004. Sending threatening or anonymous letter; classification

A person who knowingly sends or delivers to another a letter or writing, whether subscribed or not, threatening to accuse him or another of a crime, or to expose or publish his failings or infirmities, and a writer or sender of an anonymous letter or writing calculated to create distrust of another or tending to impute dishonesty, want of chastity, drunkenness or any crime or infirmity to the receiver of the letter or to any other person, is guilty of a class 2 misdemeanor.

13-3005. Interception of wire, electronic and oral communications; installation of pen register or trap and trace device; classification; exceptions

A. Except as provided in this section and section 13-3012, a person is guilty of a class 5 felony who either:
1. Intentionally intercepts a wire or electronic communication to which he is not a party, or aids, authorizes, employs, procures or permits another to so do, without the consent of either a sender or receiver thereof.
2. Intentionally intercepts a conversation or discussion at which he is not present, or aids, authorizes, employs, procures or permits another to so do, without the consent of a party to such conversation or discussion.
3. Intentionally intercepts the deliberations of a jury or aids, authorizes, employs, procures or permits another to so do.
B. Except as provided in sections 13-3012 and 13-3017, a person who intentionally and without lawful authority installs or uses a pen register or trap and trace device on the telephone lines or communications facilities of another person which are utilized for wire or electronic communication is guilty of a class 6 felony.

13-3006. Divulging communication service information; classification; exception

A person is guilty of a class 6 felony who either:
1. Intentionally and without lawful authority obtains any knowledge of the contents of a wire or electronic communication by connivance with a communication service provider or its officer or employee.
2. Is a communications service provider, officer or employee of a communications service provider and intentionally divulges to anyone but the person for whom it was intended, except with the permission of the sender or the person for whom it was intended or in any case covered by the exemption in section 13-3012, the contents or the nature of a wire or electronic communication entrusted to the communications service provider for transmission or delivery.

13-3008. Possession of interception devices; classification

A. It is unlawful for a person to have in his possession or control any device, contrivance, machine or apparatus designed or primarily useful for the interception of wire, electronic or oral communications as defined in section 13-3001 with the intent to unlawfully use or employ or allow the device, contrivance, machine or apparatus to be used or employed for the interception, or having reason to know the device, contrivance, machine or apparatus is intended to be so used.
B. All property possessed or controlled by any person in violation of this section is subject to seizure and forfeiture pursuant to chapter 39 of this title.
C. A person who violates this section is guilty of a class 6 felony.

13-3009. Duty to report to law enforcement officers; classification

It shall be the duty of every communications service provider and its officers and employees to report any violation of sections 13-3005, 13-3006 and 13-3008 coming within their knowledge to the county attorney having jurisdiction and to the attorney general. Any intentional violation of this section is a class 3 misdemeanor.

13-3010. Ex parte order for interception; definition

A. On application of a county attorney, the attorney general or a prosecuting attorney whom a county attorney or the attorney general designates in writing, any justice of the supreme court, judge of the court of appeals or superior court judge may issue an ex parte order for the interception of wire, electronic or oral communications if there is probable cause to believe both:

1. A crime has been, is being or is about to be committed.

2. Evidence of that crime or the location of a fugitive from justice from that crime may be obtained by the interception.

B. An application under subsection A shall be made in writing and upon the oath or affirmation of the applicant. It shall include:

1. The name and title of the applicant.

2. A full and complete statement of the facts and circumstances relied upon by the applicant, including the supporting oath or affirmation of the investigating peace officer of this state or any political subdivision of this state to justify the officer's belief that an order should be issued. The statement shall include:

(a) Details as to the particular crime that has been, is being or is about to be committed.

(b) The identity of the person, if known, committing the offense and whose communications are to be intercepted.

(c) A particular description of the type of communications sought to be intercepted.

(d) A particular description of the nature, identification and location of the communication facility from which or the place where the communication is to be intercepted. If the identification or specific description of the communication facility from which or the place where the communication is to be intercepted is not practical, the affidavit in support of the application must state why:

(i) Specification is impractical.

(ii) Interception from any facility or at any place where the communication may occur is necessary.

3. A full and complete statement as to whether or not other investigative procedures have been tried and failed or why they reasonably appear to be unlikely to succeed if tried or to be too dangerous.

4. A statement of the period of time for which the interception is required to be maintained. If the nature of the investigation is such that authorization to intercept should not automatically terminate when the described type of communication has been first obtained, the statement shall include a particular description of facts establishing probable cause to believe that additional communications of the same type will occur after the communication has been first obtained.

5. A full and complete statement of the facts concerning all previous applications known to the individual authorizing and making the application, made to any judge for authorization to intercept, or for approval of interceptions of communications involving any of the same persons, facilities or places specified in the application, and the action taken by the judge on each application.

6. If the application is for the extension of an order, a statement setting forth the results thus far obtained from the interception, or a reasonable explanation of the failure to obtain such results.

C. Upon proper application, a judge may enter an ex parte order authorizing interception, as requested or with any appropriate modifications, if the judge determines on the basis of the facts submitted by the applicant that:

1. There is probable cause to believe that a person is committing, has committed or is about to commit a particular crime.

2. There is probable cause to believe that particular communications concerning that offense will be obtained through the interception.

3. Normal investigative procedures have been tried and have failed or reasonably appear to be unlikely to succeed if tried or to be too dangerous.

4. There is probable cause to believe any of the following:

(a) Wire or electronic communications concerning the offense are being made or are about to be made by the person over the communication facilities for which interception authority is granted.

(b) Oral communications concerning the offense are being made or are about to be made by the person in the location for which interception authority is granted.

(c) Communications concerning the offense are being made or are about to be made by the person in different and changing locations, or from different and changing facilities.

D. Each order authorizing the interception of any wire, electronic or oral communication shall specify all of the following:

1. The identity of the person, if known, whose communications are to be intercepted.

2. The nature and location of the communication facilities as to which or the place where authority to intercept is granted. If authority is granted to intercept communications of a person wherever that person is located or from whatever communication facility is used, the order shall so state and shall include any limitations imposed by the authorizing judge as to location, time or manner of the interception. The order shall state that the interception shall not begin until the facilities from which or the place where the communication is to be intercepted is ascertained by the person implementing the interception order.

3. A particular description of the type of communication sought to be intercepted and a statement of the particular offense to which it relates.

4. The identity of the agency authorized to intercept the communications and of the person authorizing the application.

5. The period of time during which the interception is authorized, including a statement as to whether or not the interception shall automatically terminate when the described communication has been first obtained.

6. That the authorization for interception be executed as soon as practicable, that it be conducted in such a way as to minimize the interception of communications not otherwise subject to interception under this section and that it terminate upon attainment of the authorized objective or on the date specified, whichever comes first.

7. That entry may be made to service, install or remove interception devices or equipment if entry is necessary to effect the interception.

E. An order that is entered under this section may not authorize the interception of any wire or oral communication for any period that is longer than is necessary to achieve the objective of the authorization and that exceeds thirty days. This thirty day period begins on the earlier of the day on which the interception actually begins under the order or ten days after the order is signed. The court may grant extensions of any order if an application for an extension is made pursuant to subsection A and the court makes the findings required by subsection C. The period of extension shall be no longer than the authorizing judge deems necessary to achieve the purposes for which it was granted and shall not exceed thirty days.

F. Any ex parte order for interception, together with the papers on which the application was based, shall be delivered to and retained by the applicant during the duration of the interception as authority for the interception authorized in the order. The justice or judge issuing the order shall retain a true copy of the order at all times.

G. Within ten days after the termination of the authorized interception, applications made and orders granted under this section shall be returned to and sealed by the judge. Custody of the applications and orders shall be wherever the judge directs. The applications and orders shall be disclosed only on a showing of good cause before a judge of competent jurisdiction or as otherwise provided.

H. If possible, the contents of any communication that is intercepted by any means authorized by this section shall be recorded on any tape, electronic, wire or other comparable device. The recording of the contents of any wire, electronic or oral communication under this subsection shall be done in such a way as will protect the recording from editing or alterations. Within ten days after the termination of the authorized interception, the recordings shall be made available to the judge who issued the order and shall be sealed under the judge's directions. Custody of the recordings shall be maintained pursuant to court order. The recordings shall be kept for ten years and shall not be destroyed except on an order of the issuing judge or another judge of competent jurisdiction.

I. Within ninety days after an application under subsection A is denied, or the period of an order or any extension expires, the issuing or denying judge shall serve the persons named in the order or application and any other parties to the intercepted communications as the judge may determine the interests of justice require with an inventory, including notice of all of the following:

1. The fact of the entry of the order or the application.

2. The date of the entry and the period of authorized interception, or the denial of the application.

3. The fact that during the period of authorized interception wire, electronic or oral communications were or were not intercepted. On motion, the judge may make available to the person or the person's attorney for inspection such portions of the intercepted communications, applications and order as the judge determines to be in the interest of justice. On an ex parte showing of good cause to the judge, the serving of the notice required by this subsection may be postponed.

J. On request of the applicant, any order authorizing interception shall direct that the communication service provider, landlords, custodians or other persons furnish the applicant with all information, facilities and technical assistance necessary to accomplish the interception unobtrusively and with a minimum of interference with the services that these persons are according the person whose communications are to be intercepted.

K. The order may require written reports to be made to the issuing judge at specified intervals showing the progress made toward achieving the authorized objective and the need for continued interception.

L. Any order authorizing the interception of wire communications pursuant to this chapter is also deemed to authorize the interception of any electronic communication that may be made over the same equipment or by the same facility.

M. If the intercepted communication is in a code or foreign language and an expert in that code or foreign language is not reasonably available during the interception period, minimization may be accomplished as soon as practicable after the interception.

N. An interception under this chapter may be conducted in whole or in part by government personnel or by an individual operating under a contract with the government or acting under the supervision of a law enforcement officer who is authorized to conduct the interception.

O. The applicant is responsible for providing to the administrative office of the United States courts all reports on applications for or interceptions of wire, electronic or oral communications that are required by federal statutes.

P. For the purposes of this section, "crime" means murder, gaming, kidnapping, robbery, bribery, extortion, theft, an act in violation of chapter 23 of this title, dealing in narcotic drugs, marijuana or dangerous drugs, sexual exploitation of children in violation of chapter 35.1 of this title or any felony that is dangerous to life, limb or property. Crime includes conspiracy to commit any of the offenses listed in this subsection.

13-3011. Disclosing confidential information relating to ex parte order; exceptions; classification

A. Except in any trial, hearing or other judicial proceeding, a person shall not knowingly disclose to another person any information concerning either:
1. The application for or the granting or denial of orders for the interception or installation of a pen register or trap and trace device or a request for the preservation of records or evidence pursuant to section 13-3016 or a subpoena issued pursuant to section 13-3018.
2. The identity of the person or persons whose communications are the subject of an ex parte order, subpoena or records preservation request granted pursuant to sections 13-3010, 13-3015, 13-3016, 13-3017 and 13-3018.
B. Subsection A of this section does not apply to the disclosure of information to the communication service provider whose facilities are involved or to an employee or other authorized agent of the county attorney, attorney general or law enforcement agency that applies for an order permitting interception or installation of a pen register or trap and trace device or who requests the preservation of records or evidence pursuant to section 13-3016 or a subpoena issued pursuant to section 13-3018.
C. Notwithstanding subsection A of this section, a peace officer or prosecuting attorney who obtains knowledge of the contents of a wire, electronic or oral communication as authorized by sections 13-3010, 13-3015, 13-3016, 13-3017 and 13-3018 or evidence derived from that knowledge may:
1. Disclose the contents of the communication to a peace officer or prosecuting attorney to the extent the disclosure is appropriate to the proper performance of the official duties of the peace officer or prosecuting attorney making or receiving the disclosure.
2. Use the contents of the communication to the extent that the use is appropriate to the proper performance of the official duties of the peace officer or prosecuting attorney.
D. A person who violates this section is guilty of a class 1 misdemeanor.

13-3012. Exemptions

The following are exempt from the provisions of this chapter:
1. The interception of wire, electronic or oral communications, the installation and operation of a pen register or trap and trace device, the providing of information, facilities or technical assistance to an investigative or law enforcement officer pursuant to a subpoena or an ex parte order granted pursuant to sections 13-3010, 13-3015, 13-3016, 13-3017 and 13-3018 or an emergency interception made in good faith pursuant to section 13-3015, including any of the foregoing acts by a communication service provider or its officers, agents or employees.
2. The normal use of services, equipment and facilities that are provided by a communication service provider pursuant to tariffs that are on file with the Arizona corporation commission or the federal communications commission and the normal functions of any operator of a switchboard.
3. Any officer, agent or employee of a communication service provider who performs acts that are otherwise prohibited by this article in providing, constructing, maintaining, repairing, operating or using the provider's services, equipment or facilities, protecting the provider's service, equipment and facilities from illegal use in violation of tariffs that are on file with the Arizona corporation commission or the federal communications commission and protecting the provider from the commission of fraud against it.
4. Providing requested information or any other response to a subpoena or other order that is issued by a court of competent jurisdiction or on demand of any other lawful authority.
5. The interception of wire or electronic communications or the use of a pen register or trap and trace device by a communication service provider or by a person providing technical assistance at the request of the communication service provider if the interception or use either:
(a) Relates to the operation, maintenance and testing of that service, the protection of the rights or property of the provider or the protection of users of that service from fraudulent, abusive or unlawful use of that service.
(b) Records the fact that a wire or electronic communication was initiated or completed in order to protect the provider, another provider furnishing service toward the completion of the communication or a user of that service from fraudulent, unlawful or abusive use of that service.
6. The interception of any radio communication that is transmitted:
(a) By any station for the use of the general public or if the transmission relates to ships, aircraft, vehicles or persons in distress.

(b) By any government, law enforcement, civil defense, private land mobile or public safety communication system, including police and fire systems, and that is readily accessible to the general public.

(c) By any station that operates on an authorized frequency within the bands that are allocated to the amateur, citizens band or general mobile radio services.

(d) By any marine or aeronautical communications system.

(e) Through a system using frequencies that are monitored by persons who are engaged in the provision or the use of the system or by other persons who use the same frequency if the communication is not scrambled or encrypted.

7. The interception of wire or electronic communication if the transmission is causing harmful interference to any lawfully operating station or consumer electronic equipment, to the extent necessary to identify the source of the interference.

8. The use of a pen register or trap and trace device by a communication service provider for billing or recording as an incident to billing for communication services, or for cost accounting or other like purposes in the ordinary course of business.

9. The interception of any wire, electronic or oral communication by any person, if the interception is effected with the consent of a party to the communication or a person who is present during the communication, or the installation of a pen register or trap and trace device with the consent of a user or subscriber to the service.

10. Divulging the contents of a wire or electronic communication and any related records or information to a law enforcement agency by a remote computing service or communication service provider, officer or employee if either:

(a) The contents, records or information were lawfully or inadvertently obtained by the service provider and appear to pertain to the commission of a crime.

(b) The provider reasonably believes that an emergency involving immediate danger of death or serious physical injury to any person justifies the disclosure of the contents, records or information without delay.

11. Divulging records or other information that pertains to a customer or subscriber by a remote computing service or communication service provider, other than the contents of a communication, either:

(a) As authorized by section 13-3016.

(b) With the customer's or subscriber's consent.

(c) As may be necessary incident to the rendition of the service or for the protection of the rights or property of the provider of that service.

(d) To any person other than a governmental agency.

12. The interception or access of an electronic communication that is made through an electronic communication system and that is configured so that the electronic communication is readily accessible to the general public.

13. For other users of the same frequency to intercept a radio communication that is made through a system that uses frequencies that are monitored by individuals who provide or use the system, if the communication is not scrambled or encrypted.

14. The interception of oral communications by means of a child monitoring device.

13-3013. Defenses

The following constitute a complete defense to any civil or criminal action brought under this chapter or under any other law:

1. A good faith reliance on an ex parte order or subpoena that is issued pursuant to section 13-3010, 13-3015, 13-3016, 13-3017 or 13-3018.

2. Providing information pursuant to section 13-3012.

3. Providing assistance, information or facilities for an emergency interception pursuant to section 13-3015.

4. Disclosing stored electronic communications or preserving records, content or evidence pursuant to section 13-3016.

5. Providing equipment, information or assistance to render stored electronic communications in a usable form pursuant to section 13-3016.

13-3014. Communication service provider; right to compensation

Any communication service provider who furnishes information, facilities or technical assistance pursuant to this chapter shall be compensated therefor by the applicant at the prevailing rates.

13-3015. Emergency interception

A. Notwithstanding any other provision of this chapter, if the attorney general or a county attorney or such prosecuting attorneys as they may designate in writing reasonably determines that an emergency situation exists involving immediate danger of death or serious physical injury to any person, and that such death or serious physical injury may be averted by interception of wire, electronic or oral communications before an order authorizing such interception can be obtained, the attorney general or a county attorney or his designee may specially authorize a peace officer or law enforcement agency to intercept such wire, electronic or oral communications.

B. The attorney general or county attorney or his designee specially authorizing an emergency interception pursuant to subsection A of this section shall apply for an order authorizing the interception, in accordance with the provisions of section 13-3010. The application shall be made as soon as practicable, and in no event later than forty-eight hours after commencement of the emergency interception. The application shall include an explanation and summary of any interception of communications occurring before the application for authorization.

C. If the prosecuting attorney fails to obtain an authorization within forty-eight hours after commencement of the emergency interception, or if authorization to intercept communications is denied, the interception shall immediately terminate and any communications intercepted without judicial authorization may not be used as evidence in any criminal or civil proceeding against any person. In either event, the prosecuting attorney shall furnish to the court an inventory of any communications intercepted, for service pursuant to the provisions of section 13-3010, subsection I. The provisions of this subsection do not prohibit the use as evidence of any communications intercepted without judicial authorization against the persons conducting or authorizing the interceptions if such interceptions were not made in good faith reliance on this section.

13-3016. Stored oral, wire and electronic communications; agency access; backup preservation; delayed notice; records preservation request; violation; classification

A. This section applies to oral, wire and electronic communications that are entrusted to a communication service provider or remote computing service solely for the purpose of transmission, storage or processing. Oral, wire and electronic communications that are in the possession of a person who is entitled to access the contents of such communications for any purpose other than transmission, storage or processing are ordinary business records that may be obtained by subpoena or court order.

B. An agency or political subdivision of this state may require the disclosure by a communication service provider or remote computing service of the contents of an oral, wire or electronic communication that has been in electronic storage for one hundred eighty days or less in one of the following ways:

1. Without prior notice to the subscriber or party, by obtaining a search warrant issued pursuant to chapter 38, article 8 of this title.

2. With prior notice to the subscriber or party, by serving a subpoena, except that notice may be delayed pursuant to subsection D of this section.

3. With prior notice to the subscriber or party, by obtaining a court order on an application and certification that contains specific and articulable facts showing that there are reasonable grounds to believe that the communication content sought is relevant to an ongoing criminal investigation, except that notice may be delayed pursuant to subsection D of this section.

C. An agency or political subdivision of this state may require the disclosure by a communication service provider or remote computing service of the contents of an oral, wire or electronic communication that has been in electronic storage for more than one hundred eighty days in one of the following ways:

1. Without notice to the subscriber or party, by obtaining a search warrant issued pursuant to chapter 38, article 8 of this title.

2. With prior notice to the subscriber or party, by serving a subpoena, except that notice may be delayed pursuant to subsection D of this section.

3. With prior notice to the subscriber or party, by obtaining a court order on an application and certification that contains specific and articulable facts showing that there are reasonable grounds to believe that the communication content sought is relevant to an ongoing criminal investigation, except that notice may be delayed pursuant to subsection D of this section.

D. Except as provided in subsection E of this section, the notice to the subscriber or party that is required by this section may be delayed for a period of not to exceed ninety days under any of the following circumstances:

1. If the applicant for a search warrant or court order pursuant to this section requests a delay of notification and the court finds that delay is necessary to protect the safety of any person or to prevent flight from prosecution, tampering with evidence, intimidation of witnesses or jeopardizing an investigation.

2. If the investigator or prosecuting attorney proceeding by subpoena executes a written certification that there is reason to believe that notice to the subscriber or party may result in danger to the safety of any person, flight from prosecution, tampering with evidence, intimidation of witnesses or jeopardizing an investigation. The agency shall retain a true copy of the certification with the subpoena.

E. If further delay of notification is necessary, extensions of up to ninety days each may be obtained by application to the court or certification pursuant to subsection D of this section.

F. Any agency acting pursuant to this section may apply for a court order directing the communication service provider or remote computing service not to notify any other person of the existence of the subpoena, court order or warrant for such period as the court deems appropriate. The court shall grant the application if it finds that there is reason to believe that notice may cause an adverse result described in subsection D of this section. A person who violates an order issued pursuant to this subsection is guilty of a class 1 misdemeanor.

G. On the expiration of any period of delay under this section, the agency shall deliver to the subscriber or party a copy of the process used and notice including:

1. That information was requested from the service provider.

2. The date on which the information was requested.

3. That notification to the subscriber or party was delayed.

4. The identity of the court or agency ordering or certifying the delay.

5. The provision of this section by which delay was obtained.

6. That any challenge to the subpoena or order must be filed within fourteen days.

H. On the request of an agency or political subdivision of this state, a communication service provider or remote computing service shall take all necessary steps to preserve records, communication content and other evidence in its possession pending the issuance of a court order or other process. The communication service provider or remote computing service shall retain the preserved records, communication content and other evidence for ninety days. On the renewed request of an agency or political subdivision, the preservation period may be extended for an additional ninety days. Except as provided in section 13-3011, a person shall not notify the subscriber or party during the period of the preservation request.

13-3017. Ex parte order for pen register or trap and trace device

A. Any prosecuting attorney or investigating peace officer of this state or its political subdivisions may apply to any justice of the supreme court, judge of the court of appeals, judge of the superior court or magistrate for an ex parte order authorizing the installation and use of a pen register or a trap and trace device. The application shall be made in writing and under oath and shall state:

1. The name and title of the applicant.

2. The attributes of the communication, including the number or other identifier, the identity, if known, of the subscriber and, if known, the location of the telephone line or other facility to which the pen register or trap and trace device is to be attached or applied and, if the order authorizes the installation of a trap and trace device, the geographic limits of the order.

3. A certification by the applicant that the information likely to be obtained is relevant to an ongoing criminal investigation.

4. A statement of the offense to which the information likely to be obtained by the pen register or trap and trace device relates.

B. On proper application pursuant to subsection A, the judge shall issue an ex parte order authorizing the installation and use of a pen register or trap and trace device or process if the judge finds that the applicant has certified that the information likely to be obtained by the installation and use is relevant to an ongoing criminal investigation. On service, the order applies to any person or entity that provides wire or electronic communication service in this state or that does business in this state and whose assistance may facilitate the execution of the order. If an order is served on any person or entity that is not specifically named in the order and on request of the person or entity, the prosecuting attorney or peace officer who serves the order shall provide written or electronic certification that the order applies to the person or entity being served. An order that is issued under this subsection shall specify all of the following:

1. The identity, if known, of the subscriber of the communication service or telephone line to which the pen register or trap and trace device is to be attached or applied.

2. The attributes of the communication to which the order applies, including the number or other identifier and, if known, the location of the telephone line or other facility to which the pen register or trap and trace device is to be attached or applied and, if the order authorizes the installation of a trap and trace device, the geographic limits of the order.

3. A statement of the offense to which the information likely to be obtained by the pen register or trap and trace device relates.

4. That, on the request of the applicant, the communication service provider shall furnish information, facilities and technical assistance necessary to accomplish the installation of the pen register or trap and trace device and to identify subscribers of any communication facility or telephone number obtained by operation of such device.

C. An order that is issued under this section authorizes the installation and use of a pen register or trap and trace device for a period of not to exceed sixty days. Extensions of the order may be granted, but only on an application and judicial finding pursuant to subsections A and B. The period of each extension granted shall not exceed sixty days.

13-3018. Communication service records; subpoenas; application; certification; definition

A. This section applies to all communication service providers that do business in this state or that furnish communication services to persons within this state.

B. The prosecutor may issue a subpoena duces tecum to a communication service provider in order to obtain communication service records in connection with a criminal investigation or prosecution for any offense in which a prosecutor suspects that a computer or network was used. This subsection does not prevent the prosecutor from obtaining a grand jury subpoena duces tecum.

C. The prosecutor who issues a subpoena pursuant to this section shall certify in the body of the subpoena that the information likely to be obtained is relevant to an ongoing criminal investigation.

D. An authorized representative of a communication service provider may certify communication service records that are obtained by subpoena if all of the following apply:

1. The records are the regular communication service records that are used and kept by the communication service provider.

2. The records are made at or near the time the underlying communications occur in the ordinary course of business.

3. The authorized representative certifies that the record produced in response to the subpoena is an accurate copy of the communication service provider records.

E. Certified communication service records that are obtained by subpoena may be introduced in evidence at a hearing or trial and constitute prima facie evidence of the facts contained in the records.

F. If a certification of communication service provider records is acknowledged by any notary or other officer who is authorized by law to take acknowledgments, the certification shall be received in evidence without further proof of its authenticity.

G. For the purposes of this section, "communication service records" includes subscriber information, including name, billing or installation address, length of service, payment method, telephone number, electronic account identification and associated screen names, toll bills or access logs, records of the path of an electronic communication between the point of origin and the point of delivery and the nature of the communication service provided, such as caller identification, automatic number identification, voice mail, electronic mail, paging or other service features. Communication service records do not include the content of any stored oral, wire or electronic communication.

13-3019. Surreptitious photographing, videotaping, filming or digitally recording or viewing; exemptions; classification; definitions

A. It is unlawful for any person to knowingly photograph, videotape, film, digitally record or by any other means secretly view, with or without a device, another person without that person's consent under either of the following circumstances:

1. In a restroom, bathroom, locker room, bedroom or other location where the person has a reasonable expectation of privacy and the person is urinating, defecating, dressing, undressing, nude or involved in sexual intercourse or sexual contact.

2. In a manner that directly or indirectly captures or allows the viewing of the person's genitalia, buttock or female breast, whether clothed or unclothed, that is not otherwise visible to the public.

B. It is unlawful to disclose, display, distribute or publish a photograph, videotape, film or digital recording made in violation of subsection A of this section without the consent or knowledge of the person depicted.

C. This section does not apply to:

1. Photographing, videotaping, filming or digitally recording for security purposes if notice of the use of photographing, videotaping, filming or digital recording equipment is clearly posted in the location and the location is one in which the person has a reasonable expectation of privacy.

2. Photographing, videotaping, filming or digitally recording by correctional officials for security reasons or in connection with the investigation of alleged misconduct of persons on the premises of a jail or prison.

3. Photographing, videotaping, filming or digitally recording by law enforcement officers pursuant to an investigation, which is otherwise lawful.

4. The use of a child monitoring device as defined in section 13-3001.

D. A violation of subsection A or B of this section is a class 5 felony.

E. Notwithstanding subsection D of this section, a violation of subsection A or B of this section that does not involve the use of a device is a class 6 felony, except that a second or subsequent violation of subsection A or B of this section that does not involve the use of a device is a class 5 felony.

F. Notwithstanding subsection D of this section, a violation of subsection B of this section is a class 4 felony if the person depicted is recognizable.

G. For the purposes of this section, "sexual contact" and "sexual intercourse" have the same meanings prescribed in section 13-1401.

Chapter 31 Weapons and Explosives

13-3101. Definitions

A. In this chapter, unless the context otherwise requires:

1. "Deadly weapon" means anything that is designed for lethal use. The term includes a firearm.

2. "Deface" means to remove, alter or destroy the manufacturer's serial number.

3. "Explosive" means any dynamite, nitroglycerine, black powder, or other similar explosive material, including plastic explosives. Explosive does not include ammunition or ammunition components such as primers, percussion caps, smokeless powder, black powder and black powder substitutes used for hand loading purposes.

4. "Firearm" means any loaded or unloaded handgun, pistol, revolver, rifle, shotgun or other weapon that will expel, is designed to expel or may readily be converted to expel a projectile by the action of an explosive. Firearm does not include a firearm in permanently inoperable condition.

5. "Improvised explosive device" means a device that incorporates explosives or destructive, lethal, noxious, pyrotechnic or incendiary chemicals and that is designed to destroy, disfigure, terrify or harass.

6. "Occupied structure" means any building, object, vehicle, watercraft, aircraft or place with sides and a floor that is separately securable from any other structure attached to it, that is used for lodging, business, transportation, recreation or storage and in which one or more human beings either are or are likely to be present or so near as to be in equivalent danger at the time the discharge of a firearm occurs. Occupied structure includes any dwelling house, whether occupied, unoccupied or vacant.

7. "Prohibited possessor" means any person:

(a) Who has been found to constitute a danger to self or to others or to have a persistent or acute disability or grave disability pursuant to court order pursuant to section 36-540, and whose right to possess a firearm has not been restored pursuant to section 13-925.

(b) Who has been convicted within or without this state of a felony or who has been adjudicated delinquent for a felony and whose civil right to possess or carry a gun or firearm has not been restored.

(c) Who is at the time of possession serving a term of imprisonment in any correctional or detention facility.

(d) Who is at the time of possession serving a term of probation pursuant to a conviction for a domestic violence offense as defined in section 13-3601 or a felony offense, parole, community supervision, work furlough, home arrest or release on any other basis or who is serving a term of probation or parole pursuant to the interstate compact under title 31, chapter 3, article 4.1.

(e) Who is an undocumented alien or a nonimmigrant alien traveling with or without documentation in this state for business or pleasure or who is studying in this state and who maintains a foreign residence abroad. This subdivision does not apply to:

(i) Nonimmigrant aliens who possess a valid hunting license or permit that is lawfully issued by a state in the United States.

(ii) Nonimmigrant aliens who enter the United States to participate in a competitive target shooting event or to display firearms at a sports or hunting trade show that is sponsored by a national, state or local firearms trade organization devoted to the competitive use or other sporting use of firearms.

(iii) Certain diplomats.

(iv) Officials of foreign governments or distinguished foreign visitors who are designated by the United States department of state.

(v) Persons who have received a waiver from the United States attorney general.

(f) Who has been found incompetent pursuant to rule 11, Arizona rules of criminal procedure, and who subsequently has not been found competent.

(g) Who is found guilty except insane.

8. "Prohibited weapon":

(a) Includes the following:

(i) An item that is a bomb, grenade, rocket having a propellant charge of more than four ounces or mine and that is explosive, incendiary or poison gas.

(ii) A device that is designed, made or adapted to muffle the report of a firearm.

(iii) A firearm that is capable of shooting more than one shot automatically, without manual reloading, by a single function of the trigger.

(iv) A rifle with a barrel length of less than sixteen inches, or shotgun with a barrel length of less than eighteen inches, or any firearm that is made from a rifle or shotgun and that, as modified, has an overall length of less than twenty-six inches.

(v) An instrument, including a nunchaku, that consists of two or more sticks, clubs, bars or rods to be used as handles, connected by a rope, cord, wire or chain, in the design of a weapon used in connection with the practice of a system of self-defense.

(vi) A breakable container that contains a flammable liquid with a flash point of one hundred fifty degrees Fahrenheit or less and that has a wick or similar device capable of being ignited.

(vii) A chemical or combination of chemicals, compounds or materials, including dry ice, that is possessed or manufactured for the purpose of generating a gas to cause a mechanical failure, rupture or bursting or an explosion or detonation of the chemical or combination of chemicals, compounds or materials.

(viii) An improvised explosive device.

(ix) Any combination of parts or materials that is designed and intended for use in making or converting a device into an item set forth in item (i), (vi) or (viii) of this subdivision.

(b) Does not include:

(i) Any fireworks that are imported, distributed or used in compliance with state laws or local ordinances.

(ii) Any propellant, propellant actuated devices or propellant actuated industrial tools that are manufactured, imported or distributed for their intended purposes.

(iii) A device that is commercially manufactured primarily for the purpose of illumination.

9. "Trafficking" means to sell, transfer, distribute, dispense or otherwise dispose of a weapon or explosive to another person, or to buy, receive, possess or obtain control of a weapon or explosive, with the intent to sell, transfer, distribute, dispense or otherwise dispose of the weapon or explosive to another person.

B. The items set forth in subsection A, paragraph 8, subdivision (a), items (i), (ii), (iii) and (iv) of this section do not include any firearms or devices that are possessed, manufactured or transferred in compliance with federal law.

13-3102. Misconduct involving weapons; defenses; classification; definitions

A. A person commits misconduct involving weapons by knowingly:

1. Carrying a deadly weapon except a pocket knife concealed on his person or within his immediate control in or on a means of transportation:

(a) In the furtherance of a serious offense as defined in section 13-706, a violent crime as defined in section 13-901.03 or any other felony offense; or

(b) When contacted by a law enforcement officer and failing to accurately answer the officer if the officer asks whether the person is carrying a concealed deadly weapon; or

2. Carrying a deadly weapon except a pocket knife concealed on his person or concealed within his immediate control in or on a means of transportation if the person is under twenty-one years of age; or

3. Manufacturing, possessing, transporting, selling or transferring a prohibited weapon, except that if the violation involves dry ice, a person commits misconduct involving weapons by knowingly possessing the dry ice with the intent to cause injury to or death of another person or to cause damage to the property of another person; or

4. Possessing a deadly weapon or prohibited weapon if such person is a prohibited possessor; or

5. Selling or transferring a deadly weapon to a prohibited possessor; or

6. Defacing a deadly weapon; or

7. Possessing a defaced deadly weapon knowing the deadly weapon was defaced; or

8. Using or possessing a deadly weapon during the commission of any felony offense included in chapter 34 of this title; or

9. Discharging a firearm at an occupied structure in order to assist, promote or further the interests of a criminal street gang, a criminal syndicate or a racketeering enterprise; or

10. Unless specifically authorized by law, entering any public establishment or attending any public event and carrying a deadly weapon on his person after a reasonable request by the operator of the establishment or the sponsor of the event or the sponsor's agent to remove his weapon and place it in the custody of the operator of the establishment or the sponsor of the event for temporary and secure storage of the weapon pursuant to section 13-3102.01; or

11. Unless specifically authorized by law, entering an election polling place on the day of any election carrying a deadly weapon; or

12. Possessing a deadly weapon on school grounds; or

13. Unless specifically authorized by law, entering a nuclear or hydroelectric generating station carrying a deadly weapon on his person or within the immediate control of any person; or

14. Supplying, selling or giving possession or control of a firearm to another person if the person knows or has reason to know that the other person would use the firearm in the commission of any felony; or

15. Using, possessing or exercising control over a deadly weapon in furtherance of any act of terrorism as defined in section 13-2301 or possessing or exercising control over a deadly weapon knowing or having reason to know that it will be used to facilitate any act of terrorism as defined in section 13-2301; or

16. Trafficking in weapons or explosives for financial gain in order to assist, promote or further the interests of a criminal street gang, a criminal syndicate or a racketeering enterprise.

B. Subsection A, paragraph 2 of this section shall not apply to:

1. A person in his dwelling, on his business premises or on real property owned or leased by that person or that person's parent, grandparent or legal guardian.

2. A member of the sheriff's volunteer posse or reserve organization who has received and passed firearms training that is approved by the Arizona peace officer standards and training board and who is authorized by the sheriff to carry a concealed weapon pursuant to section 11-441.

3. A firearm that is carried in:

(a) A manner where any portion of the firearm or holster in which the firearm is carried is visible.

(b) A holster that is wholly or partially visible.

(c) A scabbard or case designed for carrying weapons that is wholly or partially visible.

(d) Luggage.

(e) A case, holster, scabbard, pack or luggage that is carried within a means of transportation or within a storage compartment, map pocket, trunk or glove compartment of a means of transportation.

C. Subsection A, paragraphs 2, 3, 7, 10, 11, 12 and 13 of this section shall not apply to:

1. A peace officer or any person summoned by any peace officer to assist and while actually assisting in the performance of official duties; or

2. A member of the military forces of the United States or of any state of the United States in the performance of official duties; or

3. A warden, deputy warden, community correctional officer, detention officer, special investigator or correctional officer of the state department of corrections or the department of juvenile corrections; or

4. A person specifically licensed, authorized or permitted pursuant to a statute of this state or of the United States.

D. Subsection A, paragraph 10 of this section does not apply to an elected or appointed judicial officer in the court facility where the judicial officer works if the judicial officer has demonstrated competence with a firearm as prescribed in section 13-3112, subsection N, except that the judicial officer shall comply with any rule or policy adopted by the presiding judge of the superior court while in the court facility. For the purposes of this subsection, appointed judicial officer does not include a hearing officer or a judicial officer pro tempore that is not a full-time officer.

E. Subsection A, paragraphs 3 and 7 of this section shall not apply to:

1. The possessing, transporting, selling or transferring of weapons by a museum as a part of its collection or an educational institution for educational purposes or by an authorized employee of such museum or institution, if:

(a) Such museum or institution is operated by the United States or this state or a political subdivision of this state, or by an organization described in 26 United States Code section 170(c) as a recipient of a charitable contribution; and

(b) Reasonable precautions are taken with respect to theft or misuse of such material.

2. The regular and lawful transporting as merchandise; or

3. Acquisition by a person by operation of law such as by gift, devise or descent or in a fiduciary capacity as a recipient of the property or former property of an insolvent, incapacitated or deceased person.

F. Subsection A, paragraph 3 of this section shall not apply to the merchandise of an authorized manufacturer of or dealer in prohibited weapons, when such material is intended to be manufactured, possessed, transported, sold or transferred solely for or to a dealer, a regularly constituted or appointed state, county or municipal police department or police officer, a detention facility, the military service of this or another state or the United States, a museum or educational institution or a person specifically licensed or permitted pursuant to federal or state law.

G. Subsection A, paragraph 10 of this section shall not apply to shooting ranges or shooting events, hunting areas or similar locations or activities.

H. Subsection A, paragraph 3 of this section shall not apply to a weapon described in section 13-3101, subsection A, paragraph 8, subdivision (a), item (v), if such weapon is possessed for the purposes of preparing for, conducting or participating in lawful exhibitions, demonstrations, contests or athletic events involving the use of such weapon. Subsection A, paragraph 12 of this section shall not apply to a weapon if such weapon is possessed for the purposes of preparing for, conducting or participating in hunter or firearm safety courses.

I. Subsection A, paragraph 12 of this section shall not apply to the possession of a:

1. Firearm that is not loaded and that is carried within a means of transportation under the control of an adult provided that if the adult leaves the means of transportation the firearm shall not be visible from the outside of the means of transportation and the means of transportation shall be locked.

2. Firearm for use on the school grounds in a program approved by a school.

3. Firearm by a person who possesses a certificate of firearms proficiency pursuant to section 13-3112, subsection T and who is authorized to carry a concealed firearm pursuant to the law enforcement officers safety act of 2004 (P.L. 108-277; 118 Stat. 865; 18 United States Code sections 926B and 926C).

J. Subsection A, paragraphs 2, 3, 7 and 13 of this section shall not apply to commercial nuclear generating station armed nuclear security guards during the performance of official duties or during any security training exercises sponsored by the commercial nuclear generating station or local, state or federal authorities.

K. The operator of the establishment or the sponsor of the event or the employee of the operator or sponsor or the agent of the sponsor, including a public entity or public employee, is not liable for acts or omissions pursuant to subsection A, paragraph 10 of this section unless the operator, sponsor, employee or agent intended to cause injury or was grossly negligent.

L. If a law enforcement officer contacts a person who is in possession of a firearm, the law enforcement officer may take temporary custody of the firearm for the duration of that contact.

M. Misconduct involving weapons under subsection A, paragraph 15 of this section is a class 2 felony. Misconduct involving weapons under subsection A, paragraph 9, 14 or 16 of this section is a class 3 felony. Misconduct involving weapons under subsection A, paragraph 3, 4, 8 or 13 of this section is a class 4 felony. Misconduct involving weapons under subsection A, paragraph 12 of this section is a class 1 misdemeanor unless the violation occurs in connection with conduct that violates section 13-2308, subsection A, paragraph 5, section 13-2312, subsection C, section 13-3409 or section 13-3411, in which case the offense is a class 6 felony. Misconduct involving weapons under subsection A, paragraph 1, subdivision (a) of this section or subsection A, paragraph 5, 6 or 7 of this section is a class 6 felony. Misconduct involving weapons under subsection A, paragraph 1, subdivision (b) of this section or subsection A, paragraph 10 or 11 of this section is a class 1 misdemeanor. Misconduct involving weapons under subsection A, paragraph 2 of this section is a class 3 misdemeanor.

N. For the purposes of this section:

1. "Contacted by a law enforcement officer" means a lawful traffic or criminal investigation, arrest or detention or an investigatory stop by a law enforcement officer that is based on reasonable suspicion that an offense has been or is about to be committed.

2. "Public establishment" means a structure, vehicle or craft that is owned, leased or operated by this state or a political subdivision of this state.

3. "Public event" means a specifically named or sponsored event of limited duration that is either conducted by a public entity or conducted by a private entity with a permit or license granted by a public entity. Public event does not include an unsponsored gathering of people in a public place.

4. "School" means a public or nonpublic kindergarten program, common school or high school.

5. "School grounds" means in, or on the grounds of, a school.

13-3102.01. Storage of deadly weapons; definitions

A. If an operator of a public establishment or a sponsor of a public event requests that a person carrying a deadly weapon remove the weapon, the operator or sponsor shall provide temporary and secure storage. The storage shall be readily accessible on entry into the establishment or event and allow for the immediate retrieval of the weapon on exit from the establishment or event.

B. This section does not apply to the licensed premises of any public establishment or public event with a license issued pursuant to title 4.

C. The operator of the establishment or the sponsor of the event or the employee of the operator or sponsor or the agent of the sponsor, including a public entity or public employee, is not liable for acts or omissions pursuant to this section unless the operator, sponsor, employee or agent intended to cause injury or was grossly negligent.

D. For the purposes of this section, "public establishment" and "public event" have the same meanings prescribed in section 13-3102.

13-3103. Misconduct involving explosives; classification

A. A person commits misconduct involving explosives by knowingly:
1. Keeping or storing a greater quantity than fifty pounds of explosives in or upon any building or premises within a distance of one-half mile of the exterior limits of a city or town, except in vessels, railroad cars or vehicles receiving and keeping them in the course of and for the purpose of transportation; or
2. Keeping or storing percussion caps or any blasting powder within two hundred feet of a building or premises where explosives are kept or stored; or
3. Selling, transporting or possessing explosives without having plainly marked, in a conspicuous place on the box or package containing the explosive, its name, explosive character and date of manufacture.
4. This section shall not apply to any person who legally keeps, stores or transports explosives, percussion caps or blasting powder as a part of their business.
B. Misconduct involving explosives is a class 1 misdemeanor.

13-3104. Depositing explosives; classification

A. A person commits depositing explosives if with the intent to physically endanger, injure, intimidate or terrify any person, such person knowingly deposits any explosive on, in or near any vehicle, building or place where persons inhabit, frequent or assemble.
B. Depositing explosives is a class 4 felony.

13-3105. Forfeiture of weapons and explosives

A. On the conviction of any person for a violation of any felony in this state in which a deadly weapon, dangerous instrument or explosive was used, displayed or unlawfully possessed by the person, the court shall order the article forfeited and sold within one year after its forfeiture to any business that is authorized to receive and dispose of the article under federal and state law and that shall sell the article to the public according to federal and state law, unless the article is otherwise prohibited from being sold under federal and state law, in which case it shall be destroyed or otherwise properly disposed.
B. On the conviction of any person for a violation of section 13-2904, subsection A, paragraph 6 or section 13-3102, subsection A, paragraph 1 or 8, the court may order the forfeiture of the deadly weapon or dangerous instrument involved in the offense.
C. If at any time the court finds pursuant to rule 11 of the Arizona rules of criminal procedure that a person who is charged with a violation of this title is incompetent, the court shall order that any deadly weapon, dangerous instrument or explosive used, displayed or unlawfully possessed by the person during the commission of the alleged offense be forfeited and sold within one year after its forfeiture to any business that is authorized to receive and dispose of the article under federal and state law and that shall sell the article to the public according to federal and state law, unless the article is otherwise prohibited from being sold under federal and state law, in which case it shall be destroyed or otherwise properly disposed.

13-3106. Firearm purchase in other states

A person residing in this state, or a corporation or other business entity maintaining a place of business in this state, may purchase or otherwise obtain firearms anywhere in the United States if such purchase or acquisition fully complies with the laws of this state and the state in which the purchase or acquisition is made and the purchaser and seller, prior to the sale or delivery for sale, have complied with all the requirements of the federal gun control act of 1968, Public Law 90-618, section 922, subsection (c) and the Code of Federal Regulations, volume 26, section 178.96, subsection (c).

13-3107. Unlawful discharge of firearms; exceptions; classification; definitions

A. A person who with criminal negligence discharges a firearm within or into the limits of any municipality is guilty of a class 6 felony.
B. Notwithstanding the fact that the offense involves the discharge of a deadly weapon, unless a dangerous offense is alleged and proven pursuant to section 13-704, subsection L, section 13-604 applies to this offense.
C. This section does not apply if the firearm is discharged:
1. As allowed pursuant to chapter 4 of this title.

2. On a properly supervised range.

3. To lawfully take wildlife during an open season established by the Arizona game and fish commission and subject to the limitations prescribed by title 17 and Arizona game and fish commission rules and orders. This paragraph does not prevent a city, town or county from adopting an ordinance or rule restricting the discharge of a firearm within one-fourth mile of an occupied structure without the consent of the owner or occupant of the structure. For the purposes of this paragraph:

(a) "Occupied structure" means any building in which, at the time of the firearm's discharge, a reasonable person from the location where a firearm is discharged would expect a person to be present.

(b) "Take" has the same meaning prescribed in section 17-101.

4. For the control of nuisance wildlife by permit from the Arizona game and fish department or the United States fish and wildlife service.

5. By special permit of the chief of police of the municipality.

6. As required by an animal control officer in the performance of duties as specified in section 9-499.04.

7. Using blanks.

8. More than one mile from any occupied structure as defined in section 13-3101.

9. In self-defense or defense of another person against an animal attack if a reasonable person would believe that deadly physical force against the animal is immediately necessary and reasonable under the circumstances to protect oneself or the other person.

D. For the purposes of this section:

1. "Municipality" means any city or town and includes any property that is fully enclosed within the city or town.

2. "Properly supervised range" means a range that is any of the following:

(a) Operated by a club affiliated with the national rifle association of America, the amateur trapshooting association, the national skeet association or any other nationally recognized shooting organization, or by any public or private school.

(b) Approved by any agency of the federal government, this state or a county or city within which the range is located.

(c) Operated with adult supervision for shooting air or carbon dioxide gas operated guns, or for shooting in underground ranges on private or public property.

13-3108. Firearms regulated by state; state preemption; injunction; civil penalty; cause of action; violation; classification; definition

A. Except as provided in subsection G of this section, a political subdivision of this state shall not enact any ordinance, rule or tax relating to the transportation, possession, carrying, sale, transfer, purchase, acquisition, gift, devise, storage, licensing, registration, discharge or use of firearms or ammunition or any firearm or ammunition components or related accessories in this state.

B. A political subdivision of this state shall not require the licensing or registration of firearms or ammunition or any firearm or ammunition components or related accessories or prohibit the ownership, purchase, sale or transfer of firearms or ammunition or any firearm or ammunition components, or related accessories.

C. A political subdivision of this state shall not require or maintain a record in any form, whether permanent or temporary, including a list, log or database, of any of the following:

1. Any identifying information of a person who leaves a weapon in temporary storage at any public establishment or public event, except that the operator of the establishment or the sponsor of the event may require that a person provide a government issued identification or a reasonable copy of a government issued identification for the purpose of establishing ownership of the weapon. The operator or sponsor shall store any provided identification with the weapon and shall return the identification to the person when the weapon is retrieved. The operator or sponsor shall not retain records or copies of any identification provided pursuant to this paragraph after the weapon is retrieved.

2. Except in the course of a law enforcement investigation, any identifying information of a person who owns, possesses, purchases, sells or transfers a firearm.

3. The description, including the serial number, of a weapon that is left in temporary storage at any public establishment or public event.

D. A political subdivision of this state shall not enact any rule or ordinance that relates to firearms and is more prohibitive than or that has a penalty that is greater than any state law penalty. A political subdivision's rule or ordinance that relates to firearms and that is inconsistent with or more restrictive than state law, whether enacted before or after July 29, 2010, is null and void.

E. A political subdivision of this state shall not enact any ordinance, rule or regulation limiting the lawful taking of wildlife during an open season established by the Arizona game and fish commission unless the ordinance, rule or regulation is consistent with title 17 and rules and orders adopted by the Arizona game and fish commission. This subsection does not prevent a political subdivision from adopting an ordinance or rule restricting the discharge of a firearm within one-fourth mile of an occupied structure without the consent of the owner or occupant of the structure. For the purposes of this subsection:

1. "Occupied structure" means any building in which, at the time of the firearm's discharge, a reasonable person from the location where a firearm is discharged would expect a person to be present.

2. "Take" has the same meaning prescribed in section 17-101.

F. This state, any agency or political subdivision of this state and any law enforcement agency in this state shall not facilitate the destruction of a firearm or purchase or otherwise acquire a firearm for the purpose of destroying the firearm except as authorized by section 13-3105 or 17-240.

G. This section does not prohibit a political subdivision of this state from enacting and enforcing any ordinance or rule pursuant to state law or relating to any of the following:

1. Imposing any privilege or use tax on the retail sale, lease or rental of, or the gross proceeds or gross income from the sale, lease or rental of, firearms or ammunition or any firearm or ammunition components at a rate that applies generally to other items of tangible personal property.

2. Prohibiting a minor who is unaccompanied by a parent, grandparent or guardian or a certified hunter safety instructor or certified firearms safety instructor acting with the consent of the minor's parent, grandparent or guardian from knowingly possessing or carrying on the minor's person, within the minor's immediate control or in or on a means of transportation a firearm in any place that is open to the public or on any street or highway or on any private property except private property that is owned or leased by the minor or the minor's parent, grandparent or guardian. Any ordinance or rule that is adopted pursuant to this paragraph shall not apply to a minor who is fourteen, fifteen, sixteen or seventeen years of age and who is engaged in any of the following:

(a) Lawful hunting or shooting events or marksmanship practice at established ranges or other areas where the discharge of a firearm is not prohibited.

(b) Lawful transportation of an unloaded firearm for the purpose of lawful hunting.

(c) Lawful transportation of an unloaded firearm for the purpose of attending shooting events or marksmanship practice at established ranges or other areas where the discharge of a firearm is not prohibited.

(d) Any activity that is related to the production of crops, livestock, poultry, livestock products, poultry products or ratites or storage of agricultural commodities.

3. The regulation of commercial land and structures, including a business relating to firearms or ammunition or their components or a commercial shooting range in the same manner as other commercial businesses. Notwithstanding any other law, this paragraph does not:

(a) Authorize a political subdivision to regulate the sale or transfer of firearms on property it owns, leases, operates or controls in a manner that is different than or inconsistent with state law. For the purposes of this subdivision, a use permit or other contract that provides for the use of property owned, leased, operated or controlled by a political subdivision shall not be considered a sale, conveyance or disposition of property.

(b) Authorize a political subdivision through a zoning ordinance to prohibit or otherwise regulate the otherwise lawful discharge of a firearm or maintenance or improvements directly related to the discharge on a private lot or parcel of land that is not open to the public on a commercial or membership basis.

(c) Authorize a political subdivision to regulate the otherwise lawful discharge of a firearm or maintenance or improvements directly related to the discharge on land that is used for agriculture or other noncommercial purposes.

4. Regulating employees or independent contractors of the political subdivision who are acting within the course and scope of their employment or contract. For the purposes of this paragraph, acting within the course and scope of their employment or contract does not include the lawful possession, carrying, transporting or storing of a firearm or other weapon:

(a) On real property that is owned by the employee or independent contractor.

(b) In or on a private vehicle or craft that is owned or operated by the employee or independent contractor unless the ordinance or rule violates another applicable federal or state law or regulation.

(c) Pursuant to section 12-781.

5. Limiting or prohibiting the discharge of firearms in parks and preserves except:

(a) As allowed pursuant to chapter 4 of this title.

(b) On a properly supervised range as defined in section 13-3107.

(c) In an area approved as a hunting area by the Arizona game and fish department. Any such area may be closed when deemed unsafe by the director of the Arizona game and fish department.

(d) To control nuisance wildlife by permit from the Arizona game and fish department or the United States fish and wildlife service.

(e) By special permit of the chief law enforcement officer of the political subdivision.

(f) As required by an animal control officer in performing duties specified in section 9-499.04 and title 11, chapter 7, article 6.

(g) In self-defense or defense of another person against an animal attack if a reasonable person would believe that deadly physical force against the animal is immediately necessary and reasonable under the circumstances to protect oneself or the other person.

H. Any ordinance, regulation, tax or rule that is enacted by a political subdivision in violation of this section is invalid and subject to a permanent injunction against the political subdivision from enforcing the ordinance, regulation, tax or rule. It is not a defense that the political subdivision was acting in good faith or on the advice of counsel.

I. If a court determines that a political subdivision has knowingly and wilfully violated this section, the court may assess a civil penalty of up to fifty thousand dollars against the political subdivision.

J. If a court determines that a person has knowingly and wilfully violated this section while acting in the person's official capacity through enactment of any ordinance, regulation, tax, measure, directive, rule, enactment, order or policy, the person may be subject to termination from employment to the extent allowable under state law.

K. A person or an organization whose membership is adversely affected by any ordinance, regulation, tax, measure, directive, rule, enactment, order or policy that is in violation of this section may file a civil action for declaratory and injunctive relief and actual damages against the political subdivision in any court of this state having jurisdiction over any defendant in the action. If the plaintiff prevails in the action, the court shall award both:

1. Reasonable attorney fees and costs.

2. The actual damages incurred not to exceed one hundred thousand dollars.

L. A violation of any ordinance established pursuant to subsection G, paragraph 5 of this section is a class 2 misdemeanor unless the political subdivision designates a lesser classification by ordinance.

M. For the purposes of this section, "political subdivision" includes a political subdivision acting in any capacity, including under police power, in a proprietary capacity or otherwise.

13-3109. Sale or gift of firearm to minor; classification

A. Except as provided in subsection C of this section, a person who sells or gives to a minor, without written consent of the minor's parent or legal guardian, a firearm, ammunition or a toy pistol by which dangerous and explosive substances may be discharged is guilty of a class 6 felony.

B. Nothing in this section shall be construed to require reporting sales of firearms, nor shall registration of firearms or firearms sales be required.

C. The temporary transfer of firearms and ammunition by firearms safety instructors, hunter safety instructors, competition coaches or their assistants shall be allowed if the minor's parent or guardian has given consent for the minor to participate in activities such as firearms or hunting safety courses, firearms competition or training. With the consent of the minor's parent or guardian, the temporary transfer of firearms and ammunition by an adult accompanying minors engaged in hunting or formal or informal target shooting activities shall be allowed for those purposes.

13-3110. Misconduct involving simulated explosive devices; classification; definition

A. A person commits misconduct involving simulated explosive devices by intentionally giving or sending to another person or placing in a private or public place a simulated explosive device with the intent to terrify, intimidate, threaten or harass.

B. The placing or sending of a simulated explosive device without written notice attached to the device in a conspicuous place that the device has been rendered inert and is possessed for the purpose of curio or relic collection, display or other similar purpose is prima facie evidence of intent to terrify, intimidate, threaten or harass.

C. Misconduct involving simulated explosive devices is a class 5 felony.

D. For the purposes of this section, "simulated explosive device" means a simulation of a prohibited weapon described in section 13-3101, subsection A, paragraph 8, subdivision (a), item (i), (vi) or (viii) that a reasonable person would believe is such a prohibited weapon.

13-3111. Minors prohibited from carrying or possessing firearms; exceptions; seizure and forfeiture; penalties; classification

A. Except as provided in subsection B, an unemancipated person who is under eighteen years of age and who is unaccompanied by a parent, grandparent or guardian, or a certified hunter safety instructor or certified firearms safety instructor acting with the consent of the unemancipated person's parent or guardian, shall not knowingly carry or possess on his person, within his immediate control, or in or on a means of transportation a firearm in any place that is open to the public or on any street or highway or on any private property except private property owned or leased by the minor or the minor's parent, grandparent or guardian.

B. This section does not apply to a person who is fourteen, fifteen, sixteen or seventeen years of age and who is any of the following:

1. Engaged in lawful hunting or shooting events or marksmanship practice at established ranges or other areas where the discharge of a firearm is not prohibited.

2. Engaged in lawful transportation of an unloaded firearm for the purpose of lawful hunting.

3. Engaged in lawful transportation of an unloaded firearm between the hours of 5:00 a.m. and 10:00 p.m. for the purpose of shooting events or marksmanship practice at established ranges or other areas where the discharge of a firearm is not prohibited.

4. Engaged in activities requiring the use of a firearm that are related to the production of crops, livestock, poultry, livestock products, poultry products, or ratites or in the production or storage of agricultural commodities.

C. If the minor is not exempt under subsection B and is in possession of a firearm, a peace officer shall seize the firearm at the time the violation occurs.

D. In addition to any other penalty provided by law, a person who violates subsection A shall be subject to the following penalties:

1. If adjudicated a delinquent juvenile for an offense involving an unloaded firearm, a fine of not more than two hundred fifty dollars, and the court may order the suspension or revocation of the person's driver license until the person reaches eighteen years of age. If the person does not have a driver license at the time of the adjudication, the court may direct that the department of transportation not issue a driver license to the person until the person reaches eighteen years of age.

2. If adjudicated a delinquent juvenile for an offense involving a loaded firearm, a fine of not more than five hundred dollars, and the court may order the suspension or revocation of the person's driver license until the person reaches eighteen years of age. If the person does not have a driver license at the time of the adjudication, the court may direct that the department of transportation not issue a driver license to the person until the person reaches eighteen years of age.

3. If adjudicated a delinquent juvenile for an offense involving a loaded or unloaded firearm, if the person possessed the firearm while the person was the driver or an occupant of a motor vehicle, a fine of not more than five hundred dollars and the court shall order the suspension or revocation of the person's driver license until the person reaches eighteen years of age. If the person does not have a driver license at the time of adjudication, the court shall direct that the department of transportation not issue a driver license to the person until the person reaches eighteen years of age. If the court finds that no other means of transportation is available, the driving privileges of the child may be restricted to travel between the child's home, school and place of employment during specified periods of time according to the child's school and employment schedule.

E. Firearms seized pursuant to subsection C shall be held by the law enforcement agency responsible for the seizure until the charges have been adjudicated or disposed of otherwise or the person is convicted. Upon adjudication or conviction of a person for a violation of this section, the court shall order the firearm forfeited. However, the law enforcement agency shall return the firearm to the lawful owner if the identity of that person is known.

F. If the court finds that the parent or guardian of a minor found responsible for violating this section knew or reasonably should have known of the minor's unlawful conduct and made no effort to prohibit it, the parent or guardian is jointly and severally responsible for any fine imposed pursuant to this section or for any civil actual damages resulting from the unlawful use of the firearm by the minor.

G. This section is supplemental to any other law imposing a criminal penalty for the use or exhibition of a deadly weapon. A minor who violates this section may be prosecuted and adjudicated delinquent for any other criminal conduct involving the use or exhibition of the deadly weapon.

H. A person who violates subsection A is guilty of a class 6 felony.

13-3112. Concealed weapons; qualification; application; permit to carry; civil penalty; report; applicability

A. The department of public safety shall issue a permit to carry a concealed weapon to a person who is qualified under this section. The person shall carry the permit at all times when the person is in actual possession of the concealed weapon and is required by section 4-229 or 4-244 to carry the permit. If the person is in actual possession of the concealed weapon and is required by section 4-229 or 4-244 to carry the permit, the person shall present the permit for inspection to any law enforcement officer on request.

B. The permit of a person who is arrested or indicted for an offense that would make the person unqualified under section 13-3101, subsection A, paragraph 7 or this section shall be immediately suspended and seized. The permit of a person who becomes unqualified on conviction of that offense shall be revoked. The permit shall be restored on presentation of documentation from the court if the permittee is found not guilty or the charges are dismissed. The permit shall be restored on presentation of documentation from the county attorney that the charges against the permittee were dropped or dismissed.

C. A permittee who carries a concealed weapon, who is required by section 4-229 or 4-244 to carry a permit and who fails to present the permit for inspection on the request of a law enforcement officer commits a violation of this subsection and is subject to a civil penalty of not more than three hundred dollars. The department of public safety shall be notified of all violations of this subsection and shall immediately suspend the permit. A permittee shall not be convicted of a violation of this subsection if the permittee produces to the court a legible permit that is issued to the permittee and that was valid at the time the permittee failed to present the permit for inspection.

D. A law enforcement officer shall not confiscate or forfeit a weapon that is otherwise lawfully possessed by a permittee whose permit is suspended pursuant to subsection C of this section, except that a law enforcement officer may take temporary custody of a firearm during an investigatory stop of the permittee.

E. The department of public safety shall issue a permit to an applicant who meets all of the following conditions:

1. Is a resident of this state or a United States citizen.

2. Is twenty-one years of age or older or is at least nineteen years of age and provides evidence of current military service or proof of honorable discharge or general discharge under honorable conditions from the United States armed forces, the United States armed forces reserve or a state national guard.

3. Is not under indictment for and has not been convicted in any jurisdiction of a felony unless that conviction has been expunged, set aside or vacated or the applicant's rights have been restored and the applicant is currently not a prohibited possessor under state or federal law.

4. Does not suffer from mental illness and has not been adjudicated mentally incompetent or committed to a mental institution.

5. Is not unlawfully present in the United States.

6. Has ever demonstrated competence with a firearm as prescribed by subsection N of this section and provides adequate documentation that the person has satisfactorily completed a training program or demonstrated competence with a firearm in any state or political subdivision in the United States. For the purposes of this paragraph, "adequate documentation" means:

(a) A current or expired permit issued by the department of public safety pursuant to this section.

(b) An original or copy of a certificate, card or document that shows the applicant has ever completed any course or class prescribed by subsection N of this section or an affidavit from the instructor, school, club or organization that conducted or taught the course or class attesting to the applicant's completion of the course or class.

(c) An original or a copy of a United States department of defense form 214 (DD-214) indicating an honorable discharge or general discharge under honorable conditions, a certificate of completion of basic training or any other document demonstrating proof of the applicant's current or former service in the United States armed forces as prescribed by subsection N, paragraph 5 of this section.

(d) An original or a copy of a concealed weapon, firearm or handgun permit or a license as prescribed by subsection N, paragraph 6 of this section.

F. The application shall be completed on a form prescribed by the department of public safety. The form shall not require the applicant to disclose the type of firearm for which a permit is sought. The applicant shall attest under penalty of perjury that all of the statements made by the applicant are true, that the applicant has been furnished a copy of this chapter and chapter 4 of this title and that the applicant is knowledgeable about the provisions contained in those chapters. The applicant shall submit the application to the department with any documentation prescribed by subsection E of this section, two sets of fingerprints and a reasonable fee determined by the director of the department.

G. On receipt of a concealed weapon permit application, the department of public safety shall conduct a check of the applicant's criminal history record pursuant to section 41-1750. The department of public safety may exchange fingerprint card information with the federal bureau of investigation for federal criminal history record checks.

H. The department of public safety shall complete all of the required qualification checks within sixty days after receipt of the application and shall issue a permit within fifteen working days after completing the qualification checks if the applicant meets all of the conditions specified in subsection E of this section. If a permit is denied, the department of public safety shall notify the applicant in writing within fifteen working days after the completion of all of the required qualification checks and shall state the reasons why the application was denied. On receipt of the notification of the denial, the applicant has twenty days to submit any additional documentation to the department. On receipt of the additional documentation, the department shall reconsider its decision and inform the applicant within twenty days of the result of the reconsideration. If denied, the applicant shall be informed that the applicant may request a hearing pursuant to title 41, chapter 6, article 10. For the purposes of this subsection, "receipt of the application" means the first day that the department has physical control of the application and that is presumed to be on the date of delivery as evidenced by proof of delivery by the United States postal service or a written receipt, which shall be provided by the department on request of the applicant.

I. On issuance, a permit is valid for five years, except a permit that is held by a member of the United States armed forces, including a member of the Arizona national guard or a member of the reserves of any military establishment of the United States, who is on federal active duty and who is deployed overseas shall be extended until ninety days after the end of the member's overseas deployment.

J. The department of public safety shall maintain a computerized permit record system that is accessible to criminal justice agencies for the purpose of confirming the permit status of any person who is contacted by a law enforcement officer and who claims to hold a valid permit issued by this state. This information and any other records that are maintained regarding applicants, permit holders or instructors shall not be available to any other person or entity except on an order from a state or federal court. A criminal justice agency shall not use the computerized permit record system to conduct inquiries on whether a person is a concealed weapons permit holder unless the criminal justice agency has reasonable suspicion to believe the person is carrying a concealed weapon and the person is subject to a lawful criminal investigation, arrest, detention or an investigatory stop.

K. A permit issued pursuant to this section is renewable every five years. Before a permit may be renewed, a criminal history records check shall be conducted pursuant to section 41-1750 within sixty days after receipt of the application for renewal. For the purposes of permit renewal, the permit holder is not required to submit additional fingerprints.

L. Applications for renewal shall be accompanied by a fee determined by the director of the department of public safety.

M. The department of public safety shall suspend or revoke a permit issued under this section if the permit holder becomes ineligible pursuant to subsection E of this section. The department of public safety shall notify the permit holder in writing within fifteen working days after the revocation or suspension and shall state the reasons for the revocation or suspension.

N. An applicant shall demonstrate competence with a firearm through any of the following:

1. Completion of any firearms safety or training course or class that is available to the general public, that is offered by a law enforcement agency, a junior college, a college or a private or public institution, academy, organization or firearms training school and that is approved by the department of public safety or that uses instructors who are certified by the national rifle association.

2. Completion of any hunter education or hunter safety course approved by the Arizona game and fish department or a similar agency of another state.

3. Completion of any national rifle association firearms safety or training course.

4. Completion of any law enforcement firearms safety or training course or class that is offered for security guards, investigators, special deputies or other divisions or subdivisions of law enforcement or security enforcement and that is approved by the department of public safety.

5. Evidence of current military service or proof of honorable discharge or general discharge under honorable conditions from the United States armed forces.

6. A valid current or expired concealed weapon, firearm or handgun permit or license that is issued by another state or a political subdivision of another state and that has a training or testing requirement for initial issuance.

7. Completion of any governmental police agency firearms training course and qualification to carry a firearm in the course of normal police duties.

8. Completion of any other firearms safety or training course or class that is conducted by a department of public safety approved or national rifle association certified firearms instructor.

O. The department of public safety shall maintain information comparing the number of permits requested, the number of permits issued and the number of permits denied. The department shall annually report this information to the governor and the legislature.

P. The director of the department of public safety shall adopt rules for the purpose of implementing and administering this section including fees relating to permits that are issued pursuant to this section.

Q. This state and any political subdivision of this state shall recognize a concealed weapon, firearm or handgun permit or license that is issued by another state or a political subdivision of another state if both:

1. The permit or license is recognized as valid in the issuing state.

2. The permit or license holder is all of the following:

(a) Legally present in this state.

(b) Not legally prohibited from possessing a firearm in this state.

R. For the purpose of establishing mutual permit or license recognition with other states, the department of public safety shall enter into a written agreement if another state requires a written agreement.

S. Notwithstanding the provisions of this section, a person with a concealed weapons permit from another state may not carry a concealed weapon in this state if the person is under twenty-one years of age or is under indictment for, or has been convicted of, a felony offense in any jurisdiction, unless that conviction is expunged, set aside or vacated or the person's rights have been restored and the person is currently not a prohibited possessor under state or federal law.

T. The department of public safety may issue certificates of firearms proficiency according to the Arizona peace officer standards and training board firearms qualification for the purposes of implementing the law enforcement officers safety act of 2004 (P.L. 108-277; 118 Stat. 865; 18 United States Code sections 926B and 926C). A law enforcement or prosecutorial agency shall issue to a qualified retired law enforcement officer who has honorably retired a photographic identification that states that the officer has honorably retired from the agency. A person who was a municipal, county or state prosecutor is deemed to meet the qualifications of 18 United States Code section 926C(c)(2). The chief law enforcement officer shall determine whether an officer has honorably retired and the determination is not subject to review. A law enforcement or prosecutorial agency has no obligation to revoke, alter or modify the honorable discharge photographic identification based on conduct that the agency becomes aware of or that occurs after the officer has separated from the agency. For the purposes of this subsection, "qualified retired law enforcement officer" has the same meaning prescribed in 18 United States Code section 926C.

U. The initial and renewal application fees collected pursuant to this section shall be deposited, pursuant to sections 35-146 and 35-147, in the concealed weapons permit fund established by section 41-1722.

13-3113. Adjudicated delinquents; firearm possession; classification

A person who was previously adjudicated delinquent for an offense that would be a felony if committed by an adult and who possesses, uses or carries a firearm within ten years from the date of his adjudication or his release or escape from custody is guilty of a class 5 felony for a first offense and a class 4 felony for a second or subsequent offense if the person was previously adjudicated for an offense that if committed as an adult would constitute:

1. Burglary in the first degree.
2. Burglary in the second degree.
3. Arson.
4. Any felony offense involving the use or threatening exhibition of a deadly weapon or dangerous instrument.
5. A serious offense as defined in section 13-706.

13-3114. Arizona manufactured firearms; regulation; definitions

A. Beginning October 1, 2010, a personal firearm, a firearm accessory or ammunition that is manufactured commercially or privately in this state and that remains within the borders of this state is not subject to federal law or federal regulation, including registration, under the authority of Congress to regulate interstate commerce and is not considered to have traveled in interstate commerce.

B. This section applies to a firearm, a firearm accessory or ammunition that is manufactured in this state from basic materials and that can be manufactured without the inclusion of any significant parts imported from another state.

C. The importation into this state of a firearm accessory, any generic or insignificant part that has other manufacturing or consumer product applications or any basic materials, including unmachined steel and unshaped wood that is incorporated into, attached to or used in conjunction with a firearm, firearm accessory or ammunition manufactured in this state, does not subject the firearm, firearm accessory or ammunition to federal regulation.

D. This section does not apply to:

1. A firearm that cannot be carried and used by one person.
2. A firearm that has a bore diameter of more than one and one-half inches and that uses smokeless powder as a propellant.
3. Ammunition with a projectile that explodes using an explosion of chemical energy after the projectile leaves the firearm.
4. A firearm that discharges two or more projectiles with one activation of the trigger or other firing device.

E. A firearm that is manufactured and sold in this state pursuant to this section shall have the words "made in Arizona" clearly stamped on a central metallic part such as the receiver or frame.

F. For the purposes of this section:

1. "Firearm accessory" means an item that is used in conjunction with or mounted on a firearm but that is not essential to the basic function of a firearm, including telescopic or laser sights, magazines, flash suppressors, folding or aftermarket stocks and grips, speedloaders, ammunition carriers and lights for target illumination.
2. "Generic or insignificant part" includes springs, screws, nuts and pins.
3. "Manufactured" means that a firearm, a firearm accessory or ammunition has been created from basic materials for functional usefulness, including forging, casting, machining or other processes for working materials.

13-3115. Forensics firearms identification system

The department of public safety is authorized to establish and maintain a forensics firearms identification system designed to provide investigative information on criminal street gangs and the unlawful use of firearms.

13-3116. Misconduct involving body armor; classification; definition

A. A person commits misconduct involving body armor by knowingly wearing or otherwise using body armor during the commission of any felony offense.
B. Misconduct involving body armor is a class 4 felony.
C. For purposes of this section, "body armor" means any clothing or equipment designed in whole or in part to minimize the risk of injury from a deadly weapon.

13-3117. Remote stun guns; sales records; use; classification; definitions

A. It is unlawful for a person or entity to do any of the following:
1. Sell an authorized remote stun gun without keeping an accurate sales record as to the identity of the purchaser with the manufacturer of the authorized remote stun gun. The identification that is required by this paragraph shall be verified with a government issued identification. This requirement does not apply to secondary sales.
2. Knowingly use or threaten to use a remote stun gun or an authorized remote stun gun against a law enforcement officer who is engaged in the performance of the officer's official duties.
B. This section does not:
1. Preclude the prosecution of any person for the use of a remote stun gun or an authorized remote stun gun during the commission of any criminal offense.
2. Preclude any justification defense under chapter 4 of this title.
C. The regulation of remote stun guns and authorized remote stun guns is a matter of statewide concern.
D. A violation of:
1. Subsection A, paragraph 1 is a petty offense.
2. Subsection A, paragraph 2 is a class 4 felony.
E. For the purposes of this section:
1. "Authorized remote stun gun" means a remote stun gun that has all of the following:
(a) An electrical discharge that is less than one hundred thousand volts and less than nine joules of energy per pulse.
(b) A serial or identification number on all projectiles that are discharged from the remote stun gun.
(c) An identification and tracking system that, on deployment of remote electrodes, disperses coded material that is traceable to the purchaser through records that are kept by the manufacturer on all remote stun guns and all individual cartridges sold.
(d) A training program that is offered by the manufacturer.
2. "Remote stun gun" means an electronic device that emits an electrical charge and that is designed and primarily employed to incapacitate a person or animal either through contact with electrodes on the device itself or remotely through wired probes that are attached to the device or through a spark, plasma, ionization or other conductive means emitting from the device.

13-3118. Possession, transfer or storage of firearms; restrictions prohibited; exceptions

A. Except for the legislature, this state and any agency or political subdivision of this state shall not enact or implement any law, rule or ordinance relating to the possession, transfer or storage of firearms other than as provided in statute.
B. This section does not prohibit:
1. A state, county or municipal judicial department, law enforcement agency or prosecutorial agency from prohibiting a deadly weapon pursuant to section 13-3102, subsection A, paragraph 10.
2. A political subdivision of this state from enacting any rule or ordinance requiring a business that obtains a secondhand firearm by purchase, trade or consignment to retain the firearm for a period of not more than ten days at its place of business or another storage location that is approved by the applicable law enforcement agency.

13-3119. Misconduct involving weapons in a secured area of an airport; classification; definitions

A. A person commits misconduct involving weapons by intentionally carrying, possessing or exercising control over a deadly weapon in a secured area of an airport.
B. This section does not apply to:
1. A peace officer or a federally sworn officer while in the actual performance of the officer's duties.

2. A member of the military forces of the United States or of any state of the United States in the actual performance of the member's official duties.

3. An individual who is authorized by a federal agency in the actual performance of the individual's official duties.

4. General aviation areas not included in the security identification display area or sterile area as defined in the airport security program approved by the transportation security administration.

5. The lawful transportation of deadly weapons in accordance with state and federal law.

C. A violation of this section is a class 1 misdemeanor.

D. For the purposes of this section:

1. "Deadly weapon" has the same meaning prescribed in section 13-105.

2. "Secured area of an airport" means any area of an airport specified in an airport security program that is authorized and approved by the United States transportation security administration pursuant to 49 United States Code section 44903(h)(7)(F) and defined in 49 Code of Federal Regulations section 1540.5.

13-3120. Knives regulated by state; state preemption; definitions

A. Except as provided in subsections C and D, a political subdivision of this state shall not enact any ordinance, rule or tax relating to the transportation, possession, carrying, sale, transfer, purchase, gift, devise, licensing, registration or use of a knife or knife making components in this state.

B. A political subdivision of this state shall not enact any rule or ordinance that relates to the manufacture of a knife and that is more prohibitive than or that has a penalty that is greater than any rule or ordinance that is related to the manufacture of any other commercial goods.

C. This section does not prohibit a political subdivision of this state from enacting and enforcing any ordinance or rule pursuant to state law, to implement or enforce state law or relating to imposing any privilege or use tax on the retail sale, lease or rental of, or the gross proceeds or gross income from the sale, lease or rental of, a knife or any knife components at a rate that applies generally to other items of tangible personal property.

D. This section does not prohibit a political subdivision of this state from regulating employees or independent contractors of the political subdivision who are acting within the course and scope of their employment or contract.

E. A political subdivision's rule or ordinance that relates to knives and that is inconsistent with or more restrictive than state law, whether enacted before or after the effective date of this amendment to this section, is null and void.

F. For the purposes of this section:

1. "Knife" means a cutting instrument and includes a sharpened or pointed blade.

2. "Political subdivision" includes any county, city, including a charter city, town, municipal corporation or special district, any board, commission or agency of a county, city, including a charter city, town, municipal corporation or special district or any other local public agency.

13-3121. Firearm transfers; chief law enforcement officer certification; notification; definitions

A. If a chief law enforcement officer's certification is required by federal law or regulation for the transfer of a firearm, the chief law enforcement officer, within sixty days after receipt of a request for certification by an applicant, shall provide the certification if the applicant is not prohibited by law from receiving the firearm or is not the subject of a proceeding that could result in the applicant being prohibited by law from receiving the firearm. If the chief law enforcement officer is unable to provide a certification as required by this section, the chief law enforcement officer shall notify the applicant, in writing, of the denial and the reason for this determination.

B. The chief law enforcement officer of a law enforcement agency that has fifteen peace officers or fewer may refer an applicant who is requesting a certification pursuant to this section to the county sheriff. A county sheriff who receives a request for certification from a referred applicant shall provide the certification required by this section.

C. Section 12-820.02 applies to a chief law enforcement officer who provides a certification pursuant to this section.

D. This section does not apply to a county attorney or a tribal agency. This subsection does not prohibit a county attorney or a tribal agency from providing an applicant with a certification.

E. A chief law enforcement officer is not required to provide a certification pursuant to this section that the officer knows is untrue but may not refuse to provide a certification that is based on a generalized objection to private persons or entities making, possessing or receiving firearms or any certain type of firearm the possession of which is not prohibited by law.

F. For the purposes of this section:

1. "Certification" means the participation and assent that is required by federal law for the approval of an application to transfer or make a firearm.

2. "Chief law enforcement officer" means any official that the bureau of alcohol, tobacco, firearms and explosives, or any successor agency, identifies by regulation or otherwise as eligible to provide any required certification to make or transfer a firearm.

3. "Firearm" has the same meaning prescribed in 26 United States Code section 5845(a).

4. "Proceeding" includes an ongoing criminal investigation that could result in the applicant being prohibited by law from receiving a firearm.

13-3122. Unlawful use of electronic firearm tracking technology; classification; definitions

A. It is unlawful to require a person to use or be subject to electronic firearm tracking technology or to disclose any identifiable information about the person or the person's firearm for the purpose of using electronic firearm tracking technology.

B. This section does not apply to any of the following:

1. A criminal justice employee who obtains a search warrant.

2. A pawnbroker or an employee of a pawnshop, secondhand dealer or auction house while the pawnbroker or employee uses electronic firearm tracking technology to report information to the sheriff or the sheriff's designee pursuant to section 44-1625 or a similar reporting requirement.

3. A probation, parole or surveillance officer who supervises a person who is serving a term of probation, community supervision or parole.

4. The owner of a firearm if the owner consents in writing to the use of electronic firearm tracking technology on that owner's firearm.

C. A person who violates this section is guilty of a class 6 felony.

D. For the purposes of this section:

1. "Criminal justice employee" includes a peace officer and a prosecutor and includes any employee of a law enforcement agency who is authorized in the execution of the employee's official duties to use electronic firearm tracking technology or to obtain or disclose any identifiable information about a person or a person's firearm in order to use electronic firearm tracking technology.

2. "Electronic firearm tracking technology" means a platform, system or device or a group of systems or devices that uses a shared ledger, distributed ledger or blockchain technology or any other similar form of technology or electronic database for the purpose of storing information in a decentralized or centralized way, that is not owned or controlled by any single person or entity and that is used to locate or control the use of a firearm. Electronic firearm tracking technology does not include a law enforcement database, including the adult probation enterprise tracking system, the juvenile online tracking system, the justice web interface, the Arizona criminal justice information system, the national crime information center, the national integrated ballistic information network and a local records management system that is used to manage or process stolen, lost, found, stored or evidentiary firearms.

Chapter 32 Prostitution

13-3201. Enticement of persons for purpose of prostitution; classification

A person who knowingly entices any other person into a house of prostitution, or elsewhere, for the purpose of prostitution with another person, is guilty of a class 6 felony.

13-3202. Procurement by false pretenses of person for purpose of prostitution; classification

A person who knowingly, by any false pretenses, false representations or other fraudulent means, procures any other person to have illicit carnal relation with another person, is guilty of a class 6 felony.

13-3203. Procuring or placing persons in house of prostitution; classification

A person who knowingly receives money or other valuable thing, for, or on account of, procuring or placing in a house of prostitution, or elsewhere, any person for the purpose of prostitution is guilty of a class 5 felony.

13-3204. Receiving earnings of prostitute; classification

A person who knowingly receives money or other valuable thing from the earnings of a person engaged in prostitution, is guilty of a class 5 felony.

13-3205. Causing spouse to become prostitute; classification

A person who knowingly by force, fraud, intimidation or threats, causes his or her spouse to live in a house of prostitution or to lead a life of prostitution, is guilty of a class 5 felony.

13-3206. Taking child for purpose of prostitution; classification

A person who takes away any minor from the minor's father, mother, guardian or other person having the legal custody of the minor, for the purpose of prostitution, is guilty of a class 4 felony. If the minor is under fifteen years of age, taking a child for the purpose of prostitution is a class 2 felony and is punishable pursuant to section 13-705.

13-3207. Detention of persons in house of prostitution for debt; classification

A person who knowingly detains any person in a house of prostitution because of a debt such person has contracted or is said to have contracted, is guilty of a class 5 felony.

13-3208. Keeping or residing in house of prostitution; employment in prostitution; classification

A. A person who knowingly is an employee at a house of prostitution or prostitution enterprise is guilty of a class 1 misdemeanor.
B. A person who knowingly operates or maintains a house of prostitution or prostitution enterprise is guilty of a class 5 felony.

13-3209. Pandering; methods; classification

A person is guilty of a class 5 felony who knowingly:
1. Places any person in the charge or custody of any other person for purposes of prostitution.
2. Places any person in a house of prostitution with the intent that such person become a prostitute or engage in an act of prostitution.
3. Compels, induces or encourages any person to reside with that person, or with any other person, for the purpose of prostitution.
4. Compels, induces or encourages any person to become a prostitute or engage in an act of prostitution.

13-3210. Transporting persons for purpose of prostitution or other immoral purpose; classification; venue

A person knowingly transporting by any means of conveyance, through or across this state, any other person for the purposes of prostitution or concubinage, or for any other immoral purposes, is guilty of a class 5 felony. The prosecution of such person may be in any county in which such person is apprehended.

13-3211. Definitions

In this chapter, unless the context otherwise requires:
1. "Employee" means a person who conducts lawful or unlawful business for another person under a master-servant relationship or as an independent contractor and who is compensated by wages, commissions, tips or other valuable consideration.
2. "House of prostitution" means any building, structure or place that is used for the purpose of prostitution or lewdness or where acts of prostitution occur.
3. "Operate and maintain" means to organize, design, perpetuate or control. Operate and maintain includes providing financial support by paying utilities, rent, maintenance costs or advertising costs, supervising activities or work schedules, and directing or furthering the aims of the enterprise.
4. "Oral sexual contact" means oral contact with the penis, vulva or anus.

5. "Prostitution" means engaging in or agreeing or offering to engage in sexual conduct under a fee arrangement with any person for money or any other valuable consideration.

6. "Prostitution enterprise" means any corporation, partnership, association or other legal entity or any group of individuals associated in fact although not a legal entity engaged in providing prostitution services.

7. "Sadomasochistic abuse" means flagellation or torture by or on a person who is nude or clad in undergarments or in revealing or bizarre costume or the condition of being fettered, bound or otherwise physically restrained on the part of one so clothed.

8. "Sexual conduct" means sexual contact, sexual intercourse, oral sexual contact or sadomasochistic abuse.

9. "Sexual contact" means any direct or indirect fondling or manipulating of any part of the genitals, anus or female breast.

10. "Sexual intercourse" means penetration into the penis, vulva or anus by any part of the body or by any object.

13-3212. Child sex trafficking; classification; increased punishment; definition

A. A person commits child sex trafficking by knowingly:

1. Causing any minor to engage in prostitution.

2. Using any minor for the purposes of prostitution.

3. Permitting a minor who is under the person's custody or control to engage in prostitution.

4. Receiving any benefit for or on account of procuring or placing a minor in any place or in the charge or custody of any person for the purpose of prostitution.

5. Receiving any benefit pursuant to an agreement to participate in the proceeds of prostitution of a minor.

6. Financing, managing, supervising, controlling or owning, either alone or in association with others, prostitution activity involving a minor.

7. Transporting or financing the transportation of any minor with the intent that the minor engage in prostitution.

8. Providing a means by which a minor engages in prostitution.

9. Enticing, recruiting, harboring, providing, transporting, making available to another or otherwise obtaining a minor with the intent to cause the minor to engage in prostitution or any sexually explicit performance.

10. Enticing, recruiting, harboring, providing, transporting, making available to another or otherwise obtaining a minor with the knowledge that the minor will engage in prostitution or any sexually explicit performance.

B. A person who is at least eighteen years of age commits child sex trafficking by knowingly:

1. Engaging in prostitution with a minor who is under fifteen years of age.

2. Engaging in prostitution with a minor who the person knows or should have known is fifteen, sixteen or seventeen years of age.

3. Engaging in prostitution with a minor who is fifteen, sixteen or seventeen years of age.

C. It is not a defense to a prosecution under subsection A and subsection B, paragraphs 1 and 2 of this section that the other person is a peace officer posing as a minor or a person assisting a peace officer posing as a minor.

D. Notwithstanding any other law, a sentence imposed on a person for any of the following shall be consecutive to any other sentence imposed on the person at any time:

1. A violation of subsection A or subsection B, paragraph 2 of this section involving a minor who is fifteen, sixteen or seventeen years of age.

2. A violation of subsection A, paragraph 9 or 10 of this section.

E. Child sex trafficking pursuant to subsection A of this section is a class 2 felony if the minor is under fifteen years of age and is punishable pursuant to section 13-705.

F. Child sex trafficking pursuant to subsection B, paragraph 1 of this section is a class 2 felony and is punishable pursuant to section 13-705.

G. If the minor is fifteen, sixteen or seventeen years of age, child sex trafficking pursuant to subsection A, paragraph 1, 2, 3, 4, 5, 6, 7 or 8 of this section is a class 2 felony, the person convicted shall be sentenced pursuant to this section and the person is not eligible for suspension of sentence, probation, pardon or release from confinement on any basis except as specifically authorized by section 31-233, subsection A or B until the sentence imposed by the court has been served or commuted. The presumptive term may be aggravated or mitigated within the range under this section pursuant to section 13-701, subsections C, D and E. The terms are as follows:

1. The term for a first offense is as follows:

Minimum   Presumptive Maximum
10 years   13.5 years 24 years

2. The term for a defendant who has one historical prior felony conviction is as follows:

Minimum   Presumptive Maximum

17 years   24 years   31 years

3. The term for a defendant who has two or more historical prior felony convictions is as follows:

Minimum   Presumptive Maximum

24 years   31 years   38 years

H. If the minor is fifteen, sixteen or seventeen years of age, child sex trafficking pursuant to subsection A, paragraph 9 or 10 of this section is a class 2 felony.

I. If the minor is fifteen, sixteen or seventeen years of age, child sex trafficking pursuant to subsection B, paragraph 2 of this section is a class 2 felony, the person convicted shall be sentenced pursuant to this section and the person is not eligible for suspension of sentence, probation, pardon or release from confinement on any basis except as specifically authorized by section 31-233, subsection A or B until the sentence imposed by the court has been served or commuted. The presumptive term may be aggravated or mitigated within the range under this section pursuant to section 13-701, subsections C, D and E. The terms are as follows:

1. The term for a first offense is as follows:

Minimum   Presumptive Maximum

7 years   10.5 years   21 years

2. The term for a defendant who has one historical prior felony conviction is as follows:

Minimum   Presumptive Maximum

14 years   15.75 years   28 years

3. The term for a defendant who has two or more historical prior felony convictions is as follows:

Minimum   Presumptive Maximum

21 years   28 years   35 years

J. Child sex trafficking pursuant to subsection B, paragraph 3 of this section is a class 6 felony. If the court sentences the person to a term of probation, the court shall order that as an initial term of probation the person be imprisoned in the county jail for not less than one hundred eighty consecutive days. This jail term shall commence on the date of sentencing. The court may suspend ninety days of the jail sentence if the person has not previously been convicted of a violation of this section, a violation of section 13-3214 or a violation of any city or town ordinance that prohibits prostitution and that has the same or substantially similar elements as section 13-3214 and the person successfully completes an appropriate court ordered education or treatment program.

K. This section does not preclude the state from alleging and proving any other sentencing enhancements as provided by law.

L. For the purposes of this section, "sexually explicit performance" means a live or public act or show intended to arouse or satisfy the sexual desires or appeal to the prurient interest of patrons.

13-3214. Prostitution; classification

A. It is unlawful for a person to knowingly engage in prostitution.

B. This section does not prohibit cities or towns from enacting and enforcing ordinances to suppress and prohibit prostitution that provide a punishment for misdemeanor violations that is at least as stringent as provided in this section.

C. For the purposes of sentencing under this section, a previous violation of any city or town ordinance that prohibits prostitution and that has the same or substantially similar elements as this section shall be deemed to be a previous violation of this section.

D. It is an affirmative defense to a prosecution under this section that the defendant committed the acts constituting prostitution as a direct result of being a victim of sex trafficking.

E. A person who violates this section is guilty of a class 1 misdemeanor, except that:

1. A person who is convicted of a first violation of this section shall be sentenced to serve not less than fifteen consecutive days in jail and is not eligible for probation or suspension of execution of sentence until the entire sentence is served.

2. A person who is convicted of a second violation of this section shall be sentenced to serve not less than thirty consecutive days in jail and is not eligible for probation or suspension of execution of sentence until the entire sentence is served.

3. A person who is convicted of a third violation of this section shall be sentenced to serve not less than sixty consecutive days in jail, is not eligible for probation or suspension of execution of sentence until the entire sentence is served and shall complete an appropriate court ordered education or treatment program.

4. A person who has previously been convicted of three or more violations of this section and who commits a subsequent violation of this section is guilty of a class 5 felony, shall be sentenced to serve not less than one hundred eighty consecutive days in jail and is not eligible for probation or suspension of execution of sentence until the entire sentence is served. This paragraph does not prohibit a person from being sentenced to serve a period of incarceration in the state department of corrections.

Chapter 33 Gambling

13-3301. Definitions

(Caution: 1998 Prop. 105 applies)

In this chapter, unless the context otherwise requires:
1. "Amusement gambling" means gambling involving a device, game or contest which is played for entertainment if all of the following apply:
(a) The player or players actively participate in the game or contest or with the device.
(b) The outcome is not in the control to any material degree of any person other than the player or players.
(c) The prizes are not offered as a lure to separate the player or players from their money.
(d) Any of the following:
(i) No benefit is given to the player or players other than an immediate and unrecorded right to replay which is not exchangeable for value.
(ii) The gambling is an athletic event and no person other than the player or players derives a profit or chance of a profit from the money paid to gamble by the player or players.
(iii) The gambling is an intellectual contest or event, the money paid to gamble is part of an established purchase price for a product, no increment has been added to the price in connection with the gambling event and no drawing or lottery is held to determine the winner or winners.
(iv) Skill and not chance is clearly the predominant factor in the game and the odds of winning the game based upon chance cannot be altered, provided the game complies with any licensing or regulatory requirements by the jurisdiction in which it is operated, no benefit for a single win is given to the player or players other than a merchandise prize which has a wholesale fair market value of less than ten dollars or coupons which are redeemable only at the place of play and only for a merchandise prize which has a fair market value of less than ten dollars and, regardless of the number of wins, no aggregate of coupons may be redeemed for a merchandise prize with a wholesale fair market value of greater than five hundred fifty dollars.
2. "Conducted as a business" means gambling that is engaged in with the object of gain, benefit or advantage, either direct or indirect, realized or unrealized, but not when incidental to a bona fide social relationship.
3. "Crane game" means an amusement machine which is operated by player controlled buttons, control sticks or other means, or a combination of the buttons or controls, which is activated by coin insertion into the machine and where the player attempts to successfully retrieve prizes with a mechanical or electromechanical claw or device by positioning the claw or device over a prize.
4. "Gambling" or "gamble" means one act of risking or giving something of value for the opportunity to obtain a benefit from a game or contest of chance or skill or a future contingent event but does not include bona fide business transactions which are valid under the law of contracts including contracts for the purchase or sale at a future date of securities or commodities, contracts of indemnity or guarantee and life, health or accident insurance.
5. "Player" means a natural person who participates in gambling.
6. "Regulated gambling" means either:
(a) Gambling conducted in accordance with a tribal-state gaming compact or otherwise in accordance with the requirements of the Indian gaming regulatory act of 1988 (P.L. 100-497; 102 Stat. 2467; 25 United States Code sections 2701 through 2721 and 18 United States Code sections 1166 through 1168); or
(b) Gambling to which all of the following apply:
(i) It is operated and controlled in accordance with a statute, rule or order of this state or of the United States.
(ii) All federal, state or local taxes, fees and charges in lieu of taxes have been paid by the authorized person or entity on any activity arising out of or in connection with the gambling.
(iii) If conducted by an organization which is exempt from taxation of income under section 43-1201, the organization's records are open to public inspection.
(iv) Beginning on June 1, 2003, none of the players is under twenty-one years of age.
7. "Social gambling" means gambling that is not conducted as a business and that involves players who compete on equal terms with each other in a gamble if all of the following apply:
(a) No player receives, or becomes entitled to receive, any benefit, directly or indirectly, other than the player's winnings from the gamble.

(b) No other person receives or becomes entitled to receive any benefit, directly or indirectly, from the gambling activity, including benefits of proprietorship, management or unequal advantage or odds in a series of gambles.

(c) Until June 1, 2003, none of the players is below the age of majority. Beginning on June 1, 2003, none of the players is under twenty-one years of age.

(d) Players "compete on equal terms with each other in a gamble" when no player enjoys an advantage over any other player in the gamble under the conditions or rules of the game or contest.

13-3302. Exclusions

A. The following conduct is not unlawful under this chapter:

1. Amusement gambling.

2. Social gambling.

3. Regulated gambling if the gambling is conducted in accordance with the statutes, rules or orders governing the gambling.

4. Gambling that is conducted at state, county or district fairs and that complies with section 13-3301, paragraph 1, subdivision (d).

B. An organization that has qualified for an exemption from taxation of income under section 43-1201, subsection A, paragraph 1, 2, 4, 5, 6, 7, 10 or 11 may conduct a raffle that is subject to the following restrictions:

1. The nonprofit organization shall maintain this status and no member, director, officer, employee or agent of the nonprofit organization may receive any direct or indirect pecuniary benefit other than being able to participate in the raffle on a basis equal to all other participants.

2. The nonprofit organization has been in existence continuously in this state for a five year period immediately before conducting the raffle.

3. No person except a bona fide local member of the sponsoring organization may participate directly or indirectly in the management, sales or operation of the raffle.

4. Nothing in paragraph 1 or 3 of this subsection prohibits:

(a) A licensed general hospital, a licensed special hospital or a foundation established to support cardiovascular medical research that is exempt from taxation of income under section 43-1201, subsection A, paragraph 4 or section 501(c)(3) of the internal revenue code from contracting with an outside agent who participates in the management, sales or operation of the raffle if the proceeds of the raffle are used to fund medical research, graduate medical education or indigent care and the raffles are conducted no more than three times per calendar year. The maximum fee for an outside agent shall not exceed fifteen percent of the net proceeds of the raffle.

(b) An entity that is exempt from taxation of income under section 43-1201, subsection A, paragraph 4 or section 501(c)(3) of the internal revenue code and that has at least a twenty-year history of providing comprehensive services to prevent child abuse and to provide services and advocacy for victims of child abuse from contracting with an outside agent who participates in the management, sales or operation of the raffle if the proceeds of the raffle are used to provide comprehensive services to prevent child abuse and to provide services and advocacy for victims of child abuse and the raffles are conducted no more than three times per calendar year. The maximum fee for an outside agent shall not exceed fifteen percent of the net proceeds of the raffle.

C. A state, county or local historical society designated by this state or a county, city or town to conduct a raffle may conduct the raffle subject to the following conditions:

1. No member, director, officer, employee or agent of the historical society may receive any direct or indirect pecuniary benefit other than being able to participate in the raffle on a basis equal to all other participants.

2. The historical society must have been in existence continuously in this state for a five year period immediately before conducting the raffle.

3. No person except a bona fide local member of the sponsoring historical society may participate directly or indirectly in the management, sales or operation of the raffle.

D. A nonprofit organization that is a booster club, a civic club or a political club or political organization that is formally affiliated with and recognized by a political party in this state may conduct a raffle that is subject to the following restrictions:

1. No member, director, officer, employee or agent of the club or organization may receive any direct or indirect pecuniary benefit other than being able to participate in the raffle on a basis equal to all other participants.

2. No person except a bona fide local member of the sponsoring club or organization may participate directly or indirectly in the management, sales or operation of the raffle.

3. The maximum annual benefit that the club or organization receives for all raffles is ten thousand dollars.

4. The club or organization is organized and operated exclusively for pleasure, recreation or other nonprofit purposes and no part of the club's or organization's net earnings inures to the personal benefit of any member, director, officer, employee or agent of the club or organization.

13-3303. Promotion of gambling; classification

A. Except for amusement, regulated or social gambling, a person commits promotion of gambling if he knowingly does either of the following for a benefit:
1. Conducts, organizes, manages, directs, supervises or finances gambling.
2. Furnishes advice or assistance for the conduct, organization, management, direction, supervision or financing of gambling.
B. Promotion of gambling is a class 5 felony.

13-3304. Benefiting from gambling; classification

A. Except for amusement or regulated gambling, a person commits benefiting from gambling if he knowingly obtains any benefit from gambling.
B. Benefiting from social gambling as a player is not unlawful under this section.
C. Benefiting from gambling is a class 1 misdemeanor.

13-3305. Betting and wagering; classification

A. Subject to the exceptions contained in section 5-112, no person may engage for a fee, property, salary or reward in the business of accepting, recording or registering any bet, purported bet, wager or purported wager or engage for a fee, property, salary or reward in the business of selling wagering pools or purported wagering pools with respect to the result or purported result of any race, sporting event, contest or other game of skill or chance or any other unknown or contingent future event or occurrence whatsoever.
B. A person shall not directly or indirectly knowingly accept for a fee, property, salary or reward anything of value from another to be transmitted or delivered for wagering or betting on the results of a race, sporting event, contest or other game of skill or chance or any other unknown or contingent future event or occurrence whatsoever conducted within or without this state or anything of value as reimbursement for the prior making of such a wager or bet on behalf of another person.
C. A person who violates this section is guilty of a class 1 misdemeanor.

13-3306. Possession of a gambling device; classification

A. A person commits possession of a gambling device if the person knowingly possesses, distributes or transports any implement, machine, paraphernalia, equipment or other thing that the person knows or has reason to know is used or intended to be used in violation of this chapter.
B. A person commits possession of a bingo gambling device if the person knowingly possesses any implement, machine, paraphernalia, equipment or other thing that the person knows or has reason to know is used or intended to be used in violation of this chapter.
C. Possession of a bingo gambling device shall not be the basis for a violation of section 13-3303, 13-3304 or 13-3307.
D. Possession of a bingo gambling device is a class 2 misdemeanor. Possession of any other gambling device is a class 1 misdemeanor.
E. Nothing in this section prohibits:
1. The use of gambling devices by nonprofit or charitable organizations pursuant to section 13-3302, subsection B.
2. Possession, distribution or transportation of gambling devices for purposes not prohibited by this chapter.

13-3307. Possession of gambling records; classification

A. A person commits possession of gambling records if he knowingly possesses any book, writing, paper, instrument, article, electronically-produced data, computer software and programs, discs, tapes or other tangible or intangible method of recording information knowing or having reason to know that it arises out of, or was made in connection with, gambling in violation of this chapter.

B. Possession of gambling records is a class 1 misdemeanor.

13-3308. Presumption

In a prosecution under this chapter in which it is necessary to prove the occurrence of any event that is the subject of gambling, a published report of its occurrence in a daily newspaper, a magazine or any other periodically printed publication of general circulation is admissible into evidence and, on admission, it is presumed that the event occurred. This presumption may be rebutted. Either party may use additional evidence to prove or disprove the occurrence of the event.

13-3309. Seizure; exception; definition

A. In addition to any other remedies provided by law, any monies used or intended to be used in violation of this chapter may be seized by any peace officer on probable cause that it is money used or intended to be used in violation of this chapter.

B. In addition to any other remedy provided by law, gambling records of gambling in violation of this chapter may be seized by any peace officer on probable cause that they are gambling records.

C. In addition to any other remedy provided by law, a gambling device may be seized by any peace officer on probable cause that it is a gambling device being used or intended to be used in violation of this title.

D. If a gambling device is an antique slot machine and is not used for gambling purposes or in violation of the laws of this state, possession of the antique slot machine is lawful and it shall not be confiscated or destroyed. If the gambling device is confiscated and the owner shows that the gambling device is an antique slot machine and it is not used for gambling purposes or in violation of the laws of this state, the court acquiring jurisdiction shall order the antique slot machine returned to the person from whom it was confiscated.

E. For purposes of this section, "antique slot machine" means a gambling device which is manufactured for use as a slot machine and is at least twenty-five years old.

13-3310. Forfeiture

A. In addition to any other remedies provided by law, the following property shall be forfeited pursuant to section 13-2314 or chapter 39 of this title:

1. All benefits derived from a violation of this chapter.
2. All unlawful gambling devices.
3. All things of value used or intended to be used to facilitate a violation of this chapter.

B. A person that obtains property through a violation of this chapter is an involuntary trustee. An involuntary trustee and any other person, except a bona fide purchaser for value without notice of the unlawful conduct and who has not knowingly taken part in an illegal transaction, holds the property, its proceeds and its fruits in constructive trust for the benefit of persons entitled to remedies pursuant to section 13-2314 or chapter 39 of this title.

13-3311. Amusement gambling intellectual contests or events; registration; filing of rules; sworn statement; exceptions

A. Before any person conducts an amusement gambling intellectual contest or event pursuant to section 13-3301, paragraph 1, subdivision (d), item (iii), the person shall register with the attorney general's office. The registration shall include:

1. The name and address of the person conducting the contest or event.
2. The minimum dollar amount of all prizes to be awarded.
3. The duration of the event.
4. The statutory agent or person authorized to accept service of process in Arizona for the person conducting the contest or event.
5. All rules governing the contest or event, including the rules applicable in case of a tie.
6. The name and description of the product and the established purchase price for the product.

B. Within ten days following the award of all prizes in connection with an amusement gambling intellectual contest or event, the person conducting the contest or event shall file with the attorney general's office the names and addresses of all persons who have won prizes in connection with the contest or event.

C. For each amusement gambling intellectual contest or event held, the person conducting the event shall file with the attorney general's office a sworn statement under oath that no increment has been added to the established purchase price for the product in connection with the gambling event.

D. This section does not apply to organizations that have qualified for an exemption from taxation of income under section 43-1201, paragraph 1, 2, 4, 5, 6, 7, 10 or 11 or to academic competitions conducted by school districts or charter schools that award cash, prizes or scholarships to participants.

13-3312. Crane games; prohibited acts; classification

A. It is unlawful for a person to knowingly cause or commit the following actions:

1. Altering or maintaining a crane game so that the claw is physically unable to grasp exposed prizes.

2. Displaying prizes in a crane game in a manner so that the claw is physically incapable of grasping exposed prizes.

3. Misrepresenting the value of prizes in crane games.

4. Using cash or currency as prizes in crane games or awarding prizes in crane games which are redeemable for cash or currency.

B. A person who violates this section is guilty of a class 1 misdemeanor.

Chapter 34 Drug Offenses

13-3401. Definitions

In this chapter, unless the context otherwise requires:

1. "Administer" means to apply, inject or facilitate the inhalation or ingestion of a substance to the body of a person.

2. "Amidone" means any substance identified chemically as (4-4-diphenyl-6-dimethylamine-heptanone-3), or any salt of such substance, by whatever trade name designated.

3. "Board" means the Arizona state board of pharmacy.

4. "Cannabis" means the following substances under whatever names they may be designated:

(a) The resin extracted from any part of a plant of the genus cannabis, and every compound, manufacture, salt, derivative, mixture or preparation of such plant, its seeds or its resin. Cannabis does not include oil or cake made from the seeds of such plant, any fiber, compound, manufacture, salt, derivative, mixture or preparation of the mature stalks of such plant except the resin extracted from the stalks or any fiber, oil or cake or the sterilized seed of such plant which is incapable of germination.

(b) Every compound, manufacture, salt, derivative, mixture or preparation of such resin or tetrahydrocannabinol.

5. "Coca leaves" means cocaine, its optical isomers and any compound, manufacture, salt, derivative, mixture or preparation of coca leaves, except derivatives of coca leaves which do not contain cocaine, ecgonine or substances from which cocaine or ecgonine may be synthesized or made.

6. "Dangerous drug" means the following by whatever official, common, usual, chemical or trade name designated:

(a) Any material, compound, mixture or preparation that contains any quantity of the following hallucinogenic substances and their salts, isomers, whether optical, positional or geometric, and salts of isomers, unless specifically excepted, whenever the existence of such salts, isomers and salts of isomers is possible within the specific chemical designation:

(i) Alpha-ethyltryptamine.

(ii) Alpha-methyltryptamine.

(iii) (2-aminopropyl) benzofuran (APB).

(iv) (2-aminopropyl)-2, 3-dihydrobenzofuran (APDB).

(v) Aminorex.

(vi) 4-bromo-2, 5-dimethoxyphenethylamine.

(vii) 4-bromo-2, 5-dimethoxyamphetamine.

(viii) Bufotenine.

(ix) [3-(3-carbamoylphenyl)phenyl]N-cyclohexyl carbamate (URB-597).

(x) Diethyltryptamine.

(xi) 2, 5-dimethoxyamphetamine.

(xii) Dimethyltryptamine.

(xiii) (2-ethylaminopropyl)-benzofuran (EAPB).

(xiv) 5-methoxy-alpha-methyltryptamine.

(xv) 5-methoxy-3, 4-methylenedioxyamphetamine.

(xvi) 4-methyl-2, 5-dimethoxyamphetamine.

(xvii) (2-methylaminopropyl)-benzofuran (MAPB).

(xviii) Ibogaine.

(xix) Lysergic acid amide.

(xx) Lysergic acid diethylamide.

(xxi) Mescaline.

(xxii) 4-methoxyamphetamine.

(xxiii) Methoxymethylenedioxyamphetamine (MMDA).

(xxiv) Methylenedioxyamphetamine (MDA).

(xxv) 3, 4-methylenedioxymethamphetamine.

(xxvi) 3, 4-methylenedioxy-N-ethylamphetamine.

(xxvii) N-ethyl-3-piperidyl benzilate (JB-318).

(xxviii) N-hydroxy-3, 4-methylenedioxyamphetamine.

(xxix) N-methyl-3-piperidyl benzilate (JB-336).

(xxx) N-methyltryptamine mimetic substances that are any substances derived from N-methyltryptamine by any substitution at the nitrogen, any substitution at the indole ring, any substitution at the alpha carbon, any substitution at the beta carbon or any combination of the above. N-methyltryptamine mimetic substances do not include melatonin (5-methoxy-n-acetyltryptamine). Substances in the N-methyltryptamine generic definition include AcO-DMT, Baeocystine, Bromo-DALT, DiPT, DMT, DPT, HO-DET, HO-DiPT, HO-DMT, HO-DPT, HO-MET, MeO-DALT, MeO-DET, MeO-DiPT, MeO-DMT, MeO-DPT, MeO-NMT, MET, NMT and Norbufotenin.

(xxxi) N-(1-phenylcyclohexyl) ethylamine (PCE).

(xxxii) Nabilone.

(xxxiii) 1-(1-phenylcyclohexyl) pyrrolidine (PHP).

(xxxiv) 1-(1-(2-thienyl)-cyclohexyl) piperidine (TCP).

(xxxv) 1-(1-(2-thienyl)-cyclohexyl) pyrrolidine.

(xxxvi) Para-methoxyamphetamine (PMA).

(xxxvii) Psilacetin.

(xxxviii) Psilocybin.

(xxxix) Psilocyn.

(xl) Synhexyl.

(xli) Trifluoromethylphenylpiperazine (TFMPP).

(xlii) Trimethoxyamphetamine (TMA).

(xliii) 1-pentyl-3-(naphthoyl)indole (JWH-018 and isomers).

(xliv) 1-butyl-3-(naphthoyl)indole (JWH-073 and isomers).

(xlv) 1-hexyl-3-(naphthoyl)indole (JWH-019 and isomers).

(xlvi) 1-pentyl-3-(4-chloro naphthoyl)indole (JWH-398 and isomers).

(xlvii) 1-(2-(4-(morpholinyl)ethyl))-3-(naphthoyl)indole (JWH-200 and isomers).

(xlviii) 1-pentyl-3-(methoxyphenylacetyl)indole (JWH-250 and isomers).

(xlix) (2-methyl-1-propyl-1H-indol-3-YL)-1-naphthalenyl-methanone (JWH-015 and isomers).

(l) (6AR, 10AR)-9-(hydroxymethyl)-6,6-dimethyl-3-(2-methyloctan2-YL)-6a,7,10,10a-tetrahydrobenzo[c]chromen-1-ol) (HU-210).

(li) 5-(1,1-dimethylheptyl)-2-(3-hydroxycyclohexyl)-phenol
(CP 47,497 and isomers).

(lii) 5-(1,1-dimethyloctyl)-2-(3-hydroxycyclohexyl)-phenol
(cannabicyclohexanol, CP-47,497 C8 homologue and isomers).

(b) Any material, compound, mixture or preparation that contains any quantity of cannabimimetic substances and their salts, isomers, whether optical, positional or geometric, and salts of isomers, unless specifically excepted, whenever the existence of such salts, isomers and salts of isomers is possible within the specific chemical designation. For the purposes of this subdivision, "cannabimimetic substances" means any substances within the following structural classes:

(i) 2-(3-hydroxycyclohexyl)phenol with substitution at the 5-position of the phenolic ring by alkyl or alkenyl, whether or not substituted on the cyclohexyl ring to any extent. Substances in the 2-(3-hydroxycyclohexyl)phenol generic definition include CP-47,497, CP-47,497 C8-Homolog, CP-55,940 and CP-56,667.

(ii) 3-(naphthoyl)indole or 3-(naphthylmethane)indole by substitution at the nitrogen atom of the indole ring, whether or not further substituted on the indole ring to any extent, whether or not substituted on the naphthoyl or naphthyl ring to any extent. Substances in the 3-(naphthoyl)indole generic definition include AM-678, AM-2201, JWH-004, JWH-007, JWH-009, JWH-015, JWH-016, JWH-018, JWH-019, JWH-020, JWH-046, JWH-047, JWH-048, JWH-049, JWH-050, JWH-070, JWH-071, JWH-072, JWH-073, JWH-076, JWH-079, JWH-080, JWH-081, JWH-082, JWH-094, JWH-096, JWH-098, JWH-116, JWH-120, JWH-122, JWH-148, JWH-149, JWH-175, JWH-180, JWH-181, JWH-182, JWH-184, JWH-185, JWH-189, JWH-192, JWH-193, JWH-194, JWH-195, JWH-196, JWH-197, JWH-199, JWH-200, JWH-210, JWH-211, JWH-212, JWH-213, JWH-234, JWH-235, JWH-236, JWH-239, JWH-240, JWH-241, JWH-242, JWH-262, JWH-386, JWH-387, JWH-394, JWH-395, JWH-397, JWH-398, JWH-399, JWH-400, JWH-412, JWH-413, JWH-414 and JWH-415.

(iii) 3-naphthoyl-indazole or 3-(naphthylmethane)-indazole by substitution at one or both of the nitrogen atoms of the indazole ring, whether or not further substituted on the indazole ring to any extent, whether or not substituted on the naphthoyl ring to any extent. Substances in the 3-naphthoyl-indazole or 3-(naphthylmethane)-indazole generic definition include THJ2201 and THJ-018.

(iv) 3-(naphthoyl)pyrrole by substitution at the nitrogen atom of the pyrrole ring, whether or not further substituted in the pyrrole ring to any extent, whether or not substituted on the naphthoyl ring to any extent. Substances in the 3-(naphthoyl)pyrrole generic definition include JWH-030, JWH-145, JWH-146, JWH-147, JWH-150, JWH-156, JWH-243, JWH-244, JWH-245, JWH-246, JWH-292, JWH-293, JWH-307, JWH-308, JWH-346, JWH-348, JWH-363, JWH-364, JWH-365, JWH-367, JWH-368, JWH-369, JWH-370, JWH-371, JWH-373 and JWH-392.

(v) 1-(naphthylmethylene)indene by substitution of the 3-position of the indene ring, whether or not further substituted in the indene ring to any extent, whether or not substituted on the naphthyl ring to any extent. Substances in the 1-(naphthylmethylene)indene generic definition include JWH-176.

(vi) 3-(phenylacetyl)indole or 3-(benzoyl)indole by substitution at the nitrogen atom of the indole ring, whether or not further substituted in the indole ring to any extent, whether or not substituted on the phenyl ring to any extent. Substances in the 3-(phenylacetyl)indole generic definition include AM-694, AM-2233, JWH-167, JWH-201, JWH-202, JWH-203, JWH-204, JWH-205, JWH-206, JWH-207, JWH-208, JWH-209, JWH--237, JWH-248, JWH-250, JWH-251, JWH-253, JWH-302, JWH-303, JWH-304, JWH-305, JWH-306, JWH-311, JWH-312, JWH-313, JWH-314, JWH-315, JWH-316, RCS-4, RCS-8, SR-18 and SR-19.

(vii) 3-(cyclopropylmethanone) indole or 3-(cyclobutylmethanone) indole or 3-(cyclopentylmethanone) indole by substitution at the nitrogen atom of the indole ring, whether or not further substituted in the indole ring to any extent, whether or not substituted on the cyclopropyl, cyclobutyl or cyclopentyl rings to any extent. Substances in the 3-(cyclopropylmethanone) indole generic definition include UR-144, fluoro-UR-144 and XLR-11.

(viii) 3-adamantoylindole with substitution at the nitrogen atom of the indole ring, whether or not further substituted on the indole ring to any extent, whether or not substituted on the adamantyl ring to any extent. Substances in the 3-adamantoylindole generic definition include AB-001.

(ix) N-(adamantyl)-indole-3-carboxamide with substitution at the nitrogen atom of the indole ring, whether or not further substituted on the indole ring to any extent, whether or not substituted on the adamantyl ring to any extent. Substances in the N-(adamantyl)-indole-3-carboxamide generic definition include SDB-001.

(x) Indole-3-carboxamide orIndazole-3-carboxamide with substitution at the nitrogen atom of the indole ring or by substitution at one or both of the nitrogen atoms of the indazole ring, whether or not further substituted on the indole ring or the indazole ring to any extent, whether or not substituted on the nitrogen of the carboxamide to any extent. Substances in the indole-3-carboxamide or indazole-3-carboxamide generic definition include AKB-48, fluoro-AKB-48, APINACA, AB-PINACA, AB-FUBINACA, ABICA and ADBICA.

(xi) 8-Quinolinyl-indole-3-carboxylate or 8-quinolinyl-indazole-3-carboxylate by substitution at the nitrogen atom of the indole ring or by substitution at one or both of the nitrogen atoms of the indazole ring, whether or not further substituted in the indole ring or indazole ring to any extent, whether or not substituted on the quinoline ring to any extent. Substances in the 8-quinolinyl-indole-3-carboxylate or the 8-quinolinyl-indazole-3-carboxylate generic definition include PB-22, fluoro-PB-22, NPB-22 and fluoro-NPB-22.

(xii) Naphthalenyl-indole-3-carboxylate or naphthalenyl-indazole-3-carboxylate by substitution at the nitrogen atom of the indole ring or by substitution at one or both of the nitrogen atoms of the indazole ring, whether or not further substituted in the indole or indazole ring to any extent, whether or not substituted on the naphthalenyl ring to any extent. Substances in the naphthalenyl-indole-3-carboxylate or naphthalenyl-indazole-3-carboxylate generic definition include NM2201, FDU-PB-22, SDB-005 and fluoro SDB-005.

(c) Any material, compound, mixture or preparation that contains any quantity of the following substances and their salts, isomers, whether optical, positional or geometric, and salts of isomers having a potential for abuse associated with a stimulant effect on the central nervous system:

(i) Alpha-pyrrolidinobutiophenone (Alpha-PBP).

(ii) Alpha-pyrrolidinopropiophenone (Alpha-PPP).

(iii) Alpha-pyrrolidinovalerophenone (Alpha-PVP).

(iv) Alpha-pyrrolidinovalerothiophenone (Alpha-PVT).

(v) Aminoindane mimetic substances that are derived from aminoindane by any substitution at the indane ring, replacement of the amino group with another N group or any combination of the above. Substances in the aminoindane generic definition include MDAI, MMAI, IAI and AMMI.

(vi) Amphetamine.

(vii) Benzphetamine.

(viii) Benzylpiperazine (BZP).

(ix) Beta-keto-n-methylbenzodioxolylbutanamine (Butylone).

(x) Beta-keto-n-methylbenzodioxolylpentanamine (Pentylone).

(xi) Butorphanol.

(xii) Cathine ((+)-norpseudoephedrine).

(xiii) Cathinomimetic substances that are any substances derived from cathinone, (2-amino-1-phenyl-1-propanone) by any substitution at the phenyl ring, any substitution at the 3 position, any substitution at the nitrogen atom or any combination of the above substitutions.

(xiv) Cathinone.

(xv) 2-(4-Chloro-2,5-dimethoxyphenyl)ethanamine (2C-C).

(xvi) Chlorphentermine.

(xvii) Clortermine.

(xviii) Diethylpropion.

(xix) Dihydro-5H-indeno-(5,6-d)-1,3-dioxol-6-amine) (MDAI).

(xx) 2-(2,5-Dimethoxy-4-ethylphenyl)ethanamine (2C-E).

(xxi) 2-(2,5-Dimethoxy-4-methylphenyl)ethanamine (2C-D).

(xxii) 2-(2,5-Dimethoxy-4-nitro-phenyl)ethanamine (2C-N).

(xxiii) 2-(2,5-Dimethoxy-4-(n)-propylphenyl)ethanamine (2C-P).

(xxiv) 2-(2,5-Dimethoxyphenyl)ethanamine (2C-H).

(xxv) Dimethylcathinone (Metamfepramone).

(xxvi) Ethcathinone.

(xxvii) 2-[4-(Ethylthio)-2,5-dimethoxyphenyl]ethanamine (2C-T-2).

(xxviii) Fencamfamin.

(xxix) Fenethylline.

(xxx) Fenproporex.

(xxxi) Fluoroamphetamine.

(xxxii) Fluoromethamphetamine.

(xxxiii) Fluoromethcathinone.

(xxxiv) 2-(4-Iodo-2,5-dimethoxyphenyl)ethanamine (2C-I).

(xxxv) 2-[4-(Isopropylthio)-2,5-dimethoxyphenyl]ethanamine(2C-T-4).

(xxxvi) Mazindol.

(xxxvii) Mefenorex.

(xxxviii) Methamphetamine.

(xxxix) Methcathinone.

(xl) Methiopropamine.

(xli) Methoxy-alpha-pyrrolidinopropiophenone (MOPPP).

(xlii) Methoxymethcathinone (methedrone).

(xliii) Methoxyphenethylamine mimetic substances that are any substances derived from 2, 5-dimethoxy-phenethylamine by any substitution at the phenyl ring, any substitution at the nitrogen atom, any substitutions at the carbon atoms of the ethylamine, or any combination of the above substitutions.

(xliv) 4-methylaminorex.

(xlv) Methyl-a-pyrrolidinobutiophenone (MPBP).

(xlvi) Methylenedioxy-alphapyrrolidinopropiophenone (MDPPP).

(xlvii) Methylenedioxyethcathinone (Ethylone).

(xlviii) Methylenedioxymethcathinone (Methylone).

(xlix) Methylenedioxypyrovalerone (MDPV).

(l) Methylmethcathinone (Mephedrone).

(li) Methylphenidate.

(lii) Modafinil.

(liii) Naphthylpyrovalerone (Naphyrone).

(liv) N-ethylamphetamine.

(lv) N, N-dimethylamphetamine.

(lvi) Pemoline.

(lvii) Phendimetrazine.

(lviii) Phenmetrazine.

(lix) Phentermine.

(lx) Pipradol.

(lxi) Propylhexedrine.

(lxii) Pyrovalerone.

(lxiii) Sibutramine.

(lxiv) Spa ((-)-1-dimethylamino-1,2-diphenylethane).

(d) Any material, compound, mixture or preparation that contains any quantity of the following substances having a potential for abuse associated with a depressant effect on the central nervous system:

(i) Any substance which contains any quantity of a derivative of barbituric acid, or any salt of a derivative of barbituric acid, unless specifically excepted.

(ii) Alprazolam.

(iii) Bromazepam.

(iv) Camazepam.

(v) Carisoprodol.

(vi) Chloral betaine.

(vii) Chloral hydrate.

(viii) Chlordiazepoxide.

(ix) Chlorhexadol.

(x) Clobazam.

(xi) Clonazepam.

(xii) Clorazepate.

(xiii) Clotiazepam.

(xiv) Cloxazolam.

(xv) Delorazepam.

(xvi) Diazepam.

(xvii) Dichloralphenazone.

(xviii) Estazolam.

(xix) Ethchlorvynol.

(xx) Ethinamate.

(xxi) Ethyl loflazepate.

(xxii) Etizolam.

(xxiii) Fenfluramine.

(xxiv) Fludiazepam.

(xxv) Flunitrazepam.

(xxvi) Flurazepam.

(xxvii) Gamma hydroxy butyrate.

(xxviii) Glutethimide.

(xxix) Halazepam.

(xxx) Haloxazolam.

(xxxi) Hydroxyphencyclidine (HO-PCP).

(xxxii) Ketamine.

(xxxiii) Ketazolam.

(xxxiv) Loprazolam.

(xxxv) Lorazepam.

(xxxvi) Lormetazepam.

(xxxvii) Lysergic acid.

(xxxviii) Mebutamate.

(xxxix) Mecloqualone.

(xl) Medazepam.

(xli) Meprobamate.

(xlii) Methaqualone.

(xliii) Methohexital.

(xliv) 2-(methoxyphenyl)-2-(ethylamino)cyclohexanone(Methoxetamine).

(xlv) 2-(methoxyphenyl)-2-(methylamino)cyclohexanone(Methoxyketamine).

(xlvi) Methoxyphencyclidine(MeO-PCP).

(xlvii) Methyprylon.

(xlviii) Midazolam.

(xlix) Nimetazepam.

(l) Nitrazepam.

(li) Nordiazepam.

(lii) Oxazepam.

(liii) Oxazolam.

(liv) Paraldehyde.

(lv) Petrichloral.

(lvi) Phencyclidine (PCP).

(lvii) Phencyclidine mimetic substances that are any substances derived from phenylcyclohexylpiperidine by any substitution at the phenyl ring, any substitution at the piperidine ring, any substitution at the cyclohexyl ring, any replacement of the phenyl ring or any combination of the above. Substances in the phenylcyclohexylpiperidine generic definition include Amino-PCP, BCP, Bromo-PCP, BTCP, Chloro-PCP, Fluoro-PCP, HO-PCP, MeO-PCP, Methyl-PCP, Nitro-PCP, Oxo-PCP, PCE, PCM, PCPY, TCP and TCPY.

(lviii) Pinazepam.

(lix) Prazepam.

(lx) Scopolamine.

(lxi) Sulfondiethylmethane.

(lxii) Sulfonethylmethane.

(lxiii) Sulfonmethane.

(lxiv) Quazepam.

(lxv) Temazepam.

(lxvi) Tetrazepam.

(lxvii) Tiletamine.

(lxviii) Triazolam.

(lxix) Zaleplon.

(lxx) Zolazepam

(lxxi) Zolpidem.

(lxxii) Zopiclone.

(e) Any material, compound, mixture or preparation that contains any quantity of the following anabolic steroids and their salts, isomers or esters:

(i) Boldenone.

(ii) Clostebol (4-chlorotestosterone).

(iii) Dehydrochloromethyltestosterone.

(iv) Drostanolone.

(v) Ethylestrenol.

(vi) Fluoxymesterone.

(vii) Formebulone (formebolone).

(viii) Mesterolone.

(ix) Methandriol.

(x) Methandrostenolone (methandienone).

(xi) Methenolone.

(xii) Methyltestosterone.

(xiii) Mibolerone.

(xiv) Nandrolone.

(xv) Norethandrolon.

(xvi) Oxandrolone.

(xvii) Oxymesterone.

(xviii) Oxymetholone.

(xix) Stanolone (4-dihydrotestosterone).

(xx) Stanozolol.

(xxi) Testolactone.

(xxii) Testosterone.

(xxiii) Trenbolone.

7. "Deliver" means the actual, constructive or attempted exchange from one person to another, whether or not there is an agency relationship.

8. "Director" means the director of the department of health services.

9. "Dispense" means distribute, leave with, give away, dispose of or deliver.

10. "Drug court program" means a program that is established pursuant to section 13-3422 by the presiding judge of the superior court in cooperation with the county attorney in a county for the purpose of prosecuting, adjudicating and treating drug dependent persons who meet the criteria and guidelines for entry into the program that are developed and agreed on by the presiding judge and the prosecutor.

11. "Drug dependent person" means a person who is using a substance that is listed in paragraph 6, 19, 20, 21 or 28 of this section and who is in a state of psychological or physical dependence, or both, arising from the use of that substance.

12. "Federal act" has the same meaning prescribed in section 32-1901.

13. "Isoamidone" means any substance identified chemically as (4-4-diphenyl-5-methyl-6-dimethylaminohexanone-3), or any salt of such substance, by whatever trade name designated.

14. "Isonipecaine" means any substance identified chemically as (1-methyl-4-phenyl-piperidine-4-carboxylic acid ethyl ester), or any salt of such substance, by whatever trade name designated.

15. "Ketobemidone" means any substance identified chemically as (4-(3-hydroxyphenyl)-1-methyl-4-piperidylethyl ketone hydrochloride), or any salt of such substance, by whatever trade name designated.

16. "Licensed" or "permitted" means authorized by the laws of this state to do certain things.

17. "Manufacture" means produce, prepare, propagate, compound, mix or process, directly or indirectly, by extraction from substances of natural origin or independently by means of chemical synthesis, or by a combination of extraction and chemical synthesis. Manufacture includes any packaging or repackaging or labeling or relabeling of containers. Manufacture does not include any producing, preparing, propagating, compounding, mixing, processing, packaging or labeling done in conformity with applicable state and local laws and rules by a licensed practitioner incident to and in the course of his licensed practice.

18. "Manufacturer" means a person who manufactures a narcotic or dangerous drug or other substance controlled by this chapter.

19. "Marijuana" means all parts of any plant of the genus cannabis, from which the resin has not been extracted, whether growing or not, and the seeds of such plant. Marijuana does not include the mature stalks of such plant or the sterilized seed of such plant which is incapable of germination.

20. "Narcotic drugs" means the following, whether of natural or synthetic origin and any substance neither chemically nor physically distinguishable from them:

(a) Acetyl-alpha-methylfentanyl.

(b) Acetylmethadol.

(c) Alfentanil.

(d) Allylprodine.

(e) Alphacetylmethadol.

(f) Alphameprodine.

(g) Alphamethadol.

(h) Alpha-methylfentanyl.

(i) Alpha-methylthiofentanyl.

(j) Alphaprodine.

(k) Amidone (methadone).

(l) Anileridine.

(m) Benzethidine.

(n) Benzylfentanyl.

(o) Betacetylmethadol.

(p) Beta-hydroxyfentanyl.

(q) Beta-hydroxy-3-methylfentanyl.

(r) Betameprodine.

(s) Betamethadol.

(t) Betaprodine.

(u) Bezitramide.

(v) Buprenorphine and its salts.

(w) Cannabis.

(x) Carfentanil.

(y) 4-chloro-n-[-1-[2-(4-nitrophenyl)ethyl]-2-piperidinylidene]benzenesulfonamide (W-18).

(z) 4-chloro-n-[1-(2-pheylethyl)-2-piperidinylidene] benzenesulfonamide (W-15).

(aa) Clonitazene.

(bb) Coca leaves.

(cc) 1-cyclohexyl-4-(1,2-diphenylethyl)piperazine (MT-45).

(dd) Dextromoramide.

(ee) Dextropropoxyphene.

(ff) Diampromide.

(gg) 3,4-dichloro-n-(-[1-(dimethylamino)cyclohexyl]methyl)-benzamide (AH-7921).

(hh) 3,4-dichloro-n-[2-(dimethylamino)cyclohexyl]-N-methylbenzamide (U-47700).

(ii) Diethylthiambutene.

(jj) Difenoxin.

(kk) Dihydrocodeine.

(ll) Dimenoxadol.

(mm) Dimepheptanol.

(nn) Dimethylthiambutene.

(oo) Dioxaphetyl butyrate.

(pp) Diphenidine (DEP).

(qq) Diphenoxylate.

(rr) Dipipanone.

(ss) Ephenidine.

(tt) Ethylmethylthiambutene.

(uu) Etonitazene.

(vv) Etoxeridine.

(ww) Fentanyl.

(xx) Fentanyl mimetic substances that are any substances derived from fentanyl by any substitution in the phenethyl group, any substitution in the piperidine ring, any substitution in the aniline ring, any replacement of the phenyl portion of the phenethyl group, any replacement of the N-propionyl group or any combination of the above.

(yy) Furethidine.

(zz) Hydroxypethidine.

(aaa) Isoamidone (isomethadone).

(bbb) Isophenidine.

(ccc) Pethidine (meperidine).

(ddd) Ketobemidone.

(eee) Lefetamine.

(fff) Levomethorphan.

(ggg) Levomoramide.

(hhh) Levophenacylmorphan.

(iii) Levorphanol.

(jjj) Metazocine.

(kkk) Methoxphenidine (MXP).

(lll) 3-methylfentanyl.

(mmm) 1-methyl-4-phenyl-4-propionoxypiperidine (MPPP).

(nnn) 3-methylthiofentanyl.

(ooo) Morpheridine.

(ppp) Noracymethadol.

(qqq) Norlevorphanol.

(rrr) Normethadone.

(sss) Norpipanone.

(ttt) Opium.

(uuu) Para-fluorofentanyl.

(vvv) Pentazocine.

(www) Phenadoxone.

(xxx) Phenampromide.

(yyy) Phenazocine.

(zzz) 1-(2-phenethyl)-4-phenyl-4-acetoxypiperidine (PEPAP).

(aaaa) Phenomorphan.

(bbbb) Phenoperidine.

(cccc) Piminodine.

(dddd) Piritramide.

(eeee) Proheptazine.

(ffff) Properidine.

(gggg) Propiram.

(hhhh) Racemethorphan.

(iiii) Racemoramide.

(jjjj) Racemorphan.

(kkkk) Remifentanil.

(llll) Sufentanil.

(mmmm) Thenylfentanyl.

(nnnn) Thiofentanyl.

(oooo) Tilidine.

(pppp) Tramadol, 2-[(dimethylamino)methyl]-1-(3-methoxyphenyl) cyclohexanol, and its salts, optical and geometric isomers, and its salts of isomers.

(qqqq) Trimeperidine.

21. "Opium" means any compound, manufacture, salt, isomer, salt of isomer, derivative, mixture or preparation of the following, but does not include apomorphine or any of its salts:

(a) Acetorphine.

(b) Acetyldihydrocodeine.

(c) Benzylmorphine.

(d) Codeine.

(e) Codeine methylbromide.

(f) Codeine-N-oxide.

(g) Cyprenorphine.

(h) Desomorphine.

(i) Dihydromorphine.

(j) Drotebanol.

(k) Ethylmorphine.

(l) Etorphine.

(m) Heroin.

(n) Hydrocodone.

(o) Hydromorphinol.

(p) Hydromorphone.

(q) Levo-alphacetylmethadol.

(r) Methyldesorphine.

(s) Methyldihydromorphine.

(t) Metopon.

(u) Morphine.

(v) Morphine methylbromide.

(w) Morphine methylsulfonate.

(x) Morphine-N-oxide.

(y) Myrophine.

(z) Nalorphine.

(aa) Nicocodeine.

(bb) Nicomorphine.

(cc) Normorphine.

(dd) Oxycodone.

(ee) Oxymorphone.

(ff) Pholcodine.

(gg) Thebacon.

(hh) Thebaine.

22. "Ordinary ephedrine, pseudoephedrine, (-)-norpseudoephedrine or phenylpropanolamine product" means a product that contains ephedrine, pseudoephedrine, (-)-norpseudoephedrine or phenylpropanolamine and that is all of the following:

(a) Approved for sale under the federal act.

(b) Labeled, advertised and marketed only for an indication that is approved by the federal food and drug administration.

(c) Either:

(i) A nonliquid that is sold in package sizes of not more than three grams of ephedrine, pseudoephedrine, (-)-norpseudoephedrine or phenlypropanolamine and that is packaged in blister packs containing not more than two dosage units or, if the use of blister packs is technically infeasible, that is packaged in unit dose packets or pouches.

(ii) A liquid that is sold in package sizes of not more than three grams of ephedrine, pseudoephedrine, (-)-norpseudoephedrine or phenylpropanolamine.

23. "Peyote" means any part of a plant of the genus lophophora, known as the mescal button.

24. "Pharmacy" means a licensed business where drugs are compounded or dispensed by a licensed pharmacist.

25. "Practitioner" means a person licensed to prescribe and administer drugs.

26. "Precursor chemical I" means any material, compound, mixture or preparation which contains any quantity of the following substances and their salts, optical isomers or salts of optical isomers:

(a) N-acetylanthranilic acid.

(b) Anthranilic acid.

(c) Ephedrine.

(d) Ergotamine.

(e) Isosafrole.

(f) Lysergic acid.

(g) Methylamine.

(h) N-ethylephedrine.

(i) N-ethylpseudoephedrine.

(j) N-methylephedrine.

(k) N-methylpseudoephedrine.

(l) Norephedrine.

(m) (-)-Norpseudoephedrine.

(n) Phenylacetic acid.

(o) Phenylpropanolamine.

(p) Piperidine.

(q) Pseudoephedrine.

27. "Precursor chemical II" means any material, compound, mixture or preparation which contains any quantity of the following substances and their salts, optical isomers or salts of optical isomers:

(a) 4-cyano-2-dimethylamino-4, 4-diphenyl butane.

(b) 4-cyano-1-methyl-4-phenylpiperidine.

(c) Chlorephedrine.

(d) Chlorpseudoephedrine.

(e) Ethyl-4-phenylpiperidine-4-carboxylate.

(f) 2-methyl-3-morpholino-1, 1-diphenylpropane-carboxylic acid.

(g) 1-methyl-4-phenylpiperidine-4-carboxylic acid.

(h) N-formyl amphetamine.

(i) N-formyl methamphetamine.

(j) Phenyl-2-propanone.

(k) 1-piperidinocyclohexane carbonitrile.

(l) 1-pyrrolidinocyclohexane carbonitrile.

28. "Prescription-only drug" does not include a dangerous drug or narcotic drug but means:

(a) Any drug which because of its toxicity or other potentiality for harmful effect, or the method of its use, or the collateral measures necessary to its use, is not generally recognized among experts, qualified by scientific training and experience to evaluate its safety and efficacy, as safe for use except by or under the supervision of a medical practitioner.

(b) Any drug that is limited by an approved new drug application under the federal act or section 32-1962 to use under the supervision of a medical practitioner.

(c) Every potentially harmful drug, the labeling of which does not bear or contain full and adequate directions for use by the consumer.

(d) Any drug required by the federal act to bear on its label the legend "Caution: Federal law prohibits dispensing without prescription" or "Rx only".

29. "Produce" means grow, plant, cultivate, harvest, dry, process or prepare for sale.

30. "Regulated chemical" means the following substances in bulk form that are not a useful part of an otherwise lawful product:

(a) Acetic anhydride.

(b) Hypophosphorous acid.

(c) Iodine.

(d) Sodium acetate.

(e) Red phosphorus.

(f) Gamma butyrolactone (GBL).

(g) 1, 4-butanediol.

(h) Butyrolactone.

(i) 1, 2 butanolide.

(j) 2-oxanalone.

(k) Tetrahydro-2-furanone.

(l) Dihydro-2(3H)-furanone.

(m) Tetramethylene glycol.

31. "Retailer" means either:

(a) A person other than a practitioner who sells any precursor chemical or regulated chemical to another person for purposes of consumption and not resale, whether or not the person possesses a permit issued pursuant to title 32, chapter 18.

(b) A person other than a manufacturer or wholesaler who purchases, receives or acquires more than twenty-four grams of a precursor chemical.

32. "Sale" or "sell" means an exchange for anything of value or advantage, present or prospective.

33. "Sale for personal use" means the retail sale for a legitimate medical use in a single transaction to an individual customer, to an employer for dispensing to employees from first aid kits or medicine chests or to a school for administration pursuant to section 15-344.

34. "Scientific purpose" means research, teaching or chemical analysis.

35. "Suspicious transaction" means a transaction to which any of the following applies:

(a) A report is required under the federal act.

(b) The circumstances would lead a reasonable person to believe that any person is attempting to possess a precursor chemical or regulated chemical for the purpose of unlawful manufacture of a dangerous drug or narcotic drug, based on such factors as the amount involved, the method of payment, the method of delivery and any past dealings with any participant.

(c) The transaction involves payment for precursor or regulated chemicals in cash or money orders in a total amount of more than two hundred dollars.

(d) The transaction involves a sale, a transfer or furnishing to a retailer for resale without a prescription of ephedrine, pseudoephedrine, (-)-norpseudoephedrine or phenylpropanolamine that is not an ordinary ephedrine, pseudoephedrine, (-)-norpseudoephedrine or phenylpropanolamine product.

36. "Threshold amount" means a weight, market value or other form of measurement of an unlawful substance as follows:

(a) One gram of heroin.

(b) Nine grams of cocaine.

(c) Seven hundred fifty milligrams of cocaine base or hydrolyzed cocaine.

(d) Four grams or 50 milliliters of PCP.

(e) Nine grams of methamphetamine, including methamphetamine in liquid suspension.

(f) Nine grams of amphetamine, including amphetamine in liquid suspension.

(g) One-half milliliter of lysergic acid diethylamide, or in the case of blotter dosage units fifty dosage units.

(h) Two pounds of marijuana.

(i) For any combination consisting solely of those unlawful substances listed in subdivisions (a) through (h) of this paragraph, an amount equal to or in excess of the threshold amount, as determined by the application of section 13-3420.

(j) For any unlawful substance not listed in subdivisions (a) through (h) of this paragraph or any combination involving any unlawful substance not listed in subdivisions (a) through (h) of this paragraph, a value of at least one thousand dollars.

37. "Transfer" means furnish, deliver or give away.

38. "Vapor-releasing substance containing a toxic substance" means a material which releases vapors or fumes containing any of the following:

(a) Ketones, including acetone, methyl ethyl ketone, mibk, miak, isophorone and mesityl oxide.

(b) Hydrocarbons, including propane, butane, pentane, hexane, heptane and halogenated hydrocarbons.

(c) Ethylene dichloride.

(d) Pentachlorophenol.

(e) Chloroform.

(f) Methylene chloride.

(g) Trichloroethylene.

(h) Difluoroethane.

(i) Tetrafluoroethane.

(j) Aldehydes, including formaldehyde.

(k) Acetates, including ethyl acetate and butyl acetate.

(l) Aromatics, including benzene, toluene, xylene, ethylbenzene and cumene.

(m) Alcohols, including methyl alcohol, ethyl alcohol, isopropyl alcohol, butyl alcohol and diacetone alcohol.

(n) Ether, including Diethyl ether and petroleum ether.

(o) Nitrous oxide.

(p) Amyl nitrite.

(q) Isobutyl nitrite.

39. "Weight" unless otherwise specified includes the entire weight of any mixture or substance that contains a detectable amount of an unlawful substance. If a mixture or substance contains more than one unlawful substance, the weight of the entire mixture or substance is assigned to the unlawful substance that results in the greater offense. If a mixture or substance contains lysergic acid diethylamide, the offense that results from the unlawful substance shall be based on the greater offense as determined by the entire weight of the mixture or substance or the number of blotter dosage units. For the purposes of this paragraph, "mixture" means any combination of substances from which the unlawful substance cannot be removed without a chemical process.

40. "Wholesaler" means a person who in the usual course of business lawfully supplies narcotic drugs, dangerous drugs, precursor chemicals or regulated chemicals that he himself has not produced or prepared, but not to a person for the purpose of consumption by the person, whether or not the wholesaler has a permit that is issued pursuant to title 32, chapter 18. Wholesaler includes a person who sells, delivers or dispenses a precursor chemical in an amount or under circumstances that would require registration as a distributor of precursor chemicals under the federal act.

13-3402. Possession and sale of peyote; classification

A. A person who knowingly possesses, sells, transfers or offers to sell or transfer peyote is guilty of a class 6 felony.
B. In a prosecution for violation of this section, it is a defense that the peyote is being used or is intended for use:
1. In connection with the bona fide practice of a religious belief, and
2. As an integral part of a religious exercise, and
3. In a manner not dangerous to public health, safety or morals.

13-3403. Possession and sale of a vapor-releasing substance containing a toxic substance; regulation of sale; exceptions; classification

A. A person shall not knowingly:
1. Breathe, inhale or drink a vapor-releasing substance containing a toxic substance.
2. Sell, transfer or offer to sell or transfer a vapor-releasing substance containing a toxic substance to a person under eighteen years of age.
3. Sell, transfer or offer to sell or transfer a vapor-releasing substance containing a toxic substance if such person is not, at the time of sale, transfer or offer, employed by or engaged in operating a licensed commercial establishment at a fixed location regularly offering such substance for sale and such sale, transfer or offer is made in the course of employment or operation.
B. A person making a sale or transfer of a vapor-releasing glue containing a toxic substance shall require identification of the purchaser and shall record:
1. The name of the glue.
2. The date and hour of delivery.
3. The intended use of the glue.
4. The signature and address of the purchaser.
5. The signature of the seller or deliverer.
Such record shall be kept for three years and be available to board inspectors and peace officers.
C. The operator of a commercial establishment shall keep all vapor-releasing glue containing a toxic substance in a place that is unavailable to customers without the assistance of the operator or an employee of the establishment.
D. The operator of a commercial establishment selling vapor-releasing paints and varnishes containing a toxic substance dispensed by the use of any aerosol spray device shall conspicuously display an easily legible sign of not less than eleven by fourteen inches which states: "Warning: inhalation of vapors can be dangerous".
E. This section is not applicable to the transfer of a vapor-releasing substance containing a toxic substance from a parent or guardian to his child or ward, or the sale or transfer made for manufacturing or industrial purposes.
F. Subsection A, paragraphs 2 and 3 and subsections B and C do not apply to substances certified by the department of health services as containing an additive that inhibits inhalation or induces sneezing.
G. A person who violates any provision of this section is guilty of a class 5 felony, but the court, having regard to the nature and circumstances of the offense, may enter judgment of conviction for a class 1 misdemeanor and make disposition accordingly or may place the defendant on probation in accordance with chapter 9 of this title and refrain from designating the offense as a felony or misdemeanor until the probation is terminated. The offense shall be treated as a felony for all purposes until such time as the court enters an order designating the offense a misdemeanor.
H. For the purposes of subsections A and E, "vapor-releasing substance containing a toxic substance" means paint or varnish dispensed by the use of aerosol spray, or any glue, that releases vapors or fumes containing acetone, volatile acetates, benzene, butyl alcohol, ethyl alcohol, ethylene dichloride, isopropyl alcohol, methyl alcohol, methyl ethyl ketone, pentachlorophenol, petroleum ether, toluene, volatile ketones, isophorone, chloroform, methylene chloride, mesityl oxide, xylene, cumene, ethylbenzene, trichloroethylene, mibk, miak, mek or diacetone alcohol or isobutyl nitrite.

13-3403.01. Nitrous oxide containers; sale to minors; classification

A. A person shall not knowingly sell, give or deliver to a person under eighteen years of age any container exclusively containing nitrous oxide, unless the person under eighteen years of age is delivering or accepting delivery in the person's capacity as an employee.
B. A person who violates this section is guilty of a class 5 felony unless the court does either of the following:

1. Enters a judgment of conviction for a class 1 misdemeanor and makes disposition accordingly.

2. Places the person on probation in accordance with chapter 9 of this title and refrains from designating the offense as a felony or misdemeanor until the probation is terminated. The offense shall be treated as a felony for all purposes until such time as the court may actually enter an order designating the offense as a misdemeanor.

13-3403.02. Selling or giving nitrous oxide to underage person; illegally obtaining nitrous oxide containers by underage person; classification; definition

A. An operator or employee of a commercial establishment who questions or has reason to question whether or not a person ordering, purchasing, attempting to purchase or otherwise procuring or attempting to procure the serving or delivery of a nitrous oxide container is under eighteen years of age shall require the person to exhibit a written instrument of identification and may require the person to sign the person's name, the date, and the number of the identification on a card to be retained by the operator, or may require the person to sign the person's name and the date on a photocopy of the instrument of identification to be retained by the operator. The following written instruments are the only acceptable types of identification:

1. An unexpired driver license issued by any state or by Canada, provided the license includes a picture of the licensee.

2. A nonoperating identification license issued pursuant to section 28-3165.

3. An armed forces identification card.

4. A valid passport or border crossing identification card that is issued by a government.

5. A voter card issued by the government of Mexico and that contains a photograph and the date of birth of the person.

B. An operator or employee of a commercial establishment who sells, gives, serves or furnishes a nitrous oxide container to a person who is under eighteen years of age without having recorded and retained a record of the person's age or a dated and signed photocopy of the instrument of identification exhibited as prescribed by subsection A of this section is deemed to have constructive knowledge of the person's age.

C. A person who is under eighteen years of age and who misrepresents the person's age to any person by means of a written instrument of identification with the intent to induce a person to sell, serve, give or furnish a nitrous oxide container contrary to section 13-3403.01 is guilty of a class 1 misdemeanor.

D. A person who is under eighteen years of age and who solicits another person to purchase, sell, give, serve or furnish a nitrous oxide container contrary to law is guilty of a class 3 misdemeanor.

E. A person who does not have a valid driver or nonoperating identification license and who uses a driver or nonoperating identification license of another in violation of subsection C of this section shall have that person's right to apply for a driver or nonoperating identification license suspended as provided by section 28-3309, subsection B. A person who uses a driver or nonoperating identification license in violation of subsection C of this section is subject to suspension of the driver or nonoperating identification license as provided in section 28-3309, subsection C.

F. A person who knowingly influences the selling, giving or serving of a nitrous oxide container to a person under eighteen years of age by misrepresenting the age of the person or who orders, requests, receives or procures a nitrous oxide container from an operator or employee of a commercial establishment with the intent of selling, giving or serving it to a person under eighteen years of age is guilty of a class 1 misdemeanor.

G. For purposes of this section, "nitrous oxide container" means any container or canister exclusively containing nitrous oxide.

13-3404. Sale of precursor or regulated chemicals; report; exemptions; violation; classification

A. A manufacturer, wholesaler, retailer or other person who sells, transfers or otherwise furnishes any precursor chemical or regulated chemical to any person in this state shall submit a report to the department of public safety of all of those transactions unless the entity is required to report similar transactions to a federal agency.

B. The department of public safety shall provide a common reporting form that contains at least the following information:

1. The name of the substance.

2. The proprietary name of the product, if any.

3. The quantity of the substance sold, transferred or furnished.

4. The date the substance is to be sold, transferred or furnished.

5. The name and address of the person buying or receiving the substance.

6. The name and address of the manufacturer, wholesaler, retailer or other person selling, transferring or furnishing the substance.

C. An entity that is required to report pursuant to subsection A of this section, not less than twenty-one days before delivery of the substance, shall submit a report of the transaction to the department of public safety, except that the department of public safety may authorize the submission of the reports on a monthly basis with respect to repeated, regular transactions between the furnisher and the recipient involving the same substance if the department of public safety determines that both of the following exist:

1. A pattern of regular supply of the substance exists between the manufacturer, wholesaler, retailer or other person who sells, transfers or otherwise furnishes such substance and the recipient of the substance.

2. The recipient has established a record of utilization of the substance for lawful purposes.

D. An entity that is required to report pursuant to subsection A of this section and that receives from a source outside of this state any precursor chemical or regulated chemical shall submit a report of such transaction to the department of public safety as prescribed in subsection B of this section.

E. Subsections A, B, C and D of this section do not apply to any of the following:

1. The sale, transfer or furnishing of ordinary ephedrine, pseudoephedrine, (-)-norpseudoephedrine or phenylpropanolamine products.

2. The sale for personal use of ephedrine, pseudoephedrine, (-)-norpseudoephedrine or phenylpropanolamine products totaling four packages or less.

3. The sale, transfer or furnishing of a precursor chemical or regulated chemical by a wholesaler or manufacturer if both parties to the transaction possess a valid and current permit issued pursuant to title 32, chapter 18 and a valid and current precursor list I chemical distributor registration or controlled substance distributor registration issued pursuant to the federal act.

F. Any manufacturer, wholesaler, retailer or other person who sells, transfers or otherwise furnishes any precursor chemical or regulated chemical to any person in this state in a suspicious transaction shall report the transaction in writing to the department of public safety.

G. A person who is regulated by the provisions of this chapter and who discovers the theft, disappearance or other loss of any precursor chemical II or regulated chemical or the excessive or unusual loss of any precursor chemical I shall report the theft or loss in writing to the department of public safety within three days after such discovery. Any difference between the quantity of any precursor chemical II or regulated chemical received and the quantity shipped and any excessive or unusual loss of any precursor chemical I shipped shall be reported in writing to the department of public safety within three days of actual knowledge of the discrepancy. A report made pursuant to this subsection shall also include the name of the common carrier or person who transports the substance and the date of shipment of the substance.

H. An entity that is required to report pursuant to subsection A of this section shall maintain records as described in subsection B of this section relating to all such transactions for not less than two years, except that this requirement does not apply to sales for personal use of ordinary ephedrine, pseudoephedrine, (-)-norpseudoephedrine or phenylpropanolamine products by a permitted retailer. These records shall be open for inspection and copying by peace officers in the performance of their duties. A peace officer shall not divulge pricing information obtained pursuant to this subsection except in connection with a prosecution, investigation, judicial proceeding or administrative proceeding or in response to a judicial order.

I. This section does not apply to any of the following transactions:

1. The sale, transfer or furnishing to or by any practitioner or any pharmacist acting pursuant to a prescription.

2. The sale, transfer or furnishing to or by a hospital, long-term health care provider or managed health care provider or any other licensed or permitted health care provider that administers or dispenses precursor chemical I medication under the supervision of a practitioner.

3. The sale, transfer or furnishing of iodine either:

(a) In an amount of two ounces or less by weight.

(b) To a licensed or permitted wholesaler, health care facility, pharmacy or practitioner.

(c) As a tincture of iodine or topical solution of iodine.

4. The sale, transfer or furnishing of red phosphorous in an amount of less than four ounces.

5. The movement from one facility of a licensee or permittee to another facility of the same licensee or permittee without sale.

6. The sale, transfer or furnishing of dietary supplements if all of the following apply:

(a) The dietary supplements are not otherwise prohibited by law.

(b) The dietary supplements contain naturally occurring ephedrine, ephedrine alkaloids or pseudoephedrine, or their salts, isomers or salts of isomers, or a combination of these substances that both:

(i) Are contained in the matrix of organic material in which they naturally occur.

(ii) Do not exceed five per cent of the total weight of the natural product.

(c) The dietary supplements are manufactured and distributed for legitimate use in a manner that reduces or eliminates the likelihood of abuse.

(d) The dietary supplements are labeled in compliance with the dietary supplement health and education act of 1994 (21 United States Code section 321).

J. The department of public safety shall grant an exemption from the reporting requirements under subsection C of this section to any person who supplies a precursor chemical or regulated chemical if the person can demonstrate to the department's satisfaction that the recipient requires the substance for a lawful purpose and that special circumstances prevent the supplier from reporting the transaction to the department twenty-one days or more before delivery.

K. An entity that is required to report pursuant to subsection A of this section may satisfy the reporting or record keeping requirements of this section by submitting to the department of public safety either:

1. Computer readable data from which all of the required information may be derived.

2. Copies of reports that are filed pursuant to federal law and that contain all of the information required by this section.

L. This chapter does not preclude any person, including a licensee, permittee, manufacturer, wholesaler or retailer, from instituting contact with and disclosing transactions or transaction records to appropriate federal, state or local law enforcement agencies if the person has information that may be relevant to a possible violation of any criminal statute or to the evasion or attempted evasion of any reporting or record keeping requirement of this chapter.

M. Any person, including a licensee, permittee, manufacturer, wholesaler or retailer or any officer, employee or agent of any licensee, permittee, manufacturer, wholesaler or retailer, that keeps or files a record as prescribed by this section or that communicates or discloses information or records under this section is not liable to its customer, a state or local agency or any person for any loss or damage caused in whole or in part by the making, filing or governmental use of the report or any information contained in that report.

N. Notwithstanding any other law, a county, city or town shall not enact an ordinance that is more restrictive than the requirements of this section.

O. It is unlawful for a person to knowingly:

1. Fail to submit a report that is required by this section.

2. Fail to maintain a record that is required by this section.

3. Furnish false information or omit any material information in any report or record that is required by this section.

4. Cause another person to furnish false information or to omit any material information in any report or record that is required by this section.

5. Participate in any wholesale or retail transaction or series of transactions that is structured by a person with the intent to avoid the filing by any party to the transaction of any report that is required by this section.

P. A person who violates subsection O, paragraph 3, 4 or 5 of this section is guilty of a class 5 felony. A person who violates subsection O, paragraph 1 or 2 of this section is guilty of a class 6 felony.

13-3404.01. Possession or sale of precursor chemicals, regulated chemicals, substances or equipment; exceptions; classification

A. A person shall not do any of the following:

1. Knowingly possess a precursor chemical II.

2. Knowingly possess more than twenty-four grams of pseudoephedrine, (-)-norpseudoephedrine or phenylpropanolamine without a license or permit issued pursuant to title 32, chapter 18.

3. Knowingly purchase more than three packages, not to exceed nine grams of pseudoephedrine, (-)-norpseudoephedrine or phenylpropanolamine without a valid prescription order as defined in section 32-1901 or a license or permit issued pursuant to title 32, chapter 18.

4. Knowingly possess any ephedrine that is uncombined or that is the sole active ingredient of a product or more than twenty-four grams of ephedrine that is combined with another active ingredient in any ephedrine product without a license or permit issued pursuant to title 32, chapter 18.

5. Knowingly purchase any ephedrine that is uncombined or is the sole active ingredient of a product or more than three packages, not to exceed nine grams of ephedrine that is combined with another active ingredient in any ephedrine product without a license or permit issued pursuant to title 32, chapter 18.

6. Sell, transfer or otherwise furnish any precursor chemical, regulated chemical or other substance or equipment with knowledge that the recipient will use the precursor chemical, regulated chemical, substance or equipment to unlawfully manufacture a dangerous drug or narcotic drug.

7. As a manufacturer, wholesaler or retailer, knowingly possess any precursor chemical or regulated chemical from which the label, the national drug control number or the manufacturer's lot number has been removed, altered or obliterated, except that a licensed manufacturer may relabel products as permitted under the federal act.

8. Knowingly sell, transfer or otherwise furnish more than nine grams of any precursor chemical without a license or permit issued pursuant to title 32, chapter 18.

9. Sell, transfer or furnish ephedrine, pseudoephedrine, (-)-norpseudoephedrine or phenylpropanolamine in a total amount of more than nine grams in a single transaction in this state unless the recipient possesses a valid and current permit issued by the board pursuant to title 32, chapter 18.

10. Sell, transfer or otherwise furnish a precursor chemical in violation of any rule of the board or the department of public safety.

11. As a wholesaler or retailer, purchase or otherwise acquire or receive a precursor chemical from any person who does not possess a valid and current permit issued pursuant to title 32, chapter 18.

12. Knowingly participate in any transaction or series of transactions that is structured by any person with the intent to avoid or circumvent the prohibitions or limits on sales established by this section.

B. A retailer shall not knowingly sell, transfer or otherwise furnish a precursor chemical unless:

1. The transaction occurs in the normal course of business at premises that are permitted pursuant to title 32, chapter 18.

2. The retailer has a valid and current permit that is issued pursuant to title 32, chapter 18 and that is prominently displayed at the premises where the transaction occurs.

C. A retailer shall not sell more than a total of three packages, not to exceed nine grams of ephedrine, pseudoephedrine, (-)-norpseudoephedrine or phenylpropanolamine in a single transaction unless the person has a valid prescription order as defined in section 32-1901.

D. A wholesaler shall not sell, transfer or otherwise furnish a precursor chemical to any person unless:

1. The wholesaler has a valid and current permit issued pursuant to title 32, chapter 18.

2. The recipient has a permit issued pursuant to title 32, chapter 18, is a pharmacy or is a practitioner.

3. The transaction does not involve payment in cash or money orders in an amount of more than one thousand dollars.

E. A manufacturer shall not sell, transfer or otherwise furnish a precursor chemical to any person unless:

1. The recipient is licensed or has a permit issued pursuant to title 32, chapter 18, is a pharmacy or is a practitioner.

2. The transaction does not involve payment in cash or money orders in an amount of more than one thousand dollars.

F. This section does not apply to any of the following:

1. The transfer by a licensee or permittee to a reclamation facility for destruction.

2. The movement from one facility of a licensee or permittee to another facility of the same licensee or permittee without sale.

G. Notwithstanding any other law, a county, city or town shall not enact an ordinance that is more restrictive than the requirements of this section.

H. A violation of subsection A, paragraph 1 or 6 is a class 2 felony. A violation of subsection A, paragraph 2, 3, 4, 5, 7, 9, 11 or 12 is a class 5 felony. A violation of subsection A, paragraph 8 or 10 is a class 6 felony. A violation of subsection B, D or E is a class 5 felony. A violation of subsection C is a class 5 felony, except that if the violation involves less than a total of fifty grams of ephedrine, pseudoephedrine, (-)-norpseudoephedrine or phenylpropanolamine, the first violation is a class 2 misdemeanor and the second violation is a class 1 misdemeanor. An enterprise is not criminally accountable for a violation of subsection C unless the conduct constituting the offense is engaged in, authorized, commanded or recklessly tolerated by the directors of the enterprise in any manner or by a high managerial agent acting within the scope of employment.

13-3405. Possession, use, production, sale or transportation of marijuana; classification

A. A person shall not knowingly:

1. Possess or use marijuana.

2. Possess marijuana for sale.

3. Produce marijuana.

4. Transport for sale, import into this state or offer to transport for sale or import into this state, sell, transfer or offer to sell or transfer marijuana.

B. A person who violates:

1. Subsection A, paragraph 1 of this section involving an amount of marijuana not possessed for sale having a weight of less than two pounds is guilty of a class 6 felony.

2. Subsection A, paragraph 1 of this section involving an amount of marijuana not possessed for sale having a weight of at least two pounds but less than four pounds is guilty of a class 5 felony.

3. Subsection A, paragraph 1 of this section involving an amount of marijuana not possessed for sale having a weight of four pounds or more is guilty of a class 4 felony.

4. Subsection A, paragraph 2 of this section involving an amount of marijuana having a weight of less than two pounds is guilty of a class 4 felony.

5. Subsection A, paragraph 2 of this section involving an amount of marijuana having a weight of at least two pounds but not more than four pounds is guilty of a class 3 felony.

6. Subsection A, paragraph 2 of this section involving an amount of marijuana having a weight of more than four pounds is guilty of a class 2 felony.

7. Subsection A, paragraph 3 of this section involving an amount of marijuana having a weight of less than two pounds is guilty of a class 5 felony.

8. Subsection A, paragraph 3 of this section involving an amount of marijuana having a weight of at least two pounds but not more than four pounds is guilty of a class 4 felony.

9. Subsection A, paragraph 3 of this section involving an amount of marijuana having a weight of more than four pounds is guilty of a class 3 felony.

10. Subsection A, paragraph 4 of this section involving an amount of marijuana having a weight of less than two pounds is guilty of a class 3 felony.

11. Subsection A, paragraph 4 of this section involving an amount of marijuana having a weight of two pounds or more is guilty of a class 2 felony.

C. If the aggregate amount of marijuana involved in one offense or all of the offenses that are consolidated for trial equals or exceeds the statutory threshold amount, a person who is sentenced pursuant to subsection B, paragraph 5, 6, 8, 9 or 11 of this section is not eligible for suspension of sentence, probation, pardon or release from confinement on any basis until the person has served the sentence imposed by the court, the person is eligible for release pursuant to section 41-1604.07 or the sentence is commuted.

D. In addition to any other penalty prescribed by this title, the court shall order a person who is convicted of a violation of any provision of this section to pay a fine of not less than seven hundred fifty dollars or three times the value as determined by the court of the marijuana involved in or giving rise to the charge, whichever is greater, and not more than the maximum authorized by chapter 8 of this title. A judge shall not suspend any part or all of the imposition of any fine required by this subsection.

E. A person who is convicted of a felony violation of any provision of this section for which probation or release before the expiration of the sentence imposed by the court is authorized is prohibited from using any marijuana, dangerous drug or narcotic drug except as lawfully administered by a practitioner and as a condition of any probation or release shall be required to submit to drug testing administered under the supervision of the probation department of the county or the state department of corrections as appropriate during the duration of the term of probation or before the expiration of the sentence imposed.

F. If the aggregate amount of marijuana involved in one offense or all of the offenses that are consolidated for trial is less than the statutory threshold amount, a person who is sentenced pursuant to subsection B, paragraph 4, 7 or 10 and who is granted probation by the court shall be ordered by the court that as a condition of probation the person perform not less than two hundred forty hours of community restitution with an agency or organization providing counseling, rehabilitation or treatment for alcohol or drug abuse, an agency or organization that provides medical treatment to persons who abuse controlled substances, an agency or organization that serves persons who are victims of crime or any other appropriate agency or organization.

G. If a person who is sentenced pursuant to subsection B, paragraph 1, 2 or 3 of this section is granted probation for a felony violation of this section, the court shall order that as a condition of probation the person perform not less than twenty-four hours of community restitution with an agency or organization providing counseling, rehabilitation or treatment for alcohol or drug abuse, an agency or organization that provides medical treatment to persons who abuse controlled substances, an agency or organization that serves persons who are victims of crime or any other appropriate agency or organization.

H. If a person is granted probation for a misdemeanor violation of this section, the court shall order as a condition of probation that the person attend eight hours of instruction on the nature and harmful effects of narcotic drugs, marijuana and other dangerous drugs on the human system, and on the laws related to the control of these substances, or perform twenty-four hours of community restitution.

13-3406. Possession, use, administration, acquisition, sale, manufacture or transportation of prescription-only drugs; misbranded drugs; classification; definition

A. A person shall not knowingly:

1. Possess or use a prescription-only drug unless the person obtains the prescription-only drug pursuant to a valid prescription of a prescriber who is licensed pursuant to title 32, chapter 7, 11, 13, 14, 15, 16, 17, 21, 25 or 29 or is similarly licensed in another state.

2. Unless the person holds a license or a permit issued pursuant to title 32, chapter 7, 11, 13, 14, 15, 16, 17, 18, 21, 25 or 29, possess a prescription-only drug for sale.

3. Unless the person holds a license or a permit issued pursuant to title 32, chapter 7, 11, 13, 14, 15, 16, 17, 18, 21, 25 or 29, possess equipment and chemicals for the purpose of manufacturing a prescription-only drug.

4. Unless the person holds a license or a permit issued pursuant to title 32, chapter 18, manufacture a prescription-only drug.

5. Administer a prescription-only drug to another person whose possession or use of the prescription-only drug violates this section.

6. Obtain or procure the administration of a prescription-only drug by fraud, deceit, misrepresentation or subterfuge.

7. Unless the person is authorized, transport for sale, import into this state or offer to transport for sale or import into this state, sell, transfer or offer to sell or transfer a prescription-only drug.

8. Possess or use a misbranded drug.

9. Manufacture, sell or distribute a misbranded drug.

B. A person who violates:

1. Subsection A, paragraph 9 of this section is guilty of a class 4 felony.

2. Subsection A, paragraph 2 or 7 of this section is guilty of a class 6 felony.

3. Subsection A, paragraph 1, 3, 4, 5 or 6 of this section is guilty of a class 1 misdemeanor.

4. Subsection A, paragraph 8 of this section is guilty of a class 2 misdemeanor.

C. In addition to any other penalty prescribed by this title, the court shall order a person who is convicted of a violation of this section to pay a fine of one thousand dollars. A judge shall not suspend any part or all of the imposition of any fine required by this subsection.

D. A person who is convicted of a felony violation of this section for which probation or release before the expiration of the sentence imposed by the court is authorized is prohibited from using any marijuana, dangerous drug, narcotic drug or prescription-only drug except as lawfully administered by a practitioner and as a condition of any probation or release shall be required to submit to drug testing administered under the supervision of the probation department of the county or the state department of corrections, as appropriate, during the duration of the term of probation or before the expiration of the sentence imposed.

E. If a person who is convicted of a violation of subsection A, paragraph 2 or 7 of this section is granted probation, the court shall order that as a condition of probation the person perform not less than two hundred forty hours of community restitution with an agency or organization providing counseling, rehabilitation or treatment for alcohol or drug abuse, an agency or organization that provides medical treatment to persons who abuse controlled substances, an agency or organization that serves persons who are victims of crime or any other appropriate agency or organization.

F. For the purposes of this section, "misbranded drug" means a drug that is misbranded as prescribed in section 32-1967.

13-3407. Possession, use, administration, acquisition, sale, manufacture or transportation of dangerous drugs; classification

A. A person shall not knowingly:

1. Possess or use a dangerous drug.

2. Possess a dangerous drug for sale.

3. Possess equipment or chemicals, or both, for the purpose of manufacturing a dangerous drug.

4. Manufacture a dangerous drug.

5. Administer a dangerous drug to another person.

6. Obtain or procure the administration of a dangerous drug by fraud, deceit, misrepresentation or subterfuge.

7. Transport for sale, import into this state or offer to transport for sale or import into this state, sell, transfer or offer to sell or transfer a dangerous drug.

B. A person who violates:

1. Subsection A, paragraph 1 of this section is guilty of a class 4 felony. Unless the drug involved is lysergic acid diethylamide, methamphetamine, amphetamine or phencyclidine or the person was previously convicted of a felony offense or a violation of this section or section 13-3408, the court on motion of the state, considering the nature and circumstances of the offense, for a person not previously convicted of any felony offense or a violation of this section or section 13-3408 may enter judgment of conviction for a class 1 misdemeanor and make disposition accordingly or may place the defendant on probation in accordance with chapter 9 of this

title and refrain from designating the offense as a felony or misdemeanor until the probation is successfully terminated. The offense shall be treated as a felony for all purposes until the court enters an order designating the offense a misdemeanor.

2. Subsection A, paragraph 2 of this section is guilty of a class 2 felony.

3. Subsection A, paragraph 3 of this section is guilty of a class 3 felony, except that if the offense involved methamphetamine, the person is guilty of a class 2 felony.

4. Subsection A, paragraph 4 of this section is guilty of a class 2 felony.

5. Subsection A, paragraph 5 of this section is guilty of a class 2 felony.

6. Subsection A, paragraph 6 of this section is guilty of a class 3 felony.

7. Subsection A, paragraph 7 of this section is guilty of a class 2 felony.

C. Except as provided in subsection E of this section, a person who is convicted of a violation of subsection A, paragraph 1, 3 or 6 and who has not previously been convicted of any felony or who has not been sentenced pursuant to section 13-703, section 13-704, section 13-706, subsection A, section 13-708, subsection D or any other law making the convicted person ineligible for probation is eligible for probation.

D. Except as provided in subsection E of this section, if the aggregate amount of dangerous drugs involved in one offense or all of the offenses that are consolidated for trial equals or exceeds the statutory threshold amount, a person who is convicted of a violation of subsection A, paragraph 2, 5 or 7 of this section is not eligible for suspension of sentence, probation, pardon or release from confinement on any basis until the person has served the sentence imposed by the court, the person is eligible for release pursuant to section 41-1604.07 or the sentence is commuted.

E. If the person is convicted of a violation of subsection A, paragraph 2, 3, 4 or 7 of this section and the drug involved is methamphetamine, the person shall be sentenced as follows:

Minimum	Presumptive	Maximum
5 calendar years	10 calendar years	15 calendar years

A person who has previously been convicted of a violation of subsection A, paragraph 2, 3, 4 or 7 of this section involving methamphetamine or section 13-3407.01 shall be sentenced as follows:

Minimum	Presumptive	Maximum
10 calendar years	15 calendar years	20 calendar years

F. A person who is convicted of a violation of subsection A, paragraph 4 of this section or subsection A, paragraph 2, 3 or 7 of this section involving methamphetamine is not eligible for suspension of sentence, probation, pardon or release from confinement on any basis until the person has served the sentence imposed by the court, the person is eligible for release pursuant to section 41-1604.07 or the sentence is commuted.

G. If a person is convicted of a violation of subsection A, paragraph 5 of this section, if the drug is administered without the other person's consent, if the other person is under eighteen years of age and if the drug is flunitrazepam, gamma hydroxy butrate or ketamine hydrochloride, the convicted person is not eligible for suspension of sentence, probation, pardon or release from confinement on any basis until the person has served the sentence imposed by the court, the person is eligible for release pursuant to section 41-1604.07 or the sentence is commuted.

H. In addition to any other penalty prescribed by this title, the court shall order a person who is convicted of a violation of this section to pay a fine of not less than one thousand dollars or three times the value as determined by the court of the dangerous drugs involved in or giving rise to the charge, whichever is greater, and not more than the maximum authorized by chapter 8 of this title. A judge shall not suspend any part or all of the imposition of any fine required by this subsection.

I. A person who is convicted of a violation of this section for which probation or release before the expiration of the sentence imposed by the court is authorized is prohibited from using any marijuana, dangerous drug, narcotic drug or prescription-only drug except as lawfully administered by a health care practitioner and as a condition of any probation or release shall be required to submit to drug testing administered under the supervision of the probation department of the county or the state department of corrections, as appropriate, during the duration of the term of probation or before the expiration of the sentence imposed.

J. If a person who is convicted of a violation of this section is granted probation, the court shall order that as a condition of probation the person perform not less than three hundred sixty hours of community restitution with an agency or organization that provides counseling, rehabilitation or treatment for alcohol or drug abuse, an agency or organization that provides medical treatment to persons who abuse controlled substances, an agency or organization that serves persons who are victims of crime or any other appropriate agency or organization.

K. The presumptive term imposed pursuant to subsection E of this section may be mitigated or aggravated pursuant to section 13-701, subsections D and E.

13-3407.01. Manufacturing methamphetamine under circumstances that cause physical injury to a minor; classification

A. A person shall not knowingly manufacture methamphetamine under any circumstance that causes physical injury to a minor who is under fifteen years of age.
B. A person who violates this section is guilty of a class 2 felony and is punishable as provided by section 13-705.

13-3408. Possession, use, administration, acquisition, sale, manufacture or transportation of narcotic drugs; classification

A. A person shall not knowingly:
1. Possess or use a narcotic drug.
2. Possess a narcotic drug for sale.
3. Possess equipment or chemicals, or both, for the purpose of manufacturing a narcotic drug.
4. Manufacture a narcotic drug.
5. Administer a narcotic drug to another person.
6. Obtain or procure the administration of a narcotic drug by fraud, deceit, misrepresentation or subterfuge.
7. Transport for sale, import into this state, offer to transport for sale or import into this state, sell, transfer or offer to sell or transfer a narcotic drug.
B. A person who violates:
1. Subsection A, paragraph 1 of this section is guilty of a class 4 felony.
2. Subsection A, paragraph 2 of this section is guilty of a class 2 felony.
3. Subsection A, paragraph 3 of this section is guilty of a class 3 felony.
4. Subsection A, paragraph 4 of this section is guilty of a class 2 felony.
5. Subsection A, paragraph 5 of this section is guilty of a class 2 felony.
6. Subsection A, paragraph 6 of this section is guilty of a class 3 felony.
7. Subsection A, paragraph 7 of this section is guilty of a class 2 felony.
C. A person who is convicted of a violation of subsection A, paragraph 1, 3 or 6 of this section and who has not previously been convicted of any felony or who has not been sentenced pursuant to section 13-703, section 13-704, subsection A, B, C, D or E, section 13-706, subsection A, section 13-708, subsection D or any other provision of law making the convicted person ineligible for probation is eligible for probation.
D. If the aggregate amount of narcotic drugs involved in one offense or all of the offenses that are consolidated for trial equals or exceeds the statutory threshold amount, a person who is convicted of a violation of subsection A, paragraph 2, 5 or 7 of this section is not eligible for suspension of sentence, probation, pardon or release from confinement on any basis until the person has served the sentence imposed by the court, the person is eligible for release pursuant to section 41-1604.07 or the sentence is commuted.
E. A person who is convicted of a violation of subsection A, paragraph 4 of this section is not eligible for suspension of sentence, probation, pardon or release from confinement on any basis until the person has served the sentence imposed by the court, the person is eligible for release pursuant to section 41-1604.07 or the sentence is commuted.
F. In addition to any other penalty prescribed by this title, the court shall order a person who is convicted of a violation of this section to pay a fine of not less than two thousand dollars or three times the value as determined by the court of the narcotic drugs involved in or giving rise to the charge, whichever is greater, and not more than the maximum authorized by chapter 8 of this title. A judge shall not suspend any part or all of the imposition of any fine required by this subsection.
G. A person who is convicted of a violation of this section for which probation or release before the expiration of the sentence imposed by the court is authorized is prohibited from using any marijuana, dangerous drug, narcotic drug or prescription-only drug except as lawfully administered by a health care practitioner and as a condition of any probation or release shall be required to submit to drug testing administered under the supervision of the probation department of the county or the state department of corrections, as appropriate, during the duration of the term of probation or before the expiration of the sentence imposed.
H. If a person who is convicted of a violation of this section is granted probation, the court shall order that as a condition of probation the person perform not less than three hundred sixty hours of community restitution with an agency or organization that provides counseling, rehabilitation or treatment for alcohol or drug abuse, an agency or organization that provides medical treatment to persons who abuse controlled substances, an agency or organization that serves persons who are victims of crime or any other appropriate agency or organization.

13-3409. Involving or using minors in drug offenses; classification

A. A person shall not knowingly:
1. Hire, employ or use a minor to engage in any conduct, completed or preparatory, that is prohibited by sections 13-3404, 13-3404.01, 13-3405, 13-3406, 13-3407 and 13-3408.
2. Sell, transfer or offer to sell or transfer to a minor any substance if its possession is prohibited by sections 13-3404, 13-3404.01, 13-3405, 13-3407 and 13-3408.
B. A person who violates this section is guilty of a class 2 felony and is not eligible for suspension of sentence, probation, pardon or release from confinement on any basis until the sentence imposed by the court has been served or commuted, and if the minor is under fifteen years of age it is punishable pursuant to section 13-705, subsection C.
C. In addition to any other penalty prescribed by this title, the court shall order a person who is convicted of a violation of this section to pay a fine of not less than two thousand dollars or three times the value as determined by the court of the substance involved in or giving rise to the charge, whichever is greater, and not more than the maximum authorized by chapter 8 of this title. A judge shall not suspend any part or all of the imposition of any fine required by this subsection.

13-3410. Serious drug offender; sentencing; definitions

A. A person who is at least eighteen years of age or who has been tried as an adult and who stands convicted of a serious drug offense and who committed the offense as part of a pattern of engaging in conduct prohibited by this chapter, which constituted a significant source of the person's income, shall be sentenced to life imprisonment and is not eligible for suspension of sentence, probation, pardon or release from confinement on any basis until the person has served not less than twenty-five years or the sentence is commuted.
B. A person who is at least eighteen years of age or who has been tried as an adult and who stands convicted of a serious drug offense and who committed the offense as part of the person's association with and participation in the conduct of an enterprise as defined in section 13-2301, subsection D, paragraph 2, which is engaged in dealing in substances controlled by this chapter, and who organized, managed, directed, supervised or financed the enterprise with the intent to promote or further its criminal objectives shall be sentenced to life imprisonment and is not eligible for suspension of sentence, probation, pardon or release from confinement on any basis until the person has served not less than twenty-five years or the sentence is commuted.
C. A person commits an offense as part of a pattern of engaging in conduct prohibited by this chapter if the person's conduct involves at least three criminal acts that have the same or similar purposes, results, participants, victims or methods of commission, or otherwise are interrelated by distinguishing characteristics and are not isolated events.
D. For the purposes of this section:
1. "Serious drug offense" means any violation of, including any attempt or conspiracy to commit a violation of, section 13-3404.01, section 13-3405, subsection A, paragraphs 2 through 4, section 13-3407, subsection A, paragraphs 2 through 7 or section 13-3408, subsection A, paragraphs 2 through 7 involving an amount of marijuana, dangerous drugs or narcotic drugs having a weight that equals or exceeds the statutory threshold amount, a felony violation of section 13-3406 or any violation of section 13-3409.
2. "Significant source of income" means a source of income that exceeds twenty-five thousand dollars received during a calendar year without reference to any exceptions, reductions or setoffs.

13-3411. Possession, use, sale or transfer of marijuana, peyote, prescription drugs, dangerous drugs or narcotic drugs or manufacture of dangerous drugs in a drug free school zone; violation; classification; definitions

A. It is unlawful for a person to do any of the following:
1. Intentionally be present in a drug free school zone to sell or transfer marijuana, peyote, prescription-only drugs, dangerous drugs or narcotic drugs.
2. Possess or use marijuana, peyote, dangerous drugs or narcotic drugs in a drug free school zone.
3. Manufacture dangerous drugs in a drug free school zone.
B. A person who violates subsection A of this section is guilty of the same class of felony that the person would otherwise be guilty of had the violation not occurred within a drug free school zone, except that the presumptive, minimum and maximum sentence shall be increased by one year. The additional sentence imposed under this subsection is in addition to any enhanced punishment that may

be applicable under section 13-703, section 13-704, section 13-708, subsection D or any provision in this chapter. A person is not eligible for suspension of sentence, probation, pardon or release from confinement on any basis except pursuant to section 31-233, subsection A or B until the sentence imposed by the court has been served or commuted.

C. In addition to any other penalty prescribed by this title, the court shall order a person who is convicted of a violation of this section to pay a fine of not less than two thousand dollars or three times the value as determined by the court of the drugs involved in or giving rise to the charge, whichever is greater, and not more than the maximum authorized by chapter 8 of this title. A judge shall not suspend any part or all of the imposition of any fine required by this subsection.

D. Each school district's governing board or its designee, or the chief administrative officer in the case of a nonpublic school, shall place and maintain permanently affixed signs located in a visible manner at the main entrance of each school that identifies the school and its accompanying grounds as a drug free school zone.

E. The drug free school zone map prepared pursuant to title 15 shall constitute an official record as to the location and boundaries of each drug free school zone. The school district's governing board or its designee, or the chief administrative officer in the case of any nonpublic school, shall promptly notify the county attorney of any changes in the location and boundaries of any school property and shall file with the county recorder the original map prepared pursuant to title 15.

F. All school personnel who observe a violation of this section shall immediately report the violation to a school administrator. The administrator shall immediately report the violation to a peace officer. It is unlawful for any school personnel or school administrator to fail to report a violation as prescribed in this section.

G. School personnel having custody or control of school records of a student involved in an alleged violation of this section shall make the records available to a peace officer upon written request signed by a magistrate. Records disclosed pursuant to this subsection are confidential and may be used only in a judicial or administrative proceeding. A person furnishing records required under this subsection or a person participating in a judicial or administrative proceeding or investigation resulting from the furnishing of records required under this subsection is immune from civil or criminal liability by reason of such action unless the person acted with malice.

H. A person who violates subsection F of this section is guilty of a class 3 misdemeanor.

I. For the purposes of this section:

1. "Drug free school zone" means the area within three hundred feet of a school or its accompanying grounds, any public property within one thousand feet of a school or its accompanying grounds, a school bus stop or on any school bus or bus contracted to transport pupils to any school.

2. "School" means any public or nonpublic kindergarten program, common school or high school.

13-3412. Exceptions and exemptions; burden of proof; privileged communications

(Caution: 1998 Prop. 105 applies)

A. The provisions of sections 13-3402 and 13-3403, section 13-3404.01, subsection A, paragraph 1 and sections 13-3405 through 13-3409 do not apply to:

1. Manufacturers, wholesalers, pharmacies and pharmacists under the provisions of sections 32-1921 and 32-1961.

2. Medical practitioners, pharmacies and pharmacists while acting in the course of their professional practice, in good faith and in accordance with generally accepted medical standards.

3. Persons who lawfully acquire and use such drugs only for scientific purposes.

4. Officers and employees of the United States, this state or a political subdivision of the United States or this state, while acting in the course of their official duties.

5. An employee or agent of a person described in paragraphs 1 through 4 of this subsection, and a registered nurse or medical technician under the supervision of a medical practitioner, while such employee, agent, nurse or technician is acting in the course of professional practice or employment, and not on his own account.

6. A common or contract carrier or warehouseman, or an employee of such carrier or warehouseman, whose possession of drugs is in the usual course of business or employment.

7. Persons lawfully in possession or control of controlled substances authorized by title 36, chapter 27.

8. The receipt, possession or use, of a controlled substance included in schedule I of section 36-2512, by any seriously ill or terminally ill patient, pursuant to the prescription of a doctor in compliance with the provisions of section 13-3412.01.

B. In any complaint, information or indictment and in any action or proceeding brought for the enforcement of any provision of this chapter the burden of proof of any such exception, excuse, defense or exemption is on the defendant.

C. In addition to other exceptions to the physician-patient privilege, information communicated to a physician in an effort to procure unlawfully a prescription-only, dangerous or narcotic drug, or to procure unlawfully the administration of such drug, is not a privileged communication.

13-3412.01. Prescribing controlled substances included in schedule I for seriously ill and terminally ill patients

(Caution: 1998 Prop. 105 applies)

A. Notwithstanding any law to the contrary, any medical doctor licensed to practice in this state may prescribe a controlled substance included in schedule I as prescribed by section 36-2512 to treat a disease, or to relieve the pain and suffering of a seriously ill patient or terminally ill patient, subject to the provisions of this section. In prescribing such a controlled substance, the medical doctor shall comply with professional medical standards.
B. Notwithstanding any law to the contrary, a medical doctor shall document that scientific research exists that supports the use of a controlled substance listed in schedule I as prescribed by section 36-2512 to treat a disease, or to relieve the pain and suffering of a seriously ill patient or a terminally ill patient before prescribing the controlled substance. A medical doctor prescribing a controlled substance included in schedule I as prescribed by section 36-2512 to treat a disease, or to relieve the pain and suffering of a seriously ill patient or terminally ill patient, shall obtain the written opinion of a second medical doctor that prescribing the controlled substance is appropriate to treat a disease or to relieve the pain and suffering of a seriously ill patient or terminally ill patient. The written opinion of the second medical doctor shall be kept in the patient's official medical file. Before prescribing the controlled substance included in schedule I as prescribed by section 36-2512 the medical doctor shall receive in writing the consent of the patient.
C. Any failure to comply with the provisions of this section may be the subject of investigation and appropriate disciplining action by the Arizona medical board.

13-3413. Forfeiture and disposition of drugs and evidence

A. The following items used or intended for use in violation of this chapter are subject to seizure and forfeiture pursuant to chapter 39 of this title:
1. Property, equipment, containers, chemicals, materials, money, books, records, research products, formulas, microfilm, tapes and data.
2. Vapor-releasing substances containing a toxic substance.
3. Vehicles to transport or in any manner facilitate the transportation, sale or receipt of, or in which is contained or possessed, any item or drug, except as provided in chapter 39 of this title.
B. The following property is subject to seizure and forfeiture pursuant to chapter 39 of this title:
1. All proceeds traceable to an offense that is included in this chapter and that is committed for financial gain.
2. All proceeds seized in this state and traceable to an offense that:
(a) Is chargeable or indictable under the laws of the state in which the offense occurred and, if the offense occurred in a state other than this state, would be chargeable or indictable under this chapter if the offense occurred in this state.
(b) Is punishable by imprisonment for more than one year.
(c) Involves prohibited drugs, marijuana or other prohibited chemicals or substances.
(d) Is committed for financial gain.
C. Peyote, dangerous drugs, prescription-only drugs, marijuana, narcotic drugs and plants from which such drugs may be derived which are seized in connection with any violation of this chapter or which come into the possession of a law enforcement agency are summarily forfeited.
D. When seizures of marijuana are made in excess of ten pounds or seizures of any other substance specified in subsection C of this section are made in excess of one pound in connection with any violation of this chapter the responsible law enforcement agency may retain ten pounds of the marijuana or one pound of the other substance randomly selected from the seized quantity for representation purposes as evidence. The agency may destroy the remainder of the seized marijuana or substance. Before any destruction is carried out, the responsible law enforcement agency shall photograph the material seized with identifying case numbers or other means of identification and prepare a report, identifying the seized material. The responsible law enforcement agency shall notify in writing any person arrested for a violation of this chapter or the attorney for the person at least twenty-four hours in advance that such photography will take place and that such person or the person's attorney may be present at such

photographing of the seized material. In addition to the amount of marijuana or other substance retained for representation purposes as evidence, all photographs and records made under this section and properly identified are admissible in any court proceeding for any purpose for which the seized marijuana or substance itself would be admissible. Evidence retained after trial shall be disposed of pursuant to the rules of criminal procedure, rule 28.

E. If a seizure is made of chemicals used for the manufacture of a narcotic drug or dangerous drug as defined by section 13-3401 in connection with a violation of this title, the seizing agency may apply to a magistrate or superior court judge in the application for the search warrant or as soon as reasonable after the seizure for an order allowing the proper disposal or destruction of the substances, on a showing to the magistrate or superior court judge by affidavit of both of the following:

1. The substances pose a significant safety hazard to life or property because of their explosive, flammable, poisonous or otherwise toxic nature.

2. No adequate and safe storage facility is reasonably available to the seizing agency.

F. On a proper showing pursuant to subsection E of this section, the magistrate or superior court judge shall order the substances to be properly destroyed if the containers are first photographed. In addition the magistrate or superior court judge may order that the chemicals be sampled and the samples preserved, unless the court finds either:

1. Sampling would be unnecessary or unsafe.

2. The chemicals are in labeled or factory sealed containers.

13-3414. Convicted person's information to be sent to licensing board and the department of economic security; suspension or revocation of license or registration

A. On the conviction of a person of an offense in this chapter, the court or, if directed by the court, the clerk of the court shall provide the convicted person's name, case number, date of conviction and crime convicted of and, if known, the convicted person's social security number, date of birth, address and license or registration number to all of the following:

1. The board or officer, if any, by whom the convicted defendant has been licensed or registered to practice a profession or to carry on a business. On the conviction of any such person, the court, in its discretion, may suspend or revoke the license or registration of the convicted defendant to practice the profession or to carry on the business. On the application of any person whose license or registration has been suspended or revoked, and on proper showing and for good cause, the board or officer may reinstate the license or registration.

2. If the court has knowledge that the convicted person receives temporary assistance for needy families cash benefits, the department of economic security.

B. On request of an entity listed in subsection A of this section, the court or, if directed by the court, the clerk of the court shall provide the requesting entity with a copy of the convicted person's judgment and sentence and of the opinion of the court, if any opinion is filed.

13-3415. Possession, manufacture, delivery and advertisement of drug paraphernalia; definitions; violation; classification; civil forfeiture; factors

A. It is unlawful for any person to use, or to possess with intent to use, drug paraphernalia to plant, propagate, cultivate, grow, harvest, manufacture, compound, convert, produce, process, prepare, test, analyze, pack, repack, store, contain, conceal, inject, ingest, inhale or otherwise introduce into the human body a drug in violation of this chapter. Any person who violates this subsection is guilty of a class 6 felony.

B. It is unlawful for any person to deliver, possess with intent to deliver or manufacture with intent to deliver drug paraphernalia knowing, or under circumstances where one reasonably should know, that it will be used to plant, propagate, cultivate, grow, harvest, manufacture, compound, convert, produce, process, prepare, test, analyze, pack, repack, store, contain, conceal, inject, ingest, inhale or otherwise introduce into the human body a drug in violation of this chapter. Any person who violates this subsection is guilty of a class 6 felony.

C. It is unlawful for a person to place in a newspaper, magazine, handbill or other publication any advertisement knowing, or under circumstances where one reasonably should know, that the purpose of the advertisement, in whole or in part, is to promote the sale of objects designed or intended for use as drug paraphernalia. Any person who violates this subsection is guilty of a class 6 felony.

D. All drug paraphernalia is subject to forfeiture pursuant to chapter 39 of this title. The failure to charge or acquittal of an owner or anyone in control of drug paraphernalia in violation of this chapter does not prevent a finding that the object is intended for use or designed for use as drug paraphernalia.

E. In determining whether an object is drug paraphernalia, a court or other authority shall consider, in addition to all other logically relevant factors, the following:

1. Statements by an owner or by anyone in control of the object concerning its use.

2. Prior convictions, if any, of an owner, or of anyone in control of the object, under any state or federal law relating to any drug.

3. The proximity of the object, in time and space, to a direct violation of this chapter.

4. The proximity of the object to drugs.

5. The existence of any residue of drugs on the object.

6. Direct or circumstantial evidence of the intent of an owner, or of anyone in control of the object, to deliver it to persons whom he knows, or should reasonably know, intend to use the object to facilitate a violation of this chapter.

7. Instructions, oral or written, provided with the object concerning its use.

8. Descriptive materials accompanying the object which explain or depict its use.

9. National and local advertising concerning its use.

10. The manner in which the object is displayed for sale.

11. Whether the owner, or anyone in control of the object, is a legitimate supplier of like or related items to the community, such as a licensed distributor or dealer of tobacco products.

12. Direct or circumstantial evidence of the ratio of sales of the object to the total sales of the business enterprise.

13. The existence and scope of legitimate uses for the object in the community.

14. Expert testimony concerning its use.

F. In this section, unless the context otherwise requires:

1. "Drug" means any narcotic drug, dangerous drug, marijuana or peyote.

2. "Drug paraphernalia" means all equipment, products and materials of any kind which are used, intended for use or designed for use in planting, propagating, cultivating, growing, harvesting, manufacturing, compounding, converting, producing, processing, preparing, testing, analyzing, packaging, repackaging, storing, containing, concealing, injecting, ingesting, inhaling or otherwise introducing into the human body a drug in violation of this chapter. It includes:

(a) Kits used, intended for use or designed for use in planting, propagating, cultivating, growing or harvesting any species of plant which is a drug or from which a drug can be derived.

(b) Kits used, intended for use or designed for use in manufacturing, compounding, converting, producing, processing or preparing drugs.

(c) Isomerization devices used, intended for use or designed for use in increasing the potency of any species of plant which is a drug.

(d) Testing equipment used, intended for use or designed for use in identifying or analyzing the strength, effectiveness or purity of drugs.

(e) Scales and balances used, intended for use or designed for use in weighing or measuring drugs.

(f) Diluents and adulterants, such as quinine hydrochloride, mannitol, mannite, dextrose and lactose, used, intended for use or designed for use in cutting drugs.

(g) Separation gins and sifters used, intended for use or designed for use in removing twigs and seeds from, or in otherwise cleaning or refining, marijuana.

(h) Blenders, bowls, containers, spoons and mixing devices used, intended for use or designed for use in compounding drugs.

(i) Capsules, balloons, envelopes and other containers used, intended for use or designed for use in packaging small quantities of drugs.

(j) Containers and other objects used, intended for use or designed for use in storing or concealing drugs.

(k) Hypodermic syringes, needles and other objects used, intended for use or designed for use in parenterally injecting drugs into the human body.

(l) Objects used, intended for use or designed for use in ingesting, inhaling or otherwise introducing marijuana, a narcotic drug, a dangerous drug, hashish or hashish oil into the human body, such as:

(i) Metal, wooden, acrylic, glass, stone, plastic or ceramic pipes with or without screens, permanent screens, hashish heads or punctured metal bowls.

(ii) Water pipes.

(iii) Carburetion tubes and devices.

(iv) Smoking and carburetion masks.

(v) Roach clips, meaning objects used to hold burning material, such as a marijuana cigarette, that has become too small or too short to be held in the hand.

(vi) Miniature cocaine spoons and cocaine vials.

(vii) Chamber pipes.
(viii) Carburetor pipes.
(ix) Electric pipes.
(x) Air-driven pipes.
(xi) Chillums.
(xii) Bongs.
(xiii) Ice pipes or chillers.

13-3416. Probationer; payment of costs

In addition to any other fines or assessments, persons placed on probation for a violation of this chapter with a condition to participate in community restitution, drug testing or antidrug abuse education may be required by the court to pay any reasonable costs associated with participation in these programs.

13-3417. Use of wire communication or electronic communication in drug related transactions; classification

A. It is unlawful for a person to use any wire communication or electronic communication as defined in section 13-3001 to facilitate the violation of any felony provision or to conspire to commit any felony provision of this chapter or chapter 23 of this title.
B. Any offense committed by use of a wire communication or electronic communication as set forth in this section is deemed to have been committed at the place where the transmission or transmissions originated or at the place where the transmission or transmissions were received.
C. A person who violates this section is guilty of a class 4 felony except if the felony facilitated carries a class 5 or 6 designation in which case a violation of this section shall carry the same classification as the felony facilitated.

13-3418. Ineligibility to receive public benefits; restoration; definition

A. On conviction of any offense in this chapter, the court may render the person who is convicted ineligible to receive any public benefits. The court shall determine the length of time that shall elapse before the person's eligibility is restored.
B. The court shall not deny any public benefit otherwise directly or indirectly available to any innocent person nor shall the court deny any public benefit if such denial is in conflict with the laws of the United States.
C. For the purposes of this section, "public benefits" includes any money or services provided by this state for scholarships or tuition waivers granted for state funded universities or community colleges, welfare benefits, public housing or other subsidies but does not include benefits available for drug abuse treatment, rehabilitation or counseling programs.

13-3419. Multiple drug offenses not committed on the same occasion; sentencing

A. Except for a person convicted of possession offenses pursuant to section 13-3405, subsection A, paragraph 1, section 13-3407, subsection A, paragraph 1 or section 13-3408, subsection A, paragraph 1, a person who is convicted of two or more offenses under this chapter that were not committed on the same occasion but that either are consolidated for trial purposes or are not historical prior felony convictions shall be sentenced for the second or subsequent offense pursuant to this section. The person shall not be eligible for suspension of sentence, probation, pardon or release from confinement on any basis except as specifically authorized by section 31-233, subsection A or B until the sentence imposed by the court has been served, the person is eligible for release pursuant to section 41-1604.07 or the sentence is commuted, except that a person sentenced pursuant to paragraph 1 of this subsection shall be eligible for probation. The presumptive term for paragraph 1, 2, 3 or 4 of this subsection may be aggravated under this section pursuant to section 13-701, subsections C and D. The presumptive term for paragraph 1, 2 or 3 of this subsection may be mitigated within the range under this section pursuant to section 13-701, subsections C and E. The terms are as follows:
1. For two offenses for which the aggregate amount of drugs involved in one offense or both of the offenses is less than the statutory threshold amount for the second offense:

Felony	Mitigated	Minimum	Presumptive	Maximum	Aggravated
Class 2	3 years	4 years	5 years	10 years	12.5 years
Class 3	1.8 years	2.5 years	3.5 years	7 years	8.7 years

Class 4   1.1 years   1.5 years   2.5 years   3 years   3.7 years
Class 5   .5 years   .75 years   1.5 years   2 years   2.5 years

2. For three or more offenses for which the aggregate amount of drugs involved in one offense or all of the offenses is less than the statutory threshold amount for any offense subsequent to the second offense:

Felony	Mitigated	Minimum	Presumptive	Maximum	Aggravated
Class 2	3 years	4 years	5 years	10 years	12.5 years
Class 3	1.8 years	2.5 years	3.5 years	7 years	8.7 years
Class 4	1.1 years	1.5 years	2.5 years	3 years	3.7 years
Class 5	.5 years	.75 years	1.5 years	2 years	2.5 years

3. For two offenses for which the aggregate amount of drugs involved in one offense or all of the offenses equals or exceeds the statutory threshold amount for the second offense:

Felony	Mitigated	Minimum	Presumptive	Maximum	Aggravated
Class 2	3 years	4 years	5 years	10 years	12.5 years
Class 3	1.8 years	2.5 years	3.5 years	7 years	8.7 years
Class 4	1.1 years	1.5 years	2.5 years	3 years	3.7 years
Class 5	.5 years	.75 years	1.5 years	2 years	2.5 years

4. For three or more offenses for which the aggregate amount of drugs involved in one offense or all of the offenses equals or exceeds the statutory threshold amount for any offense subsequent to the second offense:

Felony	Minimum	Presumptive	Maximum	Aggravated
Class 2	4 years	7 years	12 years	15 years
Class 3	2.5 years	5 years	9 years	11.2 years
Class 4	1.5 years	3 years	5 years	6.2 years
Class 5	.75 years	2.5 years	4 years	5 years

B. If the court increases or decreases a sentence pursuant to this section, the court shall state on the record the reasons for the increase or decrease.

C. The court shall inform all of the parties before the sentencing occurs of its intent to increase or decrease a sentence pursuant to this section. If the court fails to inform the parties, a party waives its right to be informed unless the party timely objects at the time of sentencing.

13-3420. Unlawful substances; threshold amounts

(Caution: 1998 Prop. 105 applies)

For purposes of determining if the threshold amount is equaled or exceeded in any single offense or combination of offenses, a percentage of each substance listed by weight in section 13-3401, or any fraction thereof to its threshold amount shall be established. The percentages shall be added to determine if the threshold amount is equaled or exceeded. If the total of the percentages established equals or exceeds one hundred per cent, the threshold amount is equaled or exceeded. If the threshold amount is equaled or exceeded because of the application of this subsection, the person shall be sentenced as if the combination of unlawful substances consisted entirely of the unlawful substance of the greatest proportionate amount. If there are equal proportionate amounts, the person shall be sentenced as if the unlawful substances consisted entirely of the unlawful substance constituting the highest class of offense.

13-3421. Using building for sale or manufacture of dangerous or narcotic drugs; fortification of a building, classification; definitions

A. A person who as a lessee or occupant intentionally uses a building for the purpose of unlawfully selling, manufacturing or distributing any dangerous drug or narcotic drug is guilty of a class 6 felony.

B. A person who as a lessee or occupant of a building and who with the intent to suppress law enforcement entry knowingly fortifies or allows to be fortified the building for the purpose of unlawfully selling, manufacturing or distributing any dangerous drug or narcotic drug is guilty of a class 4 felony.

C. As used in this section:

1. "Building" means any part of a building or structure, including a room, space or enclosure, that may be entered through the same outside entrance.

2. "Fortified" means the use of steel doors, wooden planking, cross bars, alarm systems, dogs or other means to prevent or impede entry into a building or structure.

13-3422. Drug court program; establishment; participation

A. The presiding judge of the superior court in each county may establish a drug court program as defined in section 13-3401.

B. Cases assigned to the drug court program may consist of defendants who are drug dependent persons and who are charged with a probation eligible offense under this chapter, including preparatory offenses.

C. A defendant may be admitted into the drug court program prior to a guilty plea or a trial only on the agreement of the court and the prosecutor.

D. A defendant is not eligible for entry into the drug court program pursuant to subsections F and H of this section if any of the following applies:

1. The defendant has been convicted of a serious offense as defined in section 13-706.

2. The defendant has been convicted of an offense under chapter 14 of this title.

3. The defendant has been convicted of a dangerous offense.

4. The defendant has completed or previously been terminated from a drug court program other than a juvenile drug court program.

5. The defendant has completed or previously been terminated from a drug diversion program other than a juvenile drug diversion program for an offense in violation of this chapter.

E. For the purposes of subsection D of this section, the age of the conviction does not matter.

F. Notwithstanding any law to the contrary, if a defendant who is assigned to the drug court program is subsequently found guilty of the offense and probation is otherwise available, the court, without entering a judgment of guilt and with the concurrence of the defendant, may defer further proceedings and place the defendant on probation. The terms and conditions of probation shall provide for the treatment of the drug dependent person and shall include any other conditions and requirements that the court deems appropriate, including the imposition of a fine, payment of fees and any other terms and conditions as provided by law which are not in violation of section 13-901.01.

G. If the defendant is placed on probation pursuant to subsection F of this section and the defendant violates a term or condition of probation, the court may terminate the defendant's participation in the drug court program, enter an adjudication of guilt and revoke the defendant's probation.

H. If the defendant is convicted of an offense listed in subsection I of this section and is placed on probation pursuant to subsection F of this section, on fulfillment of the terms and conditions of probation, the court may discharge the defendant and dismiss the proceedings against the defendant or may dispose of the case as provided by law.

I. A defendant is eligible for dismissal of proceedings as provided in subsection H of this section if the defendant is convicted of any of the following offenses:

1. Possession or use of marijuana in violation of section 13-3405, subsection A, paragraph 1.

2. Possession or use of a prescription-only drug in violation of section 13-3406, subsection A, paragraph 1.

3. Possession or use of a dangerous drug in violation of section 13-3407, subsection A, paragraph 1.

4. Possession or use of a narcotic drug in violation of section 13-3408, subsection A, paragraph 1.

5. Possession or use of drug paraphernalia in violation of section 13-3415, subsection A.

6. Any preparatory offense, as prescribed in chapter 10 of this title, to an offense listed in this subsection.

J. If the defendant is placed on probation pursuant to subsection F of this section and the defendant fails to fulfill the terms and conditions of probation, the court shall enter an adjudication of guilt and sentence the defendant as provided by law.

K. If a defendant chooses not to participate in the drug court program, the defendant shall be prosecuted as provided by law.

L. This section does not prohibit the presiding judge of the superior court from establishing a drug court program other than as defined in section 13-3401 with other terms and conditions, including requiring a defendant to participate in a drug court program subsequent to the entry of judgment of guilt and sentencing.

Chapter 34.1 Imitation Substance or Drug Offenses

13-3451. Definitions

In this chapter, unless the context otherwise requires:

1. "Controlled substance" means a drug, substance or immediate precursor in schedules I through V of title 36, chapter 27, or a dangerous drug or a narcotic drug listed in section 13-3401.

2. "Counterfeit preparation" means a preparation that has an appearance which imitates another preparation but that, in fact, is a different preparation.

3. "Distribute" means the actual, constructive or attempted transfer, delivery or sale of, or dispensing to another of, an imitation controlled substance, imitation prescription-only drug or imitation over-the-counter drug.

4. "Imitation controlled substance" means a drug, substance or immediate precursor which does or does not contain a controlled substance that by texture, consistency or color or dosage unit appearance as evidenced by color, shape, size or markings, apart from any other representations, packaging or advertisements, would lead a reasonable person to believe that the substance is a controlled substance but it is a counterfeit preparation.

5. "Imitation over-the-counter drug" means an imitation of a nonprescription drug as defined in section 32-1901 that by texture, consistency or color or dosage unit appearance as evidenced by color, shape, size or markings, apart from any other representations, packaging or advertisements, would lead a reasonable person to believe that the substance is an over-the-counter drug.

6. "Imitation prescription-only drug" means a drug, substance or immediate precursor which does or does not contain a prescription-only drug as defined by section 32-1901 that by texture, consistency or color or dosage unit appearance as evidenced by color, shape, size or markings, apart from any other representations, packaging or advertisements, would lead a reasonable person to believe that the substance is a prescription-only drug but it is a counterfeit preparation.

7. "Manufacture" means the production, preparation, compounding, processing, encapsulating, packaging or repackaging, or labeling or relabeling of an imitation controlled substance, imitation prescription-only drug or imitation over-the-counter drug.

8. "Placebo" means an inactive substance or preparation used in controlled studies to determine the effectiveness of medicinal substances or used to please or gratify a physician's patient.

13-3452. Effect of representations made in construing status of certain substances whose origin is uncertain

A. If a dosage unit is in the form of a powder or liquid or if the appearance of a dosage unit is not otherwise reasonably sufficient to establish that a substance is an imitation controlled substance, imitation prescription-only drug or imitation over-the-counter drug, the representations made in connection with the substance or drug shall be considered in addition to all other logically relevant factors in determining whether the substance or drug is an imitation controlled substance, imitation prescription-only drug or imitation over-the-counter drug.

B. For the purposes of this section, representations made in connection with any substance or drug whose status is uncertain include:

1. Statements made by an owner or by anyone else in control of the substance or drug concerning the nature of the substance or drug, or its use or effect.

2. Statements made to the recipient of the substance or drug that the substance or drug may be resold for inordinate profit.

3. Whether the substance or drug is packaged in a manner normally used for imitation controlled substances, imitation prescription-only drugs or imitation over-the-counter drugs.

4. Evasive tactics or actions utilized by the owner or person in control of the substance or drug to avoid detection by law enforcement agencies.

13-3453. Manufacture or distribution of imitation controlled substance; prohibited acts; classification

A. It is unlawful for a person to manufacture, distribute or possess with intent to distribute an imitation controlled substance.

B. It is no defense to prosecution under this section that the defendant believed the imitation controlled substance to be a legitimate controlled substance.

C. A person who violates subsection A by the manufacture, distribution or possession of with intent to distribute an imitation controlled substance as a controlled substance is guilty of a class 6 felony.

D. Any person of the age of eighteen years or older who violates subsection A with respect to any person under the age of eighteen years is guilty of a class 5 felony.

13-3454. Manufacture or distribution of imitation prescription-only drug; prohibited acts; classification

A. It is unlawful for any person to manufacture, distribute or possess with intent to distribute an imitation prescription-only drug.
B. It is no defense to prosecution under this section that the defendant believed the imitation prescription-only drug to be a legitimate prescription-only drug.
C. A person who violates subsection A by the manufacture, distribution or possession of with intent to distribute an imitation prescription-only drug is guilty of a class 6 felony.
D. A person of the age of eighteen years or older who violates subsection A with respect to any person under the age of eighteen years is guilty of a class 5 felony.

13-3455. Manufacture or distribution of imitation over-the-counter drug; prohibited acts; classification

A. It is unlawful for any person to manufacture, distribute or possess with intent to distribute an imitation over-the-counter drug.
B. It is no defense to prosecution under this section that the defendant believed the imitation over-the-counter drug to be a legitimate over-the-counter drug.
C. Any person who violates subsection A by the manufacture, distribution or possession of with intent to distribute an imitation over-the-counter drug is guilty of a class 6 felony.
D. A person of the age of eighteen years or older who violates subsection A with respect to any person under the age of eighteen years is guilty of a class 5 felony.

13-3456. Possession or possession with intent to use imitation controlled substance; violation; classification

A. It is unlawful for any person to possess or possess with intent to use an imitation controlled substance.
B. It is no defense to prosecution under this section that the defendant believed the imitation controlled substance to be a legitimate controlled substance.
C. A person who violates subsection A by the possession or the possession of with intent to use an imitation controlled substance is guilty of a class 2 misdemeanor.

13-3457. Possession or possession with intent to use an imitation prescription-only drug; violation; classification

A. It is unlawful for any person to possess or possess with intent to use an imitation prescription-only drug.
B. A person who violates subsection A by the possession or the possession of with intent to use an imitation prescription-only drug is guilty of a class 2 misdemeanor.

13-3458. Possession or possession with intent to use an imitation over-the-counter drug; violation; classification

A. It is unlawful for any person to possess or possess with intent to use an imitation over-the-counter drug.

B. A person who violates subsection A by the possession or the possession of with intent to use an imitation over-the-counter drug is guilty of a class 2 misdemeanor.

13-3459. Manufacture of certain substances and drugs by certain means; prohibited acts; classification

A. It is unlawful for any person to make, distribute or possess any punch, die, plate, stone or other thing designed to print, imprint or reproduce the trademark, trade name or other identifying mark, imprint or device relating to the authorized identification of any controlled substance, prescription-only drug or over-the-counter drug or any likeness of any of the foregoing upon any drug or container to intentionally:

1. Counterfeit a controlled substance, prescription-only drug or over-the-counter drug.

2. Duplicate substantially the physical appearance, form, package or label of a controlled substance, prescription-only drug or over-the-counter drug.

B. A person who violates any provision of subsection A is guilty of a class 1 misdemeanor.

13-3460. Civil forfeiture

All imitation controlled substances, imitation over-the-counter drugs and imitation prescription-only drugs are subject to forfeiture as provided in chapter 39 of this title.'

13-3461. Placebos; exemption from coverage

Notwithstanding any contrary statute, the manufacture, distribution, possession, possession with intent to distribute or possession with intent to use placebos in this state by the following persons is not unlawful:

1. Exempt manufacturers, wholesalers and pharmacists under sections 32-1921 and 32-1961.

2. Medical practitioners, pharmacies and pharmacists while acting in the course of their professional practice, in good faith and in accordance with generally accepted medical standards.

3. Persons who lawfully acquire placebos and use them only for scientific purposes.

4. Officers and employees of the United States, this state or a political subdivision of this state and peace officers while acting in the course of their official duties.

5. An employee or agent of a person described in paragraphs 1 through 4 of this subsection or a registered nurse or medical technician under the supervision of a medical practitioner while the employee, agent, nurse or technician is acting in the course of his professional practice or employment and not on his own account.

6. A common or contract carrier or warehouseman or an employee of such a carrier or warehouseman whose possession of placebos is in the usual course of business or employment.

Chapter 35 Obscenity

13-3501. Definitions

In this chapter, unless the context otherwise requires:

1. "Harmful to minors" means that quality of any description or representation, in whatever form, of nudity, sexual activity, sexual conduct, sexual excitement, or sadomasochistic abuse, when both:

(a) To the average adult applying contemporary state standards with respect to what is suitable for minors, it both:

(i) Appeals to the prurient interest, when taken as a whole. In order for an item as a whole to be found or intended to have an appeal to the prurient interest, it is not necessary that the item be successful in arousing or exciting any particular form of prurient interest either in the hypothetical average person, in a member of its intended and probable recipient group or in the trier of fact.

(ii) Portrays the description or representation in a patently offensive way.

(b) Taken as a whole does not have serious literary, artistic, political, or scientific value for minors.

2. "Item" means any material or performance which depicts or describes sexual activity and includes any book, leaflet, pamphlet, magazine, booklet, picture, drawing, photograph, film, negative, slide, motion picture, figure, object, article, novelty device, recording, transcription, live or recorded telephone message or other similar items whether tangible or intangible and including any performance, exhibition, transmission or dissemination of any of the above. An item also includes a live performance or exhibition which depicts sexual activity to the public or an audience of one or more persons. An item is obscene within the meaning of this chapter when all of the following apply:

(a) The average person, applying contemporary state standards, would find that the item, taken as a whole, appeals to the prurient interest. In order for an item as a whole to be found or intended to have an appeal to the prurient interest, it is not necessary that the item be successful in arousing or exciting any particular form of prurient interest either in the hypothetical average person, in a member of its intended and probable recipient group or in the trier of fact.

(b) The average person, applying contemporary state standards, would find that the item depicts or describes, in a patently offensive way, sexual activity as that term is described in this section.

(c) The item, taken as a whole, lacks serious literary, artistic, political or scientific value.

3. "Knowledge of the character" means having general knowledge or awareness, or reason to know, or a belief or ground for belief which warrants further inspection or inquiry of that which is reasonably susceptible to examination by the defendant both:

(a) That the item contains, depicts or describes nudity, sexual activity, sexual conduct, sexual excitement or sadomasochistic abuse, whichever is applicable, whether or not there is actual knowledge of the specific contents thereof. This knowledge can be proven by direct or circumstantial evidence, or both.

(b) If relevant to a prosecution for violating section 13-3506, 13-3506.01 or 13-3507, the age of the minor, provided that an honest mistake shall constitute an excuse from liability under this chapter if the defendant made a reasonable bona fide attempt to ascertain the true age of such minor.

4. "Nudity" means the showing of the human male or female genitals, pubic area or buttocks with less than a full opaque covering, or the showing of the female breast with less than a fully opaque covering of any portion thereof below the top of the nipple, or the depiction of covered male genitals in a discernibly turgid state.

5. "Sadomasochistic abuse" means flagellation or torture by or upon a person clad in undergarments, a mask or bizarre costume, or the condition of being fettered, bound or otherwise physically restrained on the part of one so clothed, for the purpose or in the context of sexual gratification or abuse.

6. "Sexual activity" means:

(a) Patently offensive representations or descriptions of ultimate sexual acts, normal or perverted, actual or simulated.

(b) Patently offensive representations or descriptions of masturbation, excretory functions, sadomasochistic abuse and lewd exhibition of the genitals.

7. "Sexual conduct" means acts of masturbation, homosexuality, sexual intercourse, or physical contact with a person's clothed or unclothed genitals, pubic area, buttocks or, if such person is a female, breast.

8. "Sexual excitement" means the condition of human male or female genitals when in a state of sexual stimulation or arousal.

9. "Ultimate sexual acts" means sexual intercourse, vaginal or anal, fellatio, cunnilingus, bestiality or sodomy. A sexual act is simulated when it depicts explicit sexual activity which gives the appearance of consummation of ultimate sexual acts.

13-3502. Production, publication, sale, possession and presentation of obscene items; classification

A person is guilty of a class 5 felony who, with knowledge of the character of the item involved, knowingly:

1. Prints, copies, manufactures, prepares, produces, or reproduces any obscene item for purposes of sale or commercial distribution.

2. Publishes, sells, rents, lends, transports or transmits in intrastate commerce, imports, sends or causes to be sent into this state for sale or commercial distribution or commercially distributes or exhibits any obscene item, or offers to do any such things.

3. Has in his possession with intent to sell, rent, lend, transport, or commercially distribute any obscene item.

4. Presents or participates in presenting the live, recorded or exhibited performance of any obscene item to the public or an audience for consideration or commercial purpose.

13-3503. Seizure of obscene things; disposition

An obscene or indecent writing, paper, book, picture, print or figure found in possession, or under control of a person arrested therefor, shall be delivered to the magistrate before whom the person arrested is required to be taken, and if the magistrate finds it is obscene or indecent, he shall deliver one copy to the county attorney of the county in which the accused is liable to prosecution, and at once destroy all other copies. The copy delivered to the county attorney shall be destroyed upon conviction of the accused.

13-3504. Coercing acceptance of obscene articles or publications; classification

A. No person, firm, association or corporation shall, as a condition to any sale, allocation, consignment or delivery for resale of any paper, magazine, book, periodical or publication require that the purchaser or consignee receive for resale any other item, article, book, or other publication which is obscene. No person, firm, association or corporation shall deny or threaten to deny any franchise or impose or threaten to impose any penalty, financial or otherwise, by reason of the failure or refusal of any person to accept such items, articles, books, or publications, or by reason of the return thereof.

B. A violation of any provision of subsection A is a class 5 felony.

13-3505. Obscene prints and articles; jurisdiction

A. The superior court has jurisdiction to enjoin the sale or distribution of obscene prints and articles, as described in subsection B of this section.

B. The county attorney of any county or the city attorney of any city in which a person, firm, association or corporation publishes, sells or distributes or is about to sell or distribute or has in his possession with intent to sell or distribute or is about to acquire possession with intent to sell or distribute any book, magazine, pamphlet, comic book, story paper, writing, paper, picture, drawing, photograph, figure, image or any written or printed matter of an indecent character, which is obscene, lewd, lascivious, filthy, indecent or disgusting, or which contains an article or instrument of indecent or immoral use or purports to be for indecent or immoral use or purpose, or in any other respect defined in section 13-3501, may maintain an action on behalf of such county or city for an injunction against such person, firm, association or corporation in the superior court to prevent the sale or further sale or the distribution or further distribution of the acquisition, publication or possession within the state of any book, magazine, pamphlet, comic book, story paper, writing, paper, picture, drawing, photographed figure or image or any written or printed matter of an indecent character, described in this subsection or in section 13-3501.

C. The person, firm, association or corporation sought to be enjoined shall be entitled to a trial of the issues within ten days after joinder of issue and a decision shall be rendered by the court within ten days of the conclusion of the trial.

D. If a final order or judgment of injunction is entered against the person, firm, association or corporation sought to be enjoined, such final order of judgment shall contain a provision directing the person, firm, association or corporation to surrender to the sheriff of the county in which the action was brought any of the matter described in subsection B of this section and such sheriff shall be directed to seize and destroy such obscene prints and articles.

E. In any action brought as provided in this section, such county attorney or city attorney bringing the action shall not be required to file any undertaking before the issuance of an injunction order provided for in subsection C of this section.

F. The sheriff directed to seize and destroy such obscene prints and articles shall not be liable for damages sustained by reason of the injunction order in cases where judgment is rendered in favor of the person, firm, association or corporation sought to be enjoined.

G. Every person, firm, association or corporation who sells, distributes, or acquires possession with intent to sell or distribute any of the matter described in subsection B of this section, after the service upon him of a summons and complaint in an action brought pursuant to this section is chargeable with knowledge of the contents thereof.

13-3506. Furnishing harmful items to minors; applicability; classification

A. It is unlawful for any person, with knowledge of the character of the item involved, to recklessly furnish, present, provide, make available, give, lend, show, advertise or distribute to minors any item that is harmful to minors.

B. This section does not apply to the transmission or sending of items over the internet.

C. A violation of this section is a class 4 felony.

13-3506.01. Furnishing harmful items to minors; internet activity; classification; definitions

A. It is unlawful for any person, with knowledge of the character of the item involved, to intentionally or knowingly transmit or send to a minor by means of electronic mail, personal messaging or any other direct internet communication an item that is harmful to minors when the person knows or believes at the time of the transmission that a minor in this state will receive the item.

B. This section does not apply to:

1. Posting material on an internet web site, bulletin board or newsgroup.

2. Sending material via a mailing list or listserv that is not administered by the sender. For the purposes of this paragraph, "mailing list" or "listserv" means a method of internet communication where a message is sent to an internet address and then is retransmitted to one or more subscribers to the mailing list or listserv.

C. It is not a defense to a prosecution for a violation of this section that the recipient of the transmission was a peace officer posing as a minor.

D. A violation of this section is a class 4 felony.

E. The failure to report a violation of this section is a class 6 felony as prescribed by section 13-3620.

F. For the purposes of this section:

1. "Internet" means the combination of computer facilities and electromagnetic transmission media, and related equipment and software, comprising the interconnected worldwide network of computer networks that employ the transmission control protocol or internet protocol or any successor protocol to transmit information.

2. "Internet web site" means a location where material placed in a computer server-based file archive is publicly accessible, over the internet, using hypertext transfer protocol or any successor protocol.

13-3507. Public display of explicit sexual materials; classification; definitions

A. It is unlawful for any person knowingly to place explicit sexual material upon public display, or knowingly to fail to take prompt action to remove such a display from property in his possession or under his control after learning of its existence.

B. A person who violates any provision of this section is guilty of a class 6 felony.

C. For the purposes of this section:

1. "Explicit sexual material" means any drawing, photograph, film negative, motion picture, figure, object, novelty device, recording, transcription or any book, leaflet, pamphlet, magazine, booklet or other item, the cover or contents of which depicts human genitalia or depicts or verbally describes nudity, sexual activity, sexual conduct, sexual excitement or sadomasochistic abuse in a way which is harmful to minors. Explicit sexual material does not include any depiction or description which, taken in context, possesses serious educational value for minors or which possesses serious literary, artistic, political or scientific value.

2. "Public display" means the placing of material on or in a billboard, viewing screen, theater marquee, newsstand, display rack, vending machine, window, showcase, display case or similar place so that material within the definition of paragraph 1 of this subsection is easily visible or readily accessible from a public thoroughfare, from the property of others, or in any place where minors are invited as part of the general public.

13-3509. Duty to report; classification

A. A person who is asked to record, film, photograph, develop or duplicate any visual or print medium depicting sexual activity, whether or not the person would be compensated, shall immediately report, or cause a report to be made of, such request to a municipal or county peace officer. The report shall include the name or names of the person, persons or business making the request, if known, and shall describe what was requested.

B. A person who knowingly violates this section is guilty of a class 6 felony.

13-3510. Evidence of obscenity

A. Expert testimony or other ancillary evidence is not required to determine obscenity if the allegedly obscene item has been placed in evidence. The item itself is the best evidence of what it represents.

B. If a person relied upon a rating given to a film or motion picture by the motion picture association of America or an equivalent rating association, the rating and evidence concerning the person's reliance on such rating shall be admissible in evidence in a trial for violation of this article.

13-3511. Exemption; broadcasts and telecasts

The provisions of this chapter shall not apply to broadcasts or telecasts through facilities licensed under the federal communications act or title 9, chapter 5, article 1.1.

13-3512. Obscene or indecent telephone communications to minors for commercial purposes; violation; classification

A. It is unlawful for any person to knowingly make by means of a telephone, directly or by a recording device, any obscene or indecent communication for commercial purposes to any person who is under the age of eighteen years. The communication is unlawful regardless of whether the maker of the communication placed the call.

B. A person who violates this section is guilty of a class 4 felony.

13-3513. Sale or distribution of material harmful to minors through vending machines; classification

A. It is unlawful for any person to knowingly display, sell or offer to sell in any coin-operated or slug-operated vending machine or mechanically or electronically controlled vending machine that is located in a public place, other than a public place from which minors are excluded, any material that is harmful to minors as defined in section 13-3501.

B. It is a defense in any prosecution for a violation of subsection A that the defendant has taken reasonable steps to ascertain that the person is eighteen years of age or older and has taken either of the following measures to restrict access to the material that is harmful to minors:

1. Required the person receiving the material that is harmful to minors to use an authorized access or identification card to use the vending machine and has established a procedure to immediately cancel the card of any person after receiving notice that the card has been lost, stolen or used by persons under eighteen years of age or that the card is no longer desired.

2. Required the person receiving the material that is harmful to minors to use a token in order to use the vending machine.

C. A person who violates this section is guilty of a class 6 felony.

Chapter 35.1 Sexual Exploitation of Children

13-3551. Definitions

In this chapter, unless the context otherwise requires:

1. "Advertising" or "advertisement" means any message in any medium that offers or solicits any person to engage in sexual conduct in this state.

2. "Communication service provider" has the same meaning prescribed in section 13-3001.

3. "Computer" has the same meaning prescribed in section 13-2301, subsection E.

4. "Computer system" has the same meaning prescribed in section 13-2301, subsection E.

5. "Exploitive exhibition" means the actual or simulated exhibition of the genitals or pubic or rectal areas of any person for the purpose of sexual stimulation of the viewer.

6. "Minor" means a person or persons who were under eighteen years of age at the time a visual depiction was created, adapted or modified.

7. "Network" has the same meaning prescribed in section 13-2301, subsection E.

8. "Producing" means financing, directing, manufacturing, issuing, publishing or advertising for pecuniary gain.

9. "Remote computing service" has the same meaning prescribed in section 13-3001.

10. "Sexual conduct" means actual or simulated:

(a) Sexual intercourse, including genital-genital, oral-genital, anal-genital or oral-anal, whether between persons of the same or opposite sex.

(b) Penetration of the vagina or rectum by any object except when done as part of a recognized medical procedure.

(c) Sexual bestiality.

(d) Masturbation, for the purpose of sexual stimulation of the viewer.

(e) Sadomasochistic abuse for the purpose of sexual stimulation of the viewer.

(f) Defecation or urination for the purpose of sexual stimulation of the viewer.

11. "Simulated" means any depicting of the genitals or rectal areas that gives the appearance of sexual conduct or incipient sexual conduct.

12. "Visual depiction" includes each visual image that is contained in an undeveloped film, videotape or photograph or data stored in any form and that is capable of conversion into a visual image.

13-3552. Commercial sexual exploitation of a minor; classification

A. A person commits commercial sexual exploitation of a minor by knowingly:

1. Using, employing, persuading, enticing, inducing or coercing a minor to engage in or assist others to engage in exploitive exhibition or other sexual conduct for the purpose of producing any visual depiction or live act depicting such conduct.

2. Using, employing, persuading, enticing, inducing or coercing a minor to expose the genitals or anus or the areola or nipple of the female breast for financial or commercial gain.

3. Permitting a minor under the person's custody or control to engage in or assist others to engage in exploitive exhibition or other sexual conduct for the purpose of producing any visual depiction or live act depicting such conduct.

4. Transporting or financing the transportation of any minor through or across this state with the intent that the minor engage in prostitution, exploitive exhibition or other sexual conduct for the purpose of producing a visual depiction or live act depicting such conduct.

5. Using an advertisement for prostitution as defined in section 13-3211 that contains a visual depiction of a minor.

B. Subsection A, paragraph 5 of this section does not apply to an act that is prohibited by section 13-3555 or to websites or internet service providers that host advertisements created and published by third parties and do not participate in creating or publishing the advertisements.

C. Commercial sexual exploitation of a minor is a class 2 felony and if the minor is under fifteen years of age it is punishable pursuant to section 13-705.

13-3553. Sexual exploitation of a minor; evidence; classification

A. A person commits sexual exploitation of a minor by knowingly:

1. Recording, filming, photographing, developing or duplicating any visual depiction in which a minor is engaged in exploitive exhibition or other sexual conduct.

2. Distributing, transporting, exhibiting, receiving, selling, purchasing, electronically transmitting, possessing or exchanging any visual depiction in which a minor is engaged in exploitive exhibition or other sexual conduct.

B. If any visual depiction of sexual exploitation of a minor is admitted into evidence, the court shall seal that evidence at the conclusion of any grand jury proceeding, hearing or trial.

C. Sexual exploitation of a minor is a class 2 felony and if the minor is under fifteen years of age it is punishable pursuant to section 13-705.

13-3554. Luring a minor for sexual exploitation; classification

A. A person commits luring a minor for sexual exploitation by offering or soliciting sexual conduct with another person knowing or having reason to know that the other person is a minor.

B. It is not a defense to a prosecution for a violation of this section that the other person is not a minor.

C. Luring a minor for sexual exploitation is a class 3 felony, and if the minor is under fifteen years of age it is punishable pursuant to section 13-705.

13-3555. Portraying adult as minor; classification

A. It is unlawful for any person depicted in a visual depiction or live act as a participant in any exploitive exhibition or sexual conduct to masquerade as a minor.

B. It is unlawful for any person knowingly to produce, record, film, photograph, develop, duplicate, distribute, transport, exhibit, electronically transmit, sell, purchase or exchange any visual depiction whose text, title or visual representation depicts a participant in any exploitive exhibition or sexual conduct as a minor even though any such participant is an adult.

C. Any person who violates this section is guilty of a class 1 misdemeanor.

13-3556. Permissible inferences

In a prosecution relating to the sexual exploitation of children, the trier of fact may draw the inference that a participant is a minor if the visual depiction or live act through its title, text or visual representation depicts the participant as a minor.

13-3557. Equipment; forfeiture

On the conviction of a person for a violation of section 13-3552, 13-3553, 13-3554 or 13-3560, the court shall order that any photographic equipment, computer system or instrument of communication that is owned or used exclusively by the person and that was used in the commission of the offense be forfeited and sold, destroyed or otherwise properly disposed.

13-3558. Admitting minors to public displays of sexual conduct; constructive knowledge of age; classification

A. It is unlawful for an owner, operator or employee to admit a person under the age of eighteen into any business establishment where persons, in the course of their employment expose their genitals or anus or the areola or nipple of the female breast.

B. An owner, operator or employee who admits a person to an establishment without evidence of the person's age as required in section 4-241, subsection A is deemed to have constructive knowledge of the person's age.

C. A person who violates this section is guilty of a class 6 felony.

13-3559. Reporting suspected visual depictions of sexual exploitation of a minor; immunity

A. Any communication service provider, remote computing service, system administrator, computer repair technician or other person who discovers suspected visual depictions of sexual exploitation of a minor on a computer, computer system or network or in any other storage medium may report that discovery to a law enforcement officer.

B. A person who on discovery in good faith reports the discovery of suspected visual depictions of sexual exploitation of a minor is immune from civil liability.

C. It is an affirmative defense to a prosecution for a violation of section 13-3553 that on discovery a person in good faith reports the discovery of unsolicited suspected visual depictions involving the sexual exploitation of a minor.

13-3560. Aggravated luring a minor for sexual exploitation; classification; definitions

A. A person commits aggravated luring a minor for sexual exploitation if the person does both of the following:

1. Knowing the character and content of the depiction, uses an electronic communication device to transmit at least one visual depiction of material that is harmful to minors for the purpose of initiating or engaging in communication with a recipient who the person knows or has reason to know is a minor.

2. By means of the communication, offers or solicits sexual conduct with the minor. The offer or solicitation may occur before, contemporaneously with, after or as an integrated part of the transmission of the visual depiction.

B. It is not a defense to a prosecution for a violation of this section that the other person is not a minor or that the other person is a peace officer posing as a minor.

C. Aggravated luring a minor for sexual exploitation is a class 2 felony, and if the minor is under fifteen years of age it is punishable pursuant to section 13-705, subsection D.

D. The defense prescribed in section 13-1407, subsection F applies to a prosecution pursuant to this section.

E. For the purposes of this section:

1. "Electronic communication device" means any electronic device that is capable of transmitting visual depictions and includes any of the following:

(a) A computer, computer system or network as defined in section 13-2301.

(b) A cellular or wireless telephone as defined in section 13-4801.

2. "Harmful to minors" has the same meaning prescribed in section 13-3501.

13-3561. Unlawful age misrepresentation; classification; definition

A. A person commits unlawful age misrepresentation if the person is at least eighteen years of age, and knowing or having reason to know that the recipient of a communication is a minor, uses an electronic communication device to knowingly misrepresent the person's age for the purpose of committing any sexual offense involving the recipient that is listed in section 13-3821, subsection A.

B. It is not a defense to a prosecution for a violation of this section that the recipient is not a minor.

C. This section does not apply to peace officers who act in their official capacity within the scope of their authority and in the line of duty.

D. Unlawful age misrepresentation is a class 3 felony, and if the minor is under fifteen years of age it is punishable pursuant to section 13-705.

E. For the purposes of this section, "electronic communication device" means any electronic device that is capable of transmitting visual depictions and includes any of the following:

1. A computer, computer system or network as defined in section 13-2301.

2. A cellular or wireless telephone as defined in section 13-4801.

13-3562. Notice to communication service provider of website hosting alleged sexual exploitation of children

A. If a law enforcement agency receives information that a communication service provider is hosting a website that contains an alleged violation of this chapter, the law enforcement agency shall notify the communication service provider by serving a notice of the alleged violation on the statutory agent of the communication service provider.

B. The notice shall include specific information on the location of the alleged violation.

Chapter 36 Family Offenses

13-3601. Domestic violence; definition; classification; sentencing option; arrest and procedure for violation; weapon seizure

A. "Domestic violence" means any act that is a dangerous crime against children as defined in section 13-705 or an offense prescribed in section 13-1102, 13-1103, 13-1104, 13-1105, 13-1201, 13-1202, 13-1203, 13-1204, 13-1302, 13-1303, 13-1304, 13-1406, 13-1425, 13-1502, 13-1503, 13-1504, 13-1602 or 13-2810, section 13-2904, subsection A, paragraph 1, 2, 3 or 6, section 13-2910, subsection A, paragraph 8 or 9, section 13-2915, subsection A, paragraph 3 or section 13-2916, 13-2921, 13-2921.01, 13-2923, 13-3019, 13-3601.02 or 13-3623, if any of the following applies:

1. The relationship between the victim and the defendant is one of marriage or former marriage or of persons residing or having resided in the same household.

2. The victim and the defendant have a child in common.

3. The victim or the defendant is pregnant by the other party.

4. The victim is related to the defendant or the defendant's spouse by blood or court order as a parent, grandparent, child, grandchild, brother or sister or by marriage as a parent-in-law, grandparent-in-law, stepparent, step-grandparent, stepchild, step-grandchild, brother-in-law or sister-in-law.

5. The victim is a child who resides or has resided in the same household as the defendant and is related by blood to a former spouse of the defendant or to a person who resides or who has resided in the same household as the defendant.

6. The relationship between the victim and the defendant is currently or was previously a romantic or sexual relationship. The following factors may be considered in determining whether the relationship between the victim and the defendant is currently or was previously a romantic or sexual relationship:

(a) The type of relationship.

(b) The length of the relationship.

(c) The frequency of the interaction between the victim and the defendant.

(d) If the relationship has terminated, the length of time since the termination.

B. A peace officer, with or without a warrant, may arrest a person if the officer has probable cause to believe that domestic violence has been committed and the officer has probable cause to believe that the person to be arrested has committed the offense, whether the offense is a felony or a misdemeanor and whether the offense was committed within or without the presence of the peace officer. In cases of domestic violence involving the infliction of physical injury or involving the discharge, use or threatening exhibition of a deadly weapon or dangerous instrument, the peace officer shall arrest a person who is at least fifteen years of age, with or without a warrant, if the officer has probable cause to believe that the offense has been committed and the officer has probable cause to believe that the person to be arrested has committed the offense, whether the offense was committed within or without the presence of the peace officer, unless the officer has reasonable grounds to believe that the circumstances at the time are such that the victim will be protected from further injury. Failure to make an arrest does not give rise to civil liability except pursuant to section 12-820.02. In order to arrest both parties, the peace officer shall have probable cause to believe that both parties independently have committed an act of domestic violence. An act of self-defense that is justified under chapter 4 of this title is not deemed to be an act of domestic violence. The release procedures available under section 13-3883, subsection A, paragraph 4 and section 13-3903 are not applicable to arrests made pursuant to this subsection.

C. A peace officer may question the persons who are present to determine if a firearm is present on the premises. On learning or observing that a firearm is present on the premises, the peace officer may temporarily seize the firearm if the firearm is in plain view or was found pursuant to a consent to search and if the officer reasonably believes that the firearm would expose the victim or another person in the household to a risk of serious bodily injury or death. A firearm that is owned or possessed by the victim shall not be seized unless there is probable cause to believe that both parties independently have committed an act of domestic violence.

D. If a firearm is seized pursuant to subsection C of this section, the peace officer shall give the owner or possessor of the firearm a receipt for each seized firearm. The receipt shall indicate the identification or serial number or other identifying characteristic of each seized firearm. Each seized firearm shall be held for at least seventy-two hours by the law enforcement agency that seized the firearm.

E. If a firearm is seized pursuant to subsection C of this section, the victim shall be notified by a peace officer before the firearm is released from temporary custody.

F. If there is reasonable cause to believe that returning a firearm to the owner or possessor may endanger the victim, the person who reported the assault or threat or another person in the household, the prosecutor shall file a notice of intent to retain the firearm in the appropriate superior, justice or municipal court. The prosecutor shall serve notice on the owner or possessor of the firearm by certified mail. The notice shall state that the firearm will be retained for not more than six months following the date of seizure. On receipt of the notice, the owner or possessor may request a hearing for the return of the firearm, to dispute the grounds for seizure or to request an earlier return date. The court shall hold the hearing within ten days after receiving the owner's or possessor's request for a hearing. At the hearing, unless the court determines that the return of the firearm may endanger the victim, the person who reported the assault or threat or another person in the household, the court shall order the return of the firearm to the owner or possessor.

G. A peace officer is not liable for any act or omission in the good faith exercise of the officer's duties under subsections C, D, E and F of this section.

H. Each indictment, information, complaint, summons or warrant that is issued and that involves domestic violence shall state that the offense involved domestic violence and shall be designated by the letters DV. A domestic violence charge shall not be dismissed or a domestic violence conviction shall not be set aside for failure to comply with this subsection.

I. A person who is arrested pursuant to subsection B of this section may be released from custody in accordance with the Arizona rules of criminal procedure or any other applicable statute. Any order for release, with or without an appearance bond, shall include pretrial release conditions that are necessary to provide for the protection of the alleged victim and other specifically designated persons and may provide for additional conditions that the court deems appropriate, including participation in any counseling programs available to the defendant.

J. When a peace officer responds to a call alleging that domestic violence has been or may be committed, the officer shall inform in writing any alleged or potential victim of the procedures and resources available for the protection of the victim including:

1. An order of protection pursuant to section 13-3602, an injunction pursuant to section 25-315 and an injunction against harassment pursuant to section 12-1809.

2. The emergency telephone number for the local police agency.

3. Telephone numbers for emergency services in the local community.

4. Websites for local resources related to domestic violence.

K. A peace officer is not civilly liable for noncompliance with subsection J of this section.

L. If a person is convicted of an offense involving domestic violence and the victim was pregnant at the time of the commission of the offense, at the time of sentencing the court shall take into consideration the fact that the victim was pregnant and may increase the sentence.

M. An offense that is included in domestic violence carries the classification prescribed in the section of this title in which the offense is classified. If the defendant committed a felony offense listed in subsection A of this section against a pregnant victim and knew that the victim was pregnant or if the defendant committed a felony offense causing physical injury to a pregnant victim and knew that the victim was pregnant, the maximum sentence otherwise authorized for that violation shall be increased by up to two years.

N. When a peace officer responds to a call alleging that domestic violence has been or may be committed, the officer shall determine if a minor is present. If a minor is present, the peace officer shall conduct a child welfare check to determine if the child is safe and if the child might be a victim of domestic violence or child abuse.

13-3601.01. Domestic violence; treatment; definition

A. The judge shall order a person who is convicted of a misdemeanor domestic violence offense to complete a domestic violence offender treatment program that is provided by a facility approved by the court pursuant to rules adopted by the supreme court, the department of health services, the United States department of veterans affairs or a probation department. If a person has previously been ordered to complete a domestic violence offender treatment program pursuant to this section, the judge shall order the person to complete a domestic violence offender treatment program unless the judge deems that alternative sanctions are more appropriate. The department of health services shall adopt and enforce guidelines that establish standards for domestic violence offender treatment program approval.

B. On conviction of a misdemeanor domestic violence offense, if a person within a period of sixty months has previously been convicted of a violation of a domestic violence offense or is convicted of a misdemeanor domestic violence offense and has previously been convicted of an act in another state, a court of the United States or a tribal court that if committed in this state would be a domestic violence offense, the judge may order the person to be placed on supervised probation and the person may be incarcerated as a condition of probation. If the court orders supervised probation, the court may conduct an intake assessment when the person begins the term of probation and may conduct a discharge summary when the person is released from probation. If the person is incarcerated and the court receives confirmation that the person is employed or is a student, the court, on pronouncement of any jail sentence, may provide in the sentence that the person, if the person is employed or is a student and can continue the person's employment or studies, may continue the employment or studies for not more than twelve hours a day nor more than five days a week. The person shall spend the remaining day, days or parts of days in jail until the sentence is served and shall be allowed out of jail only long enough to complete the actual hours of employment or studies.

C. A person who is ordered to complete a domestic violence offender treatment program shall pay the cost of the program.

D. If a person is ordered to attend a domestic violence offender treatment program pursuant to this section, the program shall report to the court whether the person has attended the program and has successfully completed the program.

E. For the purposes of this section, prior convictions for misdemeanor domestic violence offenses apply to convictions for offenses that were committed on or after January 1, 1999.

F. For the purposes of this section, "domestic violence offense" means an offense involving domestic violence as defined in section 13-3601.

13-3601.02. Aggravated domestic violence; classification; definition

A. A person is guilty of aggravated domestic violence if the person within a period of eighty-four months commits a third or subsequent violation of a domestic violence offense or is convicted of a violation of a domestic violence offense and has previously been convicted of any combination of convictions of a domestic violence offense or acts in another state, a court of the United States or a tribal court that if committed in this state would be a violation of a domestic violence offense.

B. A person who is convicted under this section and who within a period of eighty-four months has been convicted of two prior violations of a domestic violence offense or acts in another state, a court of the United States or a tribal court that if committed in this state would be a domestic violence offense is not eligible for probation, pardon, commutation or suspension of sentence or release on any other basis until the person has served not less than four months in jail.

C. A person who is convicted under this section and who within a period of eighty-four months has been convicted of three or more prior violations of a domestic violence offense or acts in another state, a court of the United States or a tribal court that if committed in this state would be a domestic violence offense is not eligible for probation, pardon, commutation or suspension of sentence or release on any other basis until the person has served not less than eight months in jail.

D. The dates of the commission of the offenses are the determining factor in applying the eighty-four month provision in subsection A of this section regardless of the sequence in which the offenses were committed. For purposes of this section, a third or subsequent violation for which a conviction occurs does not include a conviction for an offense arising out of the same series of acts.

E. For the purposes of this section, prior convictions for misdemeanor domestic violence offenses apply only to convictions for offenses that were committed on or after January 1, 1999.

F. Aggravated domestic violence is a class 5 felony.

G. For the purposes of this section, "domestic violence offense" means an offense involving domestic violence as defined in section 13-3601.

13-3602. Order of protection; procedure; contents; arrest for violation; penalty; protection order from another jurisdiction

A. A person may file a verified petition, as in civil actions, with a magistrate, justice of the peace or superior court judge for an order of protection for the purpose of restraining a person from committing an act included in domestic violence. If the person is a minor, the parent, legal guardian or person who has legal custody of the minor shall file the petition unless the court determines otherwise. The petition shall name the parent, guardian or custodian as the plaintiff and the minor is a specifically designated person for the purposes of subsection G of this section. If a person is either temporarily or permanently unable to request an order, a third party may request an order of protection on behalf of the plaintiff. After the request, the judicial officer shall determine if the third party is an appropriate requesting party for the plaintiff. For the purposes of this section, notwithstanding the location of the plaintiff or defendant, any court in this state may issue or enforce an order of protection.

B. An order of protection shall not be granted:

1. Unless the party who requests the order files a written verified petition for an order.

2. Against a person who is less than twelve years of age unless the order is granted by the juvenile division of the superior court.

3. Against more than one defendant.

C. The petition shall state the:

1. Name of the plaintiff. The plaintiff's address shall be disclosed to the court for purposes of service. If the address of the plaintiff is unknown to the defendant, the plaintiff may request that the address be protected. On the plaintiff's request, the address shall not be listed on the petition. Whether the court issues an order of protection, the protected address shall be maintained in a separate document or automated database and is not subject to release or disclosure by the court or any form of public access except as ordered by the court.

2. Name and address, if known, of the defendant.

3. Specific statement, including dates, of the domestic violence alleged.

4. Relationship between the parties pursuant to section 13-3601, subsection A and whether there is pending between the parties an action for maternity or paternity, annulment, legal separation or dissolution of marriage.

5. Name of the court in which any prior or pending proceeding or order was sought or issued concerning the conduct that is sought to be restrained.

6. Desired relief.

D. A fee shall not be charged for filing a petition under this section or for service of process. On request of the plaintiff, each order of protection that is issued by a municipal court shall be served by the police agency for that city if the defendant can be served within the city. If the defendant cannot be served within the city, the police agency in the city in which the defendant can be served shall serve the order. If the order cannot be served within a city, the sheriff shall serve the order. On request of the plaintiff, each order of protection that is issued by a justice of the peace shall be served by the constable or sheriff for that jurisdiction if the defendant can be served within the jurisdiction. If the defendant cannot be served within that jurisdiction, the constable or sheriff in the jurisdiction in which the defendant can be served shall serve the order. On request of the plaintiff, each order of protection that is issued by a superior court judge or commissioner shall be served by the sheriff of the county. If the defendant cannot be served within that jurisdiction, the sheriff in the jurisdiction in which the defendant can be served shall serve the order. Each court shall provide, without charge, forms for purposes of this section for assisting parties without counsel. The court shall make reasonable efforts to provide to both parties an appropriate information sheet on emergency and counseling services that are available in the local area.

E. The court shall review the petition, any other pleadings on file and any evidence offered by the plaintiff, including any evidence of harassment by electronic contact or communication, to determine whether the orders requested should issue without further hearing. The court shall issue an order of protection under subsection G of this section if the court determines that there is reasonable cause to believe any of the following:

1. The defendant may commit an act of domestic violence.

2. The defendant has committed an act of domestic violence within the past year or within a longer period of time if the court finds that good cause exists to consider a longer period.

F. For the purposes of determining the period of time under subsection E, paragraph 2 of this section, any time that the defendant has been incarcerated or out of this state shall not be counted. If the court denies the requested relief, it may schedule a further hearing within ten days, with reasonable notice to the defendant.

G. If a court issues an order of protection, the court may do any of the following:

1. Enjoin the defendant from committing a violation of one or more of the offenses included in domestic violence.

2. Grant one party the use and exclusive possession of the parties' residence on a showing that there is reasonable cause to believe that physical harm may otherwise result. If the other party is accompanied by a law enforcement officer, the other party may return to the residence on one occasion to retrieve belongings. A law enforcement officer is not liable for any act or omission in the good faith exercise of the officer's duties under this paragraph.

3. Restrain the defendant from contacting the plaintiff or other specifically designated persons and from coming near the residence, place of employment or school of the plaintiff or other specifically designated locations or persons on a showing that there is reasonable cause to believe that physical harm may otherwise result.

4. If the court finds that the defendant is a credible threat to the physical safety of the plaintiff or other specifically designated persons, prohibit the defendant from possessing or purchasing a firearm for the duration of the order. If the court prohibits the defendant from possessing a firearm, the court shall also order the defendant to transfer any firearm owned or possessed by the defendant immediately after service of the order to the appropriate law enforcement agency for the duration of the order. If the defendant does not immediately transfer the firearm, the defendant shall transfer the firearm within twenty-four hours after service of the order.

5. If the order was issued after notice and a hearing at which the defendant had an opportunity to participate, require the defendant to complete a domestic violence offender treatment program that is provided by a facility approved by the department of health services or a probation department or any other program deemed appropriate by the court.

6. Grant relief that is necessary for the protection of the alleged victim and other specifically designated persons and that is proper under the circumstances.

7. Grant the petitioner the exclusive care, custody or control of any animal that is owned, possessed, leased, kept or held by the petitioner, the respondent or a minor child residing in the residence or household of the petitioner or the respondent, and order the respondent to stay away from the animal and forbid the respondent from taking, transferring, encumbering, concealing, committing an act of cruelty or neglect in violation of section 13-2910 or otherwise disposing of the animal.

H. The court shall not grant a mutual order of protection. If opposing parties separately file verified petitions for an order of protection, the courts after consultation between the judges involved may consolidate the petitions of the opposing parties for hearing. This does not prohibit a court from issuing cross orders of protection.

I. At any time during the period during which the order is in effect, a party who is under an order of protection or who is restrained from contacting the other party is entitled to one hearing on written request. No fee may be charged for requesting a hearing. A hearing that is requested by a party who is under an order of protection or who is restrained from contacting the other party shall be held within ten days from the date requested unless the court finds good cause to continue the hearing. If exclusive use of the home is awarded, the hearing shall be held within five days from the date requested. The hearing shall be held at the earliest possible time. An ex parte order that is issued under this section shall state on its face that the defendant is entitled to a hearing on written request and shall include the name and address of the judicial office where the request may be filed. After the hearing, the court may modify, quash or continue the order.

J. The order shall include the following statement:

Warning

This is an official court order. If you disobey this order, you will be subject to arrest and prosecution for the crime of interfering with judicial proceedings and any other crime you may have committed in disobeying this order.

K. A copy of the petition and the order shall be served on the defendant within one year from the date the order is signed. An order of protection that is not served on the defendant within one year expires. An order is effective on the defendant on service of a copy of the order and petition. An order expires one year after service on the defendant. A modified order is effective on service and expires one year after service of the initial order and petition.

L. A supplemental information form that is utilized by the court or a law enforcement agency solely for the purposes of service of process on the defendant and that contains information provided by the plaintiff is confidential.

M. Each affidavit, acceptance or return of service shall be promptly filed with the clerk of the issuing court. This filing shall be completed in person, shall be made by fax or shall be postmarked, if sent by mail, no later than the end of the seventh court business day after the date of service. If the filing is made by fax, the original affidavit, acceptance or return of service shall be promptly filed with the court. Within twenty-four hours after the affidavit, acceptance or return of service has been filed, excluding weekends and holidays, the court from which the order or any modified order was issued shall forward to the sheriff of the county in which the court is located a copy of the order of protection and a copy of the affidavit or certificate of service of process or acceptance of service. On receiving these copies, the sheriff shall register the order. Registration of an order means that a copy of the order of protection and a copy of the affidavit or acceptance of service have been received by the sheriff's office. The sheriff shall maintain a central repository for orders of protection so that the existence and validity of the orders can be easily verified. The effectiveness of an order does not depend on its registration, and for enforcement purposes pursuant to section 13-2810, a copy of an order of the court, whether or not registered, is presumed to be a valid existing order of the court for a period of one year from the date of service of the order on the defendant.

N. A peace officer, with or without a warrant, may arrest a person if the peace officer has probable cause to believe that the person has violated section 13-2810 by disobeying or resisting an order that is issued in any jurisdiction in this state pursuant to this section, whether or not such violation occurred in the presence of the officer. Criminal violations of an order issued pursuant to this section shall be referred to an appropriate law enforcement agency. The law enforcement agency shall request that a prosecutorial agency file the appropriate charges. A violation of an order of protection shall not be adjudicated by a municipal or justice court unless a complaint has been filed or other legal process has been requested by the prosecuting agency. The provisions for release under section 13-3883, subsection A, paragraph 4 and section 13-3903 do not apply to an arrest made pursuant to this section. For the purposes of this section, any court in this state has jurisdiction to enforce a valid order of protection that is issued in this state and that has been violated in any jurisdiction in this state.

O. A person who is arrested pursuant to subsection M of this section may be released from custody in accordance with the Arizona rules of criminal procedure or any other applicable statute. An order for release, with or without an appearance bond, shall include pretrial release conditions that are necessary to provide for the protection of the alleged victim and other specifically designated persons and may provide for any other additional conditions that the court deems appropriate, including participation in any counseling programs available to the defendant. The agency with custody of the defendant shall make reasonable efforts to contact the victim and other specifically designated persons in the order of protection, if known to the custodial agency, who requested notification immediately on release of the arrested person from custody.

P. The remedies provided in this section for enforcement of the orders of the court are in addition to any other civil and criminal remedies available. The superior court shall have exclusive jurisdiction to issue orders of protection in all cases if it appears from the petition that an action for maternity or paternity, annulment, legal separation or dissolution of marriage is pending between the parties. A municipal court or justice court shall not issue an order of protection if it appears from the petition that an action for maternity or paternity, annulment, legal separation or dissolution of marriage is pending between the parties. After issuance of an order of protection, if the municipal court or justice court determines that an action for maternity or paternity, annulment, legal separation or dissolution of marriage is pending between the parties, the municipal court or justice court shall stop further proceedings in the action and forward all papers, together with a certified copy of docket entries or any other record in the action, to the superior court where they shall be docketed in the pending superior court action and shall proceed as though the petition for an order of protection had been originally brought in the superior court. Notwithstanding any other law and unless prohibited by an order of the superior court, a municipal court or justice court may hold a hearing on all matters relating to its ex parte order of protection if the hearing was requested before receiving written notice of the pending superior court action. No order of protection shall be invalid or determined to be ineffective merely because it was issued by a lower court at a time when an action for maternity or paternity, annulment, legal separation or dissolution of marriage was pending in a higher court. After a hearing with notice to the affected party, the court may enter an order requiring any party to pay the costs of the action, including reasonable attorney fees, if any. An order that is entered by a justice court or municipal court after a hearing pursuant to this section may be appealed to the superior court as provided in title 22, chapter 2, article 4, section 22-425, subsection B and the superior court rules of civil appellate procedure without regard to an amount in controversy. No fee may be charged to either party for filing an appeal. For the purposes of this subsection, "pending" means, with respect to an action for annulment, legal separation or dissolution of marriage or for maternity or paternity, either that:

1. An action has been commenced but a final judgment, decree or order has not been entered.

2. A post-decree proceeding has been commenced but a judgment, decree or order finally determining the proceeding has not been entered.

Q. A peace officer who makes an arrest pursuant to this section or section 13-3601 is not civilly or criminally liable for the arrest if the officer acts on probable cause and without malice.

R. In addition to persons authorized to serve process pursuant to rule 4(d) of the Arizona rules of civil procedure, a peace officer or a correctional officer as defined in section 41-1661 who is acting in the officer's official capacity may serve an order of protection that is issued pursuant to this section. Service of the order of protection has priority over other service of process that does not involve an immediate threat to the safety of a person.

S. A valid protection order that is related to domestic or family violence and that is issued by a court in another state, a court of a United States territory or a tribal court shall be accorded full faith and credit and shall be enforced as if it were issued in this state for as long as the order is effective in the issuing jurisdiction. For the purposes of this subsection:

1. A protection order includes any injunction or other order that is issued for the purpose of preventing violent or threatening acts or harassment against, contact or communication with or physical proximity to another person. A protection order includes temporary and final orders other than support or child custody orders that are issued by civil and criminal courts if the order is obtained by the filing of an independent action or is a pendente lite order in another proceeding. The civil order shall be issued in response to a complaint, petition or motion that was filed by or on behalf of a person seeking protection.

2. A protection order is valid if the issuing court had jurisdiction over the parties and the matter under the laws of the issuing state, a United States territory or an Indian tribe and the person against whom the order was issued had reasonable notice and an opportunity to be heard. If the order is issued ex parte, the notice and opportunity to be heard shall be provided within the time required by the laws of the issuing state, a United States territory or an Indian tribe and within a reasonable time after the order was issued.

3. A mutual protection order that is issued against both the party who filed a petition or a complaint or otherwise filed a written pleading for protection against abuse and the person against whom the filing was made is not entitled to full faith and credit if either:

(a) The person against whom an initial order was sought has not filed a cross or counter petition or other written pleading seeking a protection order.

(b) The issuing court failed to make specific findings supporting the entitlement of both parties to be granted a protection order.

4. A peace officer may presume the validity of and rely on a copy of a protection order that is issued by another state, a United States territory or an Indian tribe if the order was given to the officer by any source. A peace officer may also rely on the statement of any person who is protected by the order that the order remains in effect. A peace officer who acts in good faith reliance on a protection order is not civilly or criminally liable for enforcing the protection order pursuant to this section.

13-3603. Definition; punishment

A person who provides, supplies or administers to a pregnant woman, or procures such woman to take any medicine, drugs or substance, or uses or employs any instrument or other means whatever, with intent thereby to procure the miscarriage of such woman, unless it is necessary to save her life, shall be punished by imprisonment in the state prison for not less than two years nor more than five years.

13-3603.01. Partial-birth abortions; classification; civil action; definitions

A. Any physician who knowingly performs a partial-birth abortion and thereby kills a human fetus is guilty of a class 6 felony and shall be fined under this title or imprisoned not more than two years, or both.

B. This section does not apply to a partial-birth abortion that is necessary to save the life of a mother whose life is endangered by a physical disorder, physical illness or physical injury, including a life-endangering physical condition caused by or arising from the pregnancy itself.

C. The father of the fetus if married to the mother at the time she receives a partial-birth abortion procedure and the maternal grandparents of the fetus if the mother is not at least eighteen years of age at the time of the partial-birth abortion may bring a civil action to obtain appropriate relief unless the pregnancy resulted from the plaintiff's criminal conduct or the plaintiff consented to the partial-birth abortion. Relief pursuant to this subsection includes the following:

1. Money damages for all injuries, psychological and physical, resulting from the violation of this section.

2. Statutory damages in an amount equal to three times the cost of the partial-birth abortion.

D. This section shall not subject a woman upon whom a partial-birth abortion is performed to any criminal prosecution or civil liability.

E. A defendant who is accused of an offense under this section may seek a hearing before the Arizona medical board if the defendant is licensed pursuant to title 32, chapter 13 or the Arizona board of osteopathic examiners in medicine and surgery if the defendant is licensed pursuant to title 32, chapter 17 on whether the physician's conduct was necessary to save the life of the mother whose life was endangered by a physical disorder, physical illness or physical injury, including a life-endangering physical condition caused by or arising from the pregnancy itself. The findings on that issue are admissible, in the court's discretion, on that issue at the trial of the defendant. On a motion of the defendant, the court shall, in its discretion, delay the beginning of the trial for not more than thirty days to permit a hearing to take place.

F. For the purposes of this section:

1. "Partial-birth abortion" means an abortion in which the person performing the abortion does both of the following:

(a) Deliberately and intentionally vaginally delivers a living fetus until, in the case of a headfirst presentation, the entire fetal head is outside the body of the mother or, in the case of breech presentation, any part of the fetal trunk past the naval is outside the body of the mother for the purpose of performing an overt act that the person knows will kill the partially delivered living fetus.

(b) Performs the overt act, other than completion of delivery, that kills the partially delivered living fetus.

2. "Physician" means a doctor of medicine or a doctor of osteopathy who is licensed pursuant to title 32, chapter 13 or 17 or any other individual legally authorized by this state to perform abortions. Any individual who is not a physician or who is not otherwise legally authorized by this state to perform abortions but who nevertheless directly performs a partial-birth abortion shall be subject to this section.

13-3603.02. Abortion; sex and race selection; injunctive and civil relief; failure to report; definition

A. A person who knowingly does any of the following is guilty of a class 3 felony:

1. Performs an abortion knowing that the abortion is sought based on the sex or race of the child or the race of a parent of that child.

2. Uses force or the threat of force to intentionally injure or intimidate any person for the purpose of coercing a sex-selection or race-selection abortion.

3. Solicits or accepts monies to finance a sex-selection or race-selection abortion.

B. The attorney general or the county attorney may bring an action in superior court to enjoin the activity described in subsection A of this section.

C. The father of the unborn child who is married to the mother at the time she receives a sex-selection or race-selection abortion, or, if the mother has not attained eighteen years of age at the time of the abortion, the maternal grandparents of the unborn child, may bring a civil action on behalf of the unborn child to obtain appropriate relief with respect to a violation of subsection A of this section. The court may award reasonable attorney fees as part of the costs in an action brought pursuant to this subsection. For the purposes of this subsection, "appropriate relief" includes monetary damages for all injuries, whether psychological, physical or financial, including loss of companionship and support, resulting from the violation of subsection A of this section.

D. A physician, physician's assistant, nurse, counselor or other medical or mental health professional who knowingly does not report known violations of this section to appropriate law enforcement authorities shall be subject to a civil fine of not more than ten thousand dollars.

E. A woman on whom a sex-selection or race-selection abortion is performed is not subject to criminal prosecution or civil liability for any violation of this section or for a conspiracy to violate this section.

F. For the purposes of this section, "abortion" has the same meaning prescribed in section 36-2151.

13-3604. Soliciting abortion; punishment; exception

A woman who solicits from any person any medicine, drug or substance whatever, and takes it, or who submits to an operation, or to the use of any means whatever, with intent thereby to procure a miscarriage, unless it is necessary to preserve her life, shall be punished by imprisonment in the state prison for not less than one nor more than five years.

13-3605. Advertising to produce abortion or prevent conception; punishment

A person who wilfully writes, composes or publishes a notice or advertisement of any medicine or means for producing or facilitating a miscarriage or abortion, or for prevention of conception, or who offers his services by a notice, advertisement or otherwise, to assist in the accomplishment of any such purposes, is guilty of a misdemeanor.

13-3606. Bigamy; classification; exception

A. A person having a spouse living who knowingly marries any other person is guilty of a class 5 felony.

B. Subsection A of this section does not extend to a person whose spouse by the former marriage has been absent for five successive years without being known to such person within that time to be living, nor to any person whose former marriage has been pronounced void, annulled or dissolved by judgment of a competent court.

13-3607. Marrying spouse of another; classification

A person who knowingly marries the spouse of another, in any case in which such spouse would be guilty of bigamy, is guilty of a class 5 felony.

13-3608. Incest; classification

Persons who are eighteen or more years of age and are within the degrees of consanguinity within which marriages are declared by law to be incestuous and void, who knowingly intermarry with each other, or who knowingly commit fornication or adultery with each other are guilty of a class 4 felony.

13-3609. Child bigamy; classification; definitions

A. A person commits child bigamy if the person knowingly does any of the following:
1. Is at least eighteen years of age, has a spouse and marries a child.
2. Is at least eighteen years of age and, either alone or in association with others, directs, causes or controls the marriage of a child to a person who already has a spouse.
3. Is at least eighteen years of age and, either alone or in association with others, directs, causes or controls the marriage of a child if the child already has a spouse.
4. Is at least eighteen years of age and marries a child if the child already has a spouse.
5. Transports or finances the transportation of a child to promote marriage between the child and a person who already has a spouse.
6. Transports or finances the transportation of a child who already has a spouse to promote marriage between the child and another person.
B. This section does not apply if a person who marries a child:
1. Has a spouse who has been absent for at least five successive years without being known to the person within that time to be living.
2. Has a former marriage that has been pronounced void, annulled or dissolved by judgment of a competent court.
C. A violation of this section is a class 3 felony.
D. For the purposes of this section:
1. "Marriage" means the state of joining together as husband and wife through an agreement, promise or ceremony regardless of whether a marriage license has been issued by the appropriate authority.
2. "Marry" means to join together as husband and wife through an agreement, promise or ceremony regardless of whether a marriage license has been issued by the appropriate authority.
3. "Spouses" means two persons living together as husband and wife, including the assumption of those marital rights, duties and obligations that are usually manifested by married people, including but not necessarily dependent on sexual relations.

13-3610. Abandonment of spouse; classification

A married person, having sufficient ability to provide for his or her spouse's support or who is able to earn the means of such spouse's support, who knowingly abandons and leaves such spouse in a destitute condition, is guilty of a class 1 misdemeanor.

13-3611. Refusal or neglect to provide for spouse; classification

A married person, having sufficient ability to provide for his or her spouse's support or who is able to earn the means of such spouse's support, who knowingly fails or refuses to provide the spouse with necessary food, clothing, shelter or medical attendance, unless by such spouse's misconduct he or she was justified in so doing, is guilty of a class 1 misdemeanor.

13-3612. Definitions; contributing to dependency or delinquency

For the purposes of sections 13-3613 through 13-3618, unless the context otherwise requires:
1. "Delinquency" means any act that tends to debase or injure the morals, health or welfare of a child.
2. "Delinquent person" includes any person under the age of eighteen years who violates a law of this state, or an ordinance of a county, city or town defining crime.
3. "Dependent person" means a person under the age of eighteen years:
(a) Who is found begging, receiving or gathering alms, whether actually begging or under the pretext of selling or offering anything for sale.
(b) Who is found in a street, road or public place with the intent of begging, gathering or receiving alms.
(c) Who is a vagrant.
(d) Who is found wandering and who does not have a home, or a settled place of abode, or a guardian or any visible means of subsistence.
(e) Who has no parent or guardian willing to exercise, or capable of exercising, proper parental control over the dependent person.
(f) Who is destitute.
(g) Whose home, by reason of neglect, cruelty or depravity of the dependent person's parents, or either of them, or on the part of the dependent person's guardian, or on the part of the person in whose custody or care the dependent person may be, is an unfit place for such person.
(h) Who frequents the company of reputed criminals, vagrants or prostitutes.
(i) Who is found living or being in a house of prostitution or assignation.
(j) Who habitually visits, without a parent or guardian, a saloon or place where spirituous, vinous or malt liquors are sold, bartered or given away.
(k) Who persistently refuses to obey the reasonable orders or directions of the dependent person's parent or guardian.
(l) Who is incorrigible and who is beyond the control and power of the dependent person's parents, guardian or custodian by reason of the vicious conduct or nature of the person.
(m) Whose father or mother is dead, or has abandoned the family, or is an habitual drunkard, or whose father or mother does not provide for the person, and it appears that the person is destitute of a suitable home or adequate means of obtaining an honest living, or who is in danger of being brought up to lead an idle, dissolute and immoral life, or when both parents are dead, or the mother or father, if living, is unable to provide proper support and care of the person.
(n) Who habitually uses intoxicating liquor as a beverage, habitually smokes cigarettes or uses opium, cocaine, morphine or other similar drugs without direction of a competent physician or a qualified registered nurse practitioner.
(o) Who from any cause is in danger of growing up to lead an idle, dissolute or immoral life.

13-3613. Contributing to delinquency and dependency; classification; procedure

A. A person who by any act, causes, encourages or contributes to the dependency or delinquency of a child, as defined by section 13-3612, or who for any cause is responsible therefor is guilty of a class 1 misdemeanor.
B. The procedure and prosecution shall be the same as in other criminal cases.
C. When the charge concerns the dependency of a child or children, the offense for convenience may be termed contributory dependency, and when the charge concerns the delinquency of a child or children, the offense for convenience may be termed contributory delinquency.

13-3614. Proof of guilt

In order to find a person guilty of violating the provisions of section 13-3613, it is not necessary to prove that the child has actually become dependent or delinquent, if it appears from the evidence that through any act of neglect or omission of duty, or by any improper act or conduct on the part of such person the dependency or delinquency of a child may have been caused or merely encouraged.

13-3615. Suspension of sentence upon posting bond; custody of child; revocation of suspension

A. The sentence which may be imposed by section 13-3613, or its execution, may be suspended by the court upon condition that defendant give a good and sufficient bond to the state in such penal sum as the court determines, not exceeding one thousand dollars, conditioned for the payment of an amount the court may order, not exceeding thirty dollars per month, for the support, care and maintenance of the child to whose dependency the person has contributed, and the money shall be expended under direction of the court for such purposes.

B. In suspending the sentence, or its execution, the court may also permit the child to remain in the custody of the defendant upon conditions as the court deems proper.

C. When it appears to the court that any condition contained in the bond or imposed by the court in permitting the child to remain in custody of defendant has been breached, the court may revoke the suspension, and the sentence thereunder shall commence from the date upon which the sentence is imposed or ordered to be enforced.

13-3616. Conditions of bond; forfeiture; disposition of proceeds recovered

A. A condition of the bond provided in section 13-3615, shall be that it shall not be necessary to bring a separate action to recover the penalty of such bond if forfeited, but that the court may order a citation to issue to the sureties thereon, requiring that they appear at a time named by the court, not less than ten nor more than twenty days from issuance thereof, and show cause why a judgment should not be entered for the penalty of the bond. Upon failure to appear or failure to show sufficient cause, the court shall enter judgment in behalf of the state against the principal and sureties.

B. Any monies collected or paid upon the bond shall be paid to the clerk of the court, and applied first to the payment of all court costs, and then to the care and maintenance of the child in such manner and upon such terms as the court may direct. If the money is unnecessary for such purposes, it shall be paid within one year to the county treasurer.

13-3617. Limitation on period of suspension or stay; discharge of defendant

Sentence shall not be suspended, or execution stayed, for more than two years, and if at any time within such period, it appears to the satisfaction of the court that the person has complied with the conditions of the suspension, or is for any cause entitled to be released, the court may discharge him and exonerate the bond.

13-3618. Construction and effect of chapter

A. The provisions of sections 13-3612 through 13-3618 shall be liberally construed in favor of the state for the protection of the child from neglect or omission of parental duty toward the child, and also to protect children of the state from the effects of the improper conduct, acts or bad example of any person which may be calculated to cause, encourage or contribute to, the dependency or delinquency of children, although such person is in no way related to the child.

B. Nothing in sections 13-3612 through 13-3618 shall be construed to be in conflict with, repeal or prevent proceedings under any law of this state which may otherwise define any specific conduct of a person as a crime which might also constitute contributory dependency, or to prevent or interfere with proceedings upon any such law.

C. The provisions of sections 13-3612 through 13-3618 shall not be construed to be inconsistent with or to repeal any law providing for the support by the parent or parents of their minor children, or any law providing for punishment of cruelty to children, or taking of indecent liberties with, or selling liquor, tobacco or firearms to children, or permitting them to be in evil or disreputable places, and nothing in any such laws or similar laws shall be construed to be inconsistent with or to repeal the provisions of this chapter relating to contributing to the dependency or delinquency of a child, or prevent proceedings under this chapter.

13-3619. Permitting life, health or morals of minor to be imperiled by neglect, abuse or immoral associations; classification

A person having custody of a minor under sixteen years of age who knowingly causes or permits the life of such minor to be endangered, its health to be injured or its moral welfare to be imperiled, by neglect, abuse or immoral associations, is guilty of a class 1 misdemeanor.

13-3620. Duty to report abuse, physical injury, neglect and denial or deprivation of medical or surgical care or nourishment of minors; medical records; exception; violation; classification; definitions

A. Any person who reasonably believes that a minor is or has been the victim of physical injury, abuse, child abuse, a reportable offense or neglect that appears to have been inflicted on the minor by other than accidental means or that is not explained by the available medical history as being accidental in nature or who reasonably believes there has been a denial or deprivation of necessary medical treatment or surgical care or nourishment with the intent to cause or allow the death of an infant who is protected under section 36-2281 shall immediately report or cause reports to be made of this information to a peace officer, to the department of child safety or to a tribal law enforcement or social services agency for any Indian minor who resides on an Indian reservation, except if the report concerns a person who does not have care, custody or control of the minor, the report shall be made to a peace officer only. A member of the clergy, a Christian Science practitioner or a priest who has received a confidential communication or a confession in that person's role as a member of the clergy, as a Christian Science practitioner or as a priest in the course of the discipline enjoined by the church to which the member of the clergy, the Christian Science practitioner or the priest belongs may withhold reporting of the communication or confession if the member of the clergy, the Christian Science practitioner or the priest determines that it is reasonable and necessary within the concepts of the religion. This exemption applies only to the communication or confession and not to personal observations the member of the clergy, the Christian Science practitioner or the priest may otherwise make of the minor. For the purposes of this subsection, "person" means:

1. Any physician, physician's assistant, optometrist, dentist, osteopath, chiropractor, podiatrist, behavioral health professional, nurse, psychologist, counselor or social worker who develops the reasonable belief in the course of treating a patient.

2. Any peace officer, child welfare investigator, child safety worker, member of the clergy, priest or Christian Science practitioner.

3. The parent, stepparent or guardian of the minor.

4. School personnel, domestic violence victim advocates or sexual assault victim advocates who develop the reasonable belief in the course of their employment.

5. Any other person who has responsibility for the care or treatment of the minor.

B. A report is not required under this section either:

1. For conduct prescribed by sections 13-1404 and 13-1405 if the conduct involves only minors who are fourteen, fifteen, sixteen or seventeen years of age and there is nothing to indicate that the conduct is other than consensual.

2. If a minor is of elementary school age, the physical injury occurs accidentally in the course of typical playground activity during a school day, occurs on the premises of the school that the minor attends and is reported to the legal parent or guardian of the minor and the school maintains a written record of the incident.

C. If a physician, psychologist or behavioral health professional receives a statement from a person other than a parent, stepparent, guardian or custodian of the minor during the course of providing sex offender treatment that is not court ordered or that does not occur while the offender is incarcerated in the state department of corrections or the department of juvenile corrections, the physician, psychologist or behavioral health professional may withhold the reporting of that statement if the physician, psychologist or behavioral health professional determines it is reasonable and necessary to accomplish the purposes of the treatment.

D. Reports shall be made immediately either electronically or by telephone. The reports shall contain the following information, if known:

1. The names and addresses of the minor and the minor's parents or the person or persons having custody of the minor.

2. The minor's age and the nature and extent of the minor's abuse, child abuse, physical injury or neglect, including any evidence of previous abuse, child abuse, physical injury or neglect.

3. Any other information that the person believes might be helpful in establishing the cause of the abuse, child abuse, physical injury or neglect.

E. A health care professional who is regulated pursuant to title 32 and who, after a routine newborn physical assessment of a newborn infant's health status or following notification of positive toxicology screens of a newborn infant, reasonably believes that the newborn infant may be affected by the presence of alcohol or a drug listed in section 13-3401 shall immediately report this information, or cause a report to be made, to the department of child safety. For the purposes of this subsection, "newborn infant" means a newborn infant who is under thirty days of age.

F. Any person other than one required to report or cause reports to be made under subsection A of this section who reasonably believes that a minor is or has been a victim of abuse, child abuse, physical injury, a reportable offense or neglect may report the information to a peace officer or to the department of child safety, except if the report concerns a person who does not have care, custody or control of the minor, the report shall be made to a peace officer only.

G. A person who has custody or control of medical records of a minor for whom a report is required or authorized under this section shall make the records, or a copy of the records, available to a peace officer, child welfare investigator or child safety worker investigating the minor's neglect, child abuse, physical injury or abuse on written request for the records signed by the peace officer, child welfare investigator or child safety worker. Records disclosed pursuant to this subsection are confidential and may be used only in a judicial or administrative proceeding or investigation resulting from a report required or authorized under this section.

H. When reports are received by a peace officer, the officer shall immediately notify the department of child safety. Notwithstanding any other statute, when the department receives these reports, it shall immediately notify a peace officer in the appropriate jurisdiction.

I. Any person who is required to receive reports pursuant to subsection A of this section may take or cause to be taken photographs of the minor and the vicinity involved. Medical examinations of the involved minor may be performed.

J. A person who furnishes a report, information or records required or authorized under this section, or a person who participates in a judicial or administrative proceeding or investigation resulting from a report, information or records required or authorized under this section, is immune from any civil or criminal liability by reason of that action unless the person acted with malice or unless the person has been charged with or is suspected of abusing or neglecting the child or children in question.

K. Except for the attorney client privilege or the privilege under subsection L of this section, no privilege applies to any:

1. Civil or criminal litigation or administrative proceeding in which a minor's neglect, dependency, abuse, child abuse, physical injury or abandonment is an issue.

2. Judicial or administrative proceeding resulting from a report, information or records submitted pursuant to this section.

3. Investigation of a minor's child abuse, physical injury, neglect or abuse conducted by a peace officer or the department of child safety.

L. In any civil or criminal litigation in which a child's neglect, dependency, physical injury, abuse, child abuse or abandonment is an issue, a member of the clergy, a Christian Science practitioner or a priest shall not, without his consent, be examined as a witness concerning any confession made to him in his role as a member of the clergy, a Christian Science practitioner or a priest in the course of the discipline enjoined by the church to which he belongs. This subsection does not discharge a member of the clergy, a Christian Science practitioner or a priest from the duty to report pursuant to subsection A of this section.

M. If psychiatric records are requested pursuant to subsection G of this section, the custodian of the records shall notify the attending psychiatrist, who may excise from the records, before they are made available:

1. Personal information about individuals other than the patient.

2. Information regarding specific diagnosis or treatment of a psychiatric condition, if the attending psychiatrist certifies in writing that release of the information would be detrimental to the patient's health or treatment.

N. If any portion of a psychiatric record is excised pursuant to subsection M of this section, a court, on application of a peace officer, child welfare investigator or child safety worker, may order that the entire record or any portion of the record that contains information relevant to the reported abuse, child abuse, physical injury or neglect be made available to the peace officer, child welfare investigator or child safety worker investigating the abuse, child abuse, physical injury or neglect.

O. A person who violates this section is guilty of a class 1 misdemeanor, except if the failure to report involves a reportable offense, the person is guilty of a class 6 felony.

P. For the purposes of this section:

1. "Abuse" has the same meaning prescribed in section 8-201.

2. "Child abuse" means child abuse pursuant to section 13-3623.

3. "Neglect" has the same meaning prescribed in section 8-201.

4. "Reportable offense" means any of the following:

(a) Any offense listed in chapters 14 and 35.1 of this title or section 13-3506.01.

(b) Surreptitious photographing, videotaping, filming or digitally recording or viewing a minor pursuant to section 13-3019.

(c) Child sex trafficking pursuant to section 13-3212.

(d) Incest pursuant to section 13-3608.

(e) Unlawful mutilation pursuant to section 13-1214.

13-3620.01. False reports; violation; classification

A. A person acting with malice who knowingly and intentionally makes a false report of child abuse or neglect or a person acting with malice who coerces another person to make a false report of child abuse or neglect is guilty of a class 1 misdemeanor.

B. A person who knowingly and intentionally makes a false report that a person has violated the provisions of subsection A of this section is guilty of a class 1 misdemeanor.

13-3621. Hire or use of child under sixteen for public vocation; classification

A person having in his care, custody or control, in any capacity, a child under the age of sixteen years, who knowingly sells, apprentices or otherwise disposes of such child to any person under any name, title or pretense for the purpose of giving a performance, begging or peddling, in a public street or highway, or in any mendicant or wandering business whatsoever, or a person who receives, uses or has in his custody, a child for such purpose, is guilty of a class 2 misdemeanor.

13-3622. Furnishing of tobacco product, vapor product or tobacco or shisha instruments or paraphernalia to minor; minor accepting or receiving tobacco product, vapor product or tobacco or shisha instruments or paraphernalia; illegally obtaining tobacco product, vapor product or tobacco or shisha instruments or paraphernalia by underage person; classification; definitions

A. A person who knowingly sells, gives or furnishes a tobacco product, a vapor product or any instrument or paraphernalia that is solely designed for the smoking or ingestion of tobacco or shisha, including a hookah or waterpipe, to a minor is guilty of a petty offense.
B. A minor who buys, or has in his possession or knowingly accepts or receives from any person, a tobacco product, a vapor product or any instrument or paraphernalia that is solely designed for the smoking or ingestion of tobacco or shisha, including a hookah or waterpipe, is guilty of a petty offense, and if the offense involves any instrument or paraphernalia that is solely designed for the smoking or ingestion of tobacco or shisha, shall pay a fine of not less than one hundred dollars or perform not less than thirty hours of community restitution.
C. A minor who misrepresents the minor's age to any person by means of a written instrument of identification with the intent to induce the person to sell, give or furnish a tobacco product, a vapor product or any instrument or paraphernalia that is solely designed for the smoking or ingestion of tobacco or shisha, including a hookah or waterpipe, in violation of subsection A or B of this section is guilty of a petty offense and, notwithstanding section 13-802, shall pay a fine of not more than five hundred dollars.
D. This section does not apply to any of the following:
1. Cigars, cigarettes or cigarette papers, smoking or chewing tobacco or any instrument or paraphernalia that is solely designed for the smoking or ingestion of tobacco or shisha, including a hookah or waterpipe, if it is used or intended to be used in connection with a bona fide practice of a religious belief and as an integral part of a religious or ceremonial exercise.
2. Any instrument or paraphernalia that is solely designed for the smoking or ingestion of tobacco or shisha, including a hookah or waterpipe, that is given to or possessed by a minor if the instrument or paraphernalia was a gift or souvenir and is not used or intended to be used by the minor to smoke or ingest tobacco or shisha.
E. For the purposes of this section:
1. "Shisha" includes any mixture of tobacco leaf and honey, molasses or dried fruit or any other sweetener.
2. "Tobacco product" means any of the following:
(a) Cigars.
(b) Cigarettes.
(c) Cigarette papers of any kind.
(d) Smoking tobacco of any kind.
(e) Chewing tobacco of any kind.
3. "Vapor product" means a noncombustible tobacco-derived product containing nicotine that employs a mechanical heating element, battery or circuit, regardless of shape or size, that can be used to heat a liquid nicotine solution contained in cartridges. Vapor product does not include any product that is regulated by the United States food and drug administration under chapter V of the federal food, drug and cosmetic act.

13-3623. Child or vulnerable adult abuse; emotional abuse; classification; exceptions; definitions

A. Under circumstances likely to produce death or serious physical injury, any person who causes a child or vulnerable adult to suffer physical injury or, having the care or custody of a child or vulnerable adult, who causes or permits the person or health of the child or vulnerable adult to be injured or who causes or permits a child or vulnerable adult to be placed in a situation where the person or health of the child or vulnerable adult is endangered is guilty of an offense as follows:
1. If done intentionally or knowingly, the offense is a class 2 felony and if the victim is under fifteen years of age it is punishable pursuant to section 13-705.
2. If done recklessly, the offense is a class 3 felony.
3. If done with criminal negligence, the offense is a class 4 felony.

B. Under circumstances other than those likely to produce death or serious physical injury to a child or vulnerable adult, any person who causes a child or vulnerable adult to suffer physical injury or abuse or, having the care or custody of a child or vulnerable adult, who causes or permits the person or health of the child or vulnerable adult to be injured or who causes or permits a child or vulnerable adult to be placed in a situation where the person or health of the child or vulnerable adult is endangered is guilty of an offense as follows:

1. If done intentionally or knowingly, the offense is a class 4 felony.

2. If done recklessly, the offense is a class 5 felony.

3. If done with criminal negligence, the offense is a class 6 felony.

C. For the purposes of subsections A and B of this section, the terms endangered and abuse include but are not limited to circumstances in which a child or vulnerable adult is permitted to enter or remain in any structure or vehicle in which volatile, toxic or flammable chemicals are found or equipment is possessed by any person for the purpose of manufacturing a dangerous drug in violation of section 13-3407, subsection A, paragraph 3 or 4. Notwithstanding any other provision of this section, a violation committed under the circumstances described in this subsection does not require that a person have care or custody of the child or vulnerable adult.

D. A person who intentionally or knowingly engages in emotional abuse of a vulnerable adult who is a patient or resident in any setting in which health care, health-related services or assistance with one or more of the activities of daily living is provided or, having the care or custody of a vulnerable adult, who intentionally or knowingly subjects or permits the vulnerable adult to be subjected to emotional abuse is guilty of a class 6 felony.

E. This section does not apply to:

1. A health care provider as defined in section 36-3201 who permits a patient to die or the patient's condition to deteriorate by not providing health care if that patient refuses that care directly or indirectly through a health care directive as defined in section 36-3201, through a surrogate pursuant to section 36-3231 or through a court appointed guardian as provided for in title 14, chapter 5, article 3.

2. A vulnerable adult who is being furnished spiritual treatment through prayer alone and who would not otherwise be considered to be abused, neglected or endangered if medical treatment were being furnished.

F. For the purposes of this section:

1. "Abuse", when used in reference to a child, means abuse as defined in section 8-201, except for those acts in the definition that are declared unlawful by another statute of this title and, when used in reference to a vulnerable adult, means:

(a) Intentional infliction of physical harm.

(b) Injury caused by criminally negligent acts or omissions.

(c) Unlawful imprisonment, as described in section 13-1303.

(d) Sexual abuse or sexual assault.

2. "Child" means an individual who is under eighteen years of age.

3. "Emotional abuse" means a pattern of ridiculing or demeaning a vulnerable adult, making derogatory remarks to a vulnerable adult, verbally harassing a vulnerable adult or threatening to inflict physical or emotional harm on a vulnerable adult.

4. "Physical injury" means the impairment of physical condition and includes any skin bruising, pressure sores, bleeding, failure to thrive, malnutrition, dehydration, burns, fracture of any bone, subdural hematoma, soft tissue swelling, injury to any internal organ or any physical condition that imperils health or welfare.

5. "Serious physical injury" means physical injury that creates a reasonable risk of death or that causes serious or permanent disfigurement, serious impairment of health or loss or protracted impairment of the function of any bodily organ or limb.

6. "Vulnerable adult" means an individual who is eighteen years of age or older and who is unable to protect himself from abuse, neglect or exploitation by others because of a mental or physical impairment.

13-3623.01. Safe haven for newborn infants; definitions

A. A person is not guilty of abuse of a child pursuant to section 13-3623, subsection B solely for leaving an unharmed newborn infant with a safe haven provider.

B. A fire station and a health care institution that is classified by the department of health services pursuant to section 36-405 as a general hospital or a rural general hospital shall post a notice that it accepts a newborn infant pursuant to this section. The notice shall be placed on the exterior of the building in a location that is noticeable to the public. The words "baby safe haven" shall be printed in bold-faced capital letters that are not less than two inches in height. The notice may include an identifying logo. A fire station or hospital that does not post a notice as prescribed by this subsection is not subject to civil liability. A notice that is valid before September 30, 2009 remains valid after September 30, 2009.

C. If a parent or agent of a parent voluntarily delivers the parent's newborn infant to a safe haven provider, the safe haven provider shall take custody of the newborn infant if both of the following are true:

1. The parent did not express an intent to return for the newborn infant.

2. The safe haven provider reasonably believes that the child is a newborn infant.

D. The safe haven provider shall comply with the requirements of section 8-528 and report the receipt of a newborn infant to of the department of child safety as soon as practicable after taking custody of the newborn infant. The department shall report the number of newborn infants delivered to safe haven providers pursuant to section 8-526.

E. A parent or agent of a parent who leaves a newborn infant with a safe haven provider may remain anonymous, and the safe haven provider shall not require the parent or agent to answer any questions. A safe haven provider shall offer written information about information and referral organizations.

F. A safe haven provider who receives a newborn infant pursuant to this section is not liable for any civil or other damages for any act or omission by the safe haven provider in maintaining custody of the newborn infant if the safe haven provider acts in good faith without gross negligence.

G. This section does not preclude the prosecution of the person for any offense based on any act not covered by this section.

H. For the purposes of this section:

1. "Newborn infant" means an infant who is seventy-two hours old or younger.

2. "Safe haven provider" means any of the following:

(a) A firefighter who is on duty.

(b) An emergency medical technician who is on duty.

(c) A health care institution that is classified by the department of health services pursuant to section 36-405 as a general hospital or a rural general hospital. The parent or agent must deliver the newborn infant to a medical staff member at the health care institution.

(d) A staff member or volunteer at any of the following that posts a public notice that it is willing to accept a newborn infant pursuant to this section:

(i) A private child welfare agency licensed pursuant to title 8, chapter 4, article 4.

(ii) An adoption agency licensed pursuant to section 8-126.

(iii) A church. For the purposes of this item, "church" means a building that is erected or converted for use as a church, where services are regularly convened, that is used primarily for religious worship and schooling and that a reasonable person would conclude is a church by reason of design, signs or architectural or other features.

13-3624. Emergency orders of protection

A. In counties with a population of one hundred fifty thousand persons or more according to the most recent United States decennial census, the presiding judge of the superior court, during the hours that the courts are closed, shall make available on a rotating basis a judge, justice of the peace, magistrate or commissioner who shall issue emergency orders of protection by telephone.

B. In counties with a population of less than one hundred fifty thousand persons according to the most recent United States decennial census, a judge, justice of the peace, magistrate or commissioner may issue an emergency order by telephone. The court, within twenty-four hours after a defendant is arrested for an act of domestic violence, shall register a certified copy of the release order with the sheriff's office of the county in which the order was issued. The court shall notify the sheriff's office of material changes in the release order, if the conditions of the release order are no longer in effect and when the charges are resolved. The sheriff in each county shall maintain a central repository for release orders so that the existence and validity of the orders can be easily verified. The law enforcement agency shall advise domestic violence victims where the victim may verify the registration and conditions of a release order.

C. The judge, justice of the peace, magistrate or commissioner who is authorized to issue emergency orders of protection may issue a written or oral ex parte emergency order of protection if a peace officer states that the officer has reasonable grounds to believe that a person is in immediate and present danger of domestic violence based on an allegation of a recent incident of actual domestic violence.

D. An emergency order of protection may include any of the following:

1. The defendant may be enjoined from committing a violation of one or more of the offenses included in domestic violence.

2. One party may be granted the use and exclusive possession of the parties' residence on a showing that there is reasonable cause to believe that physical harm may otherwise result.

3. The defendant may be restrained from contacting the plaintiff, coming near the residence, place of employment or school of the plaintiff or other specifically designated locations or persons on a showing that there is reasonable cause to believe that physical harm may otherwise result.

4. If the court finds that the defendant may inflict bodily injury or death on the plaintiff, the defendant may be prohibited from possessing or purchasing a firearm for the duration of the order.

E. An emergency order of protection expires at the close of the next day of judicial business following the day of issue unless otherwise continued by the court.

F. A judge, justice of the peace, magistrate or commissioner may issue an oral emergency order of protection pursuant to subsection C of this section upon request of the alleged victim, if there is a finding that a person's life or health is in imminent danger. If a person is either temporarily or permanently unable to request an order, a third party may request an order of protection on behalf of the plaintiff. After the request, the judicial officer shall determine if the third party is an appropriate requesting party for the plaintiff. The officer who receives the verbal order shall write and sign the order. The emergency order shall be served on the respondent, and a copy shall be given to the protected party. The emergency order shall be filed as soon as practicable after its issuance. The officer shall file a certificate of service with the court and shall verbally notify the sheriff's office that the emergency order of protection has been issued. If a person who is named in the order and who has not received personal service of the order but has received actual notice of the existence and substance of the order commits an act that violates the order, the person is subject to any penalty for the violation.

G. The availability of an emergency order of protection is not affected by either party leaving the residence.

H. A law enforcement agency that has jurisdiction to enforce an emergency order of protection shall enforce the emergency order when it has reasonable cause to believe that the order has been violated.

I. Failure of a law enforcement agency to enforce an emergency order of protection pursuant to this section does not give rise to civil liability except pursuant to section 12-820.02.

13-3625. Unlawful sale or purchase of children; classification

A. Except for adoptions pursuant to title 8, chapter 1 and guardianships pursuant to title 14, chapter 5, a person shall not sell or offer to sell a child for money or other valuable consideration and shall not purchase or offer to purchase a child in exchange for money or other valuable consideration.

B. A person who violates this section is guilty of a class 5 felony.

Chapter 37 Miscellanous Offenses

13-3701. Unlawful use of food stamps; classification; definitions

A. A person commits unlawful use of food stamps if the person knowingly:
1. Uses, transfers, acquires, possesses or redeems food stamps by means of a false statement or representation, a material omission or the failure to disclose a change in circumstances or by any other fraudulent device.
2. Counterfeits, alters, uses, transfers, acquires or possesses counterfeited or altered food stamps or electronic benefit transfer cards.
3. Appropriates food stamps with which the person has been entrusted or of which the person has gained possession by virtue of a position as a public employee.
4. Buys, sells, transfers, acquires or redeems food stamps, or eligible food purchased with food stamps, in exchange for cash or consideration other than eligible food.
B. Unlawful use of food stamps under subsection A, paragraph 1 is a class 1 misdemeanor if the value of the food stamps is one hundred dollars or less, or a class 6 felony if the value is over one hundred dollars. Unlawful use of food stamps under subsection A, paragraphs 2, 3 and 4 is a class 5 felony.

C. For the purposes of this section:

1. "Eligible food" means any of the following:

(a) Any food or food product that is intended for human consumption except alcoholic beverages, tobacco and hot foods and hot food products that are prepared for immediate consumption.

(b) Seeds and plants to grow foods for the personal consumption of an eligible household.

(c) Meals that are prepared and delivered by an authorized meal delivery service to a household that is eligible to use coupons to purchase delivered meals or meals that are served by an authorized communal dining facility for the elderly or for a supplemental security income household, or both, to a household that is eligible to use coupons for communal dining.

(d) Meals that are prepared and served by a drug addict or alcoholic treatment and rehabilitation center to narcotic addicts or alcoholics and the children who live with the narcotic addict or alcoholic.

(e) Meals that are prepared and served by a group living arrangement facility to residents who are blind or who have a disability.

(f) Meals that are prepared and served by a shelter for battered women and children to the shelter's eligible residents.

(g) Meals that are prepared for and served by an authorized public or private nonprofit establishment, including a soup kitchen or temporary shelter, that is approved by an appropriate state or local agency and that feeds homeless persons.

(h) Meals that are prepared by a restaurant that contracts with an appropriate state agency to serve meals at low or reduced prices to homeless persons and households in which all persons are elderly or disabled.

2. "Food stamps" includes food stamp coupons and electronically transferred supplemental nutrition assistance program benefits.

13-3702. Defacing or damaging petroglyphs, pictographs, caves or caverns; classification

A. A person commits defacing or damaging petroglyphs, pictographs, caves or caverns if such person knowingly, without the prior written permission of the owner:

1. Breaks, breaks off, cracks, carves upon, writes or otherwise marks upon or in any manner destroys, mutilates, injures, defaces, removes, displaces, mars or harms petroglyphs, pictographs or any natural material found in any cave or cavern; or

2. Kills, harms or disturbs plant or animal life found in any cave or cavern, except for safety reasons; or

3. Disturbs or alters the natural condition of such petroglyph, pictograph, cave or cavern or takes into a cave or cavern any aerosol or other type of container containing paints, dyes or other coloring agents; or

4. Breaks, forces, tampers with, removes or otherwise disturbs a lock, gate, door or other structure or obstruction designed to prevent entrance to a cave or cavern whether or not entrance is gained.

B. As used in this section, "natural material" means stalactites, stalagmites, helictites, anthodites, gypsum flowers or needles, flowstone, draperies, columns, tufa dams, clay or mud formations or concretions or other similar crystalline mineral formations found in any cave or cavern.

C. Defacing or damaging petroglyphs, pictographs, caves or caverns is a class 2 misdemeanor.

13-3702.01. Excavating certain sites; collecting certain specimens; classification

A. A person who knowingly excavates in violation of section 41-841, subsection A without obtaining a permit as required under section 41-842 is guilty of a class 5 felony. A second or subsequent violation under this subsection is a class 3 felony.

B. A person who knowingly collects any archaeological specimen in violation of section 41-841, subsection B, is guilty of a class 1 misdemeanor.

13-3703. Abuse of venerated objects; classification

A. A person commits abuse of venerated objects by intentionally:

1. Desecrating any public monument, memorial or property of a public park; or

2. In any manner likely to provoke immediate physical retaliation:

(a) Exhibiting or displaying, placing or causing to be placed any word, figure, mark, picture, design, drawing or advertisement of any nature upon a flag or exposing or causing to be exposed to public view a flag upon which there is printed, painted or otherwise produced or to which there is attached, appended or annexed any word, figure, mark, picture, design, drawing or advertisement; or

(b) Exposing to public view, manufacturing, selling, offering to sell, giving or having in possession for any purpose any article of merchandise or receptacle for holding or carrying merchandise upon or to which there is printed, painted, placed or attached any flag in order to advertise, call attention to, decorate, mark or distinguish the article or substance; or

(c) Casting contempt upon, mutilating, defacing, defiling, burning, trampling or otherwise dishonoring or causing to bring dishonor upon a flag.

B. The provisions of this section shall not apply to:

1. Any act permitted by a statute of the United States; or

2. Any act permitted by United States military regulations; or

3. Any act where the United States government has granted permission for the use of such flag; or

4. A newspaper, periodical, book, pamphlet, circular, certificate, diploma, warrant, commission of appointment to office, ornament, picture, badge or stationery on which shall be printed, painted or placed such flag and which is disconnected from any advertisement for the purpose of sale, barter or trade.

C. For the purposes of this section:

1. "Desecrate" means defacing, damaging, polluting or otherwise doing a physical act in a manner likely to provoke immediate physical retaliation.

2. "Flag" means any emblem, banner or other symbol, of any size, composed of any substance or represented on any substance that evidently purports to be the flag of the United States or of this state.

D. Abuse of venerated objects is a class 2 misdemeanor.

13-3704. Adding poison or other harmful substance to food, drink or medicine; classification

A. A person commits adding poison or another harmful substance to water, food, drink or medicine if the person intends to harm another human being and the person knowingly:

1. Introduces, adds or mingles any poison, bacterium, virus or chemical compound into any spring, well or reservoir of water to be taken by a human being.

2. Introduces, adds or mingles any poison, bacterium, virus or chemical compound with any water, food, drink, medicine or other product to be taken by a human being or applied to the body.

3. Places a needle, razor blade or any other harmful object or substance in any water, food, drink or medicine to be taken by a human being.

B. A violation of this section is a class 6 felony.

13-3705. Unlawful copying or sale of sounds or images from recording devices; true name and address of articles; definitions; classification

A. A person commits unlawful copying or sale of sounds or images from recording devices by knowingly:

1. Manufacturing an article without the consent of the owner.

2. Distributing an article with the knowledge that the sounds thereon have been so transferred without the consent of the owner.

3. Distributing or manufacturing an article on which sounds or images have been transferred which does not bear the true name and address of the manufacturer in a prominent place on the outside cover, box, jacket or label.

4. Distributing or manufacturing the outside packaging intended for use with articles which does not bear the true name and address of the manufacturer in a prominent place on the outside cover, box, jacket or label.

5. Transferring or causing to be transferred to an article any performance, whether live before an audience or transmitted by wire or through the air by radio or television without the consent of the owner and with the intent to obtain commercial advantage or personal financial gain.

6. Distributing an article with knowledge that the performance on the article, whether live before an audience or transmitted by wire or through the air by radio or television, has been transferred without the consent of the owner.

B. This section shall not apply to any person or persons engaged in radio or television broadcasting who transfers, or causes to be transferred, any such sounds, other than from the sound track of a motion picture, intended for, or in connection with, broadcast transmission or related uses, including the making of commercials and films, or for archival purposes.

C. Subsection A, paragraphs 1 and 2 of this section apply only to recordings first fixed in a phonorecord before February 15, 1972.

D. Notwithstanding any other law and in the absence of a written agreement, the performer of a live performance is presumed to own the rights to record the performance.

E. The person who maintains custody and control over the business records of the owner is the proper witness regarding the issue of consent.

F. On conviction of a violation of this section, the court shall order:

1. The forfeiture and destruction of the articles and outside packaging.

2. The forfeiture pursuant to chapter 39 of this title of any implement, device or equipment used to manufacture or distribute the article or outside packaging.

3. The defendant to make restitution to any owner or lawful producer of a master recording, master disc, master tape, master videotape, master film or other device or article from which sounds or visual images are derived that has suffered injury resulting from the violation, or to the trade association representing the owner or lawful producer. The order of restitution shall be based on the aggregate wholesale value of lawfully manufactured and authorized recorded devices corresponding to the nonconforming recorded devices involved in the violation and shall include investigative costs relating to the violation. Proof of the specific wholesale value of each nonconforming device shall not be required.

G. In this section, unless the context otherwise requires:

1. "Aggregate wholesale value" means the average wholesale value of lawfully manufactured and authorized sound or audiovisual recordings corresponding to the nonconforming recorded devices involved in the offense.

2. "Article" means the tangible medium on which sounds or images are recorded including any original phonograph record, disc, compact disc, tape, audio or video cassette, wire, film or other medium now known or later developed on which sounds or images are or can be recorded or otherwise stored, or any copy or reproduction which duplicates in whole or in part the original.

3. "Distributing" means the actual, constructive or attempted sale, rental, delivery, possession, transportation, exhibition or advertisement of an article with intent to obtain commercial advantage or personal financial gain or to promote the sale of any goods.

4. "Fixation of sounds" means the master recording from which copies can be made of the series of sounds constituting the sound recording.

5. "Manufacturing" means transferring or causing to be transferred any sounds or images recorded on one article to another article with the intent to distribute the article.

6. "Owner" means the person who owns the original fixation of sounds or images embodied in the master phonograph record, master disc, master compact disc, master tape, master film or other device used for reproducing recorded sounds on phonograph records, discs, compact discs, tapes, films or other articles on which sound is or can be recorded, and from which the transferred recorded sounds are directly or indirectly derived, or the person who owns the rights to record or authorize the vending of a live performance.

7. "Phonorecord" means the material object in which sounds other than those accompanying a motion picture or other audiovisual work are fixed by any method now known or later developed, and from which can be perceived, reproduced or otherwise communicated directly or with the aid of a machine or device. Phonorecord includes the material object in which the sound is first fixed.

H. Unlawful copying or sale of sounds or images involving one hundred or more articles containing sound recordings or one hundred or more articles containing audiovisual recordings is a class 3 felony. Unlawful copying or sale of sounds or images involving ten or more but less than one hundred articles containing sound recordings or ten or more but less than one hundred articles containing audiovisual recordings is a class 6 felony. Unlawful copying or sale of sounds or images involving less than ten articles containing sound recordings or less than ten articles containing audiovisual recordings is a class 1 misdemeanor.

13-3706. Failure to procure or exhibit a business license; classification

A. A person commits failure to procure or exhibit a business license if such person knowingly commences or transacts any business, profession or calling, for which a license is required by any law of this state, without procuring the license prescribed for transacting such business, or who upon demand of a peace officer or magistrate, refuses to exhibit such license.

B. Failure to procure or exhibit a business license is a class 2 misdemeanor.

13-3707. Telecommunication fraud; classification; definitions

A. A person commits telecommunication fraud if the person does any of the following:

1. With the intent to defraud another of the lawful charge for telecommunication service, obtains or attempts to obtain any telecommunication service by:

(a) Charging or attempting to charge the telecommunication service either:

(i) To an existing electronic mail address, telephone number or credit card number without the authority of the person to whom issued or the subscriber to or the lawful holder of the address or number.

(ii) To a nonexistent, counterfeit, revoked or canceled credit card number.

(b) Any method of code calling.

(c) Installing, rearranging or tampering with any facility or equipment.

(d) The use of any other fraudulent means, method, trick or device.

2. With the intent that the same be used or employed to evade a lawful charge for any telecommunication service, sells, rents, lends, gives or otherwise transfers or discloses or attempts to transfer or disclose to another, or offers or advertises for sale or rental, the number or code of an existing, canceled, revoked or nonexistent electronic mail address, telephone number or credit card number or the method of numbering or coding that is employed in the issuance of telephone numbers, account identification codes or credit card numbers.

3. Knowingly makes, constructs, manufactures, fabricates, erects, assembles or possesses any software, instrument, apparatus, equipment or device, or any part of any software, instrument, apparatus, equipment or device, that is designed or adapted or that can be used either:

(a) To obtain telecommunication service by fraud in violation of this subsection.

(b) To conceal from any supplier of telecommunication service or from any lawful authority the existence or place of origin or of destination of any telecommunication in order to obtain telecommunication service by fraud in violation of this subsection.

4. Knowingly sells, rents, lends, gives, or otherwise transfers or discloses or attempts to transfer or disclose to another, or offers or advertises for sale or rental, any:

(a) Software, instrument, apparatus, equipment or device described in paragraph 3 of this subsection.

(b) Plans, specifications or instructions for making or assembling any software, instrument, apparatus, equipment or device with the intent to use or employ such software, instrument, apparatus, equipment or device, or any part of any software, instrument, apparatus, equipment or device or to allow any software, instrument, apparatus, equipment or device to be used or employed, for a purpose described in paragraph 3 of this subsection.

(c) Plans, specifications or instructions with the intent that the plans, specifications or instructions be used for making or assembling such software, instrument, apparatus, equipment or device, or any part of any software, instrument, apparatus, equipment or device.

B. Subsection A, paragraph 3 of this section does not prohibit the use or possession of any software, instrument, apparatus, equipment or device by either of the following:

1. Law enforcement officers who are acting in their official capacity within the scope of their authority and in the line of duty.

2. Employees or agents of communication service providers as defined in section 13-3001 who are acting in their official capacity within the scope of their employment for the purpose of protecting the property or legal rights of the provider.

C. This section applies when the telecommunication service originates or terminates or both originates and terminates in this state.

D. Telecommunication fraud is a class 3 felony.

E. As used in this section:

1. "Credit card number" means the card number appearing on a credit card, telephone calling card or access device as defined in section 13-2001 that is issued to a person by any supplier of telecommunication service and that permits the person to whom the card or access device has been issued to obtain telecommunication service.

2. "Telecommunication service" includes electronic communication services, subscription computer services, telephone and telegraph services and all other services that involve the transmission of information by wire, radio, cellular, wireless transmission or similar means.

13-3708. Sale or transfer of motor vehicle; lien disclosure; classification

A. A person shall not knowingly sell or transfer the person's ownership in a motor vehicle without disclosing to the purchaser or transferee that the motor vehicle is subject to a restitution lien pursuant to section 13-806.

B. A person who violates this section is guilty of a class 1 misdemeanor.

13-3709. Obtaining cable television services fraudulently; manufacturing, distributing and selling unauthorized decoding devices; classification; definition

A. Any person who with the intent to defraud another of any part of the lawful charge for services that are provided over or by a licensed cable television system as defined in section 9-505, makes any unauthorized connection, whether physically, electrically, acoustically, inductively or otherwise, or attaches any unauthorized device or devices to any cable, wire, microwave or other component of a licensed cable television system, to a television set or to any other instrument that is authorized to be attached to a cable television system is guilty of a class 2 misdemeanor.

B. Any person who manufactures, distributes, sells, rents, lends, offers or advertises for sale, rental or use any device that the person intends to be used by another person to obtain services that are provided over or by a licensed cable television system without payment of the charge for those services is guilty of a class 6 felony.

C. For the purposes of subsection B of this section it is a rebuttable presumption that the person intended that the device would be used by another person to obtain services that are provided over or by a licensed cable television system without payment of the charge for those services if, while advertising, selling, renting or lending the device, the person states that the device will enable the person who receives the device to obtain cable television or other services without payment of the charge for those services.

D. For the purposes of subsection B of this section, it is a separate violation for each individual device that is manufactured, distributed, sold, rented, lent, offered or advertised for sale, rental or use in violation of subsection B of this section.

E. A person whose business or property is injured arising out of a violation of this section may bring an action in superior court to recover damages or for an injunction, or both. The successful party to the action may recover reasonable attorney fees.

F. As used in this section "device" includes any component or combination of components capable of converting a scrambled or coded cable television signal to a signal usable on a standard television receiver.

13-3710. Obtaining subscription television services; manufacture, distribution and sale of interception and decoding devices; violation; classification; civil remedy; punitive damages

A. A person who for profit does either of the following is guilty of a class 1 misdemeanor:

1. Knowingly attaches or causes to be attached any device or devices to a television set, videotape recorder or other equipment intended to receive television transmissions or incorporates or causes to be incorporated any device into a television set, videotape recorder or other equipment intended to receive television transmissions for the purpose of intercepting or decoding any transmission by a duly licensed over-the-air subscription television service which the person is not authorized by the subscription television service to receive and decode.

2. Manufactures, distributes or sells any device, plan or kit for a device capable of intercepting or decoding transmissions by a duly licensed over-the-air subscription television service, with the intention that such device, plan or kit be used for such intercepting or decoding, unless authorized by the over-the-air subscription television service.

B. A person who suffers injury to his business or property arising out of the violation of this section may maintain an action in the superior court for the recovery of damages or for an injunction, or both. The successful party is entitled to recover reasonable attorney fees as fixed by the court.

13-3711. Unlawful commercial use of cigarette machines; civil penalties; forfeiture; classification

A. It is unlawful to possess, use or make available for use for commercial purposes a tobacco product rolling vending machine. A tobacco product rolling vending machine located in a nonresidential premises is presumed to be possessed, used or available for use for commercial purposes unless the machine is for sale. This subsection does not apply to:

1. A tobacco product rolling vending machine that is to be used exclusively for the owner's personal consumption or use if the machine is not located on a retail or other business premises.

2. Tobacco product manufacturers who have obtained a current federal manufacturer of tobacco products permit issued by the federal alcohol and tobacco tax and trade bureau to operate as a tobacco product manufacturer.

B. The department of revenue is authorized to seize the machine and all related tubes, papers, tobacco products and materials, which shall be forfeited to this state following the process prescribed in section 42-1124. All forfeited tobacco products shall also be destroyed pursuant to section 42-1124 and deemed contraband under section 42-3402.

C. A person who knowingly violates this section is guilty of a class 3 misdemeanor and is also subject to the following:

1. The revocation or termination of a license issued pursuant to section 42-3401.

2. A civil penalty not to exceed fifty thousand dollars for each violation.

3. An injunction to restrain a threatened or actual violation of this section.

4. Recovery by this state for the costs of enforcing this section or of any action or proceeding pertaining to a violation of this section, including the costs of investigation and reasonable attorney fees in the trial and appellate courts. Payments shall be deposited into the state general fund.

13-3712. Interruption of or injury to cable television systems; classification

Any person who, without the consent of the owner, knowingly tampers with, removes or injures any cable, wire, microwave or other component of a licensed cable television system as defined in section 9-505 or knowingly interrupts the service of such a licensed cable television system without the consent of the owner is guilty of a class 2 misdemeanor.

13-3713. Consideration for referral of patient, client or customer; fraud; violation; classification

A. Except for payments from a medical researcher to a physician licensed pursuant to title 32, chapter 13 or 17 in connection with identifying and monitoring patients for a clinical trial regulated by the United States food and drug administration, a person who knowingly offers, delivers, receives or accepts any rebate, refund, commission, preference or other consideration as compensation for referring a patient, client or customer to any individual, pharmacy, laboratory, clinic or health care institution providing medical or health-related services or items pursuant to title 11, chapter 2, article 7 or title 36, chapter 29, other than specifically provided for in accordance with title 11, chapter 2, article 7 or title 36, chapter 29, is guilty of:

1. A class 3 felony if the consideration had a value of one thousand dollars or more.

2. A class 4 felony if the consideration had a value of more than one hundred dollars but less than one thousand dollars.

3. A class 6 felony if the consideration had a value of one hundred dollars or less.

B. A person who knowingly presents false information or misrepresents or conceals a material fact on an application for medical or health coverage pursuant to title 36, chapter 29 or section 11-291 or who knowingly fails to notify the county of residence of a change in conditions that, if notification had been made, would have resulted in termination of eligibility or change in eligibility status for medical or health coverage pursuant to title 36, chapter 29 or section 11-291 is guilty of a class 6 felony.

C. A person who knowingly obtains or attempts to obtain medical or health coverage pursuant to title 36, chapter 29 or section 11-291 by the use of any means of identification not authorized by the Arizona health care cost containment system administration or by the use of any means of identification authorized by the Arizona health care cost containment system administration that has been or would have been fraudulently acquired is guilty of:

1. A class 5 felony if the value of the medical or health coverage or attempted coverage is one thousand dollars or more.

2. A class 6 felony if the value of the medical or health coverage or attempted coverage exceeds one hundred dollars but is less than one thousand dollars.

3. A class 1 misdemeanor if the value of the medical or health coverage or attempted coverage is one hundred dollars or less.

D. A person who knowingly counterfeits or alters any means of identification or uses, transfers, acquires or possesses counterfeited or altered identification for the purpose of fraudulently obtaining medical or health coverage pursuant to title 36, chapter 29 or section 11-291 is guilty of a class 4 felony.

E. A person lawfully entitled to medical or health coverage pursuant to title 36, chapter 29 or section 11-291 who knowingly furnishes, gives or lends that person's means of identification to any person for the purpose of fraudulently obtaining medical or health coverage pursuant to title 36, chapter 29 or section 11-291 is guilty of a class 6 felony.

F. A person who knowingly aids or abets another person pursuant to section 13-301, 13-302 or 13-303 in the commission of an offense under this section or section 36-2905.04 is guilty of a class 5 felony.

G. The county attorney of the county in which the violation occurs and the attorney general have concurrent jurisdiction to prosecute all violations specified in this section.

13-3714. Aggravated or multiple violations of insurance code; classification

A person who knowingly performs any act for which the person is required to be licensed under title 20, chapter 2, article 3, 3.1, 3.2, 3.3 or 3.5 to lawfully perform and the person has been previously licensed pursuant to title 20, chapter 2, article 3, 3.1, 3.2, 3.3 or 3.5, but whose license was suspended or revoked at the time of the act or has been convicted of violating any provision of title 20, chapter 2, article 3, 3.1, 3.2, 3.3 or 3.5, and who is not licensed at the time of the act, is guilty of a class 5 felony.

13-3715. Unauthorized manufacture, duplication, use or possession of key to a public building; classification

A. A person who knowingly causes to be manufactured or duplicated or who possesses or uses a key to any building or other area owned, operated or controlled by this state or any agency, board, commission, institution or political subdivision of this state without authorization from the person, or his designated representative, in charge of such building or area is guilty of a class 3 misdemeanor.
B. A person who manufactures or duplicates a key for himself or another to any building or other area owned, operated or controlled by this state or any agency, board, commission, institution or political subdivision of this state, with knowledge that he or the person requesting the manufacturing or duplication of such key does not have authorization from the person or his designated representative in charge of such building or area, is guilty of a class 3 misdemeanor.

13-3716. Unlawful failure to give notice of conviction of dangerous crime against children or child abuse; classification

A. It is unlawful for a person who has been convicted of a dangerous crime against children as defined in section 13-705 or child abuse pursuant to section 13-3623, subsection A or subsection B, paragraph 1 to fail to give notice of the fact of the conviction to a business institution or organization when applying for employment or volunteering for service with any business institution or organization that sponsors any activity in which adults supervise children. For the purposes of this subsection, business institutions or organizations include schools, preschools, child care providers and youth organizations.
B. A person who violates this section is guilty of a class 5 felony.

13-3717. Unlawful subleasing of motor vehicle; violation; classification; definitions

A. A person engages in an act of unlawful subleasing of a motor vehicle if all of the following conditions are met:
1. The motor vehicle is subject to a lease contract, retail installment contract or security agreement the terms of which prohibit the transfer or assignment of any right or interest in the motor vehicle or under the lease contract, retail installment contract or security agreement.
2. The person is not a party to the lease contract, retail installment contract or security agreement.
3. The person transfers or assigns, or purports to transfer or assign, any right or interest in the motor vehicle or under the lease contract, retail installment contract or security agreement to any person who is not a party to the lease contract, retail installment contract or security agreement.
4. The person does not obtain, before the transfer or assignment, written consent to the transfer or assignment from the motor vehicle's lessor, seller or secured party.

5. The person receives compensation or some other consideration for the transfer or assignment.

B. A person engages in an act of unlawful subleasing of a motor vehicle if the person is not a party to the lease contract, retail installment contract or security agreement and assists, causes or arranges an actual or purported transfer or assignment.

C. The actual or purported transfer or assignment, or the assisting, causing or arranging of an actual or purported transfer or assignment, of any right or interest in a motor vehicle or under a lease contract, retail installment contract or security agreement by an individual who is a party to the lease contract, retail installment contract or security agreement is not an act of unlawful subleasing of a motor vehicle and is not subject to prosecution.

D. This section does not affect the enforceability of any provision of any lease contract, retail installment contract, security agreement or direct loan agreement by any party to the contract or agreement.

E. The penalties under this section are in addition to any other remedies or penalties provided by law for the conduct proscribed by this section.

F. A person who violates subsection A of this section is guilty of a class 1 misdemeanor.

G. In this section, unless the context otherwise requires:

1. "Buyer" means a person who buys or hires a motor vehicle under a retail installment contract.

2. "Direct loan agreement" means an agreement between a lender and a purchaser by which the lender has advanced monies pursuant to a loan secured by the motor vehicle which the purchaser has purchased.

3. "Lease contract" means a contract for or in contemplation of the lease for the use of a motor vehicle and the purchase of services incidental to the lease by a natural person for a term exceeding four months primarily for personal, family, household, business or commercial purposes, whether or not it is agreed that the lessee bears the risk of the motor vehicle's depreciation.

4. "Lessee" includes a bailee and means a natural person who leases, offers to lease or is offered the lease of a motor vehicle under a lease contract.

5. "Lessor" includes a bailor and means a person who is engaged in the business of leasing, offering to lease or arranging the lease of a motor vehicle under a lease contract.

6. "Motor vehicle" means a motor vehicle which is required to be registered under title 28, chapter 7 and which has a gross weight, as defined in section 28-5431, of ten thousand pounds or less.

7. "Purchaser" has the same meaning prescribed in section 47-1201.

8. "Retail installment contract" has the same meaning prescribed in section 44-281 and includes the sale of a motor vehicle between a buyer and a seller primarily for business or commercial purposes.

9. "Secured party" has the same meaning prescribed in section 47-9102.

10. "Security agreement" has the same meaning prescribed in section 47-9102.

11. "Security interest" has the same meaning prescribed in section 47-1201.

12. "Seller" means a person engaged in the business of selling or leasing motor vehicles under a retail installment contract.

13-3718. Sale of ticket in excess of regular price; classification; definition

A. It is unlawful for any person to sell or offer to sell a ticket of admission to an event, which ticket was purchased for the purpose of resale, for a price in excess of the price as printed on the face of the ticket, plus lawful taxes and any other charge or assessment which is required to be paid in order to purchase the ticket from the original vendor, while being within two hundred feet of an entry to the stadium, arena, theater or other place where an event is being held, or of the entry to a contiguous parking area.

B. It is unlawful for any person to change the price printed on the face of the ticket without the written permission of the original vendor of the ticket.

C. Any person who violates this section is guilty of a petty offense.

D. For purposes of this section, "event" shall mean a theatrical production, concert, sporting event or other entertainment event.

13-3719. Obtaining wireless telecommunications services or wireless telecommunications devices fraudulently; manufacturing, distributing and selling unauthorized decoding devices; classification; definitions

A. A person who with the intent to defraud another person of any part of the lawful charge for services that are provided over or by a wireless telecommunications service or wireless telecommunications device, who makes any unauthorized connection, whether physically, electrically, acoustically, inductively or otherwise, or who attaches any unauthorized device or devices to any cable, wire, microwave or other component of a wireless telecommunications service or wireless telecommunications device, or to any other instrument that is authorized to be attached to a wireless telecommunications service or wireless telecommunications device is guilty of a class 2 misdemeanor.

B. A person who manufactures, distributes, sells, rents, lends, offers or advertises for sale, rental or use any device that the person intends to be used by another person to obtain services that are provided over or by a wireless telecommunications service or wireless telecommunications device without payment of the charge for those services is guilty of a class 6 felony.

C. For the purposes of subsection B it is a rebuttable presumption that the person intended that the device would be used by another person to obtain services that are provided over or by a wireless telecommunications service or wireless telecommunications device without payment of the charge for those services if, while advertising, selling, renting or lending the device, the person states that the device will enable the person who receives the device to obtain wireless telecommunications services or wireless telecommunications devices without payment of the charge for those services.

D. For the purposes of subsection B, it is a separate violation for each individual device that is manufactured, distributed, sold, rented, lent, offered or advertised for sale, rental or use in violation of subsection B.

E. A person whose business or property is injured arising out of a violation of this section may bring an action in superior court to recover damages or for an injunction, or both. The successful party to the action may recover reasonable attorney fees.

F. For the purposes of this section:

1. "Wireless telecommunications device" means an instrument, device, machine or equipment that is capable of transmitting or receiving telephonic, electronic or radio communications or any part of an instrument, device, machine or equipment. Wireless telecommunications device includes computer circuits, computer chips, electronic mechanisms or other components that are capable of facilitating the transmission or reception of telephonic, electronic or radio communications.

2. "Wireless telecommunications service" includes any service that is provided for a charge or compensation to facilitate the origination, transmission, emission or reception of signs, signals, data, writings, images and sounds or intelligence of any nature by wireless telephone equipment, including cellular telephone, wire, radio electromagnetic, photoelectronic or photo-optical system.

13-3720. Dropping objects from overpass; classification; definition

A. A person on an overpass who with criminal negligence drops, throws, shoots or otherwise propels an object at or on the lower level street or highway or at or on a motor vehicle that is standing or being operated on the lower level street or highway is guilty of a class 1 misdemeanor.

B. For purposes of this section, "overpass" means the upper level of a crossing, at different levels, of two streets or highways or a street or highway and a pedestrian path or railroad.

13-3721. Tattoos, brands, scarifications and piercings; minors; anesthesia; exception; defense; violation; classification; definitions

A. It is unlawful for a person:

1. To intentionally brand, scarify, implant, mutilate, tattoo or pierce the body of a person who is under eighteen years of age without the physical presence of the parent or legal guardian of the person requesting the brand, scar, tattoo, implant, mutilation or piercing.

2. Who tattoos or pierces the body of another person to use a needle or any substance that will leave color under the skin more than once or to use a needle that is not sterilized with equipment used by state licensed medical facilities pursuant to title 36, chapter 4.

3. To engage in the business of tattooing, branding, scarifying, implanting, mutilating or body piercing out of a home or an impermanent structure, including a tent, trailer, trunk or other impermanent structure.

4. Who is not licensed pursuant to title 32 to administer anesthesia during the course of any procedure involving the branding, scarifying, tattooing, implanting, mutilating or piercing of the body of another person.

B. Subsection A, paragraph 1 does not apply to the ear piercing of a person who has written or verbal permission from a parent or legal guardian or to procedures that are prescribed by a health care provider who is licensed pursuant to title 32.

C. It is a defense to a prosecution for a violation of subsection A, paragraph 1 that the person requested age identification and relied in good faith on the accuracy of the information contained in the identification.

D. A person who violates this section is guilty of a class 6 felony.

E. For the purposes of this section:

1. "Implant", "mutilate", "brand", "scarify" or "pierce" means to mark the skin or other body part with any indelible design, letter, scroll, figure, symbol or other mark that is placed by the aid of instruments on or under the skin or body part and that cannot be

removed without a surgical procedure or any design, letter, scroll, figure, symbol or other mark done by scarring on or under the skin or other body part. Implant does not include cosmetic implants.

2. "Tattoo" means to mark the skin with any indelible design, letter, scroll, figure, symbol or any other mark that is placed by the aid of needles or other instruments upon or under the skin with any substance that will leave color under the skin and that cannot be removed, repaired or reconstructed without a surgical procedure or any design, letter, scroll, figure, symbol or other mark done by scarring upon or under the skin.

13-3722. Solicitations for American veterans' organizations; approval; violation; classification

A. It is unlawful for a person to solicit money or other support in the name of American veterans unless the veterans' organization for which the person is soliciting money or other support files a registration statement with the secretary of state in a format prescribed by the secretary of state.

B. A person who violates this section is guilty of a class 3 misdemeanor.

13-3723. Unlawful operation of a recording device with the intent to record a motion picture; classification; definitions

A. It is unlawful for a person to knowingly operate an audiovisual recording function of a device in a facility in which a motion picture is being exhibited with the intent to record the motion picture when that person knew or should have known they were doing so without the consent of the owner or lessee of the facility in which the motion picture is being exhibited.

B. With reasonable cause, a person may detain on the premises in a reasonable manner and for a reasonable time any person suspected of the unlawful recording of a motion picture as prescribed in subsection A for questioning or summoning a law enforcement officer. For the purposes of this subsection, "person" means:

1. The owner or lessee of a facility in which a motion picture is being exhibited or the owner's or lessee's authorized agent or employee.

2. The licensor of the motion picture being exhibited or the licensor's authorized agent or employee.

C. This section does not prevent any federal or state law enforcement agency or officer that is engaged in any intelligence gathering activities or any other lawful investigation from operating any audiovisual recording device in any facility in which a motion picture is being exhibited.

D. This section does not prevent prosecution under any other provision of law that provides for a greater penalty.

E. A person who violates this section is guilty of a class 1 misdemeanor.

F. For the purposes of this section:

1. "Audiovisual recording function" means the capability of a device to record or transmit a motion picture or any part of a motion picture by means of any technology now known or later developed.

2. "Facility" means any theater, screening room, indoor or outdoor screening venue, auditorium, ballroom or other premises where motion pictures are publicly exhibited, regardless of whether an admission fee is charged, but does not include the lobby area of a theater or a personal residence.

13-3724. Obtaining utility service fraudulently; classification; definitions

A. It is unlawful for any customer or person to intentionally do any of the following:

1. Make a connection or reconnection with property that is owned or used by a utility to provide utility service without the authorization or consent of the utility.

2. Prevent a utility meter or other device that is used to determine the charge for utility services from accurately performing its measuring function.

3. Tamper with property that is owned or used by a utility.

4. Use, receive or otherwise divert utility services without the authorization or consent of the utility if the customer or person knows or has reason to know of the unlawful diversion, tampering or connection.

5. Divert or cause to be diverted utility services by any means.

B. There is a rebuttable presumption that the customer or person intentionally violated an act specified in this section if any of the following occurs:

1. An instrument, apparatus or device that was installed to obtain utility service without paying the full charge is found attached to the meter or other device that is used to provide the utility service on the premises controlled by the customer or by the person who uses or receives the utility service.

2. A meter was altered, tampered with or bypassed resulting in no measurement or an inaccurate measurement of utility services.

3. The customer, person or owner is an occupant of the premises or has an access to the system for delivery of the service to the premises and receives a benefit from tampered or bypassed equipment.

C. The presumption provided in subsection B shifts the burden of going forward with the evidence and does not shift the burden of proof to the defendant.

D. Obtaining utility service fraudulently is a class 6 felony.

E. For the purposes of this section:

1. "Customer" means the person in whose name a utility service is provided.

2. "Divert" means to change the intended course or path of electricity, gas or water without the authorization or consent of the utility.

3. "Reconnection" means the restoration of utility service to a customer or person after service has been legally disconnected by the utility.

4. "Tamper" means to rearrange, damage, alter, interfere with or otherwise prevent the performance of a normal or customary function, including any of the following:

(a) Connecting any wire, conduit or device to any service, distribution or transmission line that is owned or used by a utility.

(b) Defacing, puncturing, removing, reversing or altering any meter or any connections to secure unauthorized or unmeasured utility service.

(c) Preventing any meter from properly measuring or registering.

(d) Knowingly taking, receiving, using or converting to personal use or the use of another person any utility service without authorization or consent.

(e) Causing, procuring, permitting, aiding or abetting any person to do any of the acts listed in this paragraph.

5. "Utility" means any public service corporation, agricultural improvement district or other person that is engaged in the generation, transmission or delivery of electricity, water or natural gas, including this state or any political subdivision of this state.

6. "Utility service" means the provision of services or commodities by the utility for compensation.

13-3725. Interference with monitoring devices; classification

A. A person commits interference with monitoring devices by either:

1. Being required to be on electronic monitoring or global position system monitoring and removing or bypassing any device or equipment that is necessary for the electronic monitoring or global position system monitoring.

2. Assisting any person who is required to be on electronic monitoring or global position system monitoring in removing or bypassing any device or equipment that is necessary for the electronic monitoring or global position system monitoring.

B. A violation of this section is a class 4 felony.

13-3726. Unauthorized use of the name, portrait or picture of a deceased soldier; civil action; exceptions; classification; definition

A. A person shall not knowingly use the name, portrait or picture of a deceased soldier for the purpose of advertising for the sale of any goods, wares or merchandise or for the solicitation of patronage for any business without having obtained prior consent to the use by the soldier or by the soldier's spouse, immediate family member, trustee if the soldier is a minor or legally designated representative.

B. Any person who is injured by the use of the name, portrait or picture of a deceased soldier in violation of subsection A of this section may bring a civil action against the person who committed the violation pursuant to section 12-761.

C. This section does not apply to the following:

1. The use of a soldier's name, portrait or picture in an attempt to portray, describe or impersonate that soldier in a live performance, a single and original work of fine art, a play, book, article, musical work or film or on radio, television or other audio or audiovisual work if the performance, musical work, play, book, article or film does not itself constitute a commercial advertisement for any goods, wares or merchandise.

2. The use of a soldier's name, portrait or picture for noncommercial purposes, including any news, public affairs or sports broadcast or account.

3. The use of a soldier's name in truthfully identifying the soldier as the author of a particular work or program or as the performer in a particular performance.

4. Any promotional materials, advertisements or commercial announcements for a use described in paragraph 1, 2 or 3.

5. The use of photographs, video recordings and images by a person, firm or corporation practicing the profession of photography to exhibit, in or about the professional photographer's place of business or portfolio, specimens of the professional photographer's work, unless the exhibition is continued by the professional photographer after written notice objecting to the exhibition by the portrayed soldier or a person who may enforce the soldier's rights and remedies.

6. A soldier's picture or portrait that is not facially identifiable.

7. A photograph of a monument or a memorial that is placed on any goods, wares or merchandise.

D. A person who violates this section is guilty of a class 1 misdemeanor.

E. For the purposes of this section, "soldier" means any active duty member or former member of the armed forces of the United States, including any member who was killed in the line of duty.

13-3727. Unlawful residency; persons convicted of criminal offenses; exceptions; preemption; classification

A. It is unlawful for a person who has been convicted of a dangerous crime against children as defined in section 13-705 or who has been convicted of an offense committed in another jurisdiction that if committed in this state would be a dangerous crime against children as defined in section 13-705, who is required to register pursuant to section 13-3821 and who is classified as a level three offender pursuant to section 13-3825 to reside within one thousand feet of the real property comprising any of the following:

1. A private school, as defined in section 15-101, or a public school that provides instruction in kindergarten programs and any combination of kindergarten programs and grades one through eight.

2. A private school, as defined in section 15-101, or a public school that provides instruction in any combination of grades nine through twelve.

3. A child care facility as defined in section 36-881.

B. This section does not apply to any of the following:

1. A person who establishes the person's residence before September 19, 2007 or before a new school or child care facility is located.

2. A person who is a minor.

3. A person who is currently serving a term of probation.

4. A person who has had the person's civil rights restored pursuant to chapter 9 of this title.

5. A person who has not been convicted of a subsequent offense in the previous ten years, excluding any time the person was incarcerated in any federal, state, county or local jail or prison facility.

C. Notwithstanding any other law and as a matter of statewide concern, a county, city or town shall not enact an ordinance that provides for distance restrictions greater than those found in this section.

D. For the purposes of subsection A of this section, measurements shall be made in a straight line in all directions, without regard to intervening structures or objects, from the nearest point on the property line of a parcel containing the person's residence to the nearest point on the property line of a parcel containing a child care facility or a school.

E. A person who violates this section is guilty of a class 1 misdemeanor.

13-3728. Unlawful purchase or sale of used catalytic converter; classification

A. It is unlawful for a person to purchase or sell a used catalytic converter unless the purchase or sale is in the ordinary course of business by a commercial motor vehicle parts or repair business in connection with the sale or installation of a new catalytic converter.

B. This section does not apply to:

1. An automotive recycler as defined and licensed pursuant to title 28, chapter 10.

2. The purchase or sale of a used catalytic converter as prescribed by section 44-1642.01 that is acquired in a transaction with an industrial account, with another scrap metal dealer or after the used catalytic converter is authorized for release by a peace officer of the jurisdiction in which the transaction occurs.

C. A violation of this section is a class 1 misdemeanor.

13-3729. Unlawful operation of model or unmanned aircraft; state preemption; classification; definitions

A. It is unlawful for a person to operate a model aircraft or a civil unmanned aircraft if the operation:

1. Is prohibited by a federal law or regulation that governs aeronautics, including federal aviation administration regulations.

2. Interferes with a law enforcement, firefighter or emergency services operation.

B. It is unlawful for a person to operate or use an unmanned aircraft or unmanned aircraft system to intentionally photograph or loiter over or near a critical facility in the furtherance of any criminal offense.

C. Except as authorized by law, a city, town or county may not enact or adopt any ordinance, policy or rule that relates to the ownership or operation of an unmanned aircraft or unmanned aircraft system or otherwise engage in the regulation of the ownership or operation of an unmanned aircraft or an unmanned aircraft system. Any ordinance, policy or rule that violates this subsection, whether enacted or adopted by the city, town or county before or after August 6, 2016, is void.

D. This section does not:

1. Apply to a person or entity that is authorized or allowed by the federal aviation administration to operate or use an unmanned aircraft system if the person's or entity's operation or use complies with the authorization granted to the person or entity or with federal aviation administration rules.

2. Prohibit a city, town or county from enacting or adopting ordinances or rules on the operation or use of a public unmanned aircraft that is owned by the city, town or county.

3. Prohibit a city, town or county from enacting or adopting ordinances or rules that regulate the takeoff or landing of a model aircraft in a park or preserve owned by the city, town or county if:

(a) There are other parks or preserves that are within the city, town or county and that are available for model aircraft operation.

(b) The city, town or county only has one park or preserve that is within the city, town or county.

4. Apply to the operation of an unmanned aircraft, including a public unmanned aircraft, by a first responder as defined in section 36-661 while acting in the first responder's official capacity or an emergency worker while engaged in or supporting authorized emergency management activities or performing emergency functions pursuant to title 26, chapter 2.

E. A violation of subsection B of this section is a class 6 felony, except that a second or subsequent violation is a class 5 felony. A violation of subsection A of this section is a class 1 misdemeanor.

F. For the purposes of this section:

1. "Civil unmanned aircraft" means an unmanned aircraft or unmanned aircraft system that is operated by a person for any purpose other than strictly for hobby or recreational purposes, including commercial purposes, or in furtherance of or incidental to any business or media service or agency.

2. "Commercial purposes" means the use of an unmanned aircraft in return for financial compensation and includes aerial photography, aerial mapping or geospatial imaging.

3. "Critical facility" means any of the following:

(a) A petroleum or alumina refinery.

(b) A petroleum, chemical or rubber production, transportation, storage or processing facility.

(c) A chemical manufacturing facility.

(d) A water or wastewater treatment facility and water development, distribution or conveyance system, including a dam.

(e) An electric generation facility, as defined in section 42-14156, and any associated substation or switchyard.

(f) An electrical transmission or distribution substation.

(g) An electrical transmission line of at least sixty-nine thousand volts.

(h) An electronic communication station or tower.

(i) An energy control center.

(j) A distribution operating center.

(k) A facility that transfers or distributes natural gas, including a compressor station, regulator station, city gate station or pressure limiting station or a liquefied natural gas facility or supplier tap facility.

(l) Any railroad infrastructure or facility.

(m) A federal, state, county or municipal court.

(n) A public safety or emergency operation facility.

(o) A federal, state, county or municipal jail or prison or other facility in which persons are incarcerated.

(p) A federal or state military installation or facility.

(q) A hospital that receives air ambulance services.

4. "Model aircraft" has the same meaning prescribed in section 336 of the FAA modernization and reform act of 2012 (P.L. 112-95), as amended.

5. "Person" means a corporation, firm, partnership, association, individual or organization or any other group acting as a unit.

6. "Public unmanned aircraft" means an unmanned aircraft or unmanned aircraft system that is operated by a public agency for a government-related purpose.

7. "Unmanned aircraft" means an aircraft, including an aircraft commonly known as a drone, that is operated without the possibility of direct human intervention from within or on the aircraft.

8. "Unmanned aircraft system" means an unmanned aircraft and associated elements, including any communication links and components that control the unmanned aircraft.

Chapter 38 Miscellanous – Not in this Book (See "Arizona Criminal Procedure")

Chapter 39 Forfeiture

13-4301. Definitions

In this chapter, unless the context otherwise requires:

1. "Attorney for the state" means an attorney designated by the attorney general, by a county attorney or by a city attorney to investigate, commence and prosecute an action under this chapter.

2. "Commercially reasonable" means a sale or disposal that would be commercially reasonable under title 47, chapter 9, article 6.

3. "Injured person" means a person who has sustained economic loss, including medical loss, as a result of injury to his person, business or property by the conduct giving rise to the forfeiture of property, and who is not an owner of or an interest holder in the property. Injured person does not include a person who is responsible for the conduct giving rise to forfeiture or a person whose interest would not be exempt from forfeiture if the person were an owner of or interest holder in the property.

4. "Interest holder" means a person in whose favor there is a security interest or who is the beneficiary of a perfected encumbrance pertaining to an interest in property.

5. "Owner" means a person who is not a secured party within the meaning of section 47-9102 and who has an interest in property, whether legal or equitable. A person who holds property for the benefit of or as agent or nominee for another is not an owner. A purported interest which is not in compliance with any statute requiring its recordation or reflection in public records in order to perfect the interest against a bona fide purchaser for value shall not be recognized as an interest against this state in an action pursuant to this chapter. An owner with power to convey property binds other owners, and a spouse binds his spouse, by his act or omission.

6. "Person known to have an interest" means a person whose interest in property is reflected in the public records in which his interest is required by law to be recorded or reflected in order to perfect his interest. If a person's interest in property is not required by law to be reflected in public records in order to perfect his interest in the property, a person shall be known to have an interest only if his interest can be readily ascertained at the time of the commencement of the forfeiture action pursuant to this chapter.

7. "Personal property" includes all interests in property, as defined in section 13-105, in whatever form, except real property and fixtures as defined in section 47-9102.

8. "Seizing agency" means any department or agency of this state or its political subdivisions which regularly employs peace officers, and which employs the peace officer who seizes property for forfeiture, or such other agency as the seizing agency may designate in a particular case by its chief executive officer or his designee.

9. "Seizure for forfeiture" means seizure of property by a peace officer coupled with an assertion by the seizing agency or by an attorney for the state that the property is subject to forfeiture.

13-4302. Jurisdiction

The state may commence a proceeding in the superior court if the property for which forfeiture is sought is within this state at the time of the filing of the action or if the courts of this state have in personam jurisdiction of an owner of or interest holder in the property.

13-4303. Venue

A. A civil action brought pursuant to this chapter may be brought in the county in which the property is seized or in any county in which an owner or interest holder could be civilly or criminally complained against for the conduct alleged to give rise to the forfeiture of the property.

B. A claimant or defendant may obtain a change of venue only under the same circumstances under which a defendant may obtain a change of venue in a criminal case.

13-4304. Property subject to forfeiture; exemptions

(Caution: 1998 Prop. 105 applies)

All property, including all interests in such property, described in a statute providing for its forfeiture is subject to forfeiture. However:

1. No vehicle used by any person as a common carrier in the transaction of business as a common carrier may be forfeited under the provisions of this chapter unless it appears that the owner or other person in charge of the vehicle was a consenting party or privy to the act or omission giving rise to forfeiture or knew or had reason to know of it.

2. No vehicle may be forfeited under the provisions of this chapter for any act or omission established by the owner to have been committed or omitted by a person other than the owner while the vehicle was unlawfully in the possession of a person other than the owner in violation of the criminal laws of this state or of the United States.

3. No property may be forfeited pursuant to section 13-3413, subsection A, paragraph 1 or 3 if the conduct giving rise to the forfeiture both:

(a) Did not involve an amount of unlawful substance greater than the statutory threshold amount as defined in section 13-3401.

(b) Was not committed for financial gain.

4. No owner's or interest holder's interest may be forfeited under this chapter if the owner or interest holder establishes all of the following:

(a) He acquired the interest before or during the conduct giving rise to forfeiture.

(b) He did not empower any person whose act or omission gives rise to forfeiture with legal or equitable power to convey the interest, as to a bona fide purchaser for value, and he was not married to any such person or if married to such person, held the property as separate property.

(c) He did not know and could not reasonably have known of the act or omission or that it was likely to occur.

5. No owner's or interest holder's interest may be forfeited under this chapter if the owner or interest holder establishes all of the following:

(a) He acquired the interest after the conduct giving rise to forfeiture.

(b) He is a bona fide purchaser for value not knowingly taking part in an illegal transaction.

(c) He was at the time of purchase and at all times after the purchase and before the filing of a racketeering lien notice or the provision of notice of pending forfeiture or the filing and notice of a civil or criminal proceeding under this title relating to the property, whichever is earlier, reasonably without notice of the act or omission giving rise to forfeiture and reasonably without cause to believe that the property was subject to forfeiture.

13-4305. Seizure of property

A. Property subject to forfeiture under this chapter may be seized for forfeiture by a peace officer:

1. On process issued pursuant to the Arizona rules of civil procedure or this title, including a seizure warrant.

2. By making a seizure for forfeiture on property seized on process issued pursuant to law, including sections 13-3911, 13-3912, 13-3913, 13-3914 and 13-3915.

3. By making a seizure for forfeiture without court process if any of the following is true:

(a) The seizure for forfeiture is of property seized incident to an arrest or search.

(b) The property subject to seizure for forfeiture has been the subject of a prior judgment in favor of this state or any other state or the federal government in a forfeiture proceeding.

(c) The peace officer has probable cause to believe that the property is subject to forfeiture.

B. Property subject to forfeiture under this chapter may be seized for forfeiture by placing the property under constructive seizure. Constructive seizure may be made by posting notice of seizure for forfeiture on the property or by filing notice of seizure for forfeiture or notice of pending forfeiture in any appropriate public record relating to the property.

C. The court shall determine probable cause for seizure before real property may be seized for forfeiture, unless the seizure is pursuant to a constructive seizure or the filing of a racketeering lien or lis pendens. The court may make its determination ex parte if the state demonstrates that notice and an opportunity to appear would create a risk of harm to the public safety or welfare, including the risk of physical injury or the likelihood of property damage or financial loss.

D. The court shall determine probable cause for seizure before property may be seized for forfeiture as a substitute asset pursuant to section 13-2314, subsection D, E or G, or pursuant to section 13-4313, subsection A, unless the seizure is pursuant to a constructive seizure or the filing of a racketeering lien or lis pendens. The court may issue a seizure warrant for such property if it determines that there is probable cause to believe that the property is subject to forfeiture and is not available for seizure for forfeiture for any reason described in section 13-4313, subsection A. The determinations shall be made ex parte unless real property is to be seized and subsection C of this section requires notice and an opportunity to appear.

E. In establishing clear and convincing evidence and in determining probable cause for seizure and for forfeiture, a rebuttable presumption exists that the property of any person is subject to forfeiture if the state establishes all of the following by the standard of proof applicable to that proceeding:

1. Conduct giving rise to forfeiture occurred.

2. The person acquired the property during the period of the conduct giving rise to forfeiture or within a reasonable time after that period.

3. There is no likely source for the property other than the conduct giving rise to forfeiture.

F. In establishing clear and convincing evidence and in determining probable cause for seizure and for forfeiture, the fact that money or any negotiable instrument was found in proximity to contraband or to instrumentalities of an offense gives rise to an inference that the money or instrument was the proceeds of contraband or was used or intended to be used to facilitate commission of the offense.

13-4306. Powers and duties of peace officers and agencies; definition

A. In the event of a seizure for forfeiture under section 13-4305, the property is not subject to replevin, conveyance, sequestration or attachment but is deemed to be in the custody of the law enforcement agency making the seizure for forfeiture. The seizing agency or the attorney for the state may authorize the release of the seizure for forfeiture of the property if forfeiture or retention is unnecessary, may transfer the property to any other state agency or may transfer the action to another attorney for the state by discontinuing forfeiture proceedings in favor of forfeiture proceedings initiated by the other agency or attorney. Except as provided in subsections I and J of this section, the seizing agency or the attorney for the state may not transfer or refer seized property to a federal agency. An action pursuant to this chapter shall be consolidated with any other action or proceeding pursuant to this title relating to the same property on motion by the attorney for the state in either action.

B. If property is seized for forfeiture under section 13-4305, pending forfeiture and final disposition, the seizing agency may do any of the following:

1. Remove the property to a storage area for safekeeping or, if the property is a negotiable instrument or money, deposit it in an interest bearing account.

2. Remove the property to a place designated by the court.

3. Provide for another custodian or agency to take custody of the property and remove it to an appropriate location within the jurisdiction of the court.

C. As soon as practicable after seizure for forfeiture, the seizing agency shall conduct an inventory and estimate the value of the property seized. Within twenty days the seizing agency or the attorney for the state shall make reasonable efforts to provide notice of seizure for forfeiture to all persons known to have an interest in the seized property.

D. A person who acts in good faith and in a reasonable manner to comply with an order of the court or a request of a peace officer is not liable to any person for acts done in compliance with the order or request.

E. A possessory lien of a person from whose possession property is seized is not affected by the seizure.

F. In the event of a seizure for forfeiture under section 13-4305, the seizing agency shall send to an attorney for the state a written request for forfeiture within twenty days, which shall include a statement of facts and circumstances of the seizure, including the names of witnesses then known, the appraised or estimated value of the property and a summary of the facts relied on for forfeiture.

G. An owner of property seized for forfeiture may obtain the release of the seized property by posting with the attorney for the state a surety bond or cash in an amount equal to the full fair market value of the property as determined by the attorney for the state. The state may refuse to release the property if any of the following applies:

1. The bond or cash tendered is inadequate.

2. The property is retained as contraband or evidence.

3. The property is particularly altered or designed for use in conduct giving rise to forfeiture.

H. If an owner of property posts a surety bond or cash and the property is forfeited the court shall forfeit the surety bond or cash in lieu of the property.

I. The seizing agency or the attorney for the state may not enter into any agreement to transfer or refer seized property to a federal agency for the purpose of forfeiture if the property was seized pursuant to an investigation that either:

1. Did not involve a federal agency.

2. Involves a violation of a state law and no violation of a federal law is alleged.

J. Property that is seized in a joint investigation may not be transferred or referred to a federal agency for the purpose of forfeiture unless the gross estimated value of the seized property is more than seventy-five thousand dollars.

K. This section does not prohibit:

1. The federal government or any of its agencies from seizing property, seeking forfeiture pursuant to federal law and sharing property that is forfeited pursuant to federal law with a state or local law enforcement agency that participates in a joint investigation.

2. A state or local law enforcement agency from participating in a joint investigation.

L. For the purposes of this section, "joint investigation" means an investigation in which a state or local law enforcement agency directly participates in the investigation or enforcement of a federal criminal law with a federal agency and the investigation or enforcement results in a seizure.

13-4307. Notice of pending forfeiture

Whenever notice of pending forfeiture is required under this chapter it shall be given or provided in one of the following ways and is effective at the time of personal service, publication or the mailing of written notice, whichever is earlier:

1. If the owner's or interest holder's name and current address are known by either:

(a) Personal service.

(b) Mailing a copy of the notice by certified mail to the address.

2. If the owner's or interest holder's interest is required by law to be on record with a county recorder's office, the secretary of state, the department of transportation motor vehicle division, the game and fish department, or another state or federal licensing agency in order to perfect an interest in the property, but his current address is not known, by mailing a copy of the notice by certified mail to any address on the record.

3. If the owner's or interest holder's address is not known, and is not on record as provided in paragraph 2, or if his interest is not known, by publication in one issue of a newspaper of general circulation in the county in which the seizure occurs.

13-4308. Commencement of proceedings

A. The attorney for the state shall determine whether it is probable that the property is subject to forfeiture and, if so, may cause the initiation of uncontested or judicial proceedings against the property. If, on inquiry and examination, the attorney determines that the proceedings probably cannot be sustained or that justice does not require the institution of such proceedings, he shall notify the seizing agency and immediately authorize the release of the seizure for forfeiture on the property or on any specified interest in it.

B. If the state fails to initiate forfeiture proceedings against property seized for forfeiture by notice of pending forfeiture within sixty days after its seizure for forfeiture, or fails to pursue forfeiture of such property on which a timely claim has been properly filed by filing a complaint, information or indictment pursuant to section 13-4311 or 13-4312 within sixty days after notice of pending forfeiture or, if uncontested forfeiture has been made available, within sixty days after a declaration of forfeiture, whichever is later, such property shall be released from its seizure for forfeiture on the request of an owner or interest holder, pending further proceedings pursuant to this chapter, which shall be commenced within seven years after actual discovery of the last act giving rise to forfeiture.

C. If the property sought to be forfeited is real property, including fixtures, the attorney for the state may file a lis pendens or a notice of pending forfeiture with respect to the property with the county recorder of the county in which the property is located, in addition to any lien provided by section 13-2314.02, without a filing fee or other charge.

13-4309. Uncontested forfeiture

If a forfeiture is authorized by law, the attorney for the state may make uncontested civil forfeiture available to owners of and interest holders in personal property in the following manner:

1. If the attorney for the state in his discretion makes uncontested forfeiture available, he shall provide notice of pending forfeiture by giving notice within thirty days after seizure for forfeiture as provided in section 13-4307 to all persons known to have an interest who have not previously received the notice.

2. An owner of or interest holder in the property may elect to file either a claim with the court within thirty days after the notice or a petition for remission or mitigation of forfeiture with the attorney for the state within thirty days after the notice and not after a complaint has been filed, but may not file both. The claim or petition shall comply with the requirements for claims in section 13-4311, subsections E and F.

3. The following apply if one or more owners or interest holders timely file a petition for remission or mitigation:

(a) The attorney for the state shall inquire into whether the property is subject to forfeiture and the facts and circumstances surrounding petitions for remission or mitigation of forfeiture.

(b) The attorney for the state shall provide the seizing agency and the petitioner with a written declaration of forfeiture, remission or mitigation of any or all interest in the property in response to each petition within ninety days after the effective date of the notice of pending forfeiture unless one or more petitioners request an extension of time in writing or unless the circumstances of the case require additional time, in which case the attorney for the state shall notify the petitioner in writing and with specificity within the ninety day period that the circumstances of the case require additional time and further notify the petitioner of the expected decision date. In no event shall the mailing of the declaration be more than one hundred twenty days after the date of the state's notice of pending forfeiture.

(c) An owner or interest holder in any property declared forfeited may file a claim as described in section 13-4311, subsections E and F in the superior court in the county in which the uncontested forfeiture was declared within thirty days after the mailing of the declaration of forfeiture.

(d) If a declaration of forfeiture pursuant to this section is followed by a timely claim, or at any other time, the attorney for the state may elect to proceed as provided for judicial forfeitures.

(e) If no petitioner files a claim in the court within thirty days after the mailing of the declaration of forfeiture, the declaration becomes final and the attorney for the state shall proceed as provided in sections 13-4314 and 13-4315.

4. If no petitions for remission or mitigation or claims are timely filed, the attorney for the state shall proceed as provided in sections 13-4314 and 13-4315.

5. If one or more petitions for remission or mitigation and one or more claims are timely filed, no complaint for forfeiture need be filed by the state until sixty days after an uncontested declaration of forfeiture.

6. If a judicial forfeiture proceeding follows a notice of pending forfeiture making uncontested civil forfeiture available:

(a) No duplicate or repetitive notice or claim is required. The judicial proceedings shall adjudicate all timely filed claims. If a claim has been timely filed pursuant to paragraph 2 or 3 of this section it shall be determined in a judicial forfeiture proceeding after the commencement of such a proceeding pursuant to section 13-4311, subsection A or section 13-4312, subsection A.

(b) The declarations of forfeiture, remission or mitigation responsive to all petitioners who subsequently filed claims are void and shall be regarded as rejected offers to compromise.

13-4310. Judicial forfeiture proceedings; general

A. In any proceeding pursuant to this chapter, the court, on application of the state, may enter any restraining order or injunction, require the execution of satisfactory performance bonds, create receiverships, appoint conservators, appraisers, accountants or trustees or take any other action to seize, secure, maintain or preserve the availability of property subject to forfeiture under this title, including a warrant for its seizure, whether prior or subsequent to the filing of a notice of pending forfeiture, complaint, indictment or information.

B. If property is seized for forfeiture without a prior judicial determination of probable cause, an order of forfeiture or a hearing pursuant to section 13-4312, subsection D, the court, on an application filed by an owner of or interest holder in the property within fifteen days after notice of its seizure for forfeiture or actual knowledge of it, whichever is earlier, and complying with the requirements for claims in section 13-4311, subsections E and F, may issue an order to show cause to the seizing agency for a hearing on the sole issue of whether probable cause for forfeiture of the property then exists. Notice of the order to show cause hearing must be served on the attorney for the state at least five working days before the hearing is held. If the court finds that no probable cause for forfeiture of the property then exists or if the state elects not to contest the issue, the property seized for forfeiture from the applicant shall be released to the custody of the applicant pending the outcome of a judicial proceeding pursuant to this chapter. If the court finds that probable cause for the forfeiture of the property then exists, the court shall not order the property released, except as provided in section 13-4306, subsection G.

C. A defendant convicted in any criminal proceeding shall be precluded from subsequently denying the essential allegations of the criminal offense of which he was convicted in any proceeding pursuant to this chapter. For the purposes of this chapter, a conviction may result from a verdict or plea including a no contest plea.

D. In any judicial forfeiture hearing, determination or other proceeding pursuant to this chapter, the applicant, petitioner or claimant must establish by a preponderance of the evidence that he is an owner of or interest holder in the property seized for forfeiture before other evidence is taken. The burden of proving the standing of the claimant and the existence of the exemption is on the claimant or party raising the claim, and it is not necessary to negate the standing of any claimant or the existence of any exemption in any notice, application, complaint, information or indictment.

E. In hearings and determinations pursuant to this chapter:

1. The law of evidence relating to civil actions applies equally to all parties, including the state, an applicant, a petitioner, a claimant and a defendant, on all issues required to be established by a preponderance of the evidence or clear and convincing evidence.

2. The court shall receive and consider, in making any determination of probable cause or reasonable cause, all evidence and information that would be permissible in determining probable cause at a preliminary hearing, at a grand jury or by a magistrate pursuant to section 13-3913, together with inferences from the evidence and information.

F. All property, including all interests in such property, declared forfeited under this title vests in this state on the commission of the act or omission giving rise to forfeiture under this title together with the proceeds of the property after such time. Any such property or proceeds subsequently transferred to any person are subject to forfeiture and thereafter shall be ordered forfeited unless the transferee claims and establishes in a hearing pursuant to this chapter the showings set out in section 13-4304.

G. On the motion of a party and after notice to any persons who are known to have an interest in the property and an opportunity to be heard, the court may order property that has been seized for forfeiture sold, leased, rented or operated to satisfy an interest of any interest holder who has timely filed a proper claim or to preserve the interests of any party. The court may order a sale or any other disposition of the property if the property may perish, waste, be foreclosed on or otherwise be significantly reduced in value or if the expenses of maintaining the property are or will become greater than its fair market value. If the court orders a sale, the court shall designate a third party or state property manager to dispose of the property by public sale or other commercially reasonable method and shall distribute the proceeds in the following order of priority:

1. Payment of reasonable expenses incurred in connection with the sale.

2. Satisfaction of exempt interests in the order of their priority.

3. Preservation of the balance, if any, in the actual or constructive custody of the court in an interest bearing account, subject to further proceedings under this chapter.

H. If the property is disposed of pursuant to subsection G of this section, a successful claimant may apply to the court for actual monetary damages suffered, if any, as a result of the disposal of the property, but the state, a political subdivision of the state, or an officer, employee or agent of any of them shall not in any event be liable under this chapter for incidental or consequential damages or for damages either:

1. That could have been avoided if the claimant had made full and immediate disclosure to the attorney for the state of facts or evidence known or available to the claimant.

2. In excess of the fair market value of the property seized for forfeiture at the time of its seizure plus interest from the time of its seizure for forfeiture.

I. If an indictment or information is filed alleging the same conduct as the conduct giving rise to forfeiture in a civil forfeiture proceeding, the court in the civil proceeding may stay civil discovery against the criminal defendant and against the state in the civil proceeding until the defendant's criminal trial is completed. Before staying civil discovery, the court shall make adequate provision to prevent any loss or expense to any victim or party resulting from the delay, including loss or expense due to maintenance, management, insurance, storage or preservation of the availability of the property or due to depreciation in the value of the property.

J. No person claiming to be an owner of or interest holder in property seized for forfeiture under this chapter may commence or maintain any action against the state concerning the validity of the alleged interest other than as provided in this chapter.

13-4311. Judicial in rem forfeiture proceedings

A. If a forfeiture is authorized by law, it shall be ordered by a court on an action in rem brought by the state pursuant to a notice of pending forfeiture or a verified complaint for forfeiture. The state may serve the complaint in the manner provided by section 13-4307 or by the Arizona rules of civil procedure.

B. A civil in rem action may be brought by the state in addition to or in lieu of the civil and criminal in personam forfeiture procedures set forth in sections 13-4312 and 13-4313 or the uncontested civil forfeiture procedures set forth in section 13-4309. Judicial in rem forfeiture proceedings are in the nature of an action in rem and are governed by the Arizona rules of civil procedure unless a different procedure is provided by law.

C. On the filing of a civil in rem action by the state in superior court the clerk of the court in which the action is filed shall provide, and the attorney for the state may provide, the notice of pending forfeiture required by section 13-4307 unless the files of the clerk of the court reflect that such notice has previously been made.

D. An owner of or interest holder in the property may file a claim against the property, within thirty days after the notice, for a hearing to adjudicate the validity of his claimed interest in the property. The court shall hold the hearing without a jury. An owner or interest holder may not be charged a filing fee or any other charge for filing the claim.

E. The claim shall be signed by the claimant under penalty of perjury and shall set forth all of the following:

1. The caption of the proceeding as set forth on the notice of pending forfeiture or complaint and the name of the claimant.

2. The address at which the claimant will accept future mailings from the court or attorney for the state.

3. The nature and extent of the claimant's interest in the property.

4. The date, the identity of the transferor and the circumstances of the claimant's acquisition of the interest in the property.

5. The specific provisions of this chapter relied on in asserting that the property is not subject to forfeiture.

6. All facts supporting each such assertion.

7. Any additional facts supporting the claimant's claim.

8. The precise relief sought.

F. Copies of the claim shall be mailed to the seizing agency and to the attorney for the state. No extension of time for the filing of a claim may be granted.

G. Within twenty days after service of the complaint, the claimant shall file and serve the answer to the complaint and the answers to interrogatories and requests for admission if any were served with the complaint. The answer shall be signed by the owner or interest holder under penalty of perjury, shall comply with the Arizona rules of civil procedure relating to answers and shall comply with all of the requirements for claims. If no proper answer is timely filed, the attorney for the state shall proceed as provided in sections 13-4314 and 13-4315 with ten days' notice to any person who has timely filed a claim that has not been stricken by the court.

H. At the time of filing its pleadings or at any other time not less than thirty days before the hearing, the state and any claimant who has timely answered the complaint may serve discovery requests on any other party, the answers or response to which shall be due in twenty days, and may take the deposition of any person at any time after the expiration of fifteen days after the filing and service of the complaint. Any party may move for summary judgment at any time after an answer or responsive pleading is served and not less than thirty days before the hearing. The state, as the party defending against the claim, may make offers of judgment at any time more than ten days before the hearing begins.

I. An injured person may submit a request for compensation from forfeited property to the court at any time before the earlier of the entry of a final judgment or an application for an order of the forfeiture of the property, or if a hearing pursuant to subsections K, L and M of this section is held, not less than thirty days before the hearing. The request shall be signed by the requestor under penalty of perjury and shall set forth all of the following:

1. The caption of the proceeding as set forth on the notice of pending forfeiture or complaint and the name of the requestor.

2. The address at which the requestor will accept future mailings from the court or parties to the action.

3. The property subject to forfeiture from which the requestor seeks compensation.

4. The nature of the economic loss sustained by the requestor.

5. All facts supporting each such assertion.

6. Any additional facts supporting the request.

7. The amount of economic loss for which the requestor seeks compensation.

J. If a proper request for compensation from forfeited property is timely filed, the court shall hold a hearing to establish whether there is a factual basis for the request. The requestor has the burden of establishing by a preponderance of the evidence that the requestor is an injured person who sustained economic loss.

K. The hearing on the claim, to the extent practicable and consistent with the interest of justice, shall be held sixty days after all parties have complied with the disclosure required by rule 26.1 of the Arizona rules of civil procedure. The court may consolidate the hearing on the claim with a hearing on any other claim concerning the same property.

L. At the hearing, the claimant may testify, present evidence and witnesses on the claimant's own behalf and cross-examine witnesses who appear at the hearing. The state may present evidence and witnesses and cross-examine witnesses who appear at the hearing.

M. At the hearing, the state has the burden of establishing by clear and convincing evidence that the property is subject to forfeiture under section 13-4304. Any claimant who has previously established by a preponderance of the evidence that the claimant is an owner of or interest holder in the property has the burden of establishing by a preponderance of the evidence that the claimant's interest in the property is exempt from forfeiture under section 13-4304.

N. In accordance with its findings at the hearing:

1. The court shall order an interest in property returned or conveyed to a claimant, if any, who has established by a preponderance of the evidence that the claimant is an owner of or interest holder in the property if either of the following applies:

(a) The state has failed to establish by clear and convincing evidence that the interest is subject to forfeiture under section 13-4304.

(b) The claimant has established by a preponderance of the evidence that the interest is exempt from forfeiture under section 13-4304.

2. The court shall order all other property, including all interests in the property, forfeited to this state and proceed pursuant to sections 13-4314 and 13-4315.

3. If the court finds that a requestor is an injured person the court shall determine the amount of the injured person's economic loss caused by the conduct giving rise to the forfeiture of the designated property and shall require the following:

(a) If the designated property is not contraband and is not altered or designed for use in conduct giving rise to forfeiture, the attorney for the state shall sell the property as provided in section 13-4315, subsection A, paragraph 2 and shall apply the resulting balance to compensate the injured person's economic loss in the amount found by the court.

(b) If the balance is insufficient to compensate the economic loss of all injured persons the attorney for the state shall distribute the balance among the injured persons according to a method determined by the court.

(c) After compensation of all injured persons, the attorney for the state shall transmit ten percent of the remaining balance, if any, to the Arizona criminal justice commission for deposit in the victim compensation and assistance fund established by section 41-2407.

(d) The attorney for the state shall deposit the remainder of the balance, if any, in an appropriate anti-racketeering revolving fund established by section 13-2314.01 or 13-2314.03.

13-4312. Judicial in personam forfeiture proceedings

A. If a forfeiture is authorized by law, it shall be ordered by a court on proceedings by the state in an in personam civil or criminal action pursuant to section 13-2313 or 13-2314 or any other law providing for a forfeiture.
B. Any complaint, information or indictment alleging or charging one or more offenses included in section 13-2301, subsection D, paragraph 4 or a violation of section 13-2312, or any other offense giving rise to forfeiture under this title, shall set forth with reasonable particularity property that the state seeks to forfeit pursuant to this section in that action, if any. The court shall allow the allegation that particular new or different or differently described property is subject to forfeiture in an in personam criminal or civil case to be made at any time prior to the date the case is actually tried unless the allegation is filed fewer than twenty days before the case is actually tried, and the court finds on the record that the defendant was in fact prejudiced by the untimely filing and states

reasons for these findings, provided that when the allegation is filed, the state must make available to the defendant a copy of any material information concerning the allegation.

C. In any proceeding pursuant to this section, the court, on application of the state, may enter any order authorized by section 13-4310, subsection A or take any other action to seize, secure, maintain or preserve the availability of property subject to forfeiture under this title, including a warrant for its seizure, whether before or after the filing of a complaint, indictment or information.

D. Notwithstanding subsection E of this section, a temporary restraining order under this section may be entered on application of the state without notice or an opportunity for a hearing if the state demonstrates both that:

1. There is probable cause to believe that the property with respect to which the order is sought would, in the event of final judgment or conviction, be subject to forfeiture under this title.

2. Provision of notice will jeopardize the availability of the property for forfeiture. A temporary restraining order expires within ten days after the date on which it is entered unless the party against whom it is entered consents to an extension for a longer period or unless after commencing a hearing the court enters or is considering a preliminary injunction.

E. Notice of the entry of the restraining order and an opportunity for a hearing shall be afforded to persons known to have an interest in the property, whether or not a temporary restraining order is entered without notice. The hearing, however, is limited to the issues of whether both:

1. There is a probability that the state will prevail on the issue of forfeiture and that failure to enter the order will result in the property being destroyed, conveyed, encumbered or further encumbered, removed from the jurisdiction of the court, concealed or otherwise made unavailable for forfeiture.

2. The need to preserve the availability of property through the entry of the requested order outweighs the hardship on any owner, interest holder or defendant against whom the order is to be entered.

F. A hearing requested by any owner or interest holder concerning an order entered under this section shall be held at the earliest possible time and before the expiration of a temporary order.

G. On a determination of liability or the conviction of a person for conduct giving rise to forfeiture under this title, the court shall enter a judgment of forfeiture of the property described in the forfeiture statute alleged and set out in the complaint, information or indictment, as amended, and shall also authorize the county attorney or attorney general, their agents or any peace officer to seize all property ordered forfeited that was not previously seized or is not then under seizure. Following the entry of an order declaring the property forfeited, the court, on application of the state, may enter any order authorized by section 13-4310, subsection A or take any other action to protect the interest of this state or a political subdivision in the property ordered forfeited. The filing of the order of forfeiture in the appropriate public records perfects the interest of the state in the property described in the order as of the earlier of the date of the act or omission giving rise to forfeiture or the date that a notice of seizure for forfeiture or notice of pending forfeiture or racketeering lien was first filed in the records, which entitles the state to all rights of a secured party as to that property in addition to any other rights or remedies of the state in relation to the property. Any income accruing to, or derived from, an enterprise or any interest in an enterprise or other property interest that is forfeited under this chapter is also forfeited from the time of the conduct giving rise to forfeiture. It may be used pending procedures subsequent to a verdict or finding of liability to offset ordinary and necessary expenses of the enterprise or property as required by law or that are necessary to protect the interests of this state or a political subdivision.

H. Procedures subsequent to the verdict or finding of liability and order of forfeiture shall be as follows:

1. Following the entry of an order of forfeiture under this subsection the clerk of the court shall, and the attorney for the state may, give notice of pending forfeiture to all owners and interest holders who have not previously been given notice, if any, in the manner provided in section 13-4307.

2. An owner of or interest holder in property that has been ordered forfeited pursuant to such action whose claim is not precluded may file a claim as described in section 13-4311, subsections E and F in the court for a hearing to adjudicate the validity of his claimed interest in the property within thirty days after initial notice of pending forfeiture or after notice under paragraph 1 of this subsection, whichever is earlier.

3. The hearing on the claim, to the extent practicable and consistent with the interest of justice, shall be held within sixty days after the order of forfeiture. The court may consolidate the hearing on the claim with a hearing on any other claim filed by a person other than a party or defendant in the underlying action and concerning the same property.

4. The hearing shall be held by the court without a jury and conducted in the manner provided for in rem judicial forfeiture actions including the provisions of section 13-4311, subsections L and M. In addition to testimony and evidence presented at the hearing, the court shall consider the relevant portions of the record of the underlying civil or criminal action that resulted in the order of forfeiture.

5. In accordance with its findings at the hearing, the court may amend the order of forfeiture if it determines that any claimant has established by a preponderance of the evidence that the claimant is an owner of or interest holder in the property if either of the following applies:

(a) The state has failed to establish by clear and convincing evidence that the interest is subject to forfeiture under section 13-4304.

(b) The claimant has established by a preponderance of the evidence that the interest is exempt from forfeiture under section 13-4304.

I. In order to facilitate the identification or location of property declared forfeited and to facilitate the disposition of filed or subsequent claims pursuant to subsection H, paragraph 2 of this section, the court, on application of the state, may order that the testimony of any witness relating to the property forfeited or alleged to be subject to forfeiture be taken by deposition and that any designated book, paper, document, record, recording, electronic or otherwise, or other material which is not privileged be produced at the same time and place and in the same manner as that provided for the taking of depositions under the rules of civil procedure.

13-4313. Supplemental remedies

A. The court shall order the forfeiture of any other property of a claimant or an in personam civil or criminal defendant up to the value of the claimant's or defendant's property that the court finds is subject to forfeiture if any of the following circumstances apply to the property:

1. It cannot be located.

2. It has been transferred or conveyed to, sold to or deposited with a third party.

3. It has been placed beyond the jurisdiction of the court.

4. It has been substantially diminished in value by any act or omission of the defendant.

5. It has been commingled with other property which cannot be divided without difficulty.

6. It is subject to any interest that is exempt from forfeiture.

B. In addition to any other remedy provided for by law, if property subject to forfeiture is conveyed, alienated, encumbered, disposed of, received, removed from the jurisdiction of the court, concealed or otherwise rendered unavailable for forfeiture after the filing of a racketeering lien notice or provision of notice of pending forfeiture or after the filing and notice of a civil proceeding or criminal proceeding alleging forfeiture under this chapter, whichever is earlier, the state may institute an action in superior court against the person named in the racketeering lien or notice of pending forfeiture or the defendant in the civil proceeding or criminal proceeding, and the court shall enter final judgment against the person named in the racketeering lien or notice of pending forfeiture or the defendant in the civil proceeding or criminal proceeding in an amount equal to the fair market value of the property, together with reasonable investigative expenses and attorney fees. If a civil proceeding under this chapter is pending, the action shall be filed only in the court where the civil proceeding is pending.

C. This section does not limit the right of the state to obtain any order or injunction, receivership, writ, attachment, garnishment or other remedy authorized under this title or appropriate to protect the interests of the state or available under other applicable law, including title 44, chapter 8, article 1.

13-4314. Disposition by court

A. If no petitions for remission or mitigation or claims are timely filed or if no petitioner files a claim in the court within thirty days after the mailing of a declaration of forfeiture, the attorney for the state shall apply to the court for an order of forfeiture and allocation of forfeited property pursuant to section 13-4315. On the state's written application showing jurisdiction, notice and facts sufficient to demonstrate probable cause for forfeiture, and in cases brought pursuant to section 13-3413, subsection A, paragraph 1 or 3, probable cause to believe that the conduct giving rise to forfeiture involved an amount of unlawful substance greater than the statutory threshold amount as defined in section 13-3401 or was committed for financial gain, the court shall order the property forfeited to the state.

B. After the court's disposition of all claims timely filed under this chapter, the state has clear title to the forfeited property and the court shall so order. Title to the forfeited property and its proceeds is deemed to have vested in the state on the commission of the act or omission giving rise to the forfeiture under this title.

C. If, in his discretion, the attorney for the state has entered into a stipulation with an interest holder that the interest holder has an interest that is exempted from forfeiture, the court, on application of the attorney for the state, may release or convey forfeited personal property to the interest holder if all of the following are true:

1. The interest holder has an interest that was acquired in the regular course of business as a financial institution within section 13-2301, subsection D, paragraph 3.

2. The amount of the interest holder's encumbrance is readily determinable and it has been reasonably established by proof made available by the attorney for the state to the court.

3. The encumbrance held by the interest holder seeking possession is the only interest exempted from forfeiture and the order forfeiting the property to the state transferred all of the rights of the owner before forfeiture, including rights to redemption, to the state.

4. After the court's release or conveyance, the interest holder shall dispose of the property by a commercially reasonable public sale, and within ten days of disposition shall tender to the state the amount received at disposition less the amount of the interest holder's encumbrance and reasonable expense incurred by the interest holder in connection with the sale or disposal.

D. On order of the court forfeiting the subject property, the attorney for the state may transfer good and sufficient title to any subsequent purchaser or transferee, and the title shall be recognized by all courts, by this state and by all departments and agencies of this state and any political subdivision.

E. On entry of judgment for a claimant or claimants in any proceeding to forfeit property under this chapter such property or interest in property shall be returned or conveyed immediately to the claimant or claimants designated by the court. The person or seizing agency that made the seizure and the attorney for the state are not personally liable to suit or judgment on account of such seizure, suit or prosecution unless the person, seizing agency or attorney for the state intended to cause injury or was grossly negligent.

F. The court may award reasonable attorney fees, expenses and damages for loss of the use of the property to any claimant who substantially prevails by an adjudication on the merits of a claim. If the court finds that reasonable cause did not exist for the seizure for forfeiture or the filing of the notice of pending forfeiture, complaint, information or indictment and that the seizing agency or attorney for the state intended to cause injury or was grossly negligent, the court shall award the claimant treble costs or damages. The court must apportion the award for treble costs or damages between the agency that made the seizure and the office of the attorney for the state.

13-4315. Allocation of forfeited property

A. Any property, including all interests in property, forfeited to the state under this title shall be transferred as requested by the attorney for the state to the seizing agency or to the agency or political subdivision employing the attorney for the state, which may do any of the following:

1. Sell, lease, lend or transfer the property to any local or state government entity or agency or political subdivision, law enforcement agency or prosecutorial agency or any federal law enforcement agency which operates within this state for official federal, state or political subdivision use within this state, with expenses for keeping and transferring such property to be paid by the recipient. Property may not be allocated for official use if the fair market value of the property substantially exceeds the agency's probable cost of purchasing other property equally suited for the intended official use. Property that is allocated for official use may not be assigned for use by any person who supervised or exercised discretion in its forfeiture unless the use is approved in writing by the head of the agency.

2. Sell forfeited property by public or otherwise commercially reasonable sale with expenses of keeping and selling the property and the amount of all valid interests established by claimants paid out of the proceeds of the sale with the balance paid into the anti-racketeering fund of the state or of the county in which the political subdivision seizing the property or prosecuting the action is located. A sale of forfeited property may not be made to any employee of the seizing agency, any person who participated in the forfeiture, any employee of a contractor selling the property on behalf of the seizing agency or any member of the immediate family of any of these employees or persons.

3. Destroy or use for investigative purposes any illegal or controlled substances or other contraband at any time more than twenty days after seizure, on written approval of the attorney for the state, preserving only such material as may be necessary for evidence.

4. Sell, use or destroy all raw materials, products and equipment of any kind used or intended for use in manufacturing, compounding or processing a controlled substance.

5. Compromise and pay claims against property forfeited pursuant to any provision of this section.

6. Make any other disposition of forfeited property authorized by law for the disposition of property of the state, government entity, agency or political subdivision.

B. Notwithstanding subsection A of this section or any other provision of law to the contrary:

1. If the property forfeited is money, and a law enforcement agency can specifically identify monies as being from its investigative funds or as being exchanged for property from its investigative property, the monies shall be remitted to the investigative fund. If there are additional forfeited monies or monies tendered on satisfaction by an interest holder which cannot be specifically identified, the court shall order the monies returned to each law enforcement agency that makes a showing of costs or expenses which it incurred in connection with the investigation and prosecution of the matter and shall order all excess monies remaining after such

returns deposited in the anti-racketeering fund of this state or of the county in which the political subdivision seizing the monies or prosecuting the action is located, established pursuant to section 13-2314.01 or 13-2314.03.

2. If the property declared forfeited is an interest in a vehicle, the court shall order it forfeited to the local, state or other law enforcement agency seizing the vehicle for forfeiture or to the seizing agency.

C. Monies in any anti-racketeering fund established pursuant to this title may be used, in addition to any other lawful use, for:

1. The payment of any expenses necessary to seize, detain, appraise, inventory, protect, maintain, preserve the availability of, advertise or sell property that is subject to forfeiture and that is seized, detained or forfeited pursuant to this title or of any other necessary expenses incident to the seizure, detention, preservation or forfeiture of the property. The payments may include payments for contract services and payments to reimburse any federal, state or local agency for any expenditures made to perform the functions of the seizing agency.

2. The payment of awards for information or assistance leading to a civil or criminal proceeding under this title.

3. The payment of compensation from forfeited property to injured persons as provided in section 13-4311, subsection N, paragraph 3.

D. Each attorney for the state shall submit a copy of each forfeiture judgment, including each order of forfeiture, to the Arizona criminal justice commission within sixty days after the forfeiture judgment becomes final or after the conclusion of appellate review, if any.

Chapter 40 Crime Victim's Rights

13-4401. Definitions

In this chapter, unless the context otherwise requires:

1. "Accused" means a person who has been arrested for committing a criminal offense and who is held for an initial appearance or other proceeding before trial.

2. "Appellate proceeding" means any contested matter before the state court of appeals, the state supreme court, a federal court of appeals or the United States supreme court.

3. "Arrest" means the actual custodial restraint of a person or the person's submission to custody.

4. "Court" means all state, county and municipal courts in this state.

5. "Crime victim advocate" means a person who is employed or authorized by a public or private entity to provide counseling, treatment or other supportive assistance to crime victims.

6. "Criminal offense" means conduct that gives a peace officer or prosecutor probable cause to believe that a felony, a misdemeanor, a petty offense or a violation of a local criminal ordinance has occurred.

7. "Criminal proceeding" means any hearing, argument or other matter that is scheduled by and held before a trial court but does not include any deposition, lineup, grand jury proceeding or other matter that is not held in the presence of the court.

8. "Custodial agency" means any law enforcement officer or agency, a sheriff or municipal jailer, the state department of corrections or a secure mental health facility that has custody of a person who is arrested or in custody for a criminal offense.

9. "Defendant" means a person or entity that is formally charged by complaint, indictment or information of committing a criminal offense.

10. "Final disposition" means the ultimate termination of the criminal prosecution of a defendant by a trial court, including dismissal, acquittal or imposition of a sentence.

11. "Immediate family" means a victim's spouse, parent, child, sibling, grandparent or lawful guardian.

12. "Lawful representative" means a person who is designated by the victim or appointed by the court and who acts in the best interests of the victim.

13. "Post-arrest release" means the discharge of the accused from confinement on recognizance, bond or other condition.

14. "Post-conviction release" means parole, work furlough, community supervision, probation if the court waived community supervision pursuant to section 13-603, home arrest or any other permanent, conditional or temporary discharge from confinement in the custody of the state department of corrections or a sheriff or from confinement in a municipal jail or a secure mental health facility.

15. "Post-conviction relief proceeding" means a contested argument or evidentiary hearing that is held in open court and that involves a request for relief from a conviction or sentence.

16. "Prisoner" means a person who has been convicted of a criminal offense against a victim and who has been sentenced to the custody of the sheriff, the state department of corrections, a municipal jail or a secure mental health facility.

17. "Release" means no longer in the custody of a custodial agency and includes transfer from one custodial agency to another custodial agency.

18. "Rights" means any right that is granted to the victim by the laws of this state.

19. "Victim" means a person against whom the criminal offense has been committed, including a minor, or if the person is killed or incapacitated, the person's spouse, parent, child, grandparent or sibling, any other person related to the person by consanguinity or affinity to the second degree or any other lawful representative of the person, except if the person or the person's spouse, parent, child, grandparent, sibling, other person related to the person by consanguinity or affinity to the second degree or other lawful representative is in custody for an offense or is the accused.

13-4401.01. Victims' rights for neighborhood associations

A. A neighborhood association may register with the city, town or county in which the neighborhood association is located to invoke the rights that are afforded pursuant to this article. The city, town or county shall establish procedures for the registration of neighborhood associations pursuant to this section. The procedures shall require the neighborhood association to provide to the city, town or county the name and telephone number of one person who shall act on behalf of the neighborhood association and who may receive notice or invoke rights pursuant to this section. The neighborhood association shall notify the city, town or county of any changes to this information. If the neighborhood association fails to keep this information current, the neighborhood association is deemed to have waived its rights under this section.

B. Notwithstanding any law to the contrary, if a person commits an act in violation of section 13-1602, subsection A, paragraph 5, section 13-3102, subsection A, paragraph 9, section 13-3201 or 13-3204, section 13-3208, subsection B or section 13-3209, 13-3405, 13-3407, 13-3408, 13-3409, 13-3421 or 13-4702, a neighborhood association that is registered with a city, town or county pursuant to subsection A of this section may receive notice or may invoke rights pursuant to the following sections:

1. Section 13-4409.
2. Section 13-4420.
3. Section 13-4426.

C. Sections 13-4428, 13-4434 and 13-4436 apply to all matters in which a neighborhood association invokes rights under this section.

D. If the neighborhood association wishes to invoke victims' rights for a crime as prescribed in subsection B of this section that resulted in an arrest, the person who is registered with the city, town or county pursuant to subsection A of this section shall contact the law enforcement agency responsible for the arrest. The law enforcement agency shall fill out the form prescribed by section 13-4405. Thereafter the neighborhood association, through the contact person, shall be afforded all of the rights listed under subsection B of this section.

13-4402. Implementation of rights and duties

A. Except as provided in sections 13-4404 and 13-4405, the rights and duties that are established by this chapter arise on the arrest or formal charging of the person or persons who are alleged to be responsible for a criminal offense against a victim. The rights and duties continue to be enforceable pursuant to this chapter until the final disposition of the charges, including acquittal or dismissal of the charges, all post-conviction release and relief proceedings and the discharge of all criminal proceedings relating to restitution. If a defendant is ordered to pay restitution to a victim, the rights and duties continue to be enforceable by the court until restitution is paid.

B. If a defendant's conviction is reversed and the case is returned to the trial court for further proceedings, the victim has the same rights that were applicable to the criminal proceedings that led to the appeal or other post-conviction relief proceeding.

C. After the final termination of a criminal prosecution by dismissal with prejudice or acquittal, a person who has received notice and the right to be present and heard pursuant to the victims' rights act, article II, section 2.1, Constitution of Arizona, any implementing legislation or court rule is no longer entitled to such rights.

13-4402.01. Victims' rights; dismissed counts

A. If a criminal offense against a victim has been charged but the prosecution on the count or counts involving the victim has been or is being dismissed as the result of a plea agreement in which the defendant is pleading to or pled to other charges, the victim of the offenses involved in the dismissed counts, on request, may exercise all the applicable rights of a crime victim throughout the criminal justice process as though the count or counts involving the person had not been dismissed.

B. As to each count that is dismissed, the prosecutor shall notify the probation department if the victim requested the victim's rights pursuant to this chapter.

C. For each victim who is involved in the dismissed counts and who requested the victim's rights, the prosecutor shall forward to the probation department information within the prosecutor's possession that would enable the probation department to carry out its duties as prescribed by this chapter.

13-4403. Inability to exercise rights; lawful representatives; notice; definition

A. If a victim is physically or emotionally unable to exercise any right but is able to designate a lawful representative who is not a bona fide witness, the designated representative may exercise the same rights that the victim is entitled to exercise. The victim may revoke this designation at any time and exercise the victim's rights.

B. If a victim is incompetent, deceased or otherwise incapable of designating a representative to act in the victim's place, the court may appoint a lawful representative who is not a witness. If at any time the victim is no longer incompetent, incapacitated or otherwise incapable of acting, the victim may personally exercise the victim's rights.

C. If the victim is a minor or vulnerable adult the victim's parent, child or other immediate family member may exercise all of the victim's rights on behalf of the victim. If the criminal offense is alleged against a member of the minor's or vulnerable adult's immediate family, the victim's rights may not be exercised by that person but may be exercised by another member of the immediate family unless, after considering the guidelines in subsection D of this section, the court finds that another person would better represent the interests of the minor or vulnerable adult for purposes of this chapter.

D. The court shall consider the following guidelines in appointing a representative for a minor or vulnerable adult victim:

1. Whether there is a relative who would not be so substantially affected or adversely impacted by the conflict occasioned by the allegation of criminal conduct against a member of the immediate family of the minor or vulnerable adult that the relative could not represent the victim.

2. The representative's willingness and ability to do all of the following:

(a) Undertake working with and accompanying the minor or vulnerable adult victim through all proceedings, including criminal, civil and dependency proceedings.

(b) Communicate with the minor or vulnerable adult victim.

(c) Express the concerns of the minor or vulnerable adult victim to those authorized to come in contact with the minor or vulnerable adult as a result of the proceedings.

3. The representative's training, if any, to serve as a minor or vulnerable adult victim's representative.

4. The likelihood of the representative being called as a witness in the case.

E. The minor or vulnerable adult victim's representative shall accompany the minor or vulnerable adult through all proceedings, including delinquency, criminal, dependency and civil proceedings, and, before the minor's or vulnerable adult's courtroom appearance, shall explain to the minor or vulnerable adult the nature of the proceedings and what the minor or vulnerable adult will be asked to do, including telling the minor or vulnerable adult that the minor or vulnerable adult is expected to tell the truth. The representative shall be available to observe the minor or vulnerable adult in all aspects of the case in order to consult with the court as to any special needs of the minor or vulnerable adult. Those consultations shall take place before the minor or vulnerable adult testifies. The court may recognize the minor or vulnerable adult victim's representative when the representative indicates a need to address the court. A minor or vulnerable adult victim's representative shall not discuss the facts and circumstances of the case with the minor or vulnerable adult witness, unless the court orders otherwise upon a showing that it is in the best interests of the minor or vulnerable adult.

F. Any notices that are to be provided to a victim pursuant to this chapter shall be sent only to the victim or the victim's lawful representative.

G. For the purposes of this section, "vulnerable adult" has the same meaning prescribed in section 13-3623.

13-4404. Limited rights of a legal entity

A corporation, partnership, association or other legal entity which, except for its status as an artificial entity, would be included in the definition of victim in section 13-4401, shall be afforded the following rights:

1. The prosecutor shall, within a reasonable time after arrest, notify the legal entity of the right to appear and be heard at any proceeding relating to restitution or sentencing of the person convicted of committing the criminal offense against the legal entity.

2. The prosecutor shall notify the legal entity of the right to submit to the court a written statement containing information and opinions on restitution and sentencing in its case.

3. On request, the prosecutor shall notify the legal entity in a timely manner of the date, time and place of any proceeding relating to restitution or sentencing of the person convicted of committing the criminal offense against the legal entity.

4. A lawful representative of the legal entity shall have the right, if present, to be heard at any proceeding relating to the sentencing or restitution of the person convicted of committing the criminal offense against the legal entity.

13-4405. Information provided to victim by law enforcement agencies

A. As soon after the detection of a criminal offense as the victim may be contacted without interfering with an investigation or arrest, the law enforcement agency that has responsibility for investigating the criminal offense shall provide electronic forms, pamphlets, information cards or other materials to the victim:

1. That allows the victim to request or waive applicable rights to which the victim is entitled, on request, under this article.

2. That provides the victim a method to designate a lawful representative if the victim chooses pursuant to section 13-4403, subsection A or section 13-4404.

3. That provides notice to the victim of all of the following information:

(a) The victim's right under the victims' bill of rights, article II, section 2.1, Constitution of Arizona, to be treated with fairness, respect and dignity and to be free of intimidation, harassment or abuse throughout the criminal or juvenile justice process.

(b) The availability, if any, of crisis intervention services and emergency and medical services and, where applicable, that medical expenses arising out of the need to secure evidence may be reimbursed pursuant to section 13-1414.

(c) In cases of domestic violence, the procedures and resources available for the protection of the victim pursuant to section 13-3601.

(d) The names and telephone numbers of public and private victim assistance programs, including the county victim compensation program and programs that provide counseling, treatment and other support services.

(e) The police report number, if available, other identifying case information and the following statement:

If within thirty days you are not notified of an arrest in your case, you may call (the law enforcement agency's telephone number) for the status of the case.

(f) Whether the suspect is an adult or juvenile, a statement that the victim will be notified by the law enforcement agency at the earliest opportunity after the arrest of a suspect.

(g) If the suspect is an adult and has been arrested, the victim's right, on request, to be informed of the suspect's release, of the next regularly scheduled time, place and date for initial appearances in the jurisdiction and of the victim's right to be heard at the initial appearance and that, to exercise these rights, the victim is advised to contact the custodial agency regarding the suspect's release and to contact the court regarding any changes to the initial appearance schedule.

(h) If the victim chooses to exercise the right to be heard through a written statement, how that statement may be submitted to the court.

(i) That the victim or the immediate family member of the victim, if the victim is killed or incapacitated, has the right to receive one copy of the police report, including any supplements to the report, from the investigating law enforcement agency at no charge pursuant to section 39-127.

B. If at the time of contact with a law enforcement agency the victim is physically or emotionally unable to request or waive applicable rights, the law enforcement agency shall designate this in the format that is authorized by subsection A of this section and the entities that may be subsequently affected shall presume that the victim invoked the victim's right to request applicable rights to which the victim is entitled, on request, unless the victim later waives those rights.

C. The law enforcement agency shall submit a copy of the victim's request or waiver of preconviction rights form to the custodial agency and a copy to the prosecutor if a suspect is arrested, at the time the suspect is taken into custody. If there is no arrest, the form copies shall be submitted to the prosecutor at the time the case is otherwise presented to the prosecutor for review. The prosecutor shall submit a copy of the victim's request or waiver of preconviction rights form to the departments or sections of the prosecutor's office, if applicable, that are mandated by this article to provide victims' rights services on request.

D. If the suspected offender is cited and released, the law enforcement agency responsible for investigating the offense shall inform the victim of the court date and how to obtain additional information about the subsequent criminal proceedings.

E. Law enforcement agencies within a county may establish different procedures designed to efficiently and effectively provide notice of the victim's rights pursuant to this section and notice to affected entities of the victim request or waiver information. If different procedures are established, the procedures shall:

1. Be reported to the entities within a county affected by the procedures and reported to the attorney general.

2. Be designed so that custodial agencies and prosecutors within a county receive notice of the victim's request or waiver of the victim's preconviction rights at the same time that an adult suspect is arrested.

3. Be designed so that prosecutors within a county receive notice of the victim's request or waiver of the victim's preconviction rights, if there is no arrest, at the same time that the case is otherwise presented to the prosecutor for review.

4. Provide that the notice to affected entities of a victim's request or waiver of the victim's preconviction rights includes information that affords the affected entity the ability to contact the victim.

5. Be supported by use of electronic forms, brochures or other written materials that are developed by the law enforcement agencies within a county and reviewed by the attorney general pursuant to section 13-4417, subsection B.

F. If a suspect has not been arrested at the time of contact with the victim pursuant to subsection A of this section, the law enforcement agency that is responsible for investigating the offense shall notify the victim of the arrest of a suspect at the earliest opportunity after the arrest and of the time, place and date for the initial appearance.

13-4405.01. Issuance and execution of arrest warrants

A. Beginning on the effective date of this section, on the issuance of an arrest warrant, the court issuing the warrant shall state in the warrant whether the person named in the warrant is to be arrested for or is to be charged with committing a criminal offense as defined in section 13-4401 or is materially related to a criminal offense as defined in section 13-4401.

B. On receipt of notice of an arrest or an impending arrest of a suspect and if applicable pursuant to subsection A of this section, the agency that is responsible for holding the original warrant shall notify the law enforcement agency that was responsible for the original investigation of the offense of the impending incarceration of a suspect who is arrested on the law enforcement agency's warrant.

C. On receiving notice that the warrant was executed pursuant to subsection B of this section, the law enforcement agency that was responsible for the original investigation of the offense shall do all of the following if the victim has requested notice pursuant to section 13-4405:

1. Notify the victim of the arrest and of the time, place and date for the initial appearance.

2. Inform the victim of the telephone number of the custodial agency in which the arrested person is held.

3. Provide the custodial agency with the victim information pursuant to section 13-4405 so that the custodial agency may notify the victim of the release of the suspect pursuant to section 13-4412, if applicable.

D. A law enforcement agency is not required to provide victim information pursuant to Section 13-4405, subsections C and E to the custodial agency at the time a suspect is taken into custody unless the law enforcement agency that performs that warrant arrest is also the law enforcement agency that was responsible for the original investigation of the offense.

E. The victim's right to be informed of an arrest or a release after a suspect is arrested pursuant to a warrant applies to warrants that are issued on or after September 1, 1996.

F. Law enforcement, courts and custodial agencies are not liable pursuant to section 13-4437 for the failure to inform a victim of the arrest or release of a suspect on warrants that were issued before September 1, 1996.

13-4406. Notice of initial appearance

On becoming aware of the date, time and place of the initial appearance of the accused, the law enforcement agency shall inform the victim of that information unless the accused appeared in response to a summons or writ of habeas corpus. In that case, the prosecutor's office shall, on receiving that information, provide the notice to the victim.

13-4407. Notice of terms and conditions of release

On the request of the victim, the custodial agency shall provide a copy of the terms and conditions of release to the victim unless the accused appeared in response to a summons. In that case, on request of the victim, the prosecutor's office, on receiving such information, shall provide a copy of the terms and conditions of release to the victim. The copy of the terms and conditions of release may be provided to the victim in an electronic form, pamphlet, information card or other material.

13-4408. Pretrial notice

A. Within seven days after the prosecutor charges a criminal offense by complaint, information or indictment and the accused is in custody or has been served a summons, the prosecutor's office shall give the victim notice of the following:

1. The victim's rights under the victims' bill of rights, article II, section 2.1, Constitution of Arizona, any implementing legislation and court rule.

2. The charge or charges against the defendant and a clear and concise statement of the procedural steps involved in a criminal prosecution.

3. The procedures a victim shall follow to invoke his right to confer with the prosecuting attorney pursuant to section 13-4419.

4. The person within the prosecutor's office to contact for more information.

5. The victim's right to request a preconviction restitution lien pursuant to section 13-806.

B. Notwithstanding the provisions of subsection A of this section, if a prosecutor declines to proceed with a prosecution after the final submission of a case by a law enforcement agency at the end of an investigation, the prosecutor shall, before the decision not to proceed is final, notify the victim and provide the victim with the reasons for declining to proceed with the case. The notice shall inform the victim of his right on request to confer with the prosecutor before the decision not to proceed is final. Such notice applies only to violations of a state criminal statute.

13-4409. Notice of criminal proceedings

A. Except as provided in subsection B, the court shall provide notice of criminal proceedings, for criminal offenses filed by information, complaint or indictment, except initial appearances and arraignments, to the prosecutor's office at least five days before a scheduled proceeding to allow the prosecutor's office to provide notice to the victim.

B. If the court finds that it is not reasonable to provide the five days' notice to the prosecutor's office under subsection A, the court shall state in the record why it was not reasonable to provide five days' notice.

C. On receiving the notice from the court, the prosecutor's office shall, on request, give notice to the victim in a timely manner of scheduled proceedings and any changes in that schedule, including any continuances.

13-4410. Notice of conviction, acquittal or dismissal; impact statement

A. The prosecutor's office, on request, shall give to the victim within fifteen days after the conviction or acquittal or dismissal of the charges against the defendant notice of the criminal offense for which the defendant was convicted or acquitted or the dismissal of the charges against the defendant.

B. If the defendant is convicted and the victim has requested notice, the victim shall be notified, if applicable, of:

1. The function of the presentence report.

2. The name and telephone number of the probation department that is preparing the presentence report.

3. The right to make a victim impact statement under section 13-4424.

4. The defendant's right to view the presentence report.

5. The victim's right to view the presentence report except those parts excised by the court or made confidential by law and, on request, to receive a copy from the prosecutor.

6. The right to be present and be heard at any presentence or sentencing proceeding pursuant to section 13-4426.

7. The time, place and date of the sentencing proceeding.

8. If the court orders restitution, the right to:

(a) File a restitution lien pursuant to section 13-806.

(b) Request a copy of the defendant's restitution payment history from the clerk of the court pursuant to section 13-810 or 31-412.

C. The victim shall be informed that the victim's impact statement may include the following:

1. An explanation of the nature and extent of any physical, psychological or emotional harm or trauma suffered by the victim.

2. An explanation of the extent of any economic loss or property damage suffered by the victim.

3. An opinion of the need for and extent of restitution.

4. Whether the victim has applied for or received any compensation for the loss or damage.

D. Notice provided pursuant to this section does not remove the probation department's responsibility pursuant to section 12-253 to initiate the contact between the victim and the probation department concerning the victim's economic, physical, psychological or emotional harm. At the time of contact, the probation department shall advise the victim of the date, time and place of sentencing and of the victim's right to be present and be heard at that proceeding.

13-4411. Notice of post-conviction review and appellate proceedings

A. Within fifteen days after sentencing the prosecutor's office shall, on request, notify the victim of the sentence imposed on the defendant.

B. The prosecutor's office shall provide the victim with a form that allows the victim to request post-conviction notice of all post-conviction review and appellate proceedings, all post-conviction release proceedings, all probation modification proceedings that impact the victim, all probation revocation or termination proceedings, any decisions that arise out of these proceedings, all releases and all escapes.

C. The prosecutor's office shall advise the victim on how the completed request form may be filed with the appropriate agencies and departments.

D. On request of the victim, the prosecutor's office that is responsible for handling any post-conviction or appellate proceedings immediately shall notify the victim of the proceedings and any decisions that arise out of the proceedings.

E. Beginning December 1, 2007, the supreme court or court of appeals shall send a victim who requests notice pursuant to this section a copy of the memorandum decision or opinion from the issuing court concurrently with the parties. If the victim is represented by counsel, the notice shall be provided to the victim's counsel.

13-4411.01. Notice of right to request not to receive inmate mail

A. Within fifteen days after a defendant is sentenced to the state department of corrections, the prosecutor's office shall notify the victim of the right of the victim, any member of the victim's family or any member of the victim's household, to request not to receive mail from the inmate who was convicted of committing a criminal offense against the victim. The notice shall:

1. Be made on the postconviction notice request form provided by the prosecutor to the victim pursuant to section 13-4411.

2. Inform the victim of the right of the victim, or any member of the victim's family or household who is denoted by the victim on the form, to request not to receive mail from the inmate.

3. Instruct the victim how to file the completed request form with the state department of corrections.

4. Include the following statement:

"If the defendant is incarcerated in the state department of corrections, you have the right to request that the defendant not send you, members of your family or members of the victim's household mail. If the defendant sends you or your family or household members mail after you have made this request, you or the members of your family or household have the right to report the incident to the state department of corrections for sanctions against the defendant."

B. On receipt of a postconviction notice request form in which a request not to receive inmate mail is indicated, the state department of corrections shall notify the inmate of the request and that sending mail to the victim, or the family or household members who are denoted by the victim, will result in appropriate sanctions, including reduction or denial of earned release credits and review of all outgoing mail.

C. The department shall not knowingly forward mail addressed to any person who requests not to receive mail, pursuant to this section, is not to receive mail.

13-4412. Notice of release or escape

A. The sheriff or municipal jailer, on request, shall notify the victim and the prosecutor's office of the release of the accused.

B. The custodial agency shall immediately give notice to a victim and the prosecutor's office of an escape by, and again on the subsequent rearrest of, an incarcerated person who is accused or convicted of committing a criminal offense against the victim. The custodial agency shall give notice by any reasonable means.

13-4413. Notice of prisoner's status

A. If the victim has made a request for post-conviction notice, the director of the state department of corrections shall mail to the victim the following information about a prisoner in the custody of the department of corrections:

1. Within thirty days after the request, notice of the earliest release date of the prisoner if his sentence exceeds six months.

2. At least fifteen days before the prisoner's release, notice of the release.

3. Within fifteen days after the prisoner's death, notice of the death.

B. If the victim has made a request for post-conviction notice, the sheriff having custody of the prisoner shall mail to the victim notice of release at least fifteen days before the prisoner's release or notice of death within fifteen days after the prisoner's death.

13-4414. Notice of postconviction release; right to be heard; hearing; final decision; free electronic recording

A. The victim has the right to be present and be heard at any proceeding in which postconviction release from confinement is being considered pursuant to section 31-233, 31-411 or 41-1604.13.

B. If the victim has made a request for postconviction notice, the board of executive clemency shall, at least fifteen days before the hearing, give to the victim written notice of the hearing and of the victim's right to be present and be heard at the hearing.

C. If the victim has made a request for postconviction notice, the board of executive clemency shall give to the victim notice of the decision reached by the board. The notice shall be mailed within fifteen days after the board reaches its decision.

D. Any electronic recordings that are made during a postconviction release hearing shall be provided, on request, to the victim free of charge.

13-4415. Notice of probation modification, termination or revocation disposition matters; notice of arrest

A. On request of a victim who has provided an address or other contact information, the court shall notify the victim of any of the following:

1. A probation revocation disposition proceeding or any proceeding in which the court is asked to terminate the probation or intensive probation of a person who is convicted of committing a criminal offense against the victim.

2. Any hearing on a proposed modification of the terms of probation or intensive probation.

3. The arrest of a person who is on supervised probation and who is arrested pursuant to a warrant issued for a probation violation.

B. On request of a victim who has provided a current address or other current contact information, the probation department shall notify the victim of the following:

1. Any proposed modification to any term of probation if the modification affects restitution or incarceration status or the defendant's contact with or the safety of the victim.

2. The victim's right to be heard at a hearing that is set to consider any modification to be made to any term of probation.

3. Any violation of any term of probation that results in the filing with the court of a petition to revoke probation.

4. That a petition to revoke probation alleging that the defendant absconded from probation has been filed with the court.

5. Any conduct by the defendant that raises a substantial concern for the victim's safety.

C. If a victim has requested postconviction notice, the court shall provide notice of that request to the state department of corrections and the board of executive clemency if a defendant's probation is revoked and the defendant is committed to the custody of the state department of corrections.

D. On the request of a victim, the state department of corrections shall provide the victim with the notices that are required by sections 13-4412 and 13-4413.

E. On the request of the victim, the board of executive clemency shall provide the victim with the notice that is required by section 13-4414.

13-4416. Notice of release, discharge or escape from a mental health treatment agency

A. If the victim has made a request for notice, a mental health treatment agency shall mail to the victim at least ten days before the release or discharge of the person accused or convicted of committing a criminal offense against the victim, notice of the release or discharge of the person who is placed by court order in a mental health treatment agency pursuant to section 13-3994, 31-226, 31-226.01, 36-540.01, 36-541.01 or 36-3707.

B. A mental health treatment agency shall mail to the victim immediately after the escape or subsequent readmission of the person accused or convicted of committing a criminal offense against the victim, notice of the escape or subsequent readmission of the person who is placed by court order in a mental health treatment agency pursuant to section 13-3994, 31-226, 31-226.01, 36-540.01, 36-541.01 or 36-3707.

13-4417. Request for notice; forms; notice system

A. The victim shall provide to and maintain with the agency that is responsible for providing notice to the victim a request for notice on a form that is provided by that agency. The form shall include a telephone number and address. If the victim fails to keep the victim's telephone number and address current, the victim's request for notice is withdrawn. At any time the victim may request notice of subsequent proceedings by filing on a request form provided by the agency the victim's current telephone number and address.

B. All notices provided to a victim pursuant to this chapter shall be on forms developed or reviewed by the attorney general.

C. The court and all agencies that are responsible for providing notice to the victim shall establish and maintain a system for the receipt of victim requests for notice.

13-4418. Construction of chapter

This chapter shall be liberally construed to preserve and protect the rights to which victims are entitled.

13-4419. Victim conference with prosecuting attorney

A. On request of the victim, the prosecuting attorney shall confer with the victim about the disposition of a criminal offense, including the victim's views about a decision not to proceed with a criminal prosecution, dismissal, plea or sentence negotiations and pretrial diversion programs.

B. On request of the victim, the prosecuting attorney shall confer with the victim before the commencement of the trial.

C. The right of the victim to confer with the prosecuting attorney does not include the authority to direct the prosecution of the case.

13-4420. Criminal proceedings; right to be present

The victim has the right to be present throughout all criminal proceedings in which the defendant has the right to be present.

13-4421. Initial appearance

The victim has the right to be heard at the initial appearance of the person suspected of committing the criminal offense against the victim.

13-4422. Post-arrest custody decisions

The victim has the right to be heard at any proceeding in which the court considers the post-arrest release of the person accused of committing a criminal offense against the victim or the conditions of that release.

13-4423. Plea negotiation proceedings

A. On request of the victim, the victim has the right to be present and be heard at any proceeding in which a negotiated plea for the person accused of committing the criminal offense against the victim will be presented to the court.

B. The court shall not accept a plea agreement unless:

1. The prosecuting attorney advises the court that before requesting the negotiated plea reasonable efforts were made to confer with the victim pursuant to section 13-4419.

2. Reasonable efforts are made to give the victim notice of the plea proceeding pursuant to section 13-4409 and to inform the victim that the victim has the right to be present and, if present, to be heard.

3. The prosecuting attorney advises the court that to the best of the prosecutor's knowledge notice requirements of this chapter have been complied with and the prosecutor informs the court of the victim's position, if known, regarding the negotiated plea.

13-4424. Impact statement; presentence report

A. The victim may submit a written impact statement or make an oral impact statement to the probation officer for the officer's use in preparing a presentence report.

B. The probation officer shall consider the economic, physical and psychological impact that the criminal offense has had on the victim and the victim's immediate family pursuant to section 12-253.

13-4425. Inspection of presentence report

If the presentence report is available to the defendant, the court shall permit the victim to inspect the presentence report, except those parts excised by the court or made confidential by law. If the court excises any portion of the presentence report, it shall inform the parties and the victim of its decision and shall state on the record its reasons for the excision. On request of the victim, the prosecutor's office shall provide to the victim a copy of the presentence report.

13-4426. Sentencing

A. The victim may present evidence, information and opinions that concern the criminal offense, the defendant, the sentence or the need for restitution at any aggravation, mitigation, presentencing or sentencing proceeding.
B. At any disposition proceeding the victim has the right to be present and to address the court.

13-4426.01. Sentencing; victims' right to be heard

In any proceeding in which the victim has the right to be heard pursuant to article II, section 2.1, Constitution of Arizona, or this chapter, the victim's right to be heard is exercised not as a witness, the victim's statement is not subject to disclosure to the state or the defendant or submission to the court and the victim is not subject to cross-examination. The state and the defense shall be afforded the opportunity to explain, support or deny the victim's statement.

13-4427. Probation modification, revocation disposition or termination proceedings

A. The victim has the right to be present and be heard at any probation revocation disposition proceeding or any proceeding in which the court is requested to terminate the probation or intensive probation of a person who is convicted of committing a criminal offense against the victim.
B. The victim has the right to be heard at any proceeding in which the court is requested to modify the terms of probation or intensive probation of a person if the modification will substantially affect the person's contact with or safety of the victim or if the modification involves restitution or incarceration status.

13-4428. Victim's discretion; form of statement

A. It is at the victim's discretion to exercise the victim's rights under this chapter to be present and heard at a court proceeding, and the absence of the victim at the court proceeding does not preclude the court from going forth with the proceeding.
B. Except as provided in subsection C of this section, a victim's right to be heard may be exercised, at the victim's discretion, through an oral statement, submission of a written statement or submission of a statement through audiotape or videotape or any other video or digital media that is available to the court.
C. If a person against whom a criminal offense has been committed is in custody for an offense, the person may be heard by submitting a written statement to the court.

13-4429. Return of victim's property; release of evidence

A. On request of the victim and after consultation with the prosecuting attorney, the law enforcement agency responsible for investigating the criminal offense shall return to the victim any property belonging to the victim that was taken during the course of the investigation or shall inform the victim of the reasons why the property will not be returned. The law enforcement agency shall make reasonable efforts to return the property to the victim as soon as possible.
B. If the victim's property has been admitted as evidence during a trial or hearing, the court may order its release to the victim if a photograph can be substituted. If evidence is released pursuant to this subsection, the defendant's attorney or investigator may inspect and independently photograph the evidence before it is released.

13-4430. Consultation between crime victim advocate and victim; privileged information; exception

A. A crime victim advocate shall not disclose as a witness or otherwise any communication made by or with the victim, including any communication made to or in the presence of others, unless the victim consents in writing to the disclosure.

B. Unless the victim consents in writing to the disclosure, a crime victim advocate shall not disclose records, notes, documents, correspondence, reports or memoranda that contain opinions, theories or other information made while advising, counseling or assisting the victim or that are based on communications made by or with the victim, including communications made to or in the presence of others.

C. The communication is not privileged if the crime victim advocate knows that the victim will give or has given perjured testimony or if the communication contains exculpatory evidence.

D. A defendant may make a motion for disclosure of privileged information. If the court finds there is reasonable cause to believe the material is exculpatory, the court shall hold a hearing in camera. Material that the court finds is exculpatory shall be disclosed to the defendant.

E. If, with the written or verbal consent of the victim, the crime victim advocate discloses to the prosecutor or a law enforcement agency any communication between the victim and the crime victim advocate or any records, notes, documents, correspondence, reports or memoranda, the prosecutor or law enforcement agent shall disclose such material to the defendant's attorney only if such information is otherwise exculpatory.

F. Notwithstanding subsections A and B, if a crime victim consents either verbally or in writing, a crime victim advocate may disclose information to other professionals and administrative support persons that the advocate works with for the purpose of assisting the advocate in providing services to the victim and to the court in furtherance of any victim's right pursuant to this chapter.

13-4431. Minimizing victim's contacts

Before, during and immediately after any court proceeding, the court shall provide appropriate safeguards to minimize the contact that occurs between the victim, the victim's immediate family and the victim's witnesses and the defendant, the defendant's immediate family and defense witnesses.

13-4432. Motion to revoke bond or personal recognizance

If the prosecutor decides not to move to revoke the bond or personal recognizance of the defendant, the prosecutor shall inform the victim that the victim may petition the court to revoke the bond or personal recognizance of the defendant based on the victim's notarized statement asserting that harassment, threats, physical violence or intimidation against the victim or the victim's immediate family by the defendant or on behalf of the defendant has occurred.

13-4433. Victim's right to refuse an interview; applicability

A. Unless the victim consents, the victim shall not be compelled to submit to an interview on any matter, including any charged criminal offense witnessed by the victim and that occurred on the same occasion as the offense against the victim, or filed in the same indictment or information or consolidated for trial, that is conducted by the defendant, the defendant's attorney or an agent of the defendant.

B. The defendant, the defendant's attorney or an agent of the defendant shall only initiate contact with the victim through the prosecutor's office. The prosecutor's office shall promptly inform the victim of the defendant's request for an interview and shall advise the victim of the victim's right to refuse the interview.

C. The prosecutor shall not be required to forward any correspondence from the defendant, the defendant's attorney or an agent of the defendant to the victim or the victim's representative.

D. If the victim consents to an interview, the prosecutor's office shall inform the defendant, the defendant's attorney or an agent of the defendant of the time and place the victim has selected for the interview. If the victim wishes to impose other conditions on the interview, the prosecutor's office shall inform the defendant, the defendant's attorney or an agent of the defendant of the conditions. The victim has the right to terminate the interview at any time or to refuse to answer any question during the interview. The prosecutor has standing at the request of the victim to protect the victim from harassment, intimidation or abuse and, pursuant to that standing, may seek any appropriate protective court order.

E. Unless otherwise directed by the victim, the prosecutor may attend all interviews. If a transcript or tape recording of the interview is made and on request of the prosecutor, the prosecutor shall receive a copy of the transcript or tape recording at the prosecutor's expense.

F. If the defendant or the defendant's attorney comments at trial on the victim's refusal to be interviewed, the court shall instruct the jury that the victim has the right to refuse an interview under the Arizona Constitution.

G. This section applies to the parent or legal guardian of a minor child who exercises victims' rights on behalf of the minor child. Notwithstanding subsection E of this section, the defendant, the defendant's attorney or an agent of the defendant may not interview a minor child who has agreed to an interview, even if the minor child's parent or legal guardian initiates contact with the defendant, the defendant's attorney or an agent of the defendant, unless the prosecutor is actually notified at least five days in advance and the minor is informed that the prosecutor may be present at the interview.

13-4434. Victim's right to privacy; exception; definitions

A. The victim has the right at any court proceeding not to testify regarding any identifying or locating information unless the victim consents or the court orders disclosure on finding that a compelling need for the information exists. A court proceeding on the motion shall be in camera.

B. A victim's identifying and locating information that is obtained, compiled or reported by a law enforcement agency or prosecution agency shall be redacted by the originating agency and prosecution agencies from records pertaining to the criminal case involving the victim, including discovery disclosed to the defendant.

C. Subsection B of this section does not apply to:

1. The victim's name except, if the victim is a minor, the victim's name may be redacted from public records pertaining to the crime if the countervailing interests of confidentiality, privacy, the rights of the minor or the best interests of this state outweigh the public interest in disclosure.

2. Any records that are transmitted between law enforcement and prosecution agencies or a court.

3. Any records if the victim or, if the victim is a minor, the victim's representative as designated under section 13-4403 has consented to the release of the information.

4. The general location at which the reported crime occurred.

D. For the purposes of this section:

1. "Identifying information" includes a victim's date of birth, social security number and official state or government issued driver license or identification number.

2. "Locating information" includes the victim's address, telephone number, e-mail address and place of employment.

13-4435. Speedy trial; continuance; notice

A. In any criminal proceeding, the court, prosecutor and law enforcement officials shall take appropriate action to ensure a speedy trial for the victim.

B. The prosecutor shall make reasonable efforts to notify a victim of any request for a continuance, except that if the victim is represented by counsel who has filed a notice of appearance, the court, if the request for a continuance is in writing, shall make reasonable efforts to notify the victim's counsel in the same manner in which a party is notified.

C. A motion to continue shall be in writing unless the court makes a finding on the record that exigent circumstances exist to permit an oral motion.

D. The court shall grant a continuance only if extraordinary circumstances exist and the delay is indispensable to the interests of justice. A continuance may be granted only for the time necessary to serve the interests of justice.

E. Subsections B, C and D do not apply to justice of the peace and municipal courts.

F. Before ruling on a motion for a continuance, the court shall consider the victim's views and the victim's right to a speedy trial. If a continuance is granted, the court shall state on the record the specific reason for the continuance.

13-4436. Effect of failure to comply

A. The failure to comply with a victim's constitutional or statutory right is a ground for the victim to request a reexamination proceeding within ten days of the proceeding at which the victim's right was denied or with leave of the court for good cause shown. After the victim requests a reexamination proceeding and after the court gives reasonable notice, the court shall afford the victim a reexamination proceeding to consider the issues raised by the denial of the victim's right. Except as provided in subsection B, the court shall reconsider any decision that arises from a proceeding in which the victim's right was not protected and shall ensure that the victim's rights are thereafter protected.

B. The failure to use reasonable efforts to perform a duty or provide a right is not cause to seek to set aside a conviction after trial. Failure to afford a right under this chapter shall not provide grounds for a new trial. A victim who was given notice of a plea or sentencing proceeding may make a motion to reopen a plea or sentence only if the victim was not voluntarily absent from the proceeding and has asserted the right to be heard before or during the proceeding at issue and the right to be heard was denied and, in the case of a plea, the accused has not pled to the highest offense charged. This subsection does not affect the victim's right to restitution, which the victim may seek to enforce at any time.

C. Unless the prisoner is discharged from the prisoner's sentence, the failure to use reasonable efforts to provide notice and a right to be present or be heard pursuant to this chapter at a proceeding that involves a post-conviction release is a ground for the victim to seek to set aside the post-conviction release until the victim is afforded the opportunity to be present or be heard.

D. If the victim seeks to have a post-conviction release set aside pursuant to subsection C, the court, board of executive clemency or state department of corrections shall afford the victim a reexamination proceeding after the parties are given notice.

E. A reexamination proceeding conducted pursuant to this section or any other proceeding that is based on the failure to perform a duty or provide a right shall commence not more than thirty days after the appropriate parties have been given notice that the victim is exercising the right to a reexamination proceeding pursuant to this section or to another proceeding based on the failure to perform a duty or provide a right.

13-4437. Standing to invoke rights; recovery of damages; right to counsel

A. The rights enumerated in the victims' bill of rights, article II, section 2.1, Constitution of Arizona, any implementing legislation or court rules belong to the victim. The victim has standing to seek an order, to bring a special action or to file a notice of appearance in an appellate proceeding, seeking to enforce any right or to challenge an order denying any right guaranteed to victims. In asserting any right, the victim has the right to be represented by personal counsel at the victim's expense.

B. A victim has the right to recover damages from a governmental entity responsible for the intentional, knowing or grossly negligent violation of the victim's rights under the victims' bill of rights, article II, section 2.1, Constitution of Arizona, any implementing legislation or court rules. Nothing in this section alters or abrogates any provision for immunity provided for under common law or statute.

C. At the request of the victim, the prosecutor may assert any right to which the victim is entitled.

D. On the filing of a notice of appearance, counsel for the victim shall be endorsed on all pleadings and, if present, be included in all bench conferences and in chambers meetings and sessions with the trial court that directly involve a victim's right enumerated in article II, section 2.1, Constitution of Arizona.

E. Notwithstanding any other law and without limiting any rights and powers of the victim, the victim has the right to present evidence or information and to make an argument to the court, personally or through counsel, at any proceeding to determine the amount of restitution pursuant to section 13-804.

13-4438. Statement of rights

In order to assure that any victim who comes before the court has been advised of the victim's constitutional rights, the following statement shall be prominently posted in each superior, justice of the peace and municipal court in this state and shall be read out loud by a judge of the superior court at the daily commencement of the regular criminal docket at which accused persons are arraigned, appear for a status conference, make a change of plea or are sentenced:

If you are the victim of a crime with a case pending before this court, you are advised that you have rights to justice and due process under Arizona law that, among others, include the right to be treated with fairness, respect and dignity, to a speedy trial and a prompt and final conclusion of the case, to be present at court proceedings, to choose whether or not to be interviewed by the defendant or the defendant's attorney, to be heard before the court makes a decision on release, negotiation of a plea, scheduling and sentencing and to receive restitution from a person who is convicted of causing your loss. If you have not already been provided with a written statement of all victims' rights, please contact the victim services division of the prosecutor's office.

13-4439. Right to leave work; scheduled proceedings; counseling; employment rights; nondiscrimination; confidentiality; definition

A. An employer who has fifty or more employees for each working day in each of twenty or more calendar weeks in the current or preceding calendar year, and any agent of that employer, shall allow an employee who is a victim of a crime to leave work to:

1. Exercise the employee's right to be present at a proceeding pursuant to sections 13-4414, 13-4420, 13-4421, 13-4422, 13-4423, 13-4426, 13-4427 and 13-4436.

2. Obtain or attempt to obtain an order of protection, an injunction against harassment or any other injunctive relief to help ensure the health, safety or welfare of the victim or the victim's child.

B. An employer may not dismiss an employee who is a victim of a crime because the employee exercises the right to leave work pursuant to subsection A of this section.

C. An employer is not required to compensate an employee who is a victim of a crime when the employee leaves work pursuant to subsection A of this section.

D. If an employee leaves work pursuant to subsection A of this section, the employee may elect to use or an employer may require the employee to use the employee's accrued paid vacation, personal leave or sick leave.

E. An employee who is a victim of a crime shall not lose seniority or precedence while absent from employment pursuant to subsection A of this section.

F. Before an employee may leave work pursuant to subsection A of this section, the employee shall do all of the following:

1. Provide the employer with a copy of the form provided to the employee by the law enforcement agency pursuant to section 13-4405, subsection A, the information the law enforcement agency provides to the employee pursuant to section 13-4405, subsection E, a court order the employee is subject to or any other proper documentation.

2. If applicable, give the employer a copy of the notice of each scheduled proceeding that is provided to the victim by the agency that is responsible for providing notice to the victim.

G. It is unlawful for an employer or an employer's agent to refuse to hire or employ, to bar or to discharge from employment or to discriminate against an individual in compensation or other terms, conditions or privileges of employment because the individual exercises the right to leave work pursuant to subsection A of this section.

H. Employers shall keep confidential records regarding the employee's leave pursuant to this section.

I. An employer may limit the leave provided under this section if the employee's leave creates an undue hardship to the employer's business.

J. The prosecutor shall inform the victim of the victim's rights pursuant to this section. A victim may notify the prosecutor if exercising the victim's right to leave under this section would create an undue hardship for the victim's employer. The prosecutor shall communicate the notice to the court during the scheduling of proceedings where the victim has the right to be present. The court shall continue to take the victim's schedule into consideration when scheduling a proceeding pursuant to subsection A of this section.

K. For the purposes of this section, "undue hardship" means a significant difficulty and expense to a business and includes the consideration of the size of the employer's business and the employer's critical need of the employee.

13-4440. Notice of petition of factual innocence; right to be heard; hearing

A. The victim has the right to be present and be heard at any proceeding in which a person's factual innocence is being considered pursuant to section 12-771.

B. The prosecuting agency shall provide written notice of the following to the victim:

1. The date, time and location of the hearing.

2. The victim's right to be present and be heard at the hearing.

C. If the court makes a determination of factual innocence pursuant to section 12-771, the prosecuting agency shall provide the victim with a copy of the court order within fifteen days after the order is entered.

13-4441. Right to be heard on a petition to restore the right to possess a firearm; notice

A. A victim has the right to be present and be heard at any proceeding in which the defendant has filed a petition pursuant to section 13-925 to restore the defendant's right to possess a firearm.

B. If the victim has made a request for postconviction notice, the attorney for the state shall provide notice to the victim at least five days before the hearing.

13-4442. Use of a facility dog in court proceedings; definition

A. The court shall allow a victim who is under eighteen years of age to have a facility dog, if available, accompany the victim while testifying in court. A party seeking the use of a facility dog must file a notice with the court that includes the certification of the facility dog, the name of the person or entity who certified the dog and evidence that the facility dog is insured.

B. The court may allow a victim who is eighteen years of age or more or a witness to use a facility dog.

C. To ensure that the presence of a facility dog assisting a victim or a witness does not influence the jury or is not a reflection on the truthfulness of any testimony that is offered by the victim or witness, the court shall instruct the jury on the role of the facility dog and that the facility dog is a trained animal.

D. For the purposes of this section, "facility dog" means a dog that is a graduate of an assistance dog organization that is a member of an organization or entity whose main purpose is to improve the areas of training, placement and utilization of assistance dogs, staff and volunteer education and to establish and promote standards of excellence in all areas of assistance dog acquisition, training and partnership.

Chapter 41 Incompetence to Stand Trial

13-4501. Definitions

In this chapter, unless the context otherwise requires:

1. "Clinical liaison" means a mental health expert or any other individual who has experience and training in mental health or developmental disabilities and who is qualified and appointed by the court to aid in coordinating the treatment or training of individuals who are found incompetent to stand trial. If intellectual disability is an issue, the clinical liaison shall be an expert in intellectual disabilities.

2. "Incompetent to stand trial" means that as a result of a mental illness, defect or disability a defendant is unable to understand the nature and object of the proceeding or to assist in the defendant's defense. In the case of a person under eighteen years of age when the issue of competency is raised, incompetent to stand trial also means a person who does not have sufficient present ability to consult with the person's lawyer with a reasonable degree of rational understanding or who does not have a rational and factual understanding of the proceedings against the person. The presence of a mental illness, defect or disability alone is not grounds for finding a defendant incompetent to stand trial.

3. "Mental health expert" means a physician who is licensed pursuant to title 32, chapter 13 or 17 or a psychologist who is licensed pursuant to title 32, chapter 19.1 and who is:

(a) Familiar with this state's competency standards and statutes and criminal and involuntary commitment statutes.

(b) Familiar with the treatment, training and restoration programs that are available in this state.

(c) Certified by the court as meeting court developed guidelines using recognized programs or standards.

4. "Mental illness, defect or disability" means a psychiatric or neurological disorder that is evidenced by behavioral or emotional symptoms, including congenital mental conditions, conditions resulting from injury or disease and developmental disabilities as defined in section 36-551.

5. "Threat to public safety" means charged with the commission of any of the following:

(a) A crime involving the discharge, use or threatening exhibition of a deadly weapon or dangerous instrument or the infliction of physical injury on another person.

(b) A dangerous crime against children pursuant to section 13-705.

(c) Two or more nondangerous felonies within a period of twenty-four months.

13-4502. Effect of incompetency

A. A person shall not be tried, convicted, sentenced or punished for an offense if the court determines that the person is incompetent to stand trial.

B. The prosecutor or defense attorney may file any pretrial motion at any time while the defendant is incompetent to stand trial. The court shall hear and decide any issue presented by the motion if the defendant's presence is not essential for a fair hearing as determined by the court.

13-4503. Request for competency examination; jurisdiction over competency hearings; referral_

A. At any time after the prosecutor charges a criminal offense by complaint, information or indictment, any party or the court on its own motion may request in writing that the defendant be examined to determine the defendant's competency to stand trial, to enter a plea or to assist the defendant's attorney. The motion shall state the facts on which the mental examination is sought.

B. Within three working days after a motion is filed pursuant to this section, the parties shall provide all available medical and criminal history records to the court.

C. The court may request that a mental health expert assist the court in determining if reasonable grounds exist for examining a defendant.

D. Except as provided in subsection E of this section, after any court determines that reasonable grounds exist for further competency proceedings, the superior court shall have exclusive jurisdiction over all competency hearings.

E. The presiding judge of the superior court in each county, with the agreement of the justice of the peace or municipal court judge, may authorize a justice court or municipal court to exercise jurisdiction over a competency hearing in a misdemeanor case that arises out of the justice court or municipal court.

F. A justice of the peace or municipal court judge, with the approval of the presiding judge of the superior court and the justice or judge of the receiving court, may refer a competency hearing to another justice court or municipal court that is located in the county.

13-4504. Dismissal of misdemeanor charges; notice

A. Notwithstanding any law to the contrary, if the court finds that a person has been previously adjudicated incompetent to stand trial pursuant to this chapter, the court may hold a hearing to dismiss any misdemeanor charge against the incompetent person. The court shall give ten days' notice to the prosecutor and the defendant of this hearing. On receipt of the notice, the prosecutor shall notify the victim of the hearing.

B. If a misdemeanor charge is dismissed pursuant to this section, the court may order the prosecutor to initiate civil commitment or guardianship proceedings.

13-4505. Appointment of experts; costs

A. If the court determines pursuant to section 13-4503 that reasonable grounds exist for a competency examination, the court shall appoint two or more mental health experts to examine the defendant, issue a report and, if necessary, testify regarding the defendant's competency. The court, on its own motion or upon motion of any party, may order that one of the mental health experts appointed shall be a physician specializing in psychiatry and licensed pursuant to title 32, chapter 13 or 17. The state and the defendant, upon approval of the court, may stipulate to the appointment of only one expert.

B. The court may order the defendant to submit to physical, neurological or psychological examinations, if necessary, to adequately determine the defendant's mental condition.

C. The court shall order the defendant to pay the costs of the court ordered examination, except that if the court finds the defendant is indigent or otherwise unable to pay all or any part of the costs or if the prosecution requested the examination, the court shall order the county to pay the costs of the examination or, if the case is referred by a municipal court judge, the court shall order the city to pay the costs of the examination.

D. This section does not prohibit any party from retaining its own expert to conduct any additional examinations at its own expense.

E. A person who is appointed as a mental health expert or clinical liaison is entitled to immunity, except that the mental health expert or clinical liaison may be liable for intentional, wanton or grossly negligent acts that are done in the performance of the expert's or liaison's duties.

13 4506. Examination for purposes of insanity defense

A. On request of the court or any party, with the consent of the defendant and after a determination that a reasonable basis exists to support the plea of insanity, the mental health expert who is appointed pursuant to section 13-4505 shall provide a screening report that includes:

1. The mental status of the defendant at the time of the offense.

2. If the expert determines that the defendant suffered from a mental disease, defect or disability at the time of the offense, the relationship of the disease, defect or disability to the alleged offense.

B. If the defendant's state of mind at the time of the offense will be included in the examination, the court shall not appoint the expert to address this issue until the court receives the medical and criminal history records of the defendant.

C. Within ten working days after the expert is appointed, the parties shall provide any additional medical or criminal history records that are requested by the court or the expert.

13-4507. Examination of competency to stand trial

A. The court shall set and may change the conditions under which the examination is conducted.
B. The defense attorney shall be available to the mental health expert conducting the examination.
C. A proceeding to determine if a defendant is competent to stand trial shall not delay a judicial determination of the defendant's eligibility for pretrial release. A defendant who is otherwise entitled to pretrial release shall not be involuntarily confined or taken into custody solely because the issue of the defendant's competence to stand trial is raised and an examination is ordered unless the court determines that the defendant's confinement is necessary for the evaluation process.
D. If a defendant is released from custody under any pretrial release provision, the court may order the defendant to appear at a designated time and place for an outpatient examination. The court may make the appearance a condition of the defendant's pretrial release.
E. The court may order that the defendant be involuntarily confined until the examination is completed if the court determines that any of the following applies:
1. The defendant will not submit to an outpatient examination as a condition of pretrial release.
2. The defendant refuses to appear for an examination.
3. An adequate examination is impossible without the confinement of the defendant.
4. The defendant is a threat to public safety.
F. If a defendant is committed for an inpatient examination, the length of the commitment shall not exceed the period of time that is necessary for the examination. The commitment for examination shall not exceed thirty days, except that the commitment may be extended by fifteen days if the court finds that extraordinary circumstances exist. The county shall pay the costs of any inpatient examination ordered by the court, except that the city shall pay the costs of any inpatient examination that is ordered by a municipal court judge.

13-4508. Privilege against self-incrimination; sealed reports

A. The privilege against self-incrimination applies to any examination that is ordered by the court pursuant to this chapter.
B. Any evidence or statement that is obtained during an examination is not admissible at any proceeding to determine a defendant's guilt or innocence unless the defendant presents evidence that is intended to rebut the presumption of sanity.
C. Any statement made by the defendant during an examination or any evidence resulting from that statement concerning any other event or transaction is not admissible at any proceeding to determine the defendant's guilt or innocence of any other criminal charges that are based on those events or transactions, except that a statement or evidence may be used by any party in a hearing to determine whether the defendant is eligible for court-ordered treatment pursuant to title 36, chapter 5 or is a sexually violent person.
D. Any statement made by the defendant or any part of the evaluations that is obtained during an examination may not be used for any purpose without the written consent of the defendant or the defendant's guardian or a court order that is entered by the court that ordered the examination or that is conducting a dependency or severance proceeding.
E. After a plea of guilty or guilty except insane or the trial or after the defendant is found to be unable to be restored to competence, the court shall order all the reports submitted pursuant to this section sealed. The court may order that the reports be opened only as follows:
1. For use by the court or defendant, or by the prosecutor if otherwise permitted by law, for further competency or sanity evaluations or in a hearing to determine whether the defendant is eligible for court-ordered treatment pursuant to title 36, chapter 5 or is a sexually violent person.
2. For statistical analysis.
3. When the records are deemed necessary to assist in mental health treatment pursuant to section 13-502 or 13-4517.

4. For use by the probation department or the state department of corrections if the defendant is in the custody of or is scheduled to be transferred into the custody of the state department of corrections for the purposes of assessment and supervision or monitoring of the defendant by that department.

5. For use by a mental health treatment provider that provides treatment to the defendant or that assesses the defendant for treatment.

6. For data gathering.

7. For scientific study.

F. Any statement made by the defendant during an examination that is conducted pursuant to this chapter or any evidence resulting from that statement is not subject to disclosure pursuant to section 36-509.

13-4509. Expert's report

A. An expert who is appointed pursuant to section 13-4505 shall submit a written report of the examination to the court within ten working days after the examination is completed. The report shall include at least the following information:

1. The name of each mental health expert who examines the defendant.

2. A description of the nature, content, extent and results of the examination and any test conducted.

3. The facts on which the findings are based.

4. An opinion as to the competency of the defendant.

B. If the mental health expert determines that the defendant is incompetent to stand trial, the report shall also include the following information:

1. The nature of the mental disease, defect or disability that is the cause of the incompetency.

2. The defendant's prognosis.

3. The most appropriate form and place of treatment in this state, based on the defendant's therapeutic needs and potential threat to public safety.

4. Whether the defendant is incompetent to refuse treatment and should be subject to involuntary treatment.

C. If the mental health examiner determines that the defendant is currently competent by virtue of ongoing treatment with psychotropic medication, the report shall address the necessity of continuing that treatment and shall include a description of any limitations that the medication may have on competency.

13-4510. Competency hearing and orders

A. Within thirty days after the report is submitted, the court shall hold a hearing to determine a defendant's competency to stand trial. The parties may introduce other evidence regarding the defendant's mental condition or may submit the matter by written stipulation on the expert's report.

B. If the court finds that the defendant is competent to stand trial, the proceedings shall continue without delay.

C. If the court initially finds that the defendant is incompetent to stand trial, the court shall order treatment for the restoration of competency unless there is clear and convincing evidence that the defendant will not be restored to competency within fifteen months. The court may extend the restoration treatment by six months if the court determines that the defendant is making progress toward the goal of restoration.

D. All treatment orders issued by the court shall specify the following:

1. The place where the defendant will receive treatment.

2. Transportation to the treatment site.

3. The length of the treatment.

4. Transportation after treatment.

5. The frequency of reports.

13-4511. Competency to refuse treatment; length of sentence

If the court finds that a defendant is incompetent to stand trial, the court shall determine:
1. If the defendant is incompetent to refuse treatment, including medication, and should be subject to involuntary treatment.
2. The maximum sentence the defendant could have received pursuant to section 13-702, section 13-703, section 13-704, subsection A, B, C, D or E, section 13-705, section 13-706, subsection A, section 13-707, section 13-708, subsection D, section 13-710 or section 13-1406 or the sentence the defendant could have received pursuant to section 13-751, subsection A or any section for which a specific sentence is authorized. In making this determination the court shall not consider the sentence enhancements for prior convictions under section 13-703 or 13-704.

13-4512. Treatment order; commitment

A. The court may order a defendant to undergo out of custody competency restoration treatment. If the court determines that confinement is necessary for treatment, the court shall commit the defendant for competency restoration treatment to the competency restoration treatment program designated by the county board of supervisors.
B. If the county board of supervisors has not designated a program to provide competency restoration treatment, the court may commit the defendant for competency restoration treatment to the Arizona state hospital, subject to funding appropriated by the legislature to the Arizona state hospital for inpatient competency restoration treatment services, or to any other facility that is approved by the court.
C. A county board of supervisors that has designated a county restoration treatment program may enter into contracts with providers, including the Arizona state hospital, for inpatient, in custody competency restoration treatment. A county competency restoration treatment program may do the following:
1. Provide competency restoration treatment to a defendant in the county jail, including inpatient treatment.
2. Obtain court orders to transport the defendant to other providers, including the Arizona state hospital, for inpatient, in custody competency restoration treatment.
D. In determining the type and location of the treatment, the court shall select the least restrictive treatment alternative after considering the following:
1. If confinement is necessary for treatment.
2. The likelihood that the defendant is a threat to public safety.
3. The defendant's participation in and cooperation during an outpatient examination of competency to stand trial conducted pursuant to section 13-4507.
4. The defendant's willingness to submit to outpatient competency restoration treatment as a condition of pretrial release, if the defendant is eligible for pretrial release.
E. An order entered pursuant to this section shall state if the defendant is incompetent to refuse treatment, including medication, pursuant to section 13-4511.
F. A defendant shall pay the cost of inpatient, in custody competency restoration treatment unless otherwise ordered by the court. If the court finds the defendant is unable to pay all or a portion of the costs of inpatient, in custody treatment, the state shall pay the costs of inpatient, in custody competency restoration treatment at the Arizona state hospital that are incurred until:
1. Seven days, excluding Saturdays, Sundays or other legal holidays, after the hospital submits a report to the court stating that the defendant has regained competency or that there is no substantial probability that the defendant will regain competency within twenty-one months after the date of the original finding of incompetency.
2. The treatment order expires.
3. Seven days, excluding Saturdays, Sundays or other legal holidays, after the charges are dismissed.
G. The county, or the city if the competency proceedings arise out of a municipal court proceeding, shall pay the hospital costs that are incurred after the period of time designated in subsection F of this section and shall also pay for the costs of inpatient, in custody competency restoration treatment in court approved programs that are not programs at the Arizona state hospital.
H. Payment for the cost of outpatient community treatment shall be the responsibility of the defendant unless:

1. The defendant is enrolled in a program which covers the treatment and which has funding available for the provision of treatment to the defendant, and the defendant is eligible to receive the treatment. Defendants in these circumstances may be required to share in the cost of the treatment if cost sharing is required by the program in which the defendant is enrolled.

2. The court finds that the defendant is unable to pay all or a portion of treatment costs or that outpatient treatment is not otherwise available to the defendant. For defendants in these circumstances, all or a portion of the costs of outpatient community treatment shall be borne by the county or the city if the competency proceedings arise out of a municipal court proceeding.

I. A treatment order issued pursuant to this section is valid for one hundred eighty days or until one of the following occurs:

1. The treating facility submits a report that the defendant has regained competency or that there is no substantial probability that the defendant will regain competency within twenty-one months after the date of the original finding of incompetency.

2. The charges are dismissed.

3. The maximum sentence for the offense charged has expired.

4. A qualified physician who represents the Arizona state hospital determines that the defendant is not suffering from a mental illness and is competent to stand trial.

J. The Arizona state hospital shall collect census data for adult restoration to competency treatment programs to establish maximum capacity and the allocation formula required pursuant to section 36-206, subsection D. The Arizona state hospital or the department of health services is not required to provide restoration to competency treatment that exceeds the funded capacity. If the Arizona state hospital reaches its funded capacity in either or both the adult male or adult female restoration to competency treatment programs, the superintendent of the state hospital shall establish a waiting list for admission based on the date of the court order issued pursuant to this section.

13-4513. Appointment of clinical liaison

A. If the court enters a treatment order pursuant to this chapter, the court shall appoint a clinical liaison to coordinate the continuity of care following restoration. The clinical liaison may not be the defendant's treatment supervisor. The clinical liaison shall be familiar with aftercare facilities that are available in the defendant's locale and shall act as a liaison between the court and any treating facilities or correctional facilities.

B. The county, or the city if the competency proceedings are conducted in municipal court, shall pay the clinical liaison's fees.

C. The clinical liaison shall submit a written report to the court on request. The court shall distribute copies of the report to the prosecutor and the defense attorney.

D. The clinical liaison in cooperation with the treating facility shall advise the court on matters relating to the appropriateness of the form and location of treatment, including the level of security.

E. A treatment facility shall cooperate fully with the clinical liaison and shall provide the liaison with access to the defendant's records. The clinical liaison shall not direct treatment or render an opinion on the defendant's competency.

13-4514. Progress reports; rehearings

A. The person who supervises the treatment of a defendant who has been ordered to undergo treatment pursuant to section 13-4512 shall submit a written report to the court which shall make the report available to the prosecutor, the defense attorney and the clinical liaison as follows:

1. For inpatient treatment, after the first one hundred twenty days of the original treatment order and after each one hundred eighty days of treatment thereafter.

2. For outpatient treatment, every sixty days.

3. Whenever the person believes the defendant is competent to stand trial.

4. Whenever the person believes that there is no substantial probability that the defendant will regain competency within twenty-one months after the date of the original finding of incompetency.

5. Fourteen days before the expiration of the maximum time that an order issued pursuant to section 13-4512 or this section is in effect.

B. The report shall include the examiner's findings and the information required under section 13-4509. If the report states that the defendant remains incompetent, the report shall state the likelihood that the defendant will regain competency, an estimated time period for the restoration of competency and recommendations for treatment modification, if necessary. If the report states that the defendant has regained competency, the report shall state the effect, if any, of any limitations that are imposed by any medications used in the effort to restore the defendant's competency.

C. The court shall hold a hearing to determine the defendant's progress towards regaining competency as follows:

1. On the court's own motion.

2. On receipt of a report that is submitted by the treating facility pursuant to subsection A, paragraph 3, 4 or 5 of this section.

D. If at the hearing the court finds that the defendant has regained competency, the defendant shall be returned to the court and the proceedings against the defendant shall continue without delay. The court may order continued involuntary medication pursuant to section 13-4511 pending final disposition of this case in the trial court if the court finds that there is not a less intrusive alternative, the medication was medically appropriate and that it is essential for the sake of the defendant's safety or the safety of others.

E. If at the hearing the court finds that the defendant is incompetent to stand trial but that there is a substantial probability that the defendant will regain competency within the foreseeable future, the court shall renew and, if appropriate, modify the treatment order for not more than an additional one hundred eighty days. The court may make this determination without a formal hearing if all of the parties agree.

F. If at the hearing the court finds that the defendant is incompetent to stand trial and that there is not a substantial probability that the defendant will regain competency within twenty-one months after the date of the original finding of incompetency, the court shall proceed pursuant to section 13-4517.

13-4515. Duration of order; excluded time calculation; notice of dismissed charge or voided order; petitions

A. An order or combination of orders that is issued pursuant to section 13-4512 or 13-4514 shall not be in effect for more than twenty-one months or the maximum possible sentence the defendant could have received pursuant to section 13-702, section 13-703, section 13-704, subsection A, B, C, D or E, section 13-705, section 13-706, subsection A, section 13-708, subsection D or section 13-751 or any section for which a specific sentence is authorized, whichever is less. In making this determination the court shall not consider the sentence enhancements under section 13-703 or 13-704 for prior convictions.

B. The court shall only consider the time a defendant actually spends in a restoration to competency program when calculating the time requirements pursuant to subsection A of this section.

C. The court shall notify the prosecutor, the defense attorney, the medical supervisor and the treating facility if the charges against the defendant are dismissed or if an order is voided by the court. No charges shall be dismissed without a hearing prior to the dismissal.

D. If a defendant is discharged or released on the expiration of an order or orders issued pursuant to section 13-4512 or 13-4514, the medical supervisor may file a petition stating that the defendant requires further treatment pursuant to title 36, chapter 5 or appointment of a guardian pursuant to title 14.

13-4516. Notice to central state repository; records

A. The court shall notify the central state repository established by section 41-1750 of any commitment that is ordered or any release that is authorized under this chapter and of any determination that a defendant has regained competency to stand trial.

B. The court and the department of health services shall keep records of the offenses for which a defendant was charged, any court ordered examinations and treatment outcomes.

13-4517. Incompetent defendants; disposition

A. If the court finds that a defendant is incompetent to stand trial and that there is no substantial probability that the defendant will regain competency within twenty-one months after the date of the original finding of incompetency, any party may request that the court:

1. Remand the defendant to an evaluating agency for the institution of civil commitment proceedings pursuant to title 36, chapter 5. If the defendant is remanded, the prosecutor shall file a petition for evaluation and provide any known criminal history for the defendant.

2. Appoint a guardian pursuant to title 14, chapter 5.

3. Release the defendant from custody and dismiss the charges against the defendant without prejudice.

B. If the court enters an order pursuant to subsection A, paragraph 1 or 2 of this section, the court may also order an assessment of the defendant's eligibility for private insurance or public benefits that may be applied to the expenses of the defendant's medically necessary maintenance and treatment, including services pursuant to title 36, chapter 29, state-only behavioral health services, title xviii services and medicare part D prescription drug benefits, supplemental security income and supplemental security disability income.

C. The court may retain jurisdiction over the defendant until the defendant is committed for treatment pursuant to title 36, chapter 5 or a guardian is appointed pursuant to title 14, chapter 5.

D. If the court remands the defendant for the institution of civil commitment proceedings pursuant to title 36, chapter 5 and the court is notified that the defendant has not had a civil commitment evaluation, the court, if it has retained jurisdiction, may order the sheriff to take the defendant into custody so that the court may explore options pursuant to subsection A, paragraph 2 or 3 of this section.
E. If the court is notified that the defendant has not been ordered into treatment pursuant to title 36, chapter 5 and the court has retained jurisdiction, the court may order the sheriff to take the defendant into custody so that the court may explore options pursuant to subsection A, paragraph 2 or 3 of this section.

13-4518. Screening; sexually violent person; appointment of competent professional

A. If the county attorney receives a report that determines a defendant is incompetent to stand trial, the county attorney may request that the defendant be screened to determine if the defendant may be a sexually violent person, if both:
1. The report concludes that there is no substantial probability that the defendant will regain competency within twenty-one months after the date of the original finding of incompetency.
2. The defendant is charged with a sexually violent offense as defined in section 36-3701.
B. If the court orders a screening to determine if the defendant may be a sexually violent person, both of the following apply:
1. The court shall appoint a competent professional as defined in section 36-3701 to conduct the screening and submit a report to the court and the parties within thirty days after the appointment.
2. The criminal case may not be dismissed until the competent professional's report is provided to the court and the parties and a hearing is held pursuant to subsection C of this section or the county attorney files a petition pursuant to section 36-3704.
C. If the county attorney has not filed a petition pursuant to section 36-3704, the court may hold a hearing to determine if the county attorney is or will be filing a petition. If the county attorney has filed a petition or advises the court that it is or will be filing a petition, the court shall set a date on which the petition is due and further proceedings will be conducted pursuant to title 36, chapter 37. If a petition will not be filed, the court shall proceed pursuant to section 13-4517, subsection A, paragraph 1, 2 or 3.

Chapter 43 Motor Vehilce Chop Shops

13-4701. Definitions

In this chapter, unless the context otherwise requires:
1. "Chop shop" means any building, lot or other premises in which one or more persons alters, destroys, disassembles, dismantles, reassembles or stores at least one motor vehicle or watercraft or two or more motor vehicle or watercraft parts from at least one vehicle or watercraft that the person or persons knows were obtained by theft, fraud or conspiracy to defraud with the intent to:
(a) Alter, counterfeit, deface, destroy, disguise, falsify, forge, obliterate or remove the identity of the motor vehicles or motor vehicle parts, including the vehicle identification number for the purpose of misrepresenting or preventing the identification of the motor vehicles or motor vehicle parts.
(b) Sell or dispose of the motor vehicles or motor vehicle parts.
2. "Motor vehicle" means any self-propelled vehicle.
3. "Unidentifiable" means that specially trained investigative personnel who are experienced in motor vehicle theft investigative procedures and motor vehicle identification examination techniques cannot establish the uniqueness of a motor vehicle or motor vehicle part.
4. "Vehicle identification number" means the number that the manufacturer or the United States or a state department of transportation assigns to a motor vehicle for the purpose of identifying the motor vehicle or a major component part of the motor vehicle. Vehicle identification number includes any combination of numbers or letters.
5. "Watercraft" has the same meaning as prescribed in section 5-301.
113-4703. Forfeiture and disposition of motor vehicle, motor vehicle part, property and evidence

A. The following items used or intended for use in violation of section 13-4702 are subject to seizure and forfeiture pursuant to chapter 39 of this title:
1. A motor vehicle or motor vehicle part.

2. Any tool, instrument or other implement.

3. Real property.

B. The following property is subject to seizure and forfeiture pursuant to chapter 39 of this title:

1. All proceeds traceable to an offense that is included in section 13-4702 and is committed for financial gain.

2. All proceeds seized in this state and traceable to an offense that is chargeable or indictable under the laws of the state in which the offense occurred and if the offense occurred in a state other than this state would be chargeable or indictable under section 13-4702 if the offense occurred in this state and is committed for financial gain.

Chapter 44 Wireless Telephone Couterfeiting

13-4801. Definitions

In this chapter, unless the context otherwise requires:

1. "Acquire" means to electronically capture, record, reveal or otherwise access by means of any instrument, device or equipment a cellular or wireless telephone's electronic serial number or mobile identification number without the consent of the communication service provider.

2. "Cellular telephone" means a communication device that contains an electronic serial number and the operation of which depends on the transmission of that electronic serial number together with the mobile identification number in the form of radio signals through cell sites and mobile switching stations.

3. "Cloned cellular or wireless telephone" means a cellular or wireless telephone in which the manufacturer's electronic serial number has been altered.

4. "Cloning paraphernalia" means the materials that are necessary to create a cloned cellular or wireless telephone and includes scanners to intercept electronic serial numbers, cellular telephones and mobile identification numbers, wireless telephones, cables, chips, burners, software and the computers containing the software to program a cloned cellular or wireless telephone's microchip with a false electronic serial number and mobile identification number combination and lists of electronic serial number and mobile identification number combinations.

5. "Communication service provider" has the same meaning prescribed in section 13-3001.

6. "Electronic serial number" means the unique numerical algorithm that the manufacturer programs into the microchip of each wireless telephone.

7. "Mobile identification number" means the cellular or wireless telephone number that the cellular or wireless telephone carrier assigns to the wireless telephone.

8. "Wireless telephone" means a communication device that transmits radio, satellite or other mobile telephone communication.

13-4802. Possession or sale of cloned cellular or wireless telephones; exception; violation; classification

A. It is unlawful for a person to knowingly do any of the following:

1. Possess a cloned cellular or wireless telephone.

2. Possess an instrument that is capable of acquiring electronic serial number and mobile identification number combinations with the intent to clone a cellular or wireless telephone.

3. Sell a cloned cellular or wireless telephone.

B. This section does not prohibit the possession, sale or use of cloning paraphernalia or cloned cellular or wireless telephones or the acquisition of electronic serial numbers or mobile identification numbers by either of the following:

1. Law enforcement officers who are acting in their official capacity within the scope of their authority and in the line of duty.

2. Employees or agents of communication service providers who are acting in their official capacity within the scope of their employment for the purpose of protecting the property or legal rights of the provider.

C. A person who violates this section is guilty of a class 4 felony.

Chapter 45 Commercial Nuclear Generating Station

13-4901. Definitions

In this chapter, unless the context otherwise requires:

1. "Armed nuclear security guard" means a security guard who works at a commercial nuclear generating station, who is employed as part of the security plan approved by the nuclear regulatory commission and who meets the requirements mandated by the nuclear regulatory commission for carrying a firearm.

2. "Commercial nuclear generating station" means an electric power generating facility that is owned by a public service corporation, a municipal corporation or a consortium of public service corporations or municipal corporations and that produces electricity by means of a nuclear reactor and includes the property on which the facility is located.

3. "Enter" means the intrusion of any part of any instrument or any part of a person's body inside of a commercial nuclear generating station or a structure or fenced yard of a commercial nuclear generating station.

4. "Entering or remaining unlawfully" means an act by a person who enters or remains in or on a commercial nuclear generating station or a structure or fenced yard of a commercial nuclear generating station if that person's intent for entering or remaining is not licensed, authorized or otherwise privileged.

5. "Structure or fenced yard" means any structure, fenced yard, wall, building or other similar barrier or any combination of structures, fenced yards, walls, buildings or other barriers that surrounds a commercial nuclear generating station and that is posted with signage indicating it is a felony to trespass.

13-4902. Criminal trespass on commercial nuclear generating station; classification

A. A person commits criminal trespass on a commercial nuclear generating station by knowingly either:

1. Entering or remaining unlawfully in or on a commercial nuclear generating station.

2. Entering or remaining unlawfully within a structure or fenced yard of a commercial nuclear generating station.

B. Criminal trespass on a commercial nuclear generating station is a class 4 felony.

13-4903. Use of force; armed nuclear security guards

A. An armed nuclear security guard is justified in using physical force against another person at a commercial nuclear generating station or structure or fenced yard of a commercial nuclear generating station if the armed nuclear security guard reasonably believes that such force is necessary to prevent or terminate the commission or attempted commission of criminal damage under section 13-1602, subsection A, paragraph 3 and subsection B, paragraph 1 or 2, misconduct involving weapons under section 13-3102, subsection A, paragraph 13 or criminal trespass on a commercial nuclear generating station under section 13-4902.

B. Notwithstanding sections 13-403, 13-404, 13-405, 13-406, 13-408, 13-409, 13-410 and 13-411, an armed nuclear security guard is justified in using physical force up to and including deadly physical force against another person at a commercial nuclear generating station or structure or fenced yard of a commercial nuclear generating station if the armed nuclear security guard reasonably believes that such force is necessary to:

1. Prevent the commission of manslaughter under section 13-1103, second or first degree murder under section 13-1104 or 13-1105, aggravated assault under section 13-1204, subsection A, paragraph 1 or 2, kidnapping under section 13-1304, burglary in the second or first degree under section 13-1507 or 13-1508, arson of a structure or property under section 13-1703, arson of an occupied structure under section 13-1704, armed robbery under section 13-1904 or an act of terrorism under section 13-2308.01.

2. Defend oneself or a third person from the use or imminent use of deadly physical force.

C. Notwithstanding any other provision of this chapter, an armed nuclear security guard is justified in threatening to use physical or deadly physical force if and to the extent a reasonable armed nuclear security guard believes it necessary to protect oneself or others against another person's potential use of physical force or deadly physical force.

D. An armed nuclear security guard is not subject to civil liability for engaging in conduct that is otherwise justified pursuant to this chapter.

13-4904. Detention authority; armed nuclear security guards

A. An armed nuclear security guard, with reasonable belief, may detain in or on a commercial nuclear generating station or a structure or fenced yard of a commercial nuclear generating station in a reasonable manner and for a reasonable time any person who is suspected of committing or attempting to commit manslaughter under section 13-1103, second or first degree murder under section 13-1104 or 13-1105, aggravated assault under section 13-1204, subsection A, paragraph 1 or 2, kidnapping under section 13-1304, burglary in the second or first degree under section 13-1507 or 13-1508, criminal damage under section 13-1602, subsection A, paragraph 3 and subsection B, paragraph 1 or 2, arson of a structure or property under section 13-1703, arson of an occupied structure under section 13-1704, armed robbery under section 13-1904, an act of terrorism under section 13-2308.01, misconduct involving weapons under section 13-3102, subsection A, paragraph 13 or criminal trespass on a commercial nuclear generating station under section 13-4902 for the purpose of summoning a law enforcement officer.

B. Reasonable belief of an armed nuclear security guard is a defense to a civil or criminal action against an armed nuclear security guard for false arrest, false or unlawful imprisonment or wrongful detention.

Chapter 46 Military Reservations and Facilities Security

13-5001. Definitions

In this chapter, unless the context otherwise requires:

1. "Enter" means the intrusion of any part of any instrument or any part of a person's body inside of a military reservation or facility or a structure or fenced yard of a military reservation or facility.

2. "Entering or remaining unlawfully" means an act by a person who enters or remains in or on a military reservation or facility or a structure or fenced yard of a military reservation or facility if that person's intent for entering or remaining is not authorized or otherwise privileged.

3. "Military reservation or facility" means any land or facility that is owned or leased by or designated to the Arizona national guard.

4. "Structure or fenced yard" means any structure, fenced yard, wall, building or other similar barrier or any combination of structures, fenced yards, walls, buildings or other barriers that surrounds a military reservation or facility and that is posted with signage indicating it is a felony to trespass.

13-5002. Criminal trespass on military reservations and facilities; classification

A. A person commits criminal trespass on a military reservation or facility by knowingly entering or remaining unlawfully within a structure or fenced yard of a military reservation or facility.

B. Criminal trespass on a military reservation or facility is a class 6 felony.

13-5002. Criminal trespass on military reservations and facilities; classification

A. A person commits criminal trespass on a military reservation or facility by knowingly entering or remaining unlawfully within a structure or fenced yard of a military reservation or facility.

B. Criminal trespass on a military reservation or facility is a class 6 felony.

3-4702. Conducting a chop shop; exception; violation; classification

A. A person shall not knowingly:
1. Own or operate a chop shop.
2. Transport a motor vehicle or motor vehicle part to or from a chop shop.
3. Sell or transfer to or purchase or receive from a chop shop a motor vehicle or motor vehicle part.
4. Remove, destroy, deface or otherwise alter a vehicle identification number with the intent to misrepresent or prevent the identification of the motor vehicle or motor vehicle part.
5. Buy, sell, transfer or possess a motor vehicle or motor vehicle part knowing that the motor vehicle identification number, which was placed on the motor vehicle or motor vehicle part by the manufacturer, has been removed, destroyed, defaced or otherwise altered.
B. This section does not apply to law enforcement authorities and lawful owners acting in good faith, towing companies or scrap processors, licensed automotive recyclers and other businesses acting in good faith and in the normal course of business and in conformance with all applicable laws.
C. A person who violates subsection A, paragraph 1 of this section is guilty of a class 2 felony. A person who violates subsection A, paragraph 2, 3, 4 or 5 of this section is guilty of a class 4 felony.

Made in the
USA
Monee, IL